Completely Revised for the '80s

AMERICA'S BEST-LOVED BOOK ON BABY AND CHILD CARE

From Pregnancy through Your Child's 6th Year

Developed by leading practicing obstetricians, pediatricians, child-development specialists and psychologists, this book brings the latest advances in child care, psychology and training to the new generation of parents. In this one book is everything a mother and father need to know to bring up their child with happy confidence.

THE BABY CHECKUP BOOK: A PARENT'S GUIDE TO WELL
   BABY CARE by Sheila Hillman
BETTER HOMES AND GARDENS NEW BABY BOOK
CARING FOR YOUR UNBORN CHILD
   by Ronald E. Gots, M.D., Ph.D. and Barbara A. Gots, M.D.
CHILD'S BODY by The Diagram Group
CHOICES IN CHILDBIRTH by Dr. Silvia Feldman
THE COMPLETE BOOK OF BREASTFEEDING
   by Marvin Eiger, M.D. and Sally Wendkos Olds
FEED ME! I'M YOURS by Vicki Lansky
THE FIRST TWELVE MONTHS OF LIFE edited by Frank Caplan
HAVE IT YOUR WAY by Vicki E. Walton
HAVING A BABY AFTER THIRTY
   by Elisabeth Bing and Libby Colman
IMMACULATE DECEPTION by Suzanne Arms
MAKING YOUR OWN BABY FOOD
   by Mary Turner and James Turner
MAKING LOVE DURING PREGNANCY
   by Elisabeth Bing and Libby Colman
MOVING THROUGH PREGNANCY by Elisabeth Bing
MY BODY, MY HEALTH: THE CONCERNED WOMAN'S
   BOOK OF GYNECOLOGY by Felicia Stewart, M.D.,
   Felicia Guest, Gary Stewart, M.D., and Robert Hatcher, M.D.
NAME YOUR BABY by Laureina Rule
NEWBORN BEAUTY: A COMPLETE BEAUTY, HEALTH,
   AND ENERGY GUIDE TO THE NINE MONTHS OF
   PREGNANCY AND THE NINE MONTHS AFTER
   by Wende Devlin Gates and Gail Mcfarland Meckel
THE NEW PREGNANCY
   by Susan S. Lichtendorf and Phyllis L. Gillis
NINE MONTHS READING: A MEDICAL GUIDE FOR
   PREGNANT WOMEN by Robert E. Hall, M.D.
NO-NONSENSE NUTRITION FOR YOUR BABY'S FIRST YEAR
   by Jo-Ann Heslin, Annette B. Natow and Barbara C. Raven
PREGNANCY NOTEBOOK by Marcia Colman Morton
PREPARING FOR PARENTHOOD by Dr. Lee Salk
THE SECOND TWELVE MONTHS OF LIFE
   edited by Frank Caplan and Teresa Caplan
A SIGH OF RELIEF: THE FIRST-AID HANDBOOK FOR
   CHILDHOOD EMERGENCIES produced by Martin I. Green
SIX PRACTICAL LESSONS FOR AN EASY CHILDBIRTH
   by Elisabeth Bing
THE TAMING OF THE C.A.N.D.Y. MONSTER by Vicki Lansky
UNDERSTANDING PREGNANCY AND CHILDBIRTH
   by Sheldon H. Cherry, M.D.

Better Homes and Gardens®

NEW
BABY
BOOK

By **Edwin Kiester, Jr.**
and Sally Valente Kiester
and the Editors of
Better Homes & Gardens Books

Photography by
Kathryn Abbe and Frances McLaughlin-Gill
Medical Illustrations by
Elton Hoff

BANTAM BOOKS
TORONTO · NEW YORK · LONDON · SYDNEY

BETTER HOMES AND GARDENS ® NEW BABY BOOK

*A Bantam Book / published by arrangement with
Meredith Corporation*

PRINTING HISTORY

Meredith edition published March 1979

2nd printing..August 1979
3rd printing..January 1980
4th printing..August 1980

*A Selection of Better Homes & Gardens Family Book Service
July 1979*

Bantam Edition / October 1980
2nd printing..March 1981
3rd printing..July 1981
4th printing..January 1982

Meredith Editor: Michael P. Scott
Copy and Production Editor: Paul S. Kitzke
Graphic Designer: Neoma Alt West
Photograph on Page 2 by Robert L. Wolfe
*Food, Equipment, and Clothing Illustrations
by Hellman Design Associates*

Book design by Gene Siegel

ISBN 0-553-20965-5

Published simultaneously in the United States and Canada

---

*Bantam Books are published by Bantam Books, Inc. Its trademark,
consisting of the words "Bantam Books" and the portrayal of a
rooster, is Registered in U.S. Patent and Trademark Office and in
other countries. Marca Registrada. Bantam Books, Inc., 666 Fifth
Avenue, New York, New York 10103.*

PRINTED IN THE UNITED STATES OF AMERICA

13   12   11   10   9   8   7

Acknowledgments

R. M. Applebaum, M.D., Medical Advisor, LaLeche League International, Miami, Florida.

Frederick H. Berman, M.D., M.P.H., F.A.C.O.G., Attending Physician, Mount Zion Hospital, San Francisco, California.

C. Walter Brown, M.D., F.A.A.P., Attending Physician, Santa Teresa Community Hospital, San Jose, California.

David E. Carter, Director Audiovisual Services, Mercy Hospital, Cedar Rapids, Iowa.

Robert Creasy, M.D., F.A.C.O.G., Professor of Obstetrics and Gynecology, University of California, San Francisco.

John O. Dower, M.D., Professor of Pediatrics, University of California, San Francisco.

Michael Eliastam, M.D., M.P.P., Assistant Professor of Surgery and Medicine and Director of Emergency Services, Stanford University Medical Center, Stanford, California.

Carolyn Ferris, R.N., Nursing Care Coordinator, Obstetrical Complex, Mount Zion Hospital, San Francisco, California.

Oscar Frick, M.D., Professor of Pediatrics, University of California, San Francisco.

Alvin Jacobs, M.D., Professor of Dermatology and Pediatrics, Stanford University, Stanford, California.

Michael M. Kaback, M.D., Professor, Departments of Pediatrics and Medicine; Associate Chief, Division of Medical Genetics, Harbor General Hospital, UCLA School of Medicine, Torrance, California.

Jack E. Obedzinski, M.D., Assistant Clinical Professor of

Pediatrics, Child Study Unit, University of California, San Francisco.

Peggy Pipes, Assistant Chief, Nutrition Section, Child Development and Mental Retardation Center, University of Washington, Seattle.

Diana Pulsipher, R.N., Supervisor, Labor and Delivery Unit, Santa Teresa Community Hospital, San Jose, California.

Robert S. Roth, M.D., Coordinator, Newborn Services, Mount Zion Hospital, San Francisco, California.

D. Stewart Rowe, M.D., Associate Clinical Professor of Pediatrics; Acting Director, Pediatric Clinics, University of California, San Francisco.

Eugene C. Sandberg, M.D., Associate Professor of Gynecology and Obstetrics, Stanford University Medical Center, Stanford, California.

Pamela Schrock, R.P.T., M.P.H., Childbirth Educator, American Society for Psychoprophylaxis in Obstetrics, Evanston, Illinois.

Helen D. Ullrich, M.A., R.D., Executive Director, Society for Nutrition Education, Berkeley, California.

Lenox Hill Hospital, New York, New York.

Maternity Center Association, New York, New York.

New Baby Book

Two generations of Americans have been raised by the book—the *Better Homes and Gardens Baby Book*. In its 35-year history, the Baby Book has sold more than three million hardcover copies and two million paperback copies. But even these figures don't fully demonstrate its impact; families have raised three, four, or more children with the Baby Book's reassuring assistance and guidance.

The original edition grew out of a critical wartime need. In the early months of World War II, millions of young husbands and wives traveled to military bases far from the experience and wisdom of parents and relatives. And they had few doctors to rely on, because as soon as new ones were graduated, they went off to patch battlefield wounds. Thus, in 1942 the late Gladys Denny Schultz, a longtime child-care columnist, proposed that *Better Homes and Gardens* fill the gap with a new, basic, illustrated manual of child care. The editors agreed, and the book appeared the next year. It was an instant success.

With war's end, needs changed—and so did the Baby Book. Returning servicemen married and began long-delayed families—34 million births in the immediate postwar years alone. The Baby Book was reprinted five times in five years just to keep up with the baby boom. So many parents relied on it that one consultant to the present edition, whose children are now grown, recalls, "For ten years every time I went to a baby shower, someone got a copy of the *Better Homes and Gardens Baby Book*."

The Baby Book has been revised several times since to encompass new ideas in child-raising, as well as changes in society. And, over the last ten years, changes have been frequent. Today, many mothers give birth "naturally," often in the presence of the father and other children. Women who were fed by the bottle prefer to nourish their own babies at the breast. Moreover, as more women work outside the home, the lines between fathers' and mothers' duties and responsibilities become more and more blurred. Even childhood health problems have changed. Many of the old scourges are nearly extinct, thanks to immunizations—although runny noses and earaches still persist.

The *Better Homes and Gardens New Baby Book,* the edition for the 1980s, reflects these changes in families and in society. At heart, though, it differs little from the first edition published in 1943. Although the third generation of "Baby Book children" will be raised quite differently from their parents and grandparents, the basic theme of the *Better Homes and Gardens New Baby Book* is the same.

The most important ingredient in raising a child isn't knowledge, but love. There is no single, right way to raise a child—or, indeed, several children in the same family. Parents know more than they think they do, and, at the same time, are helped along by their own compassion and concern.

Literally hundreds of physicians, nurses, child-development specialists, psychologists, and others have contributed to the Baby Book throughout its history—so many that it is no longer possible to list them all individually. Those who contributed to and guided the New Baby Book are listed in acknowledgments, and, like their predecessors', their contributions—and their common sense—have been invaluable.

Contents

III. TWO TO SIX YEARS

IV. ADVICE FOR EVERY DAY

New Baby Book

SECTION
1

Before the Birth

Your baby is a miracle—
there simply is no other word.
Millions of babies are born
every year, some in riches, some
in poverty, some in cities,
some in jungles, some unwanted,
some devoutly wished for and
jubilantly welcomed. The
birth of a baby is the most
everyday event of all. Yet each
birth is an occasion of mystery,
marvel, and wonder.

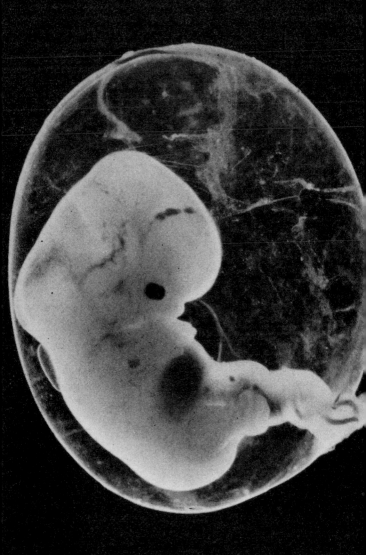

1

The Miracle of Birth

Think of your pregnancy. You certainly weren't aware of the precise moment it began. Two tiny cells, each barely distinguishable under a microscope, united into one, unnoticed even by the donors, and began the inexorable process of multiplication. Nine months later, they have produced a fantastic spectrum of specialized cells for skin, hair, fingernails, teeth, internal organs, bones—all arranged into a new seven-pound being resembling his or her parents, yet carrying a distinctive identity.

The journey from conception to birth encompasses three-fourths of a year, more or less. That period is a mysterious sequence of exquisitely orchestrated, carefully followed steps, each of which must occur precisely on schedule in order to bring on the next. Just as a symphony conductor cues first the brass, then the percussion, and finally the strings, the body signals biological and chemical changes to advance the performance. Each part of the body has a score to follow; each bodily function, a part to play.

Fifty years ago, little was known about the conception and development of human life beyond the crudest outlines. Modern research and technology have since supplied many important details. Doctors can peer into the womb itself to watch a baby grow; they can measure heartbeats, count breaths, even observe thumb sucking. They can observe and chart fetal development and extract samples of a baby's blood. Yet great gaps remain in physicians' knowledge of reproduction and the fascinating first nine months of life.

Opposite: Photograph by Robert L. Wolfe

TWO TO MAKE ONE

The woman's role in procreation is most familiar, centering on the ovaries, two walnut-size glands on either side of the pelvis, and the uterus or womb, an organ about the size and shape of a small pear. The ovaries and uterus are connected by the fallopian tubes, two tiny canals about the diameter of a soda straw (see diagram, right).

Each month, the lining of the uterus, or endometrium, prepares for the possibility of conception. Tissues thicken and enrich, nutrients accumulate, blood vessels proliferate. Midway in the month, the ovaries release an egg to be fertilized by a male sperm. If fertilization takes place, the egg embeds itself in the rich uterine wall and grows there. If it does not, the uterine bed breaks down and is flushed away in the process called menstruation.

A little girl is born with several million eggs in her ovaries. The number dwindles to a half million by puberty, still more than adequate for a lifetime of ovulating. Each month, one egg is selected from this storehouse; the ovaries are believed to take turns in furnishing the candidate. Cells surrounding the chosen egg nourish it, ripen it, and form a protective covering for the next step of its mission. When ready, the egg erupts from this follicle and travels down the fallopian tube toward the uterus.

Before fertilization, the egg is one of the largest cells in the human body but is still barely visible to the naked eye. The egg has no power to move on its own. When it is ejected from the ovary, threadlike fibers called cilia wave like blades of grass in the wind and lure the egg into the funnel-shaped opening of the fallopian tube. From there, currents of fluid and muscular contractions carry it toward the uterus. It completes the first third of the three- to five-inch journey rapidly, within a few hours. Then it halts, as if awaiting the arrival of its "date."

A sperm is one-thousandth of the egg's size, too small to be seen with unaided sight. It would take millions to fill a thimble. A sperm resembles a tadpole, with an oval-shaped head and long, whip-like tail. Unlike the egg, the sperm can move under its own power: vigorous kicks of the tail propel it forward at a rate of six inches an hour. Beginning in adolescence and continuing until old age, millions of sperm are manufactured each day by the testicles in the male scrotum, and each sperm is capable of fathering a child.

Sperm age, ripen, and then are stored until needed. At the climax of intercourse, they come tumbling from storage, are mixed with other substances to form semen, and are ejaculated

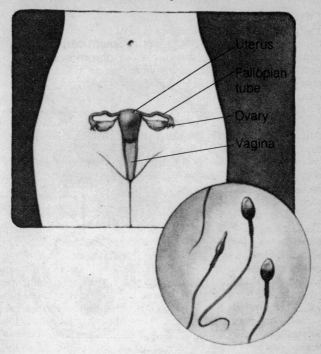

by the millions. Because only one sperm will eventually combine with the egg, the reasons for this profligacy are among reproduction's chief unknowns.

An official of the Population Council once calculated the odds of pregnancy from a given act of unprotected intercourse at 50 to one, because optimum conditions cover only a brief period each month. The egg is ripe—ready for fertilization—for no more than 12 hours, and sperm normally can survive outside the male body for only 24 hours. Against these odds, conception truly approaches the miraculous.

THE BABY'S HEREDITY

Sperm and egg approach each other carrying parts of a blueprint that will shape the new child's life. The cell nucleus of each contains an arrangement of dark-colored, rod-shaped bodies called chromosomes, composed of deoxyribonucleic acid

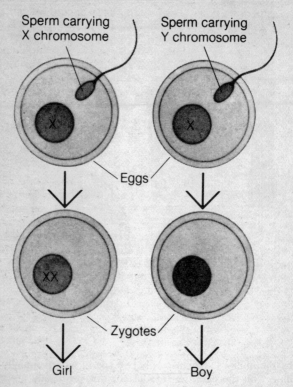

(DNA) and protein. Within the chromosomes are genes, the basic units of heredity.

These submicroscopic genes incorporate characteristics handed down from previous generations. They determine whether your baby will be blond or brunette, blue-eyed or brown, tall or short, fat or lean, even how long he or she will live. They also influence the child's personality and shape the intelligence.

There are 23 pairs of chromosomes (46) in every human cell—except in the egg and sperm. The chromosomes in the sex cells are not paired; each of them contains a single strand of 23 chromosomes. When the cells combine, the strands match up to form a new cell consisting of 23 chromosomal pairs.

Twenty-two of the chromosomes do not differ from male to

female, but the twenty-third chromosome decides the baby's sex. In the female it is called the X chromosome; in the male, either X or Y. When a sperm carrying an X chromosome unites with an egg, the XX combination produces a girl. When a Y sperm unites with an egg, the XY combination produces a boy.

Thus, it is the father who determines—involuntarily—whether a baby will be a boy or a girl. The odds are nearly equal because X and Y chromosomes are about evenly distributed among the sperm. About 106 boys are born for every 100 girls. Your baby's sex is determined at the moment of conception, and not much can be done to influence it. Like many of the fascinating aspects of reproduction, it seems to be a matter of pure chance.

THE BEGINNING OF LIFE

Appropriately, perhaps, life starts with a race. At the moment of ejaculation, millions of sperm spurt into the female body, zeroing in on the awaiting egg. Some are old and tired; they drop out early. Others head in the wrong direction or become lost in the folds of tissue. A hardy ten percent swim to the top of the uterus, where the fallopian tubes branch. Half head into the empty tube containing no fertilizable cell that month. Of the remaining sperm, perhaps only 4,000 can squeeze into the proper fallopian tube to approach the waiting egg.

Why so many sperm when only one is needed to fertilize an egg? One reason may be that they must work together to break down the defenses of the well-protected egg. The egg's nucleus, containing the chromosomal arrangement, is housed in a central core, along with necessary nourishment for the embryonic life. This mass is enclosed by a thick, transparent coating covered by a halo of follicle cells embedded in a gelatinous structure.

The sperm must make its way to the nucleus. An enzyme secreted from the cap of the sperm—or perhaps from the caps of many sperm—seems to open the way. It apparently dissolves part of the egg's outer layer, opening a pathway through the follicle cells and the outer covering of the egg. Only one sperm will pass through the opening. The egg then closes itself to all other intruders.

Now, gradually, the two cells move toward union. Following an arc-like path, the sperm penetrates into the central core of the egg. Soon both bodies are enclosed within the same envelope. They begin to combine, the two sets of chromosomes arranging themselves into a new, 46-chromosome cell called a zygote. At this moment, life has started. The whole process, from intercourse to union of the two cells, only takes about 12 hours.

When the two cells are one, a message goes out to the rest of the woman's bodily systems. Carrying the message is a hormone called human chorionic gonadotrophin (HCG). HCG is issued in minute, but unmistakable, quantities to signal that procreation has succeeded. The signal stimulates increased flows of the female hormones estrogen and progesterone, needed to support the pregnancy; the husk of the follicle left behind by the egg converts to a corpus luteum, or "yellow body," that produces more hormones; and the lining of the uterus continues to grow instead of beginning the degenerative process of menstruation. All the preparations made for a possible pregnancy are told to continue.

Meanwhile, the new life develops quickly. Within hours, the single cell divides and redivides, producing first two cells, then four, then eight, and so on until it has become an entire mass of cells, more compact, but not much larger than the original. This cluster of cells is called a morula, or "mulberry," because it resembles that fruit.

The zygote has taken shape this way in the upper half of the fallopian tube. Now it begins a slow, week-long descent toward an eventual nesting place in the wall of the uterus. Once more, it is carried along by currents of fluid and the muscular contractions of the tube.

Why does it take so many days for such a short trip? What is happening during the journey from tube to uterus? These are among the important unanswered questions about the beginning of a new life. It appears the morula requires three days to complete its voyage to the uterus. Then it apparently floats free within the uterus, for perhaps an additional four days.

At about the seventh day after fertilization, the endometrium has reached its greatest thickness and lushness. Simultaneously, the new organism has consumed most of the nourishment it started with. Now it attaches itself to the succulent uterine wall to absorb nourishment from the mother. The usual place is near the top of the uterus, although implantation may occur nearly anywhere on the uterine wall. At this point, the mother may notice a small spot of vaginal bleeding—so-called implantation bleeding.

The implanted organism looks quite different from the one that began the journey. Now called a blastocyst, it is a hollow, fluid-filled sphere. Cells have been rearranged and have begun to specialize. One clump holds those that will grow into the embryo. Around the periphery, other cells take on the mission of implanting and nourishing the embryo. These are the trophoblastic cells, or "feeding layer."

The trophoblastic cells have the ability to digest or liquefy other tissues they contact. The trophoblasts break down the cells of the endometrium and the walls of its tiny blood vessels. The cellular contents and blood nourish the blastocyst, which settles deeply into the lining. Fingerlike projections, called villi, sprout from the trophoblastic cells. Some wave freely in the blood supply, others tap new vessels, and still others form anchors to strengthen the link between the blastocyst and its nest.

These free-floating villi now begin to serve as lungs and digestive organs. From the mother, they take on oxygen, air, and simple foodstuffs, like sugar and calcium; in the opposite direction, they pass off fetal wastes. The barrier between them is permeable, but the circulations of fetus and mother never mix.

At this point, the blastocyst resembles a tiny blister surrounded by a slight pool of the mother's blood caused by the process of embedding. Soon a kind of scar tissue develops, a membrane surrounding the capsule; then a second, thicker membrane forms. The space between the two membranes fills with fluid. This is the so-called bag of waters, the sac of amniotic fluid in which the fetus will float and move about for nine months.

Meanwhile, the trophoblast and the maternal cells of the uterine lining combine to form the placenta, or "afterbirth," which will nourish the fetus through the umbilical cord, a long, coiled structure that passes through the amniotic membrane, carrying oxygen and food from the placenta to the fetus and fetal waste products out through the mother's excretory system.

THE FETUS GROWS

Doctors usually calculate fetal development in lunar months, or four-week periods—ten lunar months, also stated as 40 weeks or 280 days, is the term of pregnancy. But most of us think in terms of nine calendar months. Here is how the baby develops in those nine months.

If you could peer inside the uterus a month after conception, you would hardly believe the tiny bit of tissue before your eyes could grow into a breathing, squalling baby. The diminutive being measures only a quarter of an inch long—less than the length of a newborn's fingernail—and weighs perhaps one-

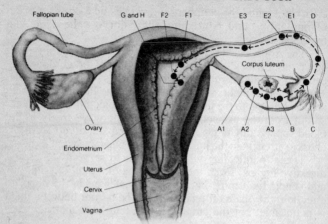

(The drawings, A to H below, correspond to the numbers and letters above.) Eggs are produced in the ovaries—more than enough for a lifetime of ovulation. Before the eggs are released and fertilized, they undergo a ripening process (A1, 2, 3). Each month, numerous eggs ripen (B), although normally only one egg does so completely. The ripened egg (C) is expelled from the ovary and is picked up by the fallopian tube. At the same time, the ruptured follicle begins its conversion into the corpus luteum. Although many sperm work to penetrate the egg (D), only one realizes that goal. After fertilization, cell division begins (E1, 2). A cluster of cells called a morula, or mulberry (E3), is formed. Next, cells rearrange to form a blastocyst (F1). A specialized layer of cells (trophoblastic cells, F2) will eventually become the placenta and unite with the mother's uterine lining. Once the blastocyst is embedded (G), the initial stages of the development of the placenta (H) take place.

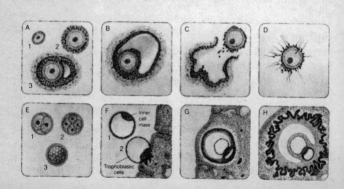

one-hundredth of an ounce. You would see no human face, no arms, no legs—just a small rudimentary tail.

Yet the most complex and vital organs already are forming. The month-old fetus has a microscopic brain, a threadlike spinal cord, and a crude nervous system. A U-shaped tube two millimeters long forms the heart and is pumping blood through primitive arteries. Another tube leading from the mouth is a rudimentary digestive tract, and a bulge midway in its length marks the spot where the stomach will develop.

A month later, there is no mistaking the human qualities. Eyes, a nose, mouth, and ears give it a decidedly human countenance. Arms and legs have developed, complete with fingers, toes, elbows, and knees. Sex organs have become apparent, though it is still difficult to distinguish male from female. And the fetus has grown. It now measures a full inch from head to heel and weighs one-thirtieth of an ounce.

At the end of the third month, the baby is three inches long and weighs a full ounce. Fingernails and toenails show; the buds of baby teeth appear in the jawbone. An observer can detect the presence or absence of a uterus. A rudimentary kidney excretes waste into the amniotic fluid. The fetus moves, but too slightly for the mother to feel.

At four months, nearly all vital organs are formed—yet the fetus is not ready to live alone. It is now about six and a half inches long and weighs about four ounces. Fine hair covers the body, and a few hairs appear on the head. More active now, the baby waggles tiny arms and legs. Using an amplified stethoscope, the doctor can hear the fetal heartbeat—a rapid 140 beats per minute, faster than that of the mother.

By five months, the fetus has developed hair, eyebrows and lashes, and even facial expressions. The father can hear the fetal heartbeat by placing an ear against the mother's abdomen. And the fetus now moves vigorously and frequently; the mother can "feel life." The baby is now nearly a foot long and weighs almost a pound and a half.

At six months, the fetus is 15 inches long, weighs two and a half pounds, and is growing rapidly. For the first time the fetus looks like a miniature human being. The skin is covered with fuzz and a creamy substance called vernix caseosa ("cheesy varnish"), a one-eighth-inch-thick layer that protects the fetus's skin from the fluid environment.

At seven months, the fetus is 16½ inches long and weighs four pounds. Development now is mainly a process of fine-tuning, the organs getting ready for independent existence. The intricate biochemistry governing many bodily functions begins to evolve: production starts on the body's 20,000 enzymes. The nerve cells mature. And the fetus fattens.

During the last two months, the fetus gains a half pound per week, accumulating layers of fat to increase its ability to survive in the outside world. At eight months, the fetus weighs six pounds and at full term, seven and one half.

The last organs to be fine-tuned are the lungs. Even though the child appears fully mature, the respiratory system may not be ready: the lungs cannot function until acted upon by chemicals that are among the last to be produced. Some doctors believe normal birth can begin only when the fetal respiratory system has completed this maturation.

Prior to the end of the seventh month, an infant has only an outside chance to survive if born prematurely. The chances increase with each additional day or week in the womb. Despite an old belief that a seven-month baby has a better chance to live than an eight-month baby, no evidence confirms that notion. However, at eight months, the chances of survival are nearly as good as if the baby had completed the full term of pregnancy.

LIFE BEFORE BIRTH

What is life like within the womb? Scientists have been able to observe and photograph it. These amazing records show that life before birth is more eventful than commonly supposed. To some extent, the bag of waters insulates the floating fetus from the outside world. Suspended in the buoyant fluid, the fetus is cushioned against sudden impacts, sharp blows, or other potential injuries. The fluid is at a constant temperature, providing additional protection against extreme heat and cold. The placental "barrier" separating maternal and fetal circulations protects against some (but by no means all) harmful foreign substances.

The fetus sleeps and wakes at irregular intervals, probably sleeping more than waking. Babies seem to have a favorite position, called a "lie," into which they settle on falling asleep; most commonly, they coil with knees drawn up and chin on chest. Awake, the fetus can move freely in the amniotic fluid, shifting frequently from side to side or even turning head over heels. The mother at first feels these movements as tiny flutters, but soon they are pronounced kicks and pokes. Occasionally, the baby will hiccup, and the mother's abdomen will twitch in a series of rhythmic jolts. Activity slows a little in the final month

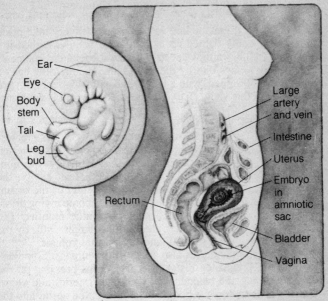

Eight weeks after fertilization, there is a noticeably human shape. Many times as large as a month ago, the fetus is an inch from head to heel and weighs 1/30 of an ounce.

of pregnancy, when the fetus occupies so much space in the sac that such movements are greatly inhibited.

The baby spends some of its time upright and some upside down. Neither position seems to bother it. Tests indicate that a fetus may be able to see and almost certainly hear. Touch and the ability to distinguish changes in temperature are sensations developed within the first few months of life. Sensitivity begins in the face and then spreads over the entire body.

An old wives' tale says a baby can be marked or affected by a mother's experiences during pregnancy. There is probably no truth to this belief; the nerves of mother and child are not connected in any way. Even so, a fetus may respond to a mother's emotional patterns. Fetal movements increase when the mother undergoes emotional stress. Apparently, these changes result from an increased secretion of maternal hormones during stress that cross the placental barrier and stimulate the fetus.

Is life inside the womb enjoyable? The unborn child seems to lead a placid, comfortable existence; hence, some doctors consider birth traumatic and advocate that delivery take place in a warm, dimly lighted room where the baby is bathed immediately in lukewarm water to re-create the fetal environment. Another view says that by the end of nine months, the baby's quarters are cramped, with a barely adequate supply of oxygen and food. In this view, an exit to the outside world is welcome.

THE MOTHER CHANGES, TOO

As the fetus grows, the mother changes, too. The greatest changes are in the reproductive system, especially the uterus. This small, muscular organ is described as having—in its non-pregnant state—a potential, rather than an actual, cavity: the front and back walls come together at the center of the organ, with only a narrow passage between. The accompanying drawings show how the uterus changes over nine months. The uterine walls thin and stretch; the cavity enlarges until, by the time of birth, it encloses 500 times its original volume.

Changes in the uterus also affect nearby organs. Some discomforts of pregnancy result from the uterus pressing on the intestinal tract, the bladder, and the major arteries and veins. Uterine pressure on the body's main artery, the aorta, and the main vein, the vena cava, restrict circulation in the lower extremities and may lead to such complaints as varicose veins, hemorrhoids, and high blood pressure.

The breasts also are changing. Almost from the beginning of pregnancy, they increase in size (most women find they need a brassiere at least one size larger). The nipples darken and increase in circumference, and tiny "blisters" develop in the areola, the dark area around each nipple. Inside the breasts, the tree-like structure of milk ducts proliferates—more branches develop and existing ones enlarge.

The volume of blood increases by one-third to nourish the organs and to help carry off the wastes of pregnancy. The heart works harder to pump the increased supply through the system.

The most noticeable change is in the posture. As the uterus distends, the abdomen expands, and the expectant mother carries a 15- to 20-pound load in front of her. To compensate, she leans backward to balance the burden.

THE ROLE OF THE HORMONES

Most of the physical changes during pregnancy result from increased amounts of the female hormones, estrogen and proges-

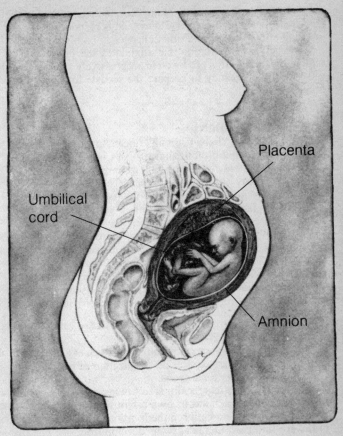

Placenta

Umbilical
cord

Amnion

At six months, the fetus truly resembles a miniature human being. The uterine walls thin and stretch, the abdomen expands as the baby demands more room.

terone. Progesterone is produced by the corpus luteum, the yellow body the egg has left behind. It helps soften and thicken the endometrium to prepare for the implantation of the fertilized egg. Later, the placenta manufactures progesterone to maintain the pregnancy, prevent premature labor, and keep all systems functioning properly.

Estrogen also causes many changes within the mother's

body. It acts on the involuntary muscles, including those of the gastrointestinal and urinary systems, and is responsible for the swelling of the breasts and other changes in bodily contours.

Prolactin is a hormone that stimulates the production of milk in the breast. It is produced in progressively greater quantities during pregnancy to prepare the breasts for feeding the infant.

BABY THE DEPENDENT

The old saying that "baby takes all" (meaning the fetus depletes the mother's supply of nourishment) isn't quite accurate. But the mother's system *does* place fetal welfare first. After all, the mother has many sources of sustenance available to her, but the fetus is totally dependent on the nourishment she provides. The fetus is—and must be—a parasite, if you define one in the strictest, most limited biological sense.

Thus, a baby feeds on the mother's store of iron to build a personal blood supply—the reason a pregnant woman must have iron replenished in her diet. The fetus also takes calcium to build bones and teeth. (However, it is not true the fetus destroys the mother's teeth in the process.) In addition, the baby has first call on glycogen, the substance that provides energy.

WILL YOU HAVE TWINS?

Normally, only one ovary per month releases an egg. But sometimes each ovary does so. Result: fertilization of two eggs and the conception of fraternal twins.

Fraternal twins technically aren't twins, just siblings born at the same time. Each has its own bag of waters and placenta; there is no connection between them. About 70 percent of twin births are fraternal. Identical twins develop from one egg that has split apart during the early stages of pregnancy. They share a placenta, although each usually has an individual sac.

Your chances of delivering twins are about one in 80. The odds of twinning increase somewhat with the mother's age, and there seems to be a tendency for identical twins to run in families. The doctor may detect two heartbeats as early as the fifth month and may then confirm the finding by ultrasonography or X ray (see Chapter 3). Twins are usually born several weeks early, with each about a pound lighter than a single baby. Otherwise, twins are equally healthy, if their lungs have matured.

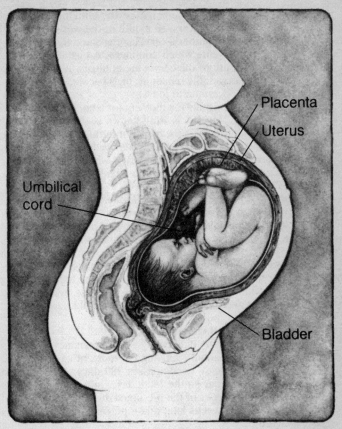

At nine months, the uterus has 500 times its original volume. The baby weighs more than seven pounds, and because this weight is carried in front, the mother leans backward to balance it.

PREPARING FOR BIRTH

Both fetus and mother normally begin preparation for birth at about the beginning of the ninth month. The baby gains weight; the lungs, nerves, and biochemical systems mature. It if hasn't already done so, the baby will assume the birth position, usually head-downward. Face turned toward the mother's back, the baby will slide lower into the pelvic cavity, with the head coming to rest against the cervix, or mouth of the womb.

Meanwhile, the mother's cervix softens and thins in a process called effacement, which continues through labor itself. Tissues at the mouth of the cervix are gradually drawn up into the sides of that organ; the remaining ones become more elastic. The pelvic joints continue to loosen.

What is it that signals the moment for labor? That question is still a mystery. All that is truly known is the uterus begins contractions that will force the baby out through the neck of the uterus. Even this explanation is challenged by some doctors who say the uterus contracts constantly—whether the woman is pregnant or not—and the contractions merely heighten with the onset of labor.

An endocrine secretion may start the process. Substances called the prostaglandins may be responsible, because they seem to trigger many bodily processes. Another explanation indicates the placenta can no longer function at its previous level. This theory is partly confirmed by the discovery of a sharp drop in hormonal secretions in the final weeks of pregnancy. Or the baby simply grows too large and too demanding for the placenta to support further. In any case, whatever the signal, mother and child receive it unmistakably.

WHEN WILL THE BABY BE BORN?

For all its precision in cuing each step of pregnancy, nature is remarkably lenient about signaling the moment of birth itself. Technically, pregnancy encompasses 280 days. But only ten percent of births occur on the 280th day. Only half of all births occur within two weeks of the presumed due date. Ten percent are more than two weeks late, and a pregnancy of 300 days is not unheard of.

Two methods can help you make a rough guess of when your baby will arrive. The first is to count *forward* nine months from the first day of your last menstrual period, then add seven days. If your last period started on January 2, for example, nine months would bring you to October 2; an additional seven days would make the presumed date of delivery October 9. The second method is to count *backward* three months from the beginning of the last period, then forward seven days. Starting from January 2 and counting back three months would be October 2; counting forward seven days would make the due date October 9.

Your doctor will probably estimate your delivery date on one of your early visits, then try to pinpoint it more exactly as time passes. The prediction may be in error partly because you have miscalculated the starting date of your previous period. Or it may just be nature's way of taking her time.

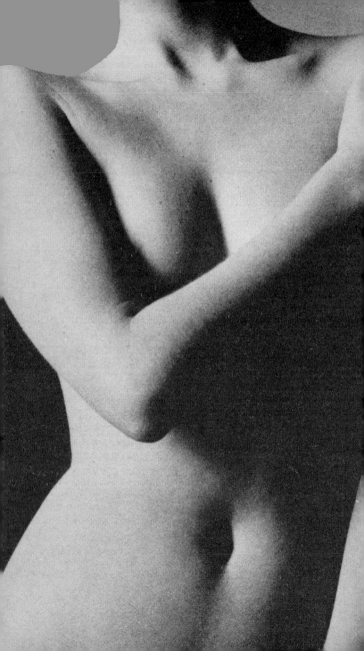

2

Nine Months of Pregnancy

Pregnancy is normal. And healthy—a fact both women and doctors sometimes forget. You *will* be a patient, you *will* have medical care, and you'll probably deliver your baby in a hospital. But that doesn't mean you're sick or need to sharply restrict your way of living.

Of course, not all pregnancies are equally easy. Nor are they all the same. Your own second pregnancy may differ greatly from your first. There are certain general rules for taking care of yourself during pregnancy, and the two best judges of what you should and shouldn't do are your doctor and yourself. Don't be guided by what other women remember about their pregnancies, or what your mother says about how it was when she was having children. *You're* having this baby.

Most doctors are more liberal than they used to be in maternity cases and acknowledge that they don't have all the answers. Bringing a healthy child into the world is not their responsibility alone, but yours and theirs together. A mother-to-be isn't expected to be passive, quiet, and obedient. Today, she's expected to be as independent in pregnancy as in other matters, to be responsible for herself, and her decisions.

Of course, giving birth to a healthy baby means being healthy yourself. Good health is a lifelong process. Habits of nutrition, physical development, freedom from disease, amount of exercise, and rest should have been established before you become pregnant. Many rules for a healthy pregnancy are merely extensions of rules for good health outside of pregnancy.

HOW DO YOU KNOW WHEN YOU'RE PREGNANT?

Usually, the first clue to a pregnancy is a missed menstrual period. If your menstrual cycle is fairly regular and ten days pass after your period is normally due, you can suspect you're pregnant. If a month passes and you miss a second period, pregnancy is practically assured—especially if you occasionally feel nauseous, visit the bathroom often, and have tender breasts.

Don't immediately rush to the doctor if your period is a few days late. Two of three women miss a period at some time in their lives, for reasons other than pregnancy. A bad cold, anemia, certain chronic conditions, even fatigue or emotional stress can disrupt a woman's menstrual cycle. The condition usually rights itself the following month. Anyway, under most circumstances, there is little a doctor can do to confirm pregnancy a few days after a missed period. You'll still have to return after you miss the second one.

TESTS FOR PREGNANCY

Sometimes, of course, it's important to know quickly if you're pregnant. Having a baby may mean a change in plans. If you can't wait a month or more to decide your future, pregnancy tests can give you a quick and usually accurate answer.

There are several types of pregnancy tests, all designed to detect human chorionic gonadotrophin (HCG), a hormonal signal of pregnancy, in the mother's urine. The woman furnishes a urine sample, collected in the morning when the hormone is most heavily concentrated. The sample will be analyzed by a laboratory or perhaps by the doctor's staff technicians.

The traditional biologic test for pregnancy is the so-called "rabbit test." It is used much less often today. Urine from the woman is injected into a laboratory animal, usually a rat or rabbit. Within two or three days, if the woman is pregnant, the animal's ovaries will change in a characteristic way. The test is accurate 95 of 100 times, providing the menstrual period is at least two weeks late when the urine sample is taken.

Immunologic tests have largely supplanted the biologic test, because they are quicker, more convenient, and equally correct (95 to 99 percent accurate two weeks after a missed menstrual period). Done in the doctor's office, these tests can give results in two minutes or two hours, depending on the test. Each test uses antibodies to HCG produced in laboratory animals.

In the shorter test, antibodies are mixed with the woman's

urine, then latex particles coated with HCG are added. If the donor *is* pregnant, there will be no reaction, because all antibodies have previously united with the HCG in the urine sample. If the donor is *not* pregnant, the HCG-coated particles and antibodies will agglutinate, or cling together.

The longer test is more sensitive to small amounts of HCG. This test measures direct agglutination. HCG antibodies and the woman's urine are placed together in a test tube. Bonding of the two substances means pregnancy.

A radioimmunoassay test can detect pregnancy even before a period has been missed, using radioactive HCG. It, too, is based on the binding of HCG to its antibodies and is sensitive to very tiny amounts. The test takes several hours to complete and sometimes produces misleading results. It is expensive, requires sophisticated equipment and trained personnel, but is steadily coming into wider use.

A radioreceptor assay test uses a mixture of animal cells and radioactive HCG, to which a woman's blood plasma is added. It can detect pregnancy as early as six days after ovulation, but it, too, is expensive and requires skilled technicians and sensitive equipment.

There are now tests you can buy over the counter at a pharmacy and administer yourself. Although you may have reasons to conduct the test privately, a laboratory test is generally considered more reliable.

THE SECONDARY SIGNS OF PREGNANCY

Besides a missed menstrual period, other bodily changes may lead you to think you're pregnant.

For many women, the first hint of pregnancy is their changing breasts. The breasts often feel full just prior to the beginning of menstruation, and the alterations in early pregnancy merely exaggerate this feeling. The breasts enlarge; they become firmer and seem tender. Sometimes they tingle, as if the skin were being stretched. The nipples and surrounding brown areas, the areolae, increase in diameter. The areolae puff, and their network of small milk glands proliferates.

Frequent urination is another indication of possible pregnancy. You may find yourself hurrying to the bathroom two or three times an hour. The reasons why this occurs aren't known precisely but seem to have a hormonal basis. Higher levels of estrogen may stimulate the pituitary gland to release additional quantities of a diuretic hormone that triggers urination. Or the estrogen may act on the smooth muscles of the ureters, the tubes carrying urine from the kidneys to the bladder. The need to urinate often decreases after the first three months but may recur later.

Morning sickness—which actually can occur at any time of day—affects two of three women in the first two to six weeks of pregnancy. It may even occur before the first missed period. It's a feeling of mild nausea, combined with lack of energy and loss of appetite. Sometimes it's worsened by nervousness and anxiety about the pregnancy. Fortunately, only one woman in three is sick enough to vomit.

Fainting is an infrequent sign that you're pregnant, although you may feel lightheaded and dizzy during the early part of the pregnancy. It can be relieved by sitting for a while with the head lower than the heart.

CHOOSING A DOCTOR

Once you're convinced you're pregnant, the next step is to plan your care. Although "alternative birth methods" described in Chapter 4 are increasing in popularity, 95 of 100 women still have their babies in hospitals, under the care of a physician. So the first step in your care is choosing a doctor.

Technically, any licensed physician is qualified to provide obstetrical care and preside at the birth of a baby. But, in practice, the task usually falls to an obstetrician-gynecologist—a doctor who specializes in maternity care and in problems of the female reproductive system. You may have already consulted one for contraceptive or other advice. If so, you'll probably want to continue seeing that doctor.

If you don't have a doctor, choose carefully, because he or she is important to you and your baby. Seek someone in whom you'll have confidence and with whom you'll have rapport. If you have a family doctor, ask him or her to recommend a specialist. Or consult friends about doctors with whom they've been pleased and satisfied. Women's health groups may have lists of obstetricians and gynecologists of both sexes whom they recommend.

You might also call a local medical school or large hospital. A community hospital usually will provide the names of members of its obstetrics staff. Or consult the local medical society.

THE FIRST VISIT

The best time for a first appointment is after you've missed a second menstrual period. Most doctors like to begin care when a woman is about eight weeks pregnant. By then the signs of pregnancy are unmistakable, but it is still early enough to outline a full program of care.

You'll probably be asked to bring a urine sample on your first visit. Expect to be with the doctor a half hour or more, although some of the time may be spent with a nurse or other member of the medical team. The examination should be thorough, yet comfortable. It's nothing to dread.

You'll be asked to provide a full medical history, including a record of all previous illnesses and any inherited conditions. In particular, you'll be asked about any previous pregnancies or miscarriages and about menstrual regularity. Your doctor will also want to know if you've been inoculated against rubella, or German measles, a mild disease that can cause serious complications for the baby if you contract it early in the pregnancy.

You'll also be weighed and measured. Your heart and pulse rate will be recorded and a blood sample taken. The doctor will also want an accurate record of blood pressure, because a sharp rise later may be the first indication of serious maternal complications.

You will have a "Pap smear" test. Named for the scientist who devised it, Dr. George Papanicolaou, this is a routine test in which certain cast-off cells are taken from the cervix and vagina with a tiny utensil, similar to a long-handled spoon or cotton-tipped applicator. The cells are then microscopically examined for changes that could be early evidence of uterine cancer. This test is important because the rate of cure is more than 75 percent in cases where the cancer is detected early.

A pelvic examination will be performed while you're lying undressed, but draped by a sheet, on an examining table. This painless internal checkup will show conclusively whether a pregnancy exists: vaginal tissues, normally pink in color, assume a bluish tinge in the early stages of pregnancy. The normally stiff cervix, or mouth of the uterus, assumes a softer feel. The uterus changes shape and consistency, too. Your pelvis also will be measured and the bone structure examined to help your doctor assess the potential difficulty or ease of a vaginal birth and to help the doctor decide whether a cesarean section may be necessary.

Often, the doctor asks about your family's medical history and may recommend that you visit a genetics counselor. This type of counseling helps identify inherited conditions that might be caused by a union of the two families. Such genetic problems are seldom a cause for concern, but both you and the doctor should be alert to them during, or after, the pregnancy.

You and the doctor also will establish a schedule for future visits. How often you see each other will depend on your condition and your doctor's practices. A common schedule calls for the second visit two weeks after the initial examination, when you should ask all the questions that have occurred to you in the meantime. Visits are usually then scheduled three weeks to a month apart until you're 32 weeks pregnant. Then you'll see the doctor twice at two-week intervals, after which you'll visit the office every week until delivery.

Don't hesitate to speak frankly with your doctor during any of your visits. There's no longer one standard, unvarying way to manage a pregnancy; as we shall see in Chapter Four, new parents must make many decisions about prenatal care, hospitalization, and delivery. You'll want to know the doctor's philosophy about anesthesia during labor, childbirth classes, the father's presence in the labor and delivery rooms, and the doctor's attitude toward breast-feeding. Discuss finances, too. Usually the doctor sets a flat fee, covering prenatal and postnatal visits, as well as the delivery. In most cases, the doctor's fee and the hospital charges will be at least partially covered by prepaid insurance, but the benefits vary from policy to policy—and they may not cover the entire bill. If you don't see eye to eye, or the fees don't fit your budget, discuss your feelings and problems. If you still aren't satisfied, feel free to seek medical care elsewhere.

Future visits to the doctor are likely to be shorter and even more routine. Usually, they are checks to confirm that the pregnancy is progressing normally. At each visit, you'll be asked to provide a urine sample, which will be tested for chemical evidence that things are going well. Your blood pressure will be taken regularly and your weight recorded. The doctor will listen to the baby's heartbeat and check the baby's position. You'll probably have an abdominal examination at each visit, although some doctors confine them to the last few months. You may have other tests, too. These are described in Chapter Three.

CAN YOU STILL WORK?

Pregnancy and childbirth are going to make changes in your life, no question about that. But these changes need not be so drastic as they were in the past. Given an uneventful pregnancy, most doctors believe a woman can continue living normally within the limits of her energy and endurance.

You may want to keep your job during pregnancy, perhaps

until the very day of delivery. Medically, there seems to be little reason not to do so. The old rule that a woman should stop work six weeks before her due date for the sake of her baby is largely disregarded now. Studies have shown that babies born to mothers who worked throughout pregnancy are just as healthy as those born to mothers who remained at home. Whether to quit and when to quit are therefore matters to be decided by you and your physician. As your pregnancy advances, you may feel too awkward and tire too easily to continue working. Or you may feel you need the stimulation of a daily job. Many doctors think the longer you work, the better it is for you emotionally.

After an extensive study, the American College of Obstetricians and Gynecologists (ACOG) concluded that women whose jobs involve sitting most of the time or resting frequently should be permitted to continue working so long as they feel able. Women who are on their feet a great deal or whose work is more strenuous should be permitted to transfer to lighter duties during pregnancy. In particular, women performing physically demanding jobs should be allowed to accept other employment during that time.

Of course, certain jobs may be riskier than others. Although evidence isn't yet clear, working in a chemical plant, for instance, may be hazardous to both mother and baby.

An employer may no longer legally dismiss you because you are pregnant, although you may be transferred to other duties. The only exception is if your condition might jeopardize customers or fellow workers. The employer may ask for a letter from your physician certifying that it is safe for you to continue working.

THE NEED FOR EXERCISE

Whether or not you continue working, regular exercise is important for you and the baby. Although pregnancy isn't the time to climb ladders and wash windows, even routine household chores can be handled readily and beneficially. Lifting, once considered taboo for pregnant women, isn't harmful if done properly. Gardening is an especially good way to get exercise and can be enjoyable as well.

At the very least, you should schedule a morning and evening walk of about 20 minutes' duration or a mile in length. Walking helps tone the muscles, boost circulation, and maintain good breathing habits that will be beneficial during labor. In addition, it's exercise you and your husband can enjoy together.

WHAT ABOUT SPORTS?

The general rule about recreation is: continue any sport in which you have participated regularly and proficiently prior to pregnancy. That includes swimming, dancing, bowling, golf, jogging, or tennis. Most doctors will advise you to discontinue any sports involving violent motion, no matter how accomplished you are. You probably should eliminate such sports as skiing, skating, motorcycle riding, water-skiing or surfing, and judo, especially in the later months of pregnancy when your expanding abdomen may cause you to lose your balance or make you unsteady on your feet. Although the baby is well-cushioned by the fluid environment against bumps and jolts, such restrictions are designed to protect you and the baby from a hard fall.

TRAVELING AND DRIVING

Until the eighth month, there's little need to restrict travel by car. The old taboo that kept expectant mothers close to home probably dated from the days when long-distance travel meant an arduous ride over bad roads. A long car trip can still be tiring, of course, so stop to rest and walk around every hour or two.

Some doctors still warn against air travel, mainly because of possible motion sickness. Most doctors consider these views exceptionally cautious, but the airlines themselves will ground you during the ninth month without a certificate from your physician stating that it is safe for you to travel. The certificate must be dated not earlier than 72 hours prior to departure and must specify the date the baby is expected; its purpose is to protect the airline in case you go into labor.

The restriction on travel after seven months is chiefly for convenience. You may unexpectedly enter labor far from home and from the physician familiar with your case. A good rule for the last two months is not to travel more than an hour from home. If you're planning to give birth in another city, move there at the end of the seventh month and remain until the baby comes.

As for driving a car, you can continue so long as you feel comfortable behind the wheel. There are no legal restrictions, and some women in the early stages of labor have actually driven themselves to the hospital. Throughout pregnancy, however, you should wear a safety restraint. A shoulder harness is preferable, because it reduces possible impact with the steering wheel. If only a lap belt is available, wear it as low on the abdomen as possible, over the pelvic bones in front and on the side.

SMOKING AND DRINKING

Women who smoke cigarettes during pregnancy run an increased risk of delivering undersized babies. A government study has shown that babies born to smokers weigh an average of 6.1 ounces less than those born to nonsmokers. The difference in weight is directly related to the number of cigarettes smoked. Women who smoke two or more packs a day during pregnancy also have an increased risk of stillbirth.

It was once believed that the placenta was a magic barrier to harmful substances, but it is known now that most drugs (including alcohol) used by the mother reach the baby. Children born to alcoholic mothers suffer from what is called the fetal-alcohol syndrome. The child is undersized and may suffer brain damage and certain deformities. These hapless victims—fortunately only a few—are born to women who drink a quart of liquor a day during pregnancy.

Possibly, even moderate drinking has slight effects on the baby. One study of 1,500 women showed that even when mothers had only two or three drinks per day, their babies weighed less at birth and had slightly smaller heads than those born to non-drinkers.

Another reason to limit drinking during pregnancy is that alcohol provides empty calories. It adds weight without providing nourishment and saps the appetite for more nutritious foods. In addition, a few drinks may make you feel unsteady on your feet, increasing the unbalanced posture and heightening the danger of falling.

DRUGS AND MEDICINES

You should not use any drugs or medications during pregnancy without first counsulting your doctor. These include over-the-counter preparations as well as prescription drugs. Aspirin, laxatives, sleeping tablets, and other medications may be prescribed by your doctor but should not be used without the physician's knowledge. If you are visiting another doctor for a condition unrelated to your pregnancy, ask him or her to check with and inform your obstetrician before prescribing any medicine and to discuss the effects of medicine already prescribed.

The so-called hard drugs are definitely taboo during pregnancy. These include not only illegal drugs, but prescription barbiturates; amphetamines (pep pills); and sleeping pills. Most doctors discourage smoking marijuana, both because its physiological effects are not fully known and because its use may cause unsteadiness and the possibility of a fall.

BATHING

During pregnancy, you'll probably prefer a shower to a bath, although either is acceptable. Many persons used to believe that pregnant women should neither bathe in a tub nor swim, but there is no evidence that immersing the body in water is harmful to the fetus in any way. If you do bathe, however, be careful while entering and leaving the bath, because of the danger of falling on the slippery surfaces. This is a particular danger in late pregnancy when movements tend to be awkward. Also, a long soak in a hot tub may sap your energy and tire you unnecessarily. You may want to substitute a shower or sponge bath in the final months before delivery.

CARE OF THE TEETH

"For every child, a tooth is lost," the saying used to go. Many persons thought the growing baby built teeth and bones by robbing the mother's system of calcium, causing her teeth to decay. The American Dental Association (ADA) says there is no evidence that pregnancy advances tooth decay in any way. The idea may have arisen because pregnancy usually occurs during that time of life when cavities are also frequent. And women may neglect their teeth during pregnancy. The ADA advises women to have dental work performed early in pregnancy or postpone it until after delivery. If X rays are needed, be sure your abdomen is covered by a lead shield. If dental work will require an anesthetic, it may be wise to postpone it until after delivery.

INTERCOURSE

How long you continue to have intercourse is strictly up to you. The only dangerous times are when vaginal bleeding occurs, when you have abnormal pain, or when the amniotic sac surrounding the baby ruptures, increasing the possibility of infection.

Your attitude toward sex may change during pregnancy. Some couples report a decrease in sexual activity, while others say they enjoy sex more than ever. Your feelings may be different, too, at different times during the nine months. During the last few months of pregnancy, you may find intercourse more comfortable if you change positions.

THE IMPORTANCE OF DIET

What you eat during pregnancy is important to both you and the baby. A successful pregnancy depends on the proper nutrients to assist the baby's development and to help your remain healthy. In fact, what you've eaten all your life will, in part, determine the baby's development. Women whose diet is poor have a higher percentage of stillbirths, undersized babies, and babies with brain damage.

Fortunately, you needn't worry quite so much about gaining weight as women—and their doctors—did in the past. In 1974, the ACOG's Committee on Nutrition revised its standards for weight gain during pregnancy.

Instead of limiting women to a gain of 20 pounds over the nine-month period, as doctors frequently did in the past, the committee now says a woman should *gain* at least 25 pounds during pregnancy, with gains up to 35 pounds considered normal. Of this amount, the baby accounts for seven pounds; the placenta, one pound; increased weight of the breasts, two pounds; increase in blood, three pounds; amniotic fluid, two

MOTHERS' WEIGHT GAIN

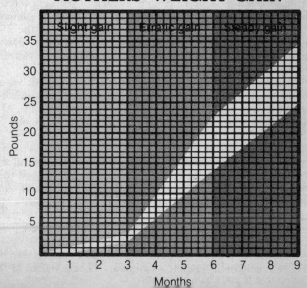

pounds; and increased size of the uterus, two pounds. The balance of the weight represents accumulated fats and fluids retained by the body during pregnancy; they will be lost after pregnancy.

Doctors once severely restricted weight gain because they believed it to be a forerunner of certain birth complications. But more recent evidence disputes this association. In fact, sharply restricting weight gain may result in low-birthweight babies, who are themselves at greater risk of complication. And other studies have shown that malnourished women generally have a higher percentage of birth complications.

Thus, if you are now underweight, your doctor probably will encourage you to gain even more than the recommended 25 pounds. If you are in your teens, he or she probably will place you on a special diet, because nourishing a new life while your own body is still growing can severely tax your system. Even if you are overweight to begin with, the doctor will probably want you to gain, or at least not attempt to lose weight until after pregnancy, lest the baby's development be jeopardized.

More important than how much you gain is how you gain it. As the chart shows, a pregnant woman normally will gain not more than three pounds in the first three months of pregnancy; she may actually lose weight or remain stationary. She then should gain about 11 or 12 pounds in each of the next three-month periods. During the last 24 weeks, she should be gaining at the rate of about a pound a week, bringing her to the 25-pound minimum. This even and regular rate of growth shows that the pregnancy is progressing normally and that the baby is developing on schedule.

A *sudden* spurt in weight, however, should be regarded as a danger signal. It may mean your body is retaining fluid, a condition sometimes associated with childbirth complications. Always discuss with your doctor any abrupt change in weight.

THERE ARE STILL LIMITS

You shouldn't interpret the new thinking to mean you can eat all you want and pile on the pounds. Gaining weight beyond the recommended limits still can be hazardous to your health. An excessive weight gain overloads the heart and circulatory system, causing the heart to work harder at pumping blood through the extra tissue. The back and leg muscles may be strained, too, by the heavy weight.

And for the sake of your own figure, you'll want to stay as close to a gain of 25 pounds as you can. Losing weight after pregnancy is never easy, but it's more manageable if the gain is kept as low as possible. Weight gains beyond 30 pounds will take plenty of work to lose afterward.

EATING THE GOOD FOODS

Unless your doctor directs otherwise, you need no longer count calories during pregnancy. "Let the calories count themselves," advises a publication of the ACOG Committee on Nutrition. "If you are taking enough protein and supplementary foods and are avoiding foods that have little nutritional value, you will not need to worry so much about calories."

Good eating in pregnancy can be summed up in a sentence: a balanced diet plus a quart of milk a day. A balanced diet means daily portions of each of the four basic food groups:

Protein—mainly meat, fish, poultry, or eggs. Organ meats, such as liver or kidneys, are very good. These also provide iron, B vitamins, and certain minerals. Shell fish, particularly oysters, are an often overlooked source of protein. Dried beans, peas, nuts, and other legumes are good vegetable sources of protein.

An adequate amount of protein comes from two or three ounces of meat—an average-size hamburger patty or a small chop. Two eggs, a cup of cooked dried beans, dried peas or lentils, a quarter cup of peanut butter, or two ounces of cheese contains as much protein as two ounces of meat. You should have three servings of protein daily.

Milk and milk products provide calcium. A pregnant woman requires four cups of milk (one quart) daily in the form of whole milk, skim milk, two percent milk, buttermilk, or reconstituted nonfat dry milk. Other milk products that can replace one cup of milk include: 1¼ cups cottage cheese, 1½ slices American cheese, 1¼ cups yogurt, or 1½ cups ice cream or ice milk.

Some of the dark, leafy green vegetables, such as collard, mustard, and turnip greens are very high in calcium, too.

Vegetables and fruits provide vitamins A and C and are subdivided into three groups. You should make it a point to have four servings from this category daily.

Group 1 includes foods rich in vitamin C—citrus fruits, cantaloupe, strawberries, papaya, and such vegetables as tomatoes, broccoli, brussels sprouts, peppers, cabbage, potatoes, and cauliflower. A medium-size orange or a four-ounce glass of citrus juice is considered a normal adult serving. A medium tomato supplies half the amount you'll need.

Group 2 includes foods rich in vitamin A, such as dark, leafy greens like romaine, beet, collard, mustard greens, and spinach. And yellow fruits and vegetables such as squash, carrots, sweet potatoes, yams, apricots, and peaches.

Group 3 includes most other vegetables and fruits, including lettuce, radishes, zucchini, cucumbers, corn, eggplant, green and wax beans, peas, beets, turnips, and such fruits as apples, peaches, cherries, berries, bananas, and pears. A half-cup of vegetables or an average-size apple or pear is a normal adult serving.

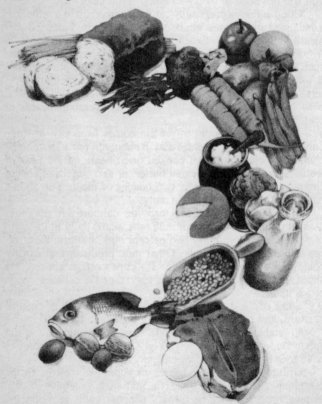

Good eating is a question of balance–daily meals with portions from each of the basic food groups: protein, milk and milk products, vegetables and fruits, and grain and grain products.

Grain and grain products provide thiamine, niacin, riboflavin, iron, phosphorus, and zinc. Whole-grain products provide more minerals than enriched breads and cereals, crackers, macaroni and spaghetti, tortillas, waffles, and pancakes. A normal serving is a slice of bread, a bowl of ready-to-eat cereal, or a half-cup of spaghetti. Include four servings a day in your diet.

THE IMPORTANCE OF PROTEIN
Of all the food groups, the most important to you and your growing baby is protein, whether consumed as meat, milk, or in vegetable form. Protein provides the actual building material for fetal tissues. The recommended daily intake is 80 to 100 grams.

Actually, most Americans—pregnant or not—probably consume sufficient amounts of protein in their diet, if it's balanced. You can assure yourself plenty of protein by eating two servings of meat and two eggs every day, plus the recommended quart of milk.

MILK FOR BONES AND TEETH
Milk and milk products furnish the minerals—especially calcium—that build your baby's bones and teeth. That's why you should sharply increase your intake of milk during pregnancy. Milk is the primary source of calcium, but it also provides other important nutrients, including proteins, carbohydrates, and vitamin A.

If you're not a milk drinker and find the consumption of a quart a day utterly unpalatable, there are trade-offs in the form of cheese, cottage cheese, and yogurt. You may substitute skimmed milk, buttermilk, low-fat milk, or diluted evaporated milk for the whole variety.

Remember, too, that you can use milk in cooking. Creamed soups, custards, and puddings or sauces are other ways to include milk. Ice cream can be substituted for milk, although it is more weight-producing. If you really "can't stand the taste of the stuff," add chocolate syrup or other flavoring to the milk. And remember, you're taking on additional calories.

You also might ask your obstetrician to prescribe calcium tablets as a partial substitute for milk, although some doctors feel that calcium in tablet form is less readily absorbed than it is in milk. Calcium tablets may be substituted in case you are allergic to milk.

In any case, milk is one of the key items in a pregnant woman's diet and should not be reduced or eliminated.

THE NUTRIENTS:
WHAT, WHY AND HOW

Nutrient	*Why we need it*	*Sources*
Protein	Builds and repairs all tissue; synthesizes hormones, antibodies, and enzymes; provides sources of energy (expensive and inefficient).	Plant: Legumes, nuts, cereal grain products. Animal: Meat, fish; poultry, eggs; milk and milk products.
Fat	Provides concentrated source of energy; carries fat-soluble vitamins (A, D, E, and K) and essential fatty acids.	Plant: Vegetable oil, margarine, salad dressings. Animal: Butter, fat meats; cream.
Carbohydrate	Provides economical and efficient sources of energy and fiber or roughage.	Plant: Cereal grain products, starchy vegetables, sugar, fruits. Animal: None

Important minerals

Calcium	Forms bone and teeth; clots blood; maintains muscle contractions.	Plant: Collards, kale; mustard greens; legumes. Animal: Milk and milk products, canned fish.
Iron	Forms hemoglobin; supplies various energy-producing enzyme systems.	Plant: Legumes, prune juice, leafy green vegetables. Animal: Liver, red meats (beef, pork, lamb).
Zinc	Maintains growth and reproductive functions; produces blood cells; promotes enzyme reactions.	Plant: Whole grain products. Animal: Shellfish, meats; liver, eggs.

Important vitamins/fat soluble

Vitamin A	Maintains mucous membranes and inner organs; enhances resistance to infections; promotes nerve and eye development.	Plant: Deep green and yellow-orange fruits and vegetables, margarine. Animal: Liver, egg yolk, butter.

Vitamin D	Facilitates absorption of calcium for strong teeth and bones.	Exposure to direct sunlight. Animal: Fortified milk and milk products, eggs, fish.
Vitamin E	Prevents oxidation of essential vitamins and fatty acids.	Plant: Vegetable oils, green leafy vegetables. Animal: None
Vitamin K	Maintains normal blood clotting and prevents hemorrhage.	Plant: Leafy greens, cereal grain products. Animal: None

Important vitamins/water soluble

Thiamin (B_1)	Promotes use of carbohydrates; provides energy and promotes good appetite and digestion.	Plant: Whole grain cereals; nuts, legumes. Animal: Meat, milk.
Riboflavin (B_2)	Maintains healthy skin and eye tissue; produces energy in cells.	Plant: Whole grain cereals, fortified grain products. Animal: Milk, fish, eggs, meat.
Niacin	Promotes use of carbohydrates; synthesizes fatty acids; maintains healthy nervous system; aids digestion and appetite.	Plant: Peanut butter, whole grain cereal, fortified cereals, leafy vegetables. Animal: Meat, poultry, fish.
Pyrodoxine (B_6)	Metabolizes protein; synthesizes hemoglobin.	Plant: Cereals, green leafy vegetables. Animal: Meats.
Folic acid (folacin)	Produces blood cells; sustains growth.	Plant: Leafy vegetables, fruits, soybeans. Animal: Liver, eggs.
Cobalamin (B_{12})	Produces blood cells; metabolizes energy; maintains functions of central nervous system.	Plant: None Animal: Meats.

| Ascorbic acid (C) | Forms connective tissues such as collagen; helps heal wounds and broken bones; metabolizes other important vitamins (folic acid, for example); maintains elasticity and strength of blood vessels. | Plant: Citrus fruits, dark green leafy vegetables, potatoes, broccoli, cabbage, tomatoes, cantaloupes, strawberries, peppers.
Animal: None |

VITAMINS AND SUPPLEMENTS

Your doctor may or may not prescribe daily doses of vitamins. Both you and the baby need vitamins, but your requirements will be satisfied if you follow a balanced diet like the one described above. However, some doctors prefer to play it safe and prescribe vitamin capsules, too.

An iron supplement is almost always required, however, because it's not readily available in most diets. Iron gives blood its red color and is an absolutely essential mineral, because it is used in the production of hemoglobin, the blood component that carries oxygen to the cells. A woman takes in iron in small amounts throughout her life and stores them in her tissues; the baby draws on this storehouse to build his or her own blood supply. Thus, you must take in much more iron during pregnancy. Some iron is present in foods like milk, meat, leafy vegetables, and fruit, but most doctors prefer to bolster this natural supply with an iron supplement.

Another supplement that may be prescribed is folic acid. This nutrient, found mainly in leafy vegetables and in vegetable sources of protein, helps to enrich the blood supply and prevent anemia. Some doctors prescribe a single capsule containing folic acid, other multiple vitamins, and iron.

WHAT YOU SHOULDN'T EAT

As a category, you should avoid "junk foods"—potato chips, pastries, candy, cookies, and other snacks that fill you up without providing nutrition. Occasional snacking isn't harmful, however. You also may find that certain foods make you uncomfortable because they produce gas that presses on the abdomen.

Fad diets should not be followed during pregnancy; indeed, some are downright dangerous. However, a vegetarian regimen including milk (lacto-vegetarian) is all right for both mother and fetus, provided sufficient protein is obtained in the choice of foods eaten.

SALT: NO LONGER A NO-NO

So long as your pregnancy is progressing normally, you can salt your food to taste, a marked departure from past obstetrical practice. Doctors formerly felt that salt caused the tissues to retain water, thus increasing the rate of complications. They urged that it be eliminated during pregnancy. Some doctors prescribed diuretics to flush the salt and other accumulated fluids from the tissues.

Another statement of the ACOG Committee on Nutrition reversed this position. Instead of a sodium-free diet, the committee said, women with a problem-free pregnancy should consume their normal amount of salt, because sodium is essential to the baby's development. The committee recommended the use of iodized salt, which provides the essential nutrient, iodine. If fluid does begin to accumulate or in cases of elevated blood pressure, the directive said, obstetricians then may wish to reduce salt intake.

For your kidneys' sake, drink fluids in addition to milk every day, especially if you substitute milk products for milk itself. Doctors differ on the recommended amount, but four glasses of water or soft drinks, or cups of tea or coffee are probably sufficient. Liquids must be increased to remove wastes, because the kidneys now function for both mother and fetus.

CHANGING YOUR EATING HABITS

Space your meals so you eat small amounts six times a day instead of three. You'll like this schedule better in early pregnancy when you may not feel like eating, and again in the final months when the growing baby presses on the digestive system and reduces your stomach's capacity. Try to eat the same quantity at each of the three main meals, and balance the size of the snacks the same way. Eating in the morning is important, even though you may not want to eat much. Experiment with different foods to vary your own breakfast menu.

The easiest way to follow a balanced diet is to include one food from each of the four basic groups at each major meal. Then you can choose one food from each of Groups 2, 3, and 4 for snacks.

Here, as recommended by the California Department of Public Health, is a sample one-day menu you might follow:

Breakfast:
½ cup orange juice
½ cup oatmeal with brown sugar
One cup milk (some of it on oatmeal)
Coffee or tea
Mid-morning snack:
1¼ ounces cheese and crackers
Lunch:
Tuna fish sandwich on whole wheat bread, with celery, lettuce, and mayonnaise to taste
A small banana or dish of prunes, figs, or other fruit
One cup milk
Afternoon snack:
An apple
⅔ cup cottage cheese

Dinner:
Three ounces lean roast beef
½ cup buttered noodles
¾ cup cut asparagus
Green salad made with spinach, sliced mushrooms, and radishes, with oil and vinegar dressing
½ cup milk
Coffee or tea
Evening snack:
Two oatmeal raisin cookies
½ cup milk

Avoid foods that fill you up but aren't nutritious (potato chips, pastries, candy). Snacking can be part of a regular daily menu: try cheese and crackers, cottage cheese, apples, oatmeal cookies, and milk.

RECORD WHAT YOU EAT

A daily food record can help you follow a balanced diet. Write in a notebook everything you eat, both by name and quantity, for two or three days. Carry the list in your purse so you can record lunches and snacks, too. Then evaluate in terms of the four food groups.

Don't worry if you can't always be precise about ingredients or amounts. But don't skip entries because the meal was not typical. If you keep the list for several days, unusual meals will average out and you'll get a balanced picture of your intake. Then, if you see your diet is deficient in some nutrients, make changes to bring it more in line with the recommendations.

CARING FOR YOUR APPEARANCE

Obviously, you want to look as attractive during pregnancy as when you're not pregnant. Some women are said to be never so beautiful as during the nine months of pregnancy. That's not automatic, however, and you probably won't always feel beautiful. Sometimes you'll feel large, lumpy, and unattractive; you'll despair of ever getting your figure back. Those feelings will pass, however. Your complexion and hair, at least, may be improved during pregnancy.

Under the effect of certain glandular secretions, your skin probably will become drier. If you ordinarily have an oily complexion, you'll have better skin tone, rosier hues, and softer skin. If your skin is normally dry, use more moisteners. Rarely, the secretions cause a skin irritation resembling acne. It can usually be dealt with by washing in warm water.

The amount of oil in your hair will decrease, too; the strands may become brittle and split, so you may need a daily shampoo to keep it fluffy and fresh. Your hair may become thinner, with less body; it may be time to change to a shorter, fuller cut. However, if you have oily hair ordinarily, the change may be a boon.

Brunettes may note certain changes in complexion. Because of stimulation of the cells governing skin pigmentation, brunettes may develop dark spots on the cheeks and forehead, even a tinge over the whole face, sometimes called "the mask of pregnancy." These changes may require additional makeup, but you can be reassured they will disappear after delivery. You may also find your facial contours changing. You may have a rounder, fuller face, calling for a different hairstyle or makeup.

ELASTIC PANEL

Your clothes will look good if they're simple, practical, and safe.
Maternity clothes should fit your changing appearance. A whole
wardrobe may be unnecessary; a few outfits will do nicely.

YOUR MATERNITY WARDROBE

Your choice of clothing should be governed by a few simple
rules: keep it simple, keep it practical, and keep it safe. Beyond
that, you'll want clothes that are loose and comfortable, clothes
that don't restrict you in any way.

You'll probably continue wearing your regular clothes until
some time during the fifth month, at which point they'll begin
feeling tight. Your new garments will have to allow for an expanding abdomen and for a waist that has all but disappeared.
Blouses and dresses will have to hang from the shoulders instead of being gathered at the waist.

You probably won't want to buy a closet full of maternity
clothes, especially if it's your first pregnancy, because they are
expensive and you'll wear them only a few months. But you'll

certainly want a few outfits for special occasions. Most cities have shops specializing in stylish maternity apparel. Also, department stores usually have maternity departments. If you plan to work throughout the pregnancy, you'll need more clothes than if you're staying home.

For casual wear, maternity clothes aren't necessary. An oversized shirt will serve as a top, or you can make do with an unbelted dress. You can cut the front out of an old pair of jeans or skirt and replace it with an elastic panel that will stretch as the baby grows. A wrap-around skirt can be worn during pregnancy, as can an unbelted jumper. In addition, a smock or tent dress also probably will fit your growing figure for the full nine months.

Maternity clothes come in the same sizes as street clothes. That is, a size 10 maternity dress is designed to fit a size 10 woman who happens to have a larger waistline. (You may, of course, need a bigger size if you've put on a lot of weight.) Most maternity clothes are designed to provide growing room for the developing baby, with tabs, elastic, or pleats for a better fit. Dark, solid colors usually are most attractive. You may want to pick designs with accents or touches at the shoulders or neckline to divert attention from your expanding waist.

Separates are usually your best bet in maternity clothes. You can choose from any number of shirts, blouses, tunics, and even T-shirts; all can be combined with skirts, jumpers, or pants. Many of them even can be worn after pregnancy. Look for slacks and jeans with a semicircular elastic panel at the waist to allow for expansion; they can be found in denim, corduroy, or linen and are both attractive and comfortable. Play outfits and even maternity bathing suits are also available. Essentially, you're limited only by your budget and taste. And if you can sew, a wide variety of patterns for both maternity dresses and blouses is available.

Underclothing must be chosen with care. It must not fit so tightly as to restrict circulation. You'll probably want snug underpants or briefs, but they should not limit blood flow in the legs. Panty girdles are taboo. A maternity girdle with an expanding panel is permissible if it has no reinforcing panels or stays. Avoid garter belts, garters, and stockings. Maternity pantyhose are good because they adapt to your movements and permit free circulation.

You'll probably wear a larger brassiere. If you regularly take a 34B, you may require a 36 or 38C by the end of the third month. Select a good bra, one that provides firm support but does not constrict the breasts nor press too hard on the nipples.

Pick shoes for comfort and safety. As your abdomen enlarges, you may lean backward and walk more flat-footed. The best shoes have a broad toe and a heel not more than an inch high. Any higher heel will cause you to pitch forward and teeter precariously. Shoes need a full back rather than a sling. Especially in late pregnancy, you may wish to purchase shoes a half-size larger, because your feet will have a tendency to swell late in the day. Avoid sneakers, ballet slippers, negative-heel shoes, flopping sandals, and shoes with slippery soles.

A PREGNANT WOMAN'S CHECKLIST

While you needn't act like an invalid during pregnancy, you should observe certain sensible precautions to ensure a safe pregnancy. Here are the most important:

1. Avoid anyone with a cold or other contagious diseases. Because a disease may be transmitted before a definite diagnosis can be made, stay away from anyone who seems to be coming down with an illness. Children's diseases are a particular hazard. Be especially careful if you have not been inoculated against rubella (German measles).

2. Get plenty of exercise—and also plenty of rest. Complicated calisthenics aren't necessary; simple walking will do. Follow a nutritious diet with plenty of good foods.

3. See your doctor at regular intervals, and notify him immediately of any unusual symptoms. Keep a close watch on yourself, and be aware of anything that seems untoward.

4. Continue your outside interests and develop new ones. Keep working as long as you feel up to it.

5. Learn all you can about pregnancy, childbirth, and child-bearing. There's no such thing as knowing too much about being a parent.

3

Minor Discomforts of Pregnancy

Some women sail through pregnancy and never feel better in their lives. Most, however, have brief, intermittent bouts of minor discomfort throughout the entire nine months—"a variety of aches and pains," one obstetrician has said, "throughout the area between the navel and the knees." Fortunately, such problems usually cure themselves or can be cleared up with simple treatment. A few rare, serious prenatal complications require a doctor's attention.

"MORNING SICKNESS"

Nausea early in the pregnancy isn't inevitable; and when it occurs, it is more a nuisance than a serious problem. Mild stomach upset and queasiness may occur at any time during the day; a few women have several episodes, morning and evening. The condition seems to be caused primarily by increased amounts of estrogen acting on the smooth muscles of the stomach and intestinal tract.

Ordinary morning sickness, even with occasional vomiting, doesn't require medical attention. It's simply one of those passing annoyances pregnant women put up with. But if you vomit persistently, be sure to tell your doctor.

There's no sure cure for morning sickness, although women (and doctors) have been seeking one for centuries. Some women cut down on eating, believing the less you put down, the less will come up. However, you'll probably feel better with some food in the stomach. Try eating six small meals during the day, rather than three full ones. (You may have little appetite, anyway.) Keep dry crackers on the night stand and eat them as soon as your eyes open, even before lifting your head from the pillow. (A glass of milk first thing in the morning may also help.) Stay in bed for 20 minutes after eating. Some women carry crackers in their purses to nibble on if they feel nauseous.

Change your diet to eliminate foods that are difficult to digest. Concentrate on starches—bread, crackers, potatoes, rice—and skip fried and fatty foods. Avoid butter, olive oil, and cream. Whole wheat toast and fruit are helpful, as are milk, tea, and carbonated beverages.

If your nausea occurs mostly in the morning, ask your doctor if you can take an antinauseant the night before. If the problem occurs later in the day, take the medicine as soon as you get up. Brief rest periods during the day also may help. Lie down or prop up your feet for 15 to 20 minutes after eating until the nausea passes.

GAS, HEARTBURN, AND INDIGESTION
In the early months of pregnancy, you may feel bloated and uncomfortable after eating, burp embarrassingly, and bring up a little sour-tasting fluid. You also may have heartburn, that hot sensation in the upper abdomen or lower chest. This discomfort probably isn't primarily a result of your diet. Like morning sickness, it results from estrogen secretion.

Antacids may bring you some relief. So may a half glass of milk or a level tablespoonful of milk of magnesia about a half hour before eating. Baking soda, the standard remedy for indigestion, usually is ruled out by doctors during pregnancy, because of the sodium content.

Just as you might for morning sickness, you can lessen the effects of heartburn and indigestion by reducing your consumption of foods that produce gas or are difficult to digest. Cut back on beans, onions, and fried foods in favor of fruits and juices. Drinking enough liquids also helps. In addition, regular exercise and good bowel habits can speed digestion.

VARICOSE VEINS
Swollen, painful veins in the legs occur because the growing uterus presses on the major arteries and veins serving the lower half of the body. Circulation slows; the blood pools. The veins must work harder to return the blood to the heart. Their walls stretch and swell, causing the unsightly and throbbing blotches.

Varicose veins are rare in first pregnancies, but the risk increases as each subsequent pregnancy further weakens the

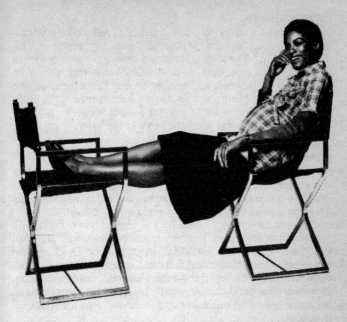

vein walls. The tendency appears to be inherited, and, fortunately, the problem does not afflict all women.

Presently, there are no methods to prevent varicose veins, but there are ways to gain relief. Support pantyhose, which look little different from ordinary pantyhose, reduce pressure and throbbing. Elastic stockings, put on before arising in the morning, may hold the swelling down. For severe cases, an elastic support bandage may be required. Start the bandage at the ankle, taking one or two turns around the instep and under the arch, then wind around the leg to just below the knee and fasten with a safety pin or special fastener. The bandage can easily be covered with hose, a leotard, or slacks.

Exercise is often a helpful treatment (or preventive) for varicose veins, too. Don't stand in one position for extended periods of time. Walk around to keep the blood flowing. Or lie on your back, feet in the air, and pump your legs as if you were riding a bicycle. Try to sit with your feet higher than your legs to speed the blood's return to the heart. If possible, lie down at intervals during the day.

HEMORRHOIDS

Another usually temporary consequence of reduced circulation in the lower part of the body is hemorrhoids, or "varicose veins of the rectum." The itching, enlarged veins may appear for the first time during pregnancy, or existing hemorrhoids may be aggravated by pregnancy. Constipation may make the condition painful. A diet of fruits and juices may help to relieve the problem, or ask your doctor to suggest a stool softener. Usually, hemorrhoids disappear after the birth of the baby.

CONSTIPATION AND IRREGULARITY

Bowel irregularity is most common in the early months, another consequence of increased estrogen. Irregularity usually is relieved by midpregnancy, only to return in the final months when the baby's head descends and presses on the bowel.

Proper diet, plenty of fluids, and regular bowel habits will help promote regularity. Follow a balanced menu,with plenty of fruits and vegetables, and drink more liquids. Drinking two glasses of water before breakfast often stimulates bowel action. A regular time for a bowel movement also reduces constipation. Mornings after breakfast are usually best, although this time can be inconvenient if you're working or have children to pack off to school.

Eating laxative foods may help. Such foods include prunes, raw, stewed, or in juice; figs, dates, or other stewed fruits; baked apples; oranges; and cereals or breads with a high fiber content. Eating fruit before retiring at night may help to establish a morning bowel movement.

A mild laxative or stool softener may be helpful. Never use laxatives, such as castor oil or enemas, without the doctor's consent.

BLEEDING AND VAGINAL DISCHARGE

A few women may have one or two episodes of slight vaginal bleeding after conception. These are usually of short duration and light flow, seldom lasting more than a day. A few women are said to "menstruate" throughout pregnancy, but such episodes are very rare. Any flow of blood from the vagina, no matter how scant, should be regarded as a possible danger signal. Report it to your doctor immediately.

Increased vaginal discharge is normal, however. Usually white or pale yellow in color, the discharge represents increased secretions of mucus from the glands of the cervix and walls of the vagina. It can be washed off, although you may wish to wear a pad to protect your clothes.

If the discharge is heavy, has an odor, or causes itching, it may represent a vaginal infection. There are several types of infections, each with a specific remedy. Report the condition to your doctor for examination and care.

ITCHY SKIN
About one pregnant woman in five develops an annoying itch in the abdominal area, especially during warm, humid weather. The itching seems to be related to increased hormonal secretion, as well as stretching of the skin. It may worsen as the pregnancy progresses and the abdomen enlarges and may be further irritated if you wear a girdle or other tight-fitting clothing.

Choose loose, nonrestrictive garments that allow the skin to "breathe" freely. Do not use lotions containing cortisone.

Abdominal itching is not related to itching around the vagina. If an irritation develops in the vaginal or anal area, see your doctor.

MUSCLE CRAMPS
Cramps in the calf, and sometimes in the thigh, occur in middle or late pregnancy. The reason is obscure. Sluggish circulation, the swaybacked maternity posture, and the amount of calcium in the diet may be causes. Shooting pains in the legs may occur during the final months of pregnancy when the baby's head presses on nerves in the pelvis that run down the back of the legs.

Massage is probably the best remedy. Hold the foot of the affected leg in your hands and bend it upwards, to tense the calf muscle. Rub the muscle itself with your hands. If the cramp persists, you can apply a heating pad or a hot-water bottle. Liniments and lotions aren't necessary, however. Shooting pains can sometimes be relieved by shifting position, or by lying on your back and drawing your knees toward your chest for a few minutes. A maternity girdle and low-heeled shoes may help correct your posture and prevent leg pains.

SWOLLEN FEET AND ANKLES
Your shoes may feel tight and your feet and ankles puffy in the last two months of pregnancy, especially if you're working at a job that requires you to sit in one position or stay on your feet all day. Again, the culprit is sluggish circulation. Fluid from the

pooled blood leaks into the tissue, causing a condition called edema.

Exercise won't prevent swelling, but it will lessen it. Continue your daily walks. When sitting, prop your feet as often as possible—the swelling will probably decrease within 15 minutes. You may find that it's worse at night and improved by morning. If, however, the swelling persists through the night and especially if your hands and face also swell, be sure to notify your doctor.

SHORTNESS OF BREATH

Late in pregnancy you may find yourself gasping and short of breath after even the slightest exertion. One explanation for this sensation may be the expanded uterus pressing on the lungs. Fortunately, the problem will be relieved just before delivery, when the baby sinks lower into the pelvis. Always choose straight-backed chairs instead of upholstered ones. Try to stand and walk straight. If you can't sleep because of shortness of breath, prop yourself with pillows into a half-sitting position.

Shortness of breath is normal, but if it becomes so severe that you cannot climb stairs without puffing heavily, notify the doctor.

CHANGES IN YOUR SKIN

Besides spots on the complexion and the so-called mask of pregnancy, other skin changes may take place. They include darkening of the nipples and the development of a dark vertical line on the abdomen between the navel and pubic hair. The facial changes usually disappear after delivery; the brown line may fade but never completely vanish.

Stretch marks—"striae"—are reddish, slightly depressed streaks on the lower abdomen and thighs. They result from tiny tears in the elastic layer beneath the skin as the abdomen stretches to accommodate the growing baby. The more weight you gain, the more the stretching. After delivery, the marks turn from red to white but do not disappear. The tendency to develop them seems to be hereditary. Stretch marks cannot be prevented, although bath oils and moisturizing lotions may keep the surrounding skin from drying out.

Vascular "spiders" are tiny red elevations radiating from a central point. They most commonly appear on the face, neck, upper chest, and arms and appear to be caused by high concentrations of estrogen. They normally disappear after delivery.

Regular exercise—walking, moderate jogging—may not prevent varicose veins or swollen ankles and feet, but such activity can help to relieve the discomfort they cause.

BACKACHE

Leaning backwards to compensate for a growing abdomen may cause chronic backache or a "catch" just below the waistline. You may get relief from massage or heat. To prevent it, wear a light maternity girdle and low-heeled shoes. Exercises learned in prenatal classes (see page 58) will also strengthen back muscles. Sleeping on a firm mattress also helps.

FOOD CRAVINGS

Folklore says you'll have sudden cravings for foods you don't ordinarily like and in odd combinations—pickles and ice cream, hot dogs, coconut, persimmons. So long as the cravings are infrequent and the choices don't interfere with a balanced diet, go ahead and satisfy them. Very rarely, some pregnant women have bizarre cravings to eat such substances as laundry starch or even dirt. This condition, called pica, should be reported to your doctor immediately.

DIZZINESS AND FAINTING

Dizziness and fainting are most common in the middle months of pregnancy. You are most vulnerable when you have been sitting or standing in one position for a long period, restricting the return of blood from the legs and feet.

If you feel faint, sit down immediately and place your head between your knees, so that it will be lower than the heart. Don't be embarrassed to do so even if you are in a public place. Remember, it is better to sit down than to fall down. Carry a bottle of aromatic spirits of ammonia in your purse, and use it if necessary.

Wearing support hose helps to stimulate circulation and so does regular exercise. If your job requires you to sit for long periods of time, pump your legs—as if you were riding a bicycle—before standing. If the fainting is frequent or if it is accompanied by blurred vision, be sure to tell your doctor.

CARE OF THE NIPPLES

About the fourth month of pregnancy, you may notice that a thick fluid, yellowish or whitish in color, called colostrum, has begun to drain from the nipples.

Drainage may continue throughout pregnancy, until milk begins to flow after birth. The substance is harmless, and if it cakes on the nipples, you may wish to wear pads inside your bra to protect your clothes.

Tender or sore nipples may be cared for by rubbing them

with a skin cream. If you plan to breast-feed your baby, you may wish to apply a special salve to toughen the nipples or stimulate them with massage. Your doctor can describe how to do this, or it may be taught in prepared childbirth classes, although many doctors consider either massage or salve unnecessary as a prelude to breast-feeding.

INSOMNIA AND OVERSLEEPING

Some women say they "slept their way through pregnancy." Most pregnant women do sleep more, especially in the early months. Your nightly slumber may stretch from eight to nine hours, and you may also find that you want to take an afternoon nap.

By contrast, in late pregnancy sleep may not come easily. The baby's movements, muscle cramps, breathing difficulties, and the frequent need to urinate may combine to keep you awake. A short walk before retiring, a warm shower, a glass of warm milk or cocoa may help you fall asleep more quickly. If insomnia persists, tell your doctor. Do not take sleeping medications unless prescribed.

MOOD SWINGS

You may have intermittent changes of mood during pregnancy—one day high, the next down in the dumps. On Monday you may feel overjoyed at the prospect of motherhood; on Tuesday you may feel depressed at how the baby will change your life. Some days you may feel big, cumbersome, and ugly; other days you may think that you have never felt so well and looked so enthusiastically to the future.

To some extent these moods have a hormonal basis; the increased secretion of estrogen and progesterone may be the cause of metabolic changes. Hormones notwithstanding, such swings are psychologically normal. Most women experience ambivalent feelings about motherhood—wanting children and the maternal role, while at the same time being aware of how profoundly different everything will be. Too, the relationship between husband and wife undergoes a change or changes during pregnancy and thereafter. Fathers, like mothers, are ambivalent about parenthood, with its added financial and ethical responsibilities. Their relationship may deepen, enrich, and strengthen, but it is definitely not the same as before.

It's common during pregnancy to laugh one minute and cry the next. These mood swings will pass. Still, it is best to discuss your feelings with someone—your doctor, your husband, a friend. You may find your worries less troublesome than you thought. Don't be upset if there are times when you wish you'd never become pregnant—it's a normal reaction to a normal event, and one that normally ends happily.

THINGS THAT WON'T HAPPEN

There are still many old fears and old wives' tales about pregnancy. Here are a few you may have heard and that appear to have no basis:

• The odor of paint will *not* cause a miscarriage. That may have been true when paints had a higher lead content, but it is not true today.

• Raising your hands over your head (to hang clothes or reach a high shelf, for example) will *not* tie a knot in the baby's umbilical cord.

• Seven-month babies are *not* more likely to survive than eight-month babies; the closer to term a baby is born, the greater the chances for his or her survival.

• A "dry" labor is *not* longer nor is it harder than a labor that begins with the bag of waters intact.

• You can't "mark" your baby by your behavior during pregnancy. Listening to music for nine months won't make your child a musician, nor will a sudden fright, or attending a funeral bring forth a terrified or grieving child.

IF YOU'RE OVER 35

Most women give birth for the first time in their teens or 20s, and their families are complete before they are 30. But the average age of a first-time mother is steadily rising. Many women do not have their first child until their mid' or late 20s, and an increasing number are past 30, or even 35.

With good medical supervision; there is no reason to fear a pregnancy at this age. You may require closer attention than a younger mother, but the pregnancy can be equally safe. Labor and delivery may be a little longer if this is your first baby. One study shows that first-time mothers 35 years or older labor 1½ to four hours longer than younger first-time mothers.

There are certain risks to motherhood when you're over 35. The older mother is more likely to bear twins. And the possibility of conceiving a child with Down's Syndrome, or mongolism, increases with age, being markedly higher at age 45 than 35. For this reason, your doctor may recommend a prenatal procedure called amniocentesis (see page 81) to determine whether this problem exists.

THE DANGER SIGNALS IN PREGNANCY

Most problems of pregnancy can wait to be reported to your doctor during your next visit.

Some symptoms can indicate an emergency and should be reported immediately. You should be sure to notify your doctor if any of the following occur:

1. Any bleeding or bloody discharge that comes from the vagina.
2. Fever of 100 degrees Fahrenheit or more, not accompanied by a common cold.
3. Severe nausea with vomiting more than three times in an hour.
4. Swelling of the hands and face, especially if it is sudden.
5. Dimness or blurring of vision, especially if you see spots or wavy lines before your eyes.
6. Strong abdominal pains that are not relieved by a bowel movement.
7. Continuous, severe headache.
8. A sudden rush or trickle of water that comes from the vagina.
9. Very frequent urination that is accompanied by burning.
10. Any accident, hard fall, or other trauma.

HOW TO CALL YOUR DOCTOR

When you phone your doctor, make sure you get the most from the call. Follow these steps:

1. If possible, call during office hours, when records are available to the staff. Report your condition to the nurse, who may be able to answer your questions or check for instructions; if the nurse can't help, leave a message for the doctor to call back.
2. Always give your full name (there may be two Mrs. Joneses), the date when you last visited the doctor, and the stage (in months) of your pregnancy.
3. Make the call yourself if possible; relaying information through your husband or a friend can lead to troublesome delay, confusion, and misinformation.
4. Describe your problem in the most specific terms possible. How much blood is being passed? More than a heavy menstrual period? Lighter? Continuous or intermittent? How long have you felt nauseous? How many times have you vomited within an hour? Specific details will help your doctor to prescribe a treatment for the problem.
5. Keep a pencil and paper near the telephone to write down the doctor's instructions. Don't trust your memory at a time when you are not feeling well.
6. Be sure you know the name, address, and phone number of your pharmacy, so you will not have to look them up if the doctor wishes to prescribe medicine.

PRENATAL EXERCISES

*Regular exercise before birth will make your delivery easier and help
you to feel better in the meantime. The exercises on these pages,
adapted from childbirth-education classes, offset the fatigue of
pregnancy and strengthen the muscles used in labor. Begin about the
fifth or sixth month, and continue until delivery.*

Breast support

Exercise in the tailor position
offsets round-shouldered posture
and pain in the upper back caused
by heavier breasts and a larger
abdomen; it also helps to open
lungs and make breathing easier.
Sit on floor in tailor, or Indian,
fashion—legs bent at the knees
and tucked under you. Lift arms
to shoulder height directly in front
of you. Rotate arms to side, then
extend directly overhead. Return
to original position. For variation,
extend right arm to full length
overhead, until you can feel the
muscles stretch along right side
from shoulder to hip. Repeat for
the left side. Do the exercise 20
times on each side, then return to
original position. The exercise
may be performed daily during the
middle months of pregnancy.

General stretch

Muscle tone, hip and knee joints, and lower back all benefit from this general loosening-up exercise. Lie on floor, knees bent, feet flat. Inhale. As you exhale, draw your knee toward your chest as far as you can over the expanding abdomen, inhale, straighten knee, stretch leg, and flex ankle. Then exhale and lower straightened leg until the foot is a few inches off the floor. Return to starting position, then repeat exercise with other leg. Do this exercise five times on each side at the beginning of your daily exercise period.

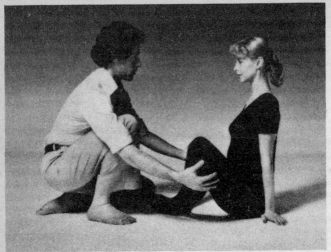

Thigh strengthener

This exercise husband and wife can do together helps strengthen the important inner thigh muscles that help the mother push during natural delivery. It also reduces fatigue if the mother's feet must be elevated in stirrups during delivery. Wife sits on the floor with knees bent, soles of feet pressed against each other. Husband kneels opposite, placing hands under wife's knees. Wife slowly pushes knees toward floor against resistance of husband's hands and holds position for a count of five. The exercise may also be done alone, with woman placing her own hands under her knees.

Thigh strengthener: a variation

In a variation of the thigh strengthener, sit on floor with legs extended in "V" position. Raise arms to shoulder height. Stretch slowly forward from the waist, keeping arms parallel to the floor. Don't try to touch the toes. Repeat exercise.

Thigh strengthener: another variation

Another way to strengthen inner thighs is to sit on the floor with legs outstretched in "V" position. Extend arms to the sides as high as shoulders. Raise left arm directly overhead. Bending from the waist, reach with the right hand toward right foot, grasping the arch if possible, the ankle or calf if arch is beyond your reach. Hold this position for a count of five, then return to original position. Repeat the exercise to left side, with your right arm extended over your head.

"Kegel" or pelvic-floor exercises

This simple exercise, at right, improves control of pelvic-floor muscles, which must be consciously relaxed during delivery.

Begin this exercise by sitting on the floor Indian fashion or with soles of feet together, keeping back straight. Relax the muscles of the genital area as if urinating. Slowly tighten the muscles and hold for a count of five. It may help to think of your muscles as an elevator: bring them slowly to the third floor, then back down. Then take the elevator to the basement, and return it to ground level.

Exercises to promote good circulation

Exercises to improve circulation are important late in pregnancy, to offset swollen feet and ankles.

Begin by sitting with back straight, legs extended. Lift the left leg, knee bent, and support it with hands behind your thighs. Alternately flex the foot backward from the ankle as far as possible, and point it forward. Flex and point 50 times with each foot, then rotate each ankle 25 times to the left and then 25 times to the right.

For a variation of this exercise, lie on the floor with a pillow under the ankles. While pointing with the left, flex the right foot 50 times. Change, and repeat exercise 50 times. Then rotate ankles 50 times—25 times to the left, 25 to the right for each ankle. Exercise should be performed morning and evening during final months of pregnancy.

In the lying position for the pelvic tilt, at right, lie on your back with the bent knees together and feet flat on the floor. Inhale and relax. Then exhale and push the small of your back toward the floor, causing the pelvis to rotate. To be fully effective, this pelvic exercise should be performed daily during the final months of pregnancy.

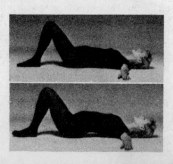

Pelvic tilt (or "rock")

This basic prenatal exercise is designed to build the back muscles, which are stretched and easily tired by the forward lean caused by the expanding abdomen.

In the "table" position, right, hands should be under the shoulders, knees under hips, with back straight. Inhale. Then exhale while arching back upward. Repeat this exercise ten times.

In the pelvic tilt exercise from a sitting position, below, sit against a wall, with your legs extended in front. Inhale. As you exhale, flatten the back against the wall, which will rotate the pel-vis forward. Relax, then repeat the exercise. The pelvic tilt also provides better support for the baby within the uterus and strengthens the mother's abdominal muscles.

4

A Time for Decisions

Each generation seems to have a different philosophy about the events leading up to that final glorious moment of childbirth. When your mother was having children, the ideal childbirth was painless and perfunctory. A woman was sedated during labor and woke up with a baby in her arms. Trusting that "doctor knows best," she left major decisions to the obstetrician.

This attitude still prevails among some women, some doctors, and in some places. But a great many other women seek greater participation and fulfillment in what is certainly a momentous event in their lives. Thus, you'll probably want a voice in where and how the birth takes place, who'll be there with you, and whether you'll be conscious to feel and watch it. Furthermore, you probably want doctors and hospitals to respect and be guided by your wishes.

These important decisions should be made early—not at the last minute on the way to the hospital. Fortunately, you'll have plenty of help in making them. Hospitals and other groups in almost every city now offer childbirth preparation classes where you can learn about the birth process, delivery techniques, and how to deal with pain. Such prenatal instruction groups will gladly furnish details on their particular methods or philosophy. And talk to your doctor—you'll find today's obstetricians more sensitive to your views. Your obstetrician may not agree with all your suggestions, but he or she will take time to discuss them, tell you why they make sense (or why they do not), and offer sound, practical advice.

THE ROLE OF THE FATHER

Today, the father has something to say about these decisions, too. Childbirth can no longer be considered exclusively a woman's domain. Both parents have an equal stake in bringing a pregnancy to a successful conclusion, just as they had in its beginning. All of the many decisions about bringing a life into the world should be arrived at jointly.

The concept of involved fatherhood is widely encouraged by doctors and hospitals. No longer is father restricted to passing out cigars and paying the bills. He has a place at your side, providing encouragement and support during pregnancy, labor, and delivery. Some hospitals insist that he have childbirth education right along with you.

Most, but not all, fathers like the idea of being included. Regardless, such matters as the use of pain relievers and their effects on you and the infant, and the father's presence in the delivery room should be brought out and fully discussed beforehand. Remember that pregnancy and childbirth are a time of stress for both parents. While you are preoccupied with your pregnancy, it's easy for the father to feel left out. The least stressful pregnancies are those that grow from mutual cooperation and responsibility—themes that cement the relationship, rather than the separation.

A VISIT TO THE HOSPITAL

Now's the time to select the hospital where you plan to deliver the baby. Usually, your choice is limited by your obstetrician's practice, although some doctors have staff privileges at more than one hospital. Discuss with your doctor his or her—and your—preference. If you're working and haven't time to visit the hospital, the doctor's staff may be able to handle necessary details before you can be admitted. You and your husband should visit the hospital about the fifth month of pregnancy, when an approximate date for your admission can be established. The main purpose of the visit is to register and reserve a bed based on a doctor's prediction of when you'll be hospitalized.

Your first stop will be the admitting office. Here you'll provide basic information about yourself, so that it won't be necessary to repeat the process when you arrive for the delivery. The hospital will want to know name, address, telephone, occupation, a limited personal and family medical history; you'll be asked your religious preference and your blood may be typed. You may also be asked to make a cash deposit or provide evidence of hospitalization insurance.

Usually, your pre-admission interview will be conducted by a member of the hospital staff. Take this opportunity to ask about certain hospital policies. (You'll want to discuss them with your doctor beforehand, too.) Among questions you may wish to ask:

1. May my husband remain with me during all stages of labor?

2. May he be present in the delivery room?

3. May photographs be taken during the birth? Are there any special rules to follow?

4. What, if any, alternative birth methods are available?

5. Will the hospital respect my wishes about alternative birth methods?

6. May my baby remain in the room with me after birth?

7. May other children, friends, or relatives visit me in the hospital and see the new baby?

Even if you're planning a conventional delivery, be sure to ask if certain specialized childbirth facilities (described below) are available. You may want to avail yourself of some features without taking advantage of the entire package. Also, ask to see the maternity ward, to look at labor and delivery rooms (if possible), patients' quarters, and the nursery. Some hospitals offer regular tours, along with an orientation for future patients. If you haven't already done so, now is a good time to ask if the hospital offers prenatal classes for parents.

You'll probably be pleasantly surprised to find the hospital more flexible—and more cheerful—than you anticipated. And so long as your obstetrician approves and your pregnancy is considered normal, with minimum risks, the hospital will probably try to accommodate any sort of delivery you suggest. You'll probably find a welcome attitude and a desire to serve.

Stung by criticisms of traditional maternity service, many hospitals have established what they call Family-Centered Maternity Care. Birth is treated as a natural, rather than a medical, happening and is conducted in a homelike, rather than an antiseptic, environment. The traditional attitude that you're a patient and not a guest is kept to a minimum and your wishes followed just so long as your own and your baby's health aren't jeopardized.

NEIGHBORHOOD BIRTH CENTERS

In the neighborhood birth center, you will find a kind of halfway house between hospital and home, combining the cozy casualness of a residence with the reserve medical facilities needed for an emergency. Reserved for low-risk patients, these centers are patterned after institutions that have operated successfully for centuries in certain European countries. Most are situated in big-city neighborhoods and function as satellites of larger hospitals.

Delivery in a birth center is usually conducted by a nurse-midwife, often with an obstetrician standing by. The father is encouraged to be present and to help in the delivery if he wishes. Drugs and medical equipment aren't used routinely but are available if needed. Afterward, you're taught how to care for the baby. You may be allowed to go home with the new baby the same day as delivery.

ALTERNATIVE BIRTH CENTERS

The whole family takes part in the birth in an alternative birth center. This concept, spreading rapidly, transfers the home atmosphere into the hospital itself. You and your family are housed in a special hospital room that resembles a hotel suite. There's usually a double bed, sleeping space for the children, cooking facilities, a television set, phonograph; and other amenities. Children are urged to bring their toys and games and act as if they were at home.

A few steps away, however, is an intensive-care nursery and a standard delivery room, ready for use in case they're necessary. You can be whisked out of the room in seconds if complications arise. All the hospital facilities and staff are available to you. The room itself has limited backup equipment, including facilities for anesthesia and an oxygen supply.

In an uncomplicated birth, both labor and delivery take place in the room. You'll be under the care of a nurse or nurse-midwife, who will remain with you throughout labor. Your private obstetrician or the nurse-midwife may deliver the baby, as you prefer. While you're waiting, you can get up and move around or even have guests. The father-to-be also will be invited to participate in the process and to be at your bedside throughout labor. Or you may ask a friend to serve as labor "coach" and to assist in the birth. The other children may gather around the bed, although most hospitals ask that there be an adult present who is charged exclusively with caring for the children.

Following the delivery, the baby remains in the room. A nurse stays to assist and provide a short course in baby care. The whole family, including the newborn, can go home within 48 hours and sometimes on the same day.

HOME BIRTH VERSUS HOSPITAL BIRTH

One important question you'll need to answer early is whether the baby *should* be born in a hospital or in your own home. Even five years ago, the idea of giving birth at home probably wouldn't have occurred to you. Ninety-five percent of babies were born in hospitals, and the proportion was rising. Recently, the trend has reversed itself slightly. Births at home are still few in number, but they are growing, even though the practice is restricted in some states.

In a home birth, you should be under the care of a nurse-midwife, who is trained to handle routine obstetrical deliveries. She should be affiliated with a nearby hospital or work under the supervision of an obstetrician. (Sometimes, obstetricians themselves make the delivery.) The midwife arrives when labor begins and remains with you until the baby is delivered. In the event of an emergency or other than routine delivery, she will summon help from the affiliated hospital. Afterward, she helps you care for the baby until you can take over yourself.

The argument for home birth is that nine of ten deliveries are normal and uncomplicated—and advocates say the rare complication can usually be identified well in advance, in time to transfer the mother to a medical facility. Proponents insist the vast (and expensive) facilities of a hospital aren't needed in most cases. Worse, they say, the hospital atmosphere is often cold, impersonal, and frightening. Nurses may be too busy to provide individual attention, leaving mothers alone and tense. By contrast, at home with a nurse-midwife, a woman gets one-on-one care in a relaxed surrounding.

Medical studies done in Europe, where home births are more common, and at least one U.S. study appear to show that complications are no more frequent in home than in hospital birth—at least when cases are identified as low risk in advance. The American College of Obstetricians and Gynecologists (ACOG), however, opposes the practice of home delivery. The ACOG says the most serious emergencies during childbirth arise very quickly, often with little warning, and the immediate medical backup of a hospital is needed to deal with them.

ROOMING-IN

In many hospitals, your newborn can now live in your room, in a bassinet beside your bed, almost from the time of delivery. He or she needn't stay in a nursery down the hall to be brought to you only at feeding time. With rooming-in, you can feed, care, and get to know the baby on your own terms.

Rooming-in arrangements vary from hospital to hospital. Some require that the practice be limited to daylight hours, especially if several women share a room. The baby remains in the nursery at night, under the observation of the nursing staff. You may actually prefer this arrangement because it lets you get more rest and gives the nurses time to spot any problems.

If this is your first baby, you'll find rooming-in an important learning experience. A nurse will spend much of the first day with you, demonstrating how to care for the baby. Under her supervision, you'll sponge-bathe the baby, change diapers, and put the baby to bed in the bassinet. She'll also help you to begin breast-feeding (if you choose this method). A major advantage to rooming-in is that you can feed the baby at your (and the baby's) convenience, rather than at a rigid feeding time.

Another advantage for a first-time mother is that rooming-in helps build confidence. You get practice caring for the baby under experienced supervision, so you're almost a veteran by the time you get home.

Too, in many hospitals the father also may participate in rooming-in care, so that he, too, gets the kind of training that will be helpful later on when the baby comes home.

FAMILY VISITING

A growing number of hospitals now permit other children in the family to visit you and see their new brother or sister in the nursery. They usually must be accompanied by another adult, and they're not permitted to hold the baby. The length of time family members may stay is also limited. In many hospitals, the father can usually visit any time he chooses. If you have a private room, he may be permitted to sleep in the hospital overnight.

IN THE LABOR AND DELIVERY ROOMS

Labor and delivery aren't something you have to go through alone, as they used to be. Now, with your obstetrician's permission, many hospitals permit your husband to remain with you throughout labor and during delivery, to provide help and support and to coach you in breathing exercises—and to share in the triumphant moment of birth. Some hospitals even permit him to watch a cesarean delivery. An additional person, such as a prepared-childbirth instructor or friend or relative, may also be permitted to watch the delivery.

Natural-light photography also may be permitted in the labor and delivery rooms, so that you have a permanent record of the happy event. The use of floodlights and flash is usually prohibited because of the very slight danger of excessive heat or anesthetic explosion touched off by a spark. The American Society for Psychoprophylaxis in Obstetrics (ASPO), the leading prepared-childbirth organization, has suggested that this danger is remote and more hospitals should allow delivery room photography. Any danger is almost nonexistent using modern equipment and fast film, ASPO says.

Ask your local camera dealer for advice whether you use black-and-white or color film. The special "spotlight" used in hospital delivery rooms, combined with fluorescent lighting and perhaps even daylight, may necessitate the use of special filters. Well in advance, check with the hospital about the lighting.

Like the captain of a ship, however, your obstetrician will be the person who has the final say over who's on board. Whether visitors (or photography, for that matter) are allowed in the labor room is considered to be a medical question, and the doctor usually reserves the right to clear the room or prohibit spectators in case of emergency.

CLASSES FOR PROSPECTIVE PARENTS

Childbirth education grew out of the natural-childbirth movement, but prenatal classes will benefit you regardless of the delivery method you choose. Many obstetricians strongly recommend that prospective mothers and fathers take these classes as a means of preparing themselves for the labor and delivery process.

If your hospital doesn't offer classes as part of its prenatal service, you may find them at a local YWCA, adult education center, or community college. You usually take six classes, beginning with the seventh month of pregnancy. (A few places also offer early-bird courses, so you can practice special breathing and relaxation techniques even further ahead of time.) Both mothers and fathers attend, usually in groups of about 20. The teacher is a specially trained childbirth education instructor.

The philosophy of childbirth education stresses learning about labor and how to deal with it so you can overcome many of the fears associated with the process. It is said women fear labor because they have been convinced it is painful. Thus, when contractions start, you grow tense, hold your breath, and fight back. This starts a vicious circle. The tighter you grit your teeth, the stronger the pain becomes and the more difficult the labor. To carry through the whole process most effectively, you must relax and breathe normally.

Childbirth preparation fosters a different attitude, advocates say. Once you've learned what's happening to your body during labor, you're able to see the experience positively—each contraction a step forward, advancing the moment when your baby will be born. Labor will no longer be a series of pains to be endured; you'll look forward to the next contraction with anticipation, not dread. And you'll want to help in the birth process, rather than fight against it. Trained to relax and work with your contractions, you'll want to forgo drugs that might dim your sensations and perception of delivery and prevent you from full participation in it.

Classes usually include the basic lessons in the anatomy and physiology of conception and labor, followed by instruction in breathing techniques and exercises to help with the labor. In the most common, the ASPO method, the following techniques are taught:

1. Relaxation, to reduce tension and permit your body to function at maximum efficiency.

2. Breathing geared to the phase of labor and aimed at teaching you to concentrate on breathing and thus reduce the perception of discomfort.

3. Abdominal exercises to help you "push" and deliver more efficiently.

4. Physical exercises designed to prepare the body for birth.

5. Instruction for a birth "coach" or partner, usually the father.

"BREATHING" EXERCISES

Proper breathing makes labor and delivery easier. Breathing exercises can be learned by enrolling in a childbirth education class. Four types of breathing are learned, corresponding to the various stages of labor. Husbands learn the exercises to coach their wives. Start exercises six weeks before due date.

Start breathing exercises from one of three basic positions:

1. Lie on back, two pillows under head, one under knees.

2. Lie on stomach, with head lower than abdomen, pillows under head, legs, abdomen.

3. Sit comfortably in chair, legs relaxed, knees bent.

Exercise 1 teaches breathing for early labor. Wife lies on back, husband kneels alongside. At his cue, "Contraction begins," she inhales deeply and exhales in a long "cleansing breath." She then begins rhythmic breathing from the chest—in through the nose, out through the mouth. The husband (or a labor "coach") times the breaths. When a rhythm of six to nine breaths per minute is achieved, the partner starts abdominal massage. Placing his cupped hands on her abdomen just above the pubic bone, he brings fingertips upward along the sides

f the abdomen, across the waistline to the midpoint, and then down the center of the abdomen to the starting point, timing the upward stroke to the inhale, downward to exhale. Massage continues until husband signals that contraction has ended, about one minute.

Exercise 2 for well-established labor, may be performed either on the back or in a sitting position. A deep, cleansing breath is followed by rapid, shallow breathing in the throat, chest barely moving; practice until it can be done for one minute. In the second stage, take a cleansing breath, then take shallow breaths at a slow rate. At the cue, "accelerate," gradually increase to rapid rate, hold pace for 30 seconds, then "decelerate." Follow with a cleansing breath.

Massage may be added, timed to the breathing rate.

Exercise 3 is for transitional labor, the period of actual delivery. On back or in a sitting position, take a cleansing breath, then follow with rapid, panting breaths—four to eight in succession—steady exhaling, followed by blowing out, as if trying to extinguish a candle. Follow the first sequence with a second pant-blow sequence, and continue for 60 seconds. Practice three times daily for four or five "contractions" of 60 to 90 seconds each.

Exercise 4 is for pushing, as the mother voluntarily helps the baby come into the world. In the sitting position, couple this exercise with the pelvic-floor exercise (see pages 61–62). Inhale and exhale normally; follow each exhalation by forcing the remaining air from lungs, while contracting the abdominal muscles and those of pelvic area. Hold for several seconds; take a deep, cleansing breath; relax; then begin exercise again.

NATURAL AND PREPARED CHILDBIRTH

Childbirth with a minimum of medication is better for you and the baby; it enables you to remain fully conscious and perceive the whole experience unhindered. Here are the most popular methods:

The Lamaze Method of Prepared Childbirth was originated in the Soviet Union by disciples of Ivan Pavlov. It was refined by a French obstetrician, Dr. Ferdinand Lamaze, and has become widespread in the U.S. during the past 15 years through the efforts of the American Society for Prophylaxis in Obstetrics (ASPO). ASPO prefers the phrase "prepared childbirth" to "natural childbirth," which the group thinks gives mothers the idea they can't have medication if they wish or require it. If the techniques are followed, however, medication frequently is not needed. Instead, discomfort is overcome by breathing, relaxation, and dissociation techniques.

Four types of breathing are taught:

• Deep-chest breathing is used in the early stages of labor. It consists of a deep, cleansing breath, taken in through the nose until the lungs swell and the abdomen rises, then exhaled through the mouth. Deep-chest breathing should be timed to coincide with contractions, which may be up to 60 seconds long. The breathing rate then should be about six per minute.

• Shallow, accelerated breathing is used as the contractions

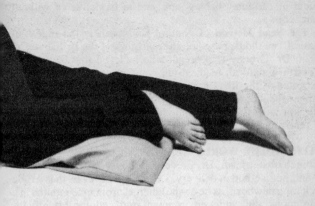

become more intense. It begins with deep breathing, followed by short, shallow breaths from the chest only. They should be fast, light, effortless, in through the nose and out through the mouth. As the contraction subsides, the pace of breathing should be slowed, followed by a deep breath.

• Panting is used when the delivery is imminent and enables the woman to hold or resist the urge to push until the appropriate time—usually when the doctor asks. Breaths are taken in and out through the mouth, in a regular panting rhythm. Exhaling should be forceful but not too forceful—like blowing out a candle. After the urge to push has abated, return to deep breathing.

• Expulsion or delivery breathing is used during pushing. It consists of two slow, deep breaths, followed by a push. During the push, the breath is held as long as possible, after which another deep breath is taken. Pushing is done only during a contraction.

The Bradley Method of Natural Childbirth differs from the Lamaze method in that it stresses abdominal (deep) breathing and teaches the woman to focus on what is happening during labor, instead of dissociating herself from it. The method, named for Dr. Robert Bradley, a Colorado obstetrician, stresses that discomfort is more tolerable when a woman participates in the whole birth process. Bradley followers also say that the woman must be totally prepared, mentally and physically, for pregnancy and delivery. Thus, Bradley also has a more intensive program of classes, beginning in the early months of pregnancy, including nutrition and exercise as well as breathing techniques. About 95 percent of "Bradley babies" are said to be delivered without medication.

The Read Method of Natural Childbirth is the oldest of "natural" methods, based on the teachings of the British obstetrician, Dr. Grantly Dick-Read, who believed that because all childbirth is natural, medical intervention should be minimal. Advocates of the Read method stress education, believing the mother will favor natural delivery once she understands what the natural process is. The Read method also emphasizes breathing and relaxation as an alternative to pain-reducing medication.

ENTERING THE WORLD GENTLY

A French obstetrician, Dr. Frederic Leboyer, is responsible for still another method of delivery. Leboyer believes birth is a rude shock for a newborn, as he or she emerges from nine months in a warm, moist, dim, quiet environment into a cooler, brightly lit, delivery room full of bustle and noise—where the baby may be immediately slapped to begin breathing independently.

The Leboyer method, therefore, recommends the delivery room be kept at warm temperatures, lighting be subdued, and medical personnel speak in hushed voices. Immediately after birth, the baby is placed on the mother's chest for the reassuring bond of skin-to-skin contact, then cleansed in a warm bath that simulates the prenatal environment. The father often does the bathing. The baby is handled gently and is allowed to begin breathing spontaneously.

Usually, the harsh lights over the delivery table are dimmed and the air conditioning turned down considerably to allow the room temperature to rise. Leboyer disciples say a baby born under these circumstances is much more alert and aware of his or her surroundings.

Medically, the most controversial aspect of Leboyer's recommendations is that the umbilical cord, the baby's lifeline throughout the first nine months of life, not be cut until it has stopped pulsating—usually a period of approximately five minutes. Normally, the cord is clamped within 60 to 90 seconds.

Many other Leboyer techniques have been adopted in part by hospitals. And although many doctors were vehemently opposed to the methods recommended by Leboyer when they were first proposed, delivery room personnel report that gentle handling in a quiet atmosphere does seem to produce a calm, alert baby.

PAIN AND PAIN-KILLERS

Probably, you'll want to limit the use of pain-reducing drugs and anesthetics during labor and delivery. A growing number of women now wish to remain fully conscious, alert, and in command of themselves throughout childbirth, so they can see, feel, and recall every aspect of the experience. Many parents are concerned, too, about the possible effects of drugs and anesthetics on mother and baby. In some hospitals, as many as 50 percent of deliveries are conducted totally without medication, and in many other births only mild pain-reducing agents or local anesthetics are used.

But pain is individual. Indeed, if you brought five women together to describe it, you'd probably hear five different descriptions. There is pain associated with labor—after all, that's how nature tells you that a new life is on the way. But how much discomfort you'll personally feel is impossible to predict. And the amount of pain one woman can tolerate cheerfully, another may find utterly unbearable. Indeed, the discomfort you felt when you delivered an earlier child may not be felt during this delivery.

There's another aspect, too, expressed by the American College of Obstetricians and Gynecologists (ACOG). "Pain relief during labor and delivery is an important aspect of modern obstetrics," states a technical bulletin published by the ACOG. "It consists of more than providing personal comfort to the mother; it is a necessary part of good obstetrical practice. Thoughtfully chosen analgesia (pain-reducing agents) can improve labor and proper anesthesia permits difficult deliveries to be accomplished with safety."

Thus, keep an open mind about pain relief. However much you want to avoid drugs and anesthetics, remember that childbirth isn't an endurance contest. If during your labor, the pain seems too great—and only you can be the judge of that—it's better to ask for relief than to go on grimly enduring what seems unendurable. And if your doctor suggests that analgesia or anesthesia might smooth the delivery, hear him or her out and respect the opinion. Remember, many healthy babies were born and enjoyed in the days when their mothers were completely anesthetized. Perhaps you may have been one of them yourself.

EFFECTS ON THE BABY

But will analgesia or anesthesia harm you or your baby? The answer is that no one knows precisely—so the tendency is to play it safe. Drugs given to the mother cross the placental barrier and reach the fetus. Some depress the baby's heart rate—although the lasting effects of the depression, if any, are not known. Some doctors say that babies born to mothers given even mild medication are sluggish and not fully alert for several days after birth. Others believe drugs may cause subtle nerve damage that may not appear for years, but their opinion has been strongly challenged. For all these reasons, however, a committee of the American Academy of Pediatrics has stated that in childbirth, probably less medication is better, and none may be best of all.

It's pointed out reassuringly, however, that millions of babies have been born to sedated mothers, and widespread effects have not been detected.

A DIRECTORY OF DRUGS

What help you'll receive for pain, if any, will depend on the circumstances of your labor and delivery. Here are the most common:

Tranquilizers don't relieve pain, but they may ease the anxiety and tension some women feel during contractions. If administered, they're usually offered early in labor.

Barbiturates may be given to bring on sleep if labor is prolonged. They do not affect pain and may slow the breathing of both mother and baby; several days may be required for the baby to overcome their effects.

Demerol, the commercial name for meperidine, is a well-known pain killer used in many situations other than labor. It is said to be given to as many as 50 percent of women during the first stage of labor. Demerol reduces pain but leaves you conscious and able to participate in labor. Its use may depress the fetal heart rate.

Morphine and scopolamine in combination (or similar drugs in combination) produce twilight sleep, a state in which the woman remains conscious but afterward has no recollection of the pain. The method is used mainly when a woman cannot cooperate with doctors because of the pain, but some doctors object that she may be psychologically harmed by the experience. In addition, a high dose may cause a reduction in the fetal heart rate.

Gas—either a combination of nitrous oxide (laughing gas) and oxygen or Trilene—is the simplest anesthesia because it is under the control of the woman herself. In the labor room, she simply places a mask over her nose and mouth when the contractions are severe and inhales deeply. The gas reduces pain, but she retains complete control of her body.

Epidural block is given at the base of the spine, carefully placed into the epidural space, an area where a network of nerves emerges from the spinal cord. Afterward, there is no sensation in the pelvic area, but muscles are not affected, so the woman can push when the doctor instructs her to do so. An epidural block is usually given during a prolonged early labor; it appears not to affect the baby's heart rate. The method requires skilled personnel and is not available in all hospitals.

Saddle block deadens sensations below the waist by means of an injection directly into the spinal canal. It gets its name from the area anesthetized, although one doctor has written that "the area is appreciably greater than that which would be in contact with a saddle." The drug is given after the cervix is fully dilated; it often is used to facilitate a forceps delivery. As with other regional anesthetics, the patient remains conscious and the baby's heart rate seems unaffected. Some women, however, suffer severe headaches afterward.

Pudendal block anesthetizes the immediate birth area. It is a simple injection, usually of novocaine, given to allow the doctor to make a small incision that widens the birth canal. It does not affect the woman's ability to feel contractions or her ability to "push" and does not affect the baby's heart rate.

General anesthesia, usually sodium pentothal, is mainly reserved for cesarean delivery, which requires the woman to be anesthetized completely. Anesthetizing the patient was once routine but now is no longer common.

Ether and chloroform are seldom used in any hospital these days, because they're volatile and because they may cause vomiting and aspiration. Hypnosis and acupuncture have been attempted by some physicians as experimental means of relieving pain during labor but are not widely employed. Some doctors say that the most important pain reliever a woman can receive is the emotional support of the husband and the obstetrical team. One widely used obstetrical text declares, "In ordinary circumstances, about 60 percent of women can go through labor with psychologic assistance and a minimum of pain-relieving drugs in a manner satisfactory to both them and their obstetrician."

Thus, the best antidote for discomfort in childbirth may be the inner strength of parents themselves.

TESTS YOU MAY HAVE

You'll have certain routine tests on each visit to the doctor; he may conduct certain others only once or send you to a laboratory to have them done. They're not a matter for concern—strictly a precaution or an effort to gain additional information about the progress of your pregnancy. Here are the most common:

Urinalysis. You'll usually furnish a urine sample on each visit, collected at home on arising or at the doctor's office. The urine will be checked for the presence of glucose, which could indicate a diabetic condition; protein, which might signal that toxemia or pre-eclampsia, two common but manageable complications of pregnancy, are developing; white blood cells, which might indicate a kidney or urinary infection; or red blood cells, which might mean a kidney problem. If any of these conditions are discovered, the doctor may decide to conduct additional tests.

Blood pressure will be measured on each visit. Elevated blood pressure may also be a warning of toxemia.

Blood tests. A small sample of blood will be taken, usually at the first or second visit, to determine whether or not you have syphilis. This test is compulsory in many states—required even though you're sure you couldn't have contracted a venereal disease. Syphilis in the mother can present grave danger to the unborn child, and because the disease frequently shows few if any symptoms, the test is important to permit prompt treatment if the disease is present and thereby reduce the risk to the unborn child.

Another portion of the urine sample will be tested for other diseases, including gonorrhea and a genital infection caused by the herpes virus that may produce no symptoms in the mother but may infect the baby during delivery. These conditions also can be controlled or eliminated with immediate treatment.

Hemoglobin concentration. Your blood also will be checked for the percentage of hemoglobin it contains; a low count indicates anemia, requiring treatment.

The Rh factor. Your blood sample also will be tested for the Rhesus, or Rh, factor. This blood constituent is found in 85 percent of the white population, who are called Rh positives. It is lacking in others, the Rh negatives. If you are found to be Rh negative, your husband's blood will be checked, too.

When an Rh-negative mother conceives by an Rh-positive father, the child is likely to be Rh positive, too—its blood incompatible with that of its mother. Although their bloodstreams are separate, some fetal blood may cross the placental barrier into the mother's system, which identifies it as an invader and produces antibodies to destroy it. This antibody production is gradual and only in very rare instances threatens the *first* pregnancy. But the antibodies remain after delivery. If the mother conceives again, the antibodies may cross back into the second baby's system, ravaging its red blood cells (a condition called erythroblastosis, or Rh disease). The amount of damage varies but can threaten the baby's life.

Fortunately, a substance called Rho-Gam can be injected into the mother shortly after delivery to neutralize the circulating antibodies and protect future babies. Rho-Gam now is given routinely to mothers known to be Rh-sensitive within 72 hours after each delivery.

A very few women carry antibodies against the Rh-factor without being aware of it. Some have received transfusions of Rh-positive blood during surgery or after an accident; others have had an early miscarriage of an Rh-positive fetus, without an injection of Rho-Gam afterward. For this reason, it is important for an Rh-negative mother to furnish her obstetrician a complete medical history, including all previous miscarriages.

In those few instances when an Rh-sensitive mother becomes pregnant without having previously received Rho-Gam, it is still sometimes possible to transfuse the fetal blood before birth, giving a tiny injection into the fetal abdomen through the mother's abdominal wall. These transfusions help the fetus survive until it is mature enough to be delivered. The infant's blood also may be totally transfused at birth.

Rubella titers. Rubella, a mild virus infection also called German measles, causes severe damage to a fetus if contracted by the mother during the first six weeks of pregnancy. For this reason, all women in the childbearing years are urged to be immunized against the disease.

Once pregnant, it's too late for immunization, however, because injecting the vaccine would have the same consequences as contracting the disease itself. Thus, if an uninoculated woman conceives, the doctor will check her blood for rubella-fighting antibodies. Chances are she may have been immunized as a child and forgotten it, or she may have had a mild case of rubella, conferring immunity, without realizing it.

If no rubella antibodies are found, the doctor will protect the mother during the critical early stages of pregnancy, usually by immunizing her family and other persons with whom she has close contact.

Amniocentesis discloses in advance the sex of the unborn baby, although it is seldom employed specifically for that purpose; it is also sometimes used in late pregnancy to determine the baby's stage of development when it is necessary to schedule a cesarean section. Its most common use, however, is to reassure parents that a fetus is free of certain, congenital problems that "run in the family" or to determine if a mother (usually over 37 years of age) carries the chromosomal abnormality that leads to Down's Syndrome, a form of retardation.

Under local anesthesia, a long, thin needle is inserted through the abdominal wall to extract a small amount of the amniotic fluid surrounding the baby. In the laboratory, cells from the fluid then are tested chemically or microscopically, depending on the information being sought. The test usually is made 16 weeks into the pregnancy.

More than 60 hereditary conditions can be detected prenatally by anmiocentesis. Genetics counselors say the test should always be conducted when family history points to sex-linked disorders such as hemophilia, certain diseases of the nervous system, inborn errors of metabolism such as Tay-Sachs disease, and muscular dystrophy. They say finding the child free of the condition brings a great relief to worried parents, and when a defect is disclosed, the doctor is immediately alerted to the need for early treatment.

Amniocentesis is a procedure done in the doctor's office and is relatively quick and painless. A nationwide government-sponsored study has disclosed that amniocentesis does not markedly increase the likelihood of miscarriage.

Ultrasonography, which resembles marine sonar, has largely replaced X rays as a means of checking the baby's growth and position, because it involves no exposure to radiation. High-frequency sound waves are transmitted through the mother's abdominal wall. Bouncing off the fetal form, their "echoes" translate into impulses that produce images on a screen, according to the distance traveled, and form a clear outline of the fetal body. Ultrasound tells doctors when the baby is developing normally; many obstetricians use it to establish whether the baby is sufficiently mature for cesarean delivery.

The challenge test begins by injecting the hormone, oxytocin, that brings on mild uterine contractions similar to those of labor. The contractions and the baby's heartbeat then are monitored electronically to determine whether the baby can withstand normal birth or would be better delivered by cesarean section. The challenge test especially is used in premature birth or when the baby's exact stage of development is uncertain.

The shake test tells whether an unborn baby's lungs are sufficiently mature for delivery. Amniotic fluid is removed by amniocentesis, diluted with alcohol, then shaken by hand or machine. After 15 minutes, bubbles at the top of the sample are examined. If they have formed a complete ring around the edge of the test tube, safe delivery is possible; if there are no bubbles, the fetal lungs are not yet mature.

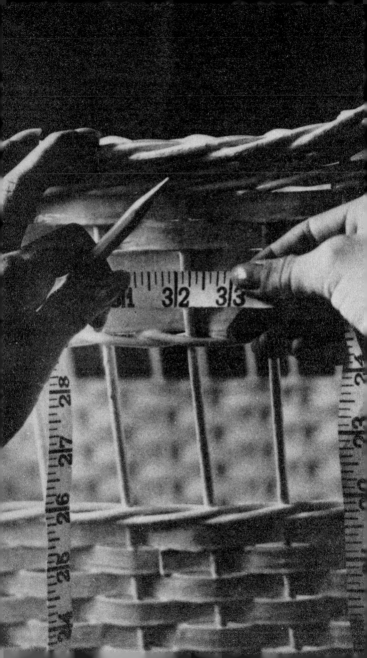

5

Getting Ready for the Baby

Outfitting a newborn can be expensive, but, fortunately, you don't have to buy everything beforehand. Beyond some basic equipment and a small wardrobe, most items can wait until the baby has arrived and you're home from the hospital. In fact, it's sensible to limit your purchases of clothes at first, because they're often outgrown before they're outworn.

Most cities have stores specializing in furniture and clothing for infants. And you can usually find a baby section in large department or discount stores. An experienced clerk can best answer your questions and give you advice on how to get the most for your money.

You need not buy everything new, of course. If you're pennywise or on a limited budget, a little searching may turn up used equipment and apparel. Garage sales are excellent sources of inexpensive nursery furnishings. With luck, they'll need only a little sprucing up or repair. School or church rummage sales are good places to pick up still usable clothing. Classified advertising sections often include baby furniture for sale. And, of course, you can expect to inherit some items from friends and relatives, in addition to baby gifts.

Try not to spend your money on frills. Furniture, in particular, should be bought to last for several years; don't be seduced by Mother Goose motifs. If you expect to work outside the home after your child is born, choose items that are easy to take care of: clothing that is simple and easily laundered and furniture that is sturdy, safe, and easily cleaned.

A ROOM FOR THE BABY

Your first impulse may be to keep the baby in your bedroom at night, to simplify feeding or just because you're worried you might not hear nocturnal cries. Resist it. A room of the baby's own is important for both of you. A baby sleeps more soundly where he or she will not be disturbed or interrupted and can develop better sleeping habits.

Meanwhile, you should live normally without tiptoeing about. During the day, you can close the door to the baby's room while he or she is taking a nap and continue with housework or other activities. At night, you'll still be able to hear the baby while retaining your own privacy.

The nursery needn't be large. All that's required is enough space for a crib or bassinet, a dresser for clothing, and a lamp. The room should be well ventilated, not drafty, and not too hot. Seventy to 72 degrees Fahrenheit is about right. In cold weather, especially, proper humidity is important, so the baby's throat and nasal membranes don't dry out—30 percent humidity is recommended. If you have a forced-air furnace or other form of dry heat, a humidifier for the furnace or a room-size humidifier may be necessary. Shallow pans of water placed near heat outlets also will add moisture to the air.

The decor in the nursery is up to you, of course, but it should be kept simple for ease of care. Pastel colors, like pink, blue, and yellow, are traditional, but any lively hue will do in this age of washable, easy-to-clean paint. Linoleum tile or a rug of synthetic fiber is best for the floor. Paint walls or secondhand furniture with a washable, nontoxic enamel. Be sure not to use lead-based paint, because teething babies may chew on it and develop lead poisoning.

BABY'S FURNITURE

A tiny newborn requires only a tiny bed, so most parents like to choose a bassinet or wicker basket on wheels. It's hip high, just right for you to bend and lift the baby, and it can easily be wheeled from one room to another or even outdoors for naps or airings. The most useful model comes in two parts: a wheeled stand that is collapsible and a basket that can be lifted off and carried separately.

The standard bassinet size is 16 inches wide by 32 long. Because the average newborn is about 21 inches long, you can see a bassinet won't be used for any length of time. After about three months, the baby will be too large, with too many kicks and squirms. Another drawback is that a bassinet is top-heavy; older

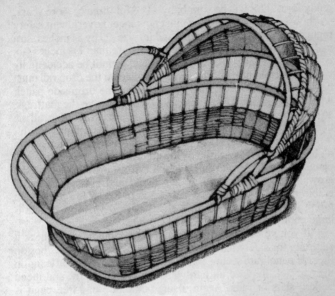

A new baby's first rest stop may well be a bassinet. About 16 inches wide and 32 inches long, it's a convenient, temporary bed for the baby. If you don't want to buy a bed, you can easily make your own.

children, in their eagerness to see the baby, may yank on the edge and turn it over.

If you can't afford a bassinet or don't want to invest in an item you'll use only for a short time, improvise one. A well-padded, good-size laundry basket makes a perfectly adequate baby bed. Or use a dresser drawer or cardboard box, lined and padded with a folded blanket. You won't have a rolling platform, of course, but you can set the box or basket on a table to reach it more easily.

You may also want to buy or borrow a rear-facing, inclined infant seat for the automobile. The best and safest models surround the baby with absorbent materials and strap to the front seat with a lap belt. They protect the baby in the event of an impact and keep him or her within your reach. In fact, such devices are recommended by the Physicians for Automotive Safety as the preferred way to transport an infant home from the hospital.

You may want to acquire a crib now or wait until the baby is ready for it. This will be your baby's bed for three or more years, so choose wisely. New cribs must now meet government safety regulations. They must be of a standard size, 27 by 54 inches, so a mattress will fit snugly; slats can be no more than 2⅜ inches (six centimeters) apart, so a newborn's head cannot be accidentally wedged between them. The locking device on the drop rail must be secure against accidental opening, and the drop-side panel, when lowered, must be at least nine inches above the mattress, so the baby cannot accidentally tumble over it. In addition, all the hardware on the crib must be safely beyond the infant's reach.

When you're buying a crib, also look for one in which panels on both sides can be raised or lowered. Be sure the lever is in a place where the baby cannot reach it from inside as he or she grows older. A model with an adjustable mattress height is preferable because the mattress may be kept raised for convenient lifting while the baby is small, then lowered when he or she is large enough to stand.

If you've bought or been given a secondhand crib, check it carefully for safety features. Be particularly sure the latches on the side panels are secure and won't pop open if the baby leans on the top rail. Replace all hardware that seems worn, and mend broken slats or rails. Again, using nontoxic, lead-free paint is particularly important if you're repainting the crib or touching it up.

If the crib rails are farther apart than the recommended space, buy a foam-rubber bumper at least six inches high and install it around the perimeter of the mattress. Make sure the mattress fits snugly on all sides. It if does not, stuff towels or sheets between mattress and side rail, up to the level of the mattress.

WHAT YOU'LL NEED FOR THE BABY'S BED

Baby's bedding needs are few. A bassinet is usually equipped with a standard-size, waterproof mattress; you can buy bassinet sheets or simply use a pillowcase, tucking excess fabric under the mattress. A flannelette or rubberized pad under the baby will protect the sheet or pillowcase. For decoration, you may want a frilly bassinet "liner," which fits inside and hangs like a skirt around the outside of the bassinet. A child this age doesn't use a pillow.

For a crib, here's what you'll need:

Mattress. Be sure it's firm—a baby's bones are still somewhat soft in the early months and good support is needed. Most new mattresses are designed with steel inner-spring coils under a thick layer of foam rubber and a waterproof plastic covering. Small vents on the sides of the mattress allow air to circulate and prevent moisture from collecting. The reversible mattress should be about four inches thick.

Older mattresses may be filled with cotton batting or horsehair. If you've inherited one of these, buy a moisture-proof sheet or mattress cover that completely covers the mattress.

Like cribs, new mattresses must meet government safety regulations. They must be of standard size, made of flame-retardant materials, and must maintain their shape. Hypoallergenic materials (those not likely to cause allergies) are recommended.

Mattress pads. A quilted mattress pad of cotton or synthetic fiber between mattress and sheet allows the mattress to "breathe" and keeps the baby cooler. You'll definitely need a quilted pad if you have an older, cotton-filled mattress. Buy at least two.

Sheets. Crib sheets, like full-size bed sheets, come with mitered (fitted) corners. Choose a soft synthetic or cotton fabric that launders easily and requires no ironing. A government regulation requires that crib sheets be flame-retardant. You can buy them in many decorative patterns and designs.

Small moisture-proof pads. One of these goes between baby and sheet for added protection. They also can go on laps, under furniture, or beneath the baby when diapers are being changed. You can buy them in several convenient sizes or in a large sheet, which you can then cut to suit your needs. A handy size is about 12 by 14 inches; it will protect most of the area around a newborn. You'll need about six.

Cotton blankets. You'll need four to six, large enough to cover the baby. They need not be tucked under the mattress.

Heavier blankets. Two are sufficient. Buy lightweight or thermal blankets or a down- or acrylic-filled comforter.

OTHER NURSERY FURNISHINGS

As mentioned earlier, a good crib will have the following features: panels (with secure latches) on each side that can be raised and lowered; an adjustable mattress height; if painted, done so with a nontoxic, lead-free paint; space for the mattress to fit snugly on all sides; constructed so that all hardware, latches, and levers are out of the baby's reach; and manufactured with slats that are no more than 2⅜ inches (six centimeters) apart, so a newborn cannot accidentally wedge his or her head between them (see page 86 for more information).

Babies are small, but they need frequent changes of clothing. A chest of drawers should have at least three roomy drawers to accommodate a growing wardrobe. If you're buying a new one, choose a durable model with washable paint and a mar-proof top that you also can use when changing the baby's diapers. If you're painting an old dresser, remember the cautions about non-toxic paint (see page 86).

A comfortable chair (many mothers and fathers prefer a rocking chair) allows you to feed the baby, nurse the baby, or just spend some relaxing moments together. A footstool placed nearby lets you prop your feet up. Add a small table beside the chair to place items needed for feeding.

A dressing table or other surface for changing the baby is handy if the dresser top isn't practical. It should be padded and moisture-proof. A bathinette-dressing table with convenient compartments below for diapers and clothing is nice but may be an unnecessary expense. Make sure that whatever you choose is the height of your hip, so bending and lifting are easier.

You'll want a shaded lamp or night light so you can occasionally peek in at your sleeping baby without disturbing him or her.

A covered pail for soiled diapers may be kept in the nursery or bathroom. If you decide to use one, a diaper service usually furnishes a deodorized container. If you launder diapers at home, buy a pail that will accept a standard-size plastic bag for soiled diapers. Even if you do neither and use disposable diapers, a

container may be preferable to flushing soiled diapers down the toilet. You can conveniently dispose of the entire bag in the garbage. To round things out, the nursery also should have a wastebasket and hamper for soiled clothes.

THE BABY'S BATH NEEDS

Now is a good time to choose a place to bathe the baby. Using the bathtub for a newborn is seldom convenient, because it requires more water than necessary and you must kneel to use it. Instead, buy an oval-shaped, plastic baby tub, big enough for the baby to kick and splash in. There's also an inflatable type of tub, which can be deflated and stored between baths.

In any case, the bathroom is warm and bath supplies handy. Be sure the sink is large enough for a newborn. If you do use a plastic tub, make sure the counter will accommodate it. In the kitchen, you can set the tub on a drainboard or use the sink itself. (Be sure to scrub it out thoroughly beforehand.) A kitchen table is convenient for diapering and dressing.

A bathinette is a tub the height of a table, with a fold-down lid for drying and dressing. It usually is equipped with towel racks, space for soap and lotions, and compartments for diapers and clothes. The tub can be lifted out to be filled or emptied.

A small tray or basket is handy to keep all the bath articles together, so they can be carried from place to place. Here's a list of bath necessities:

Mild, pure soap. Liquid soap in a bottle or tube is less wasteful. Your doctor may recommend a special soap to inhibit rash.

A soap dish or jar, if you decide to use cake soap.

Diaper pins with plastic heads. (Even if you don't use cloth diapers, you'll occasionally reclose a disposable diaper.)

Cotton balls.

Soft, terry cloth washcloths—at least two.

At least four bath towels large enough to wrap the baby completely. Some baby towels are designed with a hood to cover the head while the baby is being dried. Receiving blankets also may be substituted for towels and can be used to cover the dressing surface.

A bath apron. Babies will splash.

Powder. You need not buy the commercial variety—cornstarch is preferable.

Baby oil, cream, or lotion.

You'll want to stock a small medicine chest, including a rectal thermometer (a child's temperature is taken rectally until the age of four) and a nasal aspirator with a two-inch bulb. Most doctors discourage the use of cotton swabs to clear a baby's nose and ears because the sticks may damage delicate membranes.

THE WELL-DRESSED BABY

The baby's basic wardrobe will be partly determined by where you live and what time of year he or she is born. A baby arriving in June in Atlanta obviously won't need as many clothes immediately as one born in December in Minneapolis. Don't overstock; babies grow quickly. To start, buy the six-months' size for maximum wear.

Be prepared to bathe the baby in a bathinette or plastic tub. Necessities: mild soap and soap dish or jar; diaper pins; cotton balls; washcloth; bath towels; an apron (for you to wear); baby powder (cornstarch) and oil, cream, or lotion.

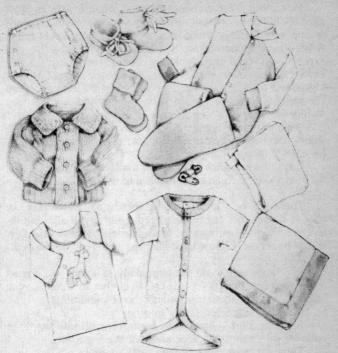

Buy clothes because they fit the baby's needs, not because they're cute. A basic wardrobe for the well-dressed baby may include: diaper and plastic pants, undershirt, a one-piece jumpsuit, booties, and light sweater.

Because most homes today are centrally heated, it's unnecessary to swathe a baby in layers and layers of clothing. Most of the time, the basic outfit consists of a diaper and plastic pants (or a disposable diaper and its own plastic cover); an undershirt; and a nightgown, a sacque, kimono, or one-piece jumpsuit. On hot days, you may even discard the outer layer. For trips outdoors or in cooler weather, the baby will need a light sweater and a blanket wrapper.

Remember, the objective is to keep a baby comfortable, not hot. Wrapping warmly won't prevent colds—infections result from exposure to other persons, not from being chilled. And overheating causes perspiration and skin rash, especially in the diaper area.

Pick clothes for convenience, not because they're cute. They should be easy to put on and remove, equipped with snaps or zippers and readily turned back or opened for diaper changing. A full-length kimono or hip-length sacque both leave the feet exposed, so you'll need socks or booties; the shorter sacque lacks a skirt and thus cuts down on the amount of wet fabric. A nightgown tied beneath the feet will keep the baby covered completely. A blanket sleeper with zipper will keep the baby warm even when he or she is active enough to kick off blankets.

A popular baby garment is the one-piece jumpsuit, which snaps from neck to ankles, allowing it to be opened completely for ease of diaper changing.

Buy these in stretch fabrics, which will expand somewhat as the baby grows and can be worn when he or she is old enough to crawl.

There will be a lot of spilling, spitting up, and soiling, so choose clothes that can be laundered easily. Synthetics, washable cottons, and permanent-press fabrics are best. Blankets should be acrylic. Choose hypoallergenic materials, where available.

If you are able to do the wash daily at home, you'll need fewer garments than if you're sending clothes to a commercial laundry or taking them to a neighborhood laundromat.

Here is a suggested first wardrobe:

Six undershirts—opening at the front, with side snaps, or pullover with adjustable neck and short sleeves.

Three kimonos, long-sleeved, with snaps.

Three sacques, short-sleeved, with snaps.

Six jumpsuits, full-length, with snaps.

Sweater, synthetic and washable. (You'll probably get one as a gift.)

Six receiving blankets.

Four plastic pants.

Two treated cotton or silk waterproof pants for dress occasions.

A dozen diaper pins, with plastic heads.

For an outer wrap, a wool or acrylic blanket usually is handier than a baby coat or baby bunting, which a newborn quickly outgrows. A baby hat is cute but seldom fits properly and won't stay on. Instead, wrap the baby in a blanket and cover the head. A quilted zipper bag with a hood will completely cover the child and protect against cold weather. If you live in a cold climate, bundle the baby in several blankets; wait until later to buy a snowsuit.

WHAT KIND OF DIAPERS?

The baby won't care about the style of diapers, but you will. There's considerable difference in cost and convenience. Disposable paper diapers are popular because they eliminate laundering, but their convenience is expensive. A diaper delivery service is also costly but particularly handy in the early months when you're especially busy. In the long run, you may find it less expensive and more convenient to own and launder your own diapers, especially if you have more than one child wearing them.

Whether you choose paper or cloth, however, you'll want some of the other kind for emergencies; even if you choose diaper delivery, you'll need about a dozen of your own.

Disposable diapers are used more than any other kind, according to their manufacturers, and can be bought in almost any drugstore or supermarket. They're made with a plastic outer liner to retain moisture and protect the clothing and an inner thickness of soft absorbent paper next to the baby's skin. The manufacturers say the paper layer can be shredded and flushed down the toilet, but the plastic must be removed and discarded. Disposables come in a variety of sizes, fitting newborn to toddler. Some brands are made with self-adhesive fasteners that eliminate the need for pins.

A diaper delivery service will bring freshly laundered diapers to your home once or twice a week, usually three dozen at a time, and will furnish a deodorized diaper container with a fitted plastic bag. Some services will wash the rest of the baby's laundry, too, for an additional fee. Diaper services now operate even in small communities, although in some places, there may be a waiting list for their services. Ask your friends which services they've been pleased with, or consult the yellow pages of the phone book.

For your own diaper supply, you can choose from three basic styles—curity, birdseye, and prefolded. The first two are made of a thin oblong fabric, which can then be folded and refolded to fit the baby. You change the folding pattern as the baby grows. Prefolded diapers are a single sheet of cloth, with an extra thickness in the diaper area. They're a little less handy for newborns, because they're made large enough to fit older children.

Automatic washers with pre-soak cycles and special diaper rinses now simplify home laundering of diapers. It's important, however, to be sure that all detergent is rinsed from the diaper during the cycle, because some detergents can cause a skin rash.

6

Your Part Before and After Delivery

The last few weeks of pregnancy are a time of eager anticipation and busy preparation. Whether you're still working outside the home or are at home counting down the days, there are a lot of last-minute chores that need to be completed before the baby arrives to take a place in the family circle. It's a hectic period, but you'll be buoyed by the realization that the countdown has almost reached zero and the nine months will soon be over.

Of course, you'll have weary times when you wish the baby would please hurry and end your discomfort; the ninth month often brings breathlessness and sleepless nights. And during these last weeks you'll begin to have waves of trepidation. How will I know when real labor starts? Will it be painful? What if I'm out shopping or away from home when the labor starts? Can I be sure to reach the hospital in time?

Be reassured. Although most women fear labor will start in the middle of the night, only about one in four pregnancies actually culminates in an early-hours race to the hospital. Studies show the number of hospital admissions are approximately evenly spaced around the clock. As many women arrive in labor between the daylight hours of noon and 6 p.m. as appear between midnight and 6 o'clock in the morning.

We already know the baby arrives at the baby's convenience, not yours, because only one baby in ten is born on the presumed due date. You probably won't be warned very far in advance, so the best idea is to be ready for a summons at any moment.

GETTING READY TO GO

About the beginning of the ninth month, pack a small suitcase for your trip to the hospital. Then, if there's a hurry-up call, you won't have to rush about looking for things at the last moment.

You won't need much. Hospital stays after delivery now average only three days, and even if you do overlook something, it can always be brought to you. The essentials are a comb and brush, toothbrush, robe and slippers, bed jacket, and cosmetics. For the first day or two, you may wear hospital gowns, but you'll probably want to discard them as quickly as possible in favor of something more attractive, so bring a few gowns from home.

If you're planning to breast-feed, you'll need a nursing brassiere. The size is sometimes difficult to gauge in advance, however; ask the hospital if they can be fitted and purchased there. If not, buy the adjustable kind. You'll also need sanitary napkins and a belt; they're usually provided by the hospital.

Wear a wristwatch (which can be checked for safekeeping during labor and delivery), but otherwise leave behind valuables, especially credit cards and more than a few dollars in cash. You may wish to bring a checkbook, tissues or handkerchiefs, pen, stationery, and stamps. Take that book you've always wanted to finish, although between caring for the baby, rest periods, visitors, and television you'll have plenty of activities to occupy you.

Pack a coming-home bag for the baby beforehand, too. Hospitals may provide disposable diapers and an undershirt or gown. Depending on climate and time of year, you'll also need a shirt, sweater, a receiving blanket, and perhaps a heavier blanket. If you haven't already done so, buy a car seat for the baby—a safer way to transport an infant from the hospital than in your arms.

You also may want to select in advance those clothes you'll wear home from the hospital. They can be brought to you on the date you're discharged. Remember that you won't yet have regained your normal shape, so the maternity clothes you wore early in your pregnancy will probably be the best bet.

If it's your first baby or you haven't a family physician, arrange now for a pediatrician to examine the baby. The pediatrician also will care for the child after the hospital stay, so you'll want to choose carefully.

If you're planning to use a diaper service, sign up now. You'll need a supply waiting when you and the baby return home.

If you're planning for a friend, relative, or visiting nurse or homemaker to live in and assist you for a few days after you return home, make arrangements at this time.

After that, there's little to do but wait.

LIGHTENING

Probably the first sign your baby is *really* on the way is one you'll greet with relief. One morning, after weeks of puffing like *The Little Engine that Could,* you'll wake up to find your breath comes easily again. If you observe yourself in the mirror, you'll see your figure has changed—the bulge is lower in the abdomen.

"Lightening" has occurred, to use the popular term. The baby has descended in the pelvic cavity. (You also may feel shooting pains down the legs, the result of pressure on nerves in the pelvic area.) A first-time mother may experience lightening at any time during the last four weeks before birth, although sometimes it does not occur until labor has started. Women who've previously borne children usually do not lighten until the last week or ten days and frequently not until just before delivery.

LABOR

If you've attended childbirth classes, the mechanics of labor probably have been explained to you. In labor, the uterine muscle contracts, like the contractions of any muscle. The contractions squeeze the baby and the bag of waters downward toward the cervical opening, where the tissues have become thinner as the result of a process called effacement, during which (see page 18) tissues of the cervix are drawn up into the uterine walls. Normally, the opening is about the diameter of a pencil lead. The pressure of repeated contractions widens the opening to many times that size to allow the baby's head to pass through. Dilation of ten centimeters, or four inches, is considered the proper measure. Your doctor or the nurses in the labor room may speak of it in terms of fingers—"five fingers dilated."

The process of labor is sometimes compared to putting on a turtleneck sweater. The opening is smaller than the head, but the head steadily pushes until it gradually widens the opening, progressing farther and farther until it ultimately pops free. As with the sweater, the opening afterward reverts to its former shape, but the process will never be so difficult again.

Labor usually is said to occur in three stages, although they actually blend together, coming one after another in a continuous sequence of events.

The first stage of labor is the longest, covering the period from the time the cervix begins to dilate until full dilation has been reached. It sometimes is further subdivided into early and late labor. Early labor is somewhat like an athlete's warmup. The muscle contracts at long intervals, loosening up for the real work during late, or hard labor, which pushes the baby little by little down through the cervix and into the birth canal. The initial contractions during this first stage of labor may be weak and 20 or more minutes apart, but they gradually become longer, stronger, and more frequent, with each one inching the baby slightly farther along the road to birth. The length of this stage is partly determined by the number of previous births. Twelve to 15 hours are not an uncommonly long period of time for the first baby. Later labors often are considerably shorter.

The second stage is sometimes called "transition" labor. It includes the period from full cervical dilation until the baby has passed through the birth canal and into the world. Contractions now are about four to five minutes apart and last almost 90 seconds each. The contractions are involuntary, and the mother assists, almost by reflex, in pushing with her abdominal muscles, as in a bowel movement. In a normal birth, the baby's head is forced out first, followed by one shoulder, then the other, then the body and legs. For a new mother, this stage of labor may last as long as an hour and a half. In later deliveries, transition labor may be over within a few minutes of full dilation.

Labor's third stage is also known as placental labor. The placenta, which has nourished and supported the budding life for nine months, is cast off by the uterus now that it is no longer needed. The placenta is often called afterbirth. There is little or no pain at this stage, and it lasts only a few minutes. The doctor may hurry the process by massaging the uterus through the abdominal wall, just above the pubic bone. Some bleeding may follow, but loss of blood throughout delivery seldom exceeds one pint.

HOW TO KNOW YOU'RE GOING INTO LABOR

Three distinct signs indicate your labor is about to begin. They may occur in any order, and you may be unaware of the first two. They are:

"**Show.**" A small amount of reddish or pink mucus tinged with blood is passed from the vagina. This material represents the plug of mucus that has closed off the uterus during pregnancy. Dilation of the cervix dislodges the plug and pushes it out the birth canal. Show may precede‚or accompany the initial contractions of labor. Once it occurs, labor commonly begins within 72 hours.

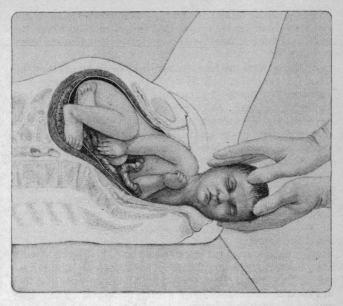

"Transition" labor ends with the baby's grand entrance into the world. Pushed along by involuntary uterine contractions and the mother's voluntary use of her abdominal muscles, the baby usually arrives head first.

Breaking of the bag of waters. Pressure from the early contractions ruptures the amniotic sac of fluid surrounding the baby. Depending on the size and location of the tear, there may be a gush or a trickle of water from the vagina. Labor usually follows within a few hours. If this happens, you should phone your doctor immediately, or, if you are not at home, proceed directly to the hospital and phone the doctor from there. The need for immediate notification doesn't mean that ruptured membranes are dangerous; many normal labors begin this way. The real reason for the haste is to get you under care quickly because the baby is no longer protected against infection.

Contractions. Everyone has these, the unmistakable signs of labor. You feel them as labor pains, but that popular term is less commonly used today because people believe it exaggerates the discomfort. Contractions first make themselves felt as a mild backache, accompanied by a weak cramp in the abdomen, somewhat like a menstrual cramp. The initial contractions may last for only ten to 20 seconds and be spaced 20 to 30 minutes apart. The interval steadily shortens, and the duration and severity increase.

Contractions are like the surf beating on an ocean shore. They rise gradually, build to a crest, break, then die away to be succeeded by another. They usually signal their coming by a twinge in the back, which then switches to the abdomen and becomes steadily stronger, holds a crescendo for a brief period, and then ebbs. In the transition stage of labor, sensations are closer together, with brief letups between.

A mother giving birth for the first time should call her physician when contractions are about five minutes apart—depending on how far she lives from the hospital and her doctor's instructions. A woman with previous children should call when she feels contractions at ten-minute intervals.

FALSE LABOR

About one woman in ten rushes to the hospital with labor seemingly begun, only to have the sensations subside after her arrival. These false alarms often resemble genuine labor, because they are uncomfortable, with pain occurring at intervals. You may be able to distinguish them from true labor, because they occur irregularly, not predictably, and do not increase in intensity. You may even find that they disappear when you change position in bed or get up and walk around—which does not happen during true labor. But don't rely on your own judgment to decide whether your labor is true or false. If there is any doubt in your mind, phone the doctor.

OFF TO THE HOSPITAL

Once you're fairly sure you're in labor, time your contractions. Wait until they've reached the appropriate interval, and then seek your doctor's instructions. Don't take medication for the pain or eat solid food, which could complicate matters if you require anesthesia later. Some doctors approve a little water or weak tea.

And don't worry—you'll reach the hospital in time. Babies arrive in the family car or the backseat of a taxi so rarely the occurrence rates coverage by the local paper or a spot on the television news. And on those infrequent occasions, a husband who's attended childbirth-preparation classes (or a policeman or paramedic) is qualified to make an emergency delivery. So just keep the car's tank filled with gas, plan your route to the hospital beforehand, and set off without delay—but not at a breakneck speed.

As Chapter Four showed, today there are many alternative methods of delivery; what'll happen when you reach the hospital depends partly on which method you've chosen. Probably, you'll be met with a wheelchair and taken to a "prep" room. If you haven't pre-registered, your husband or whoever has accompanied you may be asked to see that you're registered.

First, you'll be checked to be sure you're in labor. Your doctor or another member of the obstetrical team will conduct the first of many abdominal examinations to determine the baby's position and will listen by stethoscope to the heartbeat. Your vagina also will be examined to determine the extent of cervical dilation.

You'll be issued a hospital gown, and your temperature, blood pressure, and pulse will be taken. You also may be given an enema, although this is not always routine. Intravenous feeding may also begin at this time.

Some hospitals require that your pubic area be shaved and washed with a sterile solution. Others simply clip the hair (a poodle cut, nurses call it), which causes less itching as the hair grows back. Other hospitals ignore the practice altogether.

IN THE LABOR ROOM

When preparations have been completed, you'll be transferred to a labor room, usually a small, simply furnished cubicle equipped only with a bed, nightstand, chair, and sometimes a television. You may share the room with others, although there usually are curtains for privacy. Most hospitals now permit a husband, friend, or "labor coach" from your childbirth-preparation classes to remain with you in the labor room.

You'll be comfortable here, but you'll be left alone except for your companion. Nurses or other members of the obstetrical team will visit regularly to determine how you're progressing and may be summoned by pressing a button. The internal examinations will continue, some conducted by your doctor, some by others.

Between pains, you'll be able to converse with your visitors or even read; it's a time, too, to practice your breathing exercises (see page 72). You may even doze off between contractions. If you wish, the doctor may now give you a sedative or pain-reducing drug.

ELECTRONIC FETAL MONITORING

To provide medical attendants with an additional set of eyes and ears, some hospitals routinely use electronic fetal monitoring in the labor room. With this device, electronic sensors are placed on your abdomen and connected to a monitor at the bedside (sometimes, the signals are sent to the nursing station, too). The machine continuously records the contractions and the baby's heartbeat. If the heartbeat falters, which might indicate a decrease in the oxygen supply or that the umbilical cord has been squeezed, reducing the blood, an alarm sounds, and attendants come in a hurry.

The system is not painful, and its use does *not* indicate that yours is a problem-filled delivery, calling for extra vigilance.

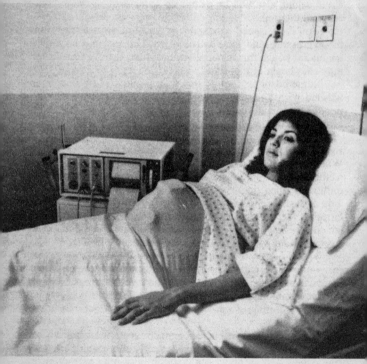

Electronic monitoring of the baby's progress toward delivery is a routine procedure in some hospitals. Sensors attached to the mother's abdomen monitor and record contractions and the baby's heartbeat.

Usually, the electrodes are held in place by a strap circling your abdomen, but in another system they are tucked inside a stockinette, which resembles a pair of pantyhose with the feet cut out. In both systems, however, you must lie on your back and cannot shift to your side.

Another system of monitoring is sometimes used when a better signal is needed. When dilation has reached about four centimeters, the bag of waters is broken, and an electrode is applied directly to the baby's scalp. This technique is more sensitive and may be substituted when a clear impulse cannot be received through the abdomen. It is also sometimes used for closer surveillance of prolonged or premature labors.

IN THE DELIVERY ROOM

When the cervix is fully dilated and you have entered the transition stage of labor, you'll be moved to the delivery room. Unless you've asked for the Leboyer method of delivery, the room will look like any operating room you've seen in the movies—bright lights, a long table, nurses and doctors in masks and gowns. An anesthesiologist may be standing by. Your own obstetrician will be there and perhaps one or more hospital staff physicians.

Your husband, friend, or labor coach may be present, too, in most hospitals, to offer encouragement and support. They may be required to wear caps and gowns, also. The number of visitors probably will be limited, and the hospital may reserve the right to ask them to leave in the event of an emergency.

Again, what happens next depends on the method of delivery you've chosen. If you have received a spinal or general anesthetic or an epidural block, you'll lie on your back during delivery. Your legs will be elevated and covered with white cotton stockings. A sheet will be draped over you, so that only your hands, face, and the birth area will show.

Or you may assume a semi-sitting position, back resting against a portion of the table that has been partially elevated. This posture enables you to push more easily, as well as to observe the birth.

This is your big moment. Your husband or labor coach will encourage you to thrust downward with the pelvic muscles, as you've learned, to help the baby emerge from the birth canal. If no companions are present, you'll get the same encouragement from nurses and medical staff, although it may not even be necessary—pushing at this stage is almost a reflex action.

At the moment of birth, the doctor will ease the baby out with gentle pressure. If you're lying down, your newborn will be lifted high for you to see and to hear the first cry. The baby will receive a name bracelet, the umbilical cord will be double-clamped, and the eyes washed out with silver nitrate to offset possible infection (gonorrhea). The baby's nose will be aspirated to clear it of mucus, and you may be able to hold your baby in your arms for the first time right at the place of delivery.

INDUCED LABOR

If labor is prolonged or delayed, the doctor may take measures to start or expedite the process. Such intervention may be particularly called for if there are indications the length of the labor is causing distress for the baby. Induced labor doesn't mean that you can have a delivery to order. It does not succeed (and, in fact, can be dangerous to both mother and baby) unless labor has already begun or is clearly about to.

Rupturing the bag of waters surrounding the baby usually will bring on labor within about 12 hours. The membranes are broken by the doctor in the hospital by puncturing them with a sterilized instrument. A few doctors perform this painless process routinely to speed up labor, but most prefer to do so only if necessary, because, as one obstetrician says, "There's no turning back once the water breaks." Also, the bag of waters appears to serve as a cushion for the baby's head during contractions of labor; in addition, breaking the waters destroys the sterile environment, allowing for possible infection.

An intravenous method of inducing labor uses a synthetic version of the natural hormone, oxytocin. Oxytocin itself is one of the hormones that increase in quantity around the time of birth, although its exact role and interaction with other substances never has been established completely. The administration of oxytocin usually will bring on labor (if it is imminent) within minutes, and it will dramatically speed up the strength and frequency of contractions if they have already begun.

Some doctors believe that births may be more difficult for both mother and baby if labor is induced. At least one study has shown more heartbeat irregularities when oxytocin is administered, and another indicates that the hormone hurries the labor to completion before the mother's systems are coordinated. In any case, a doctor is likely to use induced labor only as a last resort, and in no case should a woman attempt to bring on labor herself.

EPISIOTOMY

The vagina, which doctors describe as a "potential space," can open wide to accommodate the emerging baby, thanks to accordion-like pleats of tissue in the vaginal wall. But the canal still may not be large enough for the baby's head to exit easily. The result can be a jagged tear in the vaginal tissues. To prevent this, the doctor may widen the passage with a straight incision about two to three inches long in the perineum, just below the vagina. He uses a local anesthetic, such as novocaine, and repairs the incision by closing it with absorbable sutures, which need not be removed afterward.

This procedure, called episiotomy, is performed in about 50 percent of births in the United States but is less common in other countries. Doctors justify it on the grounds that a clean, straight incision will heal more quickly and successfully than an irregular tear. Although the stitches may cause some discomfort afterward, the procedure also will help to lessen further damage to the pelvic floor.

FORCEPS DELIVERY

Forceps—two metal blades that, joined together, look like the tongs used for serving salad—often have been called the "woman's best friend." When a labor is particularly difficult and prolonged, and natural forces seem unable to expel the child through the cervix, the doctor may remove the baby with the aid of the forceps. The two blades are shaped to fit the curve of the baby's head. First one blade is inserted into the birth canal and placed on one side of the head; the other then is placed on the other side and the handles brought together at a central joint. The doctor applies firm but gentle pressure on the handles and gradually draws the baby from the canal.

Forceps cannot be used unless the cervix is fully dilated and the baby's head is visible; under these circumstances, forceps delivery is considered safe, but it is not recommended simply as a means of shortening labor. The baby may be born with pressure marks on cheeks, but these disappear within a few days.

CESAREAN DELIVERY

Birth through the abdomen rather than the vagina—a surgical procedure called cesarean section—is nearly three times more common than it was in 1960. One of ten babies in the U.S. is now born this way.

A cesarean section usually is undertaken because the mother's pelvis is considered too small to permit easy passage of the baby's head. In a first-time mother, it is seldom conducted routinely; an obstetrician usually will attempt a normal labor first. In women who have previously had difficult or cesarean births, the operation may be anticipated and scheduled beforehand. A cesarean also may be performed under emergency circumstances, usually because of indications that the baby's life is endangered.

A cesarean section usually requires about an hour to an hour and a half. Under a regional or general anesthetic, a horizontal incision is made across the abdomen, usually at or near the pubic hair line, so the scar will be less noticeable afterward. An incision then is made in the lower quadrant of the uterus and extended until it is large enough for the baby's head to emerge. The surgeon then lifts out the baby, head first, then shoulders, trunk, and legs. The uterine incision is repaired, followed by that in the abdomen. Both usually heal quickly enough for the woman to go home within four to five days.

One reason for the increase in cesarean deliveries is that they are considerably safer than in the past. A cesarean now is considered less risky than a difficult vaginal delivery, although less safe than a normal birth. The procedure still is not consiered routine, however, because of the attendant risks of general anesthesia and major abdominal surgery.

The wider use of electronic fetal monitoring also partly accounts for more cesareans. Medical personnel now are alerted to the first indications of fetal breathing difficulties and can intervene in a hurry to save lives that might be jeopardized by allowing the labor to continue. Most hospitals now are prepared to spring into action quickly if a cesarean is needed. The American College of Obstetricians and Gynecologists' list of community hospital standards requires that a maternity ward be equipped to set up and perform a cesarean within 30 minutes.

Once a woman has been delivered by cesarean, further births often are also delivered abdominally. This precaution is undertaken because doctors fear the uterine scar may rupture during contractions. Sometimes a doctor will deliver a mother vaginally in later births but keep a team of obstetrical specialists standing by. Mothers who had been delivered by cesarean were formerly cautioned to have no more than two children. But today it is now believed that four children—or even more—can be delivered successfully by cesarean section.

OTHER TYPES OF DELIVERY

Most (95 percent) babies arrive head first, facing toward the mother's back, the easiest way to pass the pubic bone. One shoulder appears next, followed by the other shoulder, then the trunk, and finally the legs.

In a few cases, the baby is born buttocks first. The breech position presents a higher risk to the infant because the umbilical cord may be kinked or twisted, reducing the oxygen supply, and because the infant may take his or her first breath before the head has cleared the birth canal. In a breech birth, a doctor will frequently prefer to deliver the baby by cesarean section.

Rarely, the baby will "present" in other positions, such as shoulder or brow first, which also involve greater risk.

AFTER THE BIRTH

Your first stop will likely be a recovery room, where you can be watched closely for several hours. The baby will be taken to the nursery, cleaned, and bathed. You'll probably see the newcomer within a few hours and may be able to assist in caring for the baby then.

The first hour or two after delivery is critical, and you'll be visited frequently by nurses and other attendants, some of whom will wish to examine or massage your abdomen. They are checking for delayed hemorrhage, a serious postnatal complication, and to be sure the healing process has begun. You may wear a sanitary napkin to absorb blood during this period.

Even without drugs or anesthesia, you'll probably feel woozy and tired after the delivery; having a baby is hard work. Within a few hours, however, you should feel refreshed and strong enough to take a few steps, and by day's end, you'll be able to sit up and have visitors.

SECTION
2

Birth to Two Years

Now you are parents. It is
an experience as old as time
yet ever new. No one can predict
exactly how it will be for you—
how great the difficulties, how
rich the rewards. Right now the
task may seem insurmountable.
You may feel overwhelmed
and unprepared. But with time
will come skill and confidence,
fed by love, understanding,
and concern.

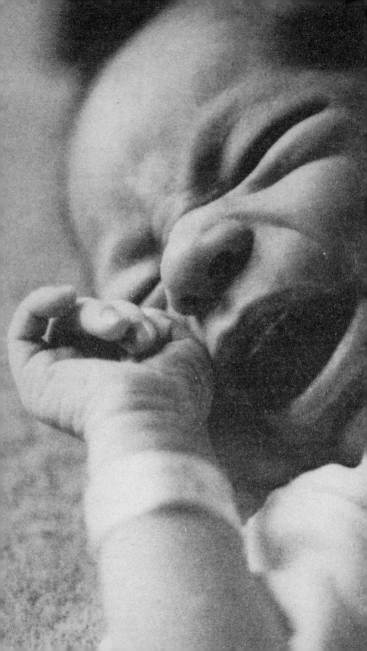

A New Life for Baby—and You

After nine months of eager anticipation, your first reaction to your new baby may be one of absolute shock. All along, you've pictured a rosy-cheeked, dimpled, brightly scrubbed infant like the one on the baby-food jar, but your newcomer will be, to put it charitably, a mess.

The baby will be wet, blood-spattered, and coated with a white, waxy substance (vernix caseosa, or cheesy varnish) that protects the skin and lubricates passage through the birth canal. Fine, downy hair—lanugo—may cover cheeks, ears, shoulders, and back. Vernix matted in it may give the baby a strange, pasted look.

You may note the baby's head looks misshapen. It may seem pointed at the back or lopsided. There may be lumps, protrusions, or swellings. The ears may look pinned back against the head or forward against the cheeks. The nose may look flattened. If yours has been a forceps delivery, there may be red marks on the baby's cheeks or temples.

Whether your own race is white, black, yellow, or brown, your baby's complexion may have a bluish tinge. It'll be particularly noticeable around the lips, nail beds, palms, and soles; white babies may be bluish from head to foot. The skin may be wrinkled and loose, perhaps with scaling in the creases of the arms and legs. The baby's legs may be so bowed that the soles actually face each other or the feet may be pointed inward, as in pigeon toes.

And the breathing! It will probably be a series of snorts, snuffles, rattles, and sneezes, punctuated by shallow breaths coming about three times as fast as your own. Small wonder parents often think, "Did we do this?"

Relax! All these characteristics are normal reminders of what the baby's been through for nine months. The vernix will dry and flake off within a few days. (Some hospitals wash it off, but most leave it to protect the baby's skin during the transition to the outside world.) The lanugo will disappear within a few months.

An asymmetrical head shape is caused by the tight squeeze through the birth canal, a passageway that is about a centimeter narrower than the diameter of the baby's head. Because the skull bones have not yet joined (hence the "soft spot" on the baby's crown), they can flex and overlap enough to facilitate the baby's passage. It'll be a week before the skull returns to a normal configuration, a year before the bones join together.

The lumps and protrusions result from the head thumping against the cervix during contractions; they're harmless and disappear in a few days, along with any marks from the forceps. The bluish tinge will vanish, too, as the baby takes more oxygen into the bloodstream and adjusts to the temperature of the outside world. The legs are bowed because they've been curled up for nine months; they'll be straight as a string within a year. As for the noisy breathing, it represents the baby's attempts to clear mucus from the respiratory system. Shortly after birth, the breathing quiets down, although several years will pass before its rapid pace slows to the adult rate.

THE BABY'S APGAR SCORE

One minute after birth and again five minutes later, a member of the obstetrical team assesses the baby's "Apgar score" and may call it out for you to hear. Named for the late pediatrician Dr. Virginia Apgar, this score is simply a quick gauge of the baby's condition at birth. The baby is given a rating (from 0 to 2) on: heart rate, respiratory effort, muscle tone, color, and response to stimuli. The maximum total for a normal baby is 10.

A very low score, especially when duplicated in the second assessment, calls for immediate medical intervention, but a score of 4 to 7 is not necessarily a cause for alarm. It simply warns the pediatrician to keep an eye on the baby during the coming days and weeks; it also may be a harbinger of conditions that may crop up in later life. Few babies achieve a rating of 10 at one minute (one doctor jokes that he only gives a 10 to children of colleagues as a professional courtesy); 8 or 9 is normal and does not indicate any deficiency in the baby.

Not all hospitals voluntarily disclose the Apgar score, but most will do so if you ask. They stress, however, that the score is not a competition and that parents should not misinterpret a less than perfect score.

WHAT IS THE BABY THINKING?

You may find your baby alert and ready to socialize from the very first minute. Especially if you haven't received medication for pain during labor and delivery, you'll notice the baby observing and absorbing this bright new world so different from the darkness left behind. If placed in your arms or on your chest in the delivery room, he or she may stare right into your eyes for up to an hour.

Babies used to be compared with newborn kittens, their senses unresponsive to their surroundings. A series of ingenious tests has shown that newborn children are much more aware of their environment than previously had been believed.

Your baby can see you, for one thing. It used to be thought that babies couldn't focus until eight weeks because they didn't smile until then. Now, tests show that even babies less than 24 hours old can discriminate clearly between images. In one test babies were propped in a box so their visual field was limited. Two images were projected, with a doctor studying the reflection of the image on the babies' pupils. The test showed that newborns preferred watching some images more than others, usually choosing bright colors and bold patterns. Above all, they were attracted to the human face.

Your baby also can hear. Ring a bell and the baby will be startled and perhaps try to locate the sound. He or she will respond to the sound of mother's voice. Films of children in the

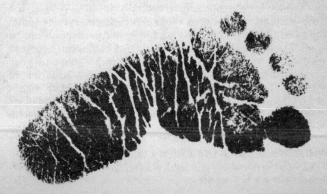

first weeks of life show that they move their arms and legs in a predictable manner when the mother speaks but not when others do so. Your baby can smell, too. He or she will react to a strong and unpleasant odor; by five days, the sense of smell is discriminating enough to distinguish mother's breast from another. And other senses are developing, too. If you prick a baby's foot, the other foot comes over and attempts to kick the offending needle away.

MOTHERING AND FATHERING

The parents' role starts at birth, and some doctors say the first hour is critical in forming the lifelong mother-child attachment called bonding—one reason many hospitals and doctors have reversed past practices and now encourage the mother to hold the baby in her arms in the delivery room for a time after birth.

This get-acquainted period gives you and the baby time to explore each other and allows you a moment to foster your maternal instincts. You'll find the baby responds to touch, warmth, skin contact, a soft voice, and gentle handling. That's why mothers the world over sing to their newborn babies and croon lullabies to soothe them.

Modern testing, too, has shown a scientific basis for the immediate interaction between mother and child. When you hold your newborn in your arms, something happens to both of you. Resting on your breast, the baby senses and reacts to the familiar heartbeat a few inches away. A baby receives from mother the reassurance of touch, of eye-to-eye contact, of warmth, and of a rhythm established by her voice that ties them together. The mother herself is stimulated by the baby's movements and responses.

Tender loving care comes naturally to most people, but some are more spontaneous about expressing it. Parents sometimes feel that newborns are very fragile and perhaps should be handled only gingerly or not at all. It's true babies can't support their heads at birth—that's why you cradle yours in your arms—but they's surprisingly durable creatures who thrive on physical affection. Some doctors believe that babies in institutions suffer most from a lack of flesh-to-flesh contact, and other studies have shown that newborns prefer physical contact to food.

WHAT WILL THE BABY LOOK LIKE?

Your newborn seven-pounder will offer some clues at birth—though not many—to his or her appearance as an adult. The arrangement of facial features, the set of the eyes, the shape of the head will not change drastically with the years. If your baby resembles father, mother, or Cousin Sally at birth, he or she will probably carry that resemblance into adulthood.

Other features, though, are less reliable—coloring, in particular. To predict the baby's future complexion, look in a mirror, because it will probably resemble the parents'. Ruddiness tinged with blue at birth will lighten gradually; by the third day, the complexion and eyes actually may appear yellow—a harmless kind of jaundice caused by an immature liver not yet completely able to cleanse itself. By the first week's end, the yellow will have given way to the pink more normally associated with babies.

Your child probably will be born with sparse dark hair—depending partly, of course, on ancestry. That won't mean much either. Baby hair will begin to drop out by the fourth month, and for a time he or she actually may appear bald. Your baby will be nearly a year old before baby hair has been replaced totally by a more permanent crop. As for future eye color, most white babies are born with blue eyes, a few with brown; brown eyes retain their color, but blue ones may change sometime during the first six months. You may get a clue to the probable change by the presence of dark flecks in the iris.

It'll be some time before the baby resembles a miniature—but well-proportioned—human being. At birth, the head comprises one fourth of the baby's length; the chest is narrow, the limbs foreshortened. Even if the baby appears fat, it's no clue he or she will be fat in maturity.

TESTS AND BIRTH CERTIFICATES

By law, your baby's birth must be recorded with state authorities. It's a simple procedure: a nurse or aide will visit your bedside and obtain pertinent data, including parents' names, nationality, citizenship, and the child's given name, length, and weight. Your obstetrician or attending physician signs the form to certify his or her presiding at the birth, and the application is filed with the state central registry. There is no fee.

You'll receive a certified copy of the document by mail, usually within a month. Always review it to be sure the information is correct, then store it in a safe place. A birth certificate is an important document in your child's life. It's required for enrolling at school, proving citizenship, and obtaining a passport, among other formalities. If you lose it, fortunately, you usually can obtain a duplicate for a few dollars.

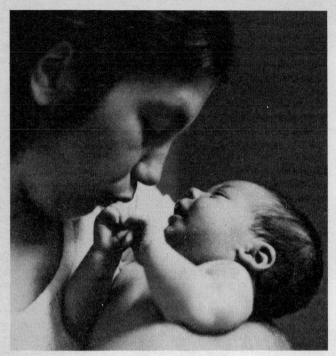

Getting to know you. The mother-child attachment called bonding begins immediately. Many hospitals and doctors now allow the mother to hold her baby in the delivery room minutes after birth.

About an hour after birth, the baby's eyes will be treated with silver nitrate or penicillin. This treatment is compulsory in most states to prevent potential blindness if gonorrheal infection is present at birth. It does not suggest that either parent has a venereal disease. The substance may cause the baby's eyes to redden and swell, which is why the procedure now usually is delayed until the baby has passed the "quiet alert" phase (the first hour after birth). In most states, the baby also receives an injection of vitamin K, which aids blood clotting and prevents internal hemorrhages.

Some states also require another test called the Guthrie test for phenylketonuria, or PKU. PKU is a rare congenital defect of the baby's metabolism that can cause retardation and death if not detected. Any problems usually can be prevented with a special diet begun shortly after birth. The simple test involves nothing more than obtaining a small blood sample from the baby's heel for immediate testing.

CIRCUMCISION

For religious or other reasons, you may wish to have your baby boy circumcised. In this minor operation, the foreskin, or movable fold at the end of the penis, is trimmed away. The operation usually is performed within three days of birth.

Circumcision has been practiced for centuries, and the overwhelming majority of American male babies today are circumcised. But, religious strictures apart, circumcision's medical value still is questioned. The procedure is usually justified on several grounds: that circumcision helps to keep the penis clean and reduce the chance of infection; that it protects against cancer of the penis; that it lowers the risks of adult prostate cancer; and that women married to circumcised men have less cervical cancer than the general population.

But in 1971, a committee of the American Academy of Pediatrics, investigating circumcision, concluded there was "no valid medical indication for routine circumcision." Four years later, the committee reviewed the subject and found no reason to change its original conclusion. The 1975 report agreed that infection and penile cancer were lower among circumcised boys but said these advantages were outweighed by the risks of the surgery. Teaching boys to keep their penises clean was safer and just as effective a preventive, the committee reported. The pediatricians found no convincing evidence that circumcision in infancy protected against prostate or cervical cancer decades later.

The committee said that circumcision should never be performed on premature babies, those with congenital defects, or those with known bleeding problems, and the committee advised that it be delayed until the boy was at least 12 hours old. The committee suggested that parents discuss the topic with the physician in advance so a thoughtful decision can be reached before delivery.

IN THE HOSPITAL

Unless delivery was by cesarean section, you'll probably remain in the hospital three days—perhaps fewer, perhaps as many as five. You won't be bedfast. You're likely to be on your feet within an hour or two of birth and ambulatory most of the time you remain in the hospital.

Most hospitals are more liberal about visitors and visiting hours than in the past, but you'll still find some restrictions. The father usually can visit without restriction throughout the day, but other visitors may be limited in number and to specified hours; they may be able to see the baby only in the nursery through a glass partition. These rules are to protect the baby against germs and infections. Children under 16, if they are permitted to visit, usually are restricted to areas outside the maternity ward.

You may not want many visitors. Although you'll rapidly regain strength, you'll probably find that you tire easily and need to rest frequently during the first few days. You may wish to postpone visits with friends until you return home.

ZIGZAGGING BACK TO NORMAL

As soon as your baby is born, the uterus begins a most remarkable vanishing act. Its function temporarily ended, this organ, which has sheltered the young life for nine months, shrinks to its normal size in a process called involution. After birth, you can feel it through the abdominal wall—a large, hard, globular mass about the size of a volleyball. Six weeks later, it will have shriveled to a mere two ounces. Sometimes, doctors inject the hormone oxytocin to hasten the process.

For four or five days after delivery, you will have a heavy discharge of blood mixed with cast-off by-products of the delivery. The flow, called lochia, usually will be deep red and about as profuse as your heaviest menstrual day. Gradually, the color will turn from red to brown; after about ten days, it will have a yellow or white tinge and will be considerably lighter. Lochia usually stops within two weeks, but there is great individual variation among women and, indeed, among deliveries. A flow of four weeks isn't unusual, but if it persists longer than this, resumes after it has stopped, has a bad odor, or exceeds your heaviest normal menstrual flow, tell your doctor.

Involution is usually painless, but some women have menstrual-like cramps that persist for a few days. They are less common among first-time mothers than among those who previously have borne children. The pains result from attempts by the uterus to expel small blood clots remaining after delivery. After-pains are seldom serious, but if they continue more than a week, notify the doctor. It may be necessary to perform a minor operation called dilation and curettage— "D and C" —to remove the clots.

If an episiotomy was performed to widen the birth canal, the stitches may make sitting a bit uncomfortable for a few days until they're absorbed by the body. You may wish to sit on an inflated cushion for comfort. Rarely, the area swells. An icepack may reduce the swelling.

Even before you leave the hospital, you may wish to begin exercises to strengthen the abdominal muscles and help regain your figure. Your physician or a nurse may demonstrate very simple exercises you can perform within a day or two of delivery. Those to be performed at home are demonstrated on page 122. You'll want to continue daily exercises at least through the first six weeks. (For more on postnatal exercises, see pages 133–135.)

THE AFTER-THE-BABY BLUES

An unexplainable bout of the blues strikes two thirds of new mothers sometime in the first six weeks of delivery. One minute you seem happy, on top of the world; the next, you may burst into tears or be plunged into what seems like bottomless gloom. Later, the episode will subside as mysteriously as it began. "It just came over me," you may explain.

Anxiety, depression, mood swings, crying, and easy distraction are some of the ways the blues manifest themselves. And when you think about it, these emotional upheavals aren't really so mysterious. You've been through quite an ordeal. A psychiatrist once compared so-called postpartum depression to combat fatigue.

There also may be a physiological explanation. After birth, secretions of the female hormones, estrogen and progesterone, drop dramatically. The amount of hormones circulating in the bloodstream affects the emotions; not coincidentally, women also feel similarly depressed when the production of female hormones drops during menopause.

WHEN WILL MENSTRUATION RESUME?

The resumption of menstruation is irregular. Periods usually begin no sooner than four to eight weeks after delivery; three to four months aren't uncommon. If you breast-feed your baby, menstruation may be delayed even longer (see page 127)—perhaps for six months or as long as the baby is only fed with breast milk. Periods usually start two to four weeks after nursing stops.

The first period after childbirth is almost always unusual—heavier than you have been accustomed to or full of clots and cellular debris. The second period—which may not occur at your regular interval—will be more normal. Several months may pass, however, before periods occur as regularly as they did before pregnancy.

Don't be fooled by the mistaken idea that you can't become pregnant until menstruation resumes or so long as you're nursing. Many women have learned to their dismay that both are incorrect. Your first menstruation signals that ovulation—the fertile period—already has taken place. Breast-feeding (see page 127) does seem to inhibit both ovulation and menstruation but usually only so long as the baby is breast-fed completely, and it is not uncommon for a woman to ovulate while breast-feeding.

EXERCISES AFTER THE DELIVERY

Exercising is important to tighten the muscles and restore your figure. You can begin the exercises on this page one or two weeks after delivery.

Abdomen strengthener (below)

To firm the abdomen, lie on your back with your knees bent. Inhale gradually, expanding the chest and abdomen. Pull in the abdomen, spreading the ribs. Then exhale. Now pull in the abdomen again, and press the lower back against the floor or bed. Hold the position for a few seconds, then exhale and relax. Repeat each phase of the exercise ten times. The exercise may be done in your hospital bed.

For the back and abdomen

Two exercises for back and abdomen top, next page, begin on hands and knees. First, lift your head and look at the ceiling, creating a hollow in your back and letting the hip muscles go slack. Repeat three times, then rest your head on your forearms. Repeat three times, four times daily. In the second exercise, pull your abdomen up toward your spine, arching the back and tightening the hip muscles. Tuck head down to look at your knees. Keep your back completely rounded. Repeat five times. Alternate the two exercises four times daily after birth.

Midriff firmer (above and right)
The exercise helps to tighten the
muscles in this area. On hands and
knees, swing hips from side to
side. Turn your head in the same
direction with each swing, so your
waistline is tucked in on the side to
which your head is turned.

For exercises after six weeks see
pages 133 through 135.

RESUMING INTERCOURSE

The old rule about resuming intercourse was: "not for six weeks," and some doctors still follow it. A more common view today limits the period to two weeks, because the cervix remains dilated for that length of time and intercourse might introduce germs to the area. (For the same reason, you should not use tampons during the first two weeks after delivery.) After that, most doctors say resumption of intercourse is strictly up to you, to resume when you feel ready. Some form of contraception should be used. If you are nursing, however, avoid oral contraceptives. Substitute another form of contraception instead.

BREAST-FEEDING IN THE HOSPITAL

You may be invited to put the baby to your breast in the delivery room. Although your breast milk won't appear for two to four days, the baby still will find the nipple and nurse through his or her rooting reflex. Immediate nursing isn't just for the baby's welfare. Nursing stimulates the secretion of oxytocin, which helps to contract the uterus, forestall hemorrhage, and promote the return of the organ to its normal size.

About one third to one half of new mothers plan to breast-feed their babies, according to LaLeche League International, the organization that has done most to revive breast-feeding. That's considerably more than the five percent of a few years ago. But because one half to two thirds of mothers do *not* wish to breast-feed and others quickly stop, the entire subject of breast-feeding is still very controversial.

The arguments on either side of the question are often quite emotional, and mothers and doctors disagree vehemently about the subject. Listen to both sides before entering the hospital, and make up your mind for yourself. Feel free to change your mind and stop nursing if your experience is less than successful. Some doctors and nurses openly or tacitly discourage women from breast-feeding, which is an acknowledged disturbance of hospital routine; sometimes other people imply the practice is old-fashioned and embarrassing. Don't be swayed by others; decide for yourself.

THE ADVANTAGES OF BREAST-FEEDING

"Human milk is for the human infant; cow's milk is for the calf." With those words, the late nutritionist, Dr. Paul Gyorgy, once derisively summed up the continuing controversy about the comparative value of breast milk and its most common substitute.

Even the commercial manufacturers of formula acknowledge that breast milk is the best nourishment for newborns. And despite conscientious efforts, manufacturers never have been able to duplicate breast milk precisely.

Breast milk confers these advantages on the newborn:

Fewer infections. The results of a study of babies in and around Cooperstown, New York, showed that breast-feeding reduced gastrointestinal infections in babies by a significant amount. Respiratory infections in breast-fed babies are fewer, too, according to another study. There also is less diarrhea, spitting up, and constipation among the breast-fed; breast-feeding seems to protect against enterocolitis, a condition that is common among bottle-fed babies. Natural immunity to polio, measles, mumps, and other viral infections appears to be prolonged when an infant is breast-feeding.

Fewer allergies. Eczema and other common skin rashes of infancy are less frequent among breast-fed babies. They also have fewer allergenic sensitivities in later childhood and adulthood, according to one study. Of course, those babies who are breast-fed are also free of infancy's most common allergy, a sensitivity to cow's milk.

More consistent growth. Human milk is used more quickly by the body, one reason breast-fed babies are fed more frequently than bottle-fed. Breast milk also provides the exact nutrients, in the proper quantities, the baby needs for growth; because breast milk is digested easily, it can be immediately put to work.

Some doctors insist that obesity in America results from early bottle-feeding, which piles up unnecessary ingredients the body cannot use immediately. The balanced diet provided by breast-feeding, according to these doctors, keeps the baby lean, and that also results in good eating habits later.

IT'S NOT JUST MILK

When it was first noticed that breast-fed babies had fewer infections, it was thought they were healthier because their supply of food was protected against contamination. More recent investigation shows that breast milk is much more than nutritious. Important constituents of breast milk are disease-fighting antibodies provided by the mother, including white blood cells that combat infection.

The flow of antibodies begins even before the milk itself arrives. Colostrum, the yellowish fluid that comes from the breast before delivery and continues after the baby is born, is a chief source of immunizing substances. It also contains a substance that has a mild laxative effect on the baby, to clear the young digestive system of meconium, the fetal waste. And it has the proper proportion of proteins and fats for the baby's early feedings.

For some mothers, the psychological side of breast-feeding is important, too. Nursing is sometimes called the very essence of mothering, and the benefits to both mother and child may go well beyond merely providing nutrition.

Studies of maternal-infant bonding have shown that much more is going on. The baby not only satisfies his or her need for food, but also for warmth, security, and love. And in a subtle way, the rhythm of the mother's movements introduces the baby to the rhythm of life. Within 24 hours of birth, the same studies demonstrate, a bond has been forged between mother and breast-feeding child that will last a lifetime.

Dr. Derrick Jellife, an international authority on the subject at the University of Southern California School of Medicine (he has studied breast-feeding in countries and cultures throughout the world where the practice is more common than in the United States), has demonstrated just such important psychological advantages. Breast-feeding, across a wide spectrum of primitive and sophisticated societies, seems to satisfy universal emotional needs.

Of course, there are more prosaic advantages to breast-feeding: it's inexpensive, it's convenient, and it's easy. You don't have to prepare formula, sterilize bottles, or clean up afterward. The supply is always on hand in the right amounts and at the right temperatures. When you travel, you don't have to pack anything—the supply travels with you. And the LaLeche League estimates that you could hire cleaning help for six months with the money you save on commercial formula and baby food!

THE BENEFITS TO MOTHER

You may think breast-feeding will spoil your figure, but the evidence is otherwise. When you nurse your child, organs involved in childbirth return more quickly to normal—and body contours with them—because of the increased flow of oxytocin. When your milk comes in, your breasts may sag; the answer is good support. But they may sag whether or not you breast-feed.

Nursing also *may* provide some protection against breast cancer. This statement has not been proved finally and is still disputed. The incidence of breast cancer *is* lower in parts of the world where nursing is customary. And one study shows American women whose babies are breast-fed at least six months appear to have less breast cancer than those who do not breast-feed.

Breast-feeding also can provide a modified form of child-spacing. Usually, so long as the baby is being *breast-fed completely,* without solid foods or supplementary formula, the mother's body secretes sufficient quantities of the hormone, prolactin, to cause lactation amenorrhea—failure to ovulate because of milk production. This protection usually ends when breast-feedings are reduced to a few a day and are supplemented by bottles or solid food.

CAN ANYONE BREAST-FEED?

The size of a woman's breasts has nothing to do with the ability to nourish her child. Milk production isn't determined by the amount of breast tissue, but by a network of vessels and canals within the breast. The woman who wears a small bra has just as extensive a network as does her more amply endowed neighbor. Some women believe they cannot breast-feed because their nipples are flat or are turned inward. Patience and special care—augmented by some relatively simple exercises—usually can overcome these difficulties for most women.

The production of milk is an intricate and self-regulating process, but almost every mother produces enough milk for her baby. Interestingly, in France before World War II, 38 percent of mothers breast-fed their babies; but during the war years when other forms of milk were scarce, 90 percent found themselves able to do so. Also, the milk you produce will almost always be rich enough for the baby's nutritional needs. And there is no evidence that because your mother or grandmother did not breast-feed, you will be unable to do so.

WHAT IF YOU DON'T BREAST-FEED?

The American Academy of Pediatrics encourages breast-feeding as a matter of policy but adds: "Normal growth and development are possible without it." Many babies have been formula-fed from birth and have thrived on it—you may have been one of them. Obviously, adopted babies, whose new mothers have no milk supply, also grow up healthy.

Some women strive valiantly to breast-feed but aren't successful despite their best efforts. Others simply don't feel able to breast-feed or don't wish to do so. Some feel they'll be tied down by breast-feeding.

There's another important reason many couples today oppose breast-feeding: it excludes the father. Bottle-feeding gives parents an opportunity to share equally in this important part of infant care.

In these cases, the hospital nurses will introduce the baby to formula feeding and show you how to give the baby a bottle, so that once you've gone home you'll be fully prepared.

Whether you feed by breast or bottle, be sure the baby gets plenty of affection. Cradle, nuzzle, talk to, and allow the baby to cling to you for support. Love and the emotional bonds of parenthood are at least as important as the nutrients contained in the milk.

BEGINNING TO BREAST-FEED

Your milk will arrive about the third day after delivery—a little earlier if you've previously had children, later if the baby's your first. (In another of those miracles of timing, the schedule will be exactly the same, even if your baby is premature.) Before the milk itself arrives, the substance colostrum will drain from the nipples, and it will continue to be an ingredient in the breast milk for about ten days.

If you're not planning to breast-feed, your doctor may give you an injection to dry up the milk. Indeed, such injections are routine in many hospitals but apparently do not seriously impair your ability to breast-feed if you continue to put the baby to your breast. When the milk arrives, your breasts may feel full, swollen, and sore. The milk may leak from the nipples onto your clothes, so you may wish to wear a folded handkerchief or pad inside your bra.

You'll probably begin nursing the baby well before you have milk to deliver. Because the nutritious and immunizing values of colostrum have been recognized, babies usually are put to the breast within four hours of birth—and, of course, sometimes immediately after delivery. You'll probably feed the baby every two to three hours after that, more frequently than if the baby were bottle-fed.

Breast-feeding comes naturally, but you'll get some advice and instruction from the nurses. Or you may wish to read LaLeche League books or pamphlets beforehand.

At first, you'll probably want to nurse the baby lying down. (Later, this will be your choice for night feedings at home, so you can doze while the baby nurses.) If you're feeding from the right breast, lie on your right side and place your right arm over the baby's head or under it, whichever is more comfortable. Use your left hand as a steering hand. Pull the baby toward you until

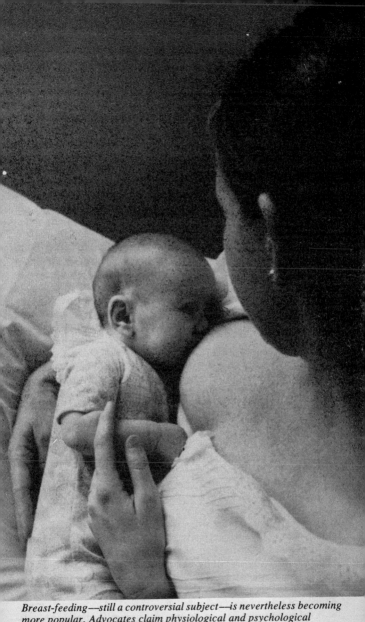

Breast-feeding—still a controversial subject—is nevertheless becoming more popular. Advocates claim physiological and psychological advantages for both mother and child.

his or her cheek touches your breast near the nipple. The baby will turn toward it instinctively, but you can give a little assistance by holding the nipple between your thumb and forefinger and guiding the baby toward it. Lift your breast from beneath, so the nipple is directed toward the mouth, and see that the baby takes the brown area around the nipple into the mouth as well. Then pull the baby's feet toward your body so the angle allows him or her to keep the nose free.

If you nurse sitting up, choose either a low, comfortable chair with arms or the corner of a sofa. Remember, you'll be there a while, so arrange yourself in a relaxed position that takes the strain off the muscles in your arms, neck, and back. A rocker is often a good choice. Sit well back in the chair, and place a pillow under your elbow on the feeding side; or double a pillow under the baby so that he or she can reach your breast without your bending forward. Hold the child in the crook of your elbow in a semi-sitting position, guiding the baby toward the nipple with your free hand. When you change breasts, shift the pillows and support to the other side.

When the baby has finished or you're changing breasts, gently press your breast away, inserting your little finger into the corner of the baby's mouth to reduce the suction on the breast. Don't yank the baby away from the breast; this may cause sore nipples. If the baby shows little interest in feeding or begins to doze, stroke the mouth or cheeks to stimulate the rooting reflex. If you can't wake the baby with gentle handling, don't worry; it won't hurt if he or she sleeps through a feeding.

A breast-fed baby usually requires less burping than a bottle-fed baby. He or she may routinely produce a bubble as you change the baby from one breast to the other; if not, burping usually can be achieved by holding the baby in a sitting position briefly.

At first, your baby may not show much interest in feeding. Appetite usually picks up when the milk itself arrives after a few days. As you gain more confidence, too, the baby may begin to eat more, because you will produce more milk. Nurses may suggest (or even automatically provide) a supplementary bottle of formula. Breast-feeding advocates discourage this practice because they say the baby becomes accustomed to the easier feeding by bottle and because the mother's milk supply is affected. The less you feed, the less milk you have and the more chance of sore or fissured nipples.

Like many aspects of mothering, breast-feeding is an individual matter. You'll probably work out your own techniques after a little practice. Usually, it's a good idea to offer both breasts at each feeding. Start the baby on one side, then stop for a rest or a change of diapers, then switch to the other breast. At the next feeding, offer the breast used last. You might attach a small safety pin to your bra to remind you which one it was.

HOW MUCH AND HOW OFTEN?

Some babies are gourmets and some are barracudas. The gourmets nurse daintily, seemingly savoring every drop, while the barracudas greedily latch onto the nipple and never let up. That's true whether the baby is breast-fed or bottle-fed. Babies' eating habits, like those of adults, are strictly individual.

Babies will tell you when they are hungry. In the hospital, he or she may be brought to you for feeding every four hours, but that interval is set more as a convenience for the staff than for any nutritional reason. Breast-fed babies want to be fed more often than their bottle-fed contemporaries, because breast milk is assimilated more quickly by the system. Fed on demand, a breast-fed baby will usually nurse every two to three hours, sometimes with one longer interval during the day.

How much depends on how soon the baby is satisfied. You'll soon be able to gauge that for yourself. About three to five minutes on each breast is a good beginning while you're in the hospital and until your nipples have become conditioned. Later, you'll probably offer the first breast for about ten minutes, the second for at least that period and perhaps longer. More than 15 minutes at each breast is probably futile and may cause soreness.

Don't worry that you won't have enough milk for the baby. Nature has its own self-regulating mechanism. The more milk the baby takes, the more the mother supplies. If you have twins, the body produces enough milk for twins. If the baby's appetite drops, the milk supply drops, too. If it drops too far, the baby will nurse more often and production will pick up again.

About a week after your milk comes in, you may lose the full feeling in your breasts, and the spontaneous leaking of milk may stop. You may think you have lost your milk. But this is simply evidence of supply adapting to demand. As nursing begins, there may be an oversupply of milk until the baby has established a daily quota. Then the supply drops to meet the baby's demands. You haven't lost your milk; just go on nursing.

At first, even though your breasts feel terribly full, you may find the baby is dissatisfied, cries, and turns away from the breast. That's because the breasts are so full the area around the nipple is swollen. The nipple then is depressed and cannot reach the baby's hard palate, which it must do in order for the baby to feed properly. You may correct this problem by hand-expressing milk from the nipple until the breast reaches a more normal configuration. Nurses can demonstrate hand-expression, or you may try it for yourself: hold nipple between thumb and forefinger and squeeze gently, but do not pull. Remember that hand-expressing milk also affects future supply; removing the milk yourself is the same as if it were consumed by the baby.

Your milk supply is governed by what is called the let-down or milk-ejection reflex. It's a psychosomatic reflex, affected by how you feel. If you're anxious about your ability to nurse, this tension interferes with milk supply and the amount the baby can receive. Doctors say anxiety is the leading cause of unsuccessful breast-feeding. On the other hand, confidence and eagerness to breast-feed enhance the milk production and flow. Some mothers find that just thinking about the baby will cause their milk to begin running.

CARE OF THE BREASTS AND NIPPLES
Having the baby tugging at your nipples can make them sore, at least until they become toughened. Then they may crack, become infected, and require special care. Soreness is one reason many women give up breast-feeding.

Before the baby is born, if you plan to breast-feed, try to condition the nipples with daily exercise, pull out the nipple several times quite firmly—until it is slightly uncomfortable but not painful. An oily lubricant may help, such as lanolin, cold cream, or baby oil.

When the milk comes in, your breasts may be tender, sore, and feel full to the point of bursting. This seems to be especially true among blondes and redheads, according to the LaLeche League. You may need to hand-express some of the milk to reduce the fullness and perhaps wear nipple shields to protect your clothes. You also need a snug-fitting brassiere, which offers good support. The best kind is the drop-front model. Wear it while you're sleeping, too.

Wash your nipples daily with warm water, but skip the soap. Soap dries the nipples, a condition that may lead to cracking and possible infection. Pat them dry. In the hospital, you may be asked to take special precautions to keep nipples sterile because of the danger of infection from other persons. Once you're home, it's less a problem. If you wear handkerchiefs or gauze pads inside your bra to absorb leaking milk, change them several times daily.

THE HUSBAND'S ROLE IN FEEDING

If your baby is formula-fed, father automatically takes part. Mother and father can alternate feedings, depending on who's available. The baby isn't likely to complain.

Breast-feeding, of course, is different. You can hand-express a relief bottle which the father can use for feeding, especially if you're planning to go out alone. Another role for the father, breast-feeding advocates say, is to provide moral support and companionship. Despite the swing to breast-feeding, many people still disparage it, and you'll have to overcome some of the comments, especially from older people. The husband's role is to defend your decision and to show that he admires you for it.

The husband also can take over a larger share of the household duties and spend more time with the other children. That leaves you free more of the time for nursing and for the routine of baby care.

EXERCISES TO BE STARTED AFTER SIX WEEKS

Routine exercises begun after six weeks will restore firmness to your midriff and abdomen, if they are performed regularly. It may take six to eight months to get your figure back.

Back builder

Sit on the floor with your right knee bent and your foot flat on the floor. Clasp your hands around the knee. Then using your back muscles, stretch your body toward the ceiling. Be sure to keep your abdomen pulled in and shoulders loose. Repeat this exercise ten times, alternating the knees after each five repetitions.

Trunk tightener (right and below)
Take position on hands and knees. Swing right arm under left side of body, reaching as far up the back as possible. Turn your head in synchronization with arm. Repeat five times per side. In second exercise below, swing arm under body, then raise toward ceiling. Lift head to look at arm. Repeat each five times daily.

Sit-ups (right)
Lie on your back, knees bent, feet flat on floor. Raise your head and shoulders off the floor. Reach forward with hands outside the left knee, then outside the right knee. Repeat three times. In second phase, lift head off floor slowly, then lower gradually. Try to raise your entire back.

High stretcher (left)

Sit on stool against the wall, with back, buttocks, and head touching wall. Tuck chin in; keep feet flat on the floor, arms at your sides. Raise arms over your head; pull in your stomach until your lower back touches the wall. Be sure your arms touch your ears on each side of the head. Repeat exercise five times.

Touch the chest (below)

To do this exercise, lie on your back with your knees pulled up and hands clasping your bent knees. Pull the knees toward your chest, touching it if possible. Hold this position, then lower your legs very slowly until your feet touch the floor. Now relax and repeat the exercise. Do the exercise six to ten times. Practice it until such time as you are able to touch your chest with your knees on each movement.

Camel walk (right)

Take a "table" position, placing your palms and feet on the floor, feet 12 to 18 inches apart. Keep your knees and elbows straight, and walk around on all fours. Repeat the exercise at least five times daily, moving around the room in this manner once on each attempt. This exercise strengthens the abdominal muscles and helps to reduce the sag that usually occurs in these muscles following delivery.

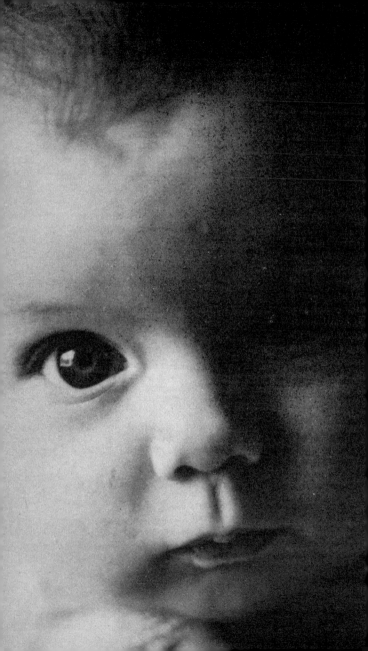

8

A New Routine at Home

The tiny bundle you bring home from the hospital can shake up your style of living far out of proportion to its modest size. The first three weeks of parenthood have often been called by new parents the longest and most depleting period of adult life, and, considering the adjustments that have to be made in your family routine, that may be no exaggeration.

The family circle may be turned topsy-turvy. Sleeping, eating, and working may be governed by when the baby wants to sleep, eat, and socialize. Family relationships, attitudes, and feelings can be knocked off stride. If the baby is your first, the household may crackle with nervousness and anxiety.

Such strain isn't surprising. For perhaps the first time in your life, another human being will be totally dependent on you. You'll face a dozen crises a day: Are we feeding enough? Are we feeding too much? Why is the baby crying? Should we pick him or her up? Is a pin sticking the child? Is the baby too warm? Is he or she too cold? Do diapers need changing?

Looking at your robust infant a year from now, you'll laugh at your beginning jitters. Babies thrive despite their parents' inexperience. The main casualties of the first six weeks are mothers' and fathers' nerves. Just relax, follow your instincts, and enjoy the baby. If you're in doubt about some detail of care for your newborn, *ask* for help—and keep asking until you get an answer that satisfies you. That's what doctors, nurses, clinics, more experienced parents—and baby books—are for.

THE LARGER FAMILY CIRCLE

Whether or not to have a friend, relative (your mother or mother-in-law, perhaps), visiting nurse, or housekeeper on hand to assist you during the first few weeks after you return from the hospital is up to you.

Some parents are made even more nervous with another person in the house; they consider a father's help plenty. But an extra pair of hands can be a godsend. First, although mothers aren't invalids, their energy levels will still be below normal. Second, temporarily delegating the household chores to another person gives parents time to get acquainted with the baby and to practice caring for the child on their own.

These first few weeks forge a lifelong bond between parents and infant; don't waste your limited energies doing the family laundry or dusting the furniture while someone else cuddles the baby. Make sure that you have a considerate helper and not a house guest.

THE OTHER CHILDREN

To you, the arrival of a new baby is a happy event, but an older—and up to now an only—child's feelings may be mixed. Once the sole occupant of the family limelight, he or she now may feel rudely shouldered aside by a demanding newcomer whose every cry brings parents running. No matter how much you reassure the older brother or sister, there's keen competition.

There are no easy answers to what psychiatrists call sibling rivalry. Preparation helps; before going to the hospital, explain about the baby to the other children, and try to emphasize that the arrival of the newcomer will not lessen your love for them. If the new baby was born at home or in the presence of the family in an alternative birth center, perhaps the lesson already has been reinforced. Yet the feeling of jealousy is a natural one for a small child, and the actual event may invoke some strong reactions.

A three-year-old may now insist on being treated like a baby—and behave like one. He or she may demand the bottle that had been given up months before. It's not uncommon for children long since past such stages to begin wetting their pants or sucking their thumbs again.

Fortunately, children adjust. You can't ignore their feelings, but don't chide or punish them. All you can do to ease the situation is assure them of your love for them, spend as much time as you can with them exclusively, and try to include them in caring for the new baby by assigning little duties that indicate they are older and more responsible. If the other child is under three, however, a word of caution: he or she should never be left alone with the baby. Whether innocently or, in psychiatric jargon, because they're acting out their aggressions, they may harm the infant by covering the baby's face with a blanket, overturning the bassinet, or even by sitting on the new brother or sister. Let the children get to know their brother or sister, but always under your watchful eye.

THE SHARING OF PARENTHOOD
Fathers take a greater part in baby care today than in the past. Most couples now share responsibility for the baby; but many

Today, fathers play a larger role in caring for the baby than ever before. The first few weeks are a time for mothers and fathers to take hold of what they know and share insights and experiences with each other.

men have never had the opportunity to change diapers or bathe an infant. Indeed, some grown men have never held a baby in their hands. Part of the mother's role is to impart her own possibly limited knowledge to her spouse. For both parents, the first few weeks must be a time of learning together.

Meanwhile, don't forget you're partners as well as parents. The stress of parenthood strains your relationship, too, as each of you may concentrate on the baby and neglect the other. Fathers often feel jealous of the little being who may monopolize the mother's time, while mothers seethe at the paternal pride that focuses on the offspring as it downplays her contribution.

These feelings are normal, and they can be overcome. As soon as you can possibly do so, spend some time by yourselves. Leave the baby with someone you can trust, and go out for the evening—even if it's only to the nearest fast-food spot. You need time to recharge your batteries and rebuild the bond between you. Strengthening your relationship benefits you as well as the baby and other family members.

BABY SETS A SCHEDULE
The first few days and nights with the baby will pass in one big blur, as one feeding blends fuzzily into the next. But soon you'll see that the baby's life (and therefore yours) falls into a regular routine.

In more dogmatic days, infants were fed every four hours, whether they were hungry or not. Now most doctors recommend a more flexible schedule. Babies eat when they announce they're hungry.

Baby's whims, unfortunately, aren't always convenient for you. Observe the baby's own pattern of eating and sleeping for a few days, and then construct your schedule accordingly.

Usually, a newborn will want to be fed six to eight times a day, about two to five hours apart. If you feed the baby at 6 a.m., you may expect to do so again at about 10 a.m., 2 p.m., 6 p.m., 10 p.m., and 2 a.m. the next morning.

But few babies are that regular. A baby may be fed at 6 a.m., ask for more at 9 a.m., then go without eating until 2 p.m. On the average, a breast-fed baby requires more frequent feedings than a bottle-fed infant; eight feedings daily at intervals of two to three hours is typical. But appetite is as individual in babies as in adults. Your bottle-feeder may feed just as frequently or infrequently as the breast-feeder next door. And some babies simply seem to be hungry all the time, eating regularly every three hours around the clock. All these patterns are normal.

As for sleeping, a newborn averages 16 hours a day and may be drowsy or half-awake several additional hours. (But some babies sleep as little as eight hours and yet are not at all deprived of sleep.)

Eventually, one nap lengthens and the number of feedings falls to five a day. This usually occurs at about five weeks or when the baby's weight reaches 11 pounds. With luck, the longer nap comes at night, and the periods when the baby is alert come during the day, when you can enjoy them.

Once you understand the baby's schedule, sometimes you can influence it. If the baby seems to sleep through a daytime feeding, wake and feed on schedule; he or she *may* take a longer nap. If the baby dozes during a feeding or falls asleep before it is finished, nudge the child so that he or she does not wake up again in two hours for refueling.

You may want to schedule the baby's bath in the morning, after the early feeding, then put the newborn to bed until another feeding is necessary. Afternoon is a good time for an airing or a stroll, when the sun is higher and the air warmer. By letting the baby catnap during the day, you may be able to keep the child awake at dinner time to socialize with the family.

Remember that the baby's welfare is important, but it can't completely dominate the family's life. When it's time for a nap, put the baby in a crib or bassinet in his or her own room, close the door, and go about your business. Do not tiptoe or caution the other children to "Hush!" Artificial silence only conditions the newcomer to wake at the slightest noise.

YOUR OWN RECOVERY

Legend says pioneer women gave birth in the morning and plowed the back 40 in the afternoon. If so, they must have been exhausted by evening. Bearing and caring for a baby are fatiguing activities.

During these early weeks, take advantage of every opportunity to rest, preferably with your feet up. Keep strenuous work to a minimum; don't set out to do the spring cleaning. Take naps when you can, because it may be difficult to get eight hours of uninterrupted sleep at night. Family finances may dictate when you return to work outside the home, of course, but many women prefer to wait at least six weeks.

The exercises on pages 133–135 will help restore your figure by tightening the abdominal muscles that stretched to accommodate the expanded uterus. Physical activity also will help trim any excessive poundage you may have accumulated during pregnancy. A girdle helps support the abdomen. If you're breast-feeding, wear a supporting brassiere during the day and while you're sleeping.

Watch your diet carefully. Breast-feeding requires that you eat for two, but if you limit junk foods and unnecessary calories, your figure won't suffer. If you're not breast-feeding, limit the food you eat. You may have eaten larger meals during pregnancy; now try fewer than 2,000 calories daily. Proper eating and exercise can restore your figure to normal within three months.

WHEN THE BABY CRIES

Babies have only one way to communicate at first: they cry. Your job is to interpret your baby's cries and decide how to respond, if at all.

In time, translation will become second nature. You'll learn to distinguish the tired cry, the hungry cry, the I'm-lonely-someone-come-and-pay-attention-to-me cry. But at first all cries may sound alike: what in the world is that child crying about?

Usually, because another feeding's in order. If the clock shows the baby hasn't eaten in three or four hours, you almost can be sure the message is, "Come and feed me."

When babies continue to cry after eating, it may mean they're not getting enough to eat. If you're breast-feeding, allow time for a longer feeding, or offer a supplementary bottle. If the baby is bottle-fed, increase the amount of formula.

Sometimes the cause of crying is obvious. It may be something as simple as a soiled diaper or the discomfort of diaper rash (see page 165). A few babies cry at sudden change, or are startled by a loud noise. Some cry when they are too warm or too cold.

Older babies may cry because they're lonely. The infant, wanting to see faces and hear voices, may call for a visitor.

The cry seldom signals a real emergency. Despite parents' fears, an open diaper pin is seldom the cause. A medical explanation is equally rare and is usually indicated by other signs, such as fever, decreased appetite, nasal congestion, vomiting and diarrhea. Thus you seldom need to drop what you're doing and respond to the baby's cries. But don't let crying continue for more than a few minutes without investigation.

THE CRYING HOUR

Some babies cry persistently without explanation. In fact, about one-fourth of the parents who visit well-baby clinics report their infants fall into this category. The crying is harmless for the baby, but nerve-wracking and exhausting for parents, particularly when they seek an explanation and cannot find one. The problem seems to get worse until age six weeks, after which it gradually decreases. It seldom lasts more than three months.

For many of these babies, a daily "crying hour" develops, mostly in late afternoon, but sometimes in the morning or late at night. The baby often reddens, draws knees up to chest, kicks and screams loudly. As each cry subsides, another begins. The length of the "crying hour" varies. Some normal infants cry six to seven hours a day.

This regular, persistent crying is sometimes called "colic," because it was previously believed to result from intestinal cramping. Most doctors now doubt this explanation. It is based on the observation that "colicky" babies draw their legs, distend their abdomens and pass gas. But babies do this at other times, too.

Intolerance of formula is sometimes blamed for colic, but changing the ingredients seldom lessens crying. (And breast-fed babies cry, too.) Other theorists, noting that the crying hour often coincides with late afternoon when parents are likely to be most frazzled, attribute the baby's crying to family emotional stress. Emotional stress may indeed exist when babies cry for hours on end, but it is difficult to determine which came first, crying or stress. Moreover, babies of experienced, calm parents are not immune from crying.

The most logical (and comforting) explanation for persistent crying is a developmental one. Babies cry because their internal nervous systems are still maturing. The regular daily pattern and the fact that the baby seems to "grow out of it" by the age of three months, no matter what steps are taken, supports this point. It is further substantiated by folklore parents have known for centuries that soothing, rhythmic sounds and motions have a calming effect on a crying baby.

To soothe a crying baby, the first step is an age-old one. Try rocking to and fro in a rhythmic, tick-tock way. Holding the baby in an upright or semi-sitting position seems to work better than cradling him or her in a horizontal posture. Other rhythmic motions in a sitting position may help. Some parents find that a car or bus ride—even a short one—will halt the crying. At home, try a mechanical wind-up swing, which will keep the baby rocking for 10 to 15 minutes.

The rhythm of music and sound helps, too. You sing to the baby—that's where lullabies originated—or play the radio or stereo. Even the regular, continuous noise of a vacuum sweeper or vaporizer may be soothing.

However, no harm is done if you simply let the baby cry until he or she stops, as he or she eventually will. Persistent crying does no physical damage. That presupposes that you can tolerate it, and that it does not disturb the neighbors.

The "crying hour" can be a great strain for parents. It is normal and natural to feel frustrated and angry at a tiny child who continues to shriek hour after hour despite your most solicitous efforts. It is particularly difficult for a parent who is left alone with the child and calls for plenty of mutual support.

THE BABY IS HUNGRY

Whether you feed by breast or bottle, baby's meals will consume time. At an average of 30 minutes per session, you'll devote three full hours to six or more daily feedings.

You won't have difficulty recognizing when it's time for a feeding. Even before the baby is fully awake, you'll hear fussing—a restless moving in the crib. Next will come a sucking, slurping noise as the baby tries to get fists into mouth and, succeeding, gnaws on them. Then there'll be a tentative cry or two, the cries coming closer together until—if you wait long enough—a series of lusty squalls will send the message in no uncertain terms.

Even if you're fast asleep, your subconscious will pick up the baby's signal. In fact, some nursing mothers say the baby's first cries unconsciously start the milk let-down reflex.

Round-the-clock feedings usually continue for approximately one to three months. Then the baby may begin to sleep through one of the feedings, lengthening that particular nap to six or more hours. Your baby may be erratic for a time, missing a feeding, then reverting to the old schedule for a night or two, then missing it again. You can induce a longer sleep by providing an extra large feeding in the evening or by waking the baby for feedings during the day, so the rest at night is a longer one.

BREAST-FEEDING AT HOME

It may not be so easy to breast-feed at home as it was in the hospital. You'll be faced by interruptions and conflicts when the baby's demands interfere with your other obligations. Many a nursing mother feels overwhelmed and gives up the project. One doctor recalls a mother whose milk dried up when she was welcomed home by a week's accumulation of dirty laundry!

For your part, this period calls for perseverance. It's a difficult time, for the baby's appetite may vary widely, leading you to feel inadequate and uncertain about your milk supply.

And being solely responsible for the baby's feeding can make you feel terribly tied down. It's important to overcome these feelings and recognize that you really needn't restrict yourself.

If breast-feeding is to succeed, your family must help, too. Your milk supply will be enhanced if you are rested and relaxed, rather than fatigued and tense. Rest is essential. So is assistance with household chores. If you haven't hired someone to help and no relatives are available, the father and any other children must pitch in, or some tasks must be postponed for a few weeks.

THE NURSING MOTHER'S DIET

As the baby's sole source of nourishment, you must eat well yourself. A nursing mother needs 2,500 calories a day—300 more than when she was pregnant and 600 more than before pregnancy. She requires an even greater number if she is under 20 and still growing herself. Of course, telling you to eat more may be gratuitous advice. You'll probably find, perhaps to your dismay, that you have a ravenous appetite.

A well-balanced diet is essential, including daily servings from each of the basic food groups of protein foods, milk and milk products, grains, and fruits and vegetables. The diet differs slightly from the one you followed during pregnancy. You need less protein and more vitamin-rich foods. The doctor may prescribe that you continue your iron supplement and multiple vitamins. The baby also may be given supplementary vitamin D.

You also need a good supply of calcium. The easiest way to get it is via a daily quart of milk, which supplies this important mineral for the baby's bones and teeth as well as providing a liquid base for the milk supply and your digestive wastes. You should take in plenty of other fluids daily. Drink a glass of water before and after each feeding.

If you're concerned about your weight, substitute low-fat or fat-free milk. Or your doctor may suggest calcium tablets. You also may use milk in puddings, custards, or soups. Other liquids may be coffee, tea, juices, or broth. Avoid carbonated drinks.

Just about anything you eat or drink may find its way into your milk supply. The flavor of onions and garlic comes through almost unchanged. Some babies will refuse to nurse if the taste is particularly strong. If you eat chocolate or nuts, it is said the baby will have diarrhea, although the relationship never has been definitely established. A meal of beans or cabbage is said to cause indigestion in the baby.

Be sparing with drugs, cigarettes, and alcohol. Aspirin or mild laxatives are probably not harmful, although you may want to ask your doctor before using them. Barbiturates, tranquilizers, and other stronger medications should be taken only for good medical reasons. Some doctors oppose the use of oral contraceptives by nursing mothers.

The potential harm of cigarette smoking by nursing mothers still is being investigated. To be on the safe side, don't smoke. Some doctors approve an occasional glass of wine to relax after a tense day and stimulate the mother's let-down reflex. But they caution that too much alcohol can make the baby woozy after breast-feeding.

You may be tempted to reduce your weight during this period, but it is not a time for strict dieting. Both you and the baby may suffer. During nursing, priority goes to building up the breast milk.

The following is a sample menu to be used during nursing:

Breakfast
Small glass orange juice
½ cup oatmeal with brown sugar
Full cup milk (some may be used on oatmeal)
Coffee or tea

Lunch
Tuna fish sandwich made with 2 slices of whole wheat bread, ½ cup tuna fish salad
1 small banana
Full cup milk

Afternoon snack
½ cup salted peanuts
Full cup milk

Dinner
Six ounces of roast beef
½ cup egg noodles
¾ cup cut asparagus
Spinach salad with oil and vinegar
Full cup milk
Coffee or tea

Evening snack
2 oatmeal raisin cookies
Full cup milk

BREAST-FEEDING AND VISITORS
You may not want many visitors during the first few weeks you are breast-feeding. Company and excitement can hold back the milk flow and result in a less than satisfactory feeding. Guests

shouldn't be allowed to interfere with the nursing schedule. For your own comfort, don't delay the feeding more than a few minutes.

Some mothers are embarrassed to nurse before other people—or feel their guests might be embarrassed. Writers who discuss etiquette divide on whether public display of this natural function is socially acceptable. But like many aspects of motherhood, the question doesn't involve protocol—it's strictly a personal question; just follow your own judgment. Nursing is natural and nothing to be ashamed of.

Regardless of your feelings, be sure to explain nursing to your other children. Make it clear that nursing is a perfectly natural phenomenon, a warm human experience between mothers and babies to be shared by the members of the entire family. In fact, it can be an early lesson in sexual differences for the older children, showing that mothers nurse babies and fathers don't.

Once you've established a regular nursing routine and feel more relaxed about it, you'll probably find no need to be isolated from the rest of the family; nursing can be a time to enjoy the other children. It provides the opportunity for conversation, for playing games with the other children, or for story-telling.

A TIME AND A PLACE

With experience, you'll be able to nurse the baby anywhere. Some mothers say they can nurse while standing or walking. But your early nursing will be more successful if you establish a relaxed, regular routine. A quiet room is best. Pick a chair with arms, bolster your elbows with pillows, and prop your feet up. Use the time exclusively to cuddle and talk to the baby, not watch television or read. At night, take the baby into bed with you, so you can rest while nursing.

For your own comfort and the baby's, nurse when the baby is ready to eat. He or she will probably follow a three-hour schedule, but if the baby wakes early, don't wait for the three hours to pass. On the other hand, if the baby oversleeps, rouse the child and begin feeding. Otherwise, your breasts may feel full and sore; and milk may begin to leak on your clothing.

Once a routine is established, you'll probably nurse about ten minutes on each breast. More than that is probably fruitless. Even slow eaters get about four fifths of their capacity in the first five minutes. Some babies are satisfied with just one breast. Remember that sucking itself is important; the baby may be kept at the breast a few minutes to satisfy this instinct. But prolonged suckling can cause sore and cracked nipples. You may wish to substitute a pacifier (see page 232).

WILL YOU HAVE ENOUGH MILK?

Only rarely does a woman have too little milk for her baby. The human breast normally manufactures one-and-one-half to two ounces of milk in each breast every three hours. A newborn only requires one to two fluid ounces per pound of body weight a day. A seven-pounder thus needs 14 to 21 ounces a day, compared to a normal output of 24 to 32 ounces.

The milk will be rich enough, too. A seven-pound baby needs about 50 calories per pound of body weight per day—350 calories daily. Breast milk measures about 22 to 25 calories per ounce, so that amounts to approximately 100 calories per feeding.

Some nursing mothers become discouraged when they first see breast milk. It just doesn't look very nourishing. It's not foamy and white, like milk you pour from a bottle, but resembles skim milk—thin, watery, and slightly blue. But that color and consistency are just right for the baby's development.

A true gauge of your milk's quality and amount is how well the baby grows. If he or she seems to be thriving and filling out, you're furnishing an ample amount of nutrition. Most babies lose a little when they first leave the hospital, but then begin to gain at the rate of about a quarter of a pound per week—noticeable even to an unpracticed eye. In any case, the doctor will weigh the baby at the first checkup, usually at about two weeks of age.

Another yardstick is how many diapers are used. More than six wet diapers a day usually indicates the baby is getting plenty of fluid.

Don't automatically assume that if your baby won't eat, there's something wrong with your milk. Bottle-fed babies also fuss, cry, spit up, or refuse to eat sometimes.

SUPPLEMENTARY AND RELIEF BOTTLES

If your baby still seems unsatisfied and continues to cry after being placed at the second breast, your doctor may suggest you offer a supplementary bottle immediately afterward. Regularly supplementing breast milk with formula is usually a last resort, however. As part of the supply-demand principle, your milk production will drop. And the baby may later resist the more difficult task of breast-feeding. Giving water isn't necessary except in hot weather.

After a few weeks, you may wish to provide a relief bottle,

For formula feeding, take a prepared bottle from refrigerator, shake, and warm in saucepan of water.

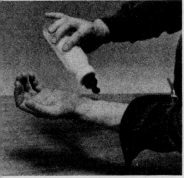

Test temperature by sprinkling a few drops on inside of wrist. It should feel warm, not hot.

Prop the baby in semi-sitting position in crook of elbow, for easier breathing and swallowing.

so the baby becomes accustomed to bottle-feeding and you can get an occasional respite. That's also a time to bring the father into the feeding routine and allow him a private period with the baby. Your own milk is the best supply. Hand-express milk from your breast, or use a breast pump to squeeze if from the nipple into a sterile bottle. Refrigerate until needed. This way you'll maintain your milk production.

When the baby is down to four or five feedings per day, relief bottles may be used more often. By then, the baby has become accomplished at nursing and may readily switch between breast and bottle; you will now be freer to leave him or her and even resume working. When you are absent from home at feeding time, you always should nurse as soon as you return, so you can relieve the fullness in your breasts and continue to produce milk. Especially in the early weeks, some milk may leak from your breasts and retard the flow. If it occurs regularly, you may wish to wear a folded handkerchief inside your nursing bra.

BOTTLE FEEDING

The majority of babies are bottle-fed, including many who started on breast milk. Babies brought up on formula thrive, too, so don't hesitate to feed yours by bottle or to switch from breast milk to formula if you find nursing unsatisfactory.

On the average, bottle-fed newborns eat less often, commonly six feedings a day, once every four hours. A newborn takes about two ounces at each feeding. The amount increases as the baby grows older, and the number of feedings decreases.

Like breast-feeding, bottle-feeding comes naturally. Because you'll be there for 30 minutes or more, pick a comfortable armchair or the corner of a sofa, with pillows to support your elbows. Hold the baby in your lap, the head in the crook of one elbow, the bottle in your other hand. The baby should be in a semi-sitting position, to keep the airway open and allow easy swallowing. Don't feed while the baby is lying on his or her back; gagging may result.

When you tickle the cheek or lips, the baby instinctively will turn, seize the nipple, and begin to suck. Hold the bottle at slightly more than a right angle to the baby's mouth, so the nipple and cap are filled with formula and not air, which causes a false fullness and makes the baby uncomfortable.

Keep the cap of the bottle slightly loose to allow air to enter. A line of bubbles will rise through the formula to indicate the baby is feeding successfully. Place a folded diaper or bib under the chin to catch dribbles.

Sometimes the baby may pull so hard that a kind of negative pressure builds up in the bottle. The nipple or plastic bottle liner collapses and shuts off the flow. The frustrated baby continues to suck but gets nothing for the effort. To prevent this, move the bottle in the baby's mouth from time to time to break the suction, or remove it entirely for a moment.

Your baby may not finish the entire bottle at each feeding. Just like adults, babies have the right not to be hungry sometimes. Don't coax him or her to finish.

On the other hand, if the baby repeatedly devours the bottle's contents and seems to want more, increase the next feeding by one-half ounce. When that amount no longer satisfies the baby, add another half ounce. Try to keep just a little ahead in matching your supply to the demands of the baby.

Don't prop the bottle and leave. That practice not only denies the baby some necessary parenting, it can be dangerous. If the milk flows too quickly, the baby may gag, vomit, or suck it into the lungs and choke. And if the bottle slips away and the baby can't recover it, the experience can be downright frustrating.

PREPARING THE FORMULA

You can mix cow's milk or evaporated milk with other ingredients to make an acceptable substitute for mother's milk, but few parents bother today. More commonly, they use commercial, premixed formulas, which cost more but are more convenient.

Sold under various brand names in supermarkets and drugstores, the formulas come in three types:

• Powdered formula is mixed with sterilized water: a scoop of formula per two ounces of water. It is the least expensive variety.

• Liquid concentrate also must be mixed, usually one part of concentrate to one of water. It is available in 13-ounce cans and must be refrigerated after opening.

• Ready-to-feed may be used directly from the can, requiring no mixing. It is the most expensive kind. Sold in cans or—the ultimate convenience—in disposable bottles, it requires only a nipple to be used for immediate feeding.

Commercial formulas are said to contain the important ingredients of mother's milk in the correct proportions, and manufacturers improve them as knowledge is gained. Most use cow's milk as the basic source of protein. Others use vegetable protein, usually from soybeans, and may be recommended for babies with allergies or for babies born into families with a history of allergy. Goat's milk and meat-based formulas are also available. The American Academy of Pediatrics recommends that formula fortified with iron be used by four months.

There are as many methods of preparing a formula as there are mothers. The traditional one is called the terminal method and enables you to mix a day's supply of formula at a time.

To prepare formula this way, you should have a set place in the kitchen, near stove, sink, and refrigerator. It should be equipped with the following, which may be bought as a kit:

- Eight eight-ounce glass or plastic bottles, with nipples, screw-on rings, and covers.
- Two or three four-ounce bottles for water.
- A quart measuring pitcher that is graduated in ounces.
- Punch can opener.
- Bottle and nipple brushes.
- Long-handled spoon for stirring.
- Funnel and tongs.
- Jar with lid for storing extra nipples.
- A sterilizer or a large pot with a tight lid. It must be deep enough so the nipples don't touch the top and the bottles can be kept off the bottom of the unit.
- A rack for the sterilizer, to keep the bottles away from the bottom of the kettle.

After a bottle has been used, rinse the formula from it with clean water. Remove and rinse the nipples, squeezing water through them to remove scum or butterfat from the holes. When ready to prepare formula, wash bottles, nipples, caps, and nipple covers in hot, sudsy water, using a detergent, which cuts scum better than soap does. Use a bottle brush to clean the insides of the bottles and nipple brush to cleanse scum or dried formula from the nipples. Also wash the measuring pitcher, can opener, tongs, and other utensils, rinsing everything in hot, clean water.

With soap, wash the top of the can containing liquid formula and rinse well.

If you are using liquid concentrate, a common proportion for a newborn is one 13-ounce can to 15 ounces of water, producing 28 ounces of formula, or a day's supply of seven four-ounce bottles. Later, the amount of water will be reduced until the proportions are equal.

Next, follow these steps:

1. Measure the prescribed number of ounces of warm water into the graduated pitcher.

2. Add a full can of concentrated formula, or specified

amount of powdered formula, and stir with the long-handled spoon. Always add concentrated or powdered formula *to* the water.

3. Pour the mixture into the clean bottles—about one more ounce per bottle than you expect the baby to drink.

4. Put nipples, rings, and caps on bottles, leaving rings loose so steam can escape.

5. Place bottles on rack in the sterilizer or kettle. Add about three inches of water.

6. Bring the water to a boil, cover, reduce heat, and allow it to boil gently for 25 minutes.

7. Remove sterilizer from heat, and allow to cool until you can touch it.

8. Remove the lid and cool the bottles gradually by adding cool water. (Gradual cooling keeps scum from forming.)

9. Remove bottles and tighten caps.

10. Store in refrigerator until ready to use.

11. Before feeding, warm the bottle by heating it in a small saucepan of water, by placing it under the hot water faucet for a few minutes, or by using a bottle warmer. Shake a few drops on your wrist to test the temperature. It should feel pleasantly warm, not too hot or cold.

A SIMPLER METHOD

With improved hygiene, a relatively pure water supply, pre-sterilized formula, and the high water temperature available in electric dishwashers, many doctors and parents consider elaborate sterilization measures unnecessary. Instead, the formula is prepared one bottle at a time.

With these methods, you first wash and dry the glass bottles in your electric dishwasher. Sterilize the nipples separately in a pot of boiling water, storing them in a jar until ready for use. If you use ready-to-feed formula, pour the prescribed amount into a bottle, cover with a nipple, and feed. Liquid concentrate or powder can be mixed with warm water directly from the faucet. Just add the right amount of liquid or powdered formula, cap with the nipple, shake the bottle, and feed.

There is a more cautious method. Wash and rinse the used bottles; fill each with the prescribed amount of water. Cover with nipples and caps, and sterilize for 25 minutes. After the bottles have cooled, remove them from the sterilizer, and store them at room temperature until needed. Then add formula, cap, shake, and use without heating. An advantage to this method is that you open formula only as necessary.

You may also sterilize one bottle at a time. Wash and rinse the bottle and nipple after use, then place them in an uncovered saucepan of water; boil for five minutes. Remove with tongs, pour in the prescribed amount of water from the saucepan in which the materials were sterilized, add formula, shake, and use.

STORING FORMULA
Bacteria grow rapidly in milk. Don't give the baby an unfinished bottle of formula unless he or she is definitely hungry again within an hour.

Be sure to refrigerate the formula as soon as it has cooled after sterilization. It will then keep as long as ordinary milk. Canned formula must always be refrigerated after opening; cover the top with aluminum foil or plastic wrap before you store it in the refrigerator.

DISPOSABLE BOTTLES
Disposable bottles are a definite convenience in busy households, and some doctors insist that babies fed with them are healthier, perhaps happier, and have less colic, too, although no one has established it scientifically.

Disposable bottles are narrow sacs of transparent plastic, bought in a roll, torn off for individual use, and thrown away afterward. A complete bottle preparation kit usually includes a roll of sacs, unbreakable plastic sac holders, nipples, retaining rings, and covers. If you've inherited an older kit, you may find a metal expander that was used before the advent of the plastic tabs that are now present on most disposable bottles.

Prepare either a day's supply or a bottle at a time. Sterilize the retaining rings, nipples, and nipple covers in a saucepan. Boil parts for at least five minutes. Then dispose of water and let nipples and rings dry until cool.

When they've cooled, tear one sac from the roll at the perforation and fold it lengthwise. Grasp it at the tabs and insert the sac in the bottle holder. Next, pull the tabs apart and slide them over the top of the holder. Pull down on the tabs (with an even motion) until they cover the retaining ring and come to rest as far down on the holder as possible (see specific instructions, page 155).

Tear off the tabs and dispose of them. Now you have a complete unit. Add sterilized water, cover with nipple and cap, and add formula when ready for use. Heating will not be necessary. Or pour formula into bottles and store in refrigerator until needed.

BOTTLE PREPARATION METHODS

Prepare a bottle of formula as you need it or a day's supply at one time. Formula and equipment are usually sterilized to kill harmful bacteria; the most popular methods are shown here. Prepared formula always should be stored in the refrigerator.

DISPOSABLE BOTTLES

To prepare formula with disposable bottles, first sterilize nipples, retainer rings, and covers in a saucepan.

Bring to full boil for at least five minutes. Pour the water off, and allow the parts to cool.

Remove single formula sac from roll, tearing at perforation. Don't touch the inside of the sac.

Slide the disposable bottle liner into holder by folding lengthwise. Hold liner by tabs only.

Separate tabs by sliding between fingers; pull over rim at top of holder. Tear off tabs; dispose.

Fill with formula; snap on nipple and cap. Or use sterilized water; add formula when ready to use.

SIMPLE METHOD

Simple method of preparing bottles kills bacteria with hot water from the dishwasher.

Sterilize nipples in saucepan of boiling water, then store them in jar until ready for use.

Fill with correct amount of tap water, cap with nipple, then add formula at feeding time.

TERMINAL METHOD

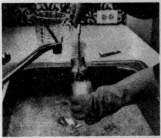

Terminal method is traditional way to sterilize. First, wash bottles and nipples in sudsy water.

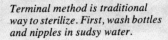

Drain bottles on cloth or paper towel; be sure to clean all caked milk from nipple openings.

Clean top of formula can with boiling water; use a sterilized punch opener to open the can.

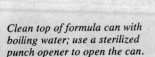

Measure the prescribed amount of warm water from the tap into a graduated pitcher that holds one quart of liquid.

To the water, add the concentrated formula or powder according to the directions, and stir with a long-handled spoon.

Pour the proper amount of liquid into each bottle. Be sure to use a funnel to prevent spilling the mixture.

Put nipples, rings, and caps on bottles. Make sure the rings remain loose so steam can escape from the bottles.

To sterilize the bottles, place them on a rack in the sterilizer. Add three inches of water. Boil gently for 25 minutes.

Remove the bottles from heat, and allow them to cool gradually for about two hours. Tighten caps. Store in refrigerator.

KEEP THE NIPPLES FLOWING

Nipple holes must be the right diameter to let the baby feed easily. If they're not large enough, the baby has to work too hard and therefore may tire of sucking too early and demand another feeding ahead of schedule. If the holes are too large, the formula streams out too fast. The baby may gag or be filled up before the sucking instinct has been satisfied.

To test the nipple, hold the bottle upside down and shake it. The formula should drip fairly rapidly, about one to three drops per second. If it drips in a steady stream, the hole is too large and the nipple should be replaced. If it is slower, you must enlarge the hole. To do this, push a red-hot needle through the nipple from the outside. It's easiest if you insert the blunt end of the needle in a cork, then heat the sharp end with a match or lighter. Enlarge the hole gradually, testing the rate of flow after each insertion until the proper diameter has been reached.

Clean nipples after each use. Butterfat in the milk causes rubber nipples to deteriorate. Wash them in warm, sudsy water, using a small nipple brush. Silicone nipples used with disposable bottles may be turned inside out for easier washing. Be sure to squeeze water through the holes. If formula has caked in the nipples or scum has formed, put a small pinch of salt in the nipple, add water to form a paste, then squeeze the nipple between your fingers to force the solution through the holes. Or boil the nipples in slightly salted water for five minutes.

TIME FOR A BURP

Both bottle- and breast-fed babies swallow air while feeding. A breast-fed child ordinarily swallows less, because the baby usually sits up to eat, allowing air to escape naturally. But either method may make a child uncomfortable if too much air is swallowed. To relieve the discomfort, the baby must be burped or bubbled.

There are three ways to get rid of the accumulated air. The most popular is to hold the baby upright, with head over your shoulder. Pat or rub the back gently until you hear a release of air. Or place the baby, stomach down, on your lap or on a mattress, turning head to the side and supporting it with your hand while you rub the back with the other hand. Third, hold the baby in a sitting position, leaning slightly forward, with your hands propping head and back. Often, simply moving the baby into that position will bring up the air.

Two burps during the feeding and one afterward are usually enough, unless the baby still seems distressed. Some nursing mothers automatically burp the baby when they switch breasts. Don't interrupt the feeding to burp the baby. Wait until there's a pause in the nursing.

After burping, place the baby in bed on the stomach. That allows for release of any additional air, and if the baby should happen to spit up, milk or mucus won't get into the lungs.

SPITTING UP

Spitting up during burping or after feeding is common. It isn't significant if the baby is gaining weight. Spitting up after feeding is seldom like the projectile vomiting of illness. Milk just seems to trickle from the mouth and usually contains a few undigested curds.

For unknown reasons, some babies seem to spit up more than others. It may indicate the baby has swallowed too much air during feeding. If spitting up persists, try burping the baby longer. More time for the baby in an inclined chair may help, too.

Some babies continue to spit up persistently despite these measures. The explanation then may not be swallowed air but immaturity of the muscles controlling the passage between

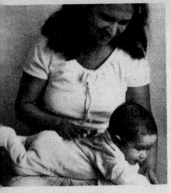

Three ways to burp the baby: newborns burp best on stomach, in your lap. Gently pat or rub back.

An older baby may be held upright, with head nestling against your shoulder. Pat back gently.

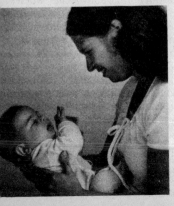

Some babies burp best when placed in a sitting position. Support head and back, then pat.

esophagus and stomach. This theory is supported by the fact that spitting up gradually lessens as the child grows older and usually ceases by the end of the first year.

Vomiting with force should be reported to the doctor, especially if it occurs after several feedings or continues for several days. Repeated vomiting may dehydrate the baby and may indicate illness or a need to change formula.

BOWEL MOVEMENTS

The baby's first bowel movements are usually greenish-black. The dark color indicates the presence of meconium, a substance in fetal wastes that continues to appear during the transition to independent life. The odorless, tarry stools last only about three to four days. Afterward, bowel movements may vary according to whether the baby is breast- or bottle-fed.

Breast-fed babies commonly have loose, watery, diarrhea-like stools during the first month. There may be as many as six to nine a day, perhaps one after each feeding. Some may be little more than a stain on the diaper. The looseness is normal and isn't true diarrhea, which is usually signaled by an abrupt change in frequency or consistency of stools.

The stools are usually yellow, orange, or even slightly green. All are normal. They also may contain undigested milk curds, because breast milk often passes rapidly through the intestinal tract before the digestive process is completed.

As the intestinal tract matures, food is used more efficiently and bowel movements are less frequent. Some breast-fed babies won't have a bowel movement for two or three days—or longer—even though they strain heartily, turn beet-red, and groan. So long as the movements are of normal consistency when they do appear, there is no cause for alarm.

Bottle-fed babies may move their bowels less frequently. Two to four movements a day are normal at first, decreasing to one or two a day after a month. The movements are usually firmer and darker, mostly yellowish or brown.

Some babies routinely may go 48 hours or longer without a bowel movement. If the final product is soft and smooth, irregularity isn't a problem. Most babies strain and groan when they have a movement, but this seldom represents bowel difficulties. Unless the movement is hard and pellet-like, the baby is not constipated.

If the baby does seem constipated, offer cool, sterilized water between feedings (not within an hour of the next feeding, however). You also might dilute the formula more or, with the doctor's approval, change brands. Don't use enemas, suppositories, or baby laxatives unless prescribed by your doctor.

Diarrhea in a small baby can be an emergency, especially if there are four or five loose, watery, or mucus-filled bowel movements in rapid succession, or even one large movement. Notify the doctor and frequently give the baby cool, sterilized water every half hour to replenish the fluids. If the baby also is vomiting, keep the amounts small. Look for other signs of pain or illness, especially if the condition continues.

CHANGING DIAPERS

Change the baby's diapers after every bowel movement and as often as practical after urination. Put on a fresh diaper after a bath and after a feeding. That usually adds up to about 12 changes a day.

A wet diaper isn't an emergency, however. Don't wake the baby to change a diaper; babies wake if they feel uncomfortable. If the baby is warm otherwise, he or she won't be chilled even if a diaper is soaked.

After a bowel movement, wipe the diaper area with soft toilet tissues, or use pre-moistened tissues that can be flushed away afterward. Cleanse the skin with a soft cloth and soap and water or with moistened cotton balls. Pat dry with a soft clean cloth, being sure to dry the creases. Apply powder or cornstarch to reduce chafing. Be careful the baby does not inhale powder.

To change a diaper, place the baby on his or her back. Unpin the diaper, placing the pins out of the baby's reach. Fold the diaper under as you unpin, and remove. Wash, dry, and powder the diaper area. Lift the baby's legs by the ankles and slip a clean diaper under, with the extra thickness in front for a boy, in the rear for a girl. Pin on each side, back overlapping front. Put your finger between diaper and skin to avoid sticking the baby. Until the baby's navel has healed, keep the diaper below it.

DIAPER CARE

Whether you launder your own diapers or subscribe to a diaper service, keep a two-gallon covered pail for soiled diapers in the bathroom. A diaper service usually will provide a deodorized pail, along with disposable liners. If it does not, buy your own.

After removing a soiled diaper, scrape or shake the stool into the toilet and flush. Rinse the diaper in the clear water until the stain is removed. Wring out and drop the diaper into the covered pail. Wet diapers may be rinsed under the faucet, wrung out completely, and placed in the diaper pail.

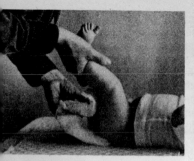

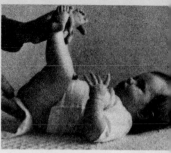

The daily dozen: to change soiled diaper, unpin and place pad under baby to catch moisture.

Wash genital area with warm, damp washcloth, including all creases and folds. Pat the area dry.

A diaper service usually will pick up soiled diapers once or twice weekly, along with your baby's other laundry. In some states, they are licensed and must meet standards that guarantee diapers are sterile.

Laundering diapers in an automatic washer at home adds up to about one tenth the price of using a diaper service but is less convenient. Adequate rinsing is critical to remove detergent, which can cause skin irritation. If the baby already has a rash, you may need to soak the diapers in a commercial purifying solution, a process described on page 167. Extra rinsing and pre-soaking also help. With proper care, home laundering achieves sterilization.

To make diapers softer, add fabric softener before the final rinse. Using a clothes dryer also makes the diapers softer, although many parents prefer hanging the diapers outdoors.

DISPOSABLE DIAPERS

Diapers you use only once and throw away are even more convenient. And using disposables also cuts down on skin rash, odor, and allergies. They're available at supermarkets and drugstores. Even if you use cloth diapers ordinarily, you'll want a supply of disposables for emergencies and for traveling.

Disposables have three layers—a porous inner layer next to the baby's skin; a waterproof outer covering; and, sandwiched between, several thicknesses of absorbent material. Moisture penetrates the inner layer and is absorbed by the center layer, keeping wetness from the baby's skin. The outer layer substitutes for plastic pants and protects clothing from getting wet.

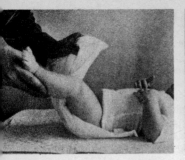 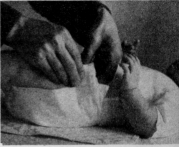

Lift baby by ankles and slide diaper under hips. Bring diaper up between the baby's legs.

Pin (or tape) diaper on each side. Always keep fingers next to baby to avoid pricking skin.

Most disposables are equipped with self-adhesive tapes that replace diaper pins.

DIAPER RASH

Diaper rash isn't a single condition. Instead, the term refers to any skin eruption in the diaper area, where heat and moisture form a natural breeding ground for bacteria. There are several varieties of diaper rash, each of which can make a small baby sore and uncomfortable. All have their own distinctive patterns, which, if recognized, let you treat them quickly and prevent further rashes.

• The most common rash affects the rounded surfaces of the diaper area, such as buttocks and lower abdomen, sparing the folds of skin. It is usually an irritation due to contact with urine. Ammonia formed by the action of bacteria on urine-soaked skin or diaper is considered the major source. Sometimes the rash consists of large red patches, sometimes of rounded, elevated areas of redness and skin breakdown. Most babies have this ammonia-related rash intermittently. It usually responds well to more frequent diaper changes and to letting the baby go without diapers as much as is practical.

• Red, raw places confined to the folds of skin in the diaper area may result from heat and friction, or from the same skin disorder that causes cradle cap. Blisters nearby indicate a secondary yeast infection. If the rash is caused by heat, remove the baby's plastic pants, because they retain heat and moisture.

• Soreness confined mainly to the rectum and genital area is usually the result of loose stools. It is more common in bottle-fed than breast-fed babies, although both are affected. It may clear without special treatment.

- Soreness in the rectal-genital area that is also accompanied by blisters and scales may result from thrush, an infection more commonly seen in the throat and mouth. Besides treating the sore places, the condition itself must be dealt with.

- A rash confined to the area of the elastic band in plastic pants at any age is the result of alternate wetting and drying. To prevent it, use diapers, without plastic pants.

- Tiny blisters and pustules covering the entire diaper area may be heat rash, or prickly heat. The blisters may be found on other parts of the body, too, but are concentrated in the diaper area because of higher temperatures. Fewer clothes will help prevent a recurrence.

- Other rashes, especially those causing large, draining blisters in the diaper area, may indicate more widespread types of skin problems or conditions affecting the entire body. They require a doctor's attention as soon as possible.

To treat all forms of diaper rash, remove diapers as soon as they are wet or soiled. As much as you can, leave the diapers off entirely until the rash heals. To help keep things dry, put two or three layers of diapers and a rubberized pad under the baby in the crib, replacing them as necessary. When you must diaper, use two or three thicknesses of cloth diapers and omit plastic or rubber pants, which may seal in moisture and keep the skin irritated.

In cases of an ammonia-related rash, petroleum jelly or a mild protective ointment may be applied after cleaning and drying, to protect the skin from further contact with urine. Zinc oxide should not be applied while the skin is inflamed but may be used after healing to prevent new inflammation. Avoid powdering with cornstarch, which can be a culture medium for bacteria. If you use baby powder, apply lightly and sparingly, not in large amounts.

An ordinary light bulb, directed toward the exposed area from a few feet away, hastens healing. Cool, wet compresses, soaked in a solution of one teaspoon salt to a pint of water, may be applied intermittently, with "air conditioning" by exposure between applications.

If these simple measures are not successful, a different form of rash may be responsible, or there may be excessive ammonia because diapers have been inadequately sterilized. A strong and persistent smell of ammonia is your first clue. If you launder diapers in an automatic washer at home, several approaches may eliminate ammonia-causing bacteria. Simply adding a cup of chlorine bleach or diaper wash to the laundry may be enough. Or you can soak the soiled diapers in a commercial ammonium compound (such as Diaperene), then wash with mild, laundry soap, repeating the rinse cycle twice. Acidify the washed and rinsed diapers by adding one cup of vinegar to half a washtub of water, soaking the diapers for 30 minutes, then spinning dry without further washing.

Finally, the simplest but most expensive course is to use a commercial laundry service.

BATHING THE BABY

A bath is an important part of the routine, but you needn't bathe the baby every day. It's strictly an individual and cultural matter. American babies, for instance, are bathed twice as often as European babies, without any difference in the health of either group.

In a warm climate, you may wish to give a bath daily, even sponging the baby off every few hours during hot summer months. In winter, cut back to a bath every other day or three times a week, because indoor heat lowers humidity and dries out the baby's skin. Frequent bathing increases chafing and itching. The number of baths also should be reduced if the baby has a skin rash. Too much bathing also bothers the baby's delicate skin.

Set a regular place and time for bathing the baby (see Chapter Five for suggestions). A bath after a feeding is a good idea, because the baby is less restless when less hungry. Many parents prefer a morning bath, so the baby is dressed in a clean wardrobe for the day. After the bath, the baby can be tucked into the crib or bassinet for a morning nap.

Almost any place that's warm, free from drafts, and a convenient height is good for bathing. The kitchen sink will do if it's large enough, or baby's own plastic tub may be placed on the drainboard. There is no special magic about a bath table except to be sure the height is right for you to bathe the baby without stooping. Most mothers prefer not to use the bathtub, which requires them to kneel.

Keep baby's bath supplies together in a tray or basket so you won't have to search for them at bath time. You won't need special toiletries. Any good, mild hand soap, preferably one without perfume, will do. Liquid soaps are good; you might want to choose a hypoallergenic product to reduce rash.

Avoid heavy use of baby oil after bathing. It may clog the baby's pores. Chafing of the baby's skin can be relieved by using lotion or cream. If you use baby powder, apply it lightly and sparingly. Don't shake the powder on lavishly because the baby may inhale it into the lungs while you're doing so. Some doctors advocate the use of cornstarch.

Until the baby's navel and circumcision are healed, give sponge rather than tub baths. (For instructions on sponge bathing, see page 169. (Afterward, the baby can graduate to a tub or a portable bathtub.

Test the temperature of the water on the inside of your elbow; it should be comfortably warm, not hot.

Whether you're giving the baby a sponge or tub bath, use your hands or a soft cloth and gentle soap. Start with the face, being careful not to get soap in the eyes. Wash the baby's head about three times a week, and rinse it with clear water at other times. Work from front to back, so soap or shampoo doesn't get into the eyes. Scrub well, using the tips of your fingers and not the fingernails; rinse thoroughly.

Clean only the outer areas of the ears, using a soft cloth or moist cotton. Don't use a cotton-tipped stick, and don't wash the insides of either nose or ears.

When you wash the baby's body, don't overlook the creases of flesh in arms and legs; rinse them well afterward and pat dry. Don't use excess powder in these areas, because it may cake and clog pores. Rinse the baby all over at least twice to prevent irritation.

Don't trim fingernails and toenails at bath time. Wait until the baby is sleeping. Cut nails straight across with a blunt scissors; a pointed scissors may poke the baby's delicate skin.

Many babies enjoy their baths immediately. They splash and kick and squeal with delight. But others find bathing traumatic, howling with protest as soon as they're wet. It may take eight or ten baths before they adjust to the water.

Introduce these reluctant bathers to the experience gradually. Soap and wash them on a towel outside the tub; then immerse them in the water for rinsing only. Be careful when you pick up the squirming, soapy infant.

Words of warning: never leave any baby unattended in the bathtub, even for a few seconds. A few inches of water can be dangerous to a newborn; when you turn away to reach soap or powder, always keep one hand firmly on the baby. If the telephone or doorbell rings, wrap the dripping baby in a towel, and take him or her with you when you respond. In a real emergency, put the child on the floor, where the baby can neither fall nor drown.

HOW TO GIVE A SPONGE BATH

Baby's first bath is usually a sponge bath. Tubless cleansing continues for the first three or four weeks, until navel and circumcision are healed. Then the baby is ready for his or her own tub.

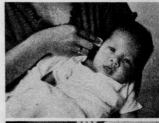

Wash only outer areas of the ears, using soft cloth or cotton. Don't use cotton-tipped stick or swab.

Shampoo scalp three times a week with mild soap. Use fingertips, not fingernails. Rinse well.

Use "football carry": your arm goes under the baby's head and back; your hand holds the head.

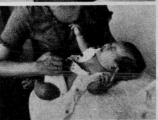

Getting prepared for a sponge bath: sit on low chair and undress baby on towel in your lap. Don't remove diaper.

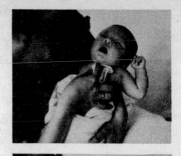

Remove shirt, but keep legs covered. Soap the baby's chest, arms, and hands, including folds and creases in the skin.

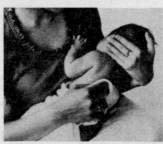

Rinse neck, chest, arms, and hands with clean, warm water. Rinse soap from folds of the skin. Pat the baby dry; don't rub.

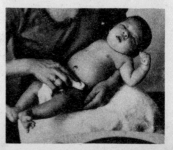

Gently, but firmly, support the head, turn the baby on right side to soap, and rinse his or her back and buttocks. Pat dry.

Remove the baby's diaper. Soap and rinse abdomen, genitals, legs, and feet. Wash gently around the navel until the area heals.

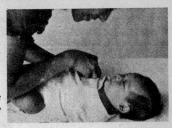

To help keep the baby dry, use powder or cornstarch in the baby's diaper area if you wish. Dress the baby quickly.

HOW TO GIVE A TUB BATH

Bathing a baby isn't a big deal. It may quickly become a highlight of the baby's schedule but needn't be done every day. Three times a week is enough. Have supplies ready before starting.

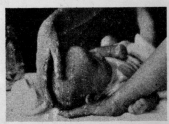

For tub bath, place baby first on soft towel. Wash face with clear water, then shampoo.

Don't forget football carry (page 169) when rinsing the head. Dry face and hair immediately.

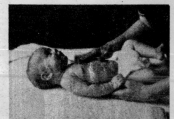

Remove shirt and soap the baby's chest and stomach. Keep the diaper unpinned but in place.

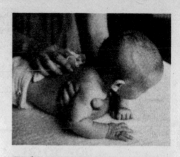

With hand under the baby's armpit, turn the baby over. Then soap back and buttocks. Make sure you have a firm grip.

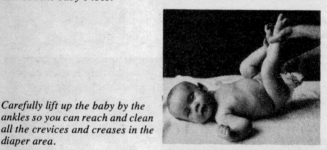

Remove diaper and soap the baby's abdomen, genital area, legs, and feet. Be sure to wash between the baby's toes.

Carefully lift up the baby by the ankles so you can reach and clean all the crevices and creases in the diaper area.

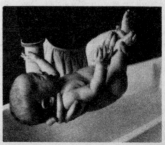

Rinse the baby in clear, warm water. One hand supports the baby's head; the other holds feet and ankles.

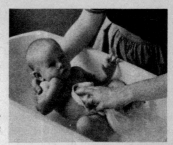

While you keep a firm grasp on the head of the sitting infant, rinse the baby quickly, but thoroughly, with a soft washcloth.

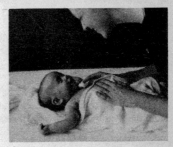

Then, carefully lift the baby out of the tub. Immediately wrap the baby in a large towel, and gently, but thoroughly, pat completely dry.

NAVEL AND CIRCUMCISION

The stump of the umbilical cord usually falls off within ten days after birth, although it may remain for three weeks. Meanwhile, the area must be kept clean and dry. Cleanse it at each diaper change, washing with a cotton ball soaked in rubbing alcohol, then drying with a clean cotton ball. Let the baby sleep on his or her back during this period if it seems more comfortable.

After the cord drops off, there may be secretions from the navel, and a spot or two of blood may appear. The spotting may continue for several days. This is normal; continue to clean the area until oozing stops. If bleeding continues more than a week, notify a doctor. It no longer is considered necessary to cover the stump with a dressing or band. Some believe a band keeps the navel from protruding in adulthood, but that has never been established.

Circumcision requires no bandage or dressing, either. Usually the circumcised area is covered with a plastic ring that drops with the skin after about 10 days. Petroleum jelly should be applied to the healing area after every sponge bath or diaper change for a week or ten days to prevent its sticking to the diaper.

If the penis swells or bleeds or does not heal within a few weeks, tell the doctor.

While the wound is healing, do not pull back the remaining foreskin for cleansing; the wound may separate. After approximately three weeks, the foreskin should be retracted at each bath for cleaning. Wash and dry carefully.

SWOLLEN BREASTS

Both boys and girls may have swollen breasts at birth—the result of maternal hormones still in the baby's bloodstream. The swelling eventually will disappear. Milk may drain from the breasts, too. It is not necessary to attempt to extract the remainder of this so-called witches' milk.

A few baby girls may have slight, blood-tinged vaginal discharge, also due to the mother's hormones. The condition is normal and requires no special treatment. It usually stops within a few days.

When a baby girl is bathed or her diaper changed, the vulva should be cleaned with moist cotton. Always work from front to back, so fecal matter does not contaminate the vaginal area.

DRESSING THE BABY

With modern central heating, swaddling the baby isn't necessary. Dress the baby in the amount of clothes that makes you comfortable. If you're not wearing long sleeves, the baby also will be hot in clothes reaching the wrists. If you're cold without a sweater, the baby also will require an outer wrap of some sort.

The baby usually wears two layers of clothing. The layer next to the skin consists of a diaper and undershirt. This first layer is covered by a kimono or gown that ties or snaps in front or back, or a one-piece jumpsuit, with full-length sleeves and built in booties. In the crib, the baby usually will be wrapped in a lightweight cotton receiving blanket.

When the temperature outdoors exceeds 75 degrees Fahrenheit, you usually can remove the receiving blanket. At 80 degrees, the baby doesn't need the outer jumpsuit or kimono. On a hot summer day, the baby will be comfortable in nothing more than a diaper.

Dressing the baby is illustrated below; Chapter Four includes a suggested newborn's wardrobe. Always dress the baby in clothes that snap or zip their full length so you can change diapers easily. Change the gown or jumpsuit and undershirt if they are wet. You can usually keep the undershirt dry by turning it back at the waist and leaving a gap between diaper and shirt. All clothes should be loose enough so they can be removed easily and so they allow the baby sufficient freedom to kick and move.

PUTTING THE BABY TO BED

While their navels are healing, babies may sleep most comfortably on their backs. Later, they usually prefer sleeping on their stomachs, with heads turned to the side. This helps to release accumulated air and later enables them to raise their heads and look about. However, you can train some babies to sleep in almost any position, and some prefer to sleep on their sides or on their backs. All these positions are safe.

While in bed, the baby should be wrapped in a receiving

The baby usually wears an undershirt next to the skin. Wrap-around shirts are easier to use than those that pull on over the head.

If you're using a jumpsuit, the baby's feet go first. Keep the undershirt dry by turning it back at the waist.

Don't try to place the sleeve over the baby's arm; put your hand inside the sleeve and pull the baby's arm through.

blanket. A second lightweight blanket may be used but should not be tucked under the mattress. If you lower the heat at night, the baby may need an additional heavier blanket. A blanket made of a synthetic fiber is preferable to one of wool, which may cause a skin rash and is more difficult to launder.

OUT FOR AN AIRING

Babies can be taken outdoors a few days after birth. It's easier in summer, when the baby does not need special clothing. But even a winter baby can go out on a chilly day, provided he or she is dressed appropriately for the weather.

When you dress the baby for an airing, follow the same rules as for indoor wear. To be warm, the baby will need approximately as many layers of clothing as you do. Indoor wardrobe, a sweater or hooded parka, a lightweight snowsuit or bunting, and a blanket may suffice on cold days. Pick a spot in the sunshine that's well protected from the wind, but don't expose the baby directly to the rays of the sun. Babies get sunburned, too.

At this age, a carriage is best for strolling; if you're just placing the baby outdoors, wheel the bassinet onto the porch. If you're taking the baby with you while shopping or walking, you may find a canvas baby tote or backpack useful.

WHEN THE BABY SEEMS ILL

Babies are immune to many childhood illnesses, including measles and mumps, but they get colds and other viral infections like the rest of us. You can protect them to some degree by discouraging visitors, avoiding obviously ill people, and keeping them from crowded places, but strict isolation isn't necessary. A cold is most contagious before any symptoms show. And a baby with older brothers and sisters is likely to be exposed to germs carried home from school.

You don't have to be a doctor to recognize when the baby is ill. A normally cheerful baby who cries continuously, fusses, won't eat, or is listless and lethargic is probably coming down with a cold or some form of infection. Such infections are seldom serious and usually clear up in a few days, but consult the doctor if a child seems ill before age six weeks.

Because the baby can't describe symptoms, your most reliable clue to illness is the rectal temperature. To measure it, you'll need a rectal thermometer—the type with a large round bulb (see page 179). Shake the thermometer until the mercury reads 96 degrees or less. Then coat the bulb with petroleum jelly. Hold the baby stomach down on your lap or bath table, face turned to one side. Spread the buttocks and insert the lubricated thermometer just beyond the bulb into the rectum. Keep the thermometer in position for two minutes, with the other hand on the baby's back so he or she won't wriggle. Then remove the thermometer and read it. Normal rectal temperatures register higher than the normal oral reading of 98.6 degrees. A rectal reading of more than 100 degrees is considered a fever. After recording the temperature, wipe the thermometer with toilet tissue, wash with warm—not hot—water, and return the thermometer to its case.

Any fever in an infant under six weeks should be brought to the pediatrician's attention. But fever alone in an older infant, in the absence of other symptoms, isn't necessarily alarming. A child who remains cheery and playful probably isn't seriously ill, regardless of the temperature. A child who is dull and draggy may need medical attention despite a low or normal temperature.

A fever by itself requires little treatment. Give plenty of fluids, remove extra clothing, and sponge face and body with cool water. If the fever makes the baby uncomfortable, ask the doctor about medicine to reduce it. Acetaminophen, an aspirin substitute, is usually preferred for children under one year. (For more on fever, see page 353.)

Regardless of precautions taken, babies usually have two or three colds their first year—maybe more if they're frequently exposed to other children. Each cold lasts a few days to two weeks. Eyes redden and appetites are lost. Noses run with a clear, watery liquid that later turns thick and sticky. Your baby will probably sniffle a lot, and you can provide relief by sucking out the material with a rubber bulb called a nasal syringe, or aspirator. But no medicine will cure the cold; you and the baby simply have to wait for it to run its course.

VISITING THE DOCTOR

You'll probably return to your obstetrician six weeks after delivery. You'll receive a routine pelvic examination to determine if the uterus and other organs involved in childbirth have returned to normal. The visit will include tests for blood pressure, pulse, and respiratory function; you also may need to give a urine specimen. The doctor will probably check your weight. If you wish it, you'll be given contraceptive advice. If you wish to discontinue breast-feeding, you may receive an injection to curtail the milk supply.

Timing of the baby's first post-hospital checkup will vary with the doctor. The doctor may wish to do a checkup two weeks after birth to see if the baby is gaining weight satisfactorily.

Otherwise, you may visit the doctor for the first time at four to six weeks. Then the baby will be weighed and measured, given a thorough examination, and appraised for proper development. The doctor usually will discuss the baby's feeding and weight gain and whether or not the formula should be altered. This is also a time to ask the doctor questions about the baby's first six weeks. Additional visits are usually scheduled at lengthening intervals for a total of about six the first year.

WHEN TO CALL THE PEDIATRICIAN

To get the maximum benefit when you call your pediatrician, follow these rules:

1. Try to call during office hours, when records are available. Some pediatricians have a period reserved for calls and telephone advice. Call after hours only if it is an emergency, such as a serious accident or injury, bleeding that cannot be stopped, unconsciousness, severe breathing difficulties, convulsions, abdominal pains lasting more than two hours, black or bloody bowel movements, or diarrhea in an infant. If you cannot reach your pediatrician in an emergency, take the baby immediately to a hospital emergency room.

2. If your child seems sick, always try to take the temperature before calling the pediatrician.

3. The person with firsthand knowledge of the child's condition should speak directly to the pediatrician. Don't relay questions or details through another party.

4. Write down pertinent information and questions in advance so you don't forget anything important.

5. Have a pencil and paper ready to write down the doctor's instructions.

6. Give information on the problem to whoever answers the doctor's phone. Sometimes you don't need to speak to the pediatrician directly. The doctor often can relay the answers to your questions through a nurse or aide.

7. Be specific in describing problems or symptoms. Instead of saying, "He has a fever," say, "He has a rectal temperature of 102.6." Instead of reporting that the baby has diarrhea, say, "She has had ten large, watery bowel movements in the last six hours." Be ready to tell the age and approximate weight of the child, how long he or she has been sick, what you think is wrong, and what you have done so far. Pinpoint the location of pains as nearly as you can; describe all symptoms, such as headache or vomiting; and, in case of injury, be ready to describe the accident.

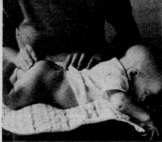

To take rectal temperature, hold baby in lap and immobilize child with hand on the back.

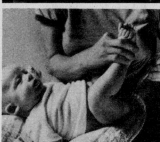

With this method, baby lies face up. Insert thermometer just beyond bulb; keep in place for two minutes.

WATCH THE BABY GROW

One of the joys of parenthood is watching your child change from a helpless infant into an active, thinking human being. It's like planting a tree and watching it gradually add leaves and branches and reach for the sky.

But babies don't grow like trees, systematically adding a ring each year. Normal children grow in spurts and leaps and at differing rates. They don't even necessarily develop sequentially, the way a tree puts out branches, which then produce other branches. Many children sit before they can stand, but a perfectly healthy minority progress directly from a horizontal posture to a vertical one and never learns to sit unsupported until the upright stance has been mastered. The usual order for ambulation is to creep, then crawl, then walk. But some children don't creep or crawl at all.

A wiry, active child may pull to a standing position at six months; a heavier, placid one, at 11. It doesn't seem to matter. No one has ever shown that a child who walks, talks, or gets teeth early grows into a more intelligent, better adjusted, healthier adult.

At the beginning of Chapters Nine through 18 lists of activities appear, brief descriptions of when your child may reach certain milestones of development. The time-tables are based on the Denver Developmental Screening Test (DDST) calculations of the chronological age at which 50 percent of normal children can perform a given act. This test will be the basis for noting what most normal babies are able to do at a given age.

It is important to note, however, that an equal number can't yet perform the act—and they are just as normal as the others. The median, too, conceals a wide range. Ten percent of normal children take their first independent step before 11 months. But another ten percent—who are also normal—aren't walking at 15 months.

Similarly, the number of words a child can speak or understand in the last four months of the first year varies widely. Some eight-month-olds repeat sounds that have meaning for them—"mama" and "dada," for example, are spoken clearly and applied regularly and consistently to the baby's parents. Other children, equally normal, will not use words in this way until later in the first year.

You'll have fun watching for your baby's firsts and recording them to be remembered later. But remember that a child's development isn't a foot race. If your child crawls earlier or later than the DDST timetable specifies, if he or she can't crawl and the neighbor's child can, indeed even if your child never crawls at all, don't worry about it. Development, to repeat the point, is strictly an individual matter. Watch your baby—not the calendar.

HEIGHT & WEIGHT
BIRTH TO ONE YEAR

Ancestry, not age, often determines a baby's height and weight. A baby with tall parents will probably be tall; one whose parents are slight may have a slim build. These charts illustrate the range of normal growth for children between birth and one year.

Tall	Heavy
Moderately tall	Moderately heavy
Average	Average
Moderately short	Moderately light
Short	Light

BOYS' HEIGHT & WEIGHT   GIRLS' HEIGHT & WEIGHT

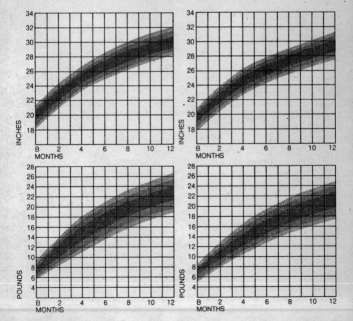

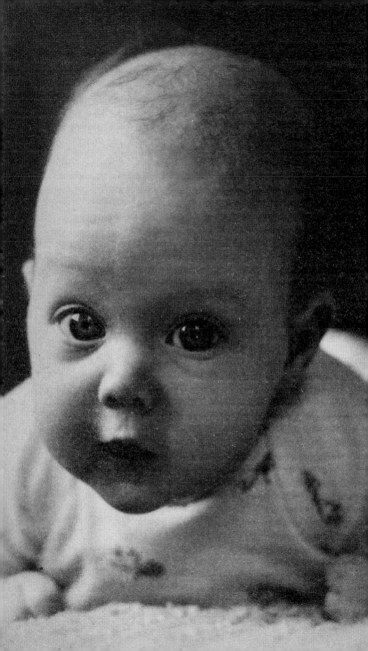

9

Six Weeks To Three Months

HOW THE BABY GROWS

Physically, the average six-week-old probably will weigh ten pounds, having gained three to four pounds since birth and grown to 21½ to 22 inches. The range of size among normal six-week-olds, however, is 7½ to 13½ pounds and 20½ to 24 inches.

The average normal baby, according to the Denver Developmental Screening Test, can achieve the following:

- hold head up at a 45-degree angle when lying on stomach;
- follow an object with eyes for a short distance;
- communicate by sounds other than crying;
- keep head erect when held in a sitting position;
- smile!

At three months, the average normal baby weighs 13 pounds and measures 24 inches, but normal weight and length may range from 9½ to 16½ pounds and 22 to 25½ inches. Here's what the average normal baby can do at three months:

- hold head and chest off bed when lying on stomach;
- sit with head steady;
- follow an object moved from one side of head to the other;
- bring hands together in front;
- laugh, squeal, and coo;
- listen to voices and recognize yours;
- smile, socialize, and respond to other people.

THAT FIRST SMILE—AND WHAT IT MEANS

One day when your baby is about six weeks old—or in many cases even sooner than that—you'll gaze into his or her crib and see a face that suddenly bursts into a bright smile. Maybe the baby will "smile" all over, legs kicking and arms waving like a windmill, wiggling body and head. Your baby—now living up to the legend of a bundle of joy—may even punctuate the smiles with a few gurgles and coos.

That first smile is a marvelous, happy moment for the baby's parents who until now have primarily thought of the baby as a hungry mouth to feed and a wet bottom to change. That smile you see and those joyful noises you hear are so spontaneous that at first you may not believe they're genuine. And some doctors still insist that infant smiling is simply a response to an upset stomach, noting that very young babies smile in their sleep, too.

But parents want to believe differently, and you'll soon see there's a pattern to the baby's smiles and that they are a definite response to the world around, especially to human faces. You'll quickly learn that you can cause a smile by your own behavior. A visit to the crib, a few words, a tickle may cause the baby to grin widely and go into the windmill act.

At first, the smiles that emanate from your baby's crib aren't directed to you. A baby beams at nearly every human face, even a strange or grumpy one. True smiles of recognition don't come until perhaps the fourth month.

Nevertheless, that first smile signals a new and challenging state of development for your fast-changing infant, who is now not only ready for social interaction and stimulation, but needs it, as well.

The factors that determine a child's I.Q. are easy to argue about. It *is* known that children who score high on intelligence tests have had (and enjoyed) a great deal of parental stimulation in infancy. Even when they were tiny—too young, seemingly, to understand—their mothers and fathers talked to them, smiled at them, played with them, listened to them, imitated them, responded to them constantly. These babies had many things to look at, listen to, and explore. Even when parents were out of the baby's sight, they chatted, cooed, and sang to the baby. Obviously, these efforts paid off.

Babies are really no different than the rest of us, they too learn from the people around them. Lying helplessly in a crib, a baby offers a smile as an invitation for attention, a way to communicate with you. If that attention is given, the smile is reinforced. The baby smiles again and then moves on to new forms of interaction and learning. If the smile and those that follow are ignored, a baby soon stops smiling—and soon stops reaching out to the world.

YOUR BABY IS AN INDIVIDUAL

A winning smile should remind you that your baby has a unique personality. From the first few days of life, a baby shows a pattern of individuality, just as adults do. You may find that temperament to be quite different from that of an older brother or sister—or from the baby next door. No one knows whether these early characteristics are inherited, are influenced by the events of pregnancy, or develop in the first days of life. It doesn't really matter. The important thing is to recognize that each baby has an individual style. Parenting will be much easier if you observe, recognize, and adapt to these characteristics.

Here are ways normal babies differ and how the differences may affect your care-taking:

Activity Level. Some babies are active; some, quiet. Yours may wriggle constantly while you change a diaper—or just lie peacefully. Both behaviors are normal. A passive baby isn't dull or retarded; an active one isn't bad or reacting negatively to you. But you may need to be extra vigilant in providing safety precautions for a growing, active baby.

Regularity. Some babies seem to have a built-in clock. They demand to be fed at precise four-hour intervals, sleep exactly so many hours, and almost always eat the same amount. Others are wildly unpredictable. Both types develop normally; but for your own peace of mind, you may need to do a little scheduling. Try to feed an irregular baby before the cries come, and put the child to bed on your timetable, not the baby's.

Adaptability. Your baby may reach eagerly for a new toy and love a bath the first time one's given. Or your baby may take a long time to enjoy anything new, kicking and splashing in terror five or six times before a bath becomes pleasant. The baby who resists change requires more patient teaching, but, once adapted, he or she won't be distracted by every new experience.

"Outgoingness." Some babies are shy and withdraw from new faces or new foods, while others immediately respond to novelty. This characteristic differs from adaptability in that it refers to the baby's reaction on first exposure, not how long it takes the child to become accustomed to a situation. Babies who quickly respond to new faces with smiles will delight relatives and visitors. But these babies may be more difficult to keep out of trouble when they're older.

Sensitivity. Some babies seem oblivious to differences in sound, light, taste, or comfort. They can sleep through the loudest noises, the brightest sunlight, the wettest diapers. Others wake at the slightest noise, crying and blinking when lights go on.

A child who is very sensitive to disturbances may make life difficult at first. But noticing small differences seems to help the baby learn faster.

Intensity of Reaction. When your child seems pleased, does he or she laugh and wriggle with delight, or just smile quietly? Does your baby merely frown a little when upset—or bellow with rage? If your baby reacts very strongly, you may later have to teach that he or she can get what is wanted without resorting to screaming and crying. Fortunately, the child's unbounded delight when he or she is happy compensates for the angry outbursts.

Distractibility. Does your baby stop feeding when another person enters the room? Or does nothing divert the baby's attention? When the baby is crying because of hunger, does a toy provide a momentary distraction, or does the crying continue? You may have to feed an easily distracted baby in a room away from other stimuli. A baby who can't be distracted from an activity, even briefly, requires persistent firmness when you're teaching him or her to change from one thing to another.

Positive or Negative Mood. Some babies are cheerful more than they are fussy or unpleasant. Any baby has good and bad moods, but, on balance, some babies seem to be in a happier frame of mind quite often, while others cry and fuss more frequently.

A baby's difficult moods certainly aren't easy to live with. But moodiness doesn't mean that your methods of child care are wrong. As parents, you must learn to accept some crying and complaining once you've established the baby doesn't really need anything—food, dry diapers, etc. Chronic negativism can wear you out, though, and you'll need more time away from the child who seems to have more bad than good days.

Attention Span and Persistence. How long will your baby continue trying to do something—even if it is frustrating or if you try to stop the attempt? Will your baby rivet his or her attention on something near the crib for long periods, or turn elsewhere within a few minutes?

True persistence is neither good nor bad. When a baby persists in activities you like or find entertaining or amusing, you'll be pleased; in activities you don't like, displeased. You'll have to be especially firm and patient in distracting a persistent child, steady and encouraging to a less persistent one.

Some babies acquire these traits in combinations that add up to a difficult or confounding personality. It takes a patient parent to deal with the so-called difficult child, for the task is strictly uphill. You need more help from other members of the family. You must be firm time after time when it might seem easier to give in, and you must learn to continue to be approving and affectionate when the child is cooperative.

Difficult babies, fortunately, can learn to be less difficult, and your devotion to this learning process during the early weeks and months may prevent trouble for the child later on. Although temperamental differences appear within the first few months of life, they are not unalterably fixed; your actions can modify them. In any case, it's important not to label the baby ("difficult," "easygoing") with a trait that may mark and follow him or her throughout life.

THE SCHEDULE CHANGES

By six weeks, the baby eats less frequently, stays awake more, and usually gives up one feeding or nursing a day. By three months, babies are usually down to four daily feedings—three

The arrival of a newborn will affect the behavior of your other children. Because the baby now has top billing, jealousy is a natural reaction. Assure the older children of your love, but never leave a baby alone with a child under three.

during the day and one at night. Capacity increases, although the total varies from baby to baby. Now the usual amount is about a quart of breast milk or formula, about 32 ounces, every 24 hours.

In addition, the three-month-old baby will let you know in short order when bigger servings are called for. Breast-feeding mothers get the message quickly, either because the baby spends more time at the breast or goes at it more eagerly. The bottle-fed baby announces an increased appetite by gulping two or three consecutive bottles down to the very last drop, then crying or gnawing his or her hands afterward and seeming to look for more. You needn't consult your pediatrician about whether or not to increase the amount of milk; just add an extra ounce at the next feeding and see if that satisfies the baby.

The baby may lie awake a total of eight hours a day, ready to play and socialize. By six weeks, sleep may come in one long stretch of seven to eight hours—fortunate is the parent when it falls between late evening and early morning—and two to four shorter stretches during the day. Some of these rest periods will be only catnaps, but others may last as long as three or four hours.

By three months, the periods of sleep are usually down to three a day, the pattern your baby will follow through most of the first year. After the last feeding of the evening, the baby now may sleep for ten consecutive hours and then take morning and afternoon naps of about two hours each.

SLEEPING POSITIONS

Between six weeks and three months, depending on size and activity, the baby should be transferred from a bassinet or small bed to a crib. And if the baby's been sleeping in the same room with you, now's the time to provide separate sleeping quarters. New-found and developing senses now enable even a sleeping baby to detect when parents are nearby, and the baby's restlessness and attempts to attract parents' attention may keep everyone awake.

By now, your baby's probably demonstrating that he or she prefers one sleeping position to another. Usually, babies like lying on their stomachs best, and many babies will even protest fussily and refuse to settle down if they are placed in some other position. Some babies seem unable to sleep until they can press their heads into a corner of the crib or against the top of the crib—some authorities believe that perhaps this position is an imitation of the secure position of the head in the womb.

Even awake, many babies may show a preference for one

side of the body over the other. For instance, they may always place the right side of their faces against the mattress when looking out through the crib bars or hold their heads to the right when propped in a sitting position. A few babies carry the favoritism to one side of the body or another so far as to favor nursing at one breast in preference to the other. Sometimes these babies actually turn away or fuss if shifted from one breast to another (although some doctors say the difference may be in the breast, not the baby).

No matter what you've heard, allowing the baby to sleep in one position or another won't cause legs or feet to develop improperly. But constantly lying on one side may cause the baby's head to seem flat and lopsided on that side. However much that may alarm you, it won't last long. The head will round out with age, and, in any case, the pressure will be relieved when the child begins to spend more time sitting than lying in his or her crib.

However, if the seeming reshaping of your child's head bothers you and if you want to do something about it, reverse the baby's crib so that he or she must look the opposite way to see into the room. Or you might try to distract the child this way: hang an attractive toy in the new direction. Another method is to tilt the mattress by placing towels or a blanket under one side of it, thus compelling the baby to turn in the direction you want.

TIME FOR THE BABY'S SHOTS

At two months, your baby is ready for a first set of immunizations. The pediatrician or baby clinic will administer a triple antigen, or DPT shot, providing combined protection against diphtheria, pertussis (whooping cough), and tetanus (lockjaw), and a first dose of live polio vaccine, given by mouth. The DPT shot will be repeated at four and six months; a second dose of polio vaccine will be given at four months. Boosters of both will be given at 18 months and four to six years.

The shots are usually more painful to the parent than the baby. After the DPT shot, a child may appear fussy or run a slight fever. To make the baby more comfortable, ask the pediatrician if you should give one-half grain of aspirin or acetaminophen (an aspirin substitute) combined with water or formula. Remember that immunizations should be postponed for a short time if the baby seems ill when they are due.

So-called children's diseases are less common and less hazardous than in the past, but it is still vitally important your child be protected against these preventable illnesses. The following general immunization schedule is recommended by the American Academy of Pediatrics:

- two months—DPT, oral polio vaccine;
- four months—DPT, oral polio vaccine;
- six months—DPT (oral polio vaccine optional);
- 12 months—tuberculin test;
- 15 months—measles, mumps, rubella (given as one shot);
- 18 months—DPT, polio boosters;
- 4 to 6 years—DPT, polio boosters.

Smallpox vaccination is no longer routine for small children. The once-dread disease is now nonexistent in the United States so risk of complications for the vaccination, though very small, is of course greater than the risk of contracting the disease. State laws requiring preschool vaccination against smallpox have been repealed or no longer are enforced. Vaccination is still necessary for visitors to some countries of the world (particularly in Asia, Africa, and South America), although many have eliminated the requirement altogether.

Inoculation against typhoid is not considered necessary, either, except when traveling to an infected area.

Protection against tetanus, however, remains important for young children. Any injury or animal bite in which the skin has been lacerated, punctured, or torn may introduce tetanus germs into the wound. Tetanus shots should always be kept up-to-date.

Because of their possible complications and devastating long-range effects, measles and mumps are serious diseases in young children. Breast-fed babies obtain prolonged immunity to them from their mothers, but this protection usually has declined by the time they are a year old. Some parents unwisely postpone these immunizations until school age because the shots may make the child uncomfortable. The recommended date for immunization is early in the second year of life, because the child may be exposed to germs by other children well before he or she begins attending school.

Rubella (German measles) is a minor disease even in small children. Immunization is given mainly to protect the mother and other women of childbearing age with whom the baby may come in contact.

Vaccines against chicken pox and certain strains of pneumonia are being tested. Ask your pediatrician if they are now available for general use.

YOUR OWN SHOT RECORD

Keep a personal record of the baby's immunizations, and have the doctor or nurse enter each shot as it is administered, along with the date. That way, you'll know when the last shots were given and when others are due, without waiting to be reminded by the doctor's office.

IMMUNIZATION RECORD			
Child's Name _____ Date of Birth _____			
_____			
Immunization	Date	Dose	Physician
DPT	_____	_____	_____
	_____	_____	_____
	_____	_____	_____
	_____	_____	_____
DT booster	_____	_____	_____
Tetanus booster	_____	_____	_____
Polio	_____	_____	_____
	_____	_____	_____
	_____	_____	_____
	_____	_____	_____
Measles	_____	_____	_____
Rubella	_____	_____	_____
Mumps	_____	_____	_____
Tuberculin test	_____	_____	_____
Others	_____	_____	_____

Also, if you change doctors or move to another community, it'll be convenient to have your own listing of shots. In the event of injury, the record can be particularly important to determine the most recent tetanus inoculation.

Most states now require that your child have a complete record of immunizations before he or she can be admitted to school—another reason to have a record that is available and up-to-date.

Your immunization record should look like an enlarged version of the one above.

SITTING UP AND GOING OUT
Now that your baby has become more social, he or she will want to spend more time in sight of you and the rest of the family.

While the baby's still in a bassinet, a simple solution is just to wheel the bassinet into the room with the other people; or an inclined infant seat will enable the baby to sit up and see you. Don't, under any circumstances, prop or place a baby alone and unsecured on a sofa or chair.

Pick a sturdy infant seat. It should be of molded fiber glass, slanted so the baby is held in a semi-sitting position by the force of gravity and can't pitch forward. It should have a secure strap and sides high enough to prevent slipping to the side, and it should be supported at the rear so it can not tip over backward.

The best place for the infant seat is on the floor. That way, an active baby won't topple far if his or her gyrations do tip the chair over (and they no doubt will). Always be sure the restraining

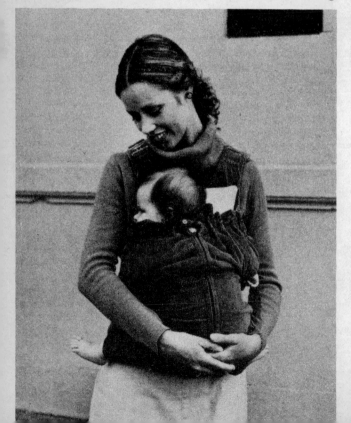

A stroller may well be the baby's first set of wheels. Lightweight, collapsible models you're able to fold with one hand are most useful. The baby rests in a sling, as pictured, secured firmly across the middle.

strap is snugly fastened, but not uncomfortably tight. The baby's hands, arms, and feet should be free, not strapped in place.

Another way many mothers keep a small baby close to them is by using a baby tote or backpack. They've been used for centuries to transport babies while mothers keep their hands and arms free to work. The baby rides in a canvas or plastic sling strapped over your shoulders and rests on your chest or back. You can talk to and nuzzle the baby while you go about your household or other duties.

A baby who holds his or her head up with little effort may also be ready for a stroller. One of the best of the new inventions is the latest model of infant strollers. A lightweight aluminum, collapsible model is most useful. The baby rests in a sling, in a semi-sitting position, and is secured firmly across the middle.

Buy one that can be opened with one hand and folds compactly. Strollers with turnable—instead of fixed—front wheels are easier to turn especially when you're steering with one hand. When driving with the baby, pack the stroller in the car until you reach your destination.

In a car, even the very young baby should have an individual seat—and should not be carried in an adult's arms. The safest model infant seat for auto travel, according to the Physicians for Automotive Safety, resembles the inclined baby rest. The baby

Until the baby can sit without support, a rear-facing seat should be used for travel in a car. Older infants and toddlers may ride in a more traditional car seat.

rides in a semi-upright position, secured with a harness and cushioned by impact-absorbing materials. The carrier is designed to face toward the rear—never forward—and is strapped to the car seat with a lap belt. Most parents install it in the front passenger's seat, so they can keep a constant watch on the baby while driving.

This type of carrier can be used until the baby is about nine months old or can sit well without support. Some models then may be converted into upright, front-facing seats for older children.

The convertible model or the traditional safety seat that is used with older infants and toddlers usually includes a harness consisting of two shoulder straps, a belt that crosses the lap, and a crotch strap.

The whole assembly is then secured by one of the car's seat belts, which either straps around the baby's middle or threads through the back of the seat to hold it in place. Some models require the use of an additional strap that is joined to a lap belt in the seat behind or fastened to an anchorage in the floor or on the rear window ledge (if the infant seat is used in the back of the car).

Another type of seat for an older child is a protective fiber glass shield that requires no harness. The padded shield acts as a cushion in the event of a crash. A lap belt circles the shield and holds it in place. A disadvantage of the shield is that an active child may climb out of it while you are driving.

ON LONGER TRIPS

Tiny babies usually are ideal traveling companions because they're light, portable, and very adaptable. They sleep a lot, don't get restless, and are easy to carry. Travel with infants is far easier than in the past because you can buy bibs, bottles, diapers, and towels that can be thrown away as they're used—even disposable plastic bags to contain the refuse.

In addition, only a small number of each is necessary; replenish the supply as you go. If you're breast-feeding, you will have no problems supplying food; bottle-feeders can purchase premixed formula at drugstores or supermarkets nearly anywhere in the country. Buy one can or bottle at a time, and don't worry about refrigeration. And if you travel a lot by automobile, there are even bottle warmers that you can plug into a car's cigarette lighter—just the thing for that first long trip to see grandparents.

In an automobile, the very young baby should travel in a safety seat, just as on shorter trips. The semi-upright position is all right for naps, too. A slightly older baby can occupy a baby rest or seat restraint. Some parents make a "wiggle platform" by padding the rear seat or deck of the station wagon, but because of the danger of being pitched forward in the event of a quick stop, the Physicians Committee for Automotive Safety frowns on any child traveling unrestrained in a moving car.

Air travel is equally simple. To transport babies under seven days old, airlines require written authorization from a physician—the restriction is left over from the old days when it was feared erratic air pressure in the cabin might damage the baby's developing lungs—but, otherwise, children under two travel free.

If you notify the airline in advance (at the time you make reservations, say), you can usually reserve the bulkhead seat, with a bassinet that attaches to the wall in front of you. Flight crews on most airlines will usually warm formula for you, and some airlines even provide an emergency supply of disposable diapers.

Bring your collapsible stroller, which will be a godsend for transporting the baby around airports, especially when you have other articles to carry. Most airlines will let you include it in your carry-on luggage. A flight attendant will stow it in the closet as you board.

CRADLE CAP

At about six weeks, a scaly crust may form in the center of the baby's scalp. So-called cradle cap results from overactivity of the oil glands and resembles adult dandruff. The oil glands are stimulated by the hormone testosterone. The overproduction of testosterone is another by-product of the hormones present in the mother's placenta.

The condition isn't a serious one, although cradle cap is usually unsightly. To control cradle cap, rub a small amount of mineral or baby oil into the scalp to loosen the flakes. Rub the oil in well. Allow it to soak in for about 30 minutes, then shampoo the baby's head vigorously with your fingertips. Use a medicated shampoo, being careful to keep the shampoo out of the baby's eyes. Then comb and brush the scalp as thoroughly as possible, making sure to use a brush with medium bristles, until all loose flakes of cradle cap are removed completely.

Cradle cap often persists because parents are afraid to massage or rub the soft spot in the baby's skull. Actually, even vigorous massage with the fingertips won't hurt the baby and is essential to remove all the scales. Usually, one or two treatments are all that's necessary to end the problem, but the treatment should be repeated if the cradle cap recurs.

TIME FOR PLAY

Babies play almost from birth. Many people are not aware of it, because it's not the organized, purposeful activity an adult considers play. At this point, though, babies begin to play with their hands. The experience of discovering those hands can be as much fun for the observer as it obviously is for the baby. Watch as they hold one hand in front of them, perhaps for minutes on end, bring it to their mouths experimentally, or inspect toys held in their hands. They'll hold up both hands, shift their gaze from one to another, and move them toward each other, watching the light and shadow. Gradually—often after several unsuccessful tries—they will bring them together until they meet and lock, then squeal with delight.

Your baby's eyes can now focus clearly and follow movement, as the hand play indicates. The baby will gaze for many minutes at a picture on a nearby wall, or at an attractive toy just out of reach, or at your face. He or she will watch as you walk back and forth through the room and follow your shadow as it falls across the bed.

The baby is now ready for toys. Lucky for most parents there's no need to buy expensive toys—because, as the hand exploration shows, enjoyment comes from something so simple as watching fingers move.

You don't need to fill the crib with costly stuffed animals or furry creatures. Instead, suspend a mobile over the crib, where it can be seen. If it is lightly suspended, it will move and jiggle when the bed moves. Soft, lightweight toys, especially if they're easy to grasp, can also be part of the learning process.

SITTERS AND CHILD CARE

How soon you leave the baby for an evening out or a visit to friends is strictly up to you. There's no reason not to leave an infant in the care of a baby-sitter right from birth, if you feel well enough and are secure about it. A baby under three months of age won't notice the difference. But be sure to choose your sitter carefully. Even a relative, friend, or neighbor can be less than fully reliable or responsible. A reliable baby-sitter can only make your evening out more enjoyable.

Some babies cry piteously when left; others take it in stride. But even at three months, it's best that the baby be awake when the sitter arrives, so the two of you can be seen together. That helps the baby make the association between parent and sitter and eases the transition. Imagine how you'd feel if you woke up in the middle of the night to find everyone you knew out of sight and a stranger standing by your bed!

In any case, invite the sitter to come before your departure to see how you hold, handle, and care for the baby. Even young babies like to be treated in a way that's familiar to them. Show your baby-sitter where things he or she will need are kept, and observe closely as she or he feeds and diapers the baby, so you are sure the sitter knows and cares about the baby.

Any time you leave your baby, no matter how briefly, make sure the sitter has the following information:
  —where you can be reached;
  —telephone numbers of the doctor, hospital and emergency room, fire department, and police (keep them posted next to the phone);
  —the name and telephone number of a responsible friend, relative, or neighbor who can be called if you can't be reached;
  —details about your house—how to regulate heat, how to lock and open the doors;
  —what and when to feed the baby;
  —when you will return;
  —what exactly you expect from the sitter while you're gone.

There are no hard-and-fast rules about when a new mother should return to a full-time or part-time job, and often the question is decided by economics. Some specialists in child behavior say there is no substitute for the natural parent in the first two years of an infant's life, although others maintain that a well-loved child can thrive in the care of another if the parents compensate for their absence during periods of reunion. In any case, the decision is not one to be reached lightly but to be planned carefully and agreed to by both parents. Once reached, however, it is not a decision to feel guilty about.

Unless the father can take over the domestic role, the mother's return to work requires some kind of professional, full-time baby care, either in your own home, in another's home, or in a day-care center. No professional baby care is inexpensive, and all require careful thought before the choice is made.

The best and least expensive full-time baby-sitters often are trusted friends or relatives. You usually know them well enough to have faith in their reliability and responsibility, you know they will have an interest in your child, and you can expect them to care for the baby the way you would do it yourself. Hiring a sitter or housekeeper and training him or her to care for the baby is a more expensive and difficult proposition. You may have to spend long hours teaching and supervising the person (however, the effort is certainly worth it). If you have several children, though, a sitter who can come to your house while you're away is often the best solution.

For a young child, care within a private home often works most satisfactorily. That's because the rhythm of home life—with the mailman coming every day, the neighbors nearby, familiar furniture always there—is nearer to the child's own experience. Care within a home also may involve smaller numbers of children, although that is no guarantee your child will get more individual attention.

In some states, private homes where children are cared for are licensed by state agencies, which inspect them for safety and also train the "day-care mother" in the essentials of home operation. Such guidelines are your best bet in selecting a home. Even with these credentials, however, you'll probably want to visit the home regularly to make sure your child is cared for according to your wishes.

Commercial day-care centers and those operated by nonprofit or charitable agencies are growing. Properly staffed and supervised, they may provide the best care, especially for children above the age of three. They also can be the most economical.

Before choosing a day-care home or center, you'll want to visit and examine it. Have these questions answered:

- Does the person or persons caring for the children seem to really care about them, or are they impersonal when handling them?

- Is the home or center clean, safe, airy, and healthful-appearing, with sufficient space for the children to play?

- Is there at least one adult for every four or five children, including the person's own children?

- Do the care-givers and the children seem to be happy and enjoying themselves?

- Are you welcome to visit the day-care center at any time, and are your suggestions for care of your child welcomed and put to practice? (And if not, are you told why?)

10

Three to Four Months

HOW THE BABY GROWS

Physically, an average normal four-month-old will weigh 14½ pounds and measure 24½ inches, a gain of 1½ pounds and an inch in length from the month before. But weight and height among normal babies will range between 11 and 17½ pounds, and between 23 and 27 inches.

Here's what half of average normal babies can do at four months:

- turn head in all directions and support self on straight arms;
- roll from front to side or back;
- grasp and hold an object; reach for and *sometimes* grab something offered;
- babble in word-like syllables; coo, gurgle, chortle, and squeal with pleasure;
- anticipate your approach and become excited;
- look at self in a mirror and smile;
- recognize mother and siblings;
- have crying quieted by a voice or music;
- bear some weight on legs when held in a standing position;
- be pulled to sitting position.

TIME OF CURIOSITY AND COMMUNICATION

In the fourth month of life your baby is no longer helpless and is fun to be around, at least most of the time. The baby likes people, enjoys life, and makes that pleasure evident. Smiles, squeals, chortles, and giggles abound. You'll notice a first attempt to "talk"—a babbling string of sounds that have no translation but are clearly attempts at speech. In the bath, the baby kicks, splashes, and laughs. Sometimes you will hear a baby in the crib, laughing aloud to no one in particular.

Your baby may even develop a "social cough." You'll quickly learn to recognize this put-on, which is just for you. Indeed, you've taught the baby to do it, probably unknowingly. One day in the past the baby coughed. You smiled. The baby liked that and coughed again. You smiled again. Because the baby quickly learned this dry little hack could provoke an enjoyable response, the cycle of cough-smile-cough was reinforced and became a game.

Smiles, laughs, and coughs are only one way a baby reaches out to the world. Your baby is now learning about surrounding events and where he or she fits in. The lesson coming across to the baby is that he or she can cause events and that those events have a somewhat predictable pattern. Watch your baby as you approach the crib and extend your arms. Your baby will wriggle and "windmill" in anticipation, having learned that outstretched arms are a prelude to being picked up. Watch, too, when you dangle an object in front of the child or place it nearby when the baby's lying down. A month ago, the baby merely would have peered at it. But now he or she immediately reaches out. There won't be many direct hits yet, but the baby's aim will keep improving as he or she explores the environment and gets ready to venture out into it. But remember babies differ. Yours may be quieter than others.

TIME FOR SOLID FOODS

How soon to feed the baby foods other than milk is a topic of continuing controversy. Some parents begin to feed their children solids within the first month of life, in the belief that the food will encourage the baby to sleep without interruption through the night. At the other end of the spectrum, some parents believe that an exclusive diet of mother's milk is perfectly adequate until the baby is nine months or even older.

Probably the most sensible compromise is to start solids sometime after three-and-a-half months and not later than six months, depending on the baby's stage of development. There are several good reasons to delay:

1. The baby's digestive system isn't developed sufficiently to accept solids unless thinned to an almost liquid consistency.

2. The baby lacks the proper tongue-and-jaw coordination to eat from a spoon rather than a nipple. If the newborn tries, the usual result is a great deal of energy and effort expended for very little nourishment.

3. Solids may lessen the appetite for milk and rob the body of essential nutrients.

4. Early consumption of solids may establish a pattern of overeating that will lead to obesity in later life.

The chief reason for continuing to feed the baby breast milk and breast milk only until late in the first year—immunity from disease transferred from mother to child—may be less important in the United States than in less developed countries of the world, where there are high rates of infant deaths.

Nutritional studies have shown that normal infants can be well nourished and grow appropriately by consuming a variety of milks, with or without the addition of solid foods. These studies show babies will thrive on either breast- or bottle-feeding exclusively, so long as they receive iron, appropriate vitamins, and fluoride supplements. According to the American Academy of Pediatrics, children who are fed semi-solids prior to four to six months of age aren't ahead nutritionally or developmentally and, in fact, may be hindered because their intake of milk is reduced.

With a few exceptions, however, most authorities agree that by the age of six months, most babies should be receiving a substantial part of their food in the form of solids, and that by nine months at least half of the caloric intake should come from those sources.

START WITH CEREAL

Cereal is usually the baby's first solid food, followed in order by fruits, vegetables, meats, and egg yolk, unless you are advised by your doctor to withhold the latter. The sequence is somewhat arbitrary, depending on your baby's tastes, and can be accelerated if the baby has started solids late. Use plain foods in the beginning, rather than mixtures, and introduce them gradually, one at a time.

Cereal usually comes first because it tastes bland and is digested easily. Precooked, dehydrated cereals, fortified with iron and vitamins, are available in rice, oatmeal, barley, wheat, and mixed varieties. To prepare, simply add warm milk, formula, or water and stir to the proper consistency. You also can cook your own whole-grain cereals.

Rice is the mildest and most readily digested cereal. Oatmeal and barley may be used interchangeably with rice after the first solid food has been introduced. If there is a family history of food allergies, wheat and mixed cereals are usually postponed until after the first year.

MIXING AND FEEDING

Start with a very small amount of cereal. One or two teaspoons is enough. Place the cereal in a clean dish and moisten with warm formula, mother's milk, sterilized cow's milk, or water. Stir until the cereal becomes semi-liquid. Some babies prefer cereal almost watery; others like a more pasty mixture. Trial and error will identify your baby's preferences.

Some parents mix cereal very thin and feed it from a bottle, using a nipple with an enlarged opening. This is often a means of feeding solids early, before the baby's head can be held erect; it's also less messy for the mother. But the method is frequently discouraged by pediatric nutritionists, who feel the baby may not receive nourishment in ample quantities.

A better way is to feed the baby tiny bites from a demitasse or other small spoon. Hold the baby in your lap, nestled in a semi-sitting position in the crook of your elbow or secured in an inclined infant rest. Fill the bowl of the spoon about half full. When you touch the baby's lips, they'll open, allowing you to insert the spoon. The upper lip and gums will guide the food into the mouth.

The first few tries will be messy, so be prepared. Wear an apron and tie a bib on the baby. Because this is a new way of doing things, the baby will use the tongue to push this strange stuff right out of the mouth. You'll probably have to scrape food off the baby's chin and bib several times and spoon it back where it belongs. Your baby may even blow or spit out the food until this new feeding is mastered.

In the beginning, feed solids just once a day, preferably in the morning. Start with a breast- or bottle-feeding, then follow with solid food, because a truly hungry baby may balk at this new taste. Later, you can reverse the order so the baby doesn't fill up on milk before the solid food is served.

A baby will let you know enough is enough by turning the head, clamping the jaws shut, or emphatically spitting the food out. Don't try to coax your baby to eat more to finish up or trick the child by spooning a bite in quickly.

ADDING OTHER FOODS

After a week of morning cereal, add an evening feeding, too. A week later, introduce another food. Fruit is the usual choice. Most parents begin with bananas, followed by applesauce, pears, and peaches.

By starting foods one at a time and serving them exclusively for a week, you can quickly learn whether they agree with the baby. If the baby suffers diarrhea, constipation, a skin rash, or any other change after the feeding of a particular food, you can immediately identify the culprit and discontinue it.

Fruit furnishes natural sugars, vitamin A, and certain minerals. It usually is served at the same meal as cereal and sometimes replaces it. A baby who rejects cereal may be given fruit first, or fruit may be mixed into the cereal. If you find the baby doesn't like either, stop offering the cereal for a while and try again later.

Vegetables, a chief source of carbohydrates, may be added to the menu about two weeks to a month after fruit. Serve vegetables separately at the midday feeding, following the same rule of introducing one at a time at regular intervals so you can watch for the baby's reactions. Begin by serving yellow vegetables with a mild flavor—squash or sweet potatoes, for example. Then progress to carrots, beans, peas. Beets and spinach may follow. Some vegetables may be unpopular, but you should acquaint your baby with all varieties.

Meat comes next, about a month after vegetables. As the baby drinks less and less milk, meat will provide most of the baby's protein, iron, and the vitamin B complex. (Vegetable sources of protein, such as beans, may be substituted for meat, according to the American Academy of Pediatrics Committee on Nutrition.) The most popular meats are beef and chicken, followed by lamb. Liver and heart have a high iron content. Many parents do not include pork until the baby is a year old.

Don't give egg yolk until the baby is at least six months old, and you should wait a year if there is any family history of food allergy. Along with meat, egg yolk eventually will supply most of the iron and protein that the growing baby will need in the months ahead.

FOODS TO AVOID

Introducing some foods too early may "sensitize" the baby and lead to allergies later. Consequently, wheat, egg white, and citrus juices are usually withheld until the baby is at least a year old. If you or the baby's brothers and sisters have shown a sensitivity to certain foods or liquids, an allergist may also recommend eliminating cow's milk and milk products.

Although orange juice is a valuable source of vitamin C, vitamin supplements can easily substitute for it. Other fruit juices enriched with vitamin C, such as apple, pear, and pineapple, may be offered. The ban on wheat not only includes wheat cereal, but bread, crackers, and teething biscuits, as well.

If other members of the family have food allergies, the baby's diet should be worked out carefully with a specialist.

Keep salt, sugar, and all seasoning to a minimum. Sugared foods not only lead to eventual tooth decay, but destroy the appetite for more nutritious foods. Using salt may be one of the causes of hypertension (high blood pressure) in adulthood; heavy use early in life may establish habits not easily broken. If a baby isn't allowed to develop a taste for large amounts of salt and sugar, he or she won't miss them. In fact, tests of infants show they accept unsalted food as readily as they do salted food.

HOW TO PREPARE YOUR OWN BABY FOOD

To prepare baby foods at home, make sure your kitchen equipment and hands are clean and all food ingredients are fresh.

Start baby meats by cutting beef chuck, lamb, chicken, or liver into cubes. Trim all the fat. Add one cup of stock per cup of meat.

On the stove bring the meat and stock to a boil over high heat, then reduce the heat and simmer until the meat is tender.

Cool, then drain, reserving liquid. Measure meat. In blender, place 1/2 cup cooking liquid for each cup of meat. Add the meat; blend.

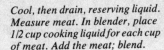

Spoon the pureed meat into ice-cube trays, cover, and place it into a freezer or the freezing compartment of the refrigerator.

When frozen, remove the cubes from the trays, and store in plastic bags for use as needed. Heat in saucepan until the meat is warm.

When fruits and vegetables are in season, prepare homemade foods for the baby. Wash fruits and vegetables well; omit all seasonings. Here are some suggestions for preparing fruits and vegetables:

Fruit.

Apples: Peel, core, and slice. Puree in blender, mixing with apple juice. Serve immediately. Or cook in a little boiling water 20 to 30 minutes, then puree into applesauce. Freeze (cooked only).

Pears: Just before serving, peel, slice, and puree pear in a blender.

Peaches: Peel and remove pit. If the fruit is very fresh and ripe, puree in a blender. If not, steam first.

Vegetables.

Acorn squash or sweet potato: Bake in 425-degree oven for 45 minutes. Allow to cool, then remove seeds and scoop out pulp. Mash or puree in blender. Add apple juice for better consistency.

Peas and green beans: Remove stems and strings of beans. Cook in a little boiling water 20 to 30 minutes; puree, adding a little milk.

White potato: Bake in skin for 45 minutes; scoop out potato, mash with fork, and add milk for thin consistency. Heat as desired. Mix with cooked, pureed carrots.

Spinach: Cook in water and puree, adding some of the water in which the vegetable was cooked.

COMMERCIAL VERSUS HOMEMADE BABY FOOD

Those tiny jars of strained baby food are a great and wonderful convenience, and they allow you a year-round choice of foods for the baby. On the other hand, commercial baby food is about double the price of homemade food—and no more nutritious.

In recent years, manufacturers of baby food have changed the ingredients of many products to make them more "natural." Flavor-enhancers and food additives have been eliminated and salt and sugar content reduced. The supermarket shelf now carries jars marked "No salt added" and "No sugar added." Fruits containing tapioca, used as a sweetener and extender, are plainly marked. Manufacturers acknowledge that in the past many ingredients were added to please the palate of the mother, not the baby, and that today's food is better for the baby.

Preparing your own baby food allows you to capitalize on the freshness of seasonal fruits and vegetables and to control seasonings and additives. And by fixing foods yourself, you can preserve more nutrients while feeding the baby the same foods given the rest of the family. However, you'll probably still want to keep a ready supply of commercial foods for convenience and quick use. In addition, you'll find that some foods are difficult to duplicate at home without extraordinary time and effort. Precooked, dehydrated cereal is the best example.

INSTANT FOODS FOR BABY

Your baby doesn't always need specially prepared foods, commercial or homemade. Thanks to modern appliances and good refrigeration, you can feed your five-month-old some of the foods you feed the rest of the family. With two minutes and the proper equipment, you can convert the family dinner of steak and peas into strained, liquefied dishes for the baby.

Of course, to prepare some foods for a baby, all you really need is a fork. Just peel and mash a banana and add a little milk for a more liquid consistency. Egg yolk, if the baby can eat it, is equally simple. After boiling the eggs, remove the shell and the white, mash the yolk with a fork, and add apple juice for moisture.

Here are some other fruits that can also be prepared quickly and easily. Peel an apple and scrape the flesh, then blend with apple juice to a liquid consistency. The result is a kind of instant applesauce. You can do the same with pears or peaches.

A blender or food processor simplifies preparation of other foods for the baby. When preparing vegetables for the rest of the family, simply scoop off a few spoonfuls before you add seasoning, place the baby's portion in the blender, set it at high speed, or puree setting, and presto! Fresh dinner for the baby. You can also make instant cereals for the baby from those you buy off the shelf. Some babies at five months of age are also ready for zwieback, arrowroot biscuits, or soft crackers, and they may eat custards or puddings.

Observe a few safety rules when preparing adult foods for babies, however. Always remove all strings and chunks from foods: they might cause the baby to gag. Avoid berries, nuts, raisins, popcorn, corn, whole peas, or other foods with small morsels, because they may become lodged in the baby's windpipe.

When offering the baby table food, it's usually best to use fresh fruits and vegetables. Frozen and canned or processed foods defeat the purpose of controlling the ingredients yourself. Always prepare the food as simply as possible, omitting seasonings and flavorings that are more suited to adult tastes. And prepare the baby's dishes separately.

Serve meat and vegetables as individual dishes. Later, after the baby has become accustomed to meat, mix it with vegetables to produce a kind of stew, which often will greatly improve the baby's appetite for meat. You can also later add noodles or spaghetti to the baby's pureed meat to provide a nutritious and tasteful dinner almost any baby will enjoy.

A CHANGE IN BOWEL MOVEMENTS

The introduction of solid food usually will also bring about a change in the baby's bowel movements. The consistency may become either pastier or thinner, depending on the food given, and may retain the food color. Carrots often produce a yellow-orange movement; peas, a greenish one. A red bowel movement following a meal of beets results from the vegetable—welcome words of reassurance to parents who sometimes think the baby is bleeding.

Some new foods may cause diarrhea, constipation, or skin rash. Watch the baby's bowel movements for a few days after each new food is tried. If there is a reaction, discontinue the food for a month and try it again.

Don't force a baby to eat a certain food. If your newborn refuses to eat it at first, try again the following day. If your baby continues to refuse it, put that food aside for a time and try it at a later date.

YOUR BABY IS MORE ACTIVE

Muscles are growing stronger and larger, and your baby now is able to twist and squirm around—no longer satisfied to lie in the crib or bassinet or even to sit and watch you contentedly from the infant seat.

A clean, carpeted floor is a safe place, if you're nearby to watch. Be sure the baby is out of traffic and won't be stepped on, and clear the surrounding area of furnishings that might be pulled or knocked over. Remove small objects that might wind up in a curious baby's mouth. The baby can't move very freely at this point, but it's difficult to predict what he or she might do, so don't leave the child alone.

At this age, you also can improvise a play space by fencing the baby into a corner with furniture and boxes. Better yet, invest now in a playpen, which the baby will use for a year or more as play space and a place for naps. A lightweight, collapsible model with mesh sides is the most useful, because it can be folded easily and moved from room to room or even outdoors in pleasant weather. The playpen should have a raised floor to keep the baby above drafts and damp ground. It should also have a moisture-proof pad for the pen's floor.

Confining the baby to a playpen early makes the idea more comfortable; he or she isn't likely to rebel when restricted later. It also keeps the baby safe while you leave the room or occupy yourself with other duties. And it enables the baby to enjoy the company of the family without someone constantly watching him or her.

Allowing the baby to lounge in a playpen will make the idea more acceptable later on. It will also keep the child safe and sound—without constant supervision.

ADD MORE TOYS

Continue to stimulate the baby with interesting and eye-catching objects. A baby's curiosity is boundless and needs to be fed constantly. Toys for babies at this age don't necessarily have to be something you buy—any safe and attractive object serves the purpose. A box, pie tins, and brightly colored blocks are all good choices. Because your baby now can reach for and often grasp toys, a rattle or other noisemaker will be especially enjoyed. Don't give the baby any toys with sharp corners or edges that might cut, or anything brittle that might shatter and cause injury. No small parts, either—they might lodge in the throat, nose, or ears. Soft toys are fine, but avoid those with ribbons or strings. They can easily become wound around the baby's neck.

Give the baby only one or two toys or objects to inspect at a time. Even babies get bored, so change toys frequently.

11

Four to Five Months

HOW THE BABY GROWS

Physically, an average normal five-month-old will weigh about 16½ pounds and measure about 25 inches, probably more than double birth weight and six inches more than length at birth. Normal babies, however, range from 12½ to 20 pounds and 24 to 27½ inches. Half of average normal five-month-olds will probably be able to:

- sit up for 30 minutes with back supported;
- lift head and shoulders while lying on back; bring feet to mouth and suck on toes;
- reach for objects and often grasp them;
- shift objects from hand to hand; may drop one deliberately to pick up another;
- "talk" to themselves and others;
- react to name;
- anticipate a whole object by seeing part of it; recognize familiar objects;
- show emotions, including anger and frustration; may protest—loudly—when something is taken away;
- raise arms to be picked up;
- may hold bottle with one or two hands; pat bottle or breast.

WHAT IS THE CHILD SAYING?

Your baby now may begin to babble a good bit of the day. Long strings of sounds formed with lips and tongue—"bababa" and "mamama" and "dadada," which, often to a mother's dismay, usually comes first. You can interpret them as the baby's first words or not, as you choose. Usually, when the baby says "dadada," he or she doesn't mean "father," but is just vocalizing. But a quick smile from daddy reinforces the association, and the baby will try it again and again.

Thus speech begins. Though not actually trying to communicate a message, a baby definitely is enchanted with the sound of his or her own voice. It's important for you to encourage these efforts wholeheartedly. You must "talk" back to the baby, smile, laugh, and help show the child that speech is the most important way people communicate.

It's perfectly all right to use baby talk, repeating the baby's own sounds. Some people say baby talk only confuses children who believe they're saying what adults are saying. There's little evidence this is true. Cultures the world over have the equivalent of baby talk. Eventually, children learn to refine their speech, making it conform to consistently normal patterns.

The baby may now—or soon—recognize a very few words. The baby begins to develop a passive vocabulary—words that are understood but can't yet be used—words that will be the basis of speech later.

The baby's conversation is so social at times that you, in fact, may have to squelch it. When you have a visitor while holding the baby in your lap, a stream of loud babble and gab from the eager child may drown out the adult voices in the room. It may be necessary to place the baby in a playpen or crib in order to be able to continue with your visit.

YOU'RE THE TEACHER

The baby is learning quickly but obviously still needs your help. Teach the baby to drink from a cup: sit behind, holding the child's hand in yours, and together lift the cup to his or her lips. Also, sit in front of the baby and demonstrate how this "complicated" procedure is done. Babies quickly learn to mimic actions they see before them. To help the baby learn how to use utensils, repeat the procedure (sitting behind and in front), and help lift the spoon to the baby's mouth. The idea will be picked up quickly, although months will pass before this trick is fully mastered.

In like manner, you can assist the development of a baby's motor skills. If your baby is trying to learn to roll from front to back, you can help by holding the stomach down with a hand on the back, then giving the child a gradual push and turn to demonstrate how it's done. Similarly, you can turn the baby from back to front. Sometimes the baby will protest your intrusion but will

Weaning baby from breast or bottle means teaching the child how to drink from a cup. Use a small one at first, with only a little liquid in the bottom. Go slowly and remember—the baby will need a bib.

soon drop the complaint as this new and fascinating trick is mastered.

Help, but don't rush the baby. Don't try to teach activities or movements your baby's not ready to learn. Look for solid clues the baby is trying to do something alone. At this age, the baby may, when you grasp his or her hands, pull erect and put weight on the balls of the feet. That doesn't mean the baby is either ready to stand independently or to walk alone, so don't press the advantage.

A FASCINATING TIME

For a parent, this period of the child's development is an undeniably wonderful and fascinating time. Your child is learning there is more to the world than just Baby—or, indeed, Baby and mother and father.

The concepts of time, space, cause and effect are being learned. When the baby's hand comes from outside the normal field of vision to an object within that field, it's a clear example of learning that things exist outside the baby's own small environment. When the child pushes a toy over the edge of a chair and watches it fall, it's a lesson in cause and effect. The baby sees your hand come around the edge of the doorway and squirms with anticipation, having learned that the part is a portion of the whole, and that soon a face—then a whole body—will come around the edge of the doorway.

CHANGING MILK FORMULAS

Bottle-fed babies usually switch from commercial formula to dairy milk shortly after they begin eating solid foods. Most babies now are given homogenized milk. Low-fat or fat-free milk is not recommended until later.

Having the baby drink the same milk as the rest of the family is a convenience and probably saves money, but, nutritionally, there's no need to rush the change. Some nutritionists think the baby will grow up leaner and healthier if whole milk is postponed until late in the first year. By then, the baby will be eating the equivalent of two or more jars of baby food a day, and their carbohydrates and sugar more than offset the additional fat in the milk. Meanwhile, the baby will thrive quite nicely on a diet of solid food and formula.

The change in milk, whenever it occurs, probably will alter the baby's bowel habits. Constipation is a common result. Dairy milk contains less sugar and carbohydrates than prepared formula does, and its protein forms a harder curd. The combination of these two facts often produces a firmer stool.

To make the bowel movements regular, feed the baby more fruit—or introduce fruit into the diet if you haven't done so. Prunes are traditionally the best remedy for constipation. Peaches and apricots also soften the stools. A time-tested remedy is adding a very small amount of dark corn syrup to the milk.

A few babies vomit or develop diarrhea or a skin rash from dairy milk. The temporary condition usually is corrected by restoring formula and trying again in a month or so. Or simmer the milk for five minutes before feeding (of course, cool it first) to break down the protein curd.

If the baby develops cramps, colic (see page 143), and digestive problems, a previously undetected allergy to milk may be the cause. Because most commercial formulas are based on cow's milk, the allergy to milk and milk products usually is discovered much earlier, but occasionally the condition does not appear until the child first encounters dairy milk. In this case, dairy milk must be withdrawn from the diet, and a nonallergenic milk, usually goat's milk or a ''milk'' made from soybeans, must be substituted in its place.

NO MORE STERILIZATION

When the baby drinks cow's milk directly from the carton, you'll no longer need to sterilize formula—if, indeed, you have been doing so. At most, sterilization is recommended only so long as the formula is stored in the bottle, as a means of killing bacteria that might multiply there. So long as you are obtaining pasteurized milk from a reputable dairy and keeping it refrigerated, you can be assured that bacteria have been killed.

The bottles and nipples still must be kept clean, however. Continue to wash disposable bottles, nipples, retaining rings and caps for preparing disposable bottles in hot, soapy water. Rinse well in hot, clear water afterward. A dishwasher also may be used for bottles and caps; nipples should be washed thoroughly by hand with a small nipple brush.

SHOULD YOU STOP NURSING?

Solid foods are a landmark for breast-fed babies, too. Many mothers consider the start of solids an appropriate time to begin weaning the baby. Studies show that two of three mothers who nursed their babies have given up nursing either wholly or partially by the end of the fifth month.

How soon to wean a breast-fed baby is another of those controversial topics in infant care with convincing arguments and recognized authorities on all sides. Again, the final decision is yours. The case for early weaning is based on the observation that solid food causes many babies to lose interest in nursing; thus, it seems a natural time to nudge the baby toward a new kind of diet. Advocates of late weaning say the loss of interest is temporary and will revive. They suggest that breast-feeding be continued until the ninth month, because mother's milk is still a complete food for babies and may continue to provide protection against disease and allergy.

Whenever it takes place, all agree that weaning should be done gradually, not abruptly, for the good of both mother and baby. You can wean your baby in a week, of course, because your milk production immediately lags as soon as the demand drops. But the sudden decline in hormonal flow can trigger a kind of blues like the postpartum depression that follows childbirth. And the emotional wrench can be severe for both mother and baby as each gives up a loving—as well as nourishing—event.

It's easier to adjust when you drop one daily feeding at a time. When the baby begins to show a lack of interest and the time seems appropriate for weaning, eliminate that feeding the following day. Usually, the noon feeding is easiest for the baby to give up. (Discontinuing the noon feeding also may allow you to return to a paid job, if you're planning to do so.) Express breast milk to relieve the discomfort caused by fullness in the breasts.

Two weeks is a decent interval to wait before eliminating another feeding, depending on how quickly you wish to wean the baby. Mothers' opinions are divided on whether to eliminate the morning or evening feeding second. Many mothers like to cling to the morning feeding because they enjoy the cozy feeling of nuzzling with the baby in bed, undistracted by household noises and other daily disturbances. On the other hand, many feel that the evening feeding, when the baby is tired, helps the infant to sleep well during the night.

There are probably as many methods of weaning as there are mothers. If you start to wean a baby at five months, you probably will want to shift from breast to a bottle of dairy milk. The usual procedure is for the baby to drink a little milk from a cup with the solids, then follow with a bottle afterward. The baby gradually will take more and more from the cup until the bottle can be eliminated. If you wait a few months, the intermediate step can be dropped. Simply substitute feeding from a cup at the meal as you cut out that feeding.

Gradual weaning shouldn't cause engorgement of the breasts or discomfort for more than a few days, because your milk supply quickly adjusts to the reduced demand. But if your breasts feel painful and full, wearing a tight-fitting brassiere that does not press on the nipples should help. If, for some reason, it becomes necessary to discontinue nursing abruptly, you may wish to ask your physician for medications that will dry up the milk quickly and completely.

A NEW TIMETABLE

Solid food also will change the baby to a more grown-up schedule of three meals a day: with solids morning, noon, and evening; a bottle- or breast-feeding following each meal; and the final bottle- or breast-feeding at bedtime. By the end of the fifth month, your baby may eat about four ounces of baby food a day and drink about 24 ounces of milk.

The baby's sleeping schedule will remain about the same, with a ten-hour sleep at night and morning and afternoon naps of about two hours each (although a few lively babies may sleep only eight hours, total). But the baby will spend much less time lying half-awake in bed. Once those eyes open, an active baby will be anxious to be up learning about the world and exploring it as completely as possible.

In fact, this wakefulness may become quite a problem. At the first crack of light, your baby may no longer lie chewing hands or fussing restlessly but may call and cry out for companionship: "Someone come and visit me!" As early as 6 a.m., your baby may serve notice that the day already has begun and that the rest of the household should be awake, too.

It's not easy to alter this inconvenient schedule, because it goes against the baby's burgeoning curiosity and interest. You can try keeping the baby up later at night so he or she awakes later in the morning. Or you can wake the child after a few hours and offer another bottle of formula or water. Exercise before bedtime, a "rough-and-tumble" with parents or brothers and sisters, or simply time to wiggle and squirm on the floor may tire the baby enough to lengthen sleeping hours sufficiently so he or she doesn't wake and call out quite so early the following morning.

It actually may be necessary to move your baby farther from the rest of the family until this period of early wakefulness ends. Such a move can be beneficial to everyone, allowing you and the others in the family more rest and giving the baby a chance to be independent a while longer. A mobile hanging over the crib will give the youngster something to look at when he or she first awakens and may keep him or her occupied for at least a short time.

HERE COME THE TEETH

Your baby's first tooth may appear at any time from the third to the twelfth month. The fifth or sixth month is the most common time, but don't be alarmed if teething occurs later (or earlier). Teething seems to be influenced by family background. If one child in the family teethes at four months, the others probably will do so, too.

The first tooth is usually a lower central incisor, right in the middle of the mouth. The second incisor follows quickly. Then come the four incisors above, followed by the two remaining incisors in the lower jaw. All eight are usually in place four months after the first appears.

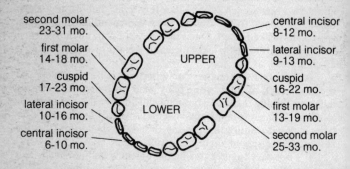

second molar
23-31 mo.

first molar
14-18 mo.

cuspid
17-23 mo.

lateral incisor
10-16 mo.

central incisor
6-10 mo.

UPPER

LOWER

central incisor
8-12 mo.

lateral incisor
9-13 mo.

cuspid
16-22 mo.

first molar
13-19 mo.

second molar
25-33 mo.

The first clue that your baby is teething may be a sudden, tiny glimmer of white—or a sudden, unexpected bite. Often, babies get teeth before parents are even aware of them. Other babies show that teeth are on the way. They drool, fuss, or are irritable. Teething can make babies uncomfortable; they'll cry continually and push away the breast or bottle no matter how hungry they are.

You can relieve the discomfort by rubbing the baby's gums with your finger or offering a clean, cool teething ring. A piece of toast to chew on may help. You also can buy a fluid-filled plastic ring that can be frozen to provide cool relief.

That first tooth will usually pop through when the baby is six months old, others appearing as a small gleam of white in the lower jaw. Teething may make the child uncomfortable and irritable, but it does not cause illness.

Many illnesses are blamed on teething, but, in fact, the process is natural and does not make the baby sick. A high fever or rash that accompanies teething probably stems from some other cause. If your child seems to be sick while teething, look for another explanation. If you cannot find one, call your pediatrician.

DRINKING FROM A CUP

Central to weaning from breast or bottle is learning to drink from a cup. Start with a small cup that fits the baby's mouth. Some have a lip, a small straw, or a narrow opening that cuts down on leaks and spills. A cup with two handles is easier for a baby to use. And don't forget a bib.

Offer only a little liquid in the bottom of the cup at first, and go slowly, a beginning drinker can take only a tiny sip at a time. Hold the cup at first, guiding the baby's hands with yours, until the idea sinks in. Encourage the baby to try it alone as soon as possible, and increase the amount as the infant becomes more dexterous.

If your baby takes a bottle, you'll probably find that he or she already pats or holds the bottle with one or both hands at feeding time. Continue to hold the child in your arms while feeding, but encourage the baby to manipulate the bottle. The sooner a baby learns independence, the better for both of you.

A NEW CHAIR AND A NEW WARDROBE

Because the baby can sit, with support, for longer periods, it's time to replace the inclined infant seat. A "bounce" chair, suspended on springs and weighted at the bottom to prevent tipping, is more suitable for restless, squirming energy. The chair will keep the lower back supported, even when the baby leans forward, and won't capsize under any normal conditions. Later, it will also help the baby learn how to stand, if the chair has a tray, it's a handy place for toys.

A four- to five-month-old also will enjoy a swing. You can buy a wind-up model or a canvas swing that can be hung from a doorway.

Remember to get a sturdier seat restraint for the car, too.

Until now, the basic wardrobe has been shirt; diaper; and kimono, sacque, or jumpsuit. These were fine so long as the baby spent most of the day lying in a crib. But as he or she sits up more and becomes more active, your baby requires different clothing. Overalls and coveralls with padded knees will enable boys and girls to creep and wriggle on the floor or in the playpen without their legs becoming uncovered. Be *sure* to buy the type that unsnap at the crotch for easier diaper changing. To make dressing a simpler task, use small pullover shirts that unbutton at the baby's shoulder or neck. At night, a five-month-old is active enough to kick off blankets and coverings; bundle the baby in a sleeper bag. The baby's not yet ready for shoes and won't be for a few months. Booties, slippers, or socks will serve for now. Be sure to buy sizes that will last for several months.

12

Five to Eight Months

HOW THE BABY GROWS

Between five and six months, the average normal baby weighs 16¼ to 17¼ pounds and measures 26 to 27 inches. But your baby may weigh as little as 12½ pounds or as much as 19½ and measure 24 to 28½ inches and still be considered within the normal range of weights and lengths.

Here are some things half of average normal babies can do between five and six months:

- sit well with support;
- get a toy that is out of reach;
- bear some weight on legs;
- pull on a toy when you pull;
- turn toward a voice;
- attempt to recover an object that falls nearby;
- recognize a familiar face.

By eight months, the average normal baby weighs 19½ pounds and is 28 inches long, but weight between 16 and 23 pounds is within the normal range. Normal length ranges from 26 to 30 inches.

Here are some things half of average normal babies can do at eight months:

- grasp objects with thumb and finger;
- play peek-a-boo;
- say "dada" and "mama";
- sit without support; get self into a sitting position;
- stand well while holding your hands;
- creep on stomach;
- be shy with strangers;
- hold a block in each hand and bang them together.

YOUR CHANGING BABY

The baby who starts this period at rest and is content to remain stationary is vastly different from the increasingly mobile baby who completes it. The time between five and eight months is marked by a tremendous spurt of physical development, highlighted by growing control of the large muscles that ultimately will transform the child's world from a lying-down to a standing-up one. At five months, the baby depends on you for transportation. At eight months, he or she can scramble about independently.

Change can come so fast during these 120 days that it is often difficult to remember what the child was doing last week. Yet at no time are the differences in pace and order of growth more apparent. Active Alice at eight months may be standing erect, clinging precariously to furniture or her playpen for support, whereas Placid Paul is content to sit for an hour in his bounce chair, playing with toys and making little effort to move about on his own.

Physical and mental development go hand in hand. An important milestone occurs when the child can reach a sitting position without help. About half can do so by the seventh month. Plopped on the buttocks, the baby can hold an object in either hand, drop one and reach for another, touch, feel, and inspect. When sitting is combined with creeping and crawling, he or she can spot an interesting object, advance on that object, reach it, then sit down and study it at a leisurely pace.

You may be surprised, though, at the number of things the baby can do easily *without* learning to sit.

As the baby gains greater independence, your own role changes. The emphasis now is on vigilance and support. With any opportunity, the baby is literally into everything. You should allow plenty of room for the baby to explore and test budding wings, while keeping your child free from potential injury or harm. And as the baby gains greater control over his or her body, twists, rolls, and quick, darting movements are commonplace. Merely changing a diaper becomes a wrestling match in which you keep offering toys to keep the writhing child's attention until the task is accomplished.

THE BABY'S DIET CHANGES

By now, you probably have introduced most simple fruits, vegetables, and meats to the diet. You can add mixtures and combinations—"baby dinners," meat-and-vegetable stews, mixed cereals, noodle dishes, simple soups. Desserts based on gelatin or milk also may be included.

Commercial baby foods offer a convenient variety of combinations for the baby's every taste, but if time permits, you may want to make your own specialties. Those baby foods you buy in a store are usually expensive for the nourishment they contain, and meat-and-noodle or meat-and-vegetable combinations may have little meat in proportion to the amount of vegetable. If you do use them, they should not substitute for a daily serving of meat.

With a blender and a little ingenuity, you can prepare your own tasty combinations, such as these two suggested by a pediatric nutritionist:

Chicken and Rice Stew
1 whole chicken breast
¾ cup water
¼ cup rice
¼ cup diced carrots or cut green beans
½ cup milk

In saucepan, cook chicken breast in the water, covered, until it is tender. Take chicken from broth. Remove chicken from bones and dice the meat. To the broth, add the ingredients listed above. Cover and cook until rice and vegetable are tender. Puree mixture in blender. Serve warm or freeze and store according to instructions on page 206.

Potato-Celery Soup
3 potatoes, peeled and quartered
1 stalk celery, chopped
½ cup chicken broth or stock
½ cup milk

Put the vegetables in a saucepan with enough liquid to cover them, and boil until tender (20 minutes). Drain, but reserve the liquid. Place vegetables in blender with a little of the liquid until they have reached a thick consistency. Return this paste to the saucepan, add stock and milk, and stir over low heat.

You also may wish to include a small, chopped onion with the vegetables, eliminate it if your baby does not like the taste.

The baby's inborn iron supply has disappeared by the sixth month, so be sure to include iron in the daily diet. Iron-fortified cereal is the best source. Meat is also a good source, as are certain leafy vegetables, including spinach. A balanced diet usually will provide the essential daily vitamins, although some doctors continue prescribing vitamin supplements. If your local water supply is not fluoridated, continue using a fluoride supplement.

There's no such thing as a set menu for a baby during this period, because individual appetites and tastes are so different. The most important rule is that the diet be balanced, although not every food group needs to be represented at every meal or even every day. Here is one suggested day's menu:

- morning—egg yolk and cereal.
- noon—vegetables and pudding or fruit.
- evening—meat and fruit or vegetables.

Breast milk, formula, or bottled milk should accompany each meal. The baby may drink some milk from a cup, but continue breast- or bottle-feedings until the baby can handle the cup without spilling much.

ADDING FINGER FOODS

With increasing dexterity, the baby is ready for self-feeding. He or she usually is accomplished enough with thumb and fingers to pick up bits of food at seven months, although some children will do so earlier and some later. The first finger foods may be bits of dry cereal, soft toast, zwieback, arrowroot biscuits or graham crackers, and tidbits of soft fruit, bananas, for instance. As feeding skills improve, add small pieces of cooked carrot or potato, scraped apple, scrambled egg, soft meats such as Vienna sausage or hamburger, scraps of cheese, or small pieces of soft bread spread with liverwurst.

Because the baby has at most only a few front teeth, be sure to pick foods of a texture that can be successfully gummed or chomped into a liquid before swallowing. Avoid chunks of raw fruit or vegetables. Give the baby only one or two bits of food at a time, so he or she doesn't cram them all into the mouth at once and choke. Keep the pieces small enough so even those swallowed whole won't become lodged in the throat.

Sensitivity to the gag reflex—which causes adults as well as babies to gag or even vomit when the back of the throat is tickled—varies among babies, and yours may react when the first finger foods are offered. If this happens, wait a few weeks and try again.

Remember that nourishment isn't the sole purpose of self-feeding. It's also a learning process, in which the baby gets an opportunity to investigate the food for texture, feel, and softness before subjecting it to the ultimate taste test. You may see your child sit for minutes on end, peering intently at each hand as he or she squeezes a morsel of food in it or—to your dismay—flattening and pounding it on the tray before eating. Table manners will probably differ greatly from those described in books of etiquette—and that's all right for now. Probably the baby will simply smash and stuff the food into the mouth with an open hand. When finished, there may be more food on face and floor than inside!

Self-feeding is also a lesson in independence, of a kind important to both babies and parents. By restraining your impulse to be neat or to see that the baby "eats enough," you're providing an opportunity for your offspring to follow his or her own appetite and pace. At the same time, you're freeing yourself for other duties while the baby eats.

DOWN WITH MILK

As the desire for solid foods increases, the appetite for breast milk or formula usually declines. The amount of intake varies from baby to baby but at seven months stabilizes at about 20 to 24 ounces. The baby's slowing growth rate is one reason for the drop. Birth weight doubles in most babies during the first three or four months of life, but the upward curve begins to taper off in the last half of the first year, and by 12 months, birth weight, on the average, has only tripled.

In addition, solids now provide much of the energy and body-building materials the baby formerly received from milk. Meat is the main source of protein; vegetables and fruits furnish the necessary carbohydrates and sugars, as well as many minerals. Meat and eggs provide iron and other nutrients.

Actually, the baby doesn't need too much milk at this point. Pediatric nutritionists say that a pint—16 ounces—of milk daily is sufficient for a seven-month-old, and some of that may be obtained from foods containing milk. Some of the liquid that used to come from milk will now come from water and fruit juices.

And unlike the earlier period when appetite was relatively consistent, the amount of milk drunk may vary considerably from interval to interval. The baby may take only an ounce or two at morning and noon feedings, then eagerly gulp three times that amount in the evening. A baby may even go one or two days with substantially lowered intake. These fluctuations are normal and not a matter of concern if the baby is healthy and thriving.

FEEDING WITHOUT PAIN

Many parents fret about the amount their babies eat and try to keep the baby filled up by coaxing, wheedling, and prodding. These not-so-subtle pressures turn mealtime into a battleground. You need to remember that when left to their own devices, babies usually eat more than enough. As growth slows, only 15 percent of their intake goes into body development. One study indicates that a baby can flourish on a daily consumption of a pint of milk, an ounce of fruit juice, a dab of vegetable, a half-jar of baby meat or its equivalent, and vitamin supplements.

Moreover, overfeeding at this time may lead to bad eating habits—and potential health problems—that will last for a lifetime. Force-feeding a baby often has counter-productive results—as many a parent discovers when suddenly splattered by a spray of strained carrots.

Unfortunately, an active and curious baby also is readily distracted at mealtime. There's just too much to be observed and learned to concentrate on something so ordinary as food. This is a good time to introduce finger foods, which will focus the baby's attention while you spoon-feed the more liquid items. Another way to keep your child's attention is to let him or her hold a cup or spoon and participate in the business of eating.

Just as the baby's appetite for milk may wax and wane now, so does the desire for solid food. Infant appetites now begin to resemble those of adults. At some meals, your baby may eagerly gobble up a half-jar of vegetables and look around for more. At another meal, he or she may take only a tentative nibble of the very same food, then firmly turn away and refuse another bite. These ups and downs, though frustrating to parents, are of little consequence if the baby appears healthy and in good spirits.

Now, your baby will begin to show likes and dislikes. Spinach is usually on the disliked list; fruits are usually a favorite. Many babies seem unable to abide the taste of meat. Providing a balanced diet is sometimes difficult under such circumstances, but you can circumvent finicky tastes by mixing a disliked food (meat, for example) with a favorite vegetable, or by spreading it on bread to form a finger food. Sometimes the baby can be persuaded to eat a disliked food by alternating spoonfuls with a popular one.

Introduce new foods at the beginning of the meal, while the baby is hungry. (But if he or she is really ravenous, the strange taste may be rejected. In that case, switch to a familiar food until the baby is satisfied, then return to the new one.) As before, try only a few spoonfuls of the new food at the first serving, then increase the amount at subsequent meals. Follow it with a food you know the baby likes.

It's usually wise to offer milk at the end of the meal rather than the beginning, because some babies fill up on fluids and are too satisfied to eat solid foods. This order is particularly important now because the baby's store of iron needs regular replenishment; if he or she concentrates on milk, an iron-deficient food, a condition called milk anemia may result.

DINNER WITH THE FAMILY

Usually, you'll feed the baby alone, before the rest of the family sits down to begin the meal. That's because it's a slow and sometimes frustratingly messy process, and the baby's schedule is somewhat less flexible than that of adults or older children. But you may still include the family's youngest member in the dinnertime circle, if you wish. If the baby is old enough to sit unsupported, he or she may be placed in a high chair or feeding table near the family table and be given a few finger foods to toy with while other family members eat their meals. If the baby can't yet sit in a high chair, he or she can inhabit a playpen not far from the dinner table, so parents and siblings can see and respond to the baby while they eat.

If the baby can sit well enough alone, it's certainly time for a high chair or feeding table. The bounce chair and swing will still be the most popular places for the baby to sit, but chairs more like those adults customarily use are better suited for the time the baby takes up eating at the dinner table.

When you buy a high chair for the baby, choose a sturdy model with a wide base that won't tip when the baby is older and more active. The type with a removable tray is probably the best choice, because it's easier to keep clean. Make sure the tray has a strong clasp that won't be dislodged if the baby leans against it. The chair also requires a crotch strap to prevent the baby from sliding under the tray or from climbing out when your back is turned. Pick a model with a tray wide enough to hold a baby dish, with a lip that will prevent inevitable spills from leaking onto the floor. If you choose a painted wooden high chair, make sure a lead-free paint has been used to cover it.

Many parents prefer to use a feeding table. A model with a seat in the center surrounds the baby with the surface of a table, thus cutting down on spills and providing a sizable area for eating and playing. As the high chair does, the table requires a strap to keep the baby from slipping or climbing out. Be sure to keep the high chair or feeding table away from stoves, electrical fixtures, the family table, appliances, or electric cords.

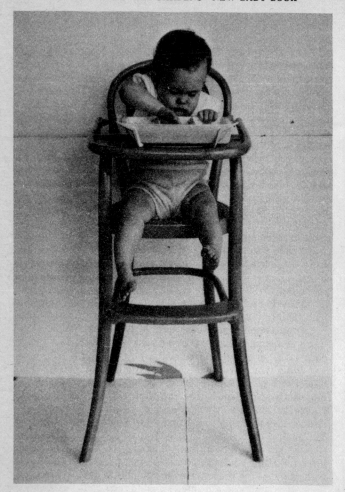

THUMBS AND PACIFIERS
Photographs of babies in the womb show them sucking their thumbs; a few are actually born with calluses as a result. Sucking is a natural instinct that helps the baby locate and consume food. Almost all babies suck their thumbs, chew on their fingers, or gnaw their fists when fussy or hungry. One study of 70 normal babies showed that 61 were thumb-suckers at such periods.

Parents often worry that teeth will be damaged, but there is little basis for the fear, especially in the early months of life. According to the American Dental Association (ADA), it is natural for an infant to suck his or her thumb up to the age of two and probably is not a matter of concern even it if persists until the child is three or four, unless done often or with heavy pressure on the jaws.

After the age of four, repeated thumb-sucking may alter the position of the permanent teeth and change the shape of the jaws, squeezing the upper teeth together. One result may be a need for expensive orthodontic work (braces) later.

If regular thumb-sucking isn't present at birth, it usually begins at six weeks and increases in frequency as the number of feedings decreases. The peak usually is reached at about seven months, when many babies seem (to their despairing parents) to have a thumb plunked in their mouths at all times. Incidentally, the peak of thumb-sucking comes as the baby becomes more mobile, and many specialists in child behavior see it as a good rather than a bad sign. As new adventures become more and more frequent and available, the baby is ambivalent about leaving behind an earlier, more secure way of living. The ever-ready thumb provides comfort.

As the child grows more confident, the amount of thumb-sucking will probably decrease, but the thumb will probably find its way back to the mouth for several years during upset, fatigue, or stress. Even a child of six years or older may revert to the comforting thumb when tired or when the demands of the world seem momentarily overwhelming.

Probably the worst course of action is to nag the child about thumb-sucking, yank the offending thumb from the mouth, or otherwise show displeasure. Any of these is likely to upset the baby further and perhaps ingrain the habit even more deeply. Most children give up the thumb—except in times of stress—by 18 months to two years; with those who don't, it should be a matter of concern only if it is a persistent part of a larger fabric of obvious psychological upset.

Pacifiers are another of those topics in child care with vehement opinion split into two camps. Some parents argue that the thumb is inexpensive, more convenient, is the proper shape, never gets lost or falls on the floor, and doesn't make the baby's mouth look like a corked bottle. Proponents of the pacifier say the device, especially new models shaped to prevent pressure on the upper jawline, is less likely to damage the teeth and jaws. And because it's removable, a pacifier is easier to get rid of when the

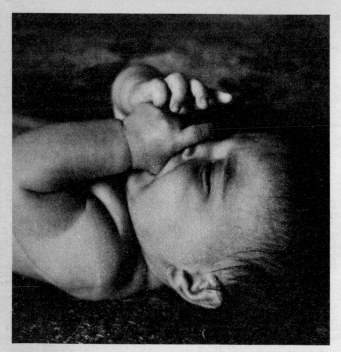

Thumb-sucking comes naturally to most babies; it's a comfortable way to deal with a rapidly expanding world. Don't bother the child about it—most children abandon the practice by the age of two.

time comes to wean the baby from it. As with thumbs, using pacifiers usually begins at or shortly after birth (some are even used in hospital nurseries to placate the baby's sucking instinct), reaches a peak about the middle of the first year, declines thereafter, and generally is voluntarily discarded sometime around the second birthday. There is no dental harm even if the baby clings to the pacifier for another year or two.

SOME SPECIAL HABITS

Comic strips have added the words "security blanket" to the language, but most parents didn't need to be told that many children become inseparably attached to a special blanket, stuffed toy, or other cuddly object. Indeed, the often disreputable appearing fabric becomes—to the parents' dismay—the baby's most cherished possession and chief source of solace, preferred over mother or father in times of stress or upset. Let the parent try to wrest the object away (even to wash it) and a tearful, poignant tug-of-war takes place.

Actually, like thumb-sucking, blanket-carrying is an important step in the baby's march to independence. Prior to about six months of age, the child depends fully on mother and father for emotional comfort and security. The older child tries to strike out alone yet still needs security and love. The blanket serves as a bridge between the total dependency of infancy and the independence of adulthood.

Some babies develop an elaborate ritual involving the treasured blanket, entwining it between the fingers or against the cheek, while sucking a thumb in just a certain way. Often the baby will maintain this posture for a half hour before bedtime, will resist being deflected from it, and will be unable to sleep until the arrangement is resumed in bed.

Despite parental worries, blanket-carrying, too, is harmless in early infancy. Although the blanket collects its own colony of germs when the baby refuses to allow laundering, no evidence exists that illness can result. After the baby is about a year old, the blanket usually will lose its favored position, although it will still be reserved for bedtime and as a refuge in moments of stress. Eventually, a child gives up the security blanket voluntarily; although even if it persists as a bedtime solace until the age of six or seven, no harm is done. Blanket-carrying requires attention only if it is accompanied by other signs of emotional upset.

Another habit that may appear at about the same time is rhythmic rocking. This usually begins when the child is able to support the body weight on all fours. Crouched in this position, he or she rocks rhythmically forward and backward, often for as long as a half hour. The tick-tock motion can actually propel a crib across an uncarpeted floor, distressing parents considerably when it collides with a wall or other furniture. Except for wear and tear on the furniture and parental nerves, consequences are minor. Specialists in child behavior theorize that the rocking soothes the baby before bedtime or that perhaps it helps prepare the child for crawling and walking. Fortunately, the habit usually disappears within a few months. Apart from moving the furniture or equipping it with rubber bumpers or the legs with rubber coasters, little can be done to stop it.

A more disturbing habit—which also, to parental relief, is usually short-lived—is head-banging. In an all-fours position, the baby rhythmically whacks the crown of his or her head against the side of the crib—sometimes using the head of the bed as the target, sometimes the side rails. The banging may continue for ten minutes or more. Parents are not unnaturally worried and try to stop the child, only to have the practice resume as soon as the baby is returned to the crib. Fortunately, the banging somehow doesn't seem to hurt the baby; on the contrary, the rhythm seems to be soothing. Head-banging seldom persists more than a few weeks, and no lasting effects have been recorded. For your own peace of mind, however, pad the crib.

A few other normal babies cultivate different rhythmic patterns upsetting to their parents. Some, for example, will sit in a bounce chair and wag the head back and forth like a metronome for as long as 15 minutes at a stretch. Others bow from the waist in the same measured, to-and-fro motion. The reasons for these rhythmic activities are not fully known but seem to serve some inner need. The erratic behavior seldom lasts more than a short time.

BABY ON THE MOVE

With greater control over their large muscles, babies as young as seven months begin to fashion their own ways of getting about. Some techniques are remarkably ingenious. Until your baby can support himself or herself on all fours, he or she may scoot along on the stomach, steering with the arms. Often the baby creeps backwards first (the muscles controlling forward movement develop more slowly), and this reverse direction may last a month before the baby masters the head-first technique.

Babies who learn to move from a prone to a sitting position often work out another method of locomotion. Propelling themselves with a hand behind them, while pulling forward with an extended foot, these "sitters" are able to bounce along on their bottoms. They can often attain a remarkable speed, however clumsy they look. Some babies, too, learn to pull with their arms before their bent legs can support them, and they inch along on their elbows and follow with their legs in a kind of modified hop. Finally, a truly adventuresome sort may bypass all these methods, pull to an erect stance by reaching overhead from a lying position, and then daringly lunge from one piece of furniture to another in a more or less upright position.

Crawling usually follows creeping—but not always. Some children creep, then stand, then drop to all fours. Usually, crawling begins during the eighth month, when the arms and legs are sturdy enough to support the baby's weight. The baby frequently will spend a week posing on hands and knees before working out the rather sophisticated and coordinated technique of making

NEW SAFETY PRECAUTIONS

Capable of quick movement and with new powers of locomotion, a seven-month-old boy or girl can reach and grab many places and objects that once seemed out of range. Additional precautions are necessary to keep the baby safe from accidents.

Here is a safety checklist for the five- to eight-month-old child:

- Install gates on all stairways, top and bottom.
- Cover all unused electrical outlets (especially those near the floor) with safety caps or tape.
- Keep electrical cords out of baby's reach; unplug lamps or appliances when the baby is on the floor.
- Keep cans, bottles, sprays, and boxes of cleaners, detergents, pesticides, laundry bleaches, liquors, medicine, and cosmetics out of low cabinets—under the kitchen sink, for instance.
- Remove matches, cigarette butts, ashtrays, small objects capable of being swallowed, sharp objects, and breakables from any room where the baby might play on the floor. Remove lamps and tables that might be pulled over.
- Keep high chair, table, or playpen away from stove, work counters, heaters and furnaces.

arms and legs work together. As with creeping, the baby may crawl backwards first. Several weeks may pass before he or she learns to move forward. Once mastered, however, crawling will be the baby's main means of progress for six months or more. Even after learning to teeter about in an upright position, crawling may be the baby's choice when it's necessary to get somewhere in a hurry.

TIME FOR FUN AND GAMES

As the baby quickly develops skills and coordination, he or she also is becoming more playful. After reaching six months of age, the baby quickly works up a repertoire of games, punctuated by laughter and excited movement.

"Peekaboo" is one of the first the baby will enjoy playing. It needs almost no explanation. Facing the baby, a parent covers eyes, uncovers them, and shouts, "Peekaboo!" The baby quickly gets the idea and imitates; he or she covers the eyes, waits for you to call, "Where is Kim?" then uncovers his or her eyes to cries of "There he (she) is!" and squeals with delight. Before long, the baby has devised all kinds of enthusiastic variations for this popular game—covering the eyes with a diaper, screwing eyes up tight, turning away and turning back.

"How big is baby?" is another six-month-old's game played over and over again. When a parent says, "How big are you?" the baby extends arms directly overhead, in a movement similar to the signal a football referee gives for a touchdown or field goal. "So big!" cries the parent, and the baby giggles with glee.

A much less popular game with parents is "I-drop-it-you-pick-it-up." Sitting in a bounce chair or high chair, the baby shoves a toy off the tray, shuts the eyes in anticipation of the loud crash, then waits expectantly for the parent to retrieve the toy (or cries until the parent does so). Once the toy has been returned, the baby promptly drops it again, and again, and again.

Actually, all three games are important stages in the baby's development, stages that indicate the child is constantly making progress. "Peekaboo" demonstrates the baby's confidence that you and the other elements of the world are fixtures, that they're here to stay and will not disappear simply by closing the eyes. "How big is baby?" helps with the lesson of spatial relationships and with verbal cues. When objects are dropped over the edge of table or chair, the delay before the expected noise shows the baby has learned about timing, that an interval passes before the crash occurs. And all three games clearly show that your child is developing a ready sense of humor, one that will stand him or her in good stead in the coming months and years.

THE SLEEP SCHEDULE CHANGES

Most babies will continue to take two daily naps, morning and afternoon, but the total time may shorten. The morning nap may be reduced to an hour or less. A rare eight-month-old will give up one nap—the morning nap, although longer, usually is abandoned first—but most retain the pattern of taking two naps a day until after their first birthday.

Like nearly everything else, the need for sleep varies widely among children. When the baby begins to stay awake longer or sleeps less than a sibling or a neighbor's child, parents sometimes worry that he or she isn't getting enough rest. That's unlikely. But if your child seems tired, grouchy, or out of sorts, don't hesitate to enforce a nap regardless of what the clock says.

A strict bedtime is another matter. Most children, even at five to eight months, don't like to be put to bed, especially if there are other children in the family who remain awake. It's simply a matter you have to be firm about. Put the baby in the crib, talk quietly for a few minutes, and then make your exit, closing the door with finality. At this age, many babies will begin to call out and cry for you to return. One such return is probably all right, if for no other reason than to convince yourself the baby isn't ill, but after that, the cries should be ignored. Otherwise, the baby will keep you trotting back and forth, back and forth for an hour or more, until both of you are exhausted and cranky.

The baby also may wake during the night and cry or call out. Some parents believe this is because the child is hungry (the practice often coincides with a decrease in milk intake), but that is rarely the case. A much more plausible explanation is simply that the child wakes to a darkened room in a silent house and cries out to be reassured that you are still nearby. The baby will usually calm down if you go to the cribside, lift him or her, and speak a few words reassuringly in soft, loving tones. Be sure that you don't give the baby a bottle to take to bed; if you want to offer a few extra ounces of milk, hold the child in your arms for the feeding. Rocking, walking the floor, or taking the baby to bed with you should be avoided.

MORE TIME FOR PLAY
Play is the baby's education, and the mobile child needs both more time and more space for it. A five- to eight-month-old may spend an hour at a time in the playpen but needs a regular unfettered period on the floor or outdoors on a grassy lawn where he or she can explore and investigate. It might be wise to invest in an expandable outdoor corral that can be formed into a circle large enough for the baby's outdoor explorations and experiments.

Toys also must keep pace with development. When the baby can sit unsupported or get about by creeping or crawling, he or she needs toys that can be pulled and pushed and that will move just as the baby does. The baby is ready for a music box, too. By now, he or she can distinguish and locate sounds, and nothing holds the attention as music does. Add a ball, too. A five- to eight-month-old delights in pushing it, watching it roll away, and then scooting after it—or in having you return it.

Toys needn't be expensive nor even labeled "toys." The baby is entranced by the ability to make noise—a handful of clattering pie tins can provide play for a half hour.

FEAR CREEPS IN
Combined with the baby's new spirit of adventure will be some new fears. Actually, the moments of fright, too, are landmarks in development—indications that the baby has become aware of the

All the world's a plaything for the growing baby, who needs both a regular time and space to explore it. Toys don't have to be expensive items bought in a store; everyday utensils can keep a child enthralled for hours.

consequences of some actions or that he or she is now conscious of differences and details that once were obscure.

Sudden loud noises, even the kind the baby has heard before, may trigger howls. Water running in the bathtub, the noise of a vacuum cleaner, a clap of thunder may bring tears and shrieks. The baby who has splashed delightedly in the bath for months may now cry as he or she watches the water run down the drain.

Be reassuring. If the noisy sweeper distresses the baby, pick up the child and talk quietly, while moving the sweeper back and forth to associate the noise and reassurance. During a thunderstorm, hold the child, and with a few words, make the point that the frightening moment is over and you are still at hand.

At this same time, shyness with people outside the immediate family may develop. Whereas once the baby ''made up'' to virtually every adult, now he or she may be wary of four or five, perhaps even including grandparents, neighbors, or the doctor whom the baby has visited many times. The baby's tears and fears may upset the grandparents who have previously been welcomed so avidly, but they only need to be reminded that the phase is temporary.

You may also find the shyness applies to baby-sitters and to visits to other homes or unfamiliar places. With sitters, you may be obliged to spend a longer time with the baby before leaving him or her, but even though the child cries, you must finally leave with firmness. (Even babies can be great actors, and the sitter will usually confirm that the baby didn't cry for long after you left.) When you visit a strange place, be sure to stay with the child and reassure him or her of your presence throughout the visit.

13

Eight to Twelve Months

HOW THE BABY GROWS

By the age of ten months, the average normal baby weighs 21¼ pounds and measures 29 inches. The range for normal babies is 17¼ to 25 pounds and 27¼ to 31 inches.

Here are some things half of average normal babies learn to do between eight and ten months.

- play pattycake;
- hold a block in each hand and bang them together;
- identify "mama" and "dada" and call them by name;
- pull to a standing position;
- stand without support for a few seconds;
- walk or sidestep, holding onto playpen or furniture;
- wave bye-bye.

The average normal baby weighs 22½ pounds and measures 30 inches on the first birthday. Normal weight ranges between 18½ and 26½ pounds and normal height between 28¼ and 32 inches.

Here's what half of average normal one-year-olds can do:

- stop a rolling ball when you push it, then roll it back to you;
- indicate wants without crying;
- drink from a cup, spilling only a little;
- take a few steps;
- stand alone, stoop, and return to a standing position;
- understand many words;
- say two to three words in addition to "mama" and "dada";
- say "no" and mean it.

YOUR BABY IS DIFFERENT

It's almost impossible to generalize about the "average" baby between eight and 12 months old. Children simply develop in too many directions at once. Statistically, half of one-year-olds can take a few steps, speak four or five recognizable words, and feed themselves reasonably well. Yet year-old Johnny may have been walking since nine months—and not say his first word until 15 months. Susan, on the other hand, may gabble a blue streak while remaining contentedly fixed in a sitting position. The range of accomplishments is truly astonishing.

Unfortunately, walking and talking bring out parental competitive urges. Mothers and fathers like to boast about how early a child walked or talked, especially if their child walked or talked before a friend's child. Parents of children who take the slow-but-sure route to transportation and communication may become frustrated and anxious. They may worry that their baby's development has been delayed and subtly try to push the baby along. Equally bad, a child's supposed slowness may make parents feel they are doing something wrong.

In children's growth, as in the Bible, there is a season to all things. Studies repeatedly show there is always an appropriate moment in development when all systems are ready for the next step forward. When a child's bones, nerves, muscles, coordination, and, most of all, ambition have matured sufficiently, the child walks; when the brain centers and the vocal muscles are ready, the child talks. Apart from providing opportunity and encouragement, you can't do much to hasten the process. If your child seems ready to walk but is wary of trying, you might try to stimulate him or her by placing a toy just out of reach as a motive to do so. But a mother who holds her nine-month-old's hands and "practices" walking may find she has gained nothing for her efforts but a sore back.

In any case, a seemingly slow child quickly makes up for lost time. The infant who walks at nine months may spend the next three months refining the movements. The child who walks later may master crawling, walking, and sitting in a week's time and two weeks later have overtaken and even surpassed the early riser.

DIFFERENCES BETWEEN THE SEXES

Apart from the obvious, boys and girls aren't terribly different. An average baby boy weighs about a half pound more and is an inch longer at birth than a baby girl, and some difference in size and weight usually persists into adulthood. But the differences in size among individual members of either sex are far greater than the differences between the sexes as a whole, either in infancy or maturity.

Temperamentally, boys and girls may seem different. Boys are thought to be more rough-and-tumble, more curious, and more outgoing, whereas girls are considered verbal, gentle, and reserved. But no one knows if these differences are actually inborn or are the product of conditioning. Films and audio recordings of parents with newborns have shown that mothers and fathers talk and behave differently toward girls than boys right from birth. A father may soften his voice and coo to his daughter and adopt a gruff, see-here-old-man tone with his son.

In any case, temperamental differences vary widely within a single sex, just as physical sizes do. You can generally expect a little girl to be more talkative and a little boy to be more active, but not always. A rambunctious girl who is into everything is just as normal as her subdued sister, and a slow-moving male just as much of a boy as a brother bent on raising the roof.

Some parents like to reinforce the presumed feminine qualities in little girls and the masculine ones in boys; others feel the child's behavior should be allowed to develop by itself without attempts to mold it into stereotypes. This is a matter of family style. More important than the approach is to be aware of your attitudes and their influence on the child. Here are some points you may wish to consider:

• Do you have different standards for boys and girls? Is your son's boisterousness considered normal behavior, your daughter's self-assertion abnormal?

• Do you push your child toward stereotyped activity? Do you buy athletic equipment for a boy, even in infancy, dolls and dishes for a girl? Do you rough-house with your son but not with your daughter?

• Do you allow both sexes equal emotional expression? When your son cries, do you tell him that's sissy stuff but expect crying and emotional displays in a daughter? Are you equally affectionate with both sons and daughters?

• Do you expect neatness from a girl, even a toddler, but excuse disorder in a boy?

• Do you pair the family by sexes? Is the father expected to have a different attitude and responsibility for a son's upbringing than a mother has for her daughter?

Most of us have qualities that we admire in children and those we don't. We reinforce those we like and ignore or criticize those we disapprove. Even in infancy, your child quickly learns to recognize which behavior is rewarded; when the reward is withheld, he or she tries to live up to your expectations.

Most parents treat their children somewhat differently, according to the child's sex. It is a perfectly human trait.

STANDING AND WALKING, STEP BY STEP

Any time after eight months, your child may enter the vertical world of grown-ups. Sitting on the floor of a playpen with legs extended, your baby may reach above his or her head, grab onto the playpen, strain sufficiently—and there, the buttocks are off the floor. The next time, a slight kink in the knees and downward pressure with the heels will elevate the baby a little higher. Another try may bring a bit more height. At last, the baby will grasp the top rail, flex the knees, tug laboriously, and finally stand triumphant and upright like the other members of the family.

Unfortunately, at first your baby won't know how to get back down. Amid terrified bleats and howls, he or she may cling to the playpen rail until little legs cave in from exhaustion and the baby drops back with an abrupt plop! If you rush to the rescue and ease the baby down gently, you may be greeted by a new protest of displeasure. No sooner is the baby sitting than he or she emphatically yanks back up again to savor some more of this newfound perspective on the world!

After a few days, the baby will be going up and down with relative ease—lowering those well-padded buttocks gently until the last few inches of free fall. Next may come a new step—actually, a sideways shuffle. Crunching toys, crackers, blankets, and bottles underfoot, the baby may sidestep around the confines of the playpen while holding onto the top rail. Released from the pen, the baby will cautiously apply the same principles to circumnavigate the furniture.

Soon the baby will learn to stand without holding. This lesson is usually accidental. One day the baby may be standing at the playpen rail, holding a toy in one hand and the rail in the other. Almost absentmindedly, he or she will relax the grip yet remain upright without being aware of the accomplishment. Balance may be maintained from a few seconds to a minute or more. Before long, the baby will be able to repeat the act deliberately, and the periods of independent stance will steadily lengthen. This, too, will quickly become routine as the baby learns new tricks, like stooping to pick up a toy and then returning to a standing position.

All these preliminaries to walking may take place within a

few weeks or be spread over several months. There is no fixed date when a baby sets sail alone. Most babies (90 percent) walk by the age of 15 months, but another ten percent, equally normal, are still sedentary at that age, either because they lack the confidence or ambition to do so or simply because they have more important things to do, like crawling.

You needn't hurry your baby to walk, either, because creeping and crawling are important steps in development.

Regardless of when they come, your baby's first independent steps are a milestone you're not likely to forget. Some babies accidentally achieve the goal themselves. Perambulating about the living room, the baby may let go of a sofa, lunge toward an inviting chair—and may "walk" without knowing it. More often than not, your help and encouragement are needed for this lesson. When the baby seems to be standing well and shows good balance in stooping and sidestepping, sit on the floor a short distance from where the baby is standing, stretch out your hands, and urge him or her to "come to me." You may have to ask several times before he or she makes the attempt. But finally, leaning strongly forward, the baby will venture toward your waiting arms. It'll be only one or two quick steps at first—almost falling forward—but the milestone will have been reached.

Once started, the baby may be hard to stop—in more ways than one. A new walker often can't get enough of his novel locomotion and may literally exhaust both self and parents lurching around the living room to refine new-found skills. Two steps increase to three and then more, until finally he or she will be able to toddle the full length of the room into your outstretched arms. Several weeks may pass, though, before the baby is able to master the more complicated technique of stopping. Like a wind-up toy, the baby will just keep going until something brings him or her to a halt.

In the jumbled sequence of development, not every child fits this model. Some learn to stand or sidestep well, then remain at this stage for several months. A few babies learn to walk backward before they can walk forward. Difficult as this seems for an adult, the baby's sequence of motor development makes it easier to do.

Meanwhile, for most babies, walking is just for fun. Crawling is for important business. Even after mastering walking, a one-year-old often will drop to all fours when the idea is to *get* somewhere. This crawling ability—often combined with climbing—can propel the baby into dangerous situations, requiring increased parental vigilance.

SAYING A FEW WORDS

By now, the baby is firmly established in the world of verbal communication. The exact number of words a child can speak or understand at this age varies widely. Each child develops speech in a unique pattern. But even the baby who has not said a word knows that vocal sounds are the way humans express their ideas and wishes and is beginning to test the notion.

Up to now, the baby has strung together repetitive sounds in a meaningless but imitative babble: "mamamama" and "dadadada." Sometime during the last few months of the first year, the sounds begin to take on meaning for most babies. "Mama" and "dada" (or the baby's version thereof) are applied regularly and consistently to the baby's parents. New words follow over the next few months. "No" is (to parents' dismay) an early addition. "Bye-bye" is another "See?" accompanied by outstretched toy, dish, or bottle to be observed, also arrives early. So do names of brothers and sisters, usually with the baby's own unique pronunciation.

Baby's first word is a landmark—but you may not be aware of it. Some babies speak their first word clearly, spontaneously, and unmistakably, as though they had been rehearsing it for weeks. More often, the baby's first attempts at speech are only partially recognizable or even completely unrecognizable to adults. Only after the baby repeatedly has used the same sound for an object or person will adults catch on that the baby has something to say.

In addition to speech, the baby's passive vocabulary—the words he or she understands but can't repeat—expands rapidly during the last part of the first year. By their first birthday, most babies recognize their own names, and many carry out simple commands like, "Give me the bottle," and respond to simple questions like, "Where is the airplane?" by pointing upward or looking toward the sky. Months may pass, however, before these words and simple sentences enter the baby's spoken vocabulary.

The baby understands nonverbal communication at this stage, too. Your moods of anger, frustration, uncertainty, or fatigue are unfailingly more clear than words.

SELF-FEEDING TIME

By now, self-feeding may be the order of the day. In fact, the baby may insist on it. You'll still have to feed the soupier, mushier fruits and vegetables, but the baby will get a lot of nourishment from finger foods and "lumps."

Much of the food will be the same as the rest of the family is

Your baby may spill a few, but practice and more practice make perfect. Real skill at using a cup and other utensils may not be apparent for another year or so. Encourage the baby's efforts—and keep paper towels handy.

eating. As the baby develops more teeth and gets the hang of chewing, he or she can eat more and more adult foods. You no longer have to strain foods; simply mash them or cut them into small and manageable pieces. By their first birthdays, babies may have anywhere from two to eight teeth, so they can pulverize most foods you serve them. Molars don't arrive until the age of one year, however, so babies can't do much grinding. That means chunks of food—raw carrots or meat that requires chewing, for example—are still off the menu. Stick to ground meat, frankfurters or Vienna sausage, lunch meat, cheese, and soft stewed meats.

Definite likes and dislikes continue to show themselves. Yet babies are surprisingly skilled at working out a balanced diet for themselves. In one historic experiment, babies barely old enough for finger foods were allowed to choose their own diet from a smorgasbord of choices. Although they sometimes ate only one food at a meal and ignored all others, over the period of observation their selections balanced out to include all the essential nutrients.

But the baby still isn't ready for fancy dishes. Restrict the menu to simple foods and combinations. Restrict seasonings, and limit salt and sugar. When preparing adult food for the baby's meals, serve the baby first, and then season it for the rest of the family.

Give the baby plenty of practice with spoon and cup. Real skill may not come for another year, but the baby gets the idea of manipulating them and gradually cuts down on the spills. Some babies can raise a cup at the proper angle to drink as early as ten months, but most aren't quite so precocious. Fifteen months is a more likely date for that achievement. If messiness at the table disturbs you, let the baby experiment with drinking from a cup in the bathtub—even if a little bathwater is swallowed in the process.

The baby's appetite for milk may continue to slacken, then stabilize at around 20 ounces. So long as the baby is healthy, the reduction is no cause for concern. As the growth rate drops, appetite naturally drops with it and will drop further in coming months.

Nine months is about the outside limit for breast-feeding, too. If you have not previously weaned the baby from the breast, the time of declining appetite may be an appropriate moment. Follow the steps outlined on page 217 to wean the baby, giving up a single feeding at a time and taking proper precautions to deal with breast engorgement. Indeed, the baby may be willing to give up breast-feeding before you do. One day he or she may simply and emphatically push the breast away in favor of other kinds of nourishment. Bottle babies, too, now may take most milk from a cup, although most will continue to cling to a nightly feeding.

SIBLING RIVALRY AGAIN

The baby's walking, talking, and cute antics may draw so much attention that competitive feelings are rekindled (see page 138) among older brothers and sisters. The rivalry may become so intense that you actually have to protect the baby, especially if the other children are younger than three or four years old.

The competition usually takes one of several forms. When the baby sets out walking on unsteady legs, the older child may "jokingly" nudge, bump, or crowd so the baby is upended. Such thumps are likely to make him or her wary and uneasy about walking and actually delay mastery of the skill. Or when the baby tries to converse with you, a sister or brother may talk louder to outshout the little rival. You also may find the older brother feeding the baby a diet of cigarette butts or paper clips or giving him or her dangerous toys to play with. And when a parent returns from work at the end of the day, the crawling baby who hurries to the door may be "accidentally" trampled by equally eager siblings.

Competing with an attractive one-year-old isn't any more fun than competing with a newborn, and you'll have to be patient with the older children. It's also true that competition isn't strictly a one-way street, and sometimes you'll have to champion the older child's rights against the younger. That means making sure the older child gets enough attention and is not constantly compelled to give in to a younger sibling. The older child's toys, for instance, should belong to him or her and be kept from the inquisitive and inadvertently destructive hands of the baby.

Older brothers and sisters are an important part of a baby's life, too. The baby can learn as much from them as from you and may actually prefer the loud and romping company of brothers and sisters. Under your watchful eye, allow them to play together and stimulate each other. Caution the older children to be careful, but remember it is also important for the baby to learn the concept of self-protection. Try to keep your interference to a minimum.

If yours is an only child, you may find that he or she shows an increasing interest in other babies. A ten-month-old may spend long minutes studying the face of another baby in a magazine. Or, being pushed around the supermarket in a stroller, your offspring may greet and reach out to other small passersby.

Babies this age, of course, don't really play together. At most, they may play side-by-side or investigate each other by looking, poking, prodding, or passing possessions back and forth. But the company of other children can stimulate a child's development. Specialists in education during early childhood have found that children less than a year old flourish and develop faster if they are repeatedly exposed to their peers and can watch and imitate them. Your one-year-old child may not be ready for a regular play group yet, but frequent outings in the park, visits to neighbors, and even time in a baby-sitter's home with other children may be valuable.

SKILL AT PLAY

The thumb-and-finger grasp is mastered at about eight months. Two to three months after that, the baby can form a neat pincers with thumb and forefinger, so that he or she can deftly scoop up objects as small as a rasin.

By now, the baby can differentiate the use of hands, carrying a bottle, for example, in the left hand while pushing a ball with the other. "Handedness," however, hasn't developed yet. The baby uses hands interchangeably and won't begin to favor one over the other until about 18 months of age.

The baby's style of play changes to complement this new skill. Now, a favorite pastime becomes skillfully retrieving dropped objects, stuffing them one by one into a can or bottle, then dumping them out again. Helped by the pincers, the baby can select one toy from many, turn the pages of a book (although he or she may do this more often with the palm of the hand), lift blocks, and even pile one on another. The baby may also be able to hold a crayon and stab marks on a piece of paper.

SEEING AND REMEMBERING

Now you may be aware that your baby takes in whole events and scenes and remembers them later. To your surprise, he or she knows the proper place for every bit of furniture in a familiar room and quickly recognizes when you've added a new chair or changed the position of another. A quick jab or gesture with the forefinger toward the misplaced object lets you know what the baby has seen and remembered.

Memory for time and events sharpens, too. Elaborating on peekaboo and drop-the-cup-and-listen-for-the-delicious-crash, the baby now recalls that last night you dangled him or her on your knee. He or she crawls up, ready to play the new game again. Hide-and-seek, infant style, played with brothers and sisters, replaces covering the eyes with the hands and playing "Guess who?" or "Peek-a-boo."

Now the baby will set down a toy and remember where it was stored. If it is placed out of the line of sight, he or she will confidently reach for it and expect it to be there. Once upon a time, each encounter with a toy was a new experience. Now the baby knows the stuffed calico dog is the same, whether found in the playpen, on the bounce chair, or behind the sofa.

An airplane roars overhead, or a car whizzes by. The baby looks up or hurries to the window, having learned from experience to link the sound and sight. When the door opens at day's end, signaling a parent's return, the baby gleefully stampedes to the door or turns in that direction, recognizing the cue and its meaning.

All these developments help your child assemble a picture of the world and a place in it. Lessons are learned that some objects are fixed and some change, that people come and go, that there is a time and order to events. Most of all, they show the child that he or she can affect these events and that they can affect the child.

SET UP A PLAY SPACE

A child needs a place to play. Not just a playpen but an area of the baby's own, with low shelves for toys and space to use them.

A play area needn't be elaborate. A corner of a room will do, if it's out of the traffic pattern. The best choice is near the living area of the house, where the baby will play more contentedly because the parents or other family members are in sight. If the play area is to be in a bedroom or nursery at the other end of the house, always leave the door open so the baby will know you're there. You can install a gate in the doorway if you want to confine the baby.

Simple equipment is enough. Durable wall-to-wall carpeting, linoleum, or tile is better than waxed floors or scatter rugs, which are hazardous footing for a novice walker. Make your own shelves or buy unpainted ones. Finish them in bright colors with a durable, lead-free plaint. Even boxes turned on their sides will serve for toy storage. Avoid toy chests with lids, which may slam down on little fingers. The baby needs to spend some time in the play space every day but also needs some time to explore and experiment in the rest of the house.

LEARNING TO SAY NO

An early entry in the baby's active vocabulary is the word, "no," and the mood that goes with it. Some time before the first birthday a spunky baby will pronounce the negative with emphasis.

When the baby isn't hungry and you try to spoon in a few vegetables, you may be admonished with a firm, "No." Take away a fragile object the baby is clutching and the child will insist, "No!" with accompanying tears. Bedtime may bring a shower of negatives—"No, no, no!"—and vigorous shakes of the head.

Being negative is just another sign the baby is growing. The message is that he or she is no longer malleable, able to be shifted about as parents choose, without a murmur of protest. As the months go on, you'll hear the word more and more as the baby makes it clear that his or her wishes are to be included in any decision.

"No" is an important addition to the child's vocabulary. As an active baby gets into everything, you'll be using it more and more. "No" spoken quickly and forcefully keeps a baby out of trouble. "That's a no-no" is a catchphrase that teaches what is permissible and what is not.

Use your "nos" judiciously, however. If the house has too many "no-nos" and too many fun things are forbidden, the word will lose its meaning; worse yet, it becomes a challenge. And, however painful for parents, some lessons are better learned the hard way. Experience may well be the most effective teacher.

AND THEN THERE'S MISCHIEF

Once your baby has learned which actions are approved and which forbidden, mischief comes to the fore. An active baby will hurry into the bathroom and suddenly flush the toilet or switch on the television and wait for the roar.

One favorite trick is to tease you into attentiveness. The baby will scuttle toward some temptation that's definitely a no-no, then pause until you're aware of where those little legs are scurrying. Once you've noticed, the baby churns into action, heading full steam for the target, only to be intercepted with squeals of delight. Or the baby may gain your attention, then move toward something that's known to be dangerous, confident that you'll be there to step in if anything goes wrong.

Sometimes you may see the baby bearing down on a vase or keepsake that's known to be forbidden, repeating "No, no, no" all the while. Odd as it may seem to you, that's a very sophisticated concept. It's the beginning of self-control, an ability that later will help the child to realize what's approved and what's disapproved.

CHANGING MOODS

The idea of "No" arrives not quite simultaneously with the idea of "Yes." Seeking your approval or hoping to avoid your disapproval are two new moods you may detect in a baby around the first birthday. Now, actions are no longer governed exclusively by the child's own obvious desires but by the reaction they may provoke in you.

Whereas crying and smiling were once the gamut of emotions, now your baby may appear sad, hurt, euphoric, tearful. When you leave, he or she may burst into tears. Chided for committing a no-no, the little transgressor may don an expression that would break the hardest heart.

Just as the baby has learned that dropping a cup from a high chair causes a noise moments later, so he or she has learned that a given action may win with a smile or frown. That doesn't mean every action is taken with the idea of manipulating you—although a one-year-old is capable of manipulation, too. It does mean that many actions are performed after carefully weighing the consequences.

A baby now can tire in a few minutes of a toy that once would have riveted concentration for a half hour. The baby performs more, too, playing for your applause in his or her accomplishments hour after hour. (But your pride and joy will probably refuse to repeat them in front of company.)

You'll also see the baby express tenderness. A doll or toy will be cuddled, loved, and carefully tended. This kind of "mothering" is the beginning of adult love—which begins with you, then is transferred to an object beyond you, and finally to persons beyond the object.

Dealing with the baby's changing moods isn't easy for many parents. Up to now, parents have seen their baby almost as an extension of themselves, to be handled or maneuvered according

KEEPING BABY SAFE

By now, the baby is so active and, often, so surprisingly strong that a new set of precautions is needed, which must strike a balance between containment for safety's sake and freedom to explore for the benefit of the baby's own development. Parents of an eight-month- to one-year-old child must be extra vigilant because changes come so fast. The time when a parent says, "Oh, he can't do that," is just the time when the baby does it.

In the supermarket, a baby this age is leaning out of the stroller, trying to snatch cans from the shelves, bending almost double in an effort to scoop papers or objects off the floor. He or she may even climb out of the stroller if left unattended. At home, the baby can climb quickly to dangerous heights, scale the stairs, or scoot outdoors if a door is temporarily left ajar. He or she can probably open drawers, closets, bottles, and packages.

Review all earlier precautions, and then add these:

• Baby-proof all closets or drawers that you think the baby can reach and some others you think he or she can't. Empty them of all small or sharp objects; possible poisons; breakables; plastic bags; and beans, peanuts, or other small bits of food that might cause the baby to choke.

• If you have pull or ring drawer handles, place a broomstick or tight rubber band between them to prevent baby from opening the drawers. Lock these areas from which you cannot remove contents.

• Do not store cleaners, cleaning fluids, detergents, or other cleaning materials where the baby can reach them.

• When cooking, always turn pot handles away from the front of the stove so the baby can't reach them and pull over the contents. Keep hot foods and items away from the baby's high chair during meals.

• Don't use dangling tablecloths. A one-year-old can pull down the cloth—dishes and all.

• Keep medicines and household products under lock and key. The ban extends to medicines like aspirin, which can harm a baby if swallowed in quantity. Be especially careful when someone is ill and medicines are out of their usual place.

• Never leave the baby alone in a bathtub or wading pool. He or she can drown in a few inches of water.

• If you have a backyard pool, make sure it is fenced and has a gate that latches firmly.

to their schedule or convenience. When the baby looks hurt, some parents melt. When a child cuts loose with anger, the parent overreacts with adult anger. For parents, the end of a child's first year is also a difficult period of growth. Now you must recognize that your offspring is not merely a helpless being to be acknowledged at your will but a personality to be dealt with in his or her own right.

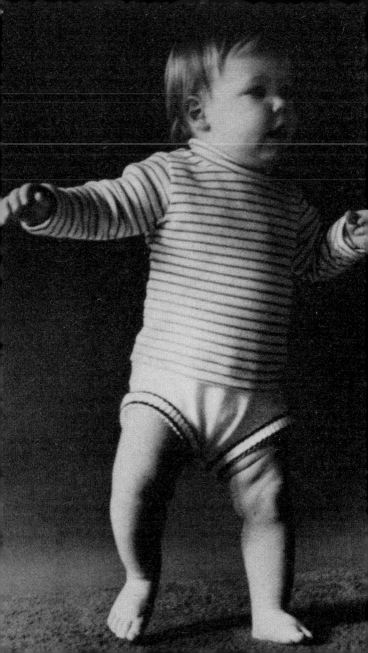

14

Twelve to Eighteen Months

HOW THE BABY GROWS

By age 15 months, the average normal baby weighs 24 pounds and measures 31 inches. The range for normal babies is 20 to 28 pounds and 29½ to 33½ inches.

Here are some things your baby may learn to do between 12 and 15 months:

- use a spoon and spill only a little;
- imitate a parent doing housework;
- build a tower with two cubes;
- scribble with a crayon;
- walk backward as well as forward.

The average normal baby grows an inch and gains a pound and a half during the next three months. At 18 months, normal weight is 25½ pounds; normal height, 32 inches. The range for normal babies is 21½ to 29½ pounds and 30½ and 34½ inches.

Here are some of the things normal babies achieve by the age of 18 months:

- remove some or all of their clothes;
- build a four-cube tower;
- walk up steps, holding rail or using wall as support;
- point to a baby's picture in a book or magazine;
- use name when referring to himself or herself.

A BLUR OF MOTION

At this age, you'll quickly learn the meaning of that expression, "the patter of tiny feet." Quick little legs and rapidly improving coordination will carry your son or daughter just about anywhere he or she wants to go. And go the tireless baby will—upstairs, downstairs, outdoors when there's an opportunity, and into every corner of the house. Once the art of walking is mastered, your baby will be on the move from morning to night—leading you on a merry chase.

At first, the pace will be hesitant and wobbly. But by the middle of the second year, your baby's steps will become quick and sure; he or she may even be able to run a little. Stairs are no longer an obstacle. A one-year-old can usually walk downstairs while holding your hand but can only crawl upstairs. Six months later, the toddler walks upstairs under his or her own steam, using a rail or the wall for support. Coming down is an all-fours, stern-first proposition. And watch out! Your toddler now can climb. The baby not only learns how to scale chairs, shelves, and tables, but also how to rearrange furniture to reach a tempting object.

Of course, toddlers' temperaments differ: some children are more content to sit and study their surroundings with their eyes; others prefer to investigate with fingers or feet. Regardless of the approach your child takes, childish curiosity now reaches its zenith. Free at last from many of the physical limitations of the first 12 months of his or her life, the baby throws all the inexhaustible energy of childhood into learning just what it is that makes the world tick.

And it's fun for you to observe this boundless drive to learn. Watch closely when you give your child something for the first time—a cookie, for instance. First there's an exploratory taste—more in the name of research than hunger. Then the baby may pound the cookie, squeeze it, hold it up to the light and eye it speculatively, trace its perimeter with a finger, roll it, set it down to inspect from various angles, rub with the palm of the hand, crumble it, and feel the texture of each crumb. Finally, having discovered every important detail about this fascinating object, the baby may actually eat what's left of the cookie—or, bored with the whole thing, abandon it.

TRYING TIMES FOR PARENTS

Another side of a one-year-old's independence is a growing sense of self. The child wants to do what he or she wants to do when he or she wants to do it and protests and resists any attempt on your part to interfere or divert attention from the goal at hand. Quickly, this tenacious me-first attitude puts little Jason or Jennifer on an unwavering collision course with the rest of the world.

Naturally, you want to give your child freedom to explore and learn to the fullest—but without danger and without trampling the rights of others. Because children at this age are frequently oblivious to danger and haven't the slightest idea what rights are, clashes are bound to occur. The important thing to realize, though, is that your one-year-old isn't being defiant, disobedient, or "bad." The concepts of right and wrong simply haven't penetrated yet and won't for several more years. When a one-year-old deliberately and carefully drops the sugar bowl on the floor after you've told him not to, it's because he wants to see what happens when it hits, not because he's a "bad boy."

Moreover, a toddler—unlike most adults—doesn't absorb a lesson in a single teaching. You may have to retrieve your young dynamo from the top shelf of the bookcase or stop him or her from stuffing towels into the toilet five or six (or more) times before the message begins to take hold clearly.

You'll never eliminate all the power struggles that may crop up at this age. But you can reduce them by diminishing the possible sources of conflict. Controlling the baby's environment is as much for the child's benefit as it is for yours. The fewer times you have to interfere, the less frazzled your nerves will be at the end of the day and the better your relationship with the baby.

First, review and reinforce the safety precautions described in earlier chapters. Try to stay one or two steps ahead of the baby: if he or she is now tall enough to reach the doorknob, assume that it will only be a matter of time until the knob is turned and your baby is toddling out the door. Install a bolt out of the child's reach.

Second, keep temptations and "no-nos" away from curious little fingers. If your child's favorite pastime is rummaging through drawers, remove valuables and replace them with toys, pans, or other harmless substitutes.

Third, don't rely on verbal warnings to check a child's disapproved behavior. If possible, take the forbidden object from the child, saying "No!" while you do it. If the child is playing with the television set, which can't be moved, take the child to another part of the house and offer him or her another toy to play with. Some determined children will quickly resume the taboo behavior, but fortunately most children have a short attention span and become absorbed by a new toy or less bothersome activity.

Of course, a slap on errant hands or whack on a diapered bottom will momentarily distract a child. But in spite of the resulting howls, a lasting lesson is seldom learned. Linking deed to punishment is still too vague an association for most toddlers to make: what the child really learns may be that parents are unpredictable and sometimes hurt you. In any case, you'll have to repeat the lesson again and again. A spontaneous vocal outburst by a terrified parent whose child has just entered a danger zone, like climbing onto the sill of an open window, can be an effective teaching tool. On the other hand, such obvious excitement on the part of mom or dad may so overwhelmingly fascinate the baby that he or she will repeat the action just to see the reaction one more time.

Even the most serene baby can leave parents exhausted by evening. The simplest, most routine act becomes a terrific and tiring tussle; you may have to learn to change diapers on the run because the baby won't lie down even for 30 seconds. The parent who remains at home with the child will need plenty of support and assistance.

AT THE SAME TIME, DEPENDENCE

You'll see it happen frequently. Striking out on some adventure of his or her own, your child will suddenly turn to look at you or even trot back to make sure you're still there. Or, off in another room out of your sight, the baby will repeatedly call out to you as a means of ensuring your continuing presence. For all the baby's bravery, he or she will cling tightly, whine, and stubbornly refuse to let go of you.

You can understand the emotional conflict. It's like dangling from a tree branch and maintaining your grip until at last you feel the ground under you. To your little adventurer, you represent safety, stability, reliability, familiarity; he or she is eager to discover the world beyond, but who knows what tigers lie out there? Should he or she give up the known to challenge the unknown? The child needs to know that if he or she ventures too far, you will still be there as a refuge and retreat.

The fear of strange places, new situations, and different people, which may have begun earlier, may continue. Where once the child cheerfully remained with any baby-sitter, he or she may now shriek and cry uncontrollably at any indication that you are leaving. If you take the child to a friend's house for a visit, the normally curious youngster will refuse to leave your lap. If the child has been cared for at home or in a day-care center while you work, you may now find that he or she refuses to enter the center or acknowledge the sitter. On the other hand, the baby-sitter may be accepted, but all others, even a favorite aunt, uncle, or grandmother, are shut out completely.

Dealing with this kind of anxiety calls for patience—both

from you and from the "strangers." Your child is still grappling with the concept of time; at 18 months or less, the baby is just beginning to learn that farewell doesn't mean forever. If he or she seems anxious about you at home, reassure the child by repeatedly calling to him or her when out of sight. Keep talking as you move about the house, even if you feel as if you're talking to yourself. If you're going out, sit with the child before leaving and reassure him or her that you'll be coming home soon.

Pick a sitter carefully. During this period, you want one who will pay attention to the child's needs and make the transition easier, not simply a custodian who will watch television while the child sleeps. Pay the sitter for an extra hour to spend with the child while you're present, so the child won't feel abandoned when you do leave.

THE CHANGING APPETITE

In the first year of life, your baby gained about 16 pounds. In the second year, the gain will only be about five. One reason will be a sharp drop in appetite. Another will be some marked changes in eating habits.

Because the baby is less hungry, he or she will pick and choose which food to eat. Some days, almost nothing will be eaten at any of the three meals; the hunger strike may even continue for several days. Then the baby will suddenly gobble every scrap and ask for more. Relieved, you may offer bigger servings at the next meal, only to have everything rejected once again.

The baby may go on binges, confining consumption to mashed potatoes or scrambled eggs or peanut butter and firmly refusing all other foods. Vegetables, for example, may be absolutely out. After a week of this, he or she may just as firmly refuse the favored food and go on to another specialty. The situation may be further complicated by the baby's inexhaustible energy and overwhelming curiosity. In the interests of science, he or she may mix all the foods together—then refuse to eat the unholy mess. Or the baby simply won't sit still long enough to down what you consider a proper meal.

This is an exasperating time for parents, who become convinced the baby will starve to death if they don't kill the child first. The objective quickly becomes to force food down the baby's throat at any price. The baby balks, the parent becomes convinced the baby is simply being disobedient and pushes harder, and the battle is on. In this way, many a lasting eating problem has begun.

The basic fact is that the year-old baby simply needs fewer calories than the six-month-old child. That may be hard for you to believe at the rate he or she is burning them off, but studies have repeatedly shown that a baby's consumption, despite the ups and downs, evens off over a period of time. Even a baby who won't eat vegetables obtains, over a period of time, the necessary vitamins, minerals, and fiber from fruit and other food. Obviously, you should worry if the baby seems not to gain weight or is clearly losing it. But most 12- to 18-month-olds thrive despite what parents consider bird-like appetites.

THE BABY'S MENU

By now, the baby can eat just about anything you eat and will feed him- or herself. Eating with a spoon will still be a somewhat messy business, and you'll have to look the other way sometimes. For the sake of convenience, you'll probably continue to offer commercially prepared baby foods on occasion. Now, most babies' milk intake will probably be down to about a pint every 24 hours or so.

One reason the baby's menu can be expanded is because more teeth have appeared. The ages when children cut primary, or "baby" teeth vary extremely, but the average child gets his or her first molars, or grinding teeth, shortly after the first birthday and by mid-year may have as many as 16 teeth—eight front incisors, four cuspids (or canine teeth), and four molars. Thus equipped, an 18-month-old can deal with many adult foods.

Among the foods on your 18-month-old's list of favorites are the following:
- Vienna sausage, in finger portions • Jelly
- Chopped hamburger • Bananas
- Lunch meats • Mashed potatoes
- Chicken, diced or chopped • Cottage cheese
- Meat loaf, lightly seasoned • Plain cookies
- Puddings • Scrambled eggs
- Smooth peanut butter • Applesauce
- Sliced orange • Cooked or canned fruits
- Macaroni and spaghetti • Bread
- Crackers • Chopped or mashed vegetables

A few foods are still off limits, primarily those that are not easily chewed and may become lodged in the throat. The list includes peanuts, popcorn, chunks or raw fruit or vegetable, fruits containing seeds or stones, and fruits with thick skins,

At this age, the baby tries for a mouthful in any way that's handy. Disregard the sloppiness and spilled food during dinnertime; they will disappear as soon as the baby learns more efficient ways to get the job done.

unless the skins have been removed beforehand. Meat should be given only if it is soft or cut into very fine pieces. Whole-kernel corn usually is withheld from babies because, unless it is well chewed, corn passes through the digestive system unchanged.

Most one-year-olds resist spicy or strongly flavored foods, including sausages, corned beef, dried beef, and such vegetables as radishes, parsnips, broccoli, and cauliflower.

In the interests of better health and sounder teeth, you may want to postpone giving the baby sugared foods or sweets. It probably is unrealistic to believe that you can keep a child away from candy or cookies forever, because he or she may encounter them in another home. Study after study has shown that even very young children prefer sweet tastes to other tastes. At the very least, you can postpone offering desserts, puddings, and other sweet foods until the end of the meal.

Basically, a toddler will eat (or at least sit down to) three major meals a day, with a break for cracker and juice at midmorning and midafternoon. At each major meal, the baby's menu should consist of one filling dish, such as cereal, eggs, potato, macaroni, or spaghetti, plus a fruit or vegetable. Meat or another high-protein food should be eaten once a day. The filling food may be a small sandwich, although babies 18 months or younger are likely to tear apart the sandwich, ignore the bread, and eat the filling.

MORE WAKING HOURS

The baby's sleeping habits will change between 12 and 18 months—and you'll probably think the change is for the worse. By this age, most children have eliminated one nap a day (usually the morning one) and sleep fewer hours at night. Despite the tremendous output of energy during the day, a 12- to 18-month-old fights being put to bed and may call and cry and thrash for an hour before dropping off to sleep. Worst of all, the baby may wake during the night and rouse the entire household with cries to be freed and permitted to resume the day's activities.

One reason for a baby's sleeplessness is "separation anxiety," that fear of being away from you even for a brief period. Another reason is simple excitement. After a day in which one thrilling discovery followed another, it takes time for the baby to unwind, just as it does for you to relax after a particularly triumphant day. A baby just can't wait to get back to the business of learning, which stimulates early rising and waking during the night.

Parents may feel that babies don't need two naps a day—but they do! You needn't worry about the baby getting enough sleep; that takes care of itself. But you'll have to take firm steps to see that *you* do. Here's how:

At naptime, place the baby in the crib, however loud the protests, and make sure he or she remains there at least an hour. Leave the bedroom door open so he or she can hear you and is aware of your presence. At night, set a regular bedtime and be relatively consistent about it. Develop a nighttime ritual that clearly means bedtime has arrived. The ritual will vary according to the baby's (and your) temperament; in some familes, it may be roughhousing followed by a quiet interlude. In others, the baby may nuzzle on your lap for a time while you talk soothingly. Or you might look at a picture book together, sing, or listen to music. This is also the time when a thumb-sucker or blanket-twister performs whatever ritual puts him or her into a sleepy mood. Regardless of the method, the message is to tell the child the curfew has arrived. When sleep seems near or the designated period has elapsed, take the baby directly to the crib, tell him or her goodnight, and leave.

You'll undoubtedly hear a few protests, cries, and squalls. You may want to return to the baby's room once, just to satisfy yourself the cries really don't signal a problem. Then you have to disentangle yourself, leave the room, and, if the cries continue, grit your teeth and ignore them—as hard as it may be to do so.

Allowing a baby to cry into sleep is easier said than done, especially if you live in cramped quarters or if the cries may disturb neighbors in an apartment. It may be necessary to put some distance between you and the baby: sleep on the sofa for a night or two, or keep the bedroom door closed until the baby is asleep.

Crying in the middle of the night can be even more distressing. Again, once you've satisfied yourself there's nothing wrong with the baby, one course is just to ride it out. If that's not practical, one parent may have to stay awake until the child becomes sleepy again.

THE INEVITABLE TEMPER TANTRUM

Even the sunniest, best-behaved baby may throw a temper tantrum during the first flush of independence. These outbursts usually begin around the first birthday and may continue intermittently until the child is three years old.

Temper tantrums result from frustration. Armed with that new independence, the child wants something or wants to do something, and the desire is thwarted. It may be a simple thing, like wanting a cookie or snack you won't permit between meals.

To adults, the fireworks that follow are far out of proportion to the cause. The child falls to the floor, screams, kicks, pounds with the fists—any physical activity to vent the rage. The ear-splitting, nerve-wracking performance can continue for minutes on end and is particularly embarrassing when it happens in the supermarket or on a downtown sidewalk.

The simple explanation for tantrums is that one-year-olds have very few ways to express emotion. They can't curse or shout as an adult can; they can't go for an angry walk around the block; they can't even argue with the parent who has refused the cookie. They aren't yet clear on the notions of time and the

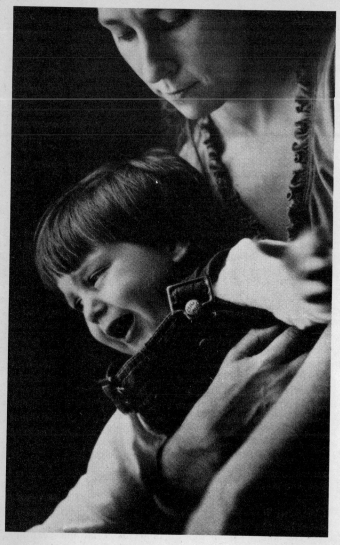

Temper tantrums are a normal response to an occasionally frustrating world. If the outburst occurs in public, you may want to take the child from the scene. Otherwise, don't fuss, and don't give in to the baby's demands.

future, either, and haven't mastered the adult concept of delayed gratification. To them, "no" means "never."

Tantrums often occur late in the day when the child and the parent are tired; sometimes they are triggered by overstimulation. The cause really isn't important. The outbursts are normal and don't reflect on your performance as a parent. The cure is to be as matter-of-fact about them as your nerves will allow.

When a tantrum occurs, you'll probably want to scoop the child out of a public place as quickly as possible, just for your own peace of mind. Otherwise, make sure the child won't be injured if he or she collides with furniture, knocks over lamps, or breaks things during the tantrum. You might place the child in a crib or playpen until the tantrum subsides, a location that will keep him or her safe and also isolated, thus conveying your disapproval of the behavior.

Make as little fuss as possible. Don't argue, plead, or reason with the child, and don't give in to the demands, even if you can recognize what they are. Surrendering only teaches the child that tantrums are an effective means to an end. Just walking away from the child may be the most graceful way of handling a tantrum. Some children require an audience for their performance.

Some diehards continue the din for up to half an hour; others begin to wind down after ten minutes or so. Loud cries will give way to whimpers; the child may look for forgiveness. Be matter-of-fact here, too. Hold the child in your lap, make comforting noises and gestures, and don't scold or lecture. A simple hug is better than showering the child with affection.

Of course, not everyone can be calm in the face of such an eruption each time it happens. Parents of a normally placid child have a particularly difficult time because the tempest seems so out of character. The startled parent is sure he or she must have done something terribly wrong to provoke such an unusual reaction and out of guilt may give in to the child's demands. A temper tantrum is seldom directed at you or anything you've done; it's a first step toward learning how to express emotion.

THE BEGINNINGS OF DISCIPLINE

No one is born with a knowledge of the rules of society or respect for the rights of others. Part of a parent's role is making clear to a child just how far he or she can go. The word for this is discipline, which most parents associate with punishment. In fact, discipline refers to teaching the child the limits of accepted behavior, the boundaries of permissible action.

Give your child plenty of freedom to develop and grow independently. But don't give in to every whim, or the child will be ill-prepared for the world outside the home where restrictions do exist. On the other hand, don't inhibit the child with restrictions or interfere in everything he or she tries to do; allow for a degree of self-education. Make a stand when it seems necessary, but don't restrict a child with too many "don'ts."

Remember that the other members of the household have rights, too. Older children are entitled to privacy from their younger brother or sister; they should have possessions of their own and time to themselves, free from the baby's demands. The exhausted parents need relief, too. The demanding child who keeps a parent shuttling back and forth to cribside must learn that parents need time for themselves.

Amazingly, repeated studies show that the most obedient child is the one who is least frequently bossed. When a rare command is given, the child understands, even at an early age, that it is important and must be followed. Children whose lives consist of an endless stream of orders and directives quickly learn to ignore them.

THE HELPFUL BABY
Helpfulness is another side to the baby nearing the middle of the second year. Although still spunkily independent, the baby also seeks your approval and looks for ways to please you. One way is to "help" around the house. The baby will begin to mimic your motions in sweeping, dusting, and cleaning.

Sometimes, you'll wish he or she weren't so helpful—as, for instance, in cleaning up after a meal by ostentatiously sweeping the crumbs and debris onto the floor. But these situations are good times to teach basic lessons. The first step toward getting a child to pick up his or her own toys begins by making a game of it—"Let's put the dolls to bed for the night" or "Let's put the cars into the garage." The game will enlist the baby's cooperation.

It's far too early, however, for the baby to be expected to do this alone or to understand the need for order.

DRESSING AND UNDRESSING
At one year to 18 months, the baby also takes the first steps toward dressing independently. Like many accomplishments, however, he or she starts backwards. A one-year-old hasn't the necessary control of small muscles to fit buttons into but-

The baby now begins to take a part in dressing independently. But you'll find that undressing is much easier and will occur at any time of the day or night. If possible, buy clothes that are hard to remove.

tonholes, snap fasteners, or close zippers. But he or she can *un*do these things and undress completely.

It'll be six months or more before the child really gets the hang of dressing. Meanwhile, you'll come into the nursery and find the baby stripped to the skin, having discovered not only how to unfasten clothes but how to remove them, including diapers. During the day, pants, shirts, and shoes may be discarded quickly. You may have considerable picking up to do for a few days—or even weeks—and it may be difficult to keep the baby in clothes, especially at night. If possible, dress him or her in clothes that can't be removed easily, such as nightclothes that snap in the back or shirts that pull over the head. Trousers or coveralls that button to shirts also are discarded less easily.

Trying as this period will be, capitalize on it by teaching the baby to cooperate. With a little encouragement, an 18-month-old will raise his or her arms for a pullover shirt or sweater and will learn to help put on trousers or jackets. A child's clothes mostly consist of a pullover shirt and trousers or coveralls.

BABY'S FIRST SHOES

The baby doesn't really need shoes until he or she begins to walk outdoors. In fact, walking barefoot strengthens the arches and the leg muscles, and a baby's feet are just as warm as the hands. Shoes are needed only to protect against rough floors or splinters.

When shoes do become necessary, nothing elaborate is required. Sneakers—canvas shoes with rubber soles—are perfectly adequate for a child's first footwear. They're also inexpensive. During this period, shoes are outgrown at the rate of about a pair every six weeks. Make sure the new shoes fit well. The toes should not be cramped, but the shoes should not slip off. The distance between the baby's toes and the end of the shoe, with full weight on the foot, should be about the thickness of your thumb. When the distance is less, discard the shoes, even though they're not worn out.

Make sure the baby's socks fit, too. They should be large enough so the toes don't curl under but not so large as to cause folds that might produce a blister. Socks that stretch to fit the baby's foot are the best buy.

Should shoes be low-cut or ankle-high? Traditionally, a baby's first shoes have been white leather high-tops, but they confer no special advantage in walking. The extra height does *not* give additional support to the ankle. However, high shoes are more difficult for the baby to remove, so you may prefer them.

NEW TOYS FOR THE BABY

Toys are the baby's learning tools, but you needn't invest in high-priced playthings labeled "educational." The baby can learn just as well from toys you make or improvise—or simply from household objects and utensils.

Some of the baby's favorite pastimes at this age are building, throwing, and putting objects into containers and pouring them out again. Given paper and a crayon, he or she will scribble spontaneously; you can hope this activity won't carry over to walls or furniture. As the child approaches 18 months, he or she can also look at pictures in books and magazines, especially likenesses of other children.

Other favorite toys are blocks, large dolls or stuffed toys, balls easily rolled or thrown, and wagons or other wheeled toys that can be pulled or pushed. The baby may also like play dishes, cooking utensils, and a mallet and pegboard for pounding.

You can also make very simple toys. A cardboard box into which he or she can pile blocks and pour them out again is a good example. Pots and pans or canned goods that can be dragged out of kitchen cupboards, piled up or clanged together, and then returned will be used as often as the most expensive toy. You may find, to your chagrin, that the child prefers treasures of the garbage can to anything you buy. Secondhand stores and garage sales are also good places to build up a child's supply of toys.

Supervised water play is also fun for children under two years of age. In warm weather, put the baby in a washtub or small plastic pool in the backyard. Allow extra time in the bathtub during the winter, and let the child play with unbreakable bottles and glasses, toys and rubber boats, and animals. Remember that most children this age like to do things themselves, rather than watch a toy in action. But even at this age, never leave a youngster unattended in the tub or pool.

A FEW MORE WORDS

Although the number of words the baby understands grows rapidly, the number he or she can pronounce grows less quickly. At 18 months, a child's vocabulary may be ten to 15 words, including names for parents, siblings, pets, and perhaps even for him- or herself. Usually, there are special versions of certain everyday words, including "bottle" or "blanket" or "truck." Not all these words will be understood by an outsider, but family members usually can translate them.

If the baby hasn't yet learned ten to 15 words, don't worry about it. Speech comes slowly for some babies, but most make up for the delay. Continue to speak to the baby in short, simple sentences. If he or she seems to understand your meaning, it will not be long until the sound is imitated.

You can help broaden your baby's vocabulary by encouraging him or her to ask for things by name, rather than point to them. You shouldn't be in too much of a hurry to satisfy your child's wants. When the baby does begin to say words in his or her own special way, don't be overly corrective; pronounce the word correctly once or twice, but let the baby get the idea independently.

HEIGHT & WEIGHT
ONE TO SIX YEARS

The growth range widens as children grow older. One two-year-old may be ten pounds lighter and half a head shorter than another—both are perfectly normal. And children don't grow as evenly as the chart's graceful curves indicate. Spurts and bursts are a normal part of growing up.

Tall	Heavy
Moderately tall	Moderately heavy
Average	Average
Moderately short	Moderately light
Short	Light

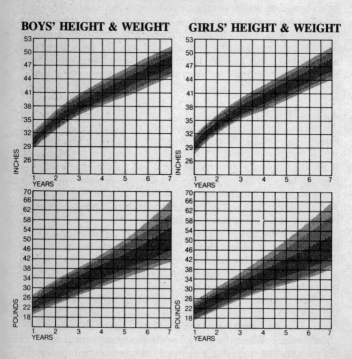

BOYS' HEIGHT & WEIGHT   **GIRLS' HEIGHT & WEIGHT**

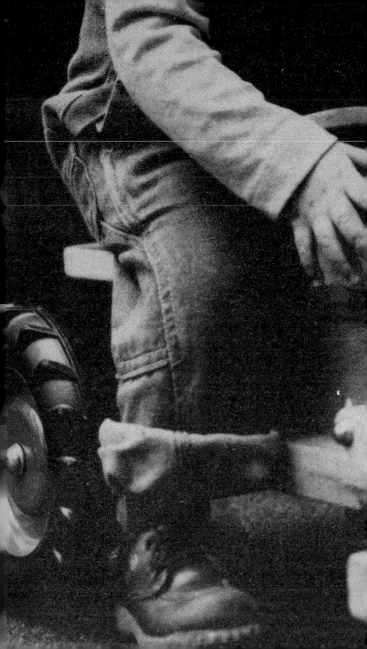

15

Eighteen Months to Two Years

HOW THE BABY GROWS

The growth rate slows considerably during the last half of the baby's second year. The average normal two-year-old weighs 28 pounds and is 34½ inches tall. The range for normal babies is 23½ to 32½ pounds and 32 to 36½ inches.

Here are some things normal babies learn to do between 18 and 24 months:

• use words in combination to make simple statements or questions;

• identify one or more parts of the body;

• follow simple directions—most of the time—if only a single step is involved;

• put on some items of clothing—but try more than succeed;

• wash and dry their hands, with parental supervision;

• identify pictures of animals by name;

• build a tower of eight blocks;

• pedal a tricycle; propel a kiddie car with feet;

• kick a ball forward or throw it overhand, neither with accuracy.

THE ART OF CONVERSATION

A two-year-old's communication is no longer limited to a few semi-intelligible words, noises, grunts, and gestures. Vocabulary increases, pronunciation improves, and the patterns of adult speech begin. The number of words—and ideas—the baby comprehends grows dramatically.

The baby may begin to speak in sentences (although many

normal babies do not combine words for another year). They're not complex, adult statements and questions: just two words put together to express basic wants and thoughts. At first, sentences will consist of just a noun and a verb, without much respect for the niceties of grammar: "Fred eat," "Mommy stay," "Go bye-bye." There will be simple questions, too: "Where Doggie?" "Who that?" But in a surprisingly short time, your son or daughter will be stringing together three or even four words into an understandable combination.

Meanwhile, as many parents are amazed (and pleased) to learn, the baby "understands everything you say!" "Passive" vocabulary grows so greatly that you can now communicate ideas that a few weeks or months ago were totally over the child's head. "Let's go in the car," you'll say, and Rachel or Ted will dash for the door—obvious proof the message has been understood. You can give simple commands or directions, confident they will be carried out: "It's time for lunch," and the baby will head for the high chair or eating table. You may even find yourself in a parent-to-child dialogue complete with statements and responses:

"Who toy?" "That's Jennifer's toy." "Where J'fer?"

"Want cookie." "No cookies until lunch." "Want cookie!"

Of course, developmental rates are erratic. Children vary in how quickly they master communications skills. Some shy, quiet children don't add words so quickly or roll them off the tongue so glibly as more outgoing, energetic personalities (although temperaments aren't always a key to verbal ability). Even the most verbally precocious may develop vocabulary in a spurt, slow down for a few weeks or months, then take another great leap forward. Girls are thought to be more fluent than boys the same age. Children in some families are more verbal than children in other families, but even children in the same family may not master speech at the same rate.

You'll find the baby has quite a storehouse of knowledge. An average 21-month-old can correctly identify one or more parts of the body. Ask, "Where is Adam's nose?" "Where is Adam's hand?" and a stubby finger may accurately point to the named part, perhaps accompanied by the emphatic declaration, "Nose!" "Hand!" or even "Adam hand!" A child nearing his or her second birthday may be able to identify the baby, horse, or dog in a book. Most children this age can tell you their names; a few can even repeat both first and last names. Family members now are all identified by name, usually with a highly personal pronunciation.

Now that the child's speech has improved, you may find that behavior and disposition improve, too. There may be fewer tantrums and temperamental outbursts when your son or daughter is able to tell you what he or she wants. You may even be able to reason with the child when things don't seem to go the right way. And the baby will now have a say in the family's affairs, not simply be a passive listener.

You can help your child develop language at this stage just by talking to him or her. In fact, you'll probably find yourself doing so almost unconsciously, just to watch the responses. "Time for lunch," you'll say, and plop him or her into the high chair. Your comments and conversations help the child to learn new words, as well as the purposes of oral communication. When you give commands or directions to a child, try to see they are carried out to strengthen the concept that words have meaning.

TIME FOR OUTDOOR PLAY

Your offspring is now ready for more play outdoors. Depending on where you live and the size of your purse, you may wish to establish his or her own area in the yard or on the porch. The best location is directly outside a window where you can keep an eye on the child and he or she can be aware of your presence.

The play area need not be large. A space fifteen by 20 feet allows plenty of room to roam. The play area should be completely enclosed, with a gate latch that resists little fingers or is beyond their reach, so you can feel free to leave the child alone.

For play equipment, a small sandbox complete with pails, shovels, spoons, and other digging implements is basic. If the baby can climb, a small slide is inexpensive fun. Swings will come a little later, although you may wish to install an entire "outdoor gym" at once. You can sometimes find these at garage sales or secondhand stores. For almost no money, you can equip the area with boxes, cubes, discarded tires, and even old tree stumps for the child to climb on, crawl over, or tunnel through. Falls will be frequent, so a grassy surface is best. Concrete or asphalt surfaces should be avoided.

Your son or daughter is also ready for more advanced toys. Some two-year-olds can pedal a tricycle or miniature auto; younger children can manipulate a kiddie car or other vehicle propelled with the feet. Indoors, a rocking horse can provide hours of fun, and building blocks become an important part of the toy chest. Most 18-month-olds have mastered the awkward art of sitting down in a small chair; it may be time for their own furniture.

If you live in an apartment or haven't room for your own play area, take the child to a park or playground often: space to run freely is important at this age. Neighborhood parks usually have a fenced toddlers' area with special equipment. Occasional supervised visits to a wading pool, lake, or seashore are also fun. But don't let the child play on the sidewalk or in an unconfined area outside the house.

TIME FOR PLAYMATES

More and more, your child will enjoy playing with children the same age. Children under two still don't really play together, but just watching each other is half the fun. Put a pair of two-year-olds side-by-side in a sandbox, and each will dig his or her own hole, fill his or her own bucket, and push his or her own truck, but there will be a good deal of pausing, observing, mimicking, and imitating. Also, toys will be grabbed, snatched, and passed back and forth. Pushing and shoving are part of the routine.

Not much time will be wasted by two-year-olds on the niceties of language, but you'll be surprised at how effectively the two youngsters manage to communicate with each other.

Some children plunge right into social situations and enjoy them; others take time to warm up. Your child may not feel comfortable with more than one playmate at a time; playground noise may be frightening. A shy, quiet child may hang back and cling to parents or be much more content to play alone within sight of the others, gradually working into the group. Other children may use the bull-in-a-china-shop approach. They may hit, poke, bite, or grab toys without giving them back. Such encounters between two-year-olds are often accompanied by a great deal of crying and complaining.

Within the limits of safety, you should try to keep hands off and let the children work things out for themselves: the tussles aren't really arguments. If one child pushes another, the second is likely to push back: the message is conveyed in a primitive way that pushing is unpopular and should be stopped. If you move in to end things too quickly and retaliation isn't allowed to take place, the aggressor doesn't have a chance to learn the consequences of aggressive behavior. In fact, your child may actually be encouraged to hit because you are inadvertently protecting him or her from the other's reaction.

If one child continues to act aggressively and the other doesn't strike back but runs away or cries and whimpers, you may be obliged to step in. If your child is the aggressor, speak firmly and sharply in disapproving tones. If the other child is the fighter, first you may have to negotiate with the child's parents. It may be necessary to separate the children.

Relationships between children are often more difficult for the parents than for the youngsters themselves. If another child repeatedly bullies your child, you may have to bring up the matter tactfully with the other parent. Parental standards differ, and it is sometimes hard for a child who has had clear, precise training to deal with a child who has not. In fact, you'll often find the other parent is giving the child a double message, vicariously enjoying the youthful aggression, while ostensibly disapproving. If so, you may have to break off the relationship with the other parent, rather than continually subject your child to a relationship that he or she is not able to handle.

LEARNING TO DRESS

The first step in dressing takes place when the child learns to name the items of clothing and the parts of the body they cover. The process of putting on clothes is usually too much for an 18-month-old, but you can begin the educational process now. Begin by naming each garment as you put it on, and then send the child to get it from the drawer or closet.

Next, enlist the child's cooperation. Teach him or her how to poke feet into trousers or hold hands in the air, so a dress can be pulled over the head. You can make a game of it: "Where is Susan?" as the shirt goes over the head; "There she is!" Finally, as your child approaches two years of age, he or she can begin to put on certain items of clothing under your supervision.

At first, it's really play; the child is just imitating adult behavior. Not much is accomplished beyond pulling on socks or shoes or worming into a jacket. You'll have to show how things go on or they'll wind up backwards, upside down, sideways or twisted, with shoes on the wrong feet. You'll also do the fastening. Buttons and zippers are still too much for little fingers; the small muscles haven't matured enough to allow that kind of dexterity. Even so, the child will be delighted with the accomplishment.

Don't expect too much of the child at this point. The objective is really to let him or her play at the idea of dressing and learn about clothes at the same time. Patiently let the child fumble with buttons or tug at shorts; don't step in too speedily to help. Eventually, of course, you'll have to do it, after allowing a brief, tolerable period for the child's education. But be sure to praise the child's efforts.

Patient supervision applies to more lessons than dressing.

You'll have to show restraint in many things as your child grows older, so he or she can learn independently.

A SENSE OF ORDER

Because the child likes to imitate grown-ups, it's now easy for you to begin helping him or her acquire a sense of order. As you work about the house, get the baby to help you with the less complicated projects at hand. At first, of course, it's only play for the baby and maybe a little extra for you, but the lesson will carry over into taking care of the child's own possessions.

When you teach in this way, simplify the child's needs. Install low hooks and hangers in closets and bedrooms so clothing can be reached easily. Assign specific places for jackets, shoes, raingear. At first, the child will be able to do little more than retrieve the garment from the hook when you ask for it. But

At this age, children don't really play together. But they do react to their companions. Watch closely and you'll see each observing the actions of the other and then trying them on for size.

once the notion is clear that clothes go in a specific place, it will be easier to teach him or her to hang them or put them away later.

The child's play area should have its own storage spaces —drawers, boxes, and shelves to hold toys. Make a nightly ritual of helping the child put the toys away for the next day's play. Of course, he or she can't do it independently at this age, but you're building a solid foundation for later behavior.

Teach the child to wash and dry hands, too. Again, training comes fairly easily because a child under two likes to imitate grown-ups. Buy a low stool or box so he or she can reach the faucet, and give him or her a personal towel, hung at an appropriately low height. Children usually prefer cold water, and you shouldn't expect a high standard of cleanliness at this point. Right now, the basic lesson is just to show how the procedure works. Teach the child to wash and dry hands before each meal—but you should expect to remind him or her for the next two or three years.

TAKING CARE OF THE TEETH

With 16 to 20 teeth, the two-year-old is more than ready for a toothbrush and a program of dental hygiene. Again, natural mimicry helps to establish good habits. Buy a small brush for the child and his or her own toothpaste and cup. At first, you must hold the brush to demonstrate how it's done. The child will quickly get the idea and want to take over. Allow him or her to do so under your supervision. Of course, a child this age can't brush adequately, and you'll have to finish up after he or she has fun with the brush.

It's true the so-called baby teeth will be lost and replaced by permanent teeth, but that doesn't mean their care should be neglected. The American Dental Association (ADA) recommends the child's first dental checkup be conducted as soon as 16 baby teeth have appeared. The ADA points out that cavities in the baby teeth or the loss of them can cause the child's permanent teeth to be pushed out of alignment. Orthodontia or other corrective measures may be necessary later. The ADA suggests a regular checkup each year after the child's first one and that dental work be done, if necessary.

Prevention, of course, is the most important ingredient of good dental care. Cavities are now recognized to be of bacterial origin; bacteria in the mouth combine with sugars, remaining on or between the teeth to produce an acid that destroys tooth enamel and eats into the heart of the tooth. Although some families seem to be more cavity-prone than others, limiting the amount of sugar can reduce cavities in many children. For better teeth, restrict chewing gum, cookies, ice cream, and sweet desserts. When sweets are eaten, the teeth should be brushed immediately, if possible, to remove the sugars that cause decay. When brushing is not convenient, the mouth should at least be rinsed with water. At the very least, the child who has eaten sweets should have his or her teeth brushed before going to bed.

The practice of letting the baby go to bed with a bottle can be potentially harmful to cavity-prone youngsters, especially if the baby keeps the bottle in the mouth throughout the night or sucks on it periodically. Sugars in formula, milk, or juice, not normally damaging, thus bathe the teeth constantly and promote tooth decay. Repeated pulling on the bottle may also damage tooth alignment. No harm seems to result when the baby drinks for a short period and the bottle is discarded or removed by parents.

If the water supply in your community is not fluoridated, your doctor or dentist may prescribe fluoride supplements for the child's teeth. These are recommended by both the ADA and the American Academy of Pediatrics.

Although not so effective as fluoridated water in preventing decay, these treatments include using chewable fluoride tablets, allowing the dentist to paint the teeth with fluoride, and brushing with fluoridated toothpaste.

EATING PROBLEMS

The baby's picky appetite continues. There are two related reasons: the child eats less because the rate of growth has slowed and less food is needed; and the body slims as the supply of baby fat is used up, so that contours begin to resemble those of an adult. Mother and father observe and conclude the child isn't eating enough. Result: they try to push more food on the child, the child resists, and each meal increasingly resembles a power struggle.

The most sensible and straightforward rule for feeding at this stage is simple: observe how much the child ordinarily eats; serve approximately that quantity or a bit more; try to balance out the nutrients over a period of time (but not necessarily at one meal or even in one day); eliminate between-meal snacks and sweets; and confine eating to three times a day, with a cracker or cookie midway in the afternoon, perhaps after the nap.

At mealtimes, let the child decide how much is enough. When he or she seems to have lost interest, try offering one bite. If it's not accepted, take the food away and let the child leave the high chair or table.

Given a choice, most children prefer sweets to other foods, so you'll have to work hard to keep him or her from concentrating on sweet desserts while neglecting other foods. There's probably no way to avoid sugar completely, but do your best to limit the child's intake of refined sugar to protect the teeth. Perhaps you can restrict it to plain cookies or simple desserts. An occasional treat, of course, is fine. Good ice cream is a nourishing food readily eaten by young children.

READY FOR TOILET TRAINING

There's no set schedule for toilet training. Most parents expect to begin when their youngster is about 18 months of age, but the child, not the calendar, tells you when the time is right. Logically, there is little point in trying until the child recognizes that he or she is having a bowel movement and can communicate that fact to you. There's wide variation as to when recognition and communication occur; even when they do, some children simply aren't interested in bowel training—they have better things to do! Studies show that four of five normal children are daytime-trained by 2½ years, but some haven't mastered the technique by the age of four.

Of course, some parents boast of a child who was bowel-trained at a year of age, or even earlier. What this usually means, however, is that the *parent* was trained. Having observed that the child had a bowel movement at a regular time each day, the alert mother or father placed the baby on the potty at the appropriate hour and "caught" the movement. The mystified child usually had no idea what he or she was doing.

When you feel your child is nearly ready for training, buy a small potty chair for the child to use. A freestanding chair with removable potty is usually better than a seat that fits the standard toilet, because it's closer to the ground and the child won't be afraid of falling or of the flushing noise. Also, you can move the potty chair to where you are, instead of isolating the child in the bathroom.

Every family has its own words for the need to urinate or defecate. It's important for a child to use these words to tell you (or if you ask) when it's time to use the toilet.

BOWEL TRAINING FIRST

Long before the child does, you'll probably notice the bowel movements follow a pattern. That's not true of all children: some are wildly irregular and may have a movement only every few days, making training more difficult. But most children have a daily movement; a common time is just after breakfast, apparently because the reflexive movements within the intestines resume their normal daytime pace. A few children have two movements a day, morning and afternoon.

Once you've discovered the appropriate time, place the baby on the potty chair for a short period as that hour approaches. Don't make the stay too long, and don't, by any means, strap the child in place. If the child produces a movement, be sure to praise the effort, so the message is clear the purpose of sitting has been fulfilled. If nothing happens, allow the child to leave the chair when he or she wants to.

Some children will sit for a time without result, then have a movement immediately after standing up. The association is clear; the timing is off. In cleaning up, try to be as matter-of-fact as you can. Remembering the child's growing vocabulary, explain that movements are to be made in the potty and that being clean is nicer than being soiled. Repeat the message when it's time to change soiled diapers. Suggest the child tell you if he or she wishes to use the potty.

READY FOR URINE TRAINING

Bowel training may be accomplished within a few days or weeks, but some months will pass before the child is reliable. Urine training takes even longer. It usually follows bowel training by up to six months. At first, sitting down is usually the appropriate posture for urination—for boys as well as girls.

The first clue that it's time for urine training comes when you notice the child's diapers remain dry for longer periods during the day, perhaps for two hours or more at a time. This usually happens some time after 18 months of age. That's because the bladder has grown and has a larger storage capacity. It also indicates the beginning of control over the bladder.

Another clue comes from the child. He or she may come to you after urinating and complain of wet diapers. The child may even hold the crotch or tug at the diaper, either before or after urinating. Again, the child's timing is off, but there's a clear association between wet diapers and the act of urinating. It also indicates the child is beginning to feel uncomfortable when wet, a fact you can take advantage of when urging him or her to urinate in the potty.

Once you're aware of these indications, begin placing the child on the potty at approximately two-hour intervals. Before and after naps, at meals, and at bedtime are appropriate moments. You'll have to set the schedule for a while. The child isn't

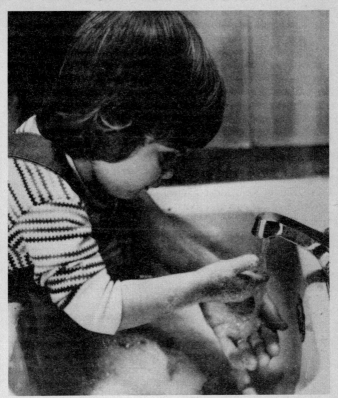

Teaching a child under two how to wash and dry hands is fairly easy. Though your son or daughter won't become proficient at it right away, the basic procedure—to be followed before and after meals—is the important lesson.

likely to be aware that he or she is ready to urinate until the last minute. As with bowel movements, the child will often urinate after leaving the potty.

Complete control of the bladder takes time to develop; once a child's bladder is full, he or she may not be able to wait even another minute to empty it. Also, boys in particular may have a more difficult time retaining urine. Some boys can't hold back urine for more than two hours until age three.

Remember, you'll also have to teach the child the proper words to tell you when he or she needs to urinate.

Training pants instead of diapers are helpful, once the baby can stay dry for two or more hours. They're not only simpler to put on and take off, but they have the psychological advantage of being "grown-up." Some doctors believe that babies feel free to urinate in diapers, whereas they exercise greater control while wearing training pants.

KEEPING THINGS CASUAL

Although many people regard it otherwise, toilet training needn't be a big deal. Like other aspects of child-rearing, training isn't a competition, and years from now, it'll make little difference that you had to launder diapers for six more months than the parents next door. Patience on your part is as important to the baby's toilet training as bladder control. You may experience a long stretch without success, even though the child clearly understands the task; nothing is so annoying to parents when they ask, "Do you have to wee-wee?" and the child solemnly denies it, while the puddle grows around his or her feet. Exasperating as the drawn-out procedure may be, scolding, shaming, or demanding immediate and perfect results doesn't help to keep diapers dry. In any case, the baby has the ultimate weapon. Nothing you can do or say will cause him or her to urinate or defecate (or withhold it) if he or she doesn't want to.

ACCIDENTS AND BREAKDOWNS

Even after the child is reasonably well trained, accidents will happen. Stress or excitement may cause the baby to urinate; some babies can't urinate on an unfamiliar potty and will wet their pants instead. Accidental urination is more common in cold weather than in warm weather. In any case, accidents should be treated routinely—but not ignored. Mention to the child that he or she would be more comfortable with clean and dry clothing.

With some children, toilet training seems to go fine for a while, then collapses. The child will return to earlier habits; you may even feel compelled to use diapers again. Often, there's an obvious reason: when a new child enters the household, for instance, an older child may revert to babyish practices. Sometimes, though, no reason can be discerned.

When that happens, treat the setback as calmly as possible. You may even drop toilet training for a time, return the child to diapers, and wait. Usually, the child will independently disclose a new readiness for further training. If the child simply balks at using the toilet at the times or places you suggest, let him or her pick the times. Sometimes, the child simply hasn't achieved full muscular control. He or she may be unable to relax while sitting on the toilet but may be able to relax while standing. But, if possible, avoid making toilet training an issue. It's a battle no parent can win.

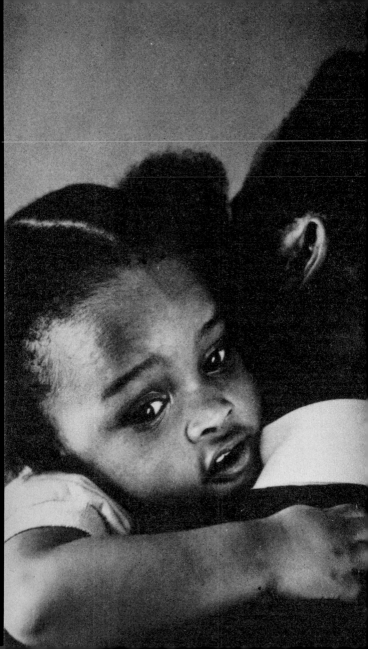

SECTION

3

Two To Six Years

Your child is a baby no more. From two to six, he or she advances rapidly toward independence. Looking back four years from now, you'll wonder where the baby went. Your own role changes just as quickly. You'll need new answers, new strengths, new skills. Just one thing will never change. These early years will strengthen the bond that unites parents and child for a lifetime.

16

Two to Three Years

HOW THE CHILD GROWS

Between the second and third birthdays, the average normal child gains four pounds and grows 3½ inches. Average weight for a three-year-old is 32½ pounds; average height, 38 inches. The range for normal children is 25½ to 38 pounds and 35 to 40½ inches.

Here are some things the average normal child learns to do between two and three years of age:
- dress with supervision and button some buttons;
- play interactive games, tag, for instance;
- tell first and last names;
- use plurals, pronouns, and prepositions in speech;
- copy a circle with a crayon;
- understand such words as "cold," "tired," "hungry";
- know where things belong and help to put them there;
- follow simple, one-step directions;
- feed him- or herself almost completely;
- be toilet-trained during the day and remain dry all night some of the time;
- recognize and identify some colors.

INCREASING SELF-RELIANCE

Day by day through the third year of life, children grow more self-reliant. Each new adventure makes them more conscious of their own individuality, their own control over their minds and bodies. Independence increases. They learn to do many things for themselves—after a fashion, at least—and, indeed, insist on it. The statement, "Me do it," is familiar to any parent.

Feeding will be strictly a "do-it-myself" project, as it should be. The child's style of eating will still lack finesse, and at the completion of a meal, the table may resemble San Francisco after the earthquake. Watery soups and runny puddings will still defeat the novice eater; sandwiches will continue to be dissected before they're digested. But with a full complement of teeth, the child can now eat most foods that were previously withheld, like raw vegetables, nuts, and popcorn.

Skill in dressing will improve steadily. As any parent can tell you, at first a two-year-old's attempts to put on clothes are little more than play, humorous imitations of what grown-ups do. Most of the actual routine of dressing a child falls to the parents. But as the months pass, your child will become more adept at wriggling into a playsuit or pulling on socks. A three-year-old may even laboriously manage a few buttons, even if the correct button doesn't match the proper buttonhole. Ironically, as mastery improves, the child loses interest in what is no longer a hill to climb—but a tedious chore.

You'll continue to establish the child's routine of eating, sleeping, and playing, but the child will want some voice in it. He or she will want to play when he or she wants to play and may stubbornly state the case with emphatic words and gestures. For your own convenience and the child's welfare, you may have to be firm about the schedule.

Increasingly, your role becomes more that of teacher than nurse. You demonstrate, the child imitates, you correct and help. Some of the imitations are just for fun at first. But you may be astonished at the amount of time and concentration your child will devote to mastering some simple task, like riding a tricycle, as he or she continues to seek new worlds to conquer.

THE LITTLE MONARCH

The two-year-old is a creature of moods, too. One of them is a kind of haughty, regal manner that is insistingly self-indulgent. With all the imperiousness of Napoleon or Catherine the Great, the two-year-old monarch will boss everybody—parents, siblings, domestic animals—and insist on having his or her own way. Nothing short of a palace revolt will overturn the royal dictum, "Gimme cookie!"

Two is also the traditional age of disobedience—although it may merely be the parents' label for the child's tendency to do as he or she pleases. It's not so much defiance; the child resents

To a two-year-old, the whole world is a private kingdom where all wishes automatically come true. Parents, siblings, and small kittens will be wrapped up by the child's desire to have it "my way."

restrictions, resents limits, and doesn't want to be told what to do. "No" will be another mainstay of the vocabulary, although you'll usually hear it as "No!" You may find yourself enforcing a number of rules with "friendly muscle" instead of "sweet reasonableness." It won't be enough to tell the child to stop doing something; you may have to physically call a halt.

Actually, you'll find a two-year-old's behavior shot full of contradictions. One day your son or daughter will be balky, contrary, cantankerous; anything you suggest will be rejected, even if it is something that delighted him or her only yesterday. Just wait: tomorrow will bring sunshine, cooperation, and agreeableness. Ann or Andrew will be a pleasure to be with. These behavioral zigzags can be exasperating to parents, who often wail, "He was so nice yesterday and so terrible today!" Consistency is simply not in the cards yet. It'll be at least a year until he or she is predictable—and closer to four before he or she obeys consistently.

All this is just another phase of growing up. The child is now learning the art of the possible—discovering the limits of behavior, what is permissible and what isn't. Still self-centered, he or she hasn't learned to distinguish between what he or she wishes would happen and what can *actually* happen. The two-year-old operates in the here and now and can't always fit present attitudes into a pattern of behavior, as an adult usually can. And many a two-year-old's attitudes really don't mean much; they're just tests. Even using the word "no" is just another way of learning what happens after refusing your request.

A FAVORITE PARENT

Part of a two-year-old's inconsistency may be attachment to one parent or the other. Some children cling to mother or father and openly dismiss the other. Boys usually attach themselves to fathers and girls to mothers; later, the preference may be for the parent of the opposite sex.

This, too, is just a phase and won't last. The best policy—for both parents—is to ignore this phase and ride it out.

That may be easier said than done: the rejected parent feels hurt; the favorite, defensive and guilty. Sometimes the rejected parent also tries to make up to the child and win back him or her. If so, the child may learn to play one parent against the other. Parents should stand together, unified in their approach to children; they shouldn't be sensitive about presumed shows of favoritism.

THOSE MADDENING RITUALS

With growing powers of observation and memory, a two-year-old knows and remembers where everything in the house belongs and how every act of daily routine is performed. Amazingly, he or she will even remember exactly where you're supposed to turn the car on the way to grandmother's house or which aisle you usually visit first in the supermarket. And, often to your dismay, you'll have to do everything in precisely the same manner and keep everything just as it was yesterday, the day before, and the day before that.

Lunch must always be served on the same plate. The teddy

bear must always be propped in the southwest corner of the crib—moving it to the northeast will bring squalls of protest. The bedtime ritual must follow exactly the same sequence—story, drink, toilet, drink, toilet, "Night-night." Change the order, omit one step, even substitute "So long" for "Night-night," and you'll hear about it. The objections will be loud and tiringly sustained.

At age two, the world is an avalanche of novel experiences and situations slightly altered from the day before. Naturally, a young learner wants some things to count on—some things to remain reliably cemented in time while he or she moves on to new, exciting matters. From your point of view, maddening though these rituals may be, they should be accepted without complaint unless they become too long, too complicated, or intrude too much on family life.

NIGHTMARES AND NIGHT FEARS

Nightmares often begin when the child is between two and three years old. But Bobby or Barbara doesn't know they're nightmares. He or she wakes, shouting in fright, to tell you that there are monsters in the room. So far as he or she is concerned, there *are* monsters lurking over behind the dresser. To a child unable to divorce fantasy from reality, even in daylight, the monsters are real.

If nightmares and night-waking are frequent, occurring every night or two, they may indicate that something else is troubling the child—the arrival of a new baby, a move to a new house. But if they occur only occasionally, then simple reassurance is enough to deal with them. Don't reason with the frightened child, explaining there are no monsters; don't turn on the light to show him or her, because he or she knows better. On the other hand, don't support the fantasy by chasing the monsters out.

Instead, distract the child as quickly as possible. Hold and soothe him or her with reassuring words until the tears stop. Then point out the familiar surroundings to ease the fears. "There's your own pillow right here"; "There's your teddy bear. Let's put him right here beside you"; "I will be in the next room and I can hear you" will usually help the scared child to settle down and return to sleep.

Don't fuss too much about the incident (attention to it only reinforces the impression), don't remain with the child so long that he or she awakens fully, and don't transfer the child to your bed; the switch may be the beginning of a pattern of nightly awakenings. If the child recalls the incident the following night and expresses fears about staying in the room, you may wish to install a night light for reassurance.

PLAYMATES AND PLAY GROUPS

The company of peers is no longer just a casual part of childish life. Your son or daughter needs regular companionship and stimulation of others the same age. Two-year-olds still play individually, rather than together, but cooperation and interaction—still sprinkled with shoving, pushing, and grabbing—steadily increase as the third birthday approaches. It's fun for parents to watch this stage, for three-year-olds' play is heavily laced with imagination and fantasy.

Your child may be fortunate enough to have playmates in the neighborhood, even a few steps away. If another two- or three-year-old is next door, the two may be together nearly all day, scampering back and forth between the houses and play areas without adult escort.

In an urban area or a neighborhood with few children, you'll have to schedule playtime. It needn't be an elaborate or formal arrangement, just an exchange of visits with a friend whose child is about the same age.

Or you may wish to set up a scheduled play group, whose members arrive to play at established times and places.

City parents often shepherd their children to a playground at a set time each day, knowing that other children the same age will probably be on hand. Often, the occasion is a social get-together for the parents, as well as a playtime for the children. In suburbs, a kaffeeklatsch may serve the same purpose. You and your friends can set a regular time to assemble with the children and rotate the meeting place.

Another informal arrangement resembles a baby-sitting cooperative. Two or three children gather at John's home one day, Martha's another, and Linda's a third. The designated parent supervises the children that day, while the other parents are free for their own pursuits.

As the children grow a little older, some play groups begin to resemble pre-school sessions. One parent is assigned to supervise the children at each gathering and to provide a program. This is usually something simple: a trip to the playground, paints and paper for fingerpainting, clay for modeling.

Charitable, governmental, and commercial organizations also sponsor play groups. These are usually more formal than those at child-care facilities and may be supervised by a certified specialist in early-childhood education. Some are operated in conjunction with an adult-education course in child development. Play groups are also operated (for a fee) in many cities and suburbs.

There aren't many rules to remember when establishing your own play group. Try to choose children of approximately the same age and temperament, children who are likely to stimulate each other and blend well together. The choice of adults is important, too. You want other parents whom you like and in whom you feel confidence. You'll also want to inquire discreetly about the other homes—if there's enough space for two or three boisterous three-year-olds, and whether normal safety precautions are observed.

Two hours a day, two days a week are a good beginning schedule for a play group. Children this age have a short attention span, so there should be plenty of activity to divert them. They need a good balance between physical play and crafts requiring the use of small muscles. The supervising parent may not be called upon to watch the children each minute but will have to look in regularly, referee disputes, and help the youngsters change directions. Three highly energetic three-year-olds are about as many as one parent can handle at a time; two parents can handle six or eight children.

Play groups work well when all children are about the same age, but it's also valuable for your child to have a mix of playmates. Playing occasionally with older children and occasionally with younger ones allows an opportunity both to follow and to lead. Don't segregate the sexes. Three-year-old boys and girls play equally well with each other.

IMAGINARY PLAYMATES

Often, a three-year-old's most devoted and beloved friend is invisible to everyone else. Boys and girls at three years of age often invent an imaginary playmate—human or animal—who in their eyes is very real indeed, someone or something to take into account as the business of the day unfolds. Your son or daughter may conduct actual conversations with "Gerald" or "Sandra," give him or her a personality, and even bring him or her into the family circle. You may have to set an extra place at the dinner table. And watch out! A terrible tragedy may take place when an unknowing visitor ignores or even sits down on the unseen friend.

In the half-magic, half-real world of the child, a friend you can talk to but not see isn't so illogical. After all, adults converse every day with people out of sight on the telephone; on television, they watch the movements and actions of people who aren't really present. The creation of a mythical playmate is one way a child works out the sometimes shifting borders of reality and learns for him- or herself what does and doesn't exist.

The imaginary playmate also fulfills another role. Your son or daughter didn't spill the milk on the new tablecloth: "Gerald did it." "Sandra," you may be told, "opened the gate," and allowed your three-year-old to escape from the yard. And if you don't buy the story of Gerald as scapegoat, you may hear the child afterward—criticizing Gerald in the same firm tones you used minutes before. Having an imaginary playmate around helps a boy or girl work out his or her own conflicts in a satisfying way. (Sometimes a stuffed toy or the family dog serves the same purpose.)

Because imaginary playmates are normal, parents should not do much about them. If Gerald begins to interfere with family life—if you have to buy an extra ice-cream cone for him, for example—you may have to put your foot down a little and suggest that Gerald come another time. Don't deny that Gerald exists; it's fruitless—his closest friend won't believe it anyway—but don't be caught up in playfully encouraging the fantasy, which will only confuse the child further. As the lyrics suggest in the children's song, *Puff, the Magic Dragon,* one day the playful fantasy will just fade away, and Gerald will disappear from the family circle forever, a welcome visitor for a time whose stay is no longer necessary. You may actually find yourself missing him more than the child does.

STORIES AND STORY TIME

Reading or telling stories to your youngster takes on special significance when he or she is about 2½ and has enough grasp of language to understand more of the tales. The first stories needn't be anything elaborate. In fact, the best ones are those you invent yourself.

A regular story hour is fun for parents, too: there's something enjoyable about snuggling up with a little one and taking him or her (and you too!) into a world of enchantment. A picture book can provide the story or just be a prop: you can point to the pictures and improvise a narrative around them. Remember what you said, though, because your listener will—and will insist that it be told the same way again. Make up stories in which your child is the central figure. And if you're artistic—or even slightly so—you can draw pictures that tell the stories.

Stories take children into the world of words and ideas. Keep them simple, with plenty of action and pictures. If possible, make the stories up yourself, reading or telling each with lots of expression and excitement.

The most popular tales among two- and three-year-olds are short on words and long on action. That's why *Mother Goose* has been such a favorite for so many years. Don't just read the stories—act them out. A mommy or daddy who can huff and puff like the Big Bad Wolf or squeal like the Three Little Pigs is the most popular storyteller. Good storytelling for a child also calls for questions, pauses for effect, and reaction from the child. "And what do you think the little pig said then?" brings a delighted, "Not by the hair of my chinny-chin-chin!"

Words to a two-year-old aren't heard just for meaning; they

also have rhythm and sound. That's why rhymes are more popular than plain old prose. Read with expression, excitement, and anticipation, and your child will enjoy it most.

AN EAR FOR MUSIC

Between two and three a child begins to like music, too. The child's a little young for Beethoven, Basie, or the Beatles; a simple tune will do. The best ones have a prominent melody and a strong beat. Nursery jingles and marches meet these qualifications—and so, you'll find, do television commercials.

William or Wanda won't yet have perfect pitch. The ability to carry a tune successfully won't develop until about the age of four. But the child will love your singing—however off-key—and will probably plunge in with his or her own little monotone. Children quickly settle on favorites, from lullabies to *She'll Be Comin' Around the Mountain*, and will insist that you provide encore after encore.

If you can play a guitar or a piano—even if you can only pick out a tune with one finger—your child will be enchanted and, being self-reliant, will want to try it alone. A windup music box that plays a simple tune is a favorite toy for many two-year-olds. A stuffed animal with its own built-in music box is a good, soothing bedtime companion.

Although a two- or three-year-old is too young to manipulate a record player, he or she will enjoy listening to records. You can buy many inexpensive children's records containing simple melodies, the old nursery rhymes, or dramatized storytelling. You'll often find these at secondhand stores or garage sales.

TELEVISION AND CHILDREN

The images and voices of the television screen capture the attention of even a two-year-old. Studies show that three-year-olds can identify television cartoon jingles before nursery rhymes and that many four-year-olds are glued to the set as much as four hours a day.

Most parents have mixed feelings about television and its influences. There seems to be little support for the belief that a heavy diet of television damages children's eyes or otherwise hurts them physically, but its effects on pliable minds are continuously disputed. Most parents despair about the drumfire commercials with their buy-buy-buy message and the heavy dose of violence on many programs, even children's programs. And no one likes to see a child passively watching a television screen when there are so many more active and exciting things to do. On the other hand, television has its positive side. Children do learn from it, as studies have repeatedly demonstrated; some of the most honored programs are aimed at the pre-school set. And, however guilty they may feel about it, almost all parents occasionally find the set to be a convenient baby-sitter. It can be a relief to a tired mother or father to plunk a youngster in front of a television, knowing that he or she will be safe from obvious harm.

One extreme way to handle the problem of television is to throw out the set. A better way is to give children some firm rules about what they can watch and when. And these rules should be taught early, when children first become aware of the television set. Here are guidelines to follow:

1. Be aware of your own viewing habits. If television is your chief entertainment, it is naive to expect the child to behave differently.

2. Monitor what the child watches. Observe the television fare frequently enough to be satisfied that content is suitable. Even familiar shows should be checked periodically, because some of these programs change approach or story line over the years.

3. Retain control of the set. That means the on-off switch. *You* decide what the child can watch and how long he or she can watch it. Call a halt when the time comes.

4. Consult television schedules or otherwise familiarize yourself with children's programs so you can influence the child's viewing. Don't automatically assume that a "children's show" is something you'd want your child to watch. Don't unthinkingly assume cartoons are children's fare. Many cartoons—especially older ones—are heavily laced with violence.

5. Discuss the programs as you would a book. Encourage the child to recall them and tell you about them. Studies show that programs are less frightening or confusing to a child if a parent is present to discuss them. In the same way, commercials have less impact if a child can question an adult about them.

6. Don't build the child's life around the television. Schedule other pastimes for weekend mornings or late afternoons. A picnic on Saturday morning is a good substitute for television; late afternoon is a good time for the story hour.

A NEW BED, A NEW CHAIR

When to move your child to a standard bed is strictly a matter for personal preference and pocketbook. Few children physically

Though few children physically outgrow a crib until the age of four, many two-year-olds can escape it with ease, even with the rail raised. Think about a "big bed," and, in the meantime, keep the rail lowered.

outgrow the crib until they're about four years old. A restless sleeper probably ought to remain in an enclosed space until he or she settles down. If you put the child to bed at one end of the crib and always find him or her wedged against the other in the morning, wait a bit longer to make the transfer. You'll probably also want to wait until the child is consistently dry at night, usually between 2½ and 3½ years old.

Most children this age can no longer be kept put by plopping them in the crib. An agile two-year-old quickly learns to scramble over the side and escape, and many evenings will be spent putting him or her into bed—and retrieving him or her again and again. Often, the young fugitive will also flee during the night or rise at the gray light of dawn to toddle into your room and wake you.

Some desperate parents try to cover the top of the crib with netting, to prevent escape, but most resign themselves and keep the crib rail in a lower position so the acrobat won't be injured crawling over. Pad the floor with pillows, too, to prevent injury.

When picking a new bed, assume, too, the child will topple from it a few times. Choose a model that is close to the floor. It'll take the child several weeks to become accustomed to the unconfined space. In the meantime, tuck in blankets and linens, and line the floor with pillows. Even though the child is usually dry all night, you'll want to place a waterproof pad between mattress and linens. Toilet accidents will continue intermittently for several years. Pick blankets of synthetic fiber: they can be washed easily, and they reduce the possibility of allergic reaction. The child is probably also ready for a pillow at this time.

The baby may also be ready to eat at the table with you—assuming, of course, you cover the table with a plastic cloth. No doubt your youngster has long since outgrown the bounce chair, and even a high chair may be confining. You may wish to substitute a booster added to an adult chair, or you may wish to remove the tray of the high chair for easier access to the adult table.

CHAPTER

17

Three To Five Years

HOW THE CHILD GROWS

The average normal four-year-old weighs 37½ pounds and stands 40½ inches, an increase of five pounds and 2½ inches from the year before. The range in size among normal children is 28 to 45 pounds, and 37½ and 43½ inches in height. Usually, girls are smaller than boys, although the height and weight of boys and girls fall within the same range.

Here are some things most normal children may learn to do before the fourth birthday:

- dress without assistance, except for difficult buttons;
- identify colors; make comparisons;
- use plurals and prepositions;
- leave parents easily and play out of their sight for long periods;
- draw a figure recognizable as a human;
- hop on one foot, and maybe skip for a few steps.

At five, an average normal child weighs 42 pounds and is 43½ inches tall. The range of height is 39½ to 46 inches, and the range in weight, 32 to 50 pounds. Here are some achievements of normal five-year-olds:

- define many words;
- catch a bounced ball;
- put on shoes, perhaps even tie them;
- sing a song with a recognizable tune;
- recognize his or her printed name, and perhaps print it.

THE INFANT ADOLESCENT

Between three and five years of age, your son or daughter goes through a transition so profound that it has been called "the adolescence of the pre-school years." As in the teens, the person who emerges from this period is quite different from the one who entered it. The three-year-old is still an infant. Your five-year-old is most clearly a child.

Your role changes, too. The three-year-old is increasingly—even demandingly—self-reliant, but many details of caring for the child still fall to you. The five-year-old can dress, eat, go to the toilet, and even bathe with little help from you; sometimes it seems that mother and dad are only called upon to cut meat and deal with difficult buttons. Even social plans may be made without you: your five-year-old will scurry off to a friend's house unescorted, play out of your sight for long periods, come and go with minimum supervision. Your child will want it that way, too, and will want a voice in many family plans.

That doesn't mean a five-year-old is a full-fledged adult, even in miniature. The child still lacks judgment. Your guidance is important—essential—to point the child in the right direction and to make decisions that are beyond childish experience. Conversely, you must not expect too much nor push too fast; though no longer a babe in arms, your offspring is still very much a child.

And the changes don't unfold at the same rate in all children, or even in the same child. A child may quickly mature physically, develop speech slowly, and change emotionally and socially by fits and starts. Your child at five will be different than your child at three, but in retrospect, it may be difficult for you to pinpoint when the transformation took place.

TALK, TALK, TALK

One of the most marked—and most erratic—areas of development is that of speech. Between three and five years of age, most children gradually master the basics of adult communication, and their speech patterns and cadences come to resemble those of grown-ups. But not all children make it over the hurdle at the same pace. Everyone knows an anecdote about a child who spoke only in monosyllables until age three and a half, then blurted out, "Please pass the butter, mother." Your child, though normal, may not have the urge to communicate as quickly as another equally normal child.

The majority of children, however, become increasingly verbal after passing their third birthday. They learn to say just about anything they want to say, and grunts and gestures fade away as a form of communication. Baby talk and mispronunciations continue, but the intricacies of sentence structure and grammar begin to creep in. Gradually, the child peppers conversation with plurals, pronouns, and prepositions. "Me do it" becomes "I'll do it," and "Mommy do it" gives way to "You do it." A four-year-old knows the proper form is "two kitties" and "three puppies" and understands the difference between "under" and "over," "in" and "on." Nearly all normal four-year-olds can define three of four prepositions, according to the Denver Developmental Screening Test, and can deal with such physically descriptive ideas as "cold," "tired," "hungry." Almost all can give their first and last names.

At the same time, the mind is stretching in other ways, too. Between three and four, your child learns the concept of number, and by the fourth birthday, he or she may be trying to count. The sequence may come out, "1, 3, 7, 2" or "1, 5, 9, 6" for a year or more yet. If you ask the child his or her age, or the number of puppies in the picture, he or she may be able to hold up three or the appropriate number of fingers. At about the age of four, many children learn to recognize their printed name; a few can even laboriously print it themselves, if the name isn't too long and the letters not too difficult. With a pencil and paper, a four-year-old may be able to draw a creditable imitation of a person.

Recognizing colors is another area of progress. Seventy-five percent of four-year-olds can identify basic colors, like "red," "blue," "yellow," and may even select a "favorite color" (although some children progress more slowly in this area than others). Many have even mastered definitions of words and can identify the opposites of "good," "fast," or "right."

The child's mastery of language may become so complete, in fact, that he or she becomes a non-stop chatterbox, driving parents to distraction with a ceaseless babble that begins at breakfast and continues to bedtime and often beyond: even after the light has been turned out, you may hear him or her in earnest conversation with the teddy bear. Most of this monologue is just practice—the child is displaying a fascination with words and sounds. Most of these endless, one-sided conversations don't require acknowledgement or reply. But through your conversation, you can help the child develop language skills, sharpen pronunciation, and learn adult cadences. Continue to talk to him or her, pronouncing words the correct way and using simple, but grown-up sentences. Don't overcorrect—but don't use baby talk—and the child will learn the lesson.

"BUT WHY, MOMMY?"

One of the favorite sentences your little talking machine will use consists of three letters: "Why?" You'll hear this inquiry from morning to night, and often after you've responded to one "Why?", you'll hear "Why?" again.

Much of the time the child doesn't really want an answer, just some verbal interaction. He or she is playing with words, testing and examining ideas. Your child likes the attention that comes with your response.

"Why?" also represents a new dimension to a child's ever-growing curiosity. Now he or she has learned there are other ways to make discoveries—tapping the accumulated wisdom of a more experienced mommy or daddy. Your child wants to know what you know and looks to you as a fountain of knowledge.

You don't have to be a walking encyclopedia to deal with these questions, and you don't have to answer them elaborately. Keep your answers simple, with a minimum of details: a child who asks about the man in the moon isn't looking for a lesson in astronomy. Nor do you need to consult reference books or authorities. A few facts are enough.

TOILET ACCIDENTS AND BED-WETTING

Even some time after a child has been successfully urine-trained during the day, accidents will periodically occur. They usually happen because the child is excited, absorbed in play, or happens to be in an unfamiliar place and doesn't know the location of the bathroom. Accidents are more frequent when the child is outdoors and hasn't time to hurry home.

Treat incidents like these as casually as you possibly can. Usually, the child is already greatly embarrassed by the whole affair—especially if other children witnessed the event—and no lecture is necessary. Just change the child's clothes, and offer a gentle reminder to start for the bathroom sooner or visit it more frequently in the future.

When a child has been successfully toilet-trained for a while and then reverts to wetting pants, an emotional cause may be suspected. The arrival of a new baby may cause an older child, especially an only child, to return to babyish behavior long since abandoned. So may a move to a new home. If you continue to treat the matter casually and pay as much attention to the child as possible, this behavior is likely to end quickly.

Repeated accidents without an obvious emotional explanation may be caused by an infection of the urinary tract. Such conditions are more common in girls than in boys. Consult your pediatrician, who can detect the infection by urinalysis and prescribe medication to treat it. A breakdown in toilet training may also be caused by an inborn structural defect in the urinary system. Such conditions can usually be corrected surgically.

About nine of ten children can remain dry through the night, most of the time, by four years of age. Night training requires much more time than daytime training, however, so don't be surprised if your youngster still has occasional accidents at night until the early school years and sometimes even beyond.

As with daytime toilet accidents, a seemingly spontaneous recurrence of bed-wetting in a child who has been reliably trained to stay dry at night may indicate an emotional or even a physical problem.

THE CHRONIC BED-WETTER

Many people think persistent bed-wetting is rare, but actually it is quite common. One study of 992 Baltimore children showed that between one-fourth and one-third of five-year-olds wet their beds once a month; two of three from this group, once a week. Ten percent of seven-year-olds were still not reliably dry, and even one in 20 12-year-olds wet the bed at least once monthly. Contrary to popular belief, boys and girls were represented in about equal numbers. The problem seemed to run in families.

Why presumably trained children wet their beds on some nights while remaining dry on others annoys parents (and the child, too) and mystifies physicians. The theory that they simply sleep more soundly than the rest of us does not stand up in laboratory tests. A child who suddenly begins to wet the bed after years of being dry may have an emotional problem, but this can usually be ruled out in the majority of cases. Infection or another physical cause is seldom an explanation, because the child is dry during the day. And it is not a matter of simply being too lazy to get up and visit the bathroom, as weary parents sometimes allege.

A popular theory today suggests a developmental lag in bladder control. Because the condition runs in families, some physicians suspect an inherited slower maturation of certain nerves. Tests have shown bed-wetters' bladders are of normal size but with a smaller "functional capacity." Even during the day, they visit the bathroom more frequently than other children.

If bed-wetting occurred nightly, it would seem less a problem; constant precautions could be taken. It's the intermittent pattern that causes such friction between child and parent. Repeatedly having to get up in the night to wrestle with wet pajamas and bedsheets leads to the conviction by parents that the child "just isn't trying." It can arouse overwhelming feelings of downright anger, even toward a small child. The first step toward a solution is acknowledging the anger, not trying to make the child feel guilty or ashamed, or calling him or her a "baby," which only complicates things further. Success against bed-wetting can only be achieved by parent and child working together.

Simple measures should be tried first. Place a plastic liner over the mattress and moistureproof sheeting between mattress and linens. Be sure the child visits the bathroom just before retiring. Limiting fluids before bedtime may help, if you don't become so obsessive about it that the child winds up thirsty. Encourage the child to go to the toilet during the night, but it's not necessary to get up with him or her. Install a night light in bedroom and bathroom to make night visits easier.

Bladder-training exercises also work for some children, usually those of school age. The child is encouraged to drink large amounts of water during the day, then is urged to wait as long as possible before using the toilet. After a few days, the intervals between visits are said to increase, and within three weeks, according to some reports, children also stay dry at night. Apparently by conditioning the bladder to hold greater volumes during the day, bladder capacity at night is also enlarged.

Your pediatrician may prescribe a medication to control bed-wetting, generally small nightly doses of an antidepressant. This treatment apparently disturbs the child's sleep just enough to rouse him or her to "calls of nature." Some doctors report this method is successful 100 percent of the time, and all studies indicate significant improvement. Unfortunately, many children return to bed-wetting when the drug is discontinued.

Another treatment the pediatrician may suggest is the use of an alarm. This pad-and-buzzer system consists of two layers of foil or wire mesh separated by a layer of cloth and connected by wires to a battery and bell or buzzer. Wetting on the cloth completes the circuit, sounds the buzzer, and wakes the child. The repeated association of bed-wetting with being rudely awakened by the buzzer presumably conditions the child to greater bladder control. The method is said to "cure" up to 90 percent of bed-wetters in about two to ten weeks, with few relapses. The drawback is inconvenience, not to mention the child's embarrassment at having the alarm announce his or her bed-wetting to the whole household.

Because the biggest problem—and greatest source of annoyance—is cleaning up, have the child take some responsibility for it, which may in turn help to motivate him or her toward dryness. A child old enough to dress and undress can be taught to change nightclothing; if the condition persists to an older age, he or she can learn to change bedding as well. A laundry hamper and linen supply in the room will help.

THE CHANGING SLEEP SCHEDULE

Children usually give up daytime naps around the fourth birthday, although many continue to take a short afternoon nap until they reach kindergarten age. If it continues, the nap may be shortened to an hour and a half.

Some children give up naps gradually. They may discontinue sleeping in the afternoon for a few months, then resume again. Others may lie down each day but sleep only on some occasions and not others. In any case, a four-year-old should continue to have a rest period or quiet time in mid-afternoon, even if he or she does not sleep. Let the child lie down with a book, pencil and paper, or a quiet toy. An afternoon rest is particularly important if the child is attending nursery school and has a full schedule of activities keeping him or her busy through-

As the child nears the fifth birthday, the number of hours spent sleeping at night usually declines to ten or 11. Schedules vary from child to child; watch yours to determine the best one.

out the morning. Even after the nap has been eliminated, insist on a rest period when the child seems overtired or keyed up.

The number of hours spent sleeping at night decreases, too, as the child approaches the fifth birthday. The duration is usually about ten to 11 hours, although the need for sleep varies tremendously. There's no best time for a four-year-old's curfew; it can be determined by family style. A common schedule is bedtime at 8 p.m., with the child arising at 6:30 or 7 in the morning, but this does not have to be rigid. Usually, the later a child retires, the later he or she will sleep. If both parents are working, you may want to enjoy the child more in the evening and allow him or her to sleep later in the morning.

HOW TO PICK A NURSERY SCHOOL

There's no set age for a child to start nursery school, assuming you want to send him or her to one. It depends on the child's temperament, personality, and maturity and your own schedule and resources. The usual beginning is sometime between the third and fourth birthday, although some children start earlier. A child usually attends two or three days a week at first and may gradually work up to a full five-day schedule. A nursery school session normally lasts about two and a half to three hours a day.

When you're trying to decide whether your child is ready for nursery school, here are some questions to ask:

1. Is he or she toilet trained during the day? Many schools insist that the child be out of diapers and know how to use the bathroom without adult assistance. The child should also be able to tell an adult when he or she needs to make a trip to the bathroom.

2. Is the child able to take care of him- or herself? In other words, can the child tell an adult when he or she is ill or hurt, get help when needed, and be self-reliant enough to play without constant adult supervision? The child should recognize personal possessions and be able to put on jackets and hats with a minimum of help.

3. Does the child leave you easily? Ease of separation doesn't usually come until after the second birthday, unless the child has become accustomed to a pre-school or child-care center. Regardless of age, the child often will cling to you during the first visit, and separation throughout the first month may be difficult.

Should your child attend nursery school? There are three main benefits:

1. Nursery schools offer encounters and social interaction

Should your son or daughter attend nursery school? One advantage is the chance each child has to adapt to other children. The nursery-schooler with a "me-first" attitude quickly learns cooperation is important.

with peers in a controlled environment. Your son or daughter learns to adapt and accept the rights and demands of other children and to adjust personal wishes to the requirements of the larger group, a process of socialization that helps mold adults.

2. The child benefits from the stimulation of early education. Nursery schools don't teach the three "R's," but they do stress learning through personal discovery, and they stress the creativity of arts and handicrafts.

3. It's good for parents. Not only does it allow you more time for yourself, but it offers an opportunity to meet other parents and exchange child-raising experiences.

Nursery schools, like play groups—and like children themselves—come in all shapes, sizes, and pedagogical philosophies. The Montessori schools, for example, stress a structured learning program leading through the entire pre-school years. Children start at two to two and a half and advance through methods of personal discovery based on special teaching materials designed by the founder, Maria Montessori. Open schools stress more freedom, with the child able to follow his or her own dictates around a series of "learning centers." Still other nursery schools emphasize arts, language, crafts, or similar activities.

The best way to discover the best choice of nursery school for your child is to visit several and observe them. Most schools have such days for parents; a few even have one-way glass viewing areas, so you can watch the children without distracting them. Here are things to look for:

Environment. Is the school structurally safe? Is the play area well enclosed, preventing easy access to the street? Is there adequate adult supervision to forestall accidents? Is the playground equipment appropriate for children of nursery-school age? Is the school satisfactorily clean by your standards? Are toilet facilities adequate for the number of children? Is medical or nursing help available or on call in case of illness or injury? Is there a place for a child who becomes ill to lie down and rest?

Most states or municipalities license or regularly inspect nursery schools, but their minimum standards may not be so high as yours.

Personnel. Do staff members regard themselves as teachers or merely custodians? How does the staff interact with children? Are the children watched or left to their own devices? If a child is hurt, does he or she get immediate attention? When snacks are offered, are the children helped to eat, or is the food simply passed out and eaten?

Situation. Are children of similar ages and sizes kept together or are three- and five-year-olds mixed indiscriminately? Some group play is fine on the playground, for instance, but each age group or level of development should have its own time. How is the school structured? Your rambunctious child may fit in well at a free-wheeling school, but your shy one may belong elsewhere.

What's expected from you? Many schools operate cooperatively to hold down costs, with one or more parents serving as teachers or teachers' assistants each day. Such economy sounds fine, but you must be sure you have the time to contribute—as well as the desire to do so. Will you have some voice in the decisions of the school—and do you want any—as in a public school, or are the structure and operation unyieldingly the same?

Expenses. Tuition for nursery school ranges widely, and there are no guidelines for what is appropriate. Some hidden expenses, however, may be: distance from school—will you need to drive the child there or take part in a car pool? Is there a bus paid for by the school? Clothing: is the school atmosphere rough-and-tumble and the equipment primitive, leading to more wear-and-tear on clothes?

Most educators now agree that children require some form of education prior to beginning formal school (about the sixth birthday). But when that starts and under what circumstances, however, are strictly up to you.

THE MARATHON RUNNY NOSE

To many parents, the years from three to five seem like one continuous runny nose. Nursery school, pre-school, or any environment filled with children brings one cold after another. You can expect that a pre-school child will have seven to eight colds a year, each lasting about two weeks. The rate is even higher in large families, with each child contributing his or her own breed of cold viruses.

Apart from passing out handkerchiefs and tissues, there's little you (or your pediatrician) can do to combat a cold. Aspirin or acetaminophen in doses appropriate for the child's age may relieve aches and pains; using a vaporizer at night may make the child's breathing easier. Cough medicines, cough drops, or over-the-counter cold preparations are expensive and their value unproved. A cough syrup made of lemon juice and honey is less expensive. The pediatrician may prescribe a decongestant to reduce nasal stuffiness. (See Chapter 20, "Common Complaints and Diseases.")

Colds are miserable but seldom life-threatening. You can't do much to help your child avoid them, and maybe you don't want to. Each exposure helps a child build immunity to that particular strain of virus, thus reducing vulnerability later. That's why a child gets so many colds in the first six years of life, when he or she encounters alien viruses for the first time, and why the rate of illnesses caused by them declines with age.

Most of the time-honored precautions seem to have little effect in preventing a cold; children whose parents observe them faithfully seem to have just as many colds as those whose parents ignore them altogether. Many people believe that drafts, wet feet, and insufficient clothing "cause" a cold, but there is no evidence for this belief. In addition, keeping a child at home to prevent a cold from spreading is unrealistic. Upper respiratory infections are contagious even before symptons appear. In any case, school is probably where he or she contracted the cold in the first place.

Be alert, however, for symptoms not normally associated with a cold. Earache, diminished hearing, or swollen glands may indicate a secondary bacterial infection complicating the original viral illness. These infections can have serious consequences, but if detected early, they may be readily subdued with antibiotics. Consult a pediatrician if any of these symptoms accompany or follow a cold. Medical attention should be sought for recurrent or persistent infections that don't subside within a few weeks.

Some parents believe that removing enlarged tonsils and adenoids will help to reduce colds and infections that often follow them, but there is no evidence this is true. Although tonsillectomy and adenoidectomy are among the most frequently performed surgical procedures in the country, doctors are not even agreed on the value of removing these bits of tissue from throat and nasal area to relieve the two conditions for which they are most commonly recommended—tonsillectomy for frequent or chronic infections of the tonsils, usually caused by the streptococcus bacteria, and adenoidectomy for repeated ear infections. Both tissues are now known to play an important part in the body's defenses against infection, and enlargement in normal children may indicate tonsils and adenoids are combating the cold virus, not that they are its victims. Removing them may actually lower resistance. As the child grows older and the number of infections decreases, the adenoids and tonsils normally shrink in size.

Although enlarged adenoids and tonsils may "squeeze" the eustachian tube connecting ear and throat—thus preventing proper drainage of fluid from the middle ear and increasing chances for infection—additional obstruction may result from slow maturation of the tube itself. If so, it's a problem that cures itself with time. Instead of adenoidectomy, some doctors advocate the insertion of tiny polyethylene tubes in the eardrum, a procedure called tympanotomy, as a means of providing proper drainage from the middle ear.

LYING, STEALING, AND DIRTY WORDS

Not all three- and four-year-olds are angels, and sometimes yours will probably behave in ways you don't approve of.

Falsehoods—you can't really call them lies—are common at this age. Nor can you call them bad—some are so transparent they're funny. A three-year-old still lives in a fantasy world, where impulses and wishes are just as real as facts and deeds. If he or she tells you an elephant ran into the room, upset the milk cup, and raced out again, it's not an attempt to mislead you nor is it said out of malice. That's what the child wishes were the explanation for the accident. Knowing you may be disappointed or angry, he or she gives you a fabricated account—or more.

Don't engage in a power struggle over an occasional lie. If you accuse the child of lying, his or her instinct is to deny it—and to believe the denial. Show that you disapprove of lying, but use the occasion as an educational experience: "Well, that sounds like a tall story to me," or "I don't care if you broke the cup or Jimmy broke the cup. In this family we don't play with the china." Your answer allows the child to save face, while you get the point across.

As the child grows older and is better able to distinguish truth from untruth, you can substitute reason. A four-year-old is sensitive to his or her own feelings, as well as those of others, and your talk can be couched in those terms. "I don't like it when you tell fibs to me" lets the child appreciate the consequences of lying in a way he or she can understand.

A five-year-old who lies habitually should cause you to reexamine *your* standards. Children usually tell lies under pressure—when they fear the truth will disappoint you or perhaps cause them to be punished. A five-year-old knows when he or she has failed or fallen short of your expectations. A sustained pattern of lying may indicate that your standards are beyond reach or that you have restricted the child too greatly.

Taking other people's possessions (and, often, lying about it) is another step in growing up. Stealing by a three-year-old is just another manifestation of the child's being dominated by wish and desire. If the child wants something, he or she takes it, because the social limitations adults understand haven't caught up with the child's self-centered impulses. It isn't a serious matter nor is it a precedent. Stealing may also recur at five. At either age, don't ignore the event; just bring it up and deal with it openly.

Don't make a major fuss, and don't directly accuse the child of stealing. If you do, the child may simply deny taking anything at all. "I don't care how it got here. That's Johnny's toy and you take it back" is better than a direct confrontation. "You stole Johnny's toy. I saw you take it" may simply encourage the child to steal more skillfully the next time.

Again, you may wish to examine your own standards. Preschoolers seldom steal because they lack personal possessions or because they are deprived. In fact, their thefts may indicate that you have not conveyed the message that other people's property must be respected.

Even a three-year-old quickly picks up blue language and may repeat it, often under embarrassing circumstances. The words sound so odd coming from a tiny mouth that you may laugh in spite of yourself. That may be the worst thing you can do: knowing such words are good for a laugh, the child may repeat them again later. Don't ignore the words, either. Just bring the matter to the child's attention by saying that words like these aren't used by anyone in your family and that they shouldn't be used again.

Mischief also becomes part of a pre-schooler's routine—and a bone of contention with parents. Exasperating as it may be when the child pours salt into the sugarbowl, you can usually endure such incidents. Even a pattern of impishness—hiding daddy's hat, smearing soap on the bathroom mirror—can be written off to harmless devilment. But if the mischief is consistently damaging or destructive, more serious intervention may be needed. Your child may be too restricted or limited. A lasting streak of destruction may also indicate the child is troubled and unhappy; an emotional explanation may be looked for.

MONEY, TOYS, ALLOWANCES

Sometime during pre-school, a child understands that money has value and can be used to obtain possessions. He or she doesn't know much about it and probably can't distinguish between a penny and a dime. By the age of four, most children know that two coins are more desirable than one coin, but they don't understand much beyond that.

Simultaneously—and with the aid of television advertising—the child begins to desire toys or other articles that appear on the screen or are seen in stores. Their desires put parents in a bind. You want to buy things for your child, but your resources are limited, and the child doesn't understand either value or limitations.

You'll find yourself saying "No" a great deal during this period—and you may find it answered with a great deal of protest and rage. It's difficult for a child to comprehend why a toy can be bought one day and not another. You'll just have to be firm, distract the child when you can, and endure the outburst when you can't. You can reason more successfully with a four- or five-year-old. By then, most children have learned they can't have everything, although they may continue to want it. You can

sometimes tell them when a gift may be bought and even set dates they can look forward to. Purchases can also be used as rewards.

A child hasn't much use for an allowance until the age of five, when it should be given in small amounts but with the proviso that the child can spend it as he or she chooses. This gets across the principle of thrift, as well as the idea of deferred gratification.

Some children respond to a special day when they can receive a reward. Saturday can become Candy Day or Treat Day, for instance, with a small budget earmarked for that day. The amount can be based on the child's age, with money subtracted for each time candy is requested in the interim.

MANNERS AND COURTESY

A three-year-old can learn to repeat the words and phrases most of us use in polite discourse, words like "please" and "thank you." No special lessons are involved in the process. If you as parents are courteous in exchanges with others, and especially with each other, the child will quickly pick them up. If you make a game of "please" and "thank you," their use will be habitual by the time the child is old enough to attend school.

In the same way, your courtesy and thoughtfulness with others will be imitated by the child. As he or she grows older, you can expand the lesson by using words, explaining that people are kind and considerate toward one another because they expect the same treatment in return. Explain simply, yet directly, that all of us are interconnected, and if we offend other people, we will lose their love and support.

Despite these lessons, some children act aggressively toward others: A three-year-old may hit, kick, or bite playmates. You can explain that people have other, better ways to express feelings. Anger is normal, you may say, but telling people you're angry is more acceptable than punching another child. As with many lessons, you can't expect the child to assimilate this stricture in a single setting. You may have to repeat the lesson several times. But remember not to lecture; keep your message short and direct.

What if other children hit your child? Youngsters quickly learn for themselves to deal with an aggressor. Usually, they just give him or her a wide berth; they will say frankly, "I don't want to play with you." This ostracism is often more effective than striking back. With some children, however, it has just the opposite effect: the aggressive child strikes out even more, hoping to gain more attention by doing so.

In such an event, you'll have to teach your child the limits of tolerance. Most of us discourage children from hitting others or striking back when attacked. But if a child allows him- or herself to be bullied continually, the pattern will continue. In this case, you must make it clear to the child that the whole world isn't reasonable; aggressive people must often be dealt with in an aggressive, physical way when they repeatedly overstep the bounds of tolerance.

OBEDIENCE, REWARD, PUNISHMENT

Obviously, you want your child to do what you say when you want it done. Always give directions with confidence they will be carried out. Don't be tentative; be firm in a way that leaves no room for argument or "Why, daddy?" But don't expect a three-year-old to obey or perform according to your expectations every time.

As your child grows older, you expect that he or she will distinguish approved behavior from the disapproved variety. Approved behavior brings reward and reinforcement; disapproved behavior brings unpleasant consequences. The relationship between behavior and consequences is the basic lesson of discipline. Those consequences must be appropriate to the act and tolerable to both parent and child.

For gaining approved behavior, reward is the best motivator. Of course, every child needs reward, in the form of positive feedback, completely apart from discipline. But rewarding a child—even with something so basic as a hug—is also a teaching technique. That doesn't mean you should give a bribe to

Reward is the best answer for good behavior. It needn't be elaborate, so long as the action and reward are linked in the child's mind. Even a simple hug will tell your son or daughter that some ways are better than others.

produce proper behavior. It does mean you should link the reward directly to the act. Reward should be bestowed for specific acts of behavior a child can understand and should be produced immediately. Asking a four-year-old to be "good" all afternoon in return for a bicycle next Christmas calls for vague behavior and a distant reward. Tell him or her to pick up toys and praise the child afterward—deed and reward are then readily and unmistakably linked.

With older children, reward need not be immediate, but steps toward an eventual reward should be taken at once. Employing a system of delayed reward, you can give the child a penny (or a gold star) for each night he or she remembers to brush the teeth.

For disapproved behavior, you want an act that communicates your displeasure. Just showing by expression or attitude your unhappiness may be enough. "Time out" is another. That means physically separating the child from you and from the scene—banishing him or her to the bedroom, bathroom, or corner. Ignoring the child's behavior, surprisingly, may also be effective. When a child persists in an annoying act, even punishment may reinforce the behavior by giving it attention: when mother screams, at least the child is being noticed.

Almost all parents resort to physical punishment occasionally. Spanking works best when directly connected to the misdeed and administered immediately. Children can understand a swat delivered in anger better than being deliberately "turned over the knee" for their own good or being punished "after daddy comes home." By school age, physical punishment is outdated. Being whacked is degrading to a five-year-old.

The least effective motivator is the unfulfilled threat. If you repeatedly tell a child, "Don't do that or I'll spank you," you must be prepared to carry out the punishment if the disapproved behavior continues. Otherwise, the only lesson the child learns is that mother or dad talks a lot but doesn't do much.

BUT WILL HE OR SHE OUTGROW IT?

Some behavior that seems attractively cute at three should be worrisome if it still persists at five. A toddler who walks unsteadily is merely amusing, but a hesitant five-year-old may legitimately concern the parents. A three-year-old who calls his sister Barbara "Babawa" gets a laugh; a five-year-old with a lisp may be the target of other children's taunts. Parents may be told (or may tell themselves), "He'll outgrow it." "She'll come around soon." But will he? Will she? When should you be concerned about your child's development?

Physical and behavioral progress covers a wide range, as this book has tried to show. Some problems that worry parents are actually well within the spectrum of normal growth; the child is simply marching to a different drummer, adhering to a personal inner rhythm. Yet early detection of a problem is important. The sooner it's discovered, the more readily it can be corrected.

Obviously, warning signals to parents may differ according

to the area of development. But here are general guidelines for intervening in developmental problems that worry you.

1. Follow your own instincts. Parents see the child most—and under the greatest variety of circumstances. Don't be swayed by your mother-in-law's diagnosis, "That child walks funny," or, conversely, by a neighbor's judgment, "My sister walked like that, too, and she grew up just fine." (On the other hand, respect the judgment of a trained outsider, a teacher or child-care specialist, for instance, who can professionally compare your child with many others.) If it looks wrong to you, by all means seek help. But don't be goaded just because it seems a child's contemporaries are ahead of him or her.

2. Consult your pediatrician, but if you are not satisfied with the verdict, ask for a consultation or seek a second opinion. If you're still concerned, try to identify the leading authority on the problem in your area, and seek his or her advice. But don't shop for doctors, which is expensive and counterproductive, and don't be put off by a doctor's "He'll outgrow it." If you're still worried, ask for any examinations or tests that may clear up the matter once and for all.

3. Once the verdict is in, be prepared to deal with it. If examinations show normal bone structure, you can be sure a child will eventually overcome a "funny walk." An exam that shows no structural defect in a lisping child's vocal organs can be similarly reassuring. Be patient in helping the child grow out of the condition. Don't call a stammer or lisp to his or her attention or urge him or her to try to walk differently. Pointing out the problem may only ingrain it more deeply and make it more difficult to overcome.

4. Be alert for possible behavioral problems, as well as those of physical development, and seek help if concerned. Most preschoolers lie sometimes, but a chronic liar may require help. Youngsters play with matches, but one who consistently sets fire needs professional assistance.

5. Don't worry about minor habits or mannerisms. Preschoolers often develop such habits as nail-biting, face-twitching, stuttering, or stammering. A few may suck their thumbs again after having given up such consolation. The less you say about these conditions the better. Unless such habits are part of a persistent pattern of emotional tension, most of them disappear within a short time.

Ninety-nine of 100 children outgrow the problems that concern their parents. But if your child does need help, get it as soon as possible.

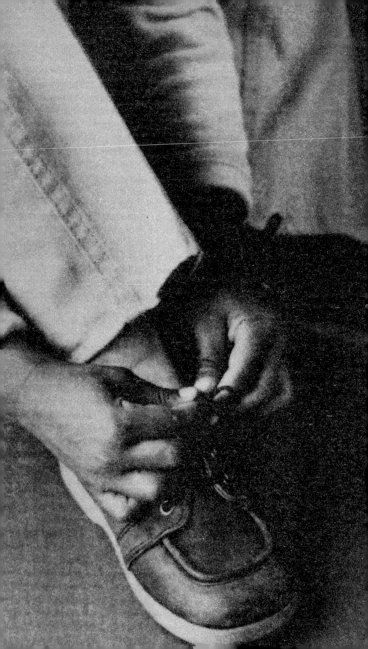

18

Five To Six Years

HOW THE CHILD GROWS

Between the fifth and sixth birthdays, the average normal child gains five pounds and grows 2½ to three inches. Average weight is 47 pounds; average height, 45½ inches. The range of normal weight is 35 to 55 pounds; the range of height, 43 to 49 inches.

Between five and six years of age, most children can do the following:

• put on and take off most clothing and probably tie shoes;

• print their first name, if it isn't too long or difficult, and recognize it;

• know both first and last names and be able to tell them to an adult;

• count from one to five in proper sequence and perhaps from one to ten;

• make a recognizable drawing of a person, including arms and legs;

• take care of toilet needs with only very rare accidents;

• wash face and hands and brush teeth with supervision;

• identify most colors;

• understand that a nickel or dime is a more valuable coin than a penny.

A CHANGE IN THE MENU

After several years of picking at food and acting as if eating it were somehow foreign to the laws of human nature, your five-year-old's appetite may suddenly begin to increase—the result of a new upturn in the growth rate.

Over the next three years, the average normal child gains 15 to 20 pounds. The change won't be an abrupt one, however, and you may not immediately notice that your child is eating more until his or her clothes begin to look too small!

Mealtime is now a family occasion, and no special diet is necessary for the growing child. The proper nutritional balance in the food you serve the rest of the family is fine for a five-year-old. He or she will still probably prefer simple foods and may reject strongly flavored or heavily seasoned dishes. Most children at this age are still leery of cooked vegetables but will eat raw carrots, celery, cucumbers, and even cauliflower. Fresh fruits provide important nutrients, and most children have several favorites. Fruit juices are popular, too.

By now, your child may have a well-developed taste for sweets and junk foods and you may have to restrict their consumption.

Milk remains a useful ingredient in a child's diet but need not be consumed in the quantities of the early bone-building years. One or two glasses a day is plenty. Any more only fills up the child and quenches the appetite for other equally useful or even more important nutrients. Skim or fat-free milk is adequate.

You don't have to give your child vitamin tablets if he or she is receiving a balanced diet, although you may wish to continue them. If the local water supply is not fluoridated, fluoride tablets may be continued as well.

A five-year-old's busy social schedule may interfere with regularly scheduled mealtimes; he or she will want to gobble on the run to resume romping with friends. You may feel you almost have to tie the child to the chair to get a decent meal eaten. Later, when everything is put away, the child may return, sniffing for snacks. Maintain your rules of regular mealtimes, but you can allow the child to leave the table as soon as he or she is finished.

THE SCHOOL BELL RINGS

Until now, home and family have been the dominant influences in your child's life. Now you'll share that responsibility with the school. A five-year-old will probably spend half a day in school five days a week.

Traditionally, a child begins kindergarten at five, first grade at six. But those starting dates aren't rigid. The spectrum of development among children is very wide, and some five-year-olds are more prepared for the social and educational experiences of kindergarten than others are. Many teachers strive to give children individual attention to bridge these differences, but this can be a demanding task. In any case, "five years old" is a nebulous term. A child who has just celebrated a fifth birthday is probably quite different from the five-year-old who is a month short of being six.

Most kindergartens now stress preparation for academic work, usually in the form of recognizing letters and preparing for reading. An astute teacher recognizes the children who will respond to such work. Unfortunately, children themselves often feel pressured to keep up with their faster-moving classmates. Despite the teacher's best effort, they may feel they're lagging behind and therefore are failures.

Many educators and psychologists recommend that some children wait a year before starting kindergarten or first grade. They may be urged to spend an additional year in nursery school. Boys, in particular, may be less ready than girls in those areas that are needed for school, and some boys are not ready for kindergarten until the age of six.

When the calendar shows your child is ready for school, you may wish to ask yourself these questions:

1. Is the child socially mature? Can he or she take care of personal needs? Does your child mix well with other children? Does he or she accept separation from you easily?

2. What are the child's strengths and weaknesses? Will he or she flourish best in a structured environment or in a more easy-going one?

3. How developed is the child's ability with language? Does he or she talk well and understand most words?

Remember the kindergarten year isn't just an academic period. It's a time of transition, as the child moves from a life in the home to one spent increasingly outside it. You want to make that transition as smooth as possible.

THE PRE-SCHOOL PHYSICAL

Although your child has probably been visiting a pediatrician or well-baby clinic regularly, he or she needs a thorough pediatric examination before starting kindergarten. (Indeed, most school districts require some sort of pre-school physical before the child can begin classes.) Schedule it well before school starts, so any problems can be handled easily.

Because senses are at the heart of learning, the eyes and ears, in particular, should be tested. Sometimes a slight impairment in vision or hearing isn't noticed by the parents and doesn't make itself evident until the child begins to struggle with classroom work. The pre-school physical examination should be more extensive than just measuring the child's ability to read the

Because sight and sound are at the center of effective learning, the preschool physical is crucial. Vision must be checked thoroughly. An audiogram, which measures hearing ability, should also be part of the examination.

eye chart posted on the doctor's wall. The doctor should, in addition, check the ability of the child's eyes to focus and, at the same time, look into the possibility of eye infections.

The hearing test should include an audiogram, which measures sensitivity to tones and frequencies as well as loudness. The doctor should also look for accumulated fluid in the middle ear, which can cause mild to moderate hearing loss.

Most doctors want to hear the child speak, too. In case of a "cute" speech pattern, the doctor may recommend the child visit a clinic or speech pathologist, because a speech impairment can hinder proper pronunciation and stand in the way of learning.

At this point, you'll also want to check the child's shots. DPT and polio boosters are due between the fourth and sixth birthdays. In many states, beginning students must produce a complete record of immunizations showing they've received all the required shots before they can be admitted to school.

SAFETY ALONG THE WAY

Safety should be the first lesson of kindergarten. If your child walks to school, be sure to cover the route with him or her beforehand. You want a five-year-old to be familiar with the route before trying it alone. If possible, escort your son or daughter to school the first few days and meet him or her for the trip home. If an older child in the neighborhood also attends the school, ask if they can walk together.

Teach the child to observe all the basic rules of pedestrian safety: stop at intersections, look both ways before crossing, and always walk within crosswalks. Teach your child always to stay on sidewalks and to follow all of the directions given by crossing guards or police who may be on the scene. Also, every child should be taught to walk through an intersection and not run across the street.

A child who rides a bus to school should learn the correct way to enter and leave the vehicle. Even if the driver escorts the child across the street after debarking, he or she should learn to look both directions before crossing. Go with the child to the bus stop the first few days, and meet him or her on the return trip, especially if the walk home covers several blocks.

School bus drivers usually control children's behavior on the bus. But tell your child to take a seat quietly, to remain in the seat throughout the ride, and not to engage in horseplay while the bus is moving.

Before joining a car pool to transport children to school, make sure that all the parents involved agree on safety regulations. Each car in the pool should have a seat belt or restraining harness for every child; belts or harnesses should not be shared. There should be no more passengers than can be seated comfortably. Children should always enter and leave the vehicle from the curb side, never the street side, and the driver or another adult should help them from the car. At the school, cars should be loaded off the street or with a teacher or other employee of the school present.

A FEELING OF SECURITY

A five-year-old usually knows his or her first and last name and can recite each of them plainly enough for an adult to understand. The child can usually also print at least his or her first name and probably can recognize his or her name if printed in block letters on paper or on the inside of clothing or boots. Before the first day at kindergarten, help your son or daughter to memorize the family phone number and your street address (or be able to describe the home), so that he or she can tell another adult when lost.

Especially in these days when many parents work or are busy with other duties during the day, schools usually require that you list the name of a friend, neighbor, or relative to be contacted in the event of an emergency when you cannot be reached. The name of the family physician or the child's pediatrician and the work telephone number of one or both parents usually must also be kept on file. However, the child should also be instructed whom to call in an emergency when you are not at home. He or she should know the phone number and address of that person (a neighbor or close relative, perhaps) and how to reach the person's home.

Always instruct the child beforehand in case the routine varies. If he or she is to go to a different home after school, make sure the plan is clear to the child before the school day begins. Many schools require that you file a written note in case of change of plans or, at least, call the child's teacher. If you're not going to be there when the child usually comes home and another person will be waiting, make sure the child expects that. Never let a five-year-old come home to an empty house—it's a scary feeling.

Mark all of the child's belongings, including jackets, hats, and overshoes, so he or she can recognize and find them easily. Try to choose garments that can easily be distinguished, even by a child who is not yet able to read a printed name. Color-code shoes and boots with green (right) and red (left) markers, so he or she can easily match the right piece of footwear to the appropriate foot. You can use a similar color key on jackets and mittens.

THE PARENTS' ROLE

You have a part to play in the child's schooling, too. Even a kindergartener brings home a blizzard of papers and handicrafts for you to inspect and admire. It might be difficult for a busy parent to review every last scrap of paper that arrives, but as

Schooltime! Safety on the way should be the first lesson. If your son or daughter will walk to school, make sure he or she knows the way. If possible, accompany the child there and back for the first few days.

often as possible, you should look at the child's work and examine it.

Always find something to praise in the child's work, however difficult it may be to decipher. The leading statement, "Tell me about your picture," is more encouraging to a fledgling artist than an incredulous, "What is that?" Avoid criticism, even constructive criticism, and try not to show amusement at the child's efforts. Laughing at him or her only makes a child feel foolish. Don't overdo the praise, though; even a child recognizes that you can say only so much about a page of printed "b's" and "d's". Try to be specific in your praise. "That's a nice tree" tells the child you really are paying attention.

Like adults, children don't always want to talk about the day's events. Don't pressure with "What did you learn today?" Just show interest and let them volunteer their recital of kindergarten happenings.

Remember that education isn't something that goes on only within school walls. Review lessons as asked by the teacher, but also help the child to review and practice what is being learned. Supply pencils and paper for printing and drawing, for example, and keep a well-stocked library of books that will help him or her reinforce reading techniques. Experiences, visits, and travel also stimulate the child's curiosity and help with informal learning.

Whether or not you join a parents' group at the child's school is strictly up to you; don't be stampeded into membership if you don't feel you have time to devote to it. But visit the classroom when possible, and discuss the child's progress with the teacher. And if you are not satisfied with the teacher or with the school program, make your opinions known.

A SENSIBLE SCHEDULE

Beginning kindergarten may dominate a child's life but shouldn't be allowed to disrupt it. A five-year-old still needs adequate rest, regular mealtimes, and a schedule that keeps activities in perspective.

The need for sleep is gradually lessening, but for most children it remains at about ten hours a night. Because school hours are consistent, bedtime should come at a fairly regular hour, too. Usually, a five-year-old should be in bed by 8:30 p.m. and awaken about 7 a.m. A kindergartener on an afternoon schedule might sleep later. The morning timetable should allow enough time for the child to eat a good breakfast before school begins.

For afternoon kindergarteners, call the child in from play sufficiently ahead of time to allow a brief rest period before school. When the child returns from school, he or she should have another period to rest and unwind, much the way an adult wants to unwind after a day at work.

Entry into kindergarten is often the signal for a flurry of other activities outside the home. Many five-year-olds are enrolled in crafts classes, gymnastics, music lessons, or swimming. These activities stimulate a child and expand his or her horizons but shouldn't be allowed to overwhelm the day. Two regular activities outside the home in addition to school are probably plenty for most children in kindergarten.

BACK TO BABYHOOD

In the first days of school, you may be dismayed to find the child returning to habits that had been given up a long time ago. A five-year-old who has long since stopped thumb-sucking may suddenly pop the thumb back into the mouth; another child may dig out the disreputable "blanky" that provided solace in infancy. Whining and crankiness are common. Some children begin to have toilet accidents or wet the bed after years of being dry and toilet trained.

These reversals are natural, temporary, and seldom related to specific events at school. Although kindergarten is usually a low-key environment, it's a new and often demanding experience for a five-year-old and quite a step up from nursery school. Youngsters themselves seem to recognize they are moving into an adult world. Although they respond to this challenge, often with eagerness, they also feel pressure that makes them—just as adults do sometimes—long for easier days.

Most children adjust to the new way of life within a few weeks. Because the change in temperament may partially be related to fatigue, you may wish to suggest that the child resume a short afternoon nap for a while. A brief quiet time after the child returns from school also may help. Of course, if the behavior persists or seems to be part of a broader pattern of emotional upset, you should seek assistance.

BACK TO WORK FOR MOTHER?

When a child begins to attend school all day, many families may want to work out new child-care arrangements that allow the mother to resume a paid job or continue her education. That means shifting responsibilities for the child who has previously been cared for exclusively in the home.

The change isn't always easy for either parents or youngsters. Many children are unhappy to learn that mother will no longer welcome them after school. "How come you have to go to work?" may be a difficult question to answer. Try to explain that although mother likes being at home, she also likes her career or schooling, just as children love their homes but have interests elsewhere. Financial reasons may persuade older children. They can understand that mother's job may enable the entire family to live more comfortably.

Any new arrangement should become a family project. It's a legitimate time for a father to share in managing the household, and everyone can pitch into domestic duties. Even young children can take a role. A five-year-old can help to keep his or her own room neat and to help handle regular, simple chores such as sweeping porches, helping with yardwork, and caring for family pets.

It's better to establish a regular child-care arrangement outside the home than set up a makeshift one or allow the child to arrive at an empty house to wait. Often, you'll find other parents in the same boat, and a cooperative child-care arrangement can be established.

Other possibilities to be explored include a child-care arrangement at your place of employment, now offered by an increasing number of employers. Sometimes local municipalities or schools offer after-school care programs or playground activities that continue until parents finish work. You may be able to find a friend who will supervise the child during the after-school hours before you return home.

Whatever course you choose, always be sure school authorities have a phone number of a friend or relative and a telephone number where you can be reached during the day. Discuss with your employer beforehand how you'll handle an emergency or a child's illness.

THE CHILD IS INDEPENDENT

More and more your child is becoming a little adult. Usually able to dial the telephone and self-reliant enough to walk to a friend's home, your son or daughter will make his or her own social plans that must be fitted into those of the rest of the family. In fact, sometimes you'll have that "empty-nest" feeling, as the child spends less time with you and more with peers. It won't be quite so easy to engage in a spontaneous family outing; the child's plans may conflict with yours.

You'll also find that even a five-year-old wants some voice in his or her life. You can't just pick out clothing for the day and expect the child to wear it docilely. Children begin to show tastes of their own—which may clash with yours—and to be adamant about them. Peer pressure and television commercials also shape their ideas of what's appropriate.

You don't have to cater to a child's every whim, but you'll have to be prepared to take them into account. You can allow latitude in picking (or buying) clothes by narrowing the selection of shirts, for example, to three and allowing the child to make the final choice of which to wear or buy. The child can follow his or her own social schedule when it doesn't conflict with the family's plans; his or her ideas should be taken into consideration but not allowed to sway the family's decision.

You're entering a stage where you'll have to be prepared to say ''No'' and be unpopular. Although your child is entering a new phase of maturity, supervision still lies with you.

SECTION
4

Advice for Every Day

Bringing up children has
rough places as well as smooth.
From bloody noses to sudden
illnesses to embarrassing
questions, difficult moments
can test your strengths and skills
as a parent. You can't foresee
everything. But the following
sections can help you understand
your child better and be ready
for some of the future needs.

19

Difficult Questions

The omnipresent "Why?" may be the easiest of an inquisitive child's questions to answer. More difficult are questions parents find embarrassing or confusing—or questions that have no simple answers. Many of these have to do with the facts of life, but others relate to style of life—your own or others—and to human differences in a changing and pluralistic society.

Although these questions deal with adult topics, children often ask them before the age of six—so you should be prepared for them. You'll see that some arise out of your child's life, but others seem to come out of a clear sky.

Children ask questions for information and for reassurance. Before answering, there are certain things to know and remember and certain rules to observe. Here are the most important:

1. Children usually don't want too much information. A few basic facts simply expressed are enough. Explaining the origins of life to a five-year-old doesn't require a biology text.

2. Children usually have some information (often inaccurate) before they ask, as well as their own feelings about the subject. Ask your own questions before you answer, then tailor your response to the child's knowledge. Make the conversation a dialogue, not a lecture.

3. Never avoid questions, postpone them ("Go ask your father"), or make jokes. Children are entitled to immediate and direct answers on subjects important to them.

4. Make it easy for your child to obtain additional information. For children who can read, simple books are available

dealing with such topics as sex, death, divorce, adoption; for those who don't yet read you can buy phonograph records. Don't push such materials on a child, but offer the book or record, and leave them where they can be found and used.

5. Answer a child's questions in a relevant way. Make it clear that the answer for your family may not apply to other families.

6. Listen for the unspoken questions as well as the spoken ones. The child who asks about a relative's death is probably also asking, "Will I die?" and "If *you* die, who will take care of me?"

7. Be concerned about the child who repeatedly asks the same question and seems never satisfied with the answer, indicating an unusual interest in the topic.

Here are just a few of the questions you may have to deal with—and possible ways you might answer, along with information to help shape your replies:

Q. Jason's dad isn't going to live with them anymore. His dad and mom are getting a divorce. Why are they doing that?

A. Sometimes grown-ups just aren't happy together. They decide that everyone in the family would be better off if they didn't live together anymore. It doesn't have anything to do with the children. Both of them still love Jason and will still take care of him.

Q. Are you and daddy happy?

A. Yes, right now we're really happy. Oh, we have quarrels sometimes, but that's like you and Jennifer. You two are happy with each other again after your quarrels.

Q. But grandma says you were married and divorced from someone before.

A. I wasn't happy then. My husband and I tried to be happy, but we had so many problems between us we just couldn't seem to solve, no matter how hard we tried. Now that I'm married to your father, we're all happy, and we're taking care of any differences very well.

The second thought may be unspoken, but it usually motivates the child's inquiry. To children, divorce is a kind of death—the end of a relationship as they know it. Divorce and death cause some of the same questions to pop into the child's mind: what will happen to me? where will I live? who will feed me? And—perhaps most important—is it my fault? Your answers to questions about divorce must reassure the child that he or she is still loved and cared for, even though the family is separated. Stress that adults, not children, cause the separation.

Q. Why did grandma die?

A. She was very old and sick, and she wasn't strong enough to go on living.

Q. Will I die, too?

A. Everyone dies at some time. It's one of those things that's bound to happen, just like we know the sun will come up in the morning. But if we are careful and take care of ourselves, it won't happen for a long time.

Q. What will happen to me if you die?

A. Daddy (or mommy) will still be with you. There will always be people to take care of you.

Questions about death frequently arise around the age of five when a child recognizes that parents are human and fallible and that the world is not permanent. This realization frightens a child, who feels that he or she may be abandoned as a result of a parent's death. First soothe the child's worries about his or her own future before discussing the biological facts.

Another question often is, "What will happen to *me* after I die?" The answer to this question depends on family beliefs about an afterlife.

Questions about religion, church, and God are among the most difficult for contemporary parents to deal with. If the parent has a certain grasp of his or her own beliefs, explaining them to a child may not be too hard, especially if the family subscribes to an organized faith with a central body of belief. Many churches have their own printed materials, books, and even records that help parents formulate answers to children's religious questions.

Many parents, however, have only a vague notion what they believe about God and religion and aren't regular churchgoers. The child's questions make them examine their own beliefs. As always, the best course is to answer in terms of your personal ideas, not a creed that others subscribe to or that you have been taught but no longer accept.

Especially with a young child, begin by determining what the child already knows or has heard. Your task may be less to answer questions than to clear up confusion resulting from what Johnny told him or her. Then try to deal with only a few simple ideas. A three-year-old with no real concept of time isn't ready for a lecture on the afterlife. Better to suggest that God represents all that is good in the world, that he is everywhere, in all things and persons including children (an idea that fascinates the young), and that he watches over the world.

Some people think you shouldn't tell a young child that God is a person or that heaven is a literal place in the sky. It probably does no harm; it helps children grasp the idea, and if you don't personally happen to hold such beliefs, you can help the child modify them later. Probably the important message is that God is responsible for the good in the world, and he is somebody to look up to.

Q. Why does Gregory have black skin and mine is white?

A. All people are different. I have brown hair, but your mommy's hair is black. Your eyes are blue but Rachel's are brown. Skins are different, too. There are a lot of different kinds of people, but they're all people and they act and feel just like you do.

Behind racial questions is often concern about difference: why am I different? why are they different from me? Young children like to resemble others; they want to be part of the crowd, yet seek a distinctiveness and individuality. Such questions often reflect a child's need to know that, despite the differences, he or she is still worthwhile.

Q. Why do you and daddy both have to work? Linda's mommy doesn't work.

A. Linda's family is different from our family. In our family, it's better for all of us when your dad and I both work. We like being with you, and we like what we do when we work. You have things you like to do—play with your friends, go to school—but that doesn't change the way you feel about your home. That's the way it is with grown-ups, too.

It's nice to earn more money, too. That helps all of us do things and buy things we all enjoy.

When children raise a question about both parents working, their fears really have to do with separation and change. Your answer to the question should be framed in terms of assuring the child that you will still spend time with him or her and that your basic relationship won't change.

If working outside the home is essential to the family's financial welfare, you should tell the child so. Otherwise, the cash benefits of a paid job should be played down. If you tell an anxious child that you're working so the family can have a new car, he or she may feel you're placing material things ahead of time spent with him or her. You may even be told, "I don't want a new car. I'd rather have you home."

In either case, the child should understand that the decision to work or not to work is for adults to make, although the child's feelings will be respected.

Q. You know Dave, the man who lives in Brian's house? He's not Brian's dad. Brian's mom and Dave aren't even married.

A. That may be fine for them. People all have their own ways of doing things. Your mom and I wanted to be married, but some people don't feel the same way. The important thing is that Dave and Brian's mother are happy with each other and happy with Brian, just like we're happy with each other and with you.

Q. Sally told me that her parents adopted her. What does that mean?

A. Children come into families in different ways. You and Adam came out of my body. But some mothers can't have babies that way, even though they want them very much. So Sally's parents let some people know that they wanted a baby very much, and these people found Sally, whose other mother couldn't take care of her. Parents love children who are adopted just as much as we love you.

Q. Why do you and mommy argue? Sometimes you don't seem to like each other very well.

A. Remember the other day when you were really angry at me? But now you're not angry, and we like each other. Or after school yesterday you were angry at Ed, but today he's your friend again. Grown-ups are like that, too. They don't agree about things, and sometimes they get angry at each other, but that doesn't mean they don't love each other.

Q. Where did Mrs. Shepard's new baby come from?

A. It grew inside of her, in a special place mothers have for babies to grow in.

Q. Did I grow in you like that?

A. You certainly did! That's where all babies live and grow until they're ready to be born.

Q. But how does the baby get in there?

A. That baby doesn't start as a baby. There's a little seed inside the mother waiting for the father to come along and start the seed growing. Then it takes almost a year for the baby to grow and come out into the world.

Q. What does the father do?

A. The most important thing he does is put the father cell inside the mother to start the baby growing. But he helps with the birth, too.

Q. How does the baby get out?

A. A mother has a special passageway made just to bring the baby out into the world. It's down between her legs. The baby grows in the mother until he or she is big enough and strong enough to live outside. Then little by little the baby comes out the passageway. The mother helps and so does the doctor.

Q. Does it hurt?

A. Only a little, and only for a while. The baby is very small, about as big as your doll (or puppy). He or she is just a little bundle. The mother's muscles stretch enough for the baby to come out.

When discussing the facts of life, keep your information simple and straightforward. During the preschool years, avoid highly technical terms for fertilization, pregnancy, and parts of the anatomy. Choose your own words and style, but try always to get across the message that babies grow inside their mothers after a cell has been planted by the father.

Children see their parents or other children without clothes, and as they grow older, they recognize the distinctions between male and female anatomy. These distinctions should be discussed directly, without embarrassment. Don't make a point of explaining the differences. Treat them casually and gradually, as they come up:

Q. What is that on Dougie?

A. That's called a penis. Little boys are made differently from little girls. Dougie's penis shows that he's a boy. A little girl has a vulva that shows she's a little girl.

Later, this knowledge will help an older child to understand in more detail how babies get started: "The father's penis fits into the inner passageway of the mother, the one the baby comes down. The father's cells are called sperm, and they pass up into the mother. When a father's cell joins with a mother's cell, or egg cell, a baby begins to grow."

Throughout childhood, you can expect your son or daughter to explore and show interest in his or her own or other human bodies. This should not be a cause for embarrassment or correction. A young child touches genitals in the same way he fondles fingers or toes; at age three or four, two children may examine each other's bodies with no motive other than curiosity. If you discover them, don't make a scene. Such explorations are harmless and—as with many other topics that embarrass adults—the more matter-of-fact the treatment, the better the result.

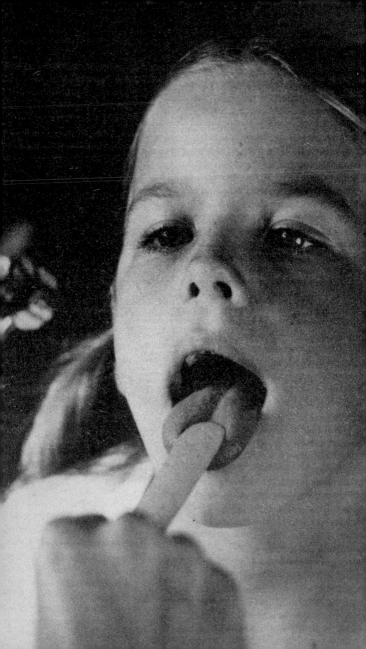

20

Common Complaints and Diseases

Most children—including your baby—are usually happy and healthy, but every normal child has occasional bouts of illness that are alarming to parents. Fortunately, these spells of sickness are seldom serious or long-lived. As parents, your first task is to recognize and treat the symptoms as quickly as possible, help the child feel better, and know when to seek medical help or advice.

Some of the more common problems of infancy and childhood have already been discussed to some extent in the earlier chapters of this book. The symptoms and treatments are described in more detail below, along with those of less frequent illnesses. Chapter Eight tells when—and, equally important, how—to call your pediatrician in the event of a child's illness.

COMMON SYMPTOMS

Abdominal pain. Sharp or dull pain in the stomach or abdomen may be mild or serious. Do not give laxatives or other medications, and do not offer solid food until the pain subsides or treatment is given.

Recurrent mild pain without apparent cause should be discussed with your physician, as should sudden, sharp pains, especially in a very young child. Appendicitis is uncommon under the age of five but should be suspected in any young child who has pain or tenderness in the abdomen, especially if it is accompanied by nausea and vomiting.

Abdominal cramps sometimes are caused by food that is difficult to digest—the "green apple" syndrome. Your suspicions may be confirmed sooner if you simply recall the child's most recent meals. Although painful for a time, such cramps usually disappear rapidly.

Colds. (See also Chapters Eight and 17.) There's no need to dwell on the symptoms of the common cold—the familiar pattern of runny nose, rattly cough, and noisy breathing. The watery discharge from the nose gradually thickens and becomes yellow, then green, before the cough subsides. The normal course of a cold, treated or untreated, is one to two weeks.

You can't shorten a cold. But you can relieve an infant's strained and noisy breathing by using a bulb aspirator to suck mucus from the nostrils. An aspirator with a rubber tip, or an ear syringe, is best for an infant's delicate membranes. If the mucus is too high in the nose to be removed successfully by suction, it may be loosened by injecting two or three drops of salt water (mix a level teaspoon of salt in a pint of lukewarm water). Dried and crusted mucus in the nasal passages may be loosened using a vaporizer at night (see Chapter Nine).

Non-prescription decongestants to relieve stuffiness are never recommended for a child under one year and should be given to an older child only on the advice of a physician. Avoid commercial cold preparations, too, unless a physician advises you to use them. The value of these medications for children is still disputed. They may cause side-effects, such as drowsiness and irritability.

The value of chest rubs and other traditional home treatments has not been proved scientifically, but some parents praise them. Do not use medicated nose drops without a physician's consent.

Constipation. Constipation, even in adults, is difficult to define. An infant may have a bowel movement only every two or three days and not be considered constipated so long as the movements are of normal consistency. Bowel movements are considered to be a problem only if they are hard enough to cause bleeding or seem to be extremely painful. Remember, however, that most infants normally strain, grunt, and turn red in the face during a bowel movement.

If the baby does seem constipated (with the above signs present), one tablespoonful of corn syrup added to each eight ounces of formula or water may loosen the stool. A child who is eating solid food may be given more fruit, especially prunes or prune juice, if he or she will accept it. Constipation in toddlers or older children may be relieved by bran cereal.

Enemas, or laxatives such as castor oil or milk of magnesia, should not be given. Your physician may prescribe a stool softener.

Cough. A cough generally accompanies any cold, as mucus drains into the throat and the child tries to clear it. Like other cold symptoms, the cough gradually subsides. Over-the-counter cough medicines should not be given, because they are expensive, probably don't help much, and can cause side-effects in young children. Make your own cough medicine by mixing equal parts of lemon juice and honey.

A persistent cough in the absence of a cold may indicate an allergy or other condition and should be reported to the physician.

Croup. Although a frequently terrifying experience for both parents and child, croup isn't necessarily a serious situation. The name comes from the deep, crowing sound a child makes while struggling for breath, the result of a narrowed larynx and trachea. It begins suddenly, usually at night when the child awakes abruptly, unable to breathe normally. The child has ordinarily had a runny nose or cough for a day or two but seemed well otherwise.

Croup is most often caused by a viral infection, which inflames the larynx and upper trachea and causes spasm of the muscles of the larynx. Cold or warm air seems to end the spasm and often brings dramatic relief. The quickest way to provide it is to place the child in a closed bathroom with the hot shower running. There are, however, other causes of breathing difficulty, so a physician should always be consulted.

Diarrhea. Like constipation, diarrhea defies definition. During the first weeks of life, bottle-fed and breast-fed infants may have six to nine liquid bowel movements daily. Thereafter, they usually decrease to three or four a day within the first year. A child normally has a consistent pattern, but it is not unusual for a child who usually has one or two movements a day suddenly to have three or four without apparent cause. They may also change considerably in consistency or color without a change of diet. Frequent loose stools in an infant are seldom significant unless other symptoms are present, like fever, irritability, or failure to gain weight.

Sudden diarrhea in a child over six months of age usually signals an intestinal viral infection. Typically, vomiting comes first, followed by diarrhea as the vomiting subsides. Both can dehydrate a child, damaging the tissues by withdrawing liquid from them. Make sure the baby continues to drink liquids.

If a child vomits more than once in an hour, stop all solid foods and substitute clear liquids, a tablespoonful every half hour at first, gradually increasing the amount. Water or apple juice may be given, along with carbonated beverages, to replace lost carbohydrates, potassium, and salt. When vomiting diminishes and diarrhea begins, continue the clear liquids but in larger amounts and less frequently. As the diarrhea subsides, give bland foods, such as cereal, bananas, and applesauce or—as our grandmothers knew—chicken broth.

Earache. Two-thirds of children under two have had at least one middle-ear infection; half of those have suffered two or more. By the age of six, one in five children has had at least six episodes. The common condition, agonizing to parents as well as children because of the difficulty of relieving the pain, usually strikes during the course of a cold and results from otitis media, an infection of the middle-ear cavity behind the tympanic membrane, or eardrum. Cold-caused stuffiness in the eustachian tube connecting ear and throat prevents proper drainage of the middle ear, allowing bacteria to proliferate. Accumulated pus and fluid press on the eardrum and cause it to bulge outward, sometimes causing excruciating pain. The pain may be accompanied by fever, or vomiting or diarrhea.

An early clue to ear infection in an infant may be refusal to take formula, accompanied by irritability or fussiness. A few infants will pull or scratch at the affected ear, as if to relieve the pain. Fever is sometimes present. If the child is recovering from a cold, you can usually guess the cause of his or her discomfort. Older children can report the pain, thus simplifying diagnosis and treatment.

The condition should be reported to a physician, because bacterial infection requires treatment with antibiotics. Aspirin or acetaminophen (an aspirin substitute) may relieve pain; a heating pad applied to the ear may comfort the child. But don't try to clear the ear by poking anything into it, and don't give decongestants, ear drops, or nose drops without consulting a physician.

Some babies are more prone than others to ear infection. The eustachian tubes in these children may be more horizontal in shape, narrower and (according to one specialist) "floppier," so they become blocked or clogged more easily. Children usually grow out of ear infections by the age of eight as the configuration of the tube changes. Recurrent ear infections may require special treatment, including control of chronic nasal congestion caused by allergies, removal of adenoids, tubes used in tympanotomy, (see Chapter 17), or daily antibiotic therapy.

Febrile seizures (convulsions). About three percent of normal children at some time have a convulsion, or generalized seizure, when fever is present. These attacks don't seem to be related to the height of the fever but may be associated with the speed with which it rises. Seizures are brief, usually subsiding within ten minutes, although they seem an eternity to terrified parents. They occur most frequently between one and two years and seldom occur before six months or after the age of five.

When a seizure begins, parents can do little except to wait it out. Remove anything in the child's mouth. The child may be held or placed on his or her back to prevent falls or collisions with furniture. See the doctor as soon as possible to determine the cause of both seizure and fever.

Usually, febrile seizures aren't damaging and do not mean the child will be seizure-prone as an adult. However, one of three children who has experienced one seizure will have a second. You may wish to discuss using anticonvulsant medication with the doctor.

Fever. The rectal technique for measuring an infant's temperature is described in Chapter Eight. After the age of four, children are old enough to have temperatures measured by the oral (mouth) or axillary (armpit) method. Keep the thermometer in place at least two minutes (measured by the clock) for an accurate reading.

In infants of two months or less, any rise in temperature above normal should be reported to the pediatrician for evaluation. Even a low-grade fever can sometimes indicate a significant infection in a newborn infant.

Otherwise, a high fever by itself often doesn't require consulting a doctor. Even a reading of 103 or 104 degrees (Fahrenheit) may have little significance if the child seems healthy in other respects and is in good spirits. The fever itself causes no damage. In fact, certain more serious conditions are marked by a slight, rather than substantial, rise in temperature. Usually, the cause of the fever is obvious. Most fevers accompany a cold or other noticeable infection. Fever persisting beyond three or four days in the absence of other symptoms should be reported to a physician.

If fever makes the child uncomfortable and achy, aspirin or an aspirin substitute (such as acetaminophen) will help. Aspirin substitutes are considered safer for children under one year of age. Recommended dosage is a half grain. After one year, the medications are considered equally safe, at recommended dosages of a grain for every year of age up to five years, given every four hours.

You can also lower temperature by removing as much of the child's clothing as possible. A diaper without an undershirt is enough for a feverish infant. A bath in lukewarm (not cold) water also helps to bring down fever.

Sore throat. Soreness in the throat with or without fever or other symptoms may represent a streptococcal ("strep") infection, particularly in a child of school age. The throat should be examined by a doctor who can obtain a throat culture and determine the need for antibiotic treatment. Rheumatic fever, which can cause damage to heart valves, is a possible consequence of untreated strep throat but is now much less common in most areas of the country and in some communities is extremely rare.

Swollen glands. Lymph nodes in the neck and at the angle of the jaw are part of the body's defense system. They enlarge during respiratory and other infections and may remain swollen weeks or even months after other symptoms have disappeared. Occasionally, the swelling may be accompanied by a sore throat.

If the glands are enlarged to a diameter of an inch or more, it could indicate a bacterial infection. Consult your pediatrician.

"CHILDHOOD DISEASES"
Chickenpox. No vaccine currently exists for chickenpox, which is now the most prevalent of the so-called childhood diseases, particularly among the nursery-school set. Highly transmissible from child to child, chickenpox usually begins with a mild fever and headache; it varies in severity, and some children have no other symptoms. More commonly, a single blister appears, often on the face, then spreads to other parts of the body, sometimes including the scalp and gums. The blisters are often preceded by small red spots or bumps. After a few hours, these develop yellow centers (pustules) and become crusted (scabs). Typically, pustules, scabs, and red spots may be seen in the same area of the body. Fever and headache usually disappear within three days of their appearance.

The most troublesome symptom is the intense itching. Because scratching may cause infection and (rarely) permanent scarring, cut the child's fingernails and give regular baths in cool water. Calamine lotion may also help. The pediatrician may prescribe antihistamines to reduce itching in severe cases. The child is most infectious before the rash appears; one case in a nursery school or kindergarten can quickly sweep the entire school. Contagion is no longer a problem after all the blisters have developed into scabs. The chickenpox rash usually disappears after about ten days.

Conjunctivitis. So-called pink eye is an inflammation of the thin membrane lining the inner eyelid and eye. It may be caused by infection (mildly contagious), allergy, or irritation caused by smog or chemicals. The eyes become sore, red, and itchy; tears flow, along with a yellow discharge. Itching and drainage can be relieved by washing the area around the eye with cotton moistened in warm water or by placing a warm, damp washcloth on the eyes. A pediatrician may prescribe eyedrops or ointment.

Measles (rubeola). Measles is preventable with a single immunization given at the age of 15 months. This potentially serious communicable viral infection begins with fever, cough, and runny nose; the eyes become red and watery. On the third or fourth day, fine white spots, circled in red, sometimes appear inside the cheeks. On the fourth day, a fine rash breaks out on the face, becomes blotchy, and spreads down neck and trunk. The fever may continue and even rise after the rash develops. The rash may last five days. The child may want to remain in bed and avoid bright light. A liquid diet is best, along with aspirin or acetaminophen to lower the fever and make the child more comfortable. A cool-mist vaporizer may relieve the cough.

Mumps. This viral infection of the salivary glands can be prevented, along with measles and rubella, with a single immunizing shot given at the age of 15 months. Transmitted by direct contact with a mumps victim, the illness usually begins with an earache and fever. About a day later, swelling begins in the angle of the jaw directly below the ear; it may spread to behind the jaw and under the chin, with one or both sides involved. The amount of swelling varies widely but usually disappears in about a week. Aspirin or acetaminophen lowers the fever and makes the patient more comfortable. Alternately applying cold and warm compresses to the swelling also may help.

Roseola. A mild viral infection with rash, it should not be mistaken for measles. It is mainly confined to babies and children under three. The illness begins with a sudden high fever of 104 to 105 degrees, fussiness, irritability, and a sharp drop in appetite. Otherwise, the child may not seem ill at all and may be playful.

The fever subsides after three days, and a blotchy red rash appears on the face and body. A liquid diet and aspirin or acetaminophen may be used to make the child more comfortable.

Rubella (German measles). German measles can be prevented by proper immunization. A mild viral infection, rubella is spread from person to person via infected droplets from the respiratory tract. The illness begins as a cold does, with mild fever, headache, runny nose, and enlarged lymph nodes. Small red spots appear first on the face, then spread to neck and trunk and frequently to the arms and legs. The rash usually lasts about three days. There is little specific treatment, beyond aspirin or acetaminophen to reduce fever. The infection's chief danger is to women in the first three months of pregnancy, whose unborn child may be affected.

Scarlet fever. This once-frightening disease is now known to be strep throat with a rash, treatable with antibiotics; scarlet fever is no more severe than strep throat without a rash. It usually begins with sore throat, chills, fever, headache, and possibly vomiting. A scarlet rash appears on the chest one to three days after the child becomes ill and spreads down the body; the child's face may become flushed but remain pale around the mouth. Aspirin or acetaminophen may be given for comfort, along with antibiotics to combat the streptococcal bacteria.

Whooping cough (pertussis). This once-common disease can readily be prevented by a series of inoculations beginning at two months. The name whooping cough graphically describes this bacterial infection's most prominent symptom. The disease is spread via droplets from the respiratory tract of an infected person and begins with a mild cough that gradually increases in severity and is more frequent at night. After about two weeks, coughing spells become so severe the child chokes, reddens, and may vomit. Each cough ends with the characteristic whoop; the spells last four to six weeks. The rare victims today are usually hospitalized.

SKIN CONDITIONS
Canker sores. This irritating viral infection of the mouth causes small painful ulcers on the gums and the inside of the cheeks, usually in the area where the two meet. The sores usually last about a week. Mouthwash or a salt-water rinse may relieve irritation, but, aside from that, there is little effective treatment.

Eczema. This condition may be a reaction to irritating substances that contact the skin or, rarely, a symptom of food allergy. Eczema is most prominent during the first two years of life and begins with patches of light red or tannish pink, rough, scaly skin often on the face, in the folds of the arms, or on the backs of the knees. The scales may flake off in a fine powder. Later, they become deep red, moist, and intensely itchy; if raw and open areas become infected, consult your pediatrician.

Fever blisters. Commonly called cold sores, fever blisters are caused by the reactivation of an earlier infection by the herpes simplex virus, to which most children are exposed. The initial infection may cause sores in the mouth or gums, fever, and malaise, or no symptoms may be apparent; afterward, the virus remains in many tissues of the body. Exposure to another virus, to sunlight, or even to emotional stress may "revive" it. The usual cold sore begins with a painful, itchy area of swelling on the lip, followed by an outbreak of oozing tiny blisters, which form a scab. The sore usually lasts about a week. There is no specific treatment, but ointments may help keep the sore from cracking or bleeding.

Hives. These raised, unbearably itchy welts may erupt anywhere on the body. Most often the cause is unknown, but in some children, they may result from sensitivity to medicines, certain foods, or other substances. The eyelids, lips, and, in extreme cases, the inside of the throat may swell. Consult your physician immediately. Usually, hives disappear in a few hours or, at most, a few days; in a sensitive child, they may recur often. Bathing the child in lukewarm water may relieve itching, or your pediatrician may prescribe antihistamines. If the hives recur, consult an allergist.

Impetigo. A common bacterial infection that is mildly contagious in children, impetigo usually starts as a small, red bump, with an oozing of thin, yellow liquid from the center. The discharge usually dries to form a light, honey-colored crust. If not treated, the blisters will spread to other parts of the body. The pediatrician may prescribe soaks in warm water and an antibiotic ointment or may give oral antibiotics. The child should have a personal washcloth and towel to prevent spread of the infection to others in the family. Impetigo seems to occur more often in summer.

Lice. These small insects infest the head and body and are more common among nursery-schoolers and kindergarteners than most parents realize. Unfortunately, lice are easily spread from child to child. The first symptom is itching in the scalp. Sometimes the lice, their eggs, or both are visible. Your pediatrician can prescribe medication that will kill lice and their eggs.

Pinworms. These are the most common intestinal worms in children and are spread by ingesting the eggs or touching infected objects and then putting the fingers into the mouth. The first symptom is usually itching around the area of the rectum, especially at night. Girls may sometimes complain of pain during urination. Sometimes the tiny, white, threadlike worms can be seen in and around the rectum, on bedclothes, or on a child's underwear. Medication is more than 90 percent effective. Usually, the entire household will be treated; it may also be necessary to sterilize bedding and clothing.

Prickly heat. Too many layers of clothes in hot weather cause this skin rash, which is most prominent in infants. The rash appears as raised, pinhead-size bumps with yellow centers on face, neck, and trunk and doesn't seem to cause itching or discomfort. Dress the child more lightly, so the rash has time to heal.

Ringworm. No worms are involved in this contagious and common fungus infection, which usually is seen on the scalp but may occur anywhere on the body. The infection may spread from child to child. Ringworm is named for the characteristic circular, itchy patches that are slightly raised around the outside. Your pediatrician may prescribe a topical medication, which clears most cases quickly.

Scabies. A skin condition caused when an itch mite buries itself under the skin and lays its eggs, scabies are characterized by inflamed areas that itch intensely and may even become infected and start to drain. The itching seems to be most severe at night and may disturb the child's sleep. Scabies are most common around the wrists, armpits, and between the fingers and toes but may be found anywhere on the body. They may last several weeks. Your pediatrician may prescribe medication to kill mites and reduce itching and may also give antibiotics in case of infection. In most cases scabies are usually contracted by contact with another child who is suffering from the condition.

Thrush. This stubborn yeast infection is most common in the mouth but may also appear in the diaper area. (See "Diaper Rash," page 165.) Thrush usually occurs (and may recur) during the first year. The first symptom of the oral variety may be a refusal to feed because of the soreness, although some babies show no discomfort. Inside the baby's mouth, you may see patchy white spots on lips, tongue, gums, palate, and cheeks that look like milk but can't be removed by wiping or scraping. The physician may prescribe an oral medication.

RESPIRATORY PROBLEMS

Bronchiolitis. A viral infection of the bronchial area, marked by rapid, labored breathing and wheezing. The area below the ribs pulls in sharply during inhalation. Bronchiolitis is most common in infants and young children, especially in winter, and seems to occur in epidemics. A cool-mist vaporizer may ease breathing. Consult your pediatrician promptly.

Bronchitis. Another viral infection of the bronchial tubes in the lower respiratory tract, it is sometimes diagnosed as a common cold and may follow one. The dry, hacking cough usually predominates, and nasal congestion is mild or absent. There may be low-grade fever. The cough usually lasts three to four weeks and is worst at night. Otherwise, the child may not act ill. There is no effective medication. Lemon-honey cough syrup and the use of a vaporizer at night may help. The condition is most common during the first three years.

Pneumonia. An inflammation of one or both lungs usually caused by either bacteria or virus. No longer so dangerous, the illness frequently develops in the aftermath of a cold, and symptoms may come on suddenly. Fever may rise sharply, accompanied by a deep, harsh cough and rapid, grunting breathing. Sometimes the child's chest hurts. The cough may be so severe that it causes the child to vomit. Call the pediatrician immediately when the disease is suspected; hospitalization is still sometimes necessary. Antibiotics, however, usually bring rapid improvement. Bed rest is necessary, along with a bland diet. Viral pneumonia is not helped by antibiotics. Vaccines for certain viruses which cause pneumonia are now being tested and may be available soon. Ask your pediatrician.

Tonsilitis. An infection of the tonsils caused either by bacteria or virus, tonsilitis may strike some young children repeatedly. Although there are usually sore throat and enlarged lymph nodes in the neck, other symptoms vary. There may be high fever and difficulty in swallowing; sometimes the child complains of a headache. The symptoms may begin abruptly or gradually. Bacterial tonsilitis can be quelled with antibiotics, but there is no effective treatment for viral infections. Salt-water gargles or sprays may relieve the soreness. In recurrent cases, the pediatrician may recommend removing tonsils.

BABY RECORDS

How could you ever forget your baby's very first step? Or the excitement of that moment when your son or daughter unmistakably called you "Mama" or "Dada"? Alas, memories fade, as new firsts succeed the old. A few months from now—but especially a year or two hence—you may be unable to completely retrieve an important landmark that was once frozen in time.

The record section provided below will help jog such memories later. For the future, mark down each shining moment in your child's present. Record each step on the child's ladder toward maturity and each achievement you will wish to cherish in years to come.

The areas of child development are arranged here according to when the majority of normal children pass each landmark. But, again, a word of caution: your child may attain these milestones sooner—or later—than other children. Exact dates mean nothing, except sentimentally. Of 20 children born on any given date, one will be walking well in seven months. But another year may pass before the other 19 are fully ambulatory. Years in the future, it will be impossible for anyone to distinguish those children who walked "early" and those children who walked "late."

As for height and weight, your child's dimensions are determined more by his or her heritage and nationality than by any given schedule of projected growth.

A "baby record" does have practical uses, of course. Charting the child's pattern of growth or development can help predict when the next hurdle may be cleared—and to show when you're expecting too much. And it may help a doctor or teacher in dealing with the child in later years.

But a baby book is primarily meant for memories and anticipation. Start now to record the highlights of your child's early years, for enjoyment both today and tomorrow.

Baby's name in full _____

Born _____
(Year, month, day, hour, and minute)

At _____ Hospital _____
(City)   (State)

Father _____
(First name   middle name   last name)

Mother _____
(First name   middle name   last name)

Address _____
(At time of baby's birth)

Subsequent addresses: _____

_____

_____

1 TO 4 MONTHS

GROWTH

	Pounds / Ounces
At one month	_____ _____
At two months	_____ _____
At three months	_____ _____
At four months	_____ _____

DEVELOPMENT

Weeks

Six weeks: Hold head up at a 45-degree angle when lying on stomach _____

Follow an object with eyes for a short distance _____

Keep head erect when held in a sitting position _____

Months

Three months: Sit with head steady. Follow an object moved from one side of head to the other _____

Bring hands together in front _____

Laugh, squeal, and coo _____

Listen to voices and recognize yours _____

Smile, socialize, and respond to people _____

Four months: Turn head in all directions and support self on arms _____

Roll over _____

Grasp and hold an object _____

Months

Babble in word-like syllables; coo, gurgle, chortle, squeal _____

Look at self in a mirror and smile _____

Recognize mother and siblings _____

Bear some weight on legs when held in a standing position _____

Be pulled to sitting position _____

5 TO 8
MONTHS

GROWTH

	Pounds / Ounces	
At five months	_____	_____
At six months	_____	_____
At seven months	_____	_____
At eight months	_____	_____

DEVELOPMENT

	Months
Five months: Sit up for 30 minutes with back supported	_____
Bring feet to mouth and suck on toes	_____
Reach for objects and often grasp them	_____
Shift objects from hand to hand; drop one to pick up another	_____
React to name	_____
Anticipate a whole object by seeing a part	_____
Show emotions; may protest—loudly—when something is taken away	_____
Six months: Sit well with support. Get a toy that is out of reach	_____
Pull back on a toy when you pull	_____
Turn toward a voice	_____
Attempt to recover an object that falls	_____

	Months
Recognize a familiar face	_____
Eight months: Grasp objects with thumb and finger	_____
Play peek-a-boo	_____
Say "dada" and "mama"	_____
Sit without support; get self into a sitting position	_____
Stand well while holding your hands	_____
Creep on stomach	_____

9 TO 12 MONTHS

GROWTH

	Pounds / Ounces	
At nine months	_____	_____
At ten months	_____	_____
At 11 months	_____	_____
At 12 months	_____	_____

DEVELOPMENT

	Months
Ten months: Play patty-cake	_____
Identify "mama" and "dada" and call them by name	_____
Pull to stand	_____
Walk or sidestep, holding onto furniture	_____
Wave bye-bye	_____
One year: Indicate want without crying	_____
Drink from a cup, spilling only a little	_____
Take a few steps	_____
Stand alone, stoop, and return to stand	_____
Understand many words	_____

1 TO 2 YEARS

GROWTH

	Pounds / Ounces	
At one year	_____	_____
At two years	_____	_____

DEVELOPMENT

	Months
15 months: Use a spoon and spill only a little	_____
Imitate a parent doing housework	_____
Scribble with a crayon	_____
18 months: Remove some or all of clothes	_____
Build a four-cube tower	_____
Walk up steps, holding rail	_____
Point to a baby's picture in a book	_____
Use name for him- or herself	_____
Two years: Combine words to make simple statements	_____
Identify one or more parts of the body	_____
Follow simple directions—if only a single step is involved	_____
Wash and dry hands, with parental supervision	_____

2 TO 3
YEARS

GROWTH

	Pounds / Ounces	
At 2½ years	_____	_____
At three years	_____	_____

DEVELOPMENT

	Months		Months
Identify pictures of animals by name	_____	Dress with supervision and button some buttons	_____
Pedal a tricycle; propel a kiddie car with feet	_____	Play interactive games, tag, for instance	_____
		Tell first and last names	_____
		Use plurals, pronouns, and prepositions in speech	_____
		Copy a circle with a crayon	_____
		Understand such words as "cold," "tired," "hungry"	_____
		Know where things belong and help to put them there	_____
		Follow simple, one-step directions	_____
		Feed him- or herself almost completely	_____
		Be toilet-trained during the day and remain dry all night some of the time	_____
		Recognize and identify some colors	_____

3 TO 4
YEARS

4 TO 5
YEARS

GROWTH

	Pounds / Ounces	
At 3½ years	_____	_____
At four years	_____	_____

DEVELOPMENT

	Months
Dress without assistance, except for difficult buttons	_____
Identify colors; make comparisons	_____
Use plurals and prepositions	_____
Leave parents easily and play out of their sight for long periods	_____
Draw a figure recognizable as a human	_____
Hop on one foot, and maybe skip for a few steps	_____

GROWTH

	Height / Weight	
At 4½ years	_____	_____
At five years	_____	_____

DEVELOPMENT

	Months
Define many words	_____
Catch a bounced ball	_____
Put on shoes, perhaps even tie them	_____
Sing a song with a recognizable tune	_____
Recognize his or her printed name, and perhaps print it	_____
Balance on one foot for ten seconds at a time	_____
Walk with a motion from heel to toe	_____

5 TO 6 YEARS

GROWTH

	Height / Weight
At 5½ years	_____ _____
At six years	_____ _____

DEVELOPMENT

Months

Put on and take off most clothing and probably tie shoes _____

Print first name, if it isn't too long or difficult, and recognize it _____

Know both first and last names and be able to tell them to an adult _____

Count from one to five in proper sequence and perhaps from one to ten _____

Make a recognizable drawing of a person, including arms and legs _____

Take care of toilet needs with only very rare accidents _____

Wash face and hands and brush teeth with supervision _____

Identify most colors _____

Understand that a nickel or dime is more valuable than a penny _____

6 TO 7 YEARS

GROWTH

	Height / Weight
At 6½ years	_____ _____
At seven years	_____ _____

DEVELOPMENT

Months

Take care of nearly all personal needs, including bathing, dressing, and going to bed _____

Define many simple words and explain simple concepts _____

Recognize most letters of the alphabet, perhaps recite them in sequence, and recognize some simple words _____

MEDICAL RECORDS

In our mobile society, it's important for you, as well as your physician, to keep family health records. If you move to another town, change doctors, or transfer to a different school, these records you keep can be important references and can be used for consultation.

The examples below will give you an idea of the records you may want to keep. Use them to devise your own, and, when possible, have your physician make the entries personally. If this cannot be done, enter the necessary information yourself immediately after the illness or health event.

This information can then be shown on request to another doctor or to authorities at your child's school. Such information should always be kept up-to-date. You may also wish to file copies of birth certificates, records of inoculation, or other important documents in this part of the book. If you did not receive this information at the time, you should obtain it now to keep your records complete and current.

FAMILY MEDICAL HISTORY

	Birth date	Illnesses
Father	_____	_____
Mother	_____	_____
Brothers	_____	_____
	_____	_____
	_____	_____
Sisters	_____	_____
	_____	_____
	_____	_____

Family illnesses, allergies, or chronic conditions _____
_____
_____
_____
_____
_____
_____
_____

ILLNESS & INJURY RECORD

Illnesses:

Nature	Date	Physician
_____	_____	_____
_____	_____	_____
_____	_____	_____
_____	_____	_____
_____	_____	_____
_____	_____	_____
_____	_____	_____
_____	_____	_____
_____	_____	_____
_____	_____	_____
_____	_____	_____
_____	_____	_____

Injuries:

_____	_____	_____
_____	_____	_____
_____	_____	_____
_____	_____	_____

BIRTH RECORD

Date of birth _____

Duration of pregnancy _____

Mother's health during pregnancy:

Illnesses _____

Drugs/medications used _____

Problems _____

Delivery:

Normal ____ Cesarean section ____

Medications during labor _____

Monitoring _____

Problems _____

_____

Birth measurements:

Weight _____

Length _____

Conditions at birth:

_____

Type of feeding:

Breast _____ Bottle _____

Duration of hospital stay (days) __

Blood type and Rh _____

Other information _____

_____

HOSPITALIZATION RECORD

Nature	Date	Physician

Allergies:

Other Information:

_____
_____
_____
_____

IMMUNIZATION RECORD

Immunization	Date	Dose	Physician
DPT	___	___	___
	___	___	___
	___	___	___
	___	___	___
DT			
booster	___	___	___
Tetanus			
booster	___	___	___
Polio	___	___	___
	___	___	___
	___	___	___
	___	___	___
Measles ..	___	___	___
Rubella ..	___	___	___
Mumps ...	___	___	___
Tuberculin			
test	___	___	___
Others ...	___	___	___
	___	___	___

DENTAL RECORD

Upper Teeth
1 central incisor
2 lateral incisor
3 cuspid
4 first molar
5 second molar

5 4 3 2 1 1 2 3 4 5

Lower Teeth
1 central incisor
2 lateral incisor
3 cuspid
4 first molar
5 second molar

5 4 3 2 1 1 2 3 4 5

Age Teeth Appeared

Upper Teeth		Lower Teeth	
Right	Left	Right	Left
1 ___	___	1 ___	___
2 ___	___	2 ___	___
3 ___	___	3 ___	___
4 ___	___	4 ___	___
5 ___	___	5 ___	___

	Age
Thumb-sucking	___
Pacifier	___
First brushed teeth	___
Brushed teeth unassisted	___
First flossed teeth	___
First visit to dentist	___
Preventive care	___
Orthodontic procedure ..	___
X-rays	___

NEWBORN GLOSSARY

Acrocyanosis
Dusky bluish color to the hands and feet of newborns present soon after birth, it persists for a few days. The circulation through the skin capillaries is not fully developed.

Bohn's Nodules *(Epstein's Pearls)*
Small pearl-white bodies toward the back of the palate of newborns that disappear in a few weeks without treatment.

Birthmarks *(Hemangiomas)*
• Capillary Hemangioma (Storkbites)
Superficial blood vessels on the back of the neck, forehead, upper eyelids, nose, and upper lip. Many fade or disappear. Some, like those on the back of the neck, may remain.
• Cavernous Hemangioma
Involve both skin and the underlying tissues. They are soft, compressible, and bluish. Overlying the cavernous hemangioma may be a capillary or strawberry hemangioma. Most will resolve spontaneously after getting larger during the first six to nine months of life. They should be watched for at least a year before attempting treatment.
• Strawberry Hemangioma
Bright red, spongy collection of elevated blood vessels. Rarely present at birth, they often appear during the first week of life. They may increase in size for the first six to nine months and then regress completely over the next year.

Breast Engorgement
Engorgement of the breasts is noticeable a few days after birth and is due to maternal hormones that cross the placenta into the baby. Milk may be secreted (witch's milk). The engorgement lasts about six to eight weeks.

Caput Succedenum

The head is misshapen and lopsided at birth, with swelling over the part of the head presented first. Small skin hemorrhages are frequent. Common among the firstborn and when the head is large. The swelling disappears within a few days.

Cephalohematoma

Localized swelling along the side (or both sides) of the head, usually to the back. Due to bleeding under the scalp, it appears a few days after birth and disappears in a few weeks. In some, calcium is deposited, and the swelling may persist for several months.

Craniotabes

The sides of the head can be indented with the finger, like a table tennis ball, but quickly spring back into place.

Erythema Toxicum *(Newborn Hives, Flea Bites)*

Benign skin condition seen frequently in newborn infants and lasting only a few days. Splotchy red areas on the trunk and extremities. Some contain a raised yellow blister in the center. Their cause is unknown.

Fontanel *(Soft Spot)*

The anterior fontanel is located at the top of the head, to the front. It is a diamond-shaped opening covered by a tough, thick membrane that closes completely with bone within 12 to 18 months. The posterior fontanel can also be felt in the newborn, at the top and to the back of the head. It closes by the age of two months.

Funnel Chest *(Pectus Excavatum)*

Hollow-like depression at the lower end of the chest bone (sternum). The mild ones require no treatment. The occasional severe cases may require surgical correction at a later age.

Harlequin Color Change

With the infant lying on a side, one side of the body may appear reddened and one side pale. The change in color occurs at the midline of the body. When the infant is placed on his or her back, the color changes disappear quickly.

Hydrocele

Swelling in the scrotum due to the collection of fluid surrounding the testicles. Fairly common in newborn males. Disappears within a few months.

Jaundice
Yellow discoloration of the skin, eyes, and membranes of the mouth seen in over 50 percent of full-term and 80 percent of premature infants. Due to the products released from the destruction of red cells in the newborn period and to immaturity of the liver. It appears about the second or third day of life and begins to disappear before the fifth day. It is usually gone by the third week.

Lanugo
A fine downy growth of hair prominent over the back, shoulders, forehead, and face. It is more noticeable in premature babies. It disappears in the first few weeks.

Laryngeal Stridor
Infant makes crowing noise when drawing breath. This common condition disappears in six to 18 months.

Milia
Obstructed sweat and oil glands appearing as pinhead-size white spots on the nose, cheeks, and chin of newborns and disappearing within a few weeks.

Mongolian Spots
Areas of bluish-gray color found over the lower back, particularly in babies with dark skin. They may be more widespread and found elsewhere on the body but tend to disappear within one to two years.

Moulding
A temporarily misshapen head caused by an overlapping of the skull bones to allow the infant to pass down the birth canal. The bones soon assume their proper position.

Nipples, Supernumerary
An accessory nipple present just below the regular breast, it may occur on one or both sides. No breast tissue develops nor does it function.

Periodic Respiration
Irregular, rapid, often shallow respiration for several seconds, followed by a few seconds when there is no breathing. Common in premature babies but may be seen in some full-term infants.

Pilondial Dimple
An indentation of the skin covering the lower end of the spine. In later life, these impressions may become infected.

Pseudotopsis
The eyelids in the newborn may operate independently. One eye may be open and the other partially or completely closed. This lasts only a short time.

Pseudostrabismus
The eyes give the impression of crossing. The epicanthus, a fold of skin at the inner angle of the eye, may be prominent, causing the band of white in one eye to appear narrower than in the other eye, producing an illusion of crossed eyes.

Reflexes
 • Grasp Reflex
Touching the palm of either of the infant's hands with a finger results in his or her grasping the finger vigorously.
 • Moro Reflex (Startle reflex)
In response to loud noises or sudden changes in position, both upper extremities are extended outward simultaneously. With the infant on his or her back on a flat surface, raising the baby a short distance and suddenly releasing him or her, elicits the startle reflex.
 • Rooting Reflex
When the cheek is stroked, the baby's head turns toward that side of the face, with mouth open for sucking.
 • Sucking Reflex
Vigorous sucking movements when lips are lightly touched.
 • Tonic Neck Reflex (Fencing position)
On the back, the head is turned to one side, causing the baby to extend the arm and leg on the side the head is turned to and flex the opposite upper and lower extremities.

Stools
 • Meconium
The newborn's bowel movements during the first few days of life. Appear greenish-black and slimy. About 70 percent of infants will have their first bowel movement within 12 hours; 95 percent, within 24 hours.
 • Transitional
Thin, loose, yellowish-green bowel movements seen from the third to fifth day of life. They contain mucus, curds of milk, and remnants of meconium.

Subconjunctival Hemorrhage
Small red spot of blood noticed in the white part of the eye due to rupture of a blood capillary during birth. It resolves quickly.

Sucking Callous
A small blister visible in the center of the upper lip of sucking infants. Condition lasts only a short time.

Tongue-tie
A condition in which the attachment from the tongue to the floor of the mouth (frenum) is located closer to the tip of the tongue than normal. In almost all cases, the frenum stretches as the infant gets older. Surgery is rarely necessary.

Umbilical Hernia
A bulge covered by skin at the naval that is most prominent with crying or straining. It often occurs around the time of birth. This is caused by a small opening in the muscles of the abdomen and contains a loop of bowel. The opening usually closes by itself during the first four to five years of life. The condition is more prominent among blacks than whites.

Undescended Testes *(Cryptorchidism)*
Both testes are found in the scrotum in a full-term male newborn. Cryptorchidism is the failure of one or both to descend normally. No treatment is necessary because the testes may descend later.

Vaginal Discharge
A white discharge from the vagina common in female newborns, it lasts a few weeks. Vaginal bleeding may also occur. This is related to maternal hormones that cross the placental barrier into the baby.

Vernix Caseosa
Cheeselike material that covers the skin of newborns and is thought to protect the infant against superficial infections.

Umbilical Cord Vessels
After it's cut, the end of the umbilical cord is carefully examined to determine the number of blood vessels. The normal number is three—two arteries and a vein. The presence of a single umbilical artery should make the physician suspicious of some congenital abnormalities, particularly abnormalities of the kidney.

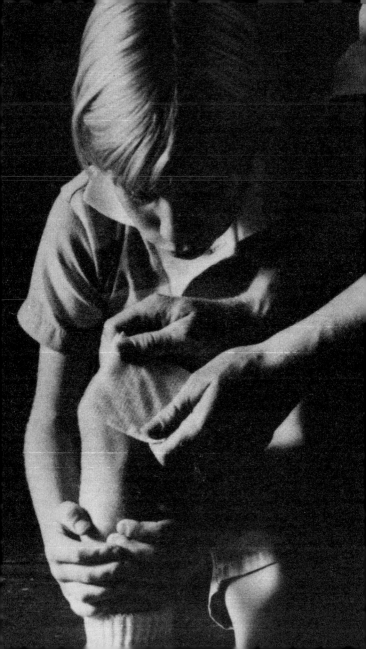

FIRST AID FOR CHILDREN

Accidents happen to young children. Fortunately, serious ones are rare. Yet each year, nearly 5,000 American boys and girls under five years of age die in mishaps—more than succumb to the seven leading fatal diseases combined. The most common causes of accidental death, in order, are automobile accidents, drowning, fires, swallowed objects, falls, poisoning, gunshot wounds, and inhalation of gas or fumes.

Earlier chapters have described safety precautions that should be taken by every household to protect young children. They include using seat belts and other restraining devices while riding in an automobile; fencing of swimming pools and close supervision in the bathtub; and "babyproofing" the house by removing from the child's reach all dangerous substances, objects small enough to be swallowed, poisons and medicines, and weapons. Close vigilance is necessary throughout infancy.

Teaching is also an important part of preventing accidents. If you do have a backyard pool or even a wading pool, make sure your child learns how to swim at the ealiest possible age. With firm but loving commands, make it clear that matches, fires, hot stoves and utensils, and cigarettes are no-nos and that dangerous play in high places where falls might occur is strictly taboo. Because you cannot watch every single minute, these lessons must be carried with a growing child. As he or she approaches school age, you'll want to teach how to ride a bicycle or tricycle safely and how to travel as a pedestrian.

No education will forestall all accidents. So be prepared. Most mishaps are minor; scrapes, bruises, bumps, and cuts are an inevitable part of growing up. Your role is to provide comfort

THE FAMILY FIRST-AID KIT

You can buy a fairly complete first-aid kit at a pharmacy or department store, but a prepared kit isn't necessary. Your own medicine cabinet already may be amply stocked. Always keep first-aid supplies together, so you won't have to hunt for them in an emergency. Check regularly to see if supplies need to be replenished. First-aid supplies for the car are necessary, too.

The list below comes from recommendations made by the American Medical Association and others concerning first-aid supplies you should have on hand.

Store these supplies in a moistureproof container; they may be transported on family outings. You may also wish to keep them in your car:

Quantity	Item
20	Paper cups, for giving fluids.
1	Flashlight.
1	Blanket.
	Newspapers (to place under the person on cold or wet ground).
10 of each	Individual ahdesive bandages in ¾-inch, 1-inch, ½-inch, and "round" spot sizes.
Box of 12	2x2 sterile first-aid dressings, individually packaged, for open wounds or burns.
Box of 12	4x4 sterile first-aid dressings.
1 roll	Roller gauze bandage, 1 inch by 5 yards.
1 roll	Roller gauze bandage, 2 inches by 5 yards.
1 roll each	Adhesive tape, 1- and 2-inch widths.
2	Triangular bandages, 36x36 inches, folded diagonally, for use as sling or to hold dressings.
6	Safety pins, 1½-inch size.
1 bar	Mild, white soap, for cleaning wounds, scratches, etc.
1 pair	Scissors with blunt tips, for cutting bandages and tape.
1 pair	Tweezers, for removing splinters.
1	Tourniquet—wide strip of cloth, at least 3 to 4 inches by 20 inches, for use when bleeding can be controlled in no other way.
1 container	Syrup of ipecac, for use in suspected poisoning.
1 3- to 4-ounce bottle	Rubbing alcohol.
1 pair	Nail clippers.
1 container	Aspirin or aspirin substitute (acetaminophen), adult strength.
1 container	Aspirin or aspirin substitute (acetaminophen), children's strength.
1 bottle	Calamine lotion, for insect bites.

and a little basic first aid. More serious emergencies call for medical intervention or trained help. However, you must be ready to take interim measures until the community rescue squad or paramedic unit arrives or the injured child can be brought to a hospital or physician.

Plan what you'll do if your child or a playmate is injured seriously. Post emergency numbers near the telephone. The list should include the common 911 number, if your community uses it, plus numbers for police, fire department, rescue squad, poison control center, and physician. Write down the numbers, and try each of them in advance to be sure they have been listed correctly. Test them periodically to be sure they haven't changed. Minutes count in an emergency, and it's no time to page through a telephone book with nervous fingers.

Know the most direct route to the doctor's office or emergency room; be able to direct someone along that route, so you can comfort the child rather than drive the car yourself. Always ask your doctor whether you should bring the child to the office or whether the doctor will meet you at the hospital.

A basic first-aid course is helpful. The local chapter of the American Red Cross or a nearby hospital may teach such courses; at the least, someone there can tell you where one is taught. Keep this book or another simple first-aid manual in a place where you can find it quickly. Some pharmacies distribute a basic one-page first-aid guide that can be posted on the family bulletin board or inside the bathroom medicine cabinet.

RULES TO REMEMBER

Regardless of the nature of an accident or injury, certain rules for treatment and care apply. Here are the most important:

1. Don't get hurt yourself. You'll be valueless to the victim if you're injured in a foolhardy attempt to help. If you cannot reach the victim without risking injury, wait for assistance.

2. If the child is in danger of further injury and you can safely move him or her, do so, but always try to keep movement to a minimum.

3. If there appears to be an injury to the head or neck, do not move the child unless absolutely necessary; then try to move the head and neck as a unit. Cushion head and neck with pillows when moving.

4. If the child is unconscious, be sure the head is turned to the side, or tilt back the head to make sure the airway is open.

5. Cover the child with a light blanket.

6. Give fluids by mouth only if the child is awake. A good

rule is to allow the child to drink only if he or she can hold a glass. If in doubt, don't, because the child may require an anesthetic or surgery later.

7. Avoid stimulants and pain killers. Minor medications, such as aspirin or aspirin substitute (acetaminophen), may be given in dosages appropriate for size and weight; they're usually listed on the container.

8. Remain with the child; send others for help. If you are alone and must go for help, make sure an unconscious child is breathing and that the airway is open.

FIRST-AID TREATMENTS
Here are basic procedures for handling common childhood injuries and emergencies.

Abscess. If a tender, inflamed, and throbbing area develops around a finger or toenail or at the site of a cut (signs of an infection), apply a warm, wet compress to relieve pain. A thick sterile bandage, clean towel, or sanitary napkin soaked in warm water will do. Change the compress as it cools. The moisture will soften the skin, allowing it to break and release the pus. An abscess is seldom an emergency but should be examined by a physician. Watch for a fever, a swelling surrounding the abscess, or red streaks that travel up the involved limb.

Animal bites. Wash the wound thoroughly with soap and water to remove saliva; hold the wounded area under running water to rinse it well. Dry with clean gauze. The wound should be examined by a physician; a tetanus shot may be recommended. Although rabies is rare among urban pets, the animal should be identified and observed for a period of ten days to see if it develops symptoms of the disease. If the bite is the result of an unprovoked attack by a wild animal, such as a skunk, bat, squirrel, or chipmunk, an attempt should be made to capture the animal; if it cannot be caught, anti-rabies shots may be necessary. In some communities, you're required to report all animal bites to health authorities. Your own domestic pets should be inoculated against rabies, and the inoculations should be kept current.

Human bites. If the skin is not broken, wash the area with mild soap and water, and dry with clean gauze. An antiseptic or dressing is not necessary. Ask your physician about any human bite that breaks the skin, because such bites frequently become infected.

Bee, wasp, and hornet stings. A cold compress or calamine lotion will relieve itching; diluted household ammonia or rubbing alcohol applied to the bite and surrounding area may also help. If the stinger—seen as a small dark object in the center of the wound—remains in place, scrape or flick it out with a fingernail; do not attempt to remove it with tweezers. The movement may inject more venom into the wound.

For intense itching or multiple bites, give the child a cool bath to break the itching cycle, and apply a soothing bath lotion. Oral antihistamines also may be given. In severe cases, a physician may prescribe an ointment to be applied to the bite.

Some children have a severe reaction to only a single bite. If the child's throat or the interior of the mouth swells, if breathing becomes difficult, or if the child becomes drowsy or unconscious, immediate medical attention is called for. Phone your physician and take the child to the emergency room of a hospital. Discuss with the doctor what to do in the event of a repeat bite.

Broken bones. Don't attempt to move a child who may have a broken bone. Speed is seldom important in the treatment of broken bones. Keep the child covered and lying down while waiting for the emergency squad or ambulance. Give nothing by mouth in case the child requires an anesthetic or surgery later.

Do not attempt to set broken bones. If the child must be moved from an exposed or dangerous place, apply an emergency splint fashioned from any rigid material, including boards, sticks, rolled newspapers, or even a folded pillow. The splint should be on both sides of the affected limb and should extend above or below the adjacent joints. To immobilize the area of the break, tie the splint with bandages above and below it. If the spine may be fractured, do not attempt to move the child under any circumstances. Wait for emergency help.

Bruises. Most require no treatment. For major bumps, apply ice or cold cloths immediately to keep down swelling. Elevating the bruised limb will also lessen swelling. If the skin is broken, treat the bruise as an open wound.

Burns. If the area is small, immerse the burned part in water or hold directly under an open faucet, to relieve pain and reduce local reaction to the burn. Wash with a mild soap. Burn ointment

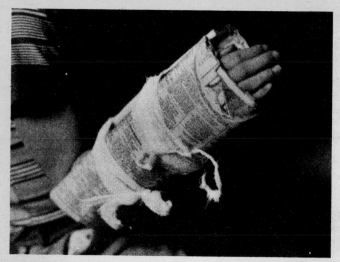

If a child with a broken bone must be moved, apply a splint made from any rigid material. Place on both sides of limb, extend above and below adjacent joints, and tie with bandages above and below break.

or butter is not necessary for minor burns. A dry, sterile dressing will keep out air and provide relief from pain.

Do not attempt to treat major burns, especially those in which the skin is broken. Never deliberately break blisters. Cover the child immediately with a clean sheet, and take him or her to a hospital; or summon the rescue squad.

Chemical burns. When the burn is caused by lye, caustic soda, or any other corrosive substance, you must flood the burned area immediately with cold water; strip off all clothing that may have come in contact with the chemical, and quickly place the child under a shower. Acid burns should also be flooded, then rinsed with a neutralizing solution of baking soda. After washing the area, you should phone a physician or the local rescue squad. Chemical burns should always be examined by medical personnel, especially if the corrosive substance has dried.

Eye injuries. If the eye is cut, torn, or damaged, do not attempt treatment; cover both eyes (the eyes work together, so cover the uninjured eye because its movement may affect the injured one), and take the child immediately to a physician or a hospital's emergency room. Bruises to the eye that cause internal bleeding should also receive immediate medical attention. If you can see bloody discoloration when looking at the child's pupil, take the victim to a hospital.

Specks in the eye. Keep the child from rubbing the eye, because the object may scratch the membrane covering the eyeball. A time-honored treatment is to draw the upper eyelid down and away from the eye, holding it by the lashes. Tears may wash out the object.

If this method fails, flush the eye with clear water or an eyewash. You may also place the child's head directly under a moderate stream of water, so the water splashes directly on the eye.

If chemicals—including cosmetics or toothpaste, as well as lime, plaster, and other caustics—enter the eye, flood with water, then call a physician or emergency department for immediate treatment.

Fainting. Rare in children, fainting is caused by a temporary deficiency in the blood supply to the brain. The child is usually pale and may crumple to the ground. Keep the victim lying down until he or she recovers consciousness, lowering the head or elevating the feet to hasten the return of blood to the brain. Make the child more comfortable by loosening tight clothing. Sprinkling water on the face to revive the victim isn't necessary.

Falls. In any fall from a high place or when the child is unconscious or seems to have suffered a severe impact, take him or her immediately for emergency treatment. Or phone the physician and report the symptoms. For infants, immediate evaluation is very important.

Even if the fall seems slight, a physician should be consulted if the child appears drowsy, acts dazed, turns pale, has memory lapses, or vomits after the accident.

Frostbite. If a child who has been outdoors in cold weather has tissue that appears blue or black and becomes painful indoors, suspect frostbite. Cover the affected area with your own hand to raise temperature and restore circulation gradually, or cover with warm—not hot—towels or blankets. Soak the affected part in lukewarm water. Do not rub the frozen area with snow or apply intense direct heat in an attempt to raise the temperature quickly.

Hiccups. These usually clear up spontaneously without treatment, but everyone has a favorite remedy for bothersome cases. Two suggestions are: 1. give the child a teaspoon of granulated sugar, to be swallowed dry; 2. use a tongue depressor or a small spoon to tickle the back of the child's throat, causing him or her to gag. Other remedies include simply ignoring them, having the child drink a glass of water as slowly as possible (some persons add a pinch of baking soda), having the child hold the breath as long as he or she can, or pulling out the tongue as far as possible to trigger the gag reflex. Persistent or recurrent hiccups lasting for several hours should be reported to a physician.

Infected wounds. Signs of infection around a cut or scrape are redness and swelling, often accompanied by a feeling of heat and throbbing pain. If possible, immerse the infected area in warm water. Repeat three or four times daily. If the area is not easily immersed, apply a bulky bandage made from a small towel or sanitary napkin, and pour the solution over it, repeating the treatment until the inflammation has disappeared. Consult a physician if the area is large or seems to be spreading.

Mouth-to-mouth resuscitation. Any time a child has stopped breathing, cardio-pulmonary resuscitation (CPR) may be necessary. Some incidents that may stop breathing include immersion in water, lack of oxygen, electric shock, or inhalation of gas. Whatever the cause, move the child to safety and begin CPR at once; if breathing is stopped for more than four to six minutes, irreversible brain damage or death may result. If more than one adult is present, one should phone for a rescue squad while the other begins treatment. If you are alone, drag the child to the phone, take the phone off the hook, dial Operator or the 911 emergency number, and give address and key information between breaths.

CPR cannot be learned from a book under emergency circumstances. Take a CPR course beforehand. The American Red Cross, the local heart association, the YMCA, or other agencies provide such instruction in many communities. At the least, a parent should become familiar with the technique by reading this book or other instructional material beforehand.

To start resuscitation, place the child on his or her back, and clean visible foreign matter from the mouth with your fingers. Tilt the head back, with chin pointed toward the ceiling, and use both hands to lift the lower jaw from behind so that it juts out, preventing the tongue from falling back. This will provide a clear

Left: For mouth-to-mouth resuscitation, tilt the head back, with chin pointed toward ceiling. Use both hands to lift the lower jaw from behind. It should jut out, preventing the tongue from falling back.

Right: Place your mouth over the child's nose and mouth to make a leak-proof seal. Breathe into the child's nose and mouth with shallow puffs of air—about 30 per minute. See text for more details.

airway. Place your mouth over the child's nose and mouth to make a leak-proof seal. Breathe into the child's nose and mouth with shallow puffs of air, at a rate of about 30 per minute; the pace should be more rapid for an infant, slower for an older child, but not as slow as the adult rate of 20 breaths per minute.

Your breath should cause the child's chest to rise and fall. If it does not and breath doesn't seem to be entering the child's body, check the position of the jaw to be sure the airway is clear. Turn the child's head to the side briefly to allow any substances to clear from the throat. If the airway still seems to be blocked, hold a small child upside down by the ankles, and give several sharp whacks between the shoulder blades. In a larger child, push with both hands at the inverted "V" of the rib cage to force the diaphragm upward, a movement that will dislodge any obstructing materials.

Also check the child's pulse and circulation. If you cannot detect a pulse, attempt to restore circulation by stimulating the heartbeat. Between two successive breaths, press down sharply on the child's chest in the middle of the breastbone for five compressions. Don't hesitate to apply pressure; children's ribs are flexible enough to withstand the shock. In any case, a few damaged ribs are a small price to pay for recovery. If two adults are present, one may apply pressure to the breastbone, while the other provides respiration at the rate of one breath after each five compressions.

For use in resuscitation, a clear plastic mask that covers both the nose and mouth may be purchased in a drugstore. One size fits adults and children. The triangular shape can be reversed for treating youngsters. Breathing tubes, formerly used, now are considered potentially damaging to children and should be discarded.

Recovery should occur quickly, usually within 15 minutes, except in cases of electric shock, drug overdose, or monoxide poisoning, which may require longer resuscitation. But treatment should be continued until help arrives.

Nosebleed. Pinch both nostrils closed between thumb and forefinger. Pressure should be applied just below the nasal bone. Keep the child in an upright position, so blood does not trickle back into the throat. Maintain the pressure with your finger for at least two minutes, then test to see if the bleeding has stopped. Another method is to place a small wedge of cotton inside the nostril, holding it there with pressure outside the nostril for five minutes. If nosebleed recurs or persists, seek medical help.

Poisoning. Drugs, medicines, cleaning fluids, and other substances are the most common causes of childhood poisoning. If you see evidence that a child has swallowed any of these, act fast. Telephone the poison control center in your community, if one exists, or your physician or hospital, and be prepared to give immediate first-aid treatment.

First, try to determine what was swallowed, because treatment differs according to the substance. But don't waste time looking for the container or for an antidote; information on bottles and cans may be out of date.

For many poisons, the doctor or poison control center may recommend syrup of ipecac to induce vomiting. Have some available—it can be purchased without prescription. The usual dose is one tablespoon of syrup of ipecac for one-year-olds and above; two teaspoons for children under one year. If vomiting has not occurred within 20 minutes, the dose may be repeated. Do not give ipecac unless instructed.

When the child vomits, hold him or her face downward in your lap so the vomited material clears the throat and is not swallowed. If vomiting does not occur within 20 to 30 minutes, the doctor may suggest a second dose of ipecac. The dose should be repeated only once.

If ipecac is not available, vomiting may be sometimes induced by feeding the child warm water or milk and then tickling the back of the throat with a tongue depressor or spoon.

Unless you're told otherwise, do not wait for vomiting to occur before getting medical help. If possible, retrieve the poisonous substance and take it with you.

Ipecac should *not* be used and vomiting should *not* be induced when the offending substance is a corrosive such as lye, cleanser, disinfectant, ammonia, or drain or toilet-bowl cleaner, because substances that burn on the way down also may burn on the way up; nor should ipecac be used for kerosene, gasoline, or turpentine. In these cases, the physician or poison-control center may administer medication to offset the effects and speed transit through the system.

Poison ivy, poison oak, and other skin poisonings. Thoroughly wash the affected area with soap and water to remove the irritating plant oils. Then repeat the lathering five or six times. Strip off all clothing that may have come into contact with the plant, and launder it immediately. Wash the area again—this time with rubbing alcohol—rinse with clear water, and dry.

Small, local patches of rash may be relieved by applying a topical drying agent (calamine lotion, for example). In extensive cases or when the outbreak oozes, appears infected, or continues to spread, consult a physician.

Shock. Shock may accompany any serious injury. It results from an injury-caused disturbance of the supply of oxygen to the tissues and inadequate blood pressure. Signs of shock are: rapid but weak pulse; pale face; cold, clammy skin; nausea; shallow breathing; and thirst. Keep in mind that not all of these symptoms will be present in every case.

Keep the patient lying flat, head level or lower than the rest of the body or with legs elevated 12 to 18 inches. Cover with a light blanket or coat to lessen the loss of body heat.

If the child is thirsty, small amounts of water may be given. Other fluids should not be given because of the possibility of anesthetic or surgery later.

Snakebite. A surprisingly large proportion of poisonous snakebite victims are small children, who are likely to be playing in suburban woodpiles or gardens where snakes may be found. But in most cases, the bite does not penetrate the skin; even when the skin is broken, rarely is the wound injected with the snake's poison. Very few children are endangered by poisonous snakebite and require anti-venom, horse-serum treatment.

Indications of venomous snakebite are severe swelling and pain at the site of the bite. Usually, two puncture wounds from the fangs can be seen. To be effective, treatment must begin immediately. Summon a physician or rescue squad, or set out for an emergency center, notifying personnel that you are en route. Begin first-aid measures in the meantime. Remove the child from the danger area; make no attempt to capture the snake to determine if it is poisonous. Carry the child; do not allow the child to walk or move about. Tie a tourniquet (see page 392) above the joint above the bite, tightly enough to restrict the blood flow but not to cut it off completely. *Do not pack the wound in ice or give the child alcohol*.

You may attempt to remove the venom from the wound by suction. Make incisions one-eighth inch long at each fang mark, and apply suction by mouth or suction cup. This must be done within 30 minutes. Suction is particularly important if the wound is on the body, neck, or head.

Because many people fear snakes and snakebite, reassurance is very important. Remain with the child, and try to reduce anxiety.

Splinters. Foreign bodies that protrude from the flesh may be removed with tweezers or the fingers. If the entire splinter has been removed, wash the area with mild soap and water, then apply antiseptic. If the splinter is completely embedded in the tissue, wash the area first. Then sterilize a needle or knife point by passing it through a flame. Remove the splinter by probing it with the sterilized point, being careful not to touch the point with your fingers. Use an antiseptic afterward.

If the object is buried deeply or is too large to be removed easily without damaging the surrounding flesh, seek emergency help, or visit your physician. A tetanus booster may be necessary if none has been given within five years.

Sprains. Injuries to a wrist, ankle, or knee may be either fractures of a bone or sprains (a stretching of the ligaments surrounding the joint). It is not always possible to determine the difference without an X ray. Both cause pain, swelling, and limited use of the joint. All such injuries should be seen by a physician or emergency personnel.

Swelling may be kept down by soaking the joint in cold water or by applying cloths soaked in ice or cold water. An icepack may also be used. Keep the limb elevated. If movement causes marked pain, immobilize the joint with a "pillow" splint. Place the limb on the pillow, fold around the affected area, and tie with a cord. Also use a pillow splint to transport the patient.

Sunburn. Babies and children have tender skin that burns easily. Sunbathing should be limited to the early morning and late afternoon when the sun is low. As with adults, exposure should be gradual. Five minutes is enough time to spend in the sun the first day, with periods gradually lengthening.

If a child is to be in the sun for an extended period, cover exposed areas with a sunscreen ointment containing PABA—paraminobenzoic acid. You will find the letters on the label.

When serious sunburn does occur, notify your physician. For mild cases, ease discomfort by placing cold, wet compresses on the affected areas or by applying cold cream, petroleum jelly, olive oil, or a baby lotion.

Swallowed objects. Most small objects swallowed by a child will pass through the system harmlessly. This is especially true of buttons and other round items, but even open safety pins, tacks, and similar sharp objects usually do not harm the stomach or bowel.

Do not give the child a laxative, and do not induce vomiting. Notify a physician, who may follow the object's progress by X ray. If the physician considers the object dangerous—and particularly if it has been ingested into the lungs—it may be extracted by inserting a flexible instrument down the windpipe.

When a small child chokes on a bit of food or other object, hold him or her upside down by the ankles, and whack several times on the back between the shoulder blades. For larger children, hold from behind with arms around the child's middle, and press sharply at the space just below the inverted "V" of the ribs. You may also press in the same manner from the front, to pressure the diaphragm and dislodge the object with a thrust of air up the windpipe.

Tick bites. Ticks are small insects that burrow into the skin; several varieties transmit serious diseases. They are common in damp grass and wooded areas during the spring and may attach themselves to small children and domestic animals, especially in the hair.

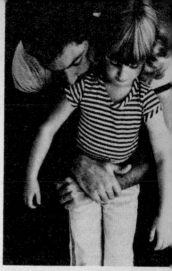

Above, left: When a small child chokes on a piece of food or other object, hold him or her upside down by the ankles, and whack forcefully several times on the back between the shoulder blades.

Above, right: If the child is too big to hold by the ankles, hold from behind with arms around the middle. Then press sharply at space just below inverted "V" of the ribs. See below for another method.

Below: As you would from behind, you may also press in the same manner from the front, applying pressure to the diaphragm and dislodging the object with a thrust of air up the windpipe.

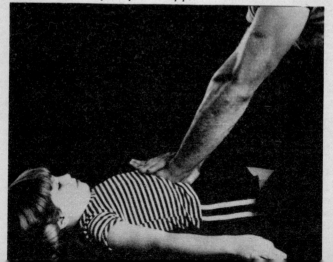

During tick season, routinely inspect small children who have been playing outdoors. If a tick is found, do not pull it off by the portion of the body protruding from the site; that may leave the head embedded in the flesh. Instead, cover the tick with petroleum jelly, facial cream, or other thick substance. After a few minutes, remove it carefully with tweezers. The wound should be treated with antiseptic.

Toothache. A child's aching tooth should be seen by a dentist as soon as possible. In the event a toothache strikes at night or when a dentist is not available, give the child aspirin or aspirin substitute (acetaminophen), appropriate for age and size; do not use stronger pain killers. If a cavity can be seen, clean it out with a toothpick tipped with cotton, then plug it with cotton dipped in oil of cloves. A heating pad, hot-water bottle, or ice pack may also relieve discomfort.

Unconsciousness. Serious accidents, such as a severe injury or burn, poisoning, gas inhalation, or electric shock, may cause unconsciousness. Rarely in children, sunstroke or heat exhaustion may also cause unconsciousness.

If breathing has stopped, begin mouth-to-mouth resuscitation at once (see page 384). If breathing appears adequate, keep the patient lying on the back, with head turned to the side to keep the airway open. Remove constricting clothing, and cover lightly. Summon emergency help; don't wait for the child to come to. Take care in moving an unconscious child because of the possibility of head injury.

Don't give water or other substances by mouth to an unconscious child, and don't shake him or her in an attempt at revival.

Wounds with minor bleeding. Clean the wound gently with a soft washcloth, using mild soap and water. Begin at the edge of the wound and wash away from it, not toward it. Most bits of dirt or other contaminating substances that remain in the wound can be removed by washing; if not, pick them out with a sterilized tweezers. Afterward, flush the wound with clean water.

Wounds with severe bleeding. Don't bother to clean the wound; stop the bleeding first. Place a sterile gauze pad, clean handkerchief, or sanitary napkin over the wound, and apply firm, steady pressure with the heel of your hand. Maintain the pressure until the bleeding stops, usually within five minutes. If bleeding is in one of the limbs, keep the limb elevated. Consult a physician about gaping wounds; sutures may be needed to promote healing.

If the bleeding does not stop, a tourniquet may be tried—but only as a last resort. Tourniquets—tight bands of cloth or rope wound around the limb above the wound to shut off the blood supply—are dangerous because tissues die if deprived of circulation for too long. If you resort to a tourniquet, write down, or tell someone, the exact time at which it was applied. Loosen it regularly to restore circulation.

Puncture wounds. Any wound caused by a sharp object that might have carried germs deep into the flesh should be seen by a physician. This is true even if the object appears to be clean. Wash the wound with mild soap and water, rinse with cold running water, cover with a bandage, and seek medical help. A tetanus booster may also be necessary if shots are not current.

INDEX

In the shadows
a color-blind photographer
can see what no one else can see...

But murder is never black and white.

THE MAGICIAN'S TALE

"...mesmerizes."
—*People*

"A strange, seductive story
[that] shows us light and dark...
reality and illusion, even good and evil,
in ways we never imagined."
—*The New York Times Book Review*

The most original and acclaimed thriller of the year

The Magician's Tale
David Hunt

"[Hunt] mesmerizes with his sleight of hand. But the book's lingering spell lies in the way its heroine's perspective enables us to see, as if for the first time, her beloved city in all its chiaroscuro splendor."

—*People*

"If you like your thrillers atmospheric, kinky, and brooding, then *The Magician's Tale* is right up your alley. David Hunt's writing is spare, savvy, and San Francisco street-smart. This is one of those books that suck you in, page by page, until you're firmly in the world created by the author. A very intense read."

—Nelson DeMille

"I read this novel at warp speed, and with great pleasure. *The Magician's Tale* is truly original— atmospheric, seductively written, and compellingly suspenseful. The world of this book is unique, as is its unusual protagonist."

—Richard North Patterson

continued . . .

"Hunt provides a gritty account of the city's darker side."

—*Booklist*

"*The Magician's Tale* is a deftly penned thriller with many attractions ... tightly assembled, cleverly paced, and as smooth as a hustler's lies in the dark."

—*Denver Post*

"Hunt knows how to create an original protagonist. His Farrow is smart, sassy and sexy ... Hunt's carefully laid out setup delivers."

—*The Hartford Courant*

"This is a melancholy and imaginative work of violence and mystery."

—*Bookman News*

"An exciting mystery that takes the reader on an intriguing tour of the foggy San Francisco underground communities."

—Harriet Klausner, *Mystery Zone*

The Magician's Tale

David Hunt

BERKLEY BOOKS,
NEW YORK

This book is a work of fiction. The events described are imaginary, and
the characters are fictitious and not intended to represent specific living
persons.

THE MAGICIAN'S TALE

A Berkley Book / published by arrangement with
the author

PRINTING HISTORY
G. P. Putnam's Sons edition / June 1997
Published simultaneously in Canada
Berkley edition / September 1998

The Penguin Putnam Inc. World Wide Web site address is
http://www.penguinputnam.com

ISBN: 0-425-16482-9

BERKLEY®
Berkley Books are published by The Berkley Publishing Group,
a member of Penguin Putnam Inc.,
375 Hudson Street, New York, New York 10014.
BERKLEY and the "B" design
are trademarks belonging to Berkley Publishing Corporation.

PRINTED IN THE UNITED STATES OF AMERICA

10 9 8 7 6 5 4 3 2 1

The Illusion

This illusion is performed out of doors, often in a dusty field. The magician works inside a circle surrounded by spectators, assisted by a young girl, his obedient daughter.

Near the end of his show, the magician suddenly and unexpectedly takes hold of the girl, pulls a dagger from beneath his cloak and slits her throat.

Blood spurts, spattering their smocks and sometimes the clothing of spectators nearby.

The magician stuffs the body of the girl into a bulb basket he has used throughout the show. Once she is inside, he covers the basket with a cloth, and mutters incantations.

Removing the cloth, he shows the audience that the basket is empty, the body of the girl gone.

Just then the spectators hear a shout from beyond the circle. They turn to see the girl gaily running through the crowd into the magician's waiting arms.

—J. M. FROST,
Strange & Extraordinary Feats of Indian Magic
(1888)

The
Magician's
Tale

One

The sun is about to set. I check myself in the mirror—glowing eyes, dark brows, small triangular face, medium-length dark hair parted on the side. I brush down some wisps so they fall across my forehead, then dress to go out—black T-shirt, jeans, black leather jacket, sneakers, Contax camera around my neck.

I wear black to blend in. My hope is that by dressing dark and with my face half concealed by my hair, I can slink along the streets, barely seen, covertly stealing images.

I pause at my living room window. Dusk is magic time, the sky still faintly lit. Streetlamps are on and lights glow from windows, making the city look mysterious and serene. The view's so spectacular it's hard to tear myself away: North Beach, Telegraph Hill, the Bay Bridge sharply defined, all still, silent, glowing behind the glass.

I move to my telescope, set the crosshairs on a penthouse terrace just below Coit Tower. The image is so clear I feel I can touch it if I reach out. Garden chairs, pots overflowing with geraniums, sliding glass doors leading to an art-filled living room behind. No lights on inside.

The Judge must be working late. I know him well. I have no lover now.

I take another moment to take in the view. I'd like to stay, watch the sky turn black, perhaps wait until the lights come on in that living room across the valley. But it's time to go out; I have an appointment with a friend.

It's chilly tonight. I turn the collar of my jacket up, peer around. A cable car is poised at the top of Lombard. Tourists disembark to descend the famous crooked street. I enter the park in front of my building, named for George Sterling, poet of the city. He composed some good lines, was eloquent on the fog, wrote "its touch is kind," described San Francisco as this "cool gray city of love." He also wrote: "At the end of our streets are stars." Not bad. Unfortunately, Sterling was no Carl Sandburg, but then San Francisco isn't a "city of the big shoulders" either.

I pause by the Alice Marble Tennis Courts, turn to look back at my building, slender in the dusk. I make out lights in some of the apartments and the glow of a Japanese paper lantern in mine. I shrug, cross the park, look for the young bearded homeless guy who sometimes sleeps amidst the bushes. Failing to find him, I take the stairs that descend the steep western slope of Russian Hill.

Polk Street: It's quiet, residential at its upper end, but as I stride south it takes on a different character. Apartment buildings give way to stores and restaurants, then, slowly, block by block, to sleaze.

Around California Street they begin to appear—the crazed, the addicts, the dispossessed. Sad, sick, broken, they perch on the sidewalk beside signs and cups, or slouch within doorways against glossy garbage bags filled with their possessions.

I pass a cavernous old movie house, a trio of junk shops, a metaphysical bookstore, cheap Chinese restaurants, funky hotels and saloons, sleazy erotic boutiques and adult-film rental joints. The strip here, called, sometimes affectionately, more often disparagingly, Polk Gulch, intersects with alleys bearing the names of beautiful trees: Fern, Hemlock, Myrtle, Olive, Willow.

In these passageways I observe young men poised alone against the sides of buildings, others lingering in small groups, twos and threes. There's a glow about them, a force field of energy. Hustlers of different races, objects of desire, they stand still, silent, awaiting clients.

I've been roaming this neighborhood since the beginning of the summer, always at night, always armed with my Contax. Those first weeks I didn't take pictures, preferring simply to look, explore, make my presence known. As I picked out probable subjects, they too began to notice me. Spotting my camera, they gave me a name, Bug, short for Shutterbug. I disliked it but pretended I didn't, since a street name here connotes acceptance.

"Hey! It's Bug. She's on the street." Word flashes down the Gulch as if by semaphore.

Some also note my affliction.

"You blind, girl?" a scrawny, tattooed kid bellowed at me yesterday as I staggered along on one of my rare daylight excursions. "What's with the shades, Bug? Drugged out?" Then, when I ignored him: "Think you're a fuckin' star?"

I know better than to respond to taunts, a lesson I learned painfully on school playgrounds years ago. But to those who become my friends, I cheerfully reveal my handicap.

I'm an achromat, which means I'm completely color-blind.

The correct name for the malady is autosomal recessive achromatopsia. It's rare; I doubt there're five thousand of us in the U.S. I lack cone function in my retinas and thus cannot see colors. My visual acuity is poor, though better than most complete achromats. My biggest problem is photophobia, the reason that in daylight I must wear heavy, dark red wraparound shades. Outside, on a brilliant sun-filled San Francisco afternoon, the rods in my eyes become saturated, the world goes white, I become lost in a dazzling blizzard—a sensation, I'm told, close to what vision normals experience as snow blindness.

But there are advantages. One is aesthetic—seeing the world uniquely in terms of gray tones instead of hues. Another is good night vision. In darkness, I like to think, I can see like a cat.

I'm searching for Tim. He called this afternoon, said he needed to talk. There was urgency in his voice, perhaps even fear. I offered to meet him at once, but he said he had to see someone first. We agreed to meet at his spot on Hemlock Alley at seven then go up to the Richmond for dinner since he didn't think he'd feel like hanging around the Gulch.

It's 7:10 now and I see no sign of him as I occupy his niche beside the Dumpster. The brick wall behind me, against which I've photographed him many times, is thickly layered with graffiti—names, symbols, dates, obscenities, most fading, a few freshly applied. I wait as the traffic thins out on Polk, but few passersby peer down the alley. It's still too early for the chicken hawks.

Tim and I met when I started taking pictures here. Of all the street people I've come to know these last months, he's the only one I think of as a real friend. He doesn't know it yet but he's also on his way to becoming the central actor in my project. All my best shots frame him—alone, surrounded by others, or on the periphery of a group. As for the formal portraits, his are the strongest. It's his eyes, I think, so large and luminous, and the fine shape of his chin and jaw that make the camera love him. He's got the cheekbones of a Greek god, the unruly hair of a savage. Whether pouting in his niche against the graffiti-scarred wall or posing bare to the waist on Angel Island with the city gleaming white behind, he emerges as a splendid modern ephebe—urban warrior, heroic, fragile, seductive. Yes, the camera loves him. The photographer loves him too.

Seven-thirty, getting cold, not a typical October night. *Where are you, Tim?*

He claims he's twenty, but barely looks seventeen, perfect disproof of the adage that a life of vice will mark your face. His unsullied beauty is his capital. Creamy of skin, fair of cheek, he's the eternal adolescent of his clients' dreams. He tells me he intends to work the street a few more years, save his money and retire. He pauses, then confides he's already got fifty thousand dollars stashed. When I stare at him in disbelief, he shows me the smile of a sphinx. Surely if you have that much, I tell him, it's time to quit right now.

Gently he shakes his head. "Not yet, Kay. I still enjoy it. The people." He laughs. "Well, most of them. The adventure too, not knowing what'll happen, who I'll meet. It's like an addiction—the money, being desired so much, people pay big-time just to touch me. And it's fun playing diamond-in-the-rough." He shows me his sweetest grin. "Or rhinestone, as the case may be."

Clever boy!

Yet even as I'm appalled by his casual disregard for my warnings—that sooner or later he'll fall into the clutches of a sociopath or be infected with HIV—I'm still beguiled by his glamour. Street hustler as psychic explorer—that has emerged as my theme. In my pictures I want to capture the lives of those who, by offering their bodies to danger and to lust, risk all and by so doing achieve a kind of stature.

"So," I ask him, "when you retire what will you do?"

"Live the good life," he says softly. He's got it all figured out. He'll move down to Mexico, a town called San Miguel de Allende. Already, he tells me, he's picked out the house.

"Yo! You there! You for sale?"

It's Tim's friend Crawford, a lean, blond Minnesotan hunk who somehow manages to maintain a permanent tan.

Crawf beams. "You look really hot there, Bug. If I had some bucks I'd buy you in a flash."

Hustler's banter . . . yet to be thirty-five and female and told one is attractive in a milieu where maleness and youth are the sole components of allure—I'm flattered.

"Waiting for Tim," I tell him.

"Saw him last night. Not since."

"If you do, tell him I'm here, okay?"

Crawf nods, smiles, tells me again how hot I look, then saunters off like a panther.

In fact, I've discovered, hustlers sometimes do purchase one another's services. Tim says it's fun to play the john once in a while, and that he's always flattered when another street kid wants to pay him for sex. When that happens, he tells me, street etiquette requires he approach the kid a few days later and reciprocate.

It's a quarter to eight and I'm getting impatient. I've never known Tim to be late. I decide to cruise the Gulch awhile, then check back. I slide over to the intersection, turn the corner, become part of the stream.

Silver-haired businessmen hauling briefcases, sweaty evening joggers in Lycra workout suits, frugal shoppers, doting couples, apprehensive tourists—we all run the gauntlet here, never certain what the street people will do.

An old Asian lady, Mao-era haircut and crazed eyes, gesticulates angrily at my camera. Stepping toward a storefront to avoid her, I nearly trip over a street vendor in swami position presiding over a display of flashlight batteries and tattered paperbacks. "Watch it, Bub!"

Is he mispronouncing my streetname, or does he think I'm a guy? No matter, I hurry on.

Nearly everyone here under twenty-five displays a piercing. I note ringed eyebrows, lips, tacked tongues. If this is what they show, I wonder, what baubles must dangle beneath their clothes?

I'm fascinated by the hustling scene, though it was fear and revulsion that originally drew me. Last spring, Maddy

Yamada, my photography coach, suggested I get out of the studio, go into the street, start photographing what I feared. Struck by her advice, I realized that for years I feared the Gulch . . . and so decided to take it on.

At first I didn't know what I was after. It's easy and glib to document commercial sex. But on the Gulch, I became aware those early weeks, there were more interesting images to be captured. Meeting hustlers, I discovered unexpected qualities—gentleness, courage, love of adventure, even a desire to heal—which gave the lie to the view that those who sell their bodies must be desperate or hold themselves cheap.

With Maddy's help, her critiques of my proof sheets, I began to sharpen my vision. It wasn't, I understood, just the hustlers I should shoot, but the reactions to them in other strollers' eyes. Not just apprehension or fear . . . also cunning, avarice, lust. So, I asked myself: Who here really are the stalkers and the prey? And I thought: Perhaps with my camera I'll find out.

I spot Knob at the corner of Polk and Bush. He's talking to a middle-aged bald guy in a cashmere turtleneck. Knob's nearly thirty, old for the Gulch, sports a goatee, has close-cropped hair and a husky fireplug build. Tonight he wears tight jeans, dark T-shirt, leather vest. Occasionally, I've heard, he'll do a session himself, but more often he acts as broker, negotiating deals for kids whom chicken hawks, fearful of jailbait, are too timid to approach.

Knob gestures, Baldy nods, the conversation appears intense. Then Baldy thrusts something into Knob's hand and moves away, casting down his eyes as I approach.

"Knob!"

"Bug!" Knob furtively sticks whatever into his pocket. I figure I've been witness to a drug deal.

"Negotiating?"

Knob sneers. "Cheap guy. Too cheap to close."

"What'd he want?"

"The usual." Knob turns away. He's wary of me,

thinks I'm a do-gooder, perhaps even an undercover cop.

I change the subject: "Seen Tim?"

He shakes his head.

"Well, if you do . . ."

He makes an imaginary pistol with his hand, aims it at me, squeezes off a shot and winks.

Eight-fifteen. Tim's more than an hour late. I'm worried—he's never stood me up before. I go to a pay phone outside the Wing Mai, call up my answering machine. No messages. Perhaps he lucked into a score. He couldn't have forgotten; his tone was too urgent. I feel something's wrong, but can't wait longer. I'm cold and hungry. I decide to get something to eat.

Two blocks south there's a Korean barbecue place I like, but tonight the smell out of the Wing Mai is good. I peer through the window, spot Alyson sitting with Doreen. The tables are linoleum and the lighting's fluorescent, which hurts my eyes, but the girls are fun. I slip on a pair of shades, enter, present myself.

"Hey, Bug!" Doreen gestures me to a chair. "We'll have a real girlie dinner now."

They're pecking with chopsticks at a whole cooked bass. I summon the waiter, order a bowl of hot-and-sour soup. As usual Alyson and Doreen are dressed hot. They have slim figures, nice breasts, wear makeup. In most ways they're more femme than I.

"How're tricks?" I ask.

Doreen moans. "You want war stories?" She's the more ironic of the two. She and Alyson refer to one another as "mates," room together, ply the same trade. I've been in their room at the Hampshire Arms—one huge bed, dirty windows, overstuffed closets, jumbles of clothes on the chairs. They rarely take clients home, prefer to perform out or, as a last resort, in cars. The clients don't mistake them for women. She-males, girls-with-cocks, are what they want.

"There was this john two nights ago."

"Monday, Doreen," Alyson corrects.

"Whatever. It was a *scene.*"

She describes an equestrian scenario they performed in a grand house on Tiburon Island: pony saddles, reins, horsetails, the works.

"See, we're supposed to be mares," Alyson explains.

"The props were pretty good."

"The john was the 'stallion'?"

They smile, exchange a look.

"More like a gelding," Doreen retorts.

Such stories fascinate me. I'm full of questions. Was it apparent that the Tiburon man had enacted the scene before, or did he strike them as a novice? And where did he get all those elaborate props?

My queries confuse them. They're not interested in the hows. It's the experience they savor, entering a client's madness, his fantasy.

"Actually, he was fine," Alyson concedes.

"If you like dead horse meat," Doreen adds.

Alyson breaks up. We share a sweet cooked banana dish for dessert. I ask if they've seen Tim.

"Yeah, yesterday," Doreen says. "He had attitude."

"How do you mean?"

"Like he was on the warpath or something. He pranced."

Alyson laughs. "That's what we did Monday—oh, Lord! we pranced! Till our tails switched up and down. 'Not side to side,' the john kept saying. Should have seen him, Bug—he was practically in tears. 'You're not flicking flies off your rumps, girls. You're horny horsies!' Eventually we got it right, made him happy."

Ten p.m. I decide to go home. I'd like to stay, perhaps take a few pictures, but because of the cold there's little going on. Also I'm feeling low. I thought Tim needed me, that confidences would be received. I was looking forward to playing the role of stand-in mom, since, until now, he and I have been mostly an older sister / kid brother routine. He's rarely spoken of his family, mentioning only that they live back east and are estranged except for an outcast gay uncle in New York. Tim is decent, loyal, soft-spoken. I'm sure there's an explanation, but I can't help but feel stood-up.

As I walk toward the Bay, I recognize a sports car, a silver Mercedes 600 SL, patrolling Polk. The driver guns his engine. He's a hawk, I know, one of the rich ones who often hang around. The car's flamboyant but the oc-cupant thinks he's invisible in darkness behind the glass.

One little-known fact about us color-blind: We can see through most camouflage. In World War II we were used as bombardiers, and many of us are good at spotting birds and snakes whose coloring conceals. The reason, of course, is that we're not distracted by color, concentrating instead on tonal values and shapes. So I'm able to make out the man in the Mercedes, not clearly but well enough to recognize him. It's Baldy, the guy I saw talking earlier with Knob.

Then, as he drives by, gunning his engine again to show off his power, I catch a glimpse of his profile and from that understand more: I've not only seen him before, I've surreptitiously photographed him several times. I didn't recognize him at first because he wasn't wearing his tou-pee.

I shiver as I climb the Chestnut Street steps. It's windy on Russian Hill. Too late now to safely venture across Sterling Park, so I follow Chestnut, turn right on Hyde, pass the crooked block of Lombard on my way up to Greenwich beside the cable car tracks and the endless ca-ble that rumbles beneath the street.

My building's at the crest. Constructed in the 1920s, slim and elegant, it offers some of the city's finest views. The rent's high; I sacrifice to live here, but have never regretted it. If by some fluke I should someday strike it rich, I'll probably buy a few things but I won't move.

I let myself in through the gilded grille door, step into

the elevator cab, push the button for the ninth floor. For me it's early. I adore the night; no photophobia, colors mean little, I don't feel caged in and my vision's at its best. I needn't blink, rarely have to squint. Horizons are limitless. It's a world of grays, a world I can roam and understand.

I enter my flat, go to the living room window. The whole city lies before me like a bejeweled carpet spread across the hills. The high-rises of the financial district glow against the inky sky. The Bay Bridge appears delicate. Coit Tower, illuminated, is a pillar of power sprouting from the peak of Telegraph Hill. Some say it resembles a giant nozzle, but I always see a phallus. The water in the Bay looks like roiling oil. Oakland, a distant galaxy, twinkles in the east.

I move to my telescope, still aimed at the penthouse. Now the living room lights over there are on.

So tell me, Judge, what are you doing tonight? Reading a brief, meditating over Justice, or perhaps bedding down some girl, young, slim and petite the way you like?

I spend half an hour gazing through the telescope, swinging it slowly across the city. Strange how the windows lit up night after night are usually the same.

There's something comforting in this. I like checking on windows I know, seeing familiar furniture, lamps, flickering TVs ... familiar people too, like the nightgowned lady on Leavenworth who putters endlessly in her kitchen, or the long-haired guy in the high-rise on Green who performs slow tai chi exercises on his terrace late at night. They're like friends, these stay-at-homes. I respect their privacy; I'm not looking to catch them in their undies. When I do stumble upon an intimate event, I usually turn my telescope away. It's not that I'm so high-principled; with a camera in hand I'm a mad-dog voyeur. But San Francisco is a city replete with telescopes, and since we must live together here, we observe a certain code.

· · ·

The lens in the lighthouse tower on Alcatraz revolves. High-masted ships, tied down at the Hyde Street Pier, creak on gently lapping waves. On the street a car passes in low gear, emitting an expensive growl. Is it Baldy in his Mercedes, unable to score, grinding out his frustration on the hill?

I'm seized by dread. I must have closed my eyes, fallen to sleep on the couch. I wake up suddenly, terrified. Did I hear something in the distance, a scream, a wail?

I listen attentively. A sound is missing. It takes me several seconds to understand: the rumble of the Hyde Street cable; they turn it off around two a.m. So . . . it was silence that woke me up.

I stretch, stand, go to my telescope, frame the Judge's penthouse once again. Now the windows are dark, the roof limned by moonlight. San Francisco is asleep.

I move to my bedroom, pull down the blackout shades, take off my clothes, slip naked beneath my sheets. I want to dream tonight, perhaps even dream in color. To do this once is my longest-held desire. To really understand what people mean when they call something blue or green, to see tomatoes as red instead of black, to see the sun as yellow instead of a shade of off-white, to understand the true meaning of such expressions as "I'm feeling blue this morning," "He's yellow, a coward," "I'm green with envy," "Look at that red-hot mama dance!" I wish!

The shrill ring of the phone cuts through my dream. I awaken with a start, grasp for the receiver, knock the apparatus to the floor.

I fumble for it, bring the handset to my ear.

"Bug?"

"Yeah?"

I hear sniffling. "It's me, Crawf."

"Crawf! Jesus, what time is it? What's going on?"

"Tim," he says. "You were waiting for him."

I check my watch. Seven a.m. "What're you telling me? That he just showed up?"

A long pause. "He's gone, Bug."

I'm silent. Then I start to tremble.

"You know that old black guy, Rory, the one sells empty soda cans?" I know the man he means. "He was messing around an hour ago, going through this Dumpster on Willow. Found these parts, you know—body parts. Got spooked, called the cops." I hold my breath. "They came right over, dug around, found a head." *No!* "It's Tim. He's dead, man." Crawf is sobbing now. "Someone wasted him . . . then cut him up."

Two

I throw on last night's clothes, pull on sneakers, grab my camera and a heavy set of shades. I don't own a car; can't get a license because of the achromatopsia. For a moment I think about phoning for a cab, then decide to go on foot. I know that if I move fast I can get over to Polk and Willow in ten minutes.

At the door I expect to be hit by harsh morning light, but soupy fog has settled over Russian Hill. The light's subdued, the tones muted, so I hang my shades around my neck and take off bare-eyed across Sterling Park.

Sorrowful foghorns resound from the Bay. I take the steps two at a time, then, on Larkin, begin to jog, causing my camera to bounce against my chest. I turn right at the Chinese church, descend to Polk, then run flat out.

Few people about. Most stores are shut. Grocery trucks are making early deliveries. Half-awake people blinking at newspapers sprawl at the tables in front of Starbucks. A lithe young woman in black sweatpants races past; except for a sports bra she's bare above the waist.

The fog's less thick here, I start picking up glare. I slow to fit on my wraparounds. Once on the Gulch, I notice a change in mood. The trash is out, the sidewalks are littered, but instead of the usual morning energy, I sense despair. Homeless men and women, reclining in doorways, peer out with haunted eyes.

I spot the patrol cars three blocks up, parked at angles, lamps whirling on their roofs. I know the lamps are red but they appear dark to me, revolving beams of charcoal light.

Crawf, in white T-shirt and jeans, sits slumped on the curb, head cradled in his arms. I settle beside him, put my arm around his shoulder. He turns to me, sobs against my jacket.

I wipe away his tears. He's freshly shaved and his long blond hair smells of coconut shampoo.

"Thanks for calling me, Crawf."

"You two were tight. Lucky I kept your card."

Gently I push back his head. I want to look into his eyes. "Tell me what happened."

Crawf blinks. "Some john, I guess. One of the bad ones. Must've been."

That much I already figured out.

"How come you're sure it's Tim?"

"Rory said so. And that old bag lady, Marge. Tim used to give her money. She went up to the cops, made them show her."

"That's what *I'm* going to do."

I stand, uncap my lens, approach a mustachioed cop standing in the intersection of the alley. His hands are linked behind his back. He rocks back rhythmically on his heels.

"Pardon me." He turns slowly. Just as he notices my camera I squeeze off a shot.

"What're you doing?"

"Taking pictures."

He puts out his hand. "Press pass?"

"Don't need one. This is a public street."

"This is a crime scene, ma'am."

I sweeten my tone. "I hear the victim was a friend. I want to see him, make sure."

He stares at me. Confused by my shades, perhaps he

wonders if I'm a druggie. "Stay here. I'll check with the detective."

He stoops under a band of tape suspended between sawhorse barriers, approaches a frizzy-haired man in a rumpled suit. They confer, Frizzy Hair turns to me, beckons. I cross the crime scene line.

"I'm Detective Shanley," he says. "Who're you?"

"Kay Farrow."

"You knew the victim?"

"I think so. I hope not."

"Yeah. . . ." He gazes at me. "Why the shades?"

I touch them lightly. "Photophobia."

His smile's slightly crooked. He looks about forty. In a few years he'll have a turkey gobbler neck.

"But you can see all right?"

"Depending on the lighting, yes."

"This isn't going to be a pretty sight," he warns.

"I've seen plenty of ugly things."

"Oh, have you now?" He guides me toward the coroner's van.

"My dad was a cop," I tell him.

He stops, peers at me. "Farrow . . . there was this Jack Farrow."

I nod.

"Jack Farrow's daughter. I'll be damned." He gazes at me. "How *is* old Jack?"

"Happy," I say. "Retired."

"Now how 'bout that!"

At the van he takes my arm. "Like I said, Kay—this is going to be rough."

I remove my shades, raise my camera to defend my eyes. I've been coping like this for years. By interposing a lens I stylize reality and by so doing shield myself from pain.

I want to shoot even as the coroner's assistant starts to lift the cloth. I'm too horrified. Seeing no body shape, I feel my knees go weak.

The hair, as always, is wild and beautiful, the oversize eyes still gorgeous. There's a terrible wound in what's left of his neck. His expression spells bewilderment.

I turn to Shanley. He's holding a handkerchief to his face.

"Well?"

"His name's Timothy Lovsey," I tell him. "On the street they call him Rain."

I start to take pictures.

"What the hell!" Shanley grabs at my camera. I evade him, squeeze off three more frames.

"I've been photographing him for months," I explain. "These'll be the last shots."

I lower the camera. He gazes at me.

"You can't take pictures anytime you feel like it."

"I think I can."

He shrugs. "Tell me about Timothy. What did he do? Did he have family? Where did he live?"

"Where's the rest of him?" I demand.

"We got his arms and legs. Haven't located his torso yet."

I glare at him. "You better fucking well find it!"

"Look, lady." Now he's pissed too.

"Don't 'Look, lady' me." I take a step back. "Scrounge around, Shanley. There're plenty of Dumpsters. He used to stand by the one on Hemlock. I'd start there if I were you."

"We already checked that one," Shanley says. "Come on, Kay, help me out."

I shake my forefinger at him. Shanley peers at me like I'm a loon. I hand him my card. "Call me when you find the rest of him," I tell him. "Then maybe I'll help."

I stalk off, turn, take a final photograph. I want to capture the hideous, lonely, sorrowful end, what it's like when you're beautiful as a Greek god, and end up beheaded, your head tossed in a rusty Dumpster on an alley littered with discarded condoms off Polk Gulch.

I grab hold of Crawf, pull him into a coffee shop—not a yuppie place with gleaming chrome machines but a hole-in-the-wall called Roy's, where the counterman's got a cough and there're stale doughnuts and wedges of pie displayed on tiers in a plastic vitrine.

"You're sweating," Crawf says. He picks up a napkin, wipes my forehead. "Shaking too."

"I feel bad," I tell him, "like I'm going to puke."

The counterman gives me water. I drain the glass, motion for a refill.

Crawf slurps his coffee. "Glad I didn't look. Couldn't take it. I got a really weak stomach."

"Who was he seeing, Crawf?"

"Johns? I don't know. Maybe someone new."

"He told you that?"

"No, but he seemed different last couple days."

"Different how?"

Crawf shrugs. "Like he was angry about something." He wipes his mouth. "I'm getting out of here, Bug. Just made up my mind. Going down to L.A., stay with my brother. Don't think I'll be back."

"It's no better down there," I warn him.

"I know. But I'm not going to work the street. I'll sign up for acting classes like I always wanted. Maybe I can make it. What do you think?"

"Maybe, sure."

So many of them, I know, share this fantasy, remember it when they get scared or fed up. A few even end up in triple-X films . . . if they have the skill to orgasm on demand.

Tim only wanted to retire. I think about what he told me. Did he really have fifty thousand saved? If so, could he have been killed for it? Where would he have kept it? In a bank? Not likely.

I grab Crawf's arm. "Let's check his place."

Crawf doesn't like the idea but changes his mind when I point out there might be something there he can use.

"I always liked his bomber jacket," he says. Then, appalled, he brings his hand up to his mouth.

•   •   •

Tim's studio is in a tenement building on Mission south of Market. The neighborhood's no treat: a needle-exchange parlor on the corner, a tough leather bar called The Tool Box, from which an odor of disinfectant permeates the morning air. But the building itself isn't bad; the stairwell graffiti's been erased. I smell cat piss and roach spray and am pleased by the sound of Verdi. Someone in the building's playing an old Callas record loud.

Tim kept his spare key in the hall molding above the fire extinguisher. I'm too short to reach it, but Crawf lunges, brings it down. He tells me he played basketball in high school.

I hesitate. What if there's someone inside? Crawf must have the same thought for he's poised to run. I meet his eyes, then knock loud. No response. I insert the key.

The room's empty, sparse, neat as a pin. Tim repainted it a month ago, also installed new vinyl tiles in the bath. I start to take pictures. I want to document his nest, which certainly doesn't appear inhabited by a man with fifty thousand dollars saved.

No phone; he used the pay phone on the corner. No stereo, just a Walkman on the dresser beside a stack of neatly folded underwear. On the floor his futon, his sleeping bag rolled and tied on top. A trestle desk supports a steam iron, a guide to Mexico and a Spanish-language workbook spread open awaiting study. I turn to the walls: a *Body Heat* poster and, opposite, a dozen prints of portraits I took of him taped to the plaster. His ravishing, large eyes meet mine. I lower my camera. My anger dissolves. I perch on his bedroll and start to bawl.

Crawf opens the closet. Six ironed denim shirts on hangers, four pressed pairs of jeans. Sneakers, shoes and boots aligned. No cowboy belt or bomber jacket. Maybe he was wearing them when . . . I choke up.

"Too weird," Crawf says. Suddenly he looks frail. "I don't know, Bug—maybe we shouldn't've come."

"You're right. It was a lousy idea. Let's get out of here."

Crawf nods; he can't wait. I lock the door and pocket

the key. If Shanley finds the torso, maybe I'll give it to him. On the stairs, opera music still pouring down, I work to compose my face.

We cut back through the Tenderloin, past malodorous curry joints protected by grilled roller screens, past a Laotian grocery and a pitiful storefront dental clinic. A woman in thigh-high boots, a regular, is out early strutting her stuff. There may be colors on these streets, but everything looks gray to me.

The Gulch is busy, cars and buses jammed up, pedestrians marching briskly to work. Some regulars are out, people who normally don't eat breakfast till afternoon. Word's spread. I see faces creased with fear: *Who's going to get it next?*

Lots of cops, but I don't see Shanley, only uniformed people climbing around Dumpsters and emptying bins. A sharp-looking female cop expedites traffic at the intersection of Sutter and Polk.

I'm sick at heart, my eyes hurt, my friend was killed. At first I loved him for his beauty, later for his gentleness. Now, I realize, I knew him hardly at all.

"I'm going home," I mutter to Crawf. He nods, probably glad to be rid of me. "Catch you later." Then I remember. "Good luck in L.A."

"I'll send you a postcard," he says.

To get away from the traffic and noise I take California over to Larkin, a residential street. I walk slowly. I want to remember Tim as he was, erase the image of his separated head. That he's gone, is dead, cuts too deep. That he was mutilated makes the loss too cruel.

Who else cared for him beside Crawf, myself and a few others on the Gulch? There was a girl he once mentioned, said he wanted to get us together. He'd told her about me, he said, and she was anxious to meet me too. He was sure I'd want to photograph her. I remember the way he smiled when I asked him why.

Then there was Uncle David in New York. Tim mentioned him a couple of times. I try to concentrate, remember his last name. I should call him so he can pass word to Tim's folks.

There's still fog on Russian Hill. Strange how this city has so many microclimates, the banana belt that cuts across Noe Valley, the chilly mists of Seacliff, the bitter-cold summer mornings on Pacific Heights. When there's an earthquake the Marina district, built on landfill, turns to jelly, while on the shale-rock hills we feel the temblors less. It can rain furiously in San Francisco, while the sun bakes Berkeley dry. Sometimes the fog clings to the Bay, other times to the peaks.

I spot Shanley standing in front of my building. He's conferring with a woman, taller than me, with short dark slick-gelled hair. I approach warily. Shanley introduces us. She's a detective, Hillary Lentz. "People call me Hilly," she says cheerfully, extending her hand.

I look hard at Shanley. "Found the rest of him?"

"Not yet."

"I told you—come see me when you do."

He's annoyed. "Christ's sake, Kay, wasn't us cut him up. Give us a break. We're doing all we can."

Hilly joins in. "If we're going to find the guy who did this, every hour counts. This is someone you cared about, right?"

A good argument, so I relent, invite them up. In the elevator Shanley asks if I have photos of Tim. I tell him I have hundreds. He asks if he can borrow one.

"What for?"

"Posters. We'll plaster the Gulch, ask for leads."

"No one there'll talk to you."

"They will if they think about it. The person who did this could easily do the same to them," Hilly says.

Suddenly I remember how decent cops can be, how a job one would think would harden people often has the opposite effect. Dad was a softy, still is. I decide to trust them. I unlock my apartment door.

"Why keep it so dark? You gotta have great views," Hilly says.

"Sunlight hurts my eyes and the views are just as good at night."

They peer around. Hilly studies my decor. "No colors except the books," she observes. "Nice effect."

"It's not an effect. I want it this way. I'm color-blind."

They stare at me. Shanley muses: "Color-blind photographer. Interesting. . . ."

"I shoot in black and white," I tell him. "You're thinking: 'I thought only boys were color-blind.' "

"Actually—" Shanley says.

"That's not color-blindness, that's red-green confusion. The inheritance pattern's different. Anything else you want to know?"

"No need to get hostile."

"Guys!" Hilly shows her palms. "We got a homicide to deal with. How 'bout we work on that?"

I take them into my office, converted from the second bedroom, open a drawer of my flat file, pull out a box of prints. I show them only the formal portraits, not the more intimate shots.

"Good looking kid," Shanley comments.

"You liked him a lot," Hilly says.

"You can tell?"

"Definitely." She picks up my Angel Island portrait. "The way you photograph him here—it shows."

It feels good to hear her say that. For the first time since Crawf woke me, I think maybe I can handle this.

"This street name, Rain," Shanley asks, "what's that all about?"

"Just a name. He had this kind of . . . I don't know . . . inner sorrow, I guess."

"Poetic," Hilly says. "Who gives out these names?"

"Someone starts it, and if you don't act offended others pick it up."

"Yours, we hear, is Bug," Shanley says.

"Great detective work. You investigating him or me?"

We go back to the living room. They want to know what Tim did. I gaze at them. Are they putting me on?

"He was a hustler."

"So we heard. How did you two get involved?"

"Involved how?"

"However," Shanley says.

I gaze at him. There's meanness there. Hilly, on the other hand, seems decent enough. Good cop / bad cop. I turn to her.

"When I started shooting on the Gulch, Tim Lovsey was one of the first people I met. We liked each other, started hanging out. I saw him maybe four, five times a week. Whenever I was up there, we'd have coffee or a drink. He called me yesterday, said there was something important he wanted to talk about. We agreed to meet at seven. I waited on Hemlock for over an hour. When he didn't show, I checked around. No one had seen him since the day before."

"What was on his mind?"

"He didn't say. I could be wrong, but I think he sounded scared."

"You think—"

"—there's a connection? Sure, otherwise I wouldn't be telling you this."

"What else can you tell us?"

Hilly, I observe, is taking notes.

"Not much. Couple weeks ago he told me he had fifty thousand stashed. You might want to look into that." Shanley nods. "What was that wound in his neck?"

"He was shot before he was beheaded."

"That's how he was killed?"

"Probably. Think it could've been a john?"

"I'd say that's a good possibility, wouldn't you?"

I stand. I've had enough of them. I give them the Angel Island print, which they like because Tim looks sexy in it and that'll draw attention to their posters. I promise to think hard and come up with his uncle's name. Finally I give them his address and hand Shanley the key. I don't mention that Crawf and I were just there.

"Let me know when you find the rest of him," I tell them at the door.

"Sure. Any particular reason?"

"I want to arrange a funeral."

I'm sitting in my office, shades down, studying photos I took of Tim. It's my way to recall him, honor his memory.

Suddenly I'm angry. He knew what he did was dangerous. At least twice we discussed the risks he took each time he went home with a stranger. I lectured him: sex workers are targets; the encounters are anonymous, giving confidence to johns who feel sadistic fury toward figures in their pasts. When the sex worker is chosen to represent that figure, he or she can end up the victim of a murderous rage.

I told him how often I'd read about slain prostitutes and about the series of homicides in Britain where the killer picked up his victims in gay bars.

Tim nodded. He knew about all that. It's dangerous too, he reminded me, to cross the street.

That was the only time I blew up at him. "Are you looking to get killed?"

He smiled at me, his special tender way. "You don't understand, Kay. Most of my johns are sweet. I tune in to the vibes. When they're bad, I pass."

"How can you tell?"

He shrugged. "You're on the street awhile you get a sixth sense for stuff like that."

I stare at a photo I took of him juggling rubber balls on the ferryboat to Sausalito. He wears a tank top and shorts; and his hair is mussed. I remember the day well, a Sunday. On the spur of the moment we decided to cross over for lunch. The water was choppy, the ferry left a churning trail, kites flew over Alcatraz, the Bay was filled with sailboats bent sharply to catch the wind.

There were kids on board and as we approached Sausalito Tim entertained them with his juggling act. He was terrific, kept four balls going. Later I asked him where he learned to do it. He said he ran away with a circus when he was ten.

He was joking of course, but he did have offbeat and engaging skills, was facile with close-up magic, pulling coins out of ears, then making them disappear. He could stick a knife down his throat, and, he told me, knew how to charm a snake. He wanted me to know he had a past, even as he refused to reveal it. Enjoying his mystifications, I played along, figuring sooner or later he'd tell me the story of his life.

I open the box that contains the nudes. I can hardly bear to look at them. Why, I wonder now, didn't we have sex? He considered himself bisexual, told me he'd had girlfriends and said he'd enjoy accommodating women if there were female takers for what he had to offer.

"There are," I assured him. "I see older women with young hunks all the time."

"Gigolos," he said with contempt. "I'm a hustler."

"Is that better?"

"Freer." He seemed certain about it. "No one controls you. You live the way you like. You hustle, make things happen, don't dance for anyone, do your thing."

It was from such conversations that I developed my notion of hustlers as free spirits and psychic explorers. A flawed perception perhaps, a romanticized view of a sordid way of life. But that was where my pictures led me. My eyes were my guide. I shot what I felt.

The phone rings. It's Shanley. He's calling on his cellular from Tim's apartment.

"Who else has keys?" he demands.

"Why?"

"Someone's been in here that's why," he says angrily. "Place is ransacked. Everything's fucking upside down."

I cry a little, then pace like a caged beast, then put on my shades and pull up the blinds and stare out at the city smothered in late-morning fog. Low-pitched horns moan from the Bay. A naval hospital ship, heading for Oakland, slips between the Embarcadero and Treasure Island. The ship is white, ghostly, and bears a huge cross which I know is red but which appears black to me.

I'm torn between grief and anger, and my anger, I fear, is gaining the upper hand. My mother shot herself when I was twenty, stuck my father's spare gun in her mouth, then pulled the trigger like a cop. That happened fifteen years ago and I still feel anger more than pain. I think anger's a way to hold on to someone who's died; if I can feel angry enough, memory of the person won't fade.

Noon. I'm trying to center myself. I keep thinking about Shanley's call. Between the time Crawf and I were at Tim's and the time Shanley got there, barely an hour passed. By then a lot of people found out what had happened. Any one of them could have broken in.

Except . . . Shanley didn't say there'd been a break-in; he asked who else had a key. So it must have been someone Tim trusted, or the person who killed him . . . since he would have had his own key with him when he died.

David Jeffrey—Uncle David's name flies into my mind. He's in the entertainment business, lives in Manhattan, is the only member of Tim's family who didn't disown him, rather took him in, helped him come to terms with his sexuality. It was Uncle David who loaned him money to move out to San Francisco. He doesn't know that Tim became a hustler, thinks he's working here as a waiter. He also doesn't know where he lives, since Tim, moving often, kept a private mailbox at one of those wrap-it / ship-it stores in the Castro.

I pick up my phone, dial New York City information. There're two David Jeffreys, three people listed as D. Jeffrey, and, using alternate spellings, half a dozen more David and D. Jefreys and Geoffreys. I take down the numbers even as I know I won't place the calls. Too many names, too many times I'll have to ask: "Are you Tim Lovsey's uncle?" Better to let Shanley do that. But then, I remember, I don't really want to talk to Shanley anymore.

I go into my darkroom, process a couple of undeveloped rolls, mechanical work that keeps me busy. After I hang up the rolls to dry, I retrieve a negative strip from my safe—the one that contains my favorite of the Angel Island shots. I place the strip on my lightbox, examine it with a magnifying glass. Seeing Tim this way, with the blacks and whites reversed, fills me with a mellow sorrow. I feel that this negative, being the piece of film upon which light he reflected actually fell, contains more of his essence than prints made from it.

Color blindness, which I once viewed as a curse, has turned out to be a gift enabling me to see the world differently than others. People think they understand color blindness: "Oh, must be like looking at black-and-white movies all day long." Perhaps it is. I have no idea. The concept of gray as a color doesn't mean anything to me either. I see black and white and shades in between, "a world cast in lead," as Greta Benning, my favorite high school art teacher, used to say. "Consider taking up drawing or etching, Kay," she advised. I tried both. All my life I wanted to be an artist, I just wasn't sure what kind.

When I started at the San Francisco Art Institute, it was with the intention of becoming a sculptor. Since sculpture materials are generally monochromatic, color perception isn't vital to success.

Everything was going fairly well, when, my second year, I took a course in studio photography. Within a week I knew I'd found my medium. My dad, responding to my enthusiasm, gave me his camera, an early-model Nikon. I started carrying it with me, shooting everything that interested me, often also using it as a telescope to see things when the rods of my retinas got saturated by brilliant light.

A camera around my neck didn't look nearly as odd as the handheld monocular most achromats carry. Soon it became a part of me—my tool, limb and shield. Since I couldn't see very well in daylight, my camera became my eyes; later, looking at my photographs, I was able to see what I had "seen."

Since I graduated from art school I've worked as a photojournalist for an alternative newspaper, a portraitist and, for five years, a studio and location fashion photographer. I've covered sports, rock concerts, political campaigns; photographed politicians, writers, dogs; shot spreads for *Details, GQ* and *Elle.*

Three years ago I went cold turkey on commercial work, determined to devote myself full-time to personal projects. I'd always wanted to be a fine-art photographer. Finally, with a little money saved, I decided to take the shot.

I've been fortunate. Last year I published a book, *Transgressions,* the best of two years' worth of pictures in which I used black-and-white studio fashion lighting techniques to glamorize and thus counterdocument the pain of battered women. The idea was to show the pride of women who, though beaten in body, were unbowed in spirit. Reviews were good though sales were not. The high priestesses of political correctness called me traitor.

The controversy helped get my pictures shown in New York. I exhibit and sell locally through the Zeitgeist Gallery. Having turned art photographer, I earn a lot less than when I did fashion work, but I get by, and most important, feel fulfilled.

My Polk Gulch project is different than *Transgressions,* executed not in the studio but, in accordance with Maddy Yamada's advice, entirely on the street. The working title is *Exposures.* Again I'm looking to glamorize what most people regard as sordid, but this time my technique is different: whatever glamour accrues to my hustler-models comes from within, not from lighting and directed poses. And the glamour portraits are only half my project; the other half is my documentation of transactions of the flesh. I've amassed hundreds of grainy images, shot candidly with available illumination at night, of my heroes interacting with johns, meeting, negotiating, driving off. The best of these, the ones I intend to use, catch the looks on the faces of hustler and john as their eyes meet, they inspect one another and forge the deals that lead to intimate acts unseen.

Three p.m. The fog has lifted. I put on my shades, grab my gym bag and walk down to Cow Hollow for aikido class. The dojo, Marina Aikido, is above a store on the corner of Laguna and Lombard, one of the most heavily traveled streets in the city. The instructor, a black woman named Rita Reese, is tough, sinewy, a former marine. Not too many mystical Zen-like utterances from her; she's more contemporary woman warrior than classic sensei.

I change quickly, then move out to the floor to stretch and practice katas. Today our class has nine women, three men. There are a couple of high-school girls, several women in their thirties, and Justine, a lithe middle-aged woman with gray bangs, an advanced student with whom I often work out. I'm one of the smallest in the group: five feet four, 114 pounds. I make no claims to being a star martial artist. I attend because I love the beauty of aikido, the clarity, the concentration, the spiritual practice. My efforts to achieve mastery make me feel powerful. And, too, I enjoy the exercise.

"You're not concentrating, Kay. Claim your space! Blend your energy!"

Rita, so elegant in her hakama, the split floor-length black skirt that, being a black belt, she's entitled to wear, is a caring instructor. But today I'm not in the mood to blend my energy; I've come here to release it.

We pair off for freestyle practice. Justine and I face one another. We bow to show respect, that we hold no anger, that it isn't hostility that drives us, but love of sport and art.

Suddenly I attack. Justine grabs my arm, turns, throws me down. I don't fall well. It hurts when I hit the mat. Aikido is not only beautiful, it can also be very painful. Today I welcome the pain. I want to fall hard, again, again and still again, want to leave class sweaty and sore.

Again I attack. Again Justine throws me. Her moves are circular, balletic, her throws nearly effortless. Rita, I see, is watching us. Up from the mat, I check myself in the mirror. I look, I think, like a rag doll, broken and spent.

By the end of practice, my jacket's drenched with my sweat, my hips and shoulders are bruised. After we bow, Justine embraces me.

"Next time I'll attack, you'll apply techniques," she promises.

Rita approaches shaking her head, causing her braided cornrows to flick. I'm breathing hard. She brushes something out of my hair. "You're a punching bag today, girlfriend," she says.

I nod.

She stares into my eyes. "I've seen you do much better. You seem vulnerable. Don't forget, Kay, on the mat all secrets are exposed."

I stare back at her, tears pulsing from my eyes. "I lost someone close," I blurt.

Suddenly she hugs me. "Oh, Kay, I'm so sorry."

I won't let this go, I decide, as I walk back up the hill. The light is dazzling; I blink even though I'm wearing heavy shades. *You can't kill someone I care about, then chop him up and throw the pieces away like trash and get away with it.*

Questions flood in: Who *was* Tim? Did he have enemies? Where did he learn to juggle and do close-up magic? Who's his Uncle David? Who's the mysterious girl he wanted me to meet? What did he want to talk about yesterday? Did he really have fifty thousand stashed? Who turned over his flat?

I want to know all these things because he was my friend and because, I've just decided, his life and death will be the subject of *Exposures*. I'll change my concept.

The book will no longer be about Gulch hustlers among whom he will be a featured player. It will be entirely about him, how he lived and died. I already have the pictures. What I need now is the story.

Three

Tonight before venturing out I wait till magic time is over, until the failing light drains away the colors from the city, colors I know are there but cannot see. Then I enter the nightscape.

This evening Polk Street is the same yet different, crawling with cops, patrol cars parked on every block. No dealers are out, few street people. The human flotsam has retreated to the alleys of the Tenderloin. With the law so visible the habitués deem the Gulch unsafe.

At the corner of Polk and Bush, I pause to examine a poster stapled to a power pole. It's my portrait of Tim, beautiful and bare-chested, the city gleaming behind. The image is mine, but the light values are not—the contrast has been pushed. Tim's skin has gone swarthy, making him appear a sunburnt soldier rather than an androgynous ephebe.

The caption below is straightforward enough:

TIMOTHY LOVESY (A.K.A. "RAIN") WAS FOUND MURDERED THURSDAY NIGHT, HIS BODY LEFT IN A DUMPSTER ON WILLOW ALLEY. TIMOTHY FREQUENTED THE POLK GULCH AREA. ANYONE WITH

INFORMATION REGARDING THIS VICTIM'S DEATH
AND/OR RECENT CONTACTS IS ASKED TO NOTIFY DE-
TECTIVES SHANLEY AND/OR LENTZ, 270-7111.
ANONYMITY GUARANTEED.

I stand back, take a shot of the poster. Suddenly I feel
a presence behind.

"Not bad, huh?"

I turn. It's Hilly, wearing dark slacks and a black
leather blouson jacket much like mine.

"Sorry, forgot to give you photo credit," she says.

I smile, ask if she and Shanley have gotten any calls.

She shakes her head. "We've only had these up since
five. Took all afternoon to get them made." She grins.
"The mills of the gods grind slowly at S.F.P.D."

"You haven't found the rest of him?"

Again she shakes her head. "I promised I'd call when
we do. I meant it."

I turn from her, peer south down Polk. Something in
her gaze upsets me. Also, I don't want her to see my eyes.

"Shanley told me Tim's studio was messed."

"Yeah, like the shit hit the fan."

"Tim was neat. He didn't have much stuff."

"Whatever he had was tossed. Futon and bedroll slit,
goose down churning in the air."

"Money?"

"If there was, it's long gone now."

I turn back to her. "What do you think about the mu-
tilation?"

Her eyes are steady on mine. "It's a goddamn shame."

"Ever seen anything like it?"

"No, but Shanley has. I've only been in Homicide
since January. Before that worked sex crimes seven
years."

"Isn't this a sex crime, Hilly?"

"Don't know that yet."

I understand what she's saying, that without Tim's
torso they can't be sure.

"We're having a little problem," she says. "We need

information, that's why we put up posters. But soon as
we put them up people rip them down. Doesn't help the
cause.''

I'm not surprised. Posters are bad for business. Life
goes on; there're livings to be made.

"Is that why so many cops are around?"

"They're more like, you know, a presence."

"Here today, gone tomorrow?"

She shrugs. "There's a great big city to patrol."

"And who cares about a murdered hustler, right?"

She stares at me, offended. "You don't think we
care?"

"I'm keeping an open mind."

"Got any suggestions?"

"Me?"

"Sure, why not?"

Our eyes meet. Is she coming on to me? I check her
ring finger for a wedding band. "Here's one suggestion—
get the uniforms off the street. You want to cover the
Gulch, do it in plainclothes, otherwise none of the hustlers'll work and none of the johns'll come around."

"Good idea. Thanks." She looks at me. "Do you live
with someone . . . have a boyfriend?"

"Not at the moment, no."

We walk a block in silence. There's traffic but not the
cruising kind. I tell her a little about my project. I don't
mention the hundreds of shots I've taken of johns.

"I care about people," she says. I wait for the other
shoe to drop. "I didn't know this kid, so I can't care about
him as much as you. But I do care, I want you to know
that." She stops, peers into my eyes, shows me her sin-
cerity. "Shanley and me—we've got a heavy caseload,
but I'm not letting this one go. We won't solve it picking
up fibers and prints. The only way's with faces, descriptions we can tie to names. We need informants with good
information. Otherwise . . ." She shrugs.

"I understand."

She smiles slightly. "I'm a lesbian. Better you hear it
from me than hear it around."

"That's fine."

"Anonymous consensual sex doesn't bother me. As for sex for money—seems like a reasonable exchange. But hurting and killing because it gets somebody off—no, Kay, this dyke doesn't stand for that." She relaxes. "I saw your book last year, liked it, even stopped by the gallery to see the originals. Beaten-up women—in Sex Crimes they were my stock-in-trade. Took Polaroids of them all the time. Not like your stuff. In mine they looked"—she shakes her head—"kinda wretched. The way they looked in yours even with the bruises and black eyes, I don't know—they seemed like movie stars almost. Which got me thinking." She smiles broadly. "Enough flattery for tonight?"

"Actually," I tell her, "I can never get enough."

She laughs. "Don't know what your angle is on this hustling scene, but you've got contacts here." I nod. "Maybe you'll pick something up."

"I don't know," I tell her. "I'll check around."

She squeezes my hand. "Thanks!" She turns, strides off.

I wander down to O'Farrell, then over to Larkin. Some of the Gulch action has moved here. I see several female streetwalkers but no hustlers. I recognize Silky, a mid-thirties black woman with huge lips, cornrows and a swagger.

I approach. "Where're the guys?"

She gives a twirl with her thumb. "Freaked out tonight, child. Try Van Ness."

I take Myrtle Alley over to Van Ness, walking quickly, spooked by the lack of people lingering against the walls. Van Ness, an avenue with a center strip, doubles here as U.S. 101, a major route that cuts through the city.

At the corner I look both ways. Cars and trucks speed by, the sidewalks are deserted. I start toward Civic Center, then catch a glimpse of a familiar form turning into Olive. I pick up my pace, follow him into the alley.

"Knob!"

It's him, I'm sure, though he speeds up, keeps his head down and doesn't turn.

"It's me, Bug!" I yell after him, then start to run. He sidesteps into the portal of a garage. When I reach him, I'm out of breath.

"Fuck you want?" he demands. His expression is surly.

"Tim and me were tight. What d'you know?"

"Fuck ask me?"

"You know the Gulch, Knob. Cops think the killer's a john."

He sniffs, then makes a gesture as if to push me back. He wants to intimidate me. I hold my ground. He's four inches taller and eighty pounds heavier; he could knock me over with a swat. In his eyes I see the calculation of a ferret.

"What's the problem?" I ask.

"Don't like cops."

"I'm not a cop."

"So you say."

We glare at one another. "I'm a photographer, Knob. Ever seen me without a camera?"

"Taking pictures—that's what a cop would do."

"*Why?*"

"Catch people."

"What kind of people?"

"People with stuff to hide."

"What kind of stuff?"

"Married guys, like that. Who they are, where they live."

"Like Baldy from last night?"

"Who?"

I find his dumb act pathetic. "The bald guy in the Mercedes," I explain. "The one you were talking to, the one who wanted chicken and wouldn't close."

"Don't know what you're talking about."

"Guy flaunts a car like that, he's asking to be noticed. Not that difficult to check out a license plate."

Knob narrows his eyes. "Fuck you want?"

"I want to know who's violent, who could've done this to Tim. I'm not a cop, but I'm going to start working with them if his friends here don't cooperate."

"I don't know nothin'."

I soften my tone: "You liked him. I know you did." I lie: "And he liked you."

Knob considers that. He's not big on human sentiment. I press him a little more.

"You're slinking around now because you're scared. And you're right. What they did to Tim, they could do to you, to anyone."

"Who says it's a 'they'?"

For the first time he surprises me. "Okay, suppose it's one guy—does that make any difference?"

"What do you mean?"

"Built-in risk, isn't it? Risk of the trade. Stop one there's always another, right?" I pause. "Or were you—" Suddenly I think I understand what's on his mind. "You're not planning on taking care of this yourself?"

He snorts, pushes me. This time I yield; the push is real, not a gesture as before.

"Tell me?" I plead as I stumble back.

"Outa my way," he says roughly. He shoves me again hard. I fall to the pavement. He walks away.

My knees are scraped. They smart as they rub against my jeans. If I hadn't needed to protect my camera I'd have used my hands to break the fall. My knees can take it; my Contax can't.

This is the first time I've been hit since coming to the Gulch. I'm more shocked than hurt. Now the security I've felt here gives way to apprehension. It's been my illusion, I realize, that this place has grace. Yes, I've witnessed moments of unexpected gentleness, but basically, I know, the Gulch is a jungle.

I pick myself up. Knob is gone. At least he didn't kick me, then stand around and gloat. I remember a book by a gonzo journalist who hung out with a motorcycle gang. He thought he'd become one of them. The day they turned on him and stomped him he learned he wasn't.

Suddenly I feel a need to take pictures. But what is there to shoot? I stride back to Polk, start blasting away at the cops. Then I stop. These shots won't get me anywhere. If Tim is to be the subject of *Exposures,* I should capture the grief of his friends.

I go into Walgreen's, purchase bandages and disinfectant, then limp my way over to the Hampshire Arms. The hotel, now seedy, has seen better days. Squares of the marble lobby floor are broken and the rough stucco walls are dark with soot. I approach the desk. A young man with bad skin is reading a comic book. He doesn't look up.

"Doreen in?"

He scratches a pimple. "Who?"

"Doreen . . . of Alyson and Doreen."

"Room three-fourteen."

I find the house phone, call upstairs.

They're both in, too brokenhearted, Doreen tells me, to play the street.

"Can I come up?"

"Sure," she says, slurring her words. "Just give us a couple minutes to straighten the joint."

I dress my wounded knees in the lobby, then take the elevator to three. I think it's more like straighten themselves, since, when Doreen opens the door, I find the joint in its usual disarray. The gals are wearing unisex underwear, not the frilly kind I'd expect.

Doreen glances at me, then at herself in the mirror. She isn't wearing makeup and her wig's askew.

"Hell with it!" she says, pulling it off. Her head, I see, is shaved. Her hands shake as she flings the wig across the room. Alyson immediately follows suit. Her head is shaved as well.

"Don't feel all that girlie tonight," Doreen explains, voice a half-octave lower. The floor is cluttered with high-heeled shoes and boots, the air pungent with stale cigarette smoke, cosmetics and gin.

"Night like this you just want to sit home and cry," Alyson says.

The two of them plop down together on the bed. I take a chair, perching atop a pile of wrinkled tutus and lingerie.

"I'm here to take your pictures," I announce.

At first they're against it, don't like the notion of being photographed unmasked. But it doesn't take long to convince them.

"When you show real feelings," I tell them, "dressup doesn't matter."

For the first few shots they assume mock-feminine poses; then they give it up. As I shoot they continue to drink straight gin, no tonic or vermouth, gulping it down like stevedores. There comes a point when I stop viewing them as she-males and begin to see them as they are: a couple of slim young skinheads who happen to have tits, getting plastered because a friend's been killed.

"Tell me about bad johns," I ask, framing Doreen against the mess in the closet.

"What'd you wanna know?" she asks.

"How bad does it get?"

Alyson lets out with a hoot. "Dearie, you got no idea!"

"They stink, some of them. You'd think they'd clean up for a date."

"They call you names—'bitch,' 'slut,' like that."

"The c-word too. Not that we mind. It's a validation really."

"Then there're the sickies." They glance at one another, click glasses, toss back great gulps.

"Some like to beat up on you. Spanking's all right— but they gotta pay extra. A few'll get carried away. Couple times I've come home with black eyes."

"When that happens what do you do?" I'm shooting now from the floor, framing them against the stained and ragged wallpaper.

"You get out of there, honey. Fast as you can. A john out of control—that can lead to real injury."

"I had one last spring." Alyson falls back on the bed. "Good-looking, middle-aged, computer-exec type. Married, lived down the peninsula somewhere. We had a few dates. He seemed nice enough. Brought me flowers, talked about earrings. Told me he liked male pussy, that was his kink."

Doreen hands Alyson a lit cigarette. Alyson props herself on an elbow, takes a long drag, then exhales in a stream.

"One night he gets loaded. We're in this motel room on Lombard. Suddenly he starts bashing me around. We're all—us, women!—we're all whores, he says. He hates us, *all* of us. I feel his rage. I'm scared. I know I gotta get out before he busts me up. I try to calm him. 'Hey, George, it's me, Alyson. I'm a guy, remember. All this is make-believe.' I'm taking a chance; these guys want to forget you're a boy. But I do it anyway, meantime wipe away my makeup and peel off my wig. So there we are, two guys commiserating over what sluts women are, how they ought to be, like—now he's getting really vicious—exterminated, eviscerated! Finally he gets up to take a piss. That's when I make my break. I shake all the way home in the cab. I never saw old Georgie again."

"Probably too scared to show his face," Doreen says. "Guy like that, we pass the word. No one else'll touch him."

"I figure he burned his bridges down in San Jose, that's why he started coming up here. Now he's probably playing in Santa Cruz. Sooner or later he'll break some girl's arm or kill her. Guys like that only get worse. We release something in them. After that . . . well, you know the saying: You can't squeeze the paste back into the tube."

By midnight Doreen and Alyson are dead drunk and I've shot out two thirty-six-frame rolls. I leave them snoring away head to toe on the bed.

On Polk the cops are gone. There's hardly a person on the street. My knees are fine now; bandaged I walk well.

I check the saloons. Most are empty. The Werewolf is closed and so is The Shillelagh.

It's strange to walk here with no one about. It's as if this place has died. Perhaps this will be Tim's memorial— a single night of silence on the Gulch.

I wander up to Jerry's All-Night Pizza, peer in through the window, notice a couple of regulars—Slick, an albino, and a kid named Remo who barely looks thirteen.

I enter, approach. "Seen Crawf?" I ask.

"Hear he left town," Slick says.

I sit. Silence. Have I interrupted a private colloquy? The harsh fluorescent lighting hurts my eyes.

I raise my camera. They tense, then relax as they remember who I am.

"Just a few shots," I promise. "I want to catch the gloom and doom."

Slick stares down at his coffee; Remo sticks out his tongue. Then, after goofing off, he offers me his profile.

"I'm collecting bad-john stories," I tell them, still shooting. "Got any good ones?" That gets them going.

The first tale is strange. Seems there's a doctor who likes to take kids to his office in Pacific Heights, where he subjects them to lengthy physical exams. As he does he whispers degrading things. "Bet a lot of cocks been down here," he says, peering into a boy's throat. "Now bend over and spread those cheeks." The culminating event is a prolonged inspection with a proctoscope.

"Physical part's not so bad," Slick says. "It's the fuckin' humiliation gets you down."

Slick's nineteen with white hair and stubble above his upper lip. He's scrawny, pale, his eyebrows and eyelashes so faint I can barely make them out. I can't read colors but Tim once told me Slick's irises are pink.

At one time or another he and most of his friends have been hired by the doctor, who, after a couple of exams, loses interest and asks for a steer to someone new. Slick affectionately chucks the point of Remo's chin. "Wouldn't send you to him, kid. Not even for a cut."

Remo's got his own story about a black van with

blacked-out windows that took him, another young hustler and two teenage girls to a play party high in the hills of Marin. The van pulled straight into a garage, from which they were taken blindfolded to a basement and told to strip. They entertained a group all night, perhaps a half-dozen men and women. They were tickled with feathers, caressed and used, for which they were paid a collective fee of a thousand dollars and deposited terrified back on Fisherman's Wharf at dawn.

There's an exuberance in the boys as they recount these adventures that reminds me a little of Tim—the camaraderie of veterans exchanging war stories at a bar.

"That Marin group's sick, the doctor too, but what about the *real* bad guys?" I ask.

They're nonplussed. Then little Remo states the obvious:

"Go with one of them you don't live to tell the tale."

Sitting on a high stool in my apartment living room peering through my telescope, I feel as though I'm in the crow's nest of a ship. The night is designed for surveillance: vistas long, horizons deep, lamps mere points of light. No blazing walls of sunlight to limit my vision. The night city lies naked to my eye.

I check the Judge's windows, find them dark . . . as are most other residence windows at this hour. I swing the telescope toward the cluster of high-rises downtown; lamps burn in offices for the night cleaning crews.

Swinging northeast, I catch the reflection of the moon on the Bay with the lights of El Cerrito flickering beyond. I observe a small but brilliant glow in the Berkeley Hills, perhaps a house on fire.

I leave my telescope, go into my office, peer out at the Golden Gate Bridge. They say that when people jump from it they nearly always face the city, perhaps because to face west, the Pacific, would be to renounce the worldly causes of their sorrows.

• • •

The eighteenth-century British chemist John Dalton was
the first scientist to properly describe color blindness,
namely his own. In truth he was a dichromatic protanope,
meaning his deficiency was a not uncommon inability to
distinguish red from green. Dalton's belief, that all color
blindness was like his, has long been disproved. But convinced of his theory that the fluid in his eyes was tinted
blue and thus absorbed red light, he willed one of his eyes
to Cambridge University, directing that it be examined
after his death.

It was, in 1844, by his friend and doctor, Joseph Ransome, who even peered through it, finding the liquid transparent and colorless. To this day the pickled eye remains
at Cambridge; Dalton's DNA was extracted from it several years ago. But it's the intimacy of the act, Ransome
actually using his close friend's eye as a lens, that comes
back to me with poignant force as I pull out the nude
photographs of Tim I took just three weeks ago.

Perhaps these pictures of his naked body will tell me
something, help me solve the enigma of his death. That,
at least, is my hope as I begin to study them, meditating
over the vulnerability of his flesh.

I hadn't planned on shooting nudes, though in retrospect, it seems a natural outgrowth of our work. Our Angel Island session, for instance, when Tim took off his
shirt to pose for the portrait now on the posters being
ripped off lampposts on the Gulch. There's something
about bare skin that lends intimacy to a photograph, which
is probably why one famous photographer is alleged to
be so adamant that her subjects strip. Nakedness, after all,
is the ultimate physical secret. In our time is there a commodity more precious than celebrity skin?

I was, I confess, aroused on Angel Island, whether by
Tim, his body, the sweetness of the air, the softness of
the lambent light or, most likely, the whole gestalt. It was
a balmy windless autumn day, the waters of the Bay were

still, gulls circled and the shoreline grasses were lustrous as pewter.

I often become aroused when work goes well. I love photography, the sense of capture, the sureness that possesses me when I'm getting at something deep. But on that day the arousal was especially intense. I remember wanting to grasp hold of Tim, roll with him in the high grass just above the island shore. I remember feeling certain he noticed my excitement, his only comment on it being a smile. It was as if he acknowledged my condition but, being the object of desire, left it to me to make the initial move . . . which, on account of pride, I did not do.

A few days later, when I showed him the Angel Island proofs, he was thrilled.

"This is how I want to look!"

"The camera doesn't lie."

"I wish I could always be so beautiful, Kay."

"Perhaps you are," I said.

He softly shook his head. "Some days are better than others." He brightened. "Would you shoot me nude? I'd like to see myself naked through your eyes, beautiful lying eyes."

I took it that he was suggesting that if the camera doesn't lie, surely the photographer does. In the face of such a challenge how could I resist?

We executed the nudes on a Sunday in my living room, beginning midmorning, working till late that afternoon. I loaded a second camera with color film, a concession to his wish for color prints. Normally I refuse to shoot color. What's the point since I can't see the hues? But no request of Tim's could be denied. I would shoot with one camera for him, with the other for myself.

I was nervous about the session, looking forward to it too. Since I'd always felt that Tim was holding something back, a nude session could be a way to break through his reserve.

Starting back in art school, I've shot numerous nudes in my career. Always as a session begins I'm filled with a sense of moral responsibility. This results from my feeling that with my camera I'm all-powerful, while my subject, of whatever gender, is defenseless before my gaze.

I felt this way waiting for Tim, and when he arrived felt his anxiety as well. Yes, he had asked for this, but he couldn't help but feel nervous too.

I was dressed skimpily, in sleeveless jersey and nylon shorts. My feet were bare. I'd turned the living room into a studio, drawn the shades, set up lights, spread a thick black velour curtain down one wall and across the floor. By so doing I'd made a conscious decision to shoot Tim in limbo against deep black. I didn't want to produce Avedon-style pictures in which he'd appear pinned against stark white walls. Rather I was after pictures that would be both luminous and romantic, emphasizing his beauty, imbuing him with glamour.

I started to shoot even as he undressed, since his manner struck me as extremely sensual. When he was naked, I discovered no surprises. Everything was as I'd imagined.

For the first rolls I had him pose against the wall, then lie down while I climbed a ladder and shot him from above. As I focused in on him I became interested in details: the way his arms met his torso, the curve of his ass, his nipples, armpits, genitals, the fuzz of hair on his chest, the musculature of his back when he lay down and extended his arms above his head. He enjoyed posing, rolling around, stretching and twisting, creating abstract forms. He did things with his body that, as I examine the proofs, seem nearly impossible unless he'd been trained as a contortionist.

I'm looking at a shot in which he's standing on his hands. His body, in profile, fills the frame. His legs curl back over him so his feet extend further forward than his head. His face though concentrated is nearly expressionless, as if to show he feels no strain.

In another shot he's leaping, arms up like a volleyball player about to execute a smash. His entire musculature is exposed, his cock has flopped up, his hard abdomen is tautly etched. At the sight of such beauty ruined I start to sob.

As the session continued, I remember now, a glaze of perspiration rose to coat his skin. He began to gleam as if he were oiled, and a fragrance, musky and saline, rose from him, the sweet aroma of his sweat. It wafted to me as I moved about, filling my nostrils, snaking deep into my lungs.

Such intimacy!

It occurs to me now that in a very special way we *were* making love that day, he the model, I the photographer, synchronized, engaged in an elaborate courtship dance. We didn't speak, rather moved slowly in relation to one another, he posing, seeming to know what I wanted, I shooting, picking up on his signals. *Yes! Kiss me here! Now over here!* his body seemed to say, and the clicks of my shutter were like licks against his flesh.

By the end, I recall, I was sweating myself, my shirt glued to my nipples and back. I remember envying him the freedom of his nudity while wishing I could tear off my own scanty clothes. The truth, of course, is that I wished he would do the tearing.

There came a moment when I actually thought that could happen. We were both poised for it, I'm sure. But the spell was broken when a slight trembling shook the building. Then it was too late, the moment dissolved and the energy lost was not regained. That night on TV a reporter announced that a mild quake of Richter magnitude 3.2 had struck the city.

We were finished. Tim pulled on his jeans; then we lay together on the velour, exhausted from eight hours of work.

He asked how I thought the session had gone.

"I'll know when I see the proofs," I said.

"Your gut feeling?"

"Great!"

"Can we do it again?"

"Sure, but not for a while. Too soon and we'll repeat ourselves."

He nodded. There was at least half a minute of silence, then he told me he had a secret wish.

"I've always wanted to be photographed a certain way," he said, "holding a special pose."

I waited for him to explain. He was nervous, I could see, perhaps even ashamed.

"Tell me," I urged.

He stared at the ceiling. He didn't want me to see his eyes.

"Saint Sebastian," he murmured in a confessional whisper. "You know who I mean?"

"The saint tied to the tree with arrows in his chest."

"Stomach too . . ."

"You want to pose like that?"

He nodded, then rolled onto his side.

I was familiar with the eroticization of the Saint Sebastian image in the work of the Japanese writer Yukio Mishima and the British filmmaker Derek Jarman. "Yes, we could set that up," I told him, "perhaps in a quiet corner of Golden Gate Park. Tie you to a tree beneath a shaft of sunlight, then glue the arrows on." I let my hand graze his bare stomach. "Do you identify with martyrdom, Tim?"

While he thought about that I stood and began to unload my cameras.

"Guess so," he said softly, "since it turns me on."

I glanced at him. "Then we'll do it," I promised, "and you'll find out if it's the image that excites you, or playing the part."

I took the rolls to my darkroom. When I returned he was fully dressed. He helped me dismantle my lights, roll up the velour, put my living room back in order; then I changed and we walked down to North Beach for pizza.

Looking at the nudes now, I see decent enough studies but nothing that strikes me as powerful. That's always the problem when you work a well-mined field, and God knows, the human nude, male and female, is well mined. Still, in these shots I see Tim's body whole, the body with which he made his living.

All those years when I was afraid of Polk Gulch, avoided it and, when obliged to cross it, strode through it as quickly as I could, it wasn't the atmosphere, buildings or even the people that frightened me, it was what they *did*.

What kind of people, I'd ask myself, rent out their bodies to strangers? And who *are* these strangers who feel they have the right to rent the body of a person they don't care about or even know? It was to answer these questions, give face to these people, that I started to explore with my camera.

When I started I had no idea how I'd feel toward them, whether I'd like them or despise them. All I knew was that I wanted to expand something within myself, overcome my fear, enlarge my sympathy for those who are reviled.

Tim more than anyone showed me the way. Through him I learned to see hustlers as fragile beings with the same yearnings as myself. I also came to understand that their bartering of their bodies was in principle not so different from the transactions between athletes and their fans. In the latter case the ticket holder has bought permission to gaze, in the former he has paid to touch.

I pick up a photograph in which Tim is facing away, posed like a Greek sculpture of a youth. With his head turned his body becomes idealized, a body beautiful— open, accessible, voluptuous. Again I feel desire for him, and as I do, am filled with regret. So many things held me back—fear of disease, ruining our friendship, being inept with such an experienced lover. Fear most of all of letting myself go.

These, of course, are selfish thoughts, considering the terrible wounds inflicted upon him. Perhaps if we had made it, everything would have been different. He would have given up his trade, he would have lived.

four

I'm standing in mud on a ridge in Wildcat Canyon Regional Park, Hilly Lentz on one side of me, a Contra Costa County deputy on the other. Shanley, cell phone in hand, stands ten paces ahead. Below us, about a hundred feet, in an area of scrub demarcated by police tape, a number of county and S.F.P.D. criminalists are combing the brush. It was here today at dawn, deep in a thicket, that a hiker spotted a male torso.

It's eight a.m., a raw, chilly morning. A slow steady rain has been falling for over an hour. I'm wearing a black slicker and boots, the cops are in ponchos, Hilly and Shanley wear nylon rain jackets with hoods, *S.F.P.D.* printed in large block letters on their backs. I hear the crackle of field radios as the criminalists communicate below. Through the surrounding mist I make out El Cerrito. San Francisco, a few miles across the Bay, is obscured by fog.

Two men from the coroner's office lug a lumpy dark rubber bag up the hill. In it is the torso which may or may not be Tim's. It's two days since I looked at the shots from our nude session, studied the curves of his body, the texture of his skin. I have not been called here to ID him;

the medical examiner will do that by matching the cuts on the limbs. They also have my Angel Island photograph which shows the freckles on his chest. Still I have come. Hilly called me as she promised and now I am here, standing on the muddy ground, camera in my hands, a witness.

Click! I shoot a long shot of the advancing men. *Click!Click!* I shoot them again as they move closer. The images will not be clear, and that's good, I think, for my feelings on this ridge are not clear either. They're dark, they concern bloodshed and carnage, and blood for me is always black.

Shanley is walking toward the men.

"How's it look?"

The older of the two wears a watch cap. He grumbles. "Rain's messing everything up."

His younger colleague nods. He's gawky, bareheaded, with stick-out ears.

"Animals've been at him," he says. He gives a little tug to the sack.

"What kind?" Shanley asks.

"Dogs maybe. There're a couple wild packs around. Maybe a mountain lion. There's one killed a lady here last spring."

I remember the story; it was on TV. The woman was walking a trail bike. The mountain lion, waiting in a tree, leapt upon her back.

Suddenly I feel sick. I think I understand Shanley's question. He wants to be sure the person who did the butchering didn't engage in a little cannibalism first.

I start down the hill. Shanley calls after me.

"Where're you going?"

"Take some pictures," I reply without looking back.

"No, you're not. No!" His voice is stern.

I ignore him.

"Halt!" he yells. I halt. "You can't enter a crime scene. Restricted area down there."

"I'll stay outside the tape, how's that?"

Hilly has reached me. She takes my arm. "Better come

back up, Kay,'' she says. ''Otherwise he'll make you leave.''

She escorts me up the hill, then goes to Shanley. They confer. Shanley, I'm certain, wants me taken home; Hilly is arguing that I be handled with care.

They're wrong, I'm not traumatized. Horrified, yes; angry, absolutely! But I'm not in the least disoriented. I know exactly what I'm doing: collecting material for *Exposures*.

The rain starts falling harder. I watch as the crew spreads plastic sheets to protect the crime scene from the elements. Is this the killing ground, the place where the body was dismembered? Has the earth here been consecrated by Tim's blood?

I take another shot so I can find this place again, revisit it when the cops are finished, leave flowers, light candles, sit and watch them burn down to pools of wax. Perhaps I will leave some kind of marker, too. I'm sure that the torso in the sack is his.

Noon. Back in San Francisco. The rain's stopped, the fog's burning off, but on Russian Hill it's still thick. Hilly has just informed me by phone that the medical examiner has matched the Wildcat Canyon torso to the arms, legs and head from the Willow Dumpster.

''It's your friend,'' she says. ''At least now he can be buried whole.''

I phone my father, tell him I need to see him.

''Love to visit with you, darlin','' he says. ''Shall we wait till after dark?''

No, I tell him, right away.

He's surprised but doesn't ask me why. We agree to meet for lunch at the Tai Yuet, a dim sum place on upper Geary.

As I arrive by bus I see him entering. He's wearing the same shapeless heavy wool sweater he's worn for years.

Soft gray locks of hair curl over his ears. I race toward
the restaurant door, reach it just in time to grab him from
behind, press my face against his back.

"Dad . . ."

He turns, hugs me hard, then kisses my forehead. As
always in his mighty arms, I feel safe.

The Tai Yuet is filled mostly with Chinese, convivial
groups seated at large round tables. Our table is small,
square, set against the wall. The waitresses stroll about
offering delicacies from trays. Dad speaks some Cantonese from the years he worked Chinatown. The girls giggle
when the big guy with the meaty Irish face tells them in
their own language he'll have a little of this, a little of
that, and could they bring over a flask of rice vinegar
please.

"Grand to see you, Kay."

His eyes sparkle through his squint. He's sixty-two, his
skin is lined, there're bags beneath his eyes. Still, he's
handsome. I think he looks like a character actor, the kind
that play old-timers in Westerns. You know the type—
they crouch around the campfire at night, sadly recalling
the way things were, grieving over the end of the open
range.

I marvel at his gentle manner. Since he retired from
S.F.P.D. and started City Stone Ground, a bread bakery
two blocks away, he's become increasingly sweet and
self-effacing.

"You look pretty relaxed," I tell him.

"Morning's over. That's the hard part of the day. Actually, I feel good," he says. "Cop work never felt right."

"Took you long enough to discover it."

"Yeah, well, some lessons are hard to learn."

He sets down his chopsticks, peers into my eyes.

"There's a sadness about you, Kay."

A waitress offers a bamboo steamer containing pork
dumplings. He mumbles "No thanks" in Cantonese without taking his eyes off mine.

I tell him about Tim. Till now he's only had the vaguest
notion of my project. I know it disturbs him to learn I've

been hanging out in such a squalid milieu, but I detect nothing judgmental, rather a deepening sympathy as he gently shakes his head, swallows and exhales. When I get to the dismemberment he despairs.

"Gotta be a copycat," he murmurs.

"What if it isn't?"

"Gotta be. Too many years."

He wants to know about Tim's torso, whether and how it was marked.

"Hilly didn't say anything about that."

"Did you ask her?"

I shake my head. "If there're marks, what would they mean?"

"If they're the same I'd say they'd mean a lot."

He stops eating. When I offer him a shrimp and chives dumpling, he shakes his head.

"Tell me about it," I urge.

"What?"

"The T case."

He groans. "That's a sorrowful ugly story."

"You're a terrific storyteller. You used to tell me great bedtime stories." I remember how much I loved the one about the little girl who couldn't see colors but could read people's minds.

"That was to help you sleep, darlin'."

"Now help me understand."

"Oh, sweet Jesus," he groans, "it seems so long ago. . . ."

There were six T case victims, he recounts, five homicides plus Robbie Sipple, the first in '76; the last, Sipple, in '81, one a year in between. After Sipple they stopped. They were called the T killings because only the torsos were found—no heads or limbs as with Tim. The victims were young males and four were never identified. No fingerprints, no dental work, and in those days DNA matching didn't exist. It was a fluke that even one besides Sipple was ID'ed; he'd been missing, his parents had filed a report, he'd recently had a gallbladder operation and the surgeon recognized the scar.

"He was gay, promiscuous." Dad says "gay" blandly, but he's of the generation that can't pronounce the word without an involuntary wince. "We learned he hit the baths every night. We assumed the others were like that too, kids who'd drifted here, gay lifestyle capital. But without heads or hands we couldn't ID them."

The five torsos showed certain common traits. They were from lean, hard, gym-toned bodies; they were all Caucasian; they'd been sodomized; their blood had been drained; their skin had been washed; they'd been left in public places (the Presidio, Point Lobos, Mount Davidson, Twin Peaks, Golden Gate Park) where they were certain to be found. That was one odd thing: that they hadn't been buried or disposed of like the limbs and heads. The other odd thing was the tattoos.

"We told the papers there were marks. We never got more specific. They were always on the back, on three victims the right shoulder area, on two the butt."

Dad pours tea into his cup, brings it to his lips, blows on it, sips.

"The tattoos weren't elaborate, the work was fair at best. We had tattooists in. They estimated the work on each took approximately three to four hours. The designs were abstract. There wasn't a picture of anything, just these curves and lines. The tattooists thought they looked like tribal markings, but they couldn't identify the tribe. We brought in an anthropologist. She said that they looked vaguely South Pacific Island. She couldn't ID them either."

"Were there colors?" I ask.

"The ink used was black."

Well, I think, *that's something.*

The case was never solved. Hundreds were interviewed: tattooists professional and prison-trained, surgeons, butchers, known homosexual sadists. There were many leads, all checked out, all dead ends. Then the killings stopped as abruptly as they began. It was one of those weird unsolved San Francisco cases, like the Zodiac killings, but in the T case there were no taunting letters to the press.

The killer remained quiet . . . as if his cutting and tattoos said it all. There was something terribly cold and cruel in Torsos that struck everyone who worked it.

"It was only once that we got even partway close. That was when I was involved."

Dad pours another cup of tea, holds it in his hands to warm them. This is the bad part of the story, I know, the part that changed his life.

"It was spring, '81. I was working the Haight, foot patrol, feeling burnt-out. I was thinking a lot those days about what to do when I retired, mulling my dream of setting up a bakery, producing and selling first-rate bread. It was around eight p.m. I was on Waller when I got the call—disturbance on Frederick just two blocks away. There's a hill there, you know, pretty steep. So I huff and puff my way up to this smallish Victorian on Frederick, and there's a middle-aged lady standing on the stoop, the room behind her lit like a Christmas tree.

"She lets me in. She's fairly panicked. Tells me she owns the house, rents out the basement and a flat upstairs. It's the basement tenant's got her worried. He's new, been there just a couple weeks. Around seven she heard strange sounds from his room, and, a few minutes before, a scream. Too scared to go down and check, she dialed nine-one-one.

"I listen hard. I can't hear anything. That tells me whatever was happening is probably over . . . and maybe it was just the TV turned on loud, a horror film, cop show, something like that. Still I go down by the outside steps and rap on the door. No answer, but I hear something faint inside like maybe an animal scratching at the wall. I turn the handle and the door opens, no lock, not even firmly shut. There's this young Caucasian male lying in the middle of the floor, wrists bound behind his back, tied to his ankles too. He's helpless, hog-tied, buck-naked except for this hood he's wearing, a full head black leather hood, kind you see in some of the gay leather stores, what they call a discipline helmet, bondage hood, whatever.

And he's moving a little but not too much, and I get the impression maybe his air's cut off.

"I rush over to him, start working on the hood straps. His body's sticky. I yell to the landlady to call for an ambulance. Hell of a time getting that hood off. All those straps and zippers—it was practically sealed to his face. Finally I yank it. This gag thing comes out with it. There's vomit inside and if he's breathing I can't hear it. But he's got a pulse so I cut the ropes, turn him over and start the old artificial respiration, pinching his nose, breathing into his lungs. He starts gurgling. By this time the medics have come. I step back. They give him oxygen."

Dad brings up his napkin, wipes his brow. It's easy for me to imagine him ministering to the kid in that basement, bringing him back to life. It's the way I like to think of him, a hero.

"After I get off him I look around. I tell you, Kay— this was one shabby pad. No bed, just a ratty couch with broken springs. No closet, just a pile of clothes in the corner. Airplane-size lav with rusty metal shower stall. Beaten-up black-and-white TV. Basically no possessions of value . . . and that makes me curious, because that hood he was wearing, it wasn't cheap.

"Lots of people in the basement now. Medics, other cops working the Haight, a sergeant from a command unit happened to be in the neighborhood. Lots of confusion too. 'Who is this kid?' 'Is he okay?' 'He sure didn't tie *himself* up like that!' 'Hey, what's this? Looks like some kind of ink.'

"They cart the kid out, ambulance him over to Cal Med on Parnassus, then the rest of us start poking around. 'Hey, look at this—amyl nitrite!' 'Wow! A syringe! Think he injected himself?' We're handling everything, passing it around, nobody thinking this has anything to do with the T case. I mean, how could it? No one's been killed, no one's been cut up, there's no torso, nothing to connect it.

"It's only the next day we find out different. The kid's name is Robbie Sipple, he's nineteen, he works as a stock clerk in a pagan-goods store on Ashbury, moved to the city from Dallas just a month before. Seems he took the afternoon off, was lingering in a gay bar when a handsome thirtyish guy picked him up. Robbie brings the guy home, they screw their brains out, then Robbie takes a little nap. When he wakes up he finds himself bound and gagged with the guy lying next to him whispering weird stuff into his ear—how's he's going to kill him, take his body to a house where he'll cut it up, then leave the pieces in various places around town. Robbie'll just disappear, the guy whispers, no one'll know he's dead 'cause there won't be any trace of him, and now, before he does all that, he's going to put some neat little decorations on Robbie's butt.

"The tattooing was about to start when somehow, terrified, Robbie spat out his gag and let out with a scream. Right away the guy wrestled the bondage helmet over his head and bound him in it so he couldn't make another sound. There was a tiny hole in the hood, to let in just enough air so he wouldn't suffocate. Robbie couldn't hear anything, couldn't see, move, could barely squirm, didn't know if the guy was still there or not. So he started to panic. Just as he passed out, certain he was going to die, I came in and pulled the helmet off."

Dad gets the check, pays, we leave the restaurant, start walking over to the bakery. The sun's shining so I put on shades. I like walking with Dad on the street.

"You get the picture, Kay. We got someone who was literally in the hands of the T killer, who barely escaped. We got someone who saw him, can describe him, work with a police sketch artist. We also got evidence, stuff that belonged to the killer: the hood, the tattoo ink, a syringe. There may even be fingerprints in the kid's apartment. In short, we got the mother lode. Except—"

Dad stops to greet a customer, a woman carrying a City Stone Ground bag. She compliments him on his bread and courteous Russian refugee staff.

"—except," Dad continues, "all that good luck suddenly turns to shit. Robbie Sipple dies. Right there in the friggin' hospital! He gets out of bed, stands, takes a deep breath and drops to the floor. Naturally they autopsy him. He's got some kind of congenital heart disease. You hear about these cases—high school kid plays basketball, suddenly keels over, he's gone. Problem was young Robbie hadn't given us a description yet. Just two words, 'handsome' and 'thirtyish.'

"And there was another problem too, a very big problem. That hood I pulled off him, the ink, the syringe—no one can find them, they're not in Robbie's apartment, not in the police property room. They're gone. Vanished. Thin air!" Dad snaps his fingers. *Click!* "Like that!"

We're standing in front of City Stone Ground. I smell the aroma of the bread. It reminds me of weekends during my childhood when Dad baked for us, trying out brands of flour, sources of spring water, new shapes, baking stones, leavenings. He was a magician with components: flour, yeast, water, salt. Our house was filled with the sweet warm fragrances of his *pain au levain,* round sourdough loaves, baguettes. Breadmaking, which started as his hobby, soon became his obsession. He was striving toward something pure and impeccable—a perfect loaf with a shattering crust. He loved working with his hands. He'd talk about kneading, how good it made him feel. Once, when I asked him why he liked breadmaking so much, he meditated on my question. "A good loaf doesn't lie," he finally said.

Dad shakes his head. He's getting to the bad part now, the part that happened after they found the evidence was gone.

"Everyone who was there that night—me, the other cops, the sergeant—we're called into a meeting with Inspector Jonathan Topper Hale, lead detective on the T case, so-called 'city's smartest cop.' We go over it with him again and again. No one can explain the loss. We all remember seeing the evidence, handling it, but everyone says he handed it off to someone else. Bottom line: No one took responsibility, secured it, bagged it, initialed and sealed the bag. But then no one had any inkling it related to a capital case. Conclusion: We must have left it in the flat, but the flat wasn't sealed. So what happened to it? Hale starts bearing down. 'Don't you remember?' 'What are you—assholes?' 'You left the stuff there like fuckin' idiots?' "

There's a gloss of sweat on Dad's forehead as he relives the humiliation.

"The top forensics team in the city went into that basement. They dusted, vacuumed, crawled around the floor with their friggin' microscopes. They found lots of prints, all sorts of hairs, but nothing they could convincingly tie to the guy who told Robbie Sipple he'd kill him and cut him up.

"You remember what happened. The I.A. investigation which was supposed to stay internal, except somehow it got leaked. The articles that came out, the way they made us look. Then the editorials, so sarcastic—the taxpayers of the city actually *paid* people to bungle a crime scene that contained the only T case evidence ever discovered.

"The sergeant, Wainy Waincroft, was demoted straightaway to patrolman. He quit. I was reassigned to a dead-end desk job. Everyone who was there that night was disciplined. They wanted to stigmatize us, make examples of us . . . and they did."

Dad wipes away the sweat.

"It hit me hard, your mother worse. You remember how she got. She couldn't take the stress, got so bad she couldn't bear to leave the house. I passed it onto her, I guess. Didn't mean to. You know that. But it just pushed her deeper into her depression. Then, what she did, Kay, I guess you could say it goes back to that night . . . though I think she was so ill she'd have probably done it anyway even if they'd promoted me, named me friggin' Commander of Patrol."

He spreads his hands.

"That's the story. Maybe now you wish you hadn't asked. How's it feel to know your old man could've been famous, the guy who cracked the T case. In law enforcement, if you're lucky, you get a chance like that once in a career. I got it and blew it ... and here I am." He smiles. "In that way at least, I like to think, it was the best thing could've happened."

He pulls me to him, kisses my forehead, then the top of my head. I tell him I want to photograph him. He's delighted, dodges into the bakery, swiftly changes into whites, plops on a baker's hat, grabs a wooden peel, steps back out.

I pose him in front of City Stone Ground, the big window through which the huge brick oven can be seen. He beams at my lens, a dusting of flour on his cheek, a gentle smile on his lips. I fire at him twice. *Click!Click!* I catch him, as in an August Sander study: the quintessential Happy Baker.

Everyone needs a coach. Mine is Maddy, also my friend, mentor, guru. I pay her for private coaching, which does not mean I go to her for lessons in technique. Basically what she does is look at my work, discuss it with me, critique it, coach me on how best to achieve my goals. Her insights are smart, penetrating, sometimes merciless. I've learned more from her about photography than from any teacher I've ever had.

She lives on Alhambra in the Marina, a flat area of art deco–period homes and apartment buildings that abuts the Bay. She's seventy now, stopped taking photographs years ago, but the walls of her flat are covered with framed prints of her work, astonishing pictures taken on city streets, some dense with life, others soft, moody, underpopulated, all poignant, full of feeling and wondrous San Francisco light. Also hanging here are many fine portraits of local artists and writers, and the famous pictures she took of GIs during the Korean War, some of the darkest, most intense combat photographs ever shot. Don't look to Maddy's work for still lifes, whimsy, charm or arty "decisive moments." She's mistress of the direct, unblinking gaze, the gaze that, in her words, probes, strips, reveals.

She greets me with a hug. A tall, thin, fragile white-haired woman, almost gaunt, she's visibly aged this past year. There're rumors she's ill, but she'll allow no discussion of her health. And even if Maddy has faded physically, her eyes are as keen as ever. People who interview her never fail to mention them. One journalist described "eyes so sharp you feel they should be registered as dangerous weapons."

We sit in her living room. Expecting me, she has thoughtfully lowered the blinds in advance.

"You're troubled, Kay." Her eyes probe mine.

How well she knows me. I tell her about Tim.

"Awful, terrible . . ." She takes my hand. "My heart aches for you, dear."

She retires to her kitchen to make tea. When she's gone I look about. A snapshot of Maddy with her late husband, Harry Yamada, sits on the lamp table beside my chair. The picture was taken aboard an ocean liner sometime in 1951. They stand at the railing, young, beautiful and in love, arms about one another, staring into the lens. Behind them the port of Yokohama glitters in the dawn. Maddy is on her way to Korea for the first time to cover the war for *Life*.

When she returns, I spread out the nudes of Tim. She fills my cup, examines them, then turns her attention to my proof sheets. It's proof sheets, she believes, that tell her most—how I work, what I was trying to do, where I made decisions good and bad.

"I'm unhappy with them," I tell her.

"You shouldn't be," she says. "There're some strong images here."

"Not strong enough."

She shakes her head. "You're wrong, Kay. I think you feel that way because all that's left of him is on film and for you now that's not enough."

Perhaps she's right.

"If these were just snaps," she goes on, "it would be a different story. But these are photographs and we don't make photographs of people to substitute for their presence. What you've brought me is a project, a session with a nude model. You're exploring him, exploring your relation to him by studying his face and body. You're even, in a way, making love to him . . . as you always do when you care about a subject. The caring here is strong, Kay. Very strong. These aren't abstract nudes. Oh, sure, a few times, you yield to the impulse to make designs. But really these are portraits of a very beautiful young man who happens to be unclothed. Interesting work. Significant. There's power here. Something tense, thrilling.''

She sits back. I'm grateful. Even if she's being kind, she has helped me understand what I did. Yes, that afternoon we took the nudes was a time of mutual exploration, perhaps as much of me by him as of him by me. There was magic between us, magic Maddy says I captured, magic I have no right now to deny.

I thank her, we stand, embrace and then I leave. Walking home, I consider how lucky I am to have her for a friend.

I call Hilly. The jerk who answers her line says she isn't there. As soon as I give my name, Shanley picks up.

"What can we do for you today?"

"Were there marks?" I ask.

"Huh?"

"On Tim's torso—marks, tattoos?"

"What kinda question's that?"

"You're saying there were?"

"I'm not saying anything. I'm asking you a question."

"I helped you. It's your turn now."

"Turn to do *what?*"

"What do you think?"

"Look, Kay, maybe I'm missing something here. I'm a cop, you're a civilian. You came forward, as you rightly should. You wanna play detective, do it on some other guy's case. Not on mine. Got it?" He hangs up.

• • •

It's twilight. I'm walking in North Beach . . . among tourists, stockbrokers, young people in love, sailors, Asian immigrants, commercial travelers seeking companionship, addicts, alcoholics, people nostalgic for the beat period, self-styled San Francisco poets.

I'm thinking about none of that, thinking instead about color blindness and the many misunderstandings that surround it. The most common is that only boys suffer from it and that they inherit it from their mothers. In fact, the defective gene that produces most color deficiencies, such as red-green confusion, *is* far more likely to affect males and *is* carried by the mother on the X chromosome. If a female child's mother is a carrier and her father is color-deficient, both her X chromosomes may carry the defect and thus cause her to suffer from the malady.

However, this inheritance pattern does not apply to autosomal recessive achromatopsia. In my case, and that of other achromats, there's usually no family history of the defect and males and females are equally affected. Furthermore, if I have children I won't pass the defect on except in the unlikely event I mate with another achromat or carrier. All of which is to say that my color blindness can't be definitively attributed to either my mom or my dad.

Why, in this cosmopolitan environment, am I thinking about inheritance patterns, chromosomes, defective genes? Because I have the chilling feeling that Dad, my closest relative on this earth, who speaks so passionately about honesty and how a good loaf of bread doesn't lie, was less than fully truthful about his involvement in the T case when he recounted it to me over lunch.

At home I search not the heavens but the city with my telescope, seeking answers in dim doorways, parked cars, lit-up rooms. San Francisco, they say, belongs to everyone—not just to its residents but also to all the visitors who travel here and come to love this place. City on the Bay, Queen of the Pacific Coast, Luminous City, Jewel of the West. It is also City of Vertigo, of Lust, of Meretricious Charms. Conan Doyle called it a "dream city" with the "glamour of literature." John Steinbeck wrote of it as a "gold and white acropolis rising wave on wave against the blue of the Pacific sky." My favorite description is Oscar Wilde's: "It's an odd thing, but anyone who disappears is said to be seen in San Francisco. It must be a delightful city and possess all the attractions of the next world."

Tonight the Judge is home: I see lights and movement through the French doors that open to his terrace. I wait patiently for him to show himself. Five minutes, ten, fifteen . . . My eyes grow weary. I pick up a fashion magazine, examine glossy black-and-white photographs of slick-haired, sleek-bodied young men and women modeling underwear. When I peer again through my telescope I'm rewarded by an appearance. The Judge leans upon his terrace balcony looking west toward me.

Does he remember that I live here across the valley? Does it occur to him that just now I may be looking straight into his eyes?

Five

I'm standing in a small crowd just outside the vault-like doors of the Main Library, due to open at nine a.m. With me are the usual suspects—early birds, scholars, nerds, as well as homeless residents of the Civic Center encampment who need to use the toilets.

Behind us, across the plaza, the dome of City Hall reflects the sun. Through the library doors we can see people moving inside. They don't acknowledge us, don't give a glance as they officiously prepare for us, the sweaty horde, hovering with growing impatience for the opening.

A Chinese intellectual, briefcase and wire-rims, checks his watch and stamps his foot.

"Always late!"

"Op-en! Op-en!" A young troublemaker with Mohawk starts the chant. Others join in. A black guard approaches the doors, stares out nervously.

"Op-en! Op-en!"

Finally, at 9:07, the great doors are unbolted. We of the sweaty horde surge inside.

• • •

I'm sitting in the periodicals room before a large black microfilm reader, unspooling a reel of the *San Francisco Examiner* vintage 1981–82. The T case is a recurring motif that year, as is the name Jonathan Topper Hale, the oft-quoted S.F.P.D. inspector, who promises the public that he and his "crack team" of investigators are "doing everything humanly possible" to solve "these horrific and hitherto intractable crimes."

Persons having knowledge of the quarry, defined as "probably a white male in his thirties who may have a meatpacking or medical background, with a possible additional interest in tattoos and/or tattooing," are urged to phone the T Case Hotline, where all tips, whether attributed or anonymous, will be promptly checked out.

"Interest in tattoos and/or tattooing"—clever that, I think. Not a word about the application of tattoos to the torsos, leaving the reader to surmise that the victims were chosen on account of tattoos already on their bodies. Yet the phrase is sufficiently enticing that if someone actually did know a person capable of both butchering and tattooing, he/she would still be likely to phone said information in.

Above several of the articles appear pictures of Inspector Hale—late forties, brooding, authoritative, canny eyes, black hair, thick eyebrows, matching black mustache. His visage announces: *I am one serious cop.*

But the more I read about Hale, the more I get a sense he isn't all that popular with colleagues. "Sure, he's a great policeman," one unnamed Department source tells the *Examiner,* "but he has this weakness—a craving for personal publicity."

Others, speaking of Hale's brilliance, also mention his arrogance. Inspector Hale, I come to learn, is no shrinking violet. But he has his defenders. Over a period of nine weeks three letters appear in the Letters to the Editor column praising "this outstanding law enforcement officer" for his "brilliant performance" and "unselfish devotion to duty." One writer goes so far as to define the inspector as "perhaps the finest of San Francisco's finest, the closest thing we've got here to a cop's cop."

On May 12, 1982, a scandal erupts, diverting attention from the T case investigation, which, in any event, is going nowhere fast. An astute *Examiner* reporter, one Jim Steele, noticing that the three letters praising Hale were written on the same typewriter, checks out the letter writers' names and finds they're fake. Increasingly suspicious, he secures a document typed by Hale on a machine in his office and has it matched by a typewriter expert to the typing on the letters.

Hale, of course, denies any knowledge of the forgeries, but voluntarily resigns "for the good of the Department." His moral breakdown is attributed by unnamed sources to everything from "work-related stress" to "a warped sense of humor." Hale's attorney, Denis Roquelle, speaks of "the immense tragedy that has overtaken this exemplary officer who is pilloried now because his brilliance has long aroused the envy of the gutless wonders who staff the upper echelons of S.F.P.D."

I gaze at a picture of Hale as he leaves the Hall of Justice for the last time. Proud, unrepentant, features set into a crooked grin, he projects himself as a man above the fray and the petty jealousies that have brought him down.

There is more. I make my way through reels from the *Chronicle* as well as the *Examiner,* sniffing around the untidy corners of the case, avoiding coverage of the Robbie Sipple incident, circling it, saving it for last . . . and not because I think it'll taste so very good. Rather I'm apprehensive it will tell me things I'd rather not know. Except that I *do* want to know those things.

Stop diddling, Kay. Confront your demons!

T VICTIM DROPS DEAD AS "DUMMY COPS" MISLAY EVIDENCE

The story is as brutal as the headline. The excoriated "dummies" are individually named: Patrolmen Jack L.

Farrow, William D. Hayes, Enrico S. Puccio, Luis Cruz Vasquez, and Sergeant Lucius D. Waincroft. Adjectives and nouns flow fast and thick: "pathetic, inept, irresponsible, incompetent; dolts, dunces, bunglers, chumps, buffoons."

I wince as I read the accompanying articles. It's hard not to think of these men as dolts. Hardest of all is to imagine Dad among them, casually handling evidence, then abandoning the basement apartment without securing it. One minute he's a hero saving Robbie Sipple's life, the next he's Prince of Fools.

I can't buy it. I ask myself why. Because Dad is the most exacting man I know, rigorously correct, even compulsive, in matters having to do with property, finances, relationships and procedures concerning everything from automobile maintenance to the making of exotic breads. He pays his bills the day he receives them, figures his taxes to the penny, promptly repays loans, conscientiously returns borrowed possessions, keeps his doors locked, his papers in order, teaches me, his child, the virtues of truthfulness and reliability. "The most important thing about a person is personal integrity," he teaches. "In fact," he adds, "it's the *only* thing."

Am I to believe that this man, who never misplaced anything, never left his house or car door unlocked, never read a set of instructions he didn't follow, never in twenty years as a cop fouled or in any way tainted a crime scene, could be party to such bungling? I cannot.

Which leaves me again with the thought that the story he told me yesterday wasn't straight. That something else happened that night at Robbie Sipple's. That Dad, alone or in complicity with others, obstructed justice. That at the very least he had knowledge of such obstruction and for some reason, which I cannot comprehend, preferred to suffer the indignity of being called a dummy rather than tell the truth.

Methodically I photocopy every relevant page of microfilm, not at all certain why I bother. No solid connection yet between Tim's dismemberment and the old T case, but, because of Tim, I've stumbled back into a mystery that for years I put out of mind.

Just before I return the reels to the desk, I search out Mom's obit. There is none, only a death notice:

FARROW, CARLOTTA RYAN—PASSED AWAY SAN FRANCISCO, OCTOBER 9, 1981, AGE 43. BELOVED WIFE OF JACK L. FARROW, LOVING MOTHER OF KAY R. FARROW, CHERISHED SISTER OF TOM RYAN AND ARLENE RYAN O'NEILL. SHE LEAVES BEHIND FEELINGS OF JOY AND LOVE THAT TOUCHED ALL SHE MET, INCLUDING HER NIECES, NEPHEWS AND NUMEROUS STUDENTS AT MARINA MIDDLE SCHOOL TO WHOM SHE TAUGHT MUSIC THROUGH THE YEARS. FRIENDS MAY VISIT FRIDAY, FROM 1 TO 5 P.M., AT TERRY SULLIVAN MORTUARY. FUNERAL ARRANGEMENTS ARE PRIVATE.

Emerging from the library onto Civic Center Plaza, I enter an arena of blinding light. Quickly I slip on shades, but even then the brilliance is nearly unendurable. As I squint and blink my way across the plaza, I feel tears forming in my eyes—whether on account of photophobia or recalling my mother's death I cannot be sure.

From home I phone the *Examiner,* ask to speak to someone on the crime desk.

"That'd be city," the operator says. She connects me to a Jason Lubow, who identifies himself as a police reporter. I complain that the killing of Timothy Lovsey has barely gotten notice.

"That Polk Gulch thing?"

"That's the one."

"We ran it."

"Six lines."

"We'll run more when there're developments."

"Such as what?" I ask.

"Arrest. Explanation. Something that wraps it up."

"Otherwise it's just another hustler homicide, right?"

"You said it, lady. Not me. But a Gulch hustler—you know, those things happen. Doesn't make for the most sympathetic victim in town."

"What about a tie-in to the T case?"

"What's that?"

Lubow never heard of it; he's only been in San Francisco six years. As I fill him in, I hear the clicking of computer keys. When I'm done he tells me he'll check it out.

"If you don't mind my asking," he asks, "who am I speaking with?"

"A concerned citizen," I tell him, and hang up.

An hour later I get a call from Hilly Lentz. There's traffic in the background, so loud I can barely hear her.

"Where are you?"

"Pay phone. You never got this call, understand?"

"What's going on?"

"Shanley's crapping in his pants."

"Something I did?"

"Your little query about tattoos."

"So tell me—*are* there tattoos?"

Her wordless breathing is my confirmation.

"What's the big secret?" I ask.

Again she doesn't respond, instead gives me her address.

"I'll be home by six," she says. "Drop by at seven and we'll talk."

She lives on Collingwood near Twentieth in the Castro. It's a nice Edwardian, renovated and well kept up. A guy with a buzz cut, Dalmatian on a leash, emerges as I mount the stoop.

"Need help?" he asks with the demeanor of a landlord.

"Looking for Hilly."

He laughs. "House cop, third floor."

I nod, kneel to meet the dog. I like Dalmatians, they're black and white. But now this one starts nosing at my groin.

"Oscar! *Oscar!*" Buzz Cut yanks at the leash, pets his pooch, grins. "He's heavy into crotch worship, dear. Can you blame him?"

"Well, who should I blame?" I ask.

Hilly's waiting for me in her doorway, dressed in a grungy gray S.F.P.D. T-shirt and baggy sweats. She laughs when I describe the encounter on the stoop.

"If Oscar takes after Jerry he's into just about everything," she says.

She shows me around. The flat is spacious, but messy like a grad student's—living room, eat-in kitchen, bedroom, bath. An aerobics class schedule and police duty roster are taped to the refrigerator door. In the half-open closet I catch sight of black leather motorcycle gear. I glance into the bedroom, notice a pair of handcuffs dangling from a bedpost.

"Standard cop-issue." Hilly giggles. "Fantasy facilitator device."

Back in the living room she clears off a place for me on a couch, opens two cans of beer. Just as she hands me one a cat leaps into my lap.

"Meet Puddy. She's an old thing, Puddy is. If she bothers you just brush her away."

I stroke the cat. "What's going on, Hilly?"

She grins. "Shanley says to kiss you off."

"Because I asked about tattoos?"

She gives a weak smile. "I gotta be careful what I say."

"Hey, you invited me here." To set her at ease I disarm myself by placing my camera on the floor. "If we're not going to talk freely, what's the point?"

She exhales.

"Why *did* you invite me?"

"I like you. You care. Few people do."

A shallow observation, but I let it pass. "Tim Lovsey was my friend."

She nods. "I know. But it's more than that. Your dad was a cop. That makes you part of the family . . . if you know what I mean."

Dysfunctional family, I think.

"Do you know anything about my dad?"

She takes a swig of beer. "Shanley does, says he was involved in the old T case."

"That's right. Yesterday we had lunch. It was the first time I heard his version. I was in art school at the time, so I never got a fix on it. Now I'm starting to. What's the connection? The tattoos the same?"

I gaze into her eyes. I can't be certain but I think they're blue. I don't know why that matters. Blue, brown, hazel—eyes to me are either light or dark.

"One thing you might be interested in—med examiner says Tim tested negative for HIV."

I sink back into the couch. He told me he was negative, got tested regularly, but a side of me wasn't sure. Perhaps if I had been I'd have made a move on him on Angel Island that idyllic afternoon.

"The tattoos?" I ask.

"No tattoos," she says.

"Then why—"

"He was marked."

I push Puddy off, sit straight. *"How?"*

She tightens her lips. "Police business. I'll get shit-canned if I say more." I wait her out, knowing she wants to tell me. "There was painting," she says finally, "black oil-based paint on his back. Abstract shapes, curves, what the med examiner calls arabesques. Like the old case, but crudely done. And something else. A number. 'Seven.' Like the T killer was starting up again from where he left off in '81."

She lets out her breath. She's crossed the line; too late now to turn back.

"Personally I don't think that's possible," she says. "It's been too long. Why would he stop so long, then

resume? And a few other things. Paint instead of tattoos.
That suggests this person doesn't have tattooing skills.
Also the limbs and head—leaving them for us, making it
possible to ID the victim. Finally, why dump them so near
the place where Tim hung out. Why do that . . . then leave
the torso on the other side of the Bay?"

She's trying to sound dispassionate but the vibrato in
her voice gives her away. Listening, I feel we're talking
about stuff that has no connection to real life.

"Maybe the heads and limbs of the earlier victims were
left in Dumpsters too," I say. "Those times, the trash was
hauled. This time a homeless guy happened to be hunting
empty soda cans."

She shrugs. "Could be."

"Butchering's a skill as much as tattooing. Isn't it a
big coincidence to have two butchers?"

"Definitely." She peers at me. "What about the
fifteen-year gap?"

"Maybe the killer was in prison."

"That's Shanley's theory. He's checking it out." She
smiles craftily, as if we're playing a mind game. "What
else?"

"The need to kill quieted down. Then something triggered it again."

"Department shrink suggested that." She shakes her
head. "Sounds like detective story crap to me."

"How do *you* explain it then?"

"Without discounting any of the above, my hunch is a
copycat. No great breakthrough, true. But it's what I
think."

"My dad's theory too."

"The question is why." Again the crafty smile.
"Someone who knows a lot about the T case . . . but not
everything. That's the key. How come he knows certain
things closely held at the time, yet doesn't know other
things the top investigators knew? He has a source. Find
the source and maybe we'll find him. That's the theory
I'll be working on."

She stands, suggests we go out, grab some food. I

watch as she goes to a mirror, checks the gel on her hair, then slips on a leather vest.

As we walk toward Castro she nudges me in the ribs.

"I shouldn't be seen with you, but we don't have to worry around here."

There're plenty of gay S.F.P.D. cops, she tells me. And the proportion of lesbians to straight women may even be greater than the proportion of gays among the men. Which is why, she confides, she moved to San Francisco. She's from L.A., member of a law enforcement family. Her father and two of her uncles are cops, one brother's with the Secret Service, the other with the F.B.I.

"Don't know why they went fed. To best the old man, I guess. In a family like ours you'd think I'd be the black sheep. But both brothers are proud of me. Like: 'Sis is great!' As for Pop—he's a little less enthusiastic. I guess he wishes his only daughter were straight."

A pair of stout diesels approach, sporting engineer's boots and Oakland A's caps backwards on their heads.

"Hey, Hilly!"

"Dina! Jude!"

They eye me slyly as they pass.

Hilly smiles. "They think we're on a date."

"They can think what they like."

"Right!"

I'm not sure how I feel about these undertones. I think I find them amusing. What interests me is why Hilly is extending herself. What does she want from me anyway?

I like the Castro, its parade of purpose and flamboyance, tank tops and tattoos, tight asses, pert tits, piercings, muscles, leather, flesh. Some call it a ghetto, but for me it's a vital portion of the city, alive with young men and women steamy with sexual energy. I believe it's that energy and the freedom it implies that ultimately enrage the bigots. I don't think they hate gay people for what they do in bed; what they can't stand is how much they enjoy it.

Hilly leads me to a solid wooden door. A discreet brass plaque identifies it as The Duchess. The moment Hilly

opens it we confront a wall of sound—loud talk, laughter,
heavy metal music. It's dark, but I can see the place is
crowded with women. I smell beer, cooking oil, cologne,
cigarette smoke, sweat.

"What do you think?" Hilly asks. "They give great
grilled tofu."

"It's not the clientele," I assure her, surveying the
crush. "But looks like it might be hard to talk."

"So true . . . and so sad!" She beams. She wants to be
agreeable. "I know another joint, quieter . . . around the
corner."

She leads me to the kind of nondescript coffee shop
you'd expect to find near a bus terminal. The patrons are
quiet, the booths are upholstered in plastic. Perhaps it sur-
vives as a refuge from the funky dives around.

"No tofu here," Hilly says, "but they make good sal-
ads."

When the waitress comes we both order low-fat Cae-
sars. After she moves away Hilly and I stare at one another. Hilly smiles first.

"Shanley told you to kiss me off," I say. "So why'd
you call me?"

"Aren't you glad?"

"Sure. But what d'you say we cut the crap?"

"Fine." She turns serious. "I don't like Shanley.
We're supposed to be partners. He treats me like an un-
derling. He's homophobic too."

"File a complaint. Isn't that what people do?"

She narrows her eyes. "I've been waiting a long time
for a case like this. Now that I've lucked into it, I'm not
about to let it go."

I stare at her.

"Don't get it, do you?"

"I'm trying," I say.

"Solve it and I'll never take shit again. Not from Shanley or any of the other assholes down on Bryant Street.
I'll be queen of the heap, one of a handful of cops who
get written up, ones the public knows and trusts. If I stay
in law enforcement I can go to the top. If I decide to get

out it's an easy move over to politics." She licks her lips. "Cops dream of stumbling into a case like this. It's cop heaven . . . and now I'm at the door."

I'm amazed by her outburst. This isn't good cop Hilly talking now, this is one tough, ambitious woman.

"I still don't—"

"Why you? Because you knew the victim. Shanley thinks you've given all you got. I think you've got more to spill."

I think about my photos of johns. *But she can't know about them.*

"Did you speak to any of Tim's friends?"

"They're not keen to talk to cops."

Her eyes twinkle. "Think they'd make an exception?"

"Because you're gay? No. You're still the law."

She shrugs. "You're the one who called Lubow, right?" I shrug in turn. "Jason Lubow. The *Examiner*. He says it was a woman who wouldn't give her name. Anyhow, he won't write anything. Shanley's got him in his pocket. He's persuaded Lubow to cooperate."

"Why're you telling me all this, Hilly?"

"I want press coverage, too. You can help me with that."

"Why should I?"

"You're pissed, Kay. I saw it in your eyes the other night. Your buddy was mutilated. You want this solved as much as me . . . and you know I'm on the right track."

"Pissed" seems a bland word for how I feel, but maybe Hilly, lost in her ambition, can't identify with my raging sorrow. Anyhow, it doesn't matter if she reads me right; what's important is that I read her.

"I might be willing to help," I tell her, "but it can't be a one-way street."

The wily smile again. "Tell me what you want."

"Photographs."

"Of what?"

"Tim's body, head, limbs, torso, the marks too, and photos of the crime scenes, Willow and Wildcat Canyon."

"Why?"

"For a book I'm doing documenting Tim's life."

She ponders. "What about copyright?"

"Police pictures are public property. Anyway, I won't use them the way they were shot. I'll blow up details, collage them, create something new."

"Interesting . . . hmmm . . . I think I could manage that. A few prints here and there won't be missed."

"There's more."

She smiles. "I figured. What?"

"Anything in the T case file on my dad."

She laughs. "Don't want much, do you?"

"Would that be so hard to get?"

"If it's in an I.A. report it'd be damn near impossible."

"Suppose it's in his personnel file?"

"Retired cop? I never asked for anything like that. Don't know if I can."

"Of course you can, Hilly." I bear down. "You've already got your justification. You're looking for the new killer's source—who knew what, who's the leak. To investigate you'll need to read the files of everyone involved—from Inspector Jonathan Topper Hale right down to Patrolman Jack L. Farrow."

I reach for the tab. Hilly mildly protests, but allows me to pick it up. She's worked a long hard day; she's tired. Our little mind game's worn her down, but it's invigorated me.

She walks me to the Muni stop at Market and Castro. We agree to think things over and let each other know. She gives me her home phone number, urges me to call whenever I like. As we wait for the bus she tries to lighten up.

"Ever make love with a woman, Kay?"

I look at her. "Now how did I know you'd get around to asking that?"

She's amused. "Doesn't seem to make you uncomfortable."

"I'm sex-positive," I tell her. "Can't be otherwise and spend time on the Gulch."

"Suppose not. . . ."

She seems disappointed. The truth is I never have slept with a woman, but I don't feel like answering her question. She's shown me a lot of herself tonight, some of it unattractive: a willingness to manipulate, to forge temporary alliances, anger, ambition, greed for success. As nice as it might be to reciprocate, I decide to follow one of Rita Reese's favorite aikido maxims: *Never let your opponent see all of your face.*

"Can I take your picture, Hilly?"

She turns a little to the side, demure. But I've already got my Contax up. *Click!* Then, as she reverts to her cocky self, I hit her again twice: *Click!Click!*

"You clever lynx!" She grins.

The bus is coming.

"Night."

"Night, Kay."

She waves as I jump aboard.

Too early to go home. I get off at Market and Polk, walk through Civic Center Plaza to the Gulch. This is my first expedition since my run-in with Knob. It's been four nights. I'm curious to see if things have changed.

On my way I think about Tim. He could have made a different life for himself if he'd settled in the Castro, found a decent job, met someone he liked and settled down. Perhaps that's what he had planned for his retirement. But then it occurs to me he did have a connection to the Castro: he kept a private mailbox there.

The first thing I notice on the Gulch is that things are back to normal. The dealers are out, the hustlers are at their stations, the street people—AIDS victims, homeless people, freaks, drugged-out adolescents—are clustered on the usual corners outside the sex stores and saloons. The second thing I notice is that there're no more Timothy Lovsey posters on the posts. Every single one has been torn down. So much for Shanley's hope of soliciting information. So much too for the first street exhibition of my photographs.

I spot Knob ahead at the corner of Fern conferring with his two favorite pretty boys, the ones I think of as his acolytes. As I approach I detach the lens from my Contax, button it up inside one jacket pocket, the camera body inside the other. Knob and I have some unfinished business. *Never advance with weakness,* Rita says.

He notices me coming, pretends he doesn't. Does he really think I'll just pass by? Disputes on the Gulch tend to get resolved. But then I'm only a girl.

Aikido is a defensive art. Before I took it up I studied karate. One step past Knob I wheel around, kick out at his stomach, then straight-arm the side of his head. As he struggles to keep balance, I smash him in the head again. As he goes down, I kick at his knees, then sweep him to the ground.

He writhes on the sidewalk. There's blood on his face. His acolytes stand over him. They gape.

"That's for skinning my knees," I tell him. "We can end it here or carry it on. Your choice, Knob. But if you want a second round, get ready to be hurt."

He stares up at me with a mixture of surprise and respect. He wipes away the blood.

"I been feeling bad about shoving you, Bug. Guess we're even now." He shows me a shit-eating grin. "You sure know how to punch."

My first inclination is to extend my hand, but I'm wary of a feint. I nod, give him a shit-eating grin of my own, then leave it to the acolytes to lift him and clean him up.

Varoom!Varoom! Between Bush and Pine I hear the roar of a car in low gear. Looking around, I spot the same Mercedes 600 SL I saw cruising the night I thought Tim stood me up. I can't see the driver through the reflecting glass, but I know it's the same bald chicken hawk. Quickly I unbutton my pockets, snap together my camera, take aim at the license plate and shoot. Just then the car swerves abruptly into Sacramento Street, then races up into Pacific Heights.

No sign of Crawf; perhaps he really did go down to L.A. I don't see any more cops than usual. The Shillelagh is back in business. Passing The Werewolf, I spot Slick standing at the bar, deep in conversation with the bartender; his albino complexion makes him prominent in the dark room of shadowy men.

On the next block I come across Alyson lingering in the doorway of The Snafu. We greet each other. Her lipstick's messy, her wig bedraggled. I ask after Doreen.

"On a date," Alyson confides.

We chat awhile. I smell gin on her breath. She confirms that Crawf left town.

"Cops been around?" I ask.

She shakes her head. "Just the first couple of nights. They don't care, you know. To them, dearie, we're trash. Just trash."

I spend a few minutes peering through my telescope: no lights on in the Judge's penthouse and nothing else interesting to be seen. Since there's still film in my camera, I set up lights and a tripod, prepare to take self-portraits. I pose against the nightscape to the east, stare into my lens as honestly as I can. Rapidly I whip off the rest of the roll: *Whap!Whap!Whap!Whap!Whap!*

I'm still wired; no way I can sleep. I take the exposed roll into the darkroom for processing. Nothing like darkroom work to quiet the mind.

I'm pleased with my results. The shots at Wildcat Canyon are appropriately moody, not surprising with all the mist and rain. The portraits of Dad are as I imagined they'd be, pictures of a solid, honest man. My second, last shot of Hilly, catching her special mix of self-centered brashness and vulnerability, is superb.

As for Baldy's license plate, it's barely legible, very small due to my wide-angle lens and blurry since he'd already started to drive away. But with a magnifying glass I can make out the first three digits. Enough to trace him,

I think, since there aren't that many twelve-cylinder Mercedes coupes around.

As for my self-portraits, I'm unimpressed. I look all right, I guess, but there's something vacant in my face; my eyes appear flat, as if I'm in a daze. In a sense, I know, I am. The events of the last week have taken their toll. I seem to have entered a dreamworld where people speak without affect of dismembered torsos, limbs and heads. I look at my self-portraits and long to see myself as fierce. I wish that like a tourist I'd handed my camera to a passerby on Polk. Then I could see how I looked when I knocked down Knob.

When Carl Sandburg wrote: "The fog comes on little cat feet," he was writing of Chicago, "hog butcher for the world." Here in San Francisco the fog has its own manner of approach, sometimes bounding through the Golden Gate like a panther leaping through a hoop, fierce, growling, ready to scrap and flay at everything within. This is the consequence of a sharp collision between very cold, deep Pacific Ocean water and hot Central Valley air that creates, then draws off mist . . . resulting in our famous teeth-chattering San Francisco summers.

It's midautumn now, normally fog-free, but there have been sporadic anomalies in our climate. Today the fog is a thick gray syrup. Since fog is a lot easier on my eyes than brilliant light, I decide to venture out.

I'm armed with my Contax and a list of seven private mailbox-service stores in the Castro, copied from the Yellow Pages. My mission: to discover Tim's box and, by so doing, discover . . . I'm not really sure. My method: to systematically visit each store and show the proprietor Tim's picture. However, on the Van Ness Avenue bus, I think up another approach, less methodical but a lot more fun. I'll try to put myself in Tim's shoes and psych out the place that would have appealed to him most.

My first stop, on Sanchez off Market, is a dreary, narrow store stuffed between a barbershop and an auto parts shop. *He wouldn't have liked it here,* I decide, and move along to the next. This is a modern well-lit full-service place on Castro, offering fax, photocopying, key cutting, the works. I don't like it, no achromat would—fluorescent light hurts our eyes. I decide Tim wouldn't like it either: too antiseptic, not welcoming enough. But the third place, on Eighteenth between Castro and Hartford, seems a likely bet. There's just something about it, including the folksy name, Mail From Home. I think: *This could be the one.*

I enter. A clean-shaven bodybuilder type in a tank top greets me with a smile. There's a stuffed teddy bear on the counter, a studded cock ring secured around one leg. Yes, I think, this is just the sort of kinky place Tim would have liked.

I introduce myself to the reception-person. His name is Gordon; he has a moon face and beautiful white teeth.

"I have a friend I think rents here. I know this is kind of weird, but would you be willing to look at his picture?"

Gordon nods, sizing me up. I'm hoping he takes me for a friendly butch.

I show him the Angel Island portrait, not from the poster but a print I made myself.

"Sure, I know him," Gordon says. "Box four-seven-five."

I nod solemnly. "Well . . . he's dead."

Gordon is stricken. "Oh, wow! Man! Was it . . ."

He means AIDS. I shake my head. I show him the tiny clipping from the *Chronicle*.

He reads it. "This is terrible," he says. "Maybe even worse than . . . you know."

"Uh-uh," I say, "nothing's worse."

I tell him I want to close down Tim's box and arrange for his mail to be forwarded. I offer two months' additional rent and whatever Gordon needs for forwarding. As he considers my request, I try to preempt his misgivings.

"Look," I tell him, "I don't have court papers. I don't even have a death certificate yet. But I was his best friend.

His family disowned him. They think he deserved what he got. So, do you think you could forget the formalities this time?''

He studies me a moment, takes down my name and address, then goes to the back of Tim's box, pulls out the contents, hands them to me, promises to forward whatever else comes in. When I try to compensate him for this gracious act, he gently waves my money away.

Back on the street, I can't believe my luck. I walk over to Castro, find a cafe, fetch a cup of cappuccino, carry it outside to a table, sit down and examine Tim's mail. There're three items. The first is a postcard bearing a post-mark from Florence, Italy. The front shows Michelan-gelo's *David*. On the back is a scrawled message:

> *Thinking of you,* Gorgeous One, *missing your silken . . . ha! Quite a little threesome we had, yes? David (see reverse) is* almost *as goodlooking as you, but, alas, is stone! I* shall *be back in Baghdad this fall ready for* heated *pleasures. Till then, G.O.,* most *fondly and devotedly,*
>
> Jerome

Second is a letter from attorney J. F. Judd strongly urging Mr. Lovsey to settle his long-overdue account of $1,250 for services rendered in connection with his July 5 arrest for loitering and solicitation. Unless prompt payment is received, the letter threatens, Mr. Judd will have no choice but to take legal action.

Third is a letter bearing a return address in New York. The sender has only affixed one name: deGeoffroy. Something about it strikes a note. It takes me a moment to make the connection. Of course! DeGeoffroy—not Jeffrey or Geoffrey. The letter must be from Uncle David.

I stir my cappuccino, take a sip, wipe my spoon and use it to slit the envelope. There's a fresh hundred-dollar bill inside and a letter written in ink on a single sheet of creamy paper:

Dear Boy!

How kind of you to write. It has been a very long time, but I have not forgotten you or A. I know (and so must you both) that I never shall.

We shared most precious times, the three of us. And then it ended, Poof! as in a puff of smoke. My fault entirely. Be assured I never blamed either one of you. Sometimes it takes a great, indeed an enormous loss to shock one into appreciating how very fortunate one has been. Sometimes, it seems to me, those cataclysmic events took place only yesterday.

I try to understand why you have sought contact after so many years. May I take your note and the good news that you are happy and well as a sign of . . . forgiveness?

I barely know San Francisco, have been there only twice. I do know it's a pretty place. How wise of you to have chosen beauty!

Please don't worry. I shall not attempt to trace you. I know better than to press myself unwanted. But if one day you should express a desire to see me again, be assured my bags are already packed.

Please, if convenient, keep me apprised of things and tell me that A. too is well and safe. I hold you both most dearly in my heart.

With great affection,
    David deG.

My hands are shaking. Whatever does this mean? Sure doesn't sound like the cuddly Uncle David I heard about. More like a tragic and passionate lover, I think, one who did a wrong and in turn was wronged. But who is A.? What *did* they do? And exactly how many years ago is "so many"?

The fog is lifting. Starting to blink, I slip on my shades and head for the bus stop on Market. There's a side of me that wants to phone Mr. deGeoffroy at once, tell him what's happened. Another side is reluctant to get involved in a relationship which appears to have been so disturbed.

But if Tim has family, they have a right to know he's dead. And I have many questions.

Manhattan directory assistance lists only one deGeoffroy. I take down the number, dial.

My opening is awkward. I introduce myself as Tim's friend. Tim, I say, always referred to Mr. deGeoffroy as "Uncle David." Babbling on, I detect impatience on the other end.

"Is something wrong?" he asks.

"Well . . ." Tongue-tied, I wish I'd rehearsed.

"Yes," he says, "something's terribly, terribly wrong."

The voice is cultured, with a British inflection. But not truly British, I decide. More stagey, like the learned theatrical English of an actor.

"Explain yourself at once!" he demands.

"He's dead," I whisper.

A gasp, a long pause and then a sob followed by a wail. Not knowing what to say, I stay quiet.

"I should ask you how this happened, I suppose. But I'm not sure I want to know just now. Or is this a trick, a canny little hoax cooked up by that naughty lad?" Dead silence, as if he's holding his breath. "Say that it is. Please say it is!"

"No, not a hoax," I tell him. "Sadly not."

"Yes . . . sadly," he murmurs, "I believe you. I don't know you, but I believe you are sincere. It would be too cruel to be otherwise."

He is weeping vigorously now. I wonder how long I can bear witness to his grief. Then I start to bawl myself. It just comes out of me in a way it hasn't till now. Delayed reaction, or is it because at last I've found someone with whom I can share my heartache, someone who also loved Tim, who truly cares? It's so strange what we're doing, total strangers sobbing together on a transcontinental call. But it feels real to me and also right. Everything else has been so crazy, so why not this?

"Forgive me," he says, choking back his tears. "I seem to have started a chain reaction." I imagine him smiling as he says it. "Now please tell me about the other. How is she?"

"I don't know who you mean."

"You don't know her?" He sounds surprised.

"Who?"

Silence, then: "Perhaps another day. Forgive me, my dear, for asking again for your name. This time I shall write it down, your number too. I'll call you back tonight if that's all right. I do want to talk more, but, if you'll forgive me, not just now. Now I must try and—how do they say it these days?—begin to process my pain."

After putting down the phone I sit still for several minutes. I'm moved and also mystified. *Who is this man?* And who is the one he calls both "the other" and "she"? Is it the "A." referred to in his letter?

I take an early aikido class. Rita puts us through our katas and then tough drills. We line up facing her; then each of us attacks with all our might. She deflects, compliments, criticizes. When it's my turn she slams me hard into the mat. The pain is sudden, harsh. I cry out. Feeling betrayed, I'm furious and scream at her: "Why me?"

Rita laughs softly as she helps me up. "Why *not* you?" she asks.

Later she pairs me with a big guy, Tom, six three, 220 pounds, long slick black hair, wiry chest hair curling out of his gi jacket. Tom's a novice. He can't believe he's been assigned to practice with a petite woman.

Rita whispers: "Nice stud muffin, huh?"

I shrug.

"Show him what we're about," she says.

Somehow Rita knows when a student needs to let off steam. She's my instructor, has instructed me to teach Tom about centrifugal force. I have no choice, I must do as sensei commands.

The first time I sweep him, he hits the floor with a thud.

In aikido the cliché is apt: the heavier they are, the faster they attack, the harder they will fall. He springs up, smiles to show me he doesn't mind, we bow to one another, then immediately I throw him down again. This time he doesn't get up so fast and his smile isn't so sweet. Since I have nothing against him, I imagine that he's Knob, and relive the glorious moments of my payback. I toy with him a little, then dump him hard. Rita helps him up, brushes him off. We bow to one another. His eyes show pain.

After class, to show there're no hard feelings, I invite him for coffee on Chestnut. He tells me he's an actor. He wants to know why Rita overmatched him.

"She wants you to understand size and strength can be a disadvantage," I tell him, "that aikido's about blending energy, not just applying techniques."

"I already knew that."

"Yeah . . . but did you *feel* it?"

He gazes at me, rubs his shoulder. "Now I do," he says.

David deGeoffroy phones back a little after six. The first thing he asks is whether he's caught me at a bad time.

"Not at all," I assure him. "I've been waiting for your call."

This time his tone is different. He sounds charming, almost merry. He's inquisitive, wants to know all about me—my age, what I do, how I knew Tim, how and when we met.

On the later point I'm cautious. Not knowing how Tim has presented himself, I don't say a word about hustling, turning tricks or johns. I simply say I've been photographing him, employing him as a model. After a while, when I feel I've revealed enough, I try to turn the conversation around.

"It's your turn," I say. "I know you're in show business. What exactly do you do?"

He seems amused. "I thought you knew. I'm the Magician."

The Magician! I didn't know there was a "the Magician" in Tim's life.

"The one who taught him to make coins disappear?"

"That . . . and a few other things." He pauses. "May I ask you a favor? I'd love to see some recent photos."

I promise to FedEx several in the morning. "What about the rest of the family?" I ask.

Another pause. "There's no one left."

"Just yourself?"

"In a manner of speaking," he says.

We banter on. He insists I call him David; in turn I request he call me Kay. Soon we're "Daviding" and "Kaying" each other like long-lost friends, a weird sort of intimacy since we've only met telephonically over a tragic loss.

When I tell him Tim's San Francisco friends called him Rain, I can almost feel David glow.

"I like that. Name suits him. He was always a bit moody. But so sweet, so very sweet." He pauses. "It's been so long since I've seen him, so many years. The silence, you know, the awful roaring silence. Then, out of the sky, like a bolt, comes his note. I have it here. I want to read it to you." He clears his throat. " 'I'm well, happy, working as a waiter, trying to make ends meet and make sense out of life and all that happened. My juggling's gotten rusty but my close-up work's still pretty good. If you get this let me know. Tim.' "

He's ready now, he tells me, to hear how Tim was killed. I decide to give it to him straight.

"Shot in the throat. Cops don't know by whom. And this is the bad part—mutilated afterwards."

A very long silence this time. "Cut up, you mean?"

But how does he know that? "You sound as if . . . like you expected it."

"I don't know quite what I expected," he says. "It occurred to me, that's all—that it would be of a piece, so to speak."

I don't know what he's talking about, and there's something detached in his tone that makes me mad.

"Well, you seem to have processed your pain quite nicely."

"Please don't think poorly of me, Kay."

There's nothing I can rejoin to that, especially as his response is so mild.

"There are things to be arranged," I tell him. "Tim's burial, cremation, whatever. What do you want me to do?"

"I never thought about it. Cremation, I suppose."

"Out here?"

"He was happy there, wasn't he? Why don't you make arrangements and let me know. Keep it simple, dignified." He asks me to choose a funeral home, have them call him. He'll put it all on his credit card. "When everything's ready let me know and I'll fly out. Then we'll meet . . . and really talk."

I prepare myself a salad, devour it, then eat an apple, then another. I stare out the window for a while, then telephone Dad to ask if he can run a license plate.

"Can't do it myself," he says, "but Rusty'll do it if I ask." Rusty Quinn is his old partner, still on the force.

I give him the first three digits from Baldy's plate, then the make and model of the car.

"What's this for, Kay? If you don't mind my asking." I tell him. "Why not turn this over to Shanley? It's his job."

"Because Shanley's kissed me off and there's probably no connection anyway."

Dad mulls that over. "Cops aren't supposed to run license plates for private parties. It's a pretty big favor to ask."

"Fine, Dad," I tell him. "I'll hire an investigator. Just thought—"

"I'll take care of it," he says.

• • •

Feeling cooped up, tired of looking out the window, I walk down the other side of Russian Hill into North Beach. I always like walking here, charmed by the neighborhood, the Old World coffeehouses populated by a mix of Italians, bohemians and tourists, the flourishing pizza parlors emitting wonderful aromas, the funky street life and the small, almost quaint district of raunchy live-action sex shows. There's something harmless about North Beach, put on and theatrical, a far cry from the desperation and danger I feel on the other side of the hill. Life on the Gulch is sour, the flesh market there for real. On North Beach it's more like a dating game, like play.

I wander, peering into cafes, then spend an hour browsing at City Lights Bookstore. I glance through the latest photography books, see work I respect but nothing that challenges my eye. What about my own project? Will *Exposures* expand people's vision? I compose a subtitle: "Life and Death of a Street Hustler." Will anyone buy it? Will anyone care? I must think they will, otherwise my work is useless.

I turn on Greenwich Street, ascend Telegraph Hill. I rarely walk here during daylight; I like the neighborhood but feel awkward blinking my way around. And there's something else: nostalgia. The Judge lives up here. I used to visit him often, arriving even before the sun had set, so anxious was I for his company. Nowadays I watch over Telegraph from my perch on Russian. To actually walk here seems like a trespass.

Greenwich dead-ends at Grant Street, but there're steps for pedestrians that lead up to Kearny, and from there it's just a few paces to the building I know so well.

It smells sweet up here; there's the fragrance of wild fennel and night-blooming shrubs mixed with the resin scent of the Monterey cypresses that compose the woods around Coit Tower. I'm so accustomed to viewing this place from a great distance through a lens that I'm surprised by the intimacy this sweet aroma conveys. Suddenly I feel heady. My pulse starts to race. It's been a while, but I recognize the sensation. I know I must leave; the feeling's too intense. I turn and run back down the hill, skidding and nearly falling on the incline.

Six

aving never arranged a cremation before, I call Sullivan's, the mortuary that took care of my mother. I speak to Randy Sullivan, grandson of the founder, explain the situation and the fact that Timothy Lovsey's body is in pieces. Randy, grasping the problem, instructs me how to get the parts released. He quotes me a price with an additional option of a boat trip to scatter the ashes at sea.

"Will you want some kind of service?" he asks.

I tell him no, nothing formal, that most likely some friends will gather, say a few words, and leave it at that.

"Sounds like just what the deceased would have wished for," Randy says.

After I hang up I wonder why he put it that way, since he obviously has no knowledge of the deceased or his preferences.

I phone Shanley. He listens politely as I tell him I've contacted David deGeoffroy in New York, that Sullivan's will be taking care of the body and that I want to wind up Tim's affairs, including termination of his lease and removal of personal effects from his studio.

Shanley's helpful. Clearly he prefers me as supplicant
to the angry shutter-happy female he's been dealing with.
I even detect a smidgen of warmth in his voice as he asks
how I'm holding up.

"Pretty good," I tell him, "considering the circumstances."

"Glad to hear it. Hilly and I were talking about you
just this morning. We think you've been great. Let me
know if there's anything I can do, not just on this—on
anything at the Hall of Justice. I don't claim to swing a
lot of weight, but there're plenty of folks here owe me
favors."

Is this the kiss-off Hilly told me about? Is this how
cops handle it these days, so nice, polite, eager to assist?
If I get a Health Department citation for improper disposal
of photochemicals, will Shanley get it fixed?

Dad's busy time starts at four in the morning and tapers
off after ten. These are the hours when he and his Russian
émigré helpers bake the loaves, deliver them to stores and
restaurants and sell the main part of the day's production
to walk-ins. Dad has one of those numbered-tag dispens-
ers on the counter so customers know whose turn it is.
He likes calling out the numbers, looking the customer in
the eye, fulfilling the order with dispatch. Fine bread is
his joy, good service is his pride. City Stone Ground, he
wants you to know, is no kind of hippie joint.

I arrive at eleven, watch him through the window. As
always, in his white apron he appears the Happy Baker.
I don't know where this tendency of mine comes from,
this need to turn people into archetypes. The Solemn
Judge, the Happy Baker and now the Enigmatic Magician.

"Dad!"

"Hey, darlin'!"

He grasps me in his arms, enveloping me in a cloud of
flour and yeast. As a girl I could never get enough of his
hugs. To this day they take me back to a time when I
knew I'd always be protected by his strength.

"Got the info for you," he whispers. He holds me back. "Bull's-eye, I think."

Arm across my shoulder, he leads me into his office off the baking floor. From his desk, neatly stacked with folders, bills, purchase orders, receipts, he extracts a slip of paper.

"Rusty ran the plate. When he called this morning he sounded impressed." He hands me the slip. "Take a look."

The first digits of the plate number and the car make and model are matched with a name: Marcus P. Crane. Something familiar there; I've read about this person but can't remember where or who he is.

"Address mean anything to you?" Dad asks.

It's in the twenty-six hundred block on Broadway, one of the fancy parts of Pacific Heights.

"Marcus Crane. Think about it," he coaxes.

"I'm thinking. Give me a hint."

"Read the society columns?"

"Not if I can help it."

"If you did you'd know Crane is husband of a local legend."

"Sarah Lashaw?"

Dad winks. "You got it, darlin'! She of the fabulous parties and the violet eyes."

I don't have to remind him I can't see violet. He knows my weakness better than anyone. But for years, like most everyone in town, I have heard about Mrs. Lashaw's eyes, their haunting beauty.

"She married Crane ten years ago," Dad says. "He's hubby number three . . . or is it four?" I'm surprised Dad knows this; evidently he *does* follow society. "Crane's a dud like the others. The difference is he's got better manners. Old San Francisco family. Holds down some kind of half-ass job in finance. Does what she tells him, holds her chair, hitches the clasp on those egg-sized emeralds she wears."

Now it starts coming back: Sarah Lashaw's violet eyes and the deep green emerald necklace she wears to complement them. The stones may not actually be egg-sized. More like quail eggs, I think.

"Is Crane bald?"

Dad shrugs. "Don't know. But from what I hear, Lashaw is one very tough lady. Best not to mess with 'em, darlin'—not unless you got 'em by the hairs."

At the Main Library I use the microfilm reader to look up references to Marcus Crane. The photos show him with a full head of hair, but his features match those of Baldy. There're many mentions but little of substance. Seems aside from being Sarah Lashaw's husband, he's known more for affability than accomplishments.

Mrs. Lashaw is another story. Reading about her one would conclude she's some kind of social goddess: grand-scale entertainments, masquerade balls on behalf of this or that worthy cause, impeccable taste, meticulously decorated homes, an apparently limitless fortune. But as I read more, what comes through is a portrait of a demanding woman, spoiled and suffused with a sense of her own entitlement.

Using the periodical index, I retrieve articles from back issues of *House & Garden, Town & Country* and *Architectural Digest*. Mrs. Lashaw, I discover, is indeed a handsome middle-aged woman whose natural good looks are bolstered by her lavish surroundings. Vases of fresh-cut flowers fill her rooms. Fine contemporary art adorns her walls. Studying pictures of the calculated interiors of her various homes, I note a horror of empty space . . . as if the filling of the rooms, their overflowing, will somehow mollify the emptiness within.

She is, moreover, an accomplished equestrian. Astride her favorite gelding, Folly, in helmet, jodhpurs and hacking jacket, she beams at the camera, a long thin dressage whip dangling carelessly from her hand. Another spread shows her and Crane picnicking with friends on the vast expanse of lawn before their Napa Valley house. The goodies (recipes courteously provided) are packed in

English wicker baskets, while the picnickers recline on Oriental carpets spread upon the grass.

Do I sound envious? I hope not, for everything in Mrs. Lashaw's ethos is the opposite of mine. She embraces the ornate while I'm drawn to the austere; she fancies gilt while I prefer black; she likes couture while I slop around in jeans. But, I remind myself, it's not she who is the object of my scrutiny, rather her suave and stylish husband whom I've seen cruising the Gulch attempting to rent underage male flesh.

From the Main Library I walk to Pacific Heights, our poshest quarter, though there are those who would argue for the enclaves at the tops of Nob and Russian hills. Stately mansions, meticulously renovated Victorians, vast art deco apartment houses. Personally I find this neighborhood boring: few contrasts, everything smooth and groomed, svelte women, perfectly behaved children, nannies with European accents pushing heirloom baby carriages. The foreign consulates are here, as well as numerous small apartment buildings with molded escutcheons above the doors. Hedge walls, lookouts, tile and slate roofs. I pass the baroque marble palace of a famous romance novelist whose diamonds are said to rival Lashaw's emeralds.

Mounting the greensward of Alta Plaza, I break a sweat. A pair of fortyish in-shape women in fashionable togs are battling it out on one of the tennis courts. Long rallies and cutting strokes—from a distance theirs appears a friendly match. But up close I hear pants and grunts, glimpse the steely eyes of fierce competitors.

From the crest of the hill I can see the whole southern portion of the city. The huge antenna on North Peak breaks the pewter sky. There are sunbathers on the slopes, people training dogs, kids playing ball. To the north is Cow Hollow and the mercurial Bay. The sun beats down; the branches are serene. A perfect afternoon in our golden City by the Bay.

Crossing Divisadero I ask myself what I'm doing here, what I expect to find. I uncap my Contax, preparing for action . . . though I expect to do nothing more than quickly view Lashaw & Crane's San Francisco home.

The houses here are huge. There is an area of mansions with grounds, not the stuck-together townhouses of eastern Pacific Heights. Two turreted Victorians, a Mediterranean villa, a timbered Tudor, a mansard-roofed Norman—the 2600 block of Broadway is a wonderland of retro architectural fantasies.

The Lashaw house lies behind an iron fence of sharp pointed bars and flamboyant double-swing gates. Surrounded by shrubs and trees, it's not easy to make out its style. It's probably my achromatopsia that's got me confused, causing shapes and textures to blend, which, to a vision normal, would be differentiated by color.

I walk along the fence, gazing through the bars not the least concerned whether I'm observed. I catch sight of an Asian gardener working with clippers on hands and knees. Though only fifty feet away, he's so intent on his work he doesn't see me.

I press up against the grate, poke my camera through, snap off three or four shots. Because my Contax is a view-finder model and not a reflex, it throws off little sound. Through it I can make out large leaded windows and a great wooden door set back within a recessed entrance. I move a few feet, peer through my viewfinder again, see that the entrance ceiling is actually a groin vault. Then, noticing that the tops of the windows are arched, I recognize the architectural style. The Lashaw house, faux ecclesiastic, is built like a rectory, a manse suitable for a prince of the church.

I walk to the end of the property, take another shot, then slowly pace back, peering in all the while. Just as I pass the main gate, I hear a mechanical sound. The gate doors begin to swing out. Then I hear a familiar growl.

Varoom!Varoom!

As I turn to the street, I bring my camera to my eye. A Mercedes 600 SL is hovering just twenty feet away, convertible top down, driver sporting full head of air-blown hair.

Varoom!Varoom!

Mr. Crane is impatient; the gates are opening too slowly for one so important as himself.

Without thinking I start taking his picture, walking backward along the side of his car. I can smell the oily heat of the engine, the finely painted metal hood baking beneath the sun. *Whap!Whap!Whap!Whap!* I'm out in the street now, taking three-quarter back views, and although the gates are now fully open, Mr. Crane is not driving in, rather he is turning in his seat giving me the eye as I move around the back of his vehicle, through the cloud of its exhaust, and approach him again from the driver's side.

Whap!Whap!Whap!Whap!

This is fun! Reveling in my outrageous conduct, I feel the same surge as when I throw down an attacker in aikido class.

"Excuse me! Miss!" *Finally the chicken hawk squawks!* He whips off his dark glasses, perhaps expecting me to do the same. I disappoint him. Then I'm surprised. He's beaming, showing me the face of a *bon vivant*.

"Ah, sorry—paparazzo at work! Or should I say 'pa-parazza'?" He grins.

"You got it!" I stick my camera in for a close-up. *Whap!* I notice faint adolescent acne scars on his cheeks.

"Why me?" His voice is calm, polite.

"Why *not* you, Mr. Crane?"

He nods, amused, guns his engine. *Varoom!Varoom!* Then he tilts his head to expose his profile. He's preening for me! I can't believe it.

"My best side," he says, grinning again.

"Thanks. I need good clear shots."

"I had no idea people find me so handsome."

I'm impressed by his sangfroid. This, I realize, is one slick customer. I lower my Contax, peer directly into his eyes. "The ones I took on Polk weren't all that clear. And of course you weren't wearing that pretty wig."

He holds the grin; then, for a second, the mask starts to crack. A glimmer of confusion, perhaps humiliation. Does he wonder who I am? A blackmailer out to expose his secret life?

Whap! I take a final shot, then step back. That'll be the good one if I caught him right. He studies me, then blinks, as if etching my features on his memory. *Varoom! Varoom!* The car lurches into the safe interior courtyard of his manse, leaving black skid marks on the pavement at my feet.

In the echoing lobby of the Hall of Justice I pick up the envelope Shanley has left for me at the reception desk. No note inside, just the key to Tim's studio. From there it's not much of a walk to his building on Mission.

I feel sad as I mount the steps. The cat-piss and roach-spray smells are the same. This time an aria from *Tosca* wafts sensuously down the stairwell from an upper floor.

On the landing I look around. The fire extinguisher is in place. As my eyes rise to the molding above, I consider leaping up to see if there's anything there. Quickly I dismiss the idea. I'm too short, and besides, I already had Crawf fetch Tim's spare key, the one I later gave to Shanley, the one I'm now holding in my hand.

There's police tape on the door. I cut it neatly, using the edge of the key, let myself in, softly close the door behind. From Hilly's description, I'm expecting a mess. But that's not what I find. Yes, the room looks different, the floor is covered with loose down from Tim's slit-up sleeping bag, the stuffing of his futon is strewn about. But his clothing and possessions have not been randomly tossed. Rather I detect a certain rigor in their arrangement—underwear in one pile, jeans in another, sweaters in a third. There's something about this sorting that touches and confuses me, something caring, perhaps even loving, I think.

I go to the kitchen, search beneath the sink, find a box of garbage bags, tote several back to the living room and start cleaning up. I throw in the torn futon and bedroll, the perishable food in the refrigerator and all the stuff in the bath—toothbrush, razor, shampoo. When I'm done with that I pitch Tim's clothes into two large nylon duffel bags and a backpack I find on the closet shelf.

Back out on the landing the *Tosca* recording seems even louder. I haul the garbage bags downstairs, stick them in one of the trash cans in back, discover some discarded cardboard boxes, carry two of them back up. These I fill with Tim's Walkman, shoes, boots and books. Then I carefully remove my photographs from the wall.

Something's wrong. One of them is missing, the Angel Island shot. Someone, it appears, has carefully removed it. I see marks where the tape previously adhered.

Now everything's packed except the *Body Heat* poster, kitchen utensils, a couple of plates, glasses, a frying pan and the paltry furnishings. Since these items have little value, I decide to leave them for the next tenant. I haul the duffels, backpack and boxes out to the landing, and prepare to relock the door.

I hesitate. I know the cops have searched the studio; I also know they're pros. But still . . . I look up at the molding again.

I go back inside, take Tim's wobbly desk chair, place it against the wall, climb onto it, start running my fingers around the molding that rings the room. This exercise takes a while; after each sweep of my hand I step down, move the chair a few feet, then step up again. I'm about to give it up when my fingers brush against something metallic. I stand on tiptoe, reach up, bring the object down. A key. To what? It's far too big for Tim's box at Mail From Home, it's clearly not a bank safety-deposit-box key and it doesn't match the key to his room. But interestingly, it's the same size and make. I pocket it and leave.

This time no music in the stairwell as I carry the duffels and boxes down. I hear a door open on an upper floor, then shut after a few seconds as if the person changed his/her mind about going out. It takes me three trips to get everything down to the front hall. I leave the stuff there while I go out to find a phone.

The Tool Box is a gloomy bar. A couple of guys in black T-shirts are playing pool. They and the bartender, a bear in tank top sporting grotesque tattoos, glance up when I walk in. Determining my gender, they smile to hide their disappointment.

I use the pay phone by the lav to call for a taxi, then start back toward the tenement. A few steps out of The Tool Box I freeze. At the end of the block a person is turning the corner. For an instant I'm certain it's Tim. The hair, bearing, walk, seem the same . . . yet something too, I know, is wrong. Perhaps it's his height, I think, as I rush up to Grace Street to check. Turning the corner myself, I'm suddenly blinded; the late-afternoon sun slams into my eyes. I blink, turn, examine the afterimage before it fades. It's not Tim, it's someone shorter, but then of course it has to be since Tim is dead. I recall how, in the months after my mother's death, I occasionally thought I saw her on the street. It took me a while to understand that I made this mistake because I wanted to see her so very much.

Waiting for my taxi I think about afterimages, a by-product of achromatopsia. Since they're a coping mechanism, achromats who wear shades from an early age generally don't experience them.

What happens, according to studies I've read, is that very bright light immediately saturates my rods, but the moment I close my eyes the light level fades to a point where my retinas are able to pick up and retain an image of what I "saw." The emergence of an afterimage is similar to the emergence of a photographic image on a sheet of exposed paper when placed in developer. But unlike the photographic variety, an afterimage is transitory, lasting only a few seconds, just long enough for me to examine and identify people or objects invisible when I try to see them with open eyes.

When my cab arrives, I load everything in, drive to my building, haul the duffels and boxes into the elevator. I have little storage space in my apartment but Tim's possessions are so meager I find room for them in the back of a closet.

I phone Tim's landlord, Murray Paulus, tell him I've cleaned out the studio, that he's free now to rerent it. When he mutters something about not being given the customary thirty days' notice, I point out that homicide victims generally don't know their fates in advance.

Paulus is caught short. "Hadn't thought of that," he says. "Guess you're right. Kinda different when the tenant's mortally sick." His voice brightens. "I got a deposit, so the hell with it!" He hangs up.

Lord praise you, Mr. Paulus!

Attorney J. F. Judd is not so kind. He still wants his $1,250.

"Tim died penniless," I tell him. "You can't get blood out of a stone."

"No, but I can go to small claims court and make trouble for his executrix."

"That's not me," I tell him. "I'm just a friend. He didn't leave a will."

"Intestate and no assets—I've heard that one. Still, someone's gotta pay. I don't work for nothing, not when it's cleaning up after someone's dirty deeds."

"Just what dirty deed did Tim do?" I ask.

"Took money from an undercover vice cop. The guy hired him to take a blow job."

"How'd you get him off?"

"Entrapment pure and simple."

"Well, Mr. Judd," I tell him without much regret, "seems this time you're going to have to eat your fee."

A little after six I phone Hilly at home.

"Hi ya," she says cheerily. "I was going to call you tonight. I got goodies!"

"Great!"

"Not the stuff on your dad—that's going to take a while. But I got a complete set of crime scene photos. Not bad, huh?"

I'm impressed. I really wanted those pictures.

"What can I do for you?" I ask.

In the short silence that follows, I imagine the gears meshing within her brain.

"I know a little about you, Kay."

"Such as?"

"Such as . . . you used to work for that free rag, *Bay Area News.*"

"That's right. Years ago. I was staff photographer."

"Still connected there?"

"What's on your mind?"

Another pause, more grinding of the gears. When she speaks again, her voice is a purr.

"I want a reporter I can trust, someone ambitious, who'll protect me as a source. I want someone, preferably female, who wants to win the fuckin' Pulitzer prize. I want—"

"I know exactly what you want, Hilly. You want what Shanley's got, a reporter in your pocket."

"You're smart, Kay. You got me figured. So—do you know someone fits the bill?"

"Actually I do. It's a 'he.' Joel Glickman. You won't find better. And he's already got a Pulitzer."

I hear the sharp, sudden intake of her breath. "Wow! Can you introduce me?"

"Maybe," I say coolly. "I'll lay the groundwork. Meanwhile see what you can turn up on my dad."

The sky's inky now, moonlight touches the roofs. I peer out my window and fiercely resolve I will never stare out and see, as so many do here, a thousand points of . . . slight.

I feel jumpy, don't know why. Perhaps I'm still spooked by that apparition on the street. Also, I feel lonely, wish I were sitting someplace busy with a group of friends, a restaurant or bar full of young people drinking, talking, laughing. I miss that kind of fun—which I used to have so often in my twenties. What I miss most, of course, is a lover, someone to hold me and to hold, to hug and lick and kiss. Wistfully I look across the valley. Then I pull on sneakers, grab my Contax and go out.

The night air is warm, surprising in November. A TV weatherperson says we're enjoying Indian summer. The trees cast sensual velvety lunar shadows on the sidewalk. The Hyde Street cable rumbles steadily beneath the street.

I cross Hyde, pause at the corner, trying to decide which way to go. Down the eastern slope into North Beach, where I can lose myself in the joyful anonymous crowds, or down the western side to the Gulch to walk among the wounded and dispossessed?

Tonight it will be the Gulch. But why I am drawn to haunt that street of damnation is a mystery I cannot solve.

I pass the Alice Marble Tennis Courts. The surrounding high steel fence cuts the moonlight into squares. I hear a dog wail in the distance. Looking to the Bay, I see a great cruise ship, decks and portholes lit, slipping between Hyde Street Pier and Alcatraz.

Walking on the gravel alley between the trees and benches of Sterling Park, I hear the snapping of a branch. I pause, listen. "Bug . . ."

A thick voice moans my street name.

I turn. Just then someone leaps at me from the shrubbery, pushing me so hard I reel into the trunk of a tree. Another, perhaps the one who called to me, straight-arms my shoulder. I fall. Then they are upon me, three of them I think, three silent males dressed in black, two turning me onto my stomach, holding me down, grinding my face into the dirt, while the third climbs onto my back, pulls some kind of fabric sack over my head, then starts beating at the sides of my face with his fists.

I hear their breathing, sense their gloat, smell their excitement, their bodies, their foul breaths. My camera is trapped beneath me. The metal bites into my breast. I squirm and scream. The fists rain on my ears and cheeks.

The gravel of the walkway crushes against my mouth. I taste blood. The beating doesn't last long, perhaps fifteen or twenty seconds, but to me it seems an eternity.

They get off me. One of them kicks me. The point of his sneaker catches my flank. "Nosy fuckin' bitch!" I squirm to protect myself. "Hurt the bitch, make her howl," orders the thick voice that called to me before. Another kick. I try to howl but can't. The breath's been knocked out of me. I gasp for air.

Then they are on me again, turning me onto my back. I try to look at them but, head bagged, can see nothing through the cloth.

One of them grasps at my camera, rips it away. Then they run off down the path. I roll and shake and cry. Tearing the bag off my head, a pillowcase, I hear the pat-pat-pat of their receding steps. Silence. I growl, hug myself, snort out my pain. "Help! Help me!" I cry, but I don't recognize my voice.

He is holding me, a young man, carefully wiping the dirt and blood from my face with a moist cloth. He sits on a park bench; I lie on it with my head in his lap. I look at him and know immediately who he is: the strange homeless youth with the long hair and beard who has been living in the park for months.

"Hospital," I whisper. My throat is raw.

His huge eyes stare into mine. Perhaps he doesn't understand.

"Get me to . . . hospital," I whisper again. There's dirt in my mouth. I choke, then try to spit it out.

"Police."

Fear in his eyes as he shakes his head.

"Doctor." He nods. "Hospital." He shrugs. "St. Francis. Hyde Street. Close."

Then I pass out.

•   •   •

The handsome black-haired resident standing above me smiles down, the ironic smile of a cynic. There's no pity in his face but lots of curiosity. I'm a case. He's had me X-rayed and scanned. He's seen my insides. His skin is dark, his eyes liquid, lustrous.

"They sure did a job on you," he says. He speaks with the accent of an Oxford don.

I peer about. The E.R. walls are white. Medical equipment gleams. The gurney I'm on is narrow and hard. Phones ring. Nurses stride briskly past. Every so often I hear soft chimes followed by softly uttered cryptic announcements on the hospital P.A.

I look back up at the resident. He is Indian. A stethoscope is nicely draped about his neck. I read his name off the little bar pinned to his white coat: Dr. C. Patel. "They call me Sasha," he says. Sasha Patel. Nice name, multicultural. I smile. He smiles. He likes me. He tells me I'll be fine.

"Two black eyes, cut and swollen ears and cheeks, contusions, abrasions, two ribs very tender but not quite cracked. They're going to hurt, those ribs. I wouldn't laugh too much if I were you. Try not to cough either. Better still, don't yawn. You're on morphine now. The Tylox I'll give you may cause a headache. I don't think there's a concussion, but if you feel dizzy or strange, come back right away. Understand?"

"You're not keeping me?"

He smiles, shakes his head. "I'm sending you home."

"How did I get here?"

"By taxi. The driver told the nurse some bum bundled you in."

"That bum, as you call him, cleaned me up. He saved my ass."

"No," Dr. Patel says, taking my hand. "I cleaned you, I saved your ass."

I look up at him. I wouldn't mind kissing him. The most I can offer now is a grin.

"See, that didn't hurt so much." He turns serious. "Who did this to you?"

"Three men."

"Not a spouse?"

"I don't have a spouse."

"What did they want?"

"My camera."

He's a skeptic, Dr. Patel is. "A beating like this just for that?"

"Well, it was a very fine camera," I tell him, "and I think there was something else."

"What?"

"A message, a warning—to stay away."

"Good God! Why not send a letter?"

"A beating's more emphatic, I think."

He raises his eyebrows. He's an ironist, I can tell. He's also solicitous. The hospital, he informs me, must report the incident to the cops. He plies me with painkillers, three kinds, two for fallback in case the side effects of the Tylox are too severe. He tells me I have a good supple body which helped prevent more serious injuries. He tells me I'll feel pain for a few days, but that the more I move about, the better. Finally he asks me for a date on one of his evenings off. I gently decline. The nurse who escorts me to a cab tells me Dr. Patel is a ladies' man. "And we love him for it," she adds, "this town being . . . well, you know how it is."

Back in the sweet cocoon I call home, I take my sore body to bed. I'm lucky. Bones could have been broken, I could have been raped and sodomized. And that may yet happen, I think, for I have no intention of heeding such a tastelessly delivered message. From this point I shall be on guard; I shall not be taken again by surprise. My greatest concern is my camera. I have several spares but my Contax and I were as one. Well, you win a few, lose a few, better to lose a camera than to end up in traction. Perhaps one day soon I'll buy myself a new one. Till then I'll manage with what I've got.

• • •

It takes me four full days to recuperate, and even then, in the mirror my face looks like shit. Like a boxer's after a brutal fight, I think, but of course I wasn't in a boxing match. I was attacked from behind.

I go out a couple of times, slowly walk a block, then return home. The rest of the time I spend in the darkroom, or on the phone, or despairing over my soreness and marveling over my luck.

What, I ask myself, is the worst thing that could happen to me short of premature death? The answer's simple: to lose my vision. Without my eyes, defective though they are, my life would be an empty torment.

My snaps of Marcus Crane are great. I'm thrilled I took the time to unload the roll; better to have lost my camera than these precious images. It's the full sequence that makes them work, me and my camera circling him while he twists to keep me in view, at first unperturbed, debonair, finally breaking as he understands I'm a threat. This, for me, is the beauty of black-and-white vision and photography—the way it can distill the essence of an individual, cut through the mask, reveal the person's core. I see much evil in my final image of Marcus Crane. I shall print the entire sequence in *Exposures:* "Cornered Chicken Hawk."

Was it Crane who had me beaten? I think so, though it could also have been Knob acting on his own. Anyhow, I know Crane and Knob are pals, that Knob brokers Crane's chicken dinners. I also know Knob hates me, and I'm almost certain he was the one who called "Bug . . ." to make me turn. Later, instructing the others to "hurt the bitch, make her howl," Knob's particular intonation came through. Yes, it was his show, perhaps just payback for dumping him in front of his boys. If Crane was involved it was strictly as paymaster. If so, I think, he probably wasn't Tim's killer, since in that event, he'd most likely have ordered me killed.

•   •   •

David deGeoffroy is due in tomorrow. We're to meet at his hotel. Sullivan's has everything arranged for a Friday scattering of the ashes. It's up to me to get some of Tim's friends to come along.

Before I do that, however, there's someone I want to find, the strange boy who lives in Sterling Park. Walking with trepidation into the Greenwich Street cul-de-sac, I start searching for the place where I was mauled.

It isn't hard to find. The alley of trees is gorgeous as ever, the gravel has been freshly raked, the resin aroma of Monterey pine perfumes the warm autumn air.

I caress the side of the tree against which I was thrown, then kneel in the dirt. How miserable I was, yet exhilarated too, all my senses alert. During those painful seconds, I believe, my thought processes went dead. It was pure feeling that suffused me: helplessness and terror.

Carefully I lie down in the position in which I was held, then twist and turn allowing the sensations to flow back. I feel weird doing this, but believe it's necessary for my recovery. When I stand up again, I feel purged. Nietzsche, I believe, had it right: what does not kill me can only make me stronger.

The youth is standing before me now, not twenty feet away. He has appeared silently out of the shrubbery. He stands still as a statue, his beard so wild it hangs down like a tangle of vines. His huge eyes meet mine, not sharply, but in wonderment. He sends me a signal that he has come in peace but that he will feel more comfortable if I don't approach.

"Hi," I say shyly.

He nods. From our last meeting I know he's not exactly talkative.

"I came here to find you—to thank you," I tell him. "You took good care of me. Thanks for putting me in that cab."

"You were asleep," he says, voice sonorous. I smile; these are the first words I've heard him speak.

"I guess I passed out. You were kind to me. I live close by. I've seen you many times."

He nods again, as if to say he has seen me too. I wonder: Has he observed me standing naked in my bedroom window at night staring out at the Golden Gate?

"Can I bring you something? Food?" He shakes his head. "Drink?" Again he declines. I was wrong about him; I thought he'd ask for whiskey. "Are you sure? Nothing at all?"

He smiles again, sweetly shakes his head, then withdraws back into the shrubbery like a ghost.

At nine p.m. I prepare to go out. My ribs are still sore, my cheekbones are still bruised, my eyes are still black, but I don't put on makeup to cover my marks. I also make a point of carrying a camera, the old Nikon Dad gave me when I first took up photography. I want this trek up the Gulch to be a statement.

I cheat a little, take the bus as far as Sacramento Street. Since walking's still painful, there's no point in strutting if no one's around. Dismounting, I peer about. I don't see anyone I know . . . which is fine since I felt less than stylish stepping off the bus.

On the next corner, California, I run into Slick and Remo. They look closely at me, but don't say anything about my bruises. Still, it's clear they've heard what happened. News has spread by Gulch telegraph. Now word will spread that Bug is back, undaunted by her ordeal . . . with a different camera too, a big black one, twice as big as the old one.

Soon others surround me: Doreen and Alyson, Scott, Silky, Fizz, Toad and Wrench. I tell them about the scattering of Tim's ashes, invite them all to come along. They nod but I doubt any of them will show. It's one thing to regret the murder of a friend, another to engage in public mourning.

"Where's Knob?" I ask innocently, looking around.

Eyes are lowered. Slick says he saw him in The Werewolf.

"Well, remember," I announce, "I'm still working on

my book. So you'll still be seeing me around."

"You're always welcome here, Bug," Doreen says.

A chorus of approving nods. Heart thoroughly warmed, I thank them and continue on my way.

Outside The Werewolf, I question my sanity. Yes, I want to show these people class, but I've been injured and am in no condition for a fight. I don't think Knob will pick one in public, but I can't be sure. Still, I know, I must complete my mission, so I straighten up and shoulder my way inside.

The Werewolf's a shadowy place, far more frightening to me than The Tool Box. Combination meat rack, gay bar, piss stop for the street, it's a place to trash out, choose a piece of chicken, or just shoot up in the toilets. There're females in here, some of indeterminate genitalia, preops, postops, a few girls looking to become boys. This is also a place where elegant pervs and goths come on weekends to slum.

I push my way through the crowd. Brushing against people does no wonders for my bruised ribs. Trying not to wince, I put on a stoic face. I spot Knob over by the wall, hanging out with the acolytes who witnessed his humiliation at my hands. Did they join him in the ambush? If so, are they proud to have gone three-on-one against a woman?

"Knob."

"Bug."

Our greetings are strained. I nod slightly to the acolytes. They smirk.

"Been looking for you, Knob."

"Here I am."

"We're going to have a little ceremony for Tim. Thought maybe you'd like to show, being one of the leaders on the Gulch."

Knob grins, then guffaws. The acolytes follow suit. Yet the eyes of all three appear uneasy; they don't know what to make of me, what I intend.

An unctuous grin. "Looks like someone roughed you, Bug."

"Yeah, someone tried to, three of them in fact. Jumped me from behind. Brave boys, very brave."

"Too bad." He lowers his eyes to my Nikon. "Camera's not so nice. Lost the other one, did you?"

I meet his eyes. "It's not the camera that's important, Knob. It's the film inside. You know—the *evidence*." I raise Dad's Nikon, trip the shutter. *Whap!* Knob is stunned. *Whap!Whap!Whap!* Finally the steely eyes blink before my gaze.

Enough! I tell myself. *Cut it off.*

And so I do, turning my back, casually shouldering my way out through the smoke to the street. I leave high-pitched squeals of laughter behind, but I don't think they're directed at me.

Seven

Until I discover his real name, I think of my park inhabitant neighbor as the Youth. And though he's declined my offer of food and drink, I nonetheless fix him a picnic. I place several containers of prepared tofu, a package of sliced cooked ham, a packet of pretzels, three apples, two bananas and a can of Coke in a square Styrofoam carton, which I tie up with ribbon. All this I deliver to the very place where I was sandbagged. No sign of him, but I'm pretty sure he's near, watching over his domain. I place the carton on the bench where he cleaned me up, scrawl "From Kay" on top, pirouette and depart.

The Magician: I'm not sure what I expect as I sit in the lobby of the Mark Hopkins Hotel awaiting Uncle David's entrance. We've arranged recognition signals; I'll be dressed in black with a camera around my neck, he'll wear a polka-dot ascot. Our rendezvous is set for three p.m. Already he's a quarter-hour late.

When finally he appears I'm amused. The man perfectly matches his voice. If ever in the future I need a "dapper gentleman" for a shoot, I'll seek one as debonair as David deGeoffroy. Tall, ramrod-straight, his soft gray hair beautifully cut into overlapping locks, he has a Clark Gable pencil-line mustache, wears the requisite ascot plus matching handkerchief in the breast pocket of his blazer, sports brilliantly polished English shoes and, to top off the effect, carries an ivory-headed walking stick which he twirls jauntily as he surveys the lobby.

Spotting me he raises his eyebrows. I smile; he advances.

"My dear Kay—at last!"

He surprises me by bowing and bringing my hand to his lips. Old World manners. I feel ridiculous standing before him in leather jacket, T-shirt, sneakers and jeans.

Instantly I like him. He's handsome, his grooming's impeccable, his smile engaging. He looks to be in his late forties, but in excellent condition, reminding me of the sleek sort of man my mother used to call a "racing tout."

"Shall we stroll?" he asks. Again I notice the theatrical accent. "Or would you prefer a drink?"

"A walk sounds good."

As we leave the hotel, he salutes the doorman with his stick.

I guide him around the Pacific-Union Club into Huntington Park. Since it's a dazzling day and I wish to conceal my bruises, I am wearing my darkest wraparound shades. The dark red lenses activate the rods in my eyes by tricking them into thinking it's night.

When David asks if my eyes are weak, I briefly explain my malady.

"So you don't see colors?"

"None," I tell him. "Just the lightness and darkness of things."

"Must be a bit like experiencing the world in grisaille."

I'm pleased by this remark, which demonstrates a knowledge of art.

"Can you tell what color an object is by the particular shade of gray?"

"Sometimes but not always. To me colors take on different values in different kinds of light."

Either that satisfies him or he's too polite to query further. He compliments me on the portraits I sent of Tim.

"Beautiful pictures, Kay—full of affection. He looks as I'd imagined. I keep seeing glimmers of the boy."

He stops before a park bench. "Shall we sit?"

He props his stick against the seat. An elderly Chinese man performs elegant tai chi katas on the grass.

David touches his finger to his line mustache. "This may be painful for you, but I'd like you to tell me what happened. Not just the bare bones, but the whole story, ugly though it may be. I know this is a great deal to ask, but I'd be most grateful, my dear. I truly would."

How can I deny him? I nod, then tell him the story, not glossing over the more sordid facts.

He winces as I describe the hustling scene on the Gulch, mutters "Poor boy" beneath his breath. By the time I finish with the gory details of dismemberment, I see tears forming in his eyes.

"Shot in the throat, then cut up! My God! That's so . . ." He brings his hand to his mouth. Like many of his gestures, this one's overwrought though not, I feel, insincere.

"I'd almost say appropriate," he adds, "though it isn't, of course. In no possible way *could* it be." He turns to me, again touches his mustache. "You don't know what I'm talking about, do you?"

Over the next several hours, David deGeoffroy and I roam the city, stopping every so often for a restroom visit or for tea. We walk awhile, then sit, then get up and walk some more. Our pace is measured. There's a trancelike aspect to the afternoon, the way we move among people in the parks and streets yet seem to exist on a separate plane. My rib cage is sore but I steel myself against pain. I don't want to lose the thread. David's story has everything a good tale should: energy and mystery, passion and regret. Listening, I think of it as the Magician's Tale:

"This, Kay, I confess—straight out of college I was a middling magician, a so-so practitioner of legerdemain. My close-up work was adequate: card tricks, flying coins, cups and balls, sometimes salt and pepper shakers and stubbed-out, then reconstructed cigarettes. I was good enough to bum my way around Europe for a couple years working street cafes. Whenever I was broke I'd sit at a table, take my saucer from beneath my cup, place a couple coins in it, then practice tricks as if for myself. Sooner or later someone would ask if he could watch. I'd nod at the saucer, and would resume when he added coins of his own. In two or three hours I could make enough to buy myself a simple dinner and rent a humble room."

David pauses, flutters his hands. "Maybe I was better than mediocre. No question, after a while I got slick. My patter was good, movements smooth. Still, I was no master magician, not by any stretch."

One thing I notice as he talks: his extensive repertory of gestures. Touching his forefinger to his mustache, shooting his cuffs, fluttering, then dry-washing his hands—every move seems calculated to divert attention from something else, some devious bit of sleight of hand.

"It was only when I returned to New York that I started getting serious. First thing I worked up a persona—top hat, black cape, cane, white gloves, the works. I became"—David winks—"'The Great deGeoffroy.'" He laughs. "No, not my real name. That's Hyman Goldstein, Brooklyn born and bred. My father was a milliner. Later he and my uncle started a company, Novelties Unlimited. Basically they produced low-end powder puffs. . . ."

Offering these background notes, he gives his stick a stylish twirl.

"I ran an advertisement and started to pick up work, kids' birthday parties mostly, affairs such as that. Soon word spread that I was good. It got to the point where I turned engagements down.

"I was making decent money then, spending it too, not just on personal luxuries, though I've always had a taste for the finer things, but most of it on better tricks and lessons in technique. I wanted to become a real magician and that meant constructing an hour-long cabaret act. I wasn't at the grand stage illusion level yet, but would soon be headed that way.

"I took a class with a carnival conjurer, learned juggling, fire-eating, swallowing swords. I wasn't particularly interested in doing these things in public but wanted to master them as a discipline. I also spent a lot on private lessons with a retired vaudeville magician." David smiles. "The Great Alexis! He *was* great. He'd come out with a saber dressed like a cossack about to launch a pogrom, then bluff through his act using this marvelous throaty Russky accent. Pretty funny, considering his original name was Terry O'Higgins. But he was effective. Good illusionist too. Taught me a lot—the Needle Trick, Chinese Linked Rings, torn newspapers, silks and billiard ball multiplications.

"Slowly, as I mastered these effects, I incorporated them into my routine. Mind you, everything I did was classical magic, nothing novel or extraordinary, nothing people hadn't seen before. That was my problem. I was too ambitious to settle for the standard repertory of tricks. I wanted to show people something new, stand out from the herd.

"It was then that I started doing serious research, hanging out with the old-timers, delving into old books. One day, in the main reading room of the Forty-second Street Library, I came upon a sector of magic I had previously known nothing about—Indian and Malay magic, which amazes by means of bizarre, shocking and bloodcurdling effects involving such grotesquerie as self-lacerations, even the decapitation of small creatures such as fowl. I remember putting down that book, closing my eyes and thinking about what I'd read. And then, as in a vision, I saw myself in a turban with black beard and coppery skin, doing those very things."

He gives me a glance to measure the effect of his

words. *Decapitation:* I wince at the memory of what happened to Tim.

"Sounds awful, Kay, I know, but remember, back then we weren't in the age of the touchy-feely magician or, for that matter, animal rights. What I wanted was to truly astound people, shock them out of self-satisfied contentment. I'm sure as an artist you can understand. *Épater le bourgeois!* Right?"

He chuckles, then kicks out with his well-shod foot— a demonstration, I gather, of a fond desire to put the boot to the middle class.

"Yes, I think in those days I was pretty violent, not on the surface—there I was smooth as glass—but underneath where the raging anger roils. I promise you I'm not like that anymore. Look at me—I'm a dandy! But peering back fourteen years, I see myself as an angry kid."

He pauses. "There was something else. It went like this: If I could not be as great a mentalist as Dunninger, as great an escape artist as Houdini, as great a stage illusionist as Blackstone, then I would become something none of them had been—a violent, flesh-cutting magician-personage, reincarnation of the conjurers who worked the villages of South Asia leaving astonishment, terror, nightmares in their wakes."

At this point we're sipping green tea in an upstairs Japanese tea parlor near Fillmore and Bush. The window is open; bitter smells permeate the air. I look at David and see a man lost in a mist of tormented memories. I decide not to interrupt. Better for us both if I simply let him speak. Perhaps he senses my anxiety, for suddenly he smiles.

"Maybe you know this, Kay." He speaks calmly. "The true magician's grail, the ultimate act of magic, is an illusion called the Indian Rope Trick."

I nod.

"No one has ever seen it convincingly performed . . . though huge sums have been offered to anyone who can. Even indoors it presents a series of complex problems: the rope, the child's climb, the fakir's subsequent climb with the sword, the disappearances, the rain of dismembered limbs, the fakir's reappearance, the child's reappearance at the end. In fact the trick can be done reasonably well in a theater with the help of motorized rope, stage smoke, catwalks, split-second timing and lots of skill. But to mount it in the open air as originally described—there's not a respectable illusionist who thinks that's possible.

"The Rope Trick has always baffled magicians. Most believe it exists only in legend. Still, the deeper I looked into Hindu and Malay magic, a sort of hybrid illusion of my own began to take shape. Mind you, nowhere near as astonishing as the Rope Trick, perhaps more like a poor second cousin. But if it could be done (and I had no doubt it could), it would be a *tour de force:* shocking, astounding and appalling all at once . . . with the added bonus of a healing finale."

David sips from his cup, then sits back. Knowing he has me spellbound, he becomes expansive, reveling in his control:

"It took me over a year to work it out, to practice my part of it and devise the rest. And then I began my search for confederates. I consulted theatrical agents, placed advertisements, even sought people out on the street. My confederates, you see, had to possess a certain appearance and, more difficult, had to be available and willing to obey. You'd think it wouldn't be all that hard to find people happy to work with a magician, earn good wages and experience fascinating travel. But what I wanted my confederates to do was extremely off-putting to those I approached, repulsing them on account of the nature of the performance and because basically what I wanted was to borrow and employ their precious kids."

Again I feel troubled. Too many of David's words cut close: "decapitation," "flesh-cutting" . . . and now the awful phrase from his description of the Rope Trick: "rain of dismembered limbs." Jesus! What the hell is he talking about? Who are these children? And if, as I suspect, one of them was Tim, in what awful bloody rites were he and David involved?

We are walking rapidly up Fillmore toward the Washington Street–Broadway crest, past pricey restaurants and boutiques purveying elegant housewares and apparel. David is once again his jaunty self, twirling his stick. The words gush from him, yet now his saga takes on an edge. It's as if in the telling he's reliving the particular moment he's about to describe, the moment when, as he puts it, he first laid eyes on *"them"*:

"I'd been searching for a set of identical female twins. They'd have to be intelligent, possess an innate flair, little show-offs if you will. They'd also have to have extremely pliant bodies, as at least one of them would be trained as a contortionist. Finally there was the matter of size: I wanted little kids, small and lean, preferably no older than five or six. That way, if they didn't grow too fast, they could, after training, perform with me for at least four years. According to my plan, when they grew too big, I'd simply replace them with another pair.

"But, as it turned out, *not* so simply. Stage parents were delighted when I'd ask to see their little darlings, but when they learned the criteria—rigorous training, devotion and discipline, long road trips, dyeing of the skin— they'd become alarmed. And if not by all that, then surely by the nature of the little play their cherished sweethearts would perform. When they understood what was involved they'd turn furious: 'What are you—a *monster?* You expect our twins to do something so disgusting as *that?*' "

He lowers his voice. "It was at a birthday party in Fairfield County that I saw them. A glorious October day. A beautiful house set within a garden bounded by a millpond with classic red horse barn behind. The setting was a fantasy. Wherever you walked you heard the tinkle of water and the crunch of fallen leaves beneath your feet. The party was held outdoors, and it was there that I performed, setting up my table between the pond and the house portico, the children seated before me on the grass.

"The birthday kid, a snooty little thing turning eight,

struck me as incredibly spoiled. I remember the obnoxious way her parents showered her with gifts, accessories for her pony, a bridle from Gucci, a saddle specially made by Hermès.

"Bored with her, I looked around. There were twenty-five or thirty children. As usual I tried to choose one or two toward whom I could direct portions of my act. I saw the usual all-American freckle-faced boys, suburban sugar-and-spice-type girls. Not an interesting face in the lot, I thought . . . until my eyes alighted on *them.*

"A striking pair, the girl with long blond hair, the boy with his hair cut short. Because they were differently dressed I took them for brother and sister, not grasping at first that they were twins. You see, it was their eyes, not their twinship, that attracted me—huge, live, sensuous eyes, fascinated and fascinating, boring into mine, eager, greedy for my magic. Powerful eyes. Burning eyes. The kind of rapturous eyes that, when you see them, you know they can devour you alive."

David stops, turns to me.

"Oh, Kay! The thrill of it! Remember, by that time I'd been performing for kids for several years. My hunt for suitable twins was more than a year old. Yet never in all that time had I seen anything like these two—their sparkle, mesmerizing beauty. Had I been a pedophile I'd have fallen into lust! As it was I merely fell in love. . . ."

As David again steps out he changes his tone, taking on the part of a cool stalker on the hunt.

"Remember what I was seeking: a pair of six-year-old identical females. A pair of eight-year-old opposite-sex fraternals had never occurred to me. With good reason. I didn't think such a pair could accomplish what I had in mind. But watching this pair as I performed—and I performed by rote that afternoon though not, apparently, to the detriment of my act; afterwards, receiving the congratulations of parents, I was informed several times my show had never been better!—watching them, attentive to them, noting how attentive they were to me, I began to calculate if there was some way I could adapt them to my trick.

"One thing was clear—even if they weren't literally identical, they looked amazingly alike. Eyes, faces, even their heights, were the same. I tried to imagine them with duplicate haircuts. Then, it seemed to me, they'd be almost perfectly matched. And the matching loose-fitting garments I had in mind would well disguise the difference in gender. What struck me most, apart from their eyes, were the identical expressions on their faces, alertness and also something sorrowful which I felt would boost the trick by arousing spectator sympathy. By the time I'd finished amazing that party of spoiled little brats, I'd concluded not only that I could adapt these two, but that no other pair I would ever find would possibly do for me as well."

We are at the top of the ridge that runs along Pacific Heights separating it from Cow Hollow below. At one time an area of slaughterhouses, Cow Hollow is now a neighborhood of fine shops, chichi restaurants, real estate brokerages dealing in the city's finer properties. Here we pause, David to gasp at the beauty of the Bay, I to take his picture. As a performer he knows well how to pose. Perhaps later I can seduce him into showing vulnerability. But shooting him now, I wonder if the pleasure in his eyes can be accounted for less by the stunning view before us than the memory of his good fortune that golden Connecticut afternoon.

Descending into Cow Hollow, he describes how, after the magic show, he schemed to meet the pair and learn their names. He carried a bunch of *The Great deGeoffroy* business cards depicting a little drawing of a magician pulling a rabbit from a hat. He wanted very much to get one of these into their hands, and so began to hand them out to everyone, kids and attending parents alike, finally reaching the coveted glowing twins.

The girl, he understood immediately, was the leader, the boy shier, submissive to his sister. Even then he knew she would be the one who would learn contortion and thus star in the crucial first portion of the act, while the boy, disguised to look like her, would emerge only for the finale.

Both were full of praise for his performance. Listening he was struck at once by their intelligence and poise.

"How can we learn to do these tricks?" the girl asked.

David could barely believe his ears. *Perhaps,* he thought, *this is a fateful meeting, one that will forever change three lives.* Taking a certain risk, he knelt until his head was level with theirs. He whispered: "You *will* learn to do them, both of you. I will *teach* you how!"

A risk, of course, because such a statement could be taken as a come-on . . . which, indeed, it was. David didn't see himself as the proverbial bogeyman of the suburbs, the one kids are warned against from the time they're old enough to play alone outside. He would not be the dark stranger with candy canes in hand who would hang around the back of the schoolyard. David de-Geoffroy was no kind of kidnapper, merely a talented magician with an ambitious plan. But if ever he was tempted to spirit kids away, it was at the instant he first felt the collective breath of those two on his cheek, saw the sparkle that lit within their eyes as they learned that they too could be taught to mystify, dazzle and astound.

He asked their names. The boy was Timmy, the girl Ariane. When he asked if their parents were around, as he would like to meet them, Ariane responded that their parents had passed away in an accident two years before, and that they now lived with their Aunt Molly but a hop, skip and jump down the road.

By this time, nervous about paying them so much attention, David glanced around. No one, he was pleased to discover, seemed even to have noticed. In fact the party had broken up into a melee, kids laughing and playing, adults dishing out wedges of birthday cake and globs of multicolored ice cream.

Kneeling between them again, he said: "If you really want to learn magic, have your aunt give me a call. I'll come out from the city and give you lessons in your home. But remember, whatever I teach must be kept between us. Magic, you understand, is a *secret* craft.''

And as at this their eyes enlarged, he knew that he would have them, that he *must*.

He was elated as he drove back to New York. All the portents were right. And in his short exchange with the twins, he had divined a possible weakness: if it was true that both blood parents were deceased, then perhaps Aunt Molly was the kind of surrogate whose feelings were founded more in obligation than parental love.

He sweated out the next few days wondering if she would call. He had decided that if she didn't he would take the initiative himself. However, on the fourth day after the party, he found a message on his machine from a Mrs. Molly Kerrigan responding, she said, to an offer to teach magic which her godchildren, Timmy and Ariane Lovsey, had reported he'd made. If in fact his offer was real, she'd appreciate it if he'd be so kind as to call her back.

At the first meeting, wishing to inspire confidence, he dressed like a schoolteacher in tweed jacket and regimental tie. He also made a point of addressing himself to Aunt Molly, maintaining eye contact with her while throwing occasional soft glances and friendly remarks to the kids, who, eyes glowing, sat together on the rug, arms wrapped about their knees.

It was in the family room of a nondescript split-level that the meeting took place. Aunt Molly offered cookies and coffee, with soft drinks for the twins. She was a good-natured, slightly disheveled, plump fifty-year-old woman with a head of tight untrained gray curls, who worked as voting registrar in the local town hall.

As David spoke about magic, he did not forget that his sole purpose was to sell himself. He was, he wanted to convey, a responsible adult who would teach not only an exotic craft, but also something that would remain with his students all their lives—discipline, commitment to excellence, the rewards of practice, the very things they would learn if they took up a musical instrument.

Molly, he quickly understood, was overwhelmed by the twins. A widow, she had three grown children of her own, one a travel agent, one a bus driver, the youngest just finishing a stint in the Marines. Having exhausted herself bringing up three ordinary kids only to find herself suddenly burdened in middle age with two more, both brilliant, intense, most likely conniving and very difficult to please—David sensed her desperation.

That night a deal was struck: he would come out once a week on Tuesday afternoons to teach magic to the twins for less than a music teacher would have charged, providing props and apparatus at wholesale prices with no profit to himself. By the end of the evening everyone was satisfied, not least of all Timmy and Ariane.

He could barely wait for that first Tuesday. In the intervening days he worked out a strategy. He would play it absolutely straight for several months, coaching the twins, measuring their abilities, building up trust which, according to his plan, would lead in time to deep complicity. He would turn them into little magicians and, with the bonding power of magic, make them his allies. He already loved them; if he could make them love him, then nothing, he felt, would be impossible.

The lessons went well. The twins were talented. Ariane was delighted at the prospect of becoming a contortionist, and Timmy soon became skilled at juggling and manipulating coins and cards. During the lessons, which he kept informal, David carefully built their confidence, teaching them how to recoup after a mistake, delighting them with special games by which he tested their talent for theatrics.

They constantly surprised him. They adored deception. And they lacked the most obvious flaw in a child magician, the desire to flaunt their secrets by revealing them to friends. Ordinarily when children are mystified by a trick, their first query is: "How did you do that?" From Ariane and Timmy the first question always was: "Please, David, *teach* us how!"

Confusion, bedazzlement, mystification—the Lovsey twins were natural adepts. They loved waving the wand, rubbing the ring, conjuring spirits from the dark. They reveled in hocus-pocus and abracadabra, liked nothing better than to pull a coin out of an ear or force it up through the surface of a table. Wine that turns to water, then back to wine, flying cards, the levitation of balls—David had never seen such quick, deceptive little hands. And being kids, they delighted in scatological variations such as pulling colorful scarves out of each other's rear ends to the accompaniment of rude noises simulated by their mouths.

But what they liked even more than prestidigitation were the sword box illusions: the Scimitars of Baghdad, the Decapitated Princess, the Mismade Lady, the Headless Chinaman in the Mysterious Trunk. These illusions, which David introduced after several months, fascinated them on account of their ability to horrify. He explained the principle: how by severely shocking people one can make them vulnerable to effects which, in a normal state, they would never accept.

It was seven months before he broached to them the special trick. He told them he had invented it uniquely for the three of them, and it was only because they were twins that it could be made to work.

David deGeoffroy and I sit in the great San Francisco bar, Top of the Mark, on the nineteenth floor of the Mark Hopkins Hotel, he nursing a martini in a perfect conical glass, I refreshing myself with a lemonade. The views here are spectacular, encompassing the city. The sun is low, the mood mellow. I'm underdressed, but David doesn't seem to mind. However, when I remove my shades, he comments on the bruises on my upper cheeks and shiners around my eyes.

"Do you live with someone, Kay?"

"No. And I wasn't battered by a lover. I was jumped the other night, probably because I stuck my camera where it didn't belong."

"This has something to do with Tim?"

I nod.

"You're a brave girl."

"Less brave than pissed off. Listen, David, the suspense is killing me. Isn't it getting time for you to, you know . . ."

"Describe the trick?"

"Yep, the trick."

He nods, takes a careful sip, folds his hands. First, he says, he will describe it from the audience point of view, then explain how it is done.

The illusion is best performed outdoors, preferably in an open field. The Great deGeoffroy is dressed and made up as an Indian fakir—turban, robe, dark skin, black beard and mustache. He is assisted by his daughter, Zamantha, a small, lean, dark-haired girl with flashing dark eyes and coppery skin. She's a spunky little thing, cloaked like an Indian in an immaculate white pleated smock. Through the performance she acts as a jill-of-all-trades, handing apparatus to the fakir, juggling balls, performing cartwheels, passing the hat to the assembled crowd. Being eager and affectionate, she quickly wins its collective heart; thus the crowd is shocked when, near the end of the performance, the fakir suddenly turns on her on account of some minuscule error.

"Idiot! Haven't I taught you *never* to do that?"

Zamantha squeals an apology, but that's not good enough. The fakir is working up to a rage. He slaps Zamantha hard. She cries out, cringes from him in fear. He grabs her by her hair, drags her to the edge of the circle, threatens her with severe punishment, while she begs feverishly for mercy.

"Enough!" the fakir retorts. "I'll teach you a lesson you won't forget!"

And with that he draws a dagger from beneath his robe, brings it to Zamantha's neck and, with a single swipe, slashes her fragile throat.

Immediately blood spurts, drenching Zamantha's pristine smock, staining the fakir's robe. A few drops may spatter too on the clothing of people seated nearby. The audience goes into collective shock. Mass confusion, screams, as blood bubbles from the dying Zamantha's throat.

But despite the chaos the fakir, projecting the confidence he has shown throughout, persuades the audience that no harm has actually been done, meanwhile placing the apparently dead Zamantha into a large bulbous wicker basket which he has employed earlier in other tricks.

He has great difficulty stuffing her inside. The mouth of the basket is narrow and Zamantha is bigger than she looks. When he finally gets her in, he covers the mouth of the basket with a cloth, then, proceeding to calm the audience, changes out of his bloody robe.

Now come the incantations, pronounced in a language no human can understand. However, a few choice words of English are interspersed to the effect that the fakir is evoking the Lords of Darkness to restore to life his beloved daughter, whom, due to some terrible flaw of character, he has wrongly killed.

A pause while the fakir allows the suspense to build. The audience holds its collective breath. Can he bring little Zamantha back? She was so sweet, endearing. The fakir swears that if he cannot, he will immediately hang himself before their very eyes.

With a flourish he suddenly tears away the cloth cover from the basket, which he then tilts and revolves so the entire audience can see inside. It's empty! Zamantha's gone, disappeared! And then, just as the audience gasps, they hear the voice of a little girl crying "Papa! Papa!" from far beyond the circle. Collectively they turn. It's Zamantha, alive and well, in spotless garb, skipping gaily toward them from the distance. The crowd parts to let her through. She runs to her father, throws her arms about him while he in turn hugs her. They kiss, embrace, then take their bows, acknowledging thunderous applause and a rain of coins and bills thrown in appreciation for the fabulous illusion just performed.

David takes another sip of his martini. "Now is that a good trick or not?"

"It's good," I say. In fact damn good, I think . . . if not also bloody and cruel.

"By now you've figured it out."

"I know the part of Zamantha is played by both kids." David nods.

"But there's plenty I don't understand."

He smiles. "I'll break it down for you, mystification by mystification. First, the slitting of the throat and the explosion of blood. That's done with stage blood, bloody meat entrails and liver. The effect's so repugnant and the audience so shocked that most members turn away. Those who don't can't bear to look too closely.

"Second, the stuffing into the basket: Due to the use of the loose-fitting smock, Zamantha appears a good deal larger than she is. I fake it when I appear to have trouble getting her in. There's actually lots of room, but I want the audience to think she barely fits.

"Third, her disappearance: In fact she's in the basket the entire time, even as I rotate it so everyone can see she's not. This is where the contortionist training comes in. The basket interior is lined; Zamantha curls herself inside the lining against the round middle of the container and thus becomes invisible. By the way, when we perform outdoors there's no question of a tunnel. Indoors, to show there's no trapdoor, we set the basket on a legged stand off the floor.

"Last, the reappearance. The second Zamantha, as you rightly figured out, is played by her twin. With identical garments, haircuts and flashing eyes, plus effeminate gestures in which Timmy's been carefully rehearsed, the audience believes it sees the girl I 'killed.' So you see, Kay, once it's explained, like all stage illusions, it's simple . . . at least in theory."

He asks if I'll join him for dinner. I accept but suggest I go home first and change. He pooh-poohs that, insisting I look fine, pointing out we're in a city known for its informal style. We adjourn downstairs to the dining room, where David orders a bottle of Opus One to accompany our food. Once settled in and eating, he continues his tale.

"The moment I described the trick, the twins were entranced, eager to start rehearsals at once. Except that there was some unhappiness on Timmy's part, his feeling that he was being shortchanged. After all, he pointed out, as much to Ariane as myself, *she* would have most of the fun participating throughout the show, while *he* would only make an entrance at the end and until then remain hidden from view. ·

"Although I hadn't anticipated his objection, I knew at once I'd have to deal with it. Any anger or jealousy between the twins and my plan could fall apart. I was trying to think up a solution when Ariane came up with her own—she and Timmy would each perfect both parts, Zamantha I and II, then alternate the roles."

David laughs. "Think about it. The twins were all of eight years old at the time, yet already highly assertive. Ariane especially—she had this disingenuous way of taking charge, consulting Timmy and myself, yet controlling the dialogue so in the end she'd get her way. There I was, a mature (or perhaps not so mature) adult sometimes having to approach an eight-year-old as supplicant. In addition she constantly took on the role of Timmy's protector, as in this case, with her proposal that they split the Zamantha part.

"Frankly, I was wary. She was the better contortionist, and body contortion was essential to the trick. I also didn't think Timmy could sustain the part of a girl. It was one thing to play Zamantha at the end, quite another to make her believable throughout. But Ariane had no such qualms. *She* would coach her brother until he could give a faultless imitation. Meanwhile they'd have fun switching off.

"As it turned out, she was right. Although to my eyes she was slightly better as Zamantha I, our audiences were dazzled no matter which twin played the role."

By this time David and the twins had grown close. He had won their confidence; they adored him as a father. Thus he left it to them to bring Aunt Molly around to the idea that they be allowed to work with him full-time over the summer. The kids were clever little manipulators; they knew exactly which of their aunt's buttons to push. They had a lot going for them: her pity for them as orphans, an intelligence far superior to hers, a polished heartbreaking manner when making a request, an iron will in pursuit of their goals.

One Tuesday afternoon in May, after David had finished giving his lesson for the week, Aunt Molly sent the twins outdoors to play, then invited him into the living room to talk. Would he consider, she asked, taking the twins on for the summer? They so loved magic, he had told her many times that they were talented, they could assist him during performances, and she'd be willing to pay a reasonable fee for his trouble. David said he'd give the matter some thought and get back to her the following day.

When he did he proposed that they draw up a contract regarding the rights and obligations of the parties, necessary protection since he would be taking responsibility for two minor children. As for a fee, none would be required; the twins would earn their keep by assisting at performances. A good deal all around, he said, since they'd have a great summer learning experience and he'd have two charming child confederates with whom to expand his act.

Within a week the contract was signed. The day after school let out, the twins joined him in New York. Thus began a five-year relationship which lasted until they were thirteen years old.

Summer stretched into fall. At that time a new contract was drawn naming David as full-time guardian. A private tutor, a young woman named Beverly Jenkins (David's then girlfriend, an aspiring magician in her own right) was engaged to keep the twins current on schoolwork, act as sitter and chaperon, and stage-manage the show. Meantime all obligations to Molly Kerrigan were rigorously met—at David's insistence, since Ariane and Timmy showed little interest: weekly phone calls, frequent letters, occasional visits home. A fine arrangement by which Aunt

Molly was relieved of the stress of bringing up two difficult children, while the Lovsey twins, liberated from a stultifying home life, were free to discover their natures while seeing the world.

By the end of August the Zamantha Illusion had been thoroughly rehearsed. The three of them performed it publicly for the first time on a carnival ground near Camden, Maine. The show was taut with energy. Audience response was tremendous. Afterward a vacationing Broadway producer approached to say he'd never seen a magic act so bold.

Thus began years of travel that took the Great deGeoffroy and his little troupe from one end of the country to the other, on to Europe for a two-year tour, then on to Australia, New Zealand and Japan. There were other illusions in the act, of course, but the Zamantha was its signature. The posters featured it: a little Indian girl with bleeding throat being stuffed into a basket by a fierce-eyed fakir. The caption read: *See The Great deGeoffroy Bring Zamantha Back to Life.* Even professional magicians who understood the mechanics were dazzled by the execution.

It was three years into the relationship, in the midst of their grand European tour, that the first serious difficulties arose. As the twins grew taller, certain modifications were made, but there came a point where the gender difference became too pronounced to be ignored. Timmy's voice began to change and he starting shooting up, while Ariane's hips began to widen and breasts began to bud. A falsetto, elevator shoes and floppy garments could only go so far. As the twins passed their eleventh birthday it became clear the Zamantha Illusion would have to be dropped.

They worked up new tricks, some quite excellent, including an Indian livestock illusion involving a cobra and a mongoose, the Double Sawing-in-Half Illusion, the Torture Harness Escape and a violent illusion called Pillars of Fear. But nothing could equal the Zamantha, which depended on the interchangeability of twins. Thus the twins' relationship with David entered a new phase; later, in retrospect, David would call it "our Baroque."

Around this time David turned to Beverly Jenkins. In the classic tradition, in which a pretty young woman acts as confederate to an all-powerful magician, David began to center his show on complicated illusions in which he cut her in half and/or made her disappear, while Ariane and Timmy were relegated to minor roles, performing flips and cartwheels along the fringes of the stage, juggling balls and swallowing knives while apparatus was hauled in and out. When David was ready to perform a new illusion he'd reappear and, in an amusing leitmotif, swat at the twins and shoo them off.

This did not go down well with two exceptionally brilliant children who'd grown accustomed to being the center of attention in a bloodcurdling heart-stopping display. Why couldn't David come up with something new for them, something extraordinary instead of these degrading stunts? But David could not and tried to explain to them why—that their value to the show lay in their ability to appear identical, and now that they no longer did, a return to a stable home life was probably in order.

He did not put it so bluntly, but the twins quickly grasped their situation. Since there was no hope of ever again playing in a substitution trick, their future as child magicians was bleak; on the other hand, any humiliation was better than resuming life with tiresome Aunt Molly.

It was Ariane who came up with a solution, albeit a temporary one. She suggested to David that she and Timmy recruit and train a new set of twins.

David was extremely fond of the Lovseys, and he was not without compassion and loyalty, but he recognized that the twins charmed him less as they approached adolescence than they had as graceful young innocents. He also felt responsible for them and a measure of guilt for having used them to further his ambitions. It would soon be time, he knew, to cut them loose, but since Ariane's proposal enabled him to keep them on awhile longer, he agreed to set them the task of finding substitute twins without thinking through the fallacy.

It was a ploy, of course, a manipulation; Ariane had no intention of finding a suitable pair. Oh, she turned up twins, several sets of female identicals, and at first things would seem to go well. But then always a problem would arise—insufficient commitment, lack of suppleness, recalcitrance, stupidity or, Ariane's favorite bugaboo, equivocal parents. Each failed involvement would waste a couple of months. Meantime Ariane and Tim (he no longer cared to be called Timmy) were secretly working up an act of their own—an act so good, fated to become so popular, it would guarantee their position in the troupe.

"It *was* fabulous," David tells me, as we sip coffee after dinner. By this time the hotel dining room has nearly emptied out. "A mentalist routine, extraordinary because it was performed by kids. Mentalism, you understand, depends upon charisma. A top-notch mentalist has to be bigger than life. So to see a girl twelve years old command a stage entirely by herself—the effect was tremendous. And Ariane brought it off. She had grown that powerful. I was amazed.

"Actually what they did was a classic second-sight routine, Ariane blindfolded sitting on a stool in the center of the stage, Timmy roaming the house, asking audience members to show him objects such as watches, jewelry, banknotes and coins. Ariane would then divine what was being shown, describing the objects in great detail. In the case of banknotes she would give the serial numbers, in the case of coins the denominations and dates.

"Such feats are accomplished by a complex set of signals having to do with the first letters of the words the confederate employs to frame his questions to the medium. Questions such as, 'What does the gentleman have?' or, 'Tell us what the lady is holding up,' convey detailed information, which is then further refined in regard to color, size and so on by such follow-up comments as: 'Hurry now!' 'Come on, Ariane!' 'Surely you see it in your mind's eye!' The codes are complicated. Mastering them requires a major feat of memorization. Yet the twins, by rigorous practice and intense concentration during their routine, could dazzle audiences even more than when I sliced Beverly into sections, recombined them and at the end brought her back smiling and whole.''

I look closely at David. ''You sound like you were jealous.''

He nods. ''I was! They prepared their act behind my back, sprung it on me as a surprise. It was polished, professional. They were prodigies. I was overwhelmed. Then as soon as they started performing, it created tremendous word of mouth. Crowds thronged the theater. I felt eclipsed.''

David beckons to a waiter, orders a cognac. I settle for a second coffee.

''They had something powerful going. Call it twinship. Their rapport was so finely tuned, their need to stay on the stage so great, that they brought off one of the most demanding of all routines. Yes, I was jealous. I was also proud. It was I, after all, who had trained them, and now was being surpassed.''

Listening I see wonderment in David's eyes, the mixture of pride and envy, amazement and dismay he's just described. The memory of Ariane's power still disturbs him. But where, I interrupt to ask, was Tim in all of this? Was he merely his sister's stooge, or did he acquire power of his own?

''Certainly,'' David says, ''he was a fine magician. He had talent and his juggling and sleight-of-hand were better than hers. But she was the one with presence, who radiated authority, so I'd say she was the superior, the one for whom magic was nourishment. Reaching the top in magic, as in music or sports, calls for more than talent. It requires mental toughness, inner strength, a will to power. Ariane had those traits, Timmy didn't. What I grasped, and even feared in her, was a potential to go all the way.''

This kind of self-knowledge came later to David; during the Baroque he was only aware of his unease. There were moments, he remembered, when he considered devoting his life to the twins, stepping down from his role as The Great deGeoffroy to become their full-time manager. He even thought up a new name for Ariane—he'd anoint her The Amazing Amoretto, meaning "Little Cupid"—not to be confused with the bitter almond-flavored Italian liqueur of similar name. But these were daydreams. David was still too young to renounce his ambitions and become a stepping-stone for a child.

By the time they reached Japan he'd made up his mind: the twins would have to go. But then something unexpected, news that Aunt Molly, felled by a stroke, had been placed in a nursing home by her grown kids.

David was upset; the twins were not. They pretended to be, engaged in some whimpering, enough to get them by. Seeing through their act, he was appalled by their coldness, wondering if he was now responsible for a pair of minor sociopaths.

"They scared me, really did. Now I understand it was just Ariane. I realize I've been talking all afternoon about them as if they were one person when in fact there were two distinct personalities involved. She was powerful, he was easygoing. She was dominant, he submissive. She was fearless, and now that I think of it, cool, distant and very strange. He, though similar in many respects, was warmer, more like a normal child.

"At the time all this happened, remember, they were at the age when kids get, you know"—David smiles—"sexualized. Hormones raging through their bodies. Hair sprouting up in odd places. Loss of innocence, not that they ever had much of it . . . but they looked as if they did. Now suddenly they were horny, and, if that weren't enough, were turning rebellious. Not on the stage—there they were smooth as country cream. But offstage they started making demands for what Ariane referred to as their fair share of the earnings. They wanted to stay out late, eat out in restaurants, go dancing, do as they pleased. What could I do with them? Couldn't send them home— there was no longer a home to send them to. Couldn't abandon them to their own devices—they were still far too young. But I couldn't control them anymore. They refused to accept my discipline. It was obvious things couldn't go on this way, that we were headed for a crisis.''

The waiters, restless and forlorn, no longer hide their irritation. David suggests we adjourn to the lobby, where, he promises, he will finish up his tale.

"I've barely mentioned Bev. That's a saga in itself. But you should know she was sensitive to what was happening and very affectionate with the twins. She'd been tutoring them for five years, so well that when she took them to an American school in Japan, they tested at an eleventh-grade level. She'd grown close to them, was concerned for them . . . and also for me. She didn't think the twins and I were good for each other anymore. We discussed this a lot, agreed a separation was in order. A year or two apart, we felt, would be in the best interests of all concerned. When she came up with the idea of enrolling them in a private boarding school, I agreed this was our only remedy.

"She set out at once to find them a proper school, one that would provide guidance and discipline while still nurturing their creativity. She sent out letters. Catalogues came back. At first the twins were scornful. They'd glance at a catalogue, then toss it aside. The school looked like a prison, the teachers looked stupid, the kids looked like nerds. But Bev was patient. Gradually she got them involved. Perhaps there was a decent place somewhere in the world, she said, where they could spend a couple of happy years studying, preparing for college, participating in sports, making friends.

"On this later point Ariane was quite resistant. She got angry whenever we'd suggest she and Tim make friends their own age. 'We don't want friends our own age,' she'd say. 'We've far more in common with adults.' And she was right.

"Finally, after months of prodding, we narrowed the choice to three schools. I sent out letters. The first to come back requested grade transcripts and recommendations. That left two. Both were interested. The head of the American School of Tangier wrote of its exceptional drama program, while the principal of the Piñon Valley School in Scottsdale, Arizona, mentioned its progressive policies and, in view of the twins' unusual background, offered them three-quarter scholarships. Needless to say, Piñon Valley was our choice.''

David and I occupy one of those formal furniture groupings that adorn hotel lobbies, a square composed of couches and easy chairs arranged about a low marble table. David, reclining against soft cushions, has dropped his busy mannerisms of the afternoon, flutterings of the hands and touchings of the mustache, the diversionary tactics of a magician. He sits still, his voice, previously so theatrical, now sounding weary and also, finally, real.

"We had a lot of fun getting them ready for school," he says, "buying them proper clothes, shoes, luggage, heaping them with gifts—cameras, backpacks, tennis rackets, Walkmans, everything we thought prep school kids ought to have. We got them fresh passports, made airline reservations, air-shipped ahead trunks filled with sheets, pillows, blankets and towels. We even sent a crate of magical apparatus so they could amuse and astound their schoolmates.

"The night before their departure, we had a lavish farewell dinner in a private room at the best restaurant in Osaka. Lots of talk, laughter, they seemed so happy and relaxed. We reminisced about the last five years, recalling our successes, the great days of the Zamantha Illusion, our many misadventures too. They seemed so normal that night, natural, at ease. When we said goodnight we embraced and kissed. In the morning, at the airport, I found myself shedding tears. I hoped, I told them, in the spring to bring the act back to the States. Then we would see them often. Their last words to me were thanks for everything I'd done, the precious world I'd opened for them, the tricks and life lessons I'd taught. Then they were off. Bev and I stayed past the takeoff, until the great plane disappeared. Then we returned to the city and walked around feeling relieved but also empty, the way I imagine all parents feel the day they first send their kids off into the world.''

David looks down, shakes his head. ''We never saw them again. We know they got to L.A. Immigration and customs records confirmed that much. They were to change planes for Phoenix, but they never checked in for their flight. We didn't even know they were missing until two days past the time they were due, when we received a telegram from the school informing us they hadn't arrived. We were worried sick. Could they have been abducted? That didn't seem likely at their age. Perhaps they'd taken a little vacation, gone off on their own for a couple of days. Surely, I thought, they'd turn up. But then I remembered the odd formality of their goodbyes. There was something final about their manner, something in the nature of a permanent farewell. It was then that it occurred to me they'd flown the coop.''

Now another change of demeanor as the chuckle fades and hurt creases David's face. ''Yes, they'd flown, and, more than that, they'd absconded with half my funds.''

Being an itinerant magician, David received his earnings in local currency, either from theater managers or direct from audiences when he performed outdoors. Since the troupe lived in hotels and ate in restaurants, he paid all expenses out of pocket, converting the surplus into money orders which, from time to time and from wherever he happened to be, he mailed off to his bank in New York. There the savings accumulated in various accounts, adding up after three years abroad to not inconsiderable sums.

In one money market account alone, there was fifty thousand dollars. As David later reconstructed the scam, most certainly masterminded by Ariane, the twins prepared a series of documents authorizing the bank to transfer that money to an account they set up at the Tokyo branch of an L.A. bank. The documents, which he later saw, bore his actual signature. The twins had tricked him into writing it by a classic sleight-of-hand substitution with a school parental permission form. Since the docu-

ments were in order, the signature correct and the transfer
bank-to-bank, David's New York bank obliged. Having
moved the money to Japan, the twins intercepted the confirmation letter, withdrew the funds in cash, which they
took with them on their flight to the States, in the process
committing several serious felonies, not the least of which
was wire fraud.

David moans. "They only took half my savings, their
way, I suppose, of acknowledging all the fine things they
thanked me for as they left. A few weeks later we received
a postcard from Mexico City, short and sweet. I remember
it well: 'Dear David and Bev: We're happy, healthy and
safe. Sorry about the money, but what else could we do?
We figure we earned it and you can easily make more . . .
which we cannot. We miss you both. Love, A. and T.' "
David looks at me. "Can you imagine?" He shakes his
head. *"They were just thirteen years old."*

On my way home in a taxi, my mind whirls. I'm amazed
by what I've heard. I could have stayed on at the Mark
Hopkins to talk all night; David as much as asked me to.
But after eight hours of nonstop listening I was too exhausted. Also, I needed time to assimilate his story.

I now understand many things—how Tim learned to
juggle and do card tricks; the identity of the person David
called "the other" and "she" and referred to as "A." in
his letter. I wonder: Is Ariane still around? Is she the
mysterious girl Tim wanted me to photograph? Is she
the person I momentarily mistook for him on the street
the day I cleaned out his flat?

For that matter, was the fifty thousand he told me he'd
saved the same fifty he and Ariane ripped off? Finally,
what if anything does all this have to do with the way
Tim was killed?

Downstairs, in the lobby of my building, I find the same
Styrofoam box, ribbon neatly retied, that I left for the

Youth in Sterling Park. Inside I find the ham and Coke untouched, and a "Dear Kay" note signed "Drake" handwritten in large round letters thanking me for the provisions. So . . . now I know my homeless savior's name and that he's a vegetarian who prefers organic food. *Only in San Francisco,* I think. I resolve to leave a fresh package for him soon.

The blinking light on my answering machine greets me as I open my door. I rewind the tape, find two messages, one from Hilly saying she's got what I want, the other from Dr. Sasha Patel expressing concern over my health and inquiring whether I'm free to go out with him Saturday night.

After a shower, dressed only in my robe, I spend half an hour with my telescope snooping around. Lights are on in the Judge's penthouse. I think I see people moving behind the glass doors. Perhaps he's hosting a dinner party, one of those intimate candlelit affairs for six he likes so much. Good talk, good wine, a rich French stew, followed by salad accompanied by a cheese soufflé, with fresh ripe fruit for dessert. Among the guests perhaps the dance critic from the *Chronicle,* the stunning assistant U.S. attorney who argued so brilliantly before him the week before, his old law school roommate and charming wife, and the Judge's latest Special Friend, who works at the Butterfield & Butterfield auction house and has the body of a swimsuit model.

Flickering light illuminates the table. The talk turns mellow as the candles burn down. Talk of art and theater, the latest production at Berkeley Rep, the mayoral race, the future of the Presidio and such as that. Even as I watch, four of the guests rise to leave. Air is kissed, bodies are hugged, then a long lingering farewell at the door. Finally the Judge and Special Friend are left alone. He turns to her, reaches out with his arms. Their faces draw close. Their glistening lips are about to touch . . .

Savagely I jerk my telescope away. It takes me a moment to realize I've actually seen none of this, have been looking through the eyepiece with closed eyes, indulging in a fantasy.

Just as I fall to sleep I'm struck by a thought: Could Tim's androgyny, which I found so engaging, so attractive, be accounted for by the fact that in the Zamantha Illusion he played a girl?

Eight

Only four of us attend the scattering of Tim's ashes, Doreen and Alyson in full drag, David deGeoffroy and myself. It's a sour morning, the sea fog hangs like a canopy above the Bay. Once through the Golden Gate and in open sea the water turns rough, we shiver beneath the metallic sky, the boat isn't large, we're all uncomfortable and Alyson looks as if she'll maybe puke.

We do the job quickly, David holding out the urn, allowing the ashes to be caught by the wind ... which blows them north toward the Marin headlands. Chrysopylae was the original name given to these straits in 1846, Greek for "Golden Gate," an attempt to mirror Chrysoceras or Golden Horn, the Byzantine name for the harbor of Constantinople. *Chrysopylae:* I love the sound of that word, mutter it several times to myself as the ashes spin into the air. Once they're gone, we return to San Francisco, David pays off the captain, we find a cab at the wharf, drop the girls at the Hampshire Arms, then drive on to my building on Russian Hill.

The purpose is for David to pick up Tim's belongings, but upstairs he looks so sad I play good hostess and offer him a glass of Chardonnay.

"Beautiful place you got here, Kay," he says, despite the fact that fog obscures the views. "And I like your black and white decor. Austere." He peers at me. "A bit like you."

I haul out Tim's stuff. We sit on the floor and go through it. David smiles at the clothes. "Hard to imagine him so tall." He holds up Tim's Walkman. "I wonder—is this the one I bought him in Japan?"

There's something maudlin about him today. The dandified clothing's the same, but the manner is not. He's moody, disturbed. The mawkishness, I decide, is a cover-up.

Casually I pick up my camera, start taking pictures. David performs for me, makes a few faces, then, giving up control, resumes his examination of Tim's things. He thinks, quite wrongly, that I'll stop. He can't imagine I'd want to continue photographing him unposed. How poorly he understands. I want to find the vulnerable person hiding behind the double subterfuge, the imperious magician and the grief-stricken "uncle." I want the truth.

"Quite the little shutterbug, aren't we, dear?" he enunciates in a brittle, irritated tone. Then, when I make no motion to stop: "Click-click-click! You know, dear, it does get boring after a while."

I pause. He looks up at me. *Whap! Whap!*

"Will you please fucking stop it!"

"I won't," I tell him. "This is how I see."

He spreads his arms, relents. "Sorry, Kay. Just edgy today, I guess."

"Not because of Tim. You've known for a week he's dead. There's something else. What?"

"It's her," he says. "She's nearby. I feel it."

"Ariane?"

He nods.

"They could have split up. He never told me about her, didn't mention her to you in his note."

He looks at the array of possessions. "Something missing here. Where's his passport, his address book?"

David's right. "Maybe the cops have it. I'll check."

He listens as I call Shanley. After I shrug and hang up, he shakes his head. "I still think she's around."

"For all you know, she's married with kids in Kalamazoo. Or beating the bushes as an itinerant magician."

"She's definitely not doing professional magic. That I've already checked."

I study him as he sits on my floor surrounded by Tim's jeans, shirts, boots. "She was the one you loved," I say.

"I loved them both."

"But her most." I take another shot. *Whap!* "There's more to it, isn't there?"

He lowers his eyes. He can't bring himself to confess.

"They didn't just up and leave because you were sending them off to school. *Did they,* David? There was something else."

He stands. He wants to leave. I've no intention of letting him go. If there's more, I mean to find out what it is.

"Better tell me, David. You'll feel a lot better if you do."

He sits down again amidst the scattered clothing. "Please, no more pictures," he begs.

I set down my camera. He's silent. I sit beside him, prepared to listen.

"Yes, I loved her," he admits. "Very much. I—" He shakes his head. "She felt my desire. She was so powerful, seductive. She came on to me. I couldn't resist." He pauses. "I'm still ashamed."

"How long did this go on?"

"Couple of months. We started just before the end."

"Did Tim know?"

"Probably. They confided everything. Also, they planned their escape so well. The stealing, fraud—later when I learned the dates, I realized they started on it shortly after she and I—" He shuts his eyes. "They probably figured that gave them the right, and . . . well . . . maybe it did. I never brought charges. It never occurred to me. I thought I'd wait them out, be patient, and sooner or later they'd come back. I made it easy for them, returned to New York, opened a mail-order magic house, took out ads in all the magic journals and magazines. A couple of years ago I started running a personal ad: 'Info Wanted on Zamantha Illusion.' I figured since magic was in their blood, eventually they'd see it, then they'd call or write. And so finally Tim did. Too late. He never got my reply.''

David interpreted Tim's note as a test to determine if David was searching for them to get his money back. They had to know that much before they risked a call. And Tim, being less emotionally involved, was the logical one to make the overture. The bland tone of his note was effective and sly.

'' 'Working as a waiter, trying to make ends meet'— his way of telling me the money was long gone and he was working at an honest job. The hundred dollars I sent back was my way of telling him money wouldn't be an issue. I figured we'd write back and forth for a time, send each other these kinds of messages. Eventually, I hoped, he'd trust me enough to call. Then, perhaps, he'd allow me to see him, see them both.''

He shrugs, not, I understand, to dismiss the possibility, but the way a man might shrug when a great opportunity has been lost.

''She's here. I'm certain. She may have seen us yesterday while we walked.''

''If that's true why didn't she contact the cops, take responsibility for his body?''

Again David shrugs, turns his palms to the ceiling. ''I just don't know,'' he says.

He takes only Tim's Walkman, leaves the rest of the stuff with me to give away. After he goes, to check out of his hotel and catch his plane, I ask myself why I didn't tell him that Tim had spoken to me about a girl he knew, whom, for reasons never explained, I would very much want to photograph. Or the apparition I saw near the corner of Mission and Grace the day I cleaned out his studio.

Or the mysterious person who entered with a key and tossed the studio between Crawf's and my visit and Shanley's. Or the fifty thousand dollars Tim claimed he'd saved. Or about Tim's dream of retiring to San Miguel de Allende—since the postcard from the twins had been mailed from Mexico City.

Why did I deprive him of so many clues which might have given him hope? Should I call him tomorrow, confide? Having been so candid with me, hasn't he earned my confidence?

The truth, I decide, is that I still don't trust him, feel there's more to his story, yet another layer he didn't reveal. And, too, I'm out for bigger game than a reunion with a girl whose life David so radically bent. I want to complete *Exposures,* and to do that I must discover who killed my friend.

The *Bay Area News*, being an alternative newspaper, is appropriately situated in a cutting-edge neighborhood—on Folsom in SoMa, surrounded by other alternative enterprises: a used record store called Psychosis, an erotic boutique called Marquis de Suede, a dance club called ATF (Alcohol, Tobacco & Firearms) famous for its orgiastic fetishwear blowouts where the dress code is strictly enforced. There are stores that specialize in furniture of the 1950s, photographers' studios, numerous pubs including the infamous adjoining BoyBar and GirlBar (never the twain shall meet), and a half-dozen basement and storefront avant-garde theaters.

The *News* takes up the top floor of a four-story warehouse. There are only two ways up, freight elevator or fire stairs. I take the stairs.

I came to work here straight out of the Art Institute willing to shoot most anything in return for pay. The wages were lousy, barely enough to get me by. I ended up sharing a ratty Edwardian on Cole Street with three *News* colleagues. But the work was fun, we were young, high-spirited, priding ourselves on breaking stories the mainstream press wouldn't touch. Even more we enjoyed smashing taboos, inserting obscene words into articles, praising alternative rock bands with names like Genitorture and, for the hell of it, kicking the Establishment in the butt.

Memories flood back as I mount the stairs. The stairwell walls are embellished with graffiti—a scrawled one-liner, *Camille Paglia is smarter than Gloria Steinem,* an obscene reference to Kierkegaard, a Dykes on Bikes poster adorning the landing. The blended pizza-and-pot aroma is also the same. I remember attacking these stairs with unprocessed film, trying to beat impossible deadlines. "Kay! Get over to the Clift. Mick Jagger's checking out." "Joey! Drive Kay round to the back of the Hall of Justice, we need a shot of the Trailside Killer in manacles."

Most of my old newsroom colleagues have long since moved on. Because the *News* is the sort of place that burns you out, it's nearly impossible to work here past the age of thirty. But there're a few who've made the paper their home. One is Joel Glickman. He originally came out from Brooklyn for the Summer of Love, lived on the Haight, balled and grooved. He joined the *News* at its founding years before I arrived, and is still here a dozen after I left. In the meantime he's won a Pulitzer for his exposé of corruption in the city assessor's office. Since then he's received numerous offers, including one to be San Francisco bureau chief for *Time.* But Joel is happy at the *News.* Here he can do what he wants. He's even paid a decent middle-class wage, probably the only reporter on the paper who is.

The spiky-haired receptionist peers at me. "How may I help you?" she asks.

"Kay Farrow to see Joel Glickman."

Her squint grows intense. "Is Joel expecting you?"

I nod. In my day they weren't nearly so protective.

Joel's office is a cubicle, but he's got a window. Even if the glass is streaked, that's a sign of status. His desk is piled with papers, his walls covered with old cartoons.

His Pulitzer certificate, cheaply framed, hangs cockeyed to show how little he expects you to be impressed. Joel, now balding, drooping mustache and goatee tinged with gray, beams up at me through what look to be the same steel-frame grannies he was wearing when we met.

"Hey, kiddo! You look great!"

I pull off my shades, flaunt my shiners. "Little beaten-up, that's all."

His forehead furrows. "Serious?"

"Not as bad as it looks."

I tell him I was jumped, and that the reason's probably connected to the purpose of my visit.

"So what's the reason, kiddo?"

I shrug the question off. "Still got good sources in the cops?"

"A few," he says. "Most are afraid to talk to me."

"Afraid you won't protect them?"

He smiles. "They figure I'm being watched."

"Are you, Joel?"

He laughs. "Imagine how much it would cost and how paltry the pickings?"

He's right. It would be exceedingly unprofitable, not to mention illegal, to keep Joel under permanent surveillance.

"I may have a new cop source for you," I tell him. "She's working on something hot and ready to leak."

"Interesting. What does she want?"

"Her name in lights—when it's over."

"Corruption?" Joel licks his lips.

"No, so don't salivate. But it's a good story. I'm working on it myself."

We go around the corner to the Transcendental Cafe, where, in my youth, I wasted more hours than I like to recall. The walls here have been laboriously papered with old tarot cards. The resident swami sits at the window table staring goggle-eyed into his crystal ball.

We order herbal tea, then I tell Joel my story. I leave out the background stuff I got from David, but am frank about my own interest and Dad's involvement in the old T case.

"I remember Torsos," he says when I finish. "Particularly that wacko inspector, what's-his-name, Hale—the one wrote all those lovely letters of self-praise. City's 'Top Cop' they called him. But there was something rotten in the cotton."

Joel's smart. He knows there's more to the equation.

"Okay, you're setting me up with Hilly. So tell me, kiddo—what do *you* get out of all of this?"

"She's getting me some information out of police files."

"That's illegal." I nod. "She must want this bad."

"She does. Because she's a woman, because she's a lesbian and because the guy she works with treats her like shit. Her partner's got his own reporter, by the way."

"Who?"

"Lubow at the *Examiner.*"

"Good man."

"But no Joel Glickman."

"No." Joel grins. "Surely not." He studies me. His eyes grow serious. He turns slightly so the light glints off his grannies. "This information—it wouldn't be *personnel* information, would it?" I nod. "About your dad?" I nod again. "Want to tell me more?"

I hesitate . . . then decide to spill. Joel, after all, is like family. "Remember, years ago, I told you how my mom shot herself?" He nods. "That was the same year Dad took abuse for the lost T case evidence. I have this feeling there's a connection there."

"Fine, suppose there is—why go back to all that pain?"

"I've got to know where I came from, Joel."

He measures me, nods. "Just wanted to see how much you care."

He says he thinks the story's worth pursuing whether it connects to the original T case or not.

"Just the idea," Joel says, "that there's this kid living that way up on Polk Gulch, then he gets killed and nobody cares, and there're forty, fifty other kids doing the same thing, taking the same risk—that's important in itself. I also like the subplot, that there're all these closeted rich guys—lawyers, stockbrokers, whatever—who swoop down in their cars from Pacific Heights and Marin basically to plunder young bodies." He nods. "Yeah, I like it a lot."

We agree to divide it up—he'll pursue it as an investigative piece for the *News* while I'll make it the subject of my book. Meantime we'll pool our information, credit one another in our respective work, and I'll supply Gulch photographs for his piece.

He thinks my calling Hilly at home is a mistake.

"Once I start asking indelicate questions around the Hall of Justice, the big shots'll figure there's a leak. Hilly'll be suspect. They'll start watching her, maybe even tap her phone."

"Aren't you being a little paranoid, Joel?"

He shakes his head. "Uh-uh, kiddo. I've been through this too many times. People who blow whistles tend to get burned. We need a contact code, for her protection as well as ours."

When he describes what he has in mind the intrigue excites me: calls from phone booths, alternate safe meeting places designated A and B; chalk marks on a mailbox in the Castro when we want to meet with Hilly or she with us.

"I also want you to buy a micro tape recorder. From now on, tape all important conversations. In a story like this there're always disputes. If you can produce a tape, ninety percent of the time you're off the hook."

"I'm glad I brought this to you," I tell him. "I feel like I've been floundering."

"I'm glad you brought it to me too," he says. "Just like old times, kiddo, right?"

I walk him back to his office. He shows me pictures of his new live-in love, Kirstin, the Scandinavian Ice Goddess, showing off in a bikini on Stinson Beach. Also photos of his daughters, one enrolled in a postgrad marine biology program at Scripps, the other majoring in English lit at Cal.

Joel, I suddenly realize, is nearly fifty years old. Before I leave I photograph him at his desk, the mishung Pulitzer above his head. *Whap!Whap!* Another archetype for my collection: the Intrepid Investigative Journalist.

Sasha Patel is not to be denied, his proprietary interest possibly explained by his having viewed my insides via X rays and scans, not to mention his hands-on acquaintance with my anatomy. I always thought doctors were detached, that clinical fleshly contacts had no power to arouse. Such, apparently, is not the case. After considerable prodding on the phone, I agree to meet him at the Buena Vista tonight after his shift. But I make it clear this will be a one-off, that I'm not in a dating mode.

I turn up after lunch at Marina Aikido, wary of combat but determined to get a workout. I show Rita my bruises. She agrees I shouldn't spar.

"Just katas today and the rest of the week," she instructs. "Keep it slow. Concentrate on form."

I appreciate that she doesn't ask whether I've been battered by a lover. After class I describe the attack, and how, once on the ground, with my attacker on my back, I was powerless against his fists.

Rita demonstrates some randori moves I might have made. "Create a whirlwind," she says. But once thrown, she agrees, I could do little but take the beating. Except, of course, if my legs were free below the knee, in which case I could have kicked back against the base of my attacker's spine.

Right! Why didn't I think of that? But then I remember: there were three of them, the second holding down my legs, the third my arms. In fact, I should never have fallen, and think the only reason I did was out of fear of damage to my camera . . . which they took anyway.

"Next time don't try and protect it," Rita advises. "Use it as a weapon, a ball and chain. Merge with it. Let your energy flow into it. Remember, Kay, a camera can be replaced." She lightly touches a bruise on my cheek. "Shattered bones take time to mend."

Walking home, on Union Street, I'm attracted by a poster in the window of a children's bookstore. *RAINBOWS!* it proclaims, and then: *COLOR!COLOR!COLOR!* Numerous books for kids are on display, all having the word "color" in their titles. *Colors; Naming Colors; Know the Colors; Colors Everywhere . . .*

I study the window for a time, then enter the store. A friendly smile from the proprietress. I pick up one of the color books, leaf through. There are photographs of farm animals and swatches in the margins, which I assume match the colors of the animals.

A second book contains plastic overlays enabling a child to create secondary colors by mixing primaries. Familiar words leap from the pages: "yellow," "magenta," "cyan" . . . all Greek to me.

A third book also bears color swatches, along with exotic words: plum, mint, crimson, poppy, absinthe, azure, robin's-egg blue, aquamarine. The names of the colors dazzle me: hyacinth, lilac, quince, saffron. I savor the sounds: salmon, indigo, mocha, flax, ocher, Pompeian red, burnt sienna.

There's a vast world here of which I have no optical knowledge. But I can dream, extrapolate, for there are words listed for the shades I do know and see. The whites, for instance, composed of all other colors: antimony, bismuth, oyster, ivory, zinc, Dutch, Chinese. The grays: charcoal, dove, gunmetal, mouse, pearl, plumbago. And, my favorites, the blacks or achromatics: bone, aniline, ink, japan, raven, soot and slate.

So yes, I decide, though there is an unknown universe here, there is also one I can distinguish quite well. The spectrum I know, the one of tones light and dark, is to

me exquisite. I may not see the rainbow or know autumnal
colors, but let no one say I cannot revel in the beauties
of the world.

Hilly loves Joel's contact code: "Secret codes, secret
rings—brings back my tomboy days."

We're sitting in a corner of The Duchess. Hilly's idea;
she figures no cop will follow her into a dyke bar. It's
smoky and noisy, but this time I don't mind. Now that
we're acquainted there's no special need for quiet.

"In my family," she reminds me, "I was the only girl,
born between two boys. My brothers were my buddies.
We'd fight and scrap. Now one's a T-man, one's a G-
man and I'm a city dick. So see, Kay, the contest still
goes on. I wanna zoom past them. I wanna be family
champ."

There's a special pungency in the air here, women oozing desire. I notice Hilly twitching. This hothouse atmosphere turns her on.

"Check her out." She gestures toward a short-haired
brunette standing at the bar. Her biceps are ringed by a
coiled snake tattoo, her midriff is bare, she wears nothing
but clingy Lycra shorts and a black leather halter bra.
"Hot, huh!"

I shrug.

"Gimme a break, Kay! Girl goes to the trouble of making herself yummy like that, you can't just *not* respond."

I shrug again. "What can I do, Hilly? I'm just a vanilla
square."

"Hey, the culture's queer! Get with it, babe!"

"Yeah . . . now about that stuff you brought me."

She nods, unfurls her copy of the *Bay Area News,* extracts a sheaf of photocopy paper. "I couldn't get your
dad's personnel file. That's held too close. And since he's
retired it's over in dead records anyway, which means
it's basically in a vault." She taps the papers. "What I
do have is the confidential I.A.D. report on the Sipple

fiasco—Waincroft, Hayes, Puccio, Vasquez and, of course, your pop.''

I hold out my hand. She passes the bundle.

''Not pretty reading, Kay.''

''Life's not pretty either.'' I thank her, tell her to expect a call from Joel. ''You'll like him,'' I tell her. ''He's a '67-vintage hippie turned serious.''

She grins. ''Sure you don't wanna stay, meet some of my buds?''

''Thanks anyway, Hilly, but I've got a date with a man.''

''Ouch!'' she says. And then, an afterthought: ''Woof!''

The Buena Vista is one of my favorite drinking holes, even if it's too often thronged with tourists. Something about the joint at the bottom of Hyde and Beach, where the Hyde Street cable car ends, that brings back happy memories of Art Institute days, meeting friends here on Sunday mornings, throwing back Irish coffees while arguing about sex and art. I like the neon sign outside, the way the letters are formed, the long bar with its tiled base, the bottles arrayed before the long beveled mirror. I like the ceiling fans and the earthy waitresses and the handsome bartender dressed in crisp white mess jacket. Best of all I like the alcoholic coffee.

Sasha is waiting for me, occupying a round wood table by the window. I haven't seen him since the night he took care of me at St. Francis Memorial, when I was morphined up.

Checking him out, I decide he still looks good, with his dark skin, brilliant black hair and large lustrous liquid eyes. A ladies' man, the nurses called him. It's pretty obvious why. It's his alluring smile, so charming and seductive. Also, I assume, so false.

''You're looking good, Kay,'' he comments as I sit down. He reaches over, removes my shades, peers at the bruises around my eyes. He touches one lightly.

"What do you want me to do next?" I ask. "Open my mouth and say 'Aaahhh'?"

"Not unless you're prepared to strip to the waist," he warns. "I want to check your rib cage." Again he touches me. "Tender?"

"A little."

He grins. "I'll be tender too."

Quite the jocular fellow is Dr. C. Patel, though I must say I like his accent.

"You talk like a Brit. How come?"

"Because I am," he says. "Born and raised over there. My parents came from India, but I'm a British subject . . . though most true-blue Brits consider me a wog."

"What's that?"

"A person of color. What you Americans call a nigger. Or 'one of our little brown brothers' when you want to show how sensitive you are."

"Are you bitter, Sasha?"

"Actually, no. I love it here. Home of the Free, Land of the Brave. I especially like American women." He shows me a grin so charming it could light the world. "And of course, you Yanks have the best medical practice in the world."

I find it difficult not to like him. He's polished, smart, has a fast mouth . . . and always those gorgeous liquid eyes toward which any girl in her right mind would crawl through splintered glass.

"Tell me something," he says suddenly. "Who *is* Kay Farrow?"

I laugh. "My life story?"

"A few high points will do."

I offer him a few high points. While I do he gazes into my eyes as if smitten by every word.

"Enough about me," I say. "Your turn now. You can start by explaining your interesting first name."

"My actual name's Clarence. They started calling me Sasha in school."

"How come?"

He smiles. "Because I wanted them to. I was reading

Russian novels at the time and fell in love with the name. Something moody about it, also romantic.'' He gazes at me. ''Tell me, Kay—do you like to dance?''

''I'm a crummy dancer,'' I say.

''I'm sure you could improve.''

''Under your tutelage?''

''Why not?''

''I think I'll wait until my rib cage heals.'' I smile at him. ''There's something you don't know about me yet.''

''Tell me.''

''I don't own a single dress.''

He laughs. ''Jeans girl! Terrific! You do own shorts?''

''Numerous pairs.''

''I love shorts and slacks, close-fitting garb.'' He wets his lips.

''You know, Sasha—I just realized something.''

''What's that?''

''We're flirting, both of us. And flirting's against my principles.''

''Mercy!'' he says.

''This is fun, but I gotta go.'' I stand. ''Please let me pay my share.''

''Absolutely not. And I'm very sorry you're leaving— just as we were starting to get on.''

I wait while he takes care of the check, then permit him to escort me up the hill. Hyde Street is steep between Bay and Chestnut. By the time we reach the top of crooked Lombard, we're both slightly out of breath.

He makes his move just inside the front alcove of my building. As we kiss, I feel like a college girl getting smooched in the doorway of her dorm. He tastes good. Must be the Irish coffee. Then I hear myself sigh. He presses upon me. I feel his hardness . . . and then myself becoming wet. He presses harder until I'm flat against the granite portal wall, brings his mouth to my ear, licks it, whispers, ''I want to make love to you, Kay.''

I move my hands so that they embrace his butt, pull him closer. ''I'd like that too,'' I whisper dreamily.

• • •

The night passes quickly. Sasha is tender. I relinquish my aggressive manner, lie back, yield, let him fill me, have his way. I'd have thought he'd be a selfish lover. He surprises me. Unlike a prototypal ladies' man, he's caring, solicitous, attentive to my every pleasure and need.

I love his dark silken skin, the fine texture of it, its taste. I ravish him with my mouth, lick him everywhere. Then he licks me and I explode. Sweet explosion!

Always with a new lover I pray that colors will show themselves, little splinters, sparks, showering off the fireworks of my rapture. Tonight they come, not the colors the rest of the world sees so easily, but colors of my imagination, colors of singers, painters, poets: cinnabar, wine-dark vermilion, carnelian, aerugo, chrome primrose, bistre, jonquil, jouvence, piccolopasso, tartrazine, solferino, roccellin. The colors of Veronese, Matisse, Vincent van Gogh (who may have been dyschromatopsic). The colors of the passionate unfurling flower of my labia. The colors of orgasm. The colors of love. All the secret colors of my inner penetrated self . . . for though we are all born color blind, we each have within us the ability to someday see the hues.

He leaves me shortly after three-thirty a.m. He must, he tells me, get back to his room at the hospital, for he is on call beginning at four. After he dresses, he leans over me, then kneels to kiss my breasts.

"Wonderful to be with you, Kay. I hope this isn't going to be a one-off like you said."

I look up at him. "I don't understand you, Sasha. You're Don Juan. One-offs are your stock and trade."

He laughs. "How sorely you've misjudged me!"

"I did have fun," I admit.

"Can I see you again tonight?"

I groan. "Let's wait a couple days. But don't worry, I doubt my ardor will cool."

• • •

I awaken late. The sun's burning in. I put on shades, go to the window, wave naked to the goggle-eyed house-painter working on the building across the street. I think of something the artist Willem de Kooning once said: that he dreamed of creating a painting that would contain all the colors of the world. Such too is a dream of mine: to partake of an act of love so vivid with colors I will never afterward miss them in my daily life.

In the bathroom I inspect my body. My bruises are fading. The smudges are fainter. If I could see colors, I would note that they're turning from blue to beige. This morning there are new marks on me, strawberry-shaped love bites. They decorate the front of one shoulder, and there are two big ones on my collarbone.

I stretch, feel luxurious, tensions relieved. Sex is great and I've forsworn it too long. Last night I relearned something I seemed to have forgotten along the way—that there are other men besides the Judge who can make my body sing.

I take a shower, put on my robe, sit down to read the papers I got from Hilly. The Internal Affairs Division report on the Robbie Sipple attack echoes every smear I found in back issues of the *Chronicle* and the *Examiner.*

Dad was right: clearly the report was leaked. Inept, incompetent—the only pejoratives lacking are the *ad hominems*: dummies, dunces, dolts, chumps, buffoons. But the report is all the more scathing for the absence of insults, calling into question the professionalism of the officers involved. Sergeant Lucius Waincroft takes particular abuse for "the shocking breakdown in the command structure that led to this debacle." And patrolman Jack Farrow, as the officer first on the scene, is held accountable for his "abysmal failure to collect and preserve vital evidence which, even at cursory viewing, was clearly relevant to a widely known ongoing investigation of a series of capital crimes."

Poor Dad! But there are ambiguities in the report which

escaped the newspapers, hints and phrases that make me take notice. The possibility, for instance, of a conspiracy among the incompetents, dismissed as being improbable, yet considered nonetheless:

"... despite these conclusions, the Division Committee cannot wholly exclude several other potential explanations of the debacle: (a) one or more officers sought to conceal the mishandling of evidence by themselves and/or their colleagues, by deliberately destroying and/or mislaying the discovered materials; (b) one or more of the officers returned to the crime scene after it was clear, and deliberately removed the discovered materials for reasons of their own."

Translation: A screwup and then a cover-up, or worse, the evidence was deliberately lost because it implicated someone inside S.F.P.D.

Another ambiguity concerns the behavior of Inspector Jonathan Topper Hale in his meeting with the patrolmen and sergeant prior to the assignment of the matter to I.A.D.:

"... Hale's abuse intimidated the officers, leaving them with little choice but to remain silent lest their careers in the Department be further jeopardized. In accordance with good management practice, Hale should have cajoled these officers into remembering clearly what transpired, rather than berating them for compromising his own opportunities to solve the case. In this matter, at least, Hale appears to have overstepped, showing more concern for personal aggrandizement than the recovery of the missing evidence. The Committee points out that this is just the sort of abuse of command authority that can occur when an investigator becomes too closely identified with a high-profile case...."

Translation: Hale scared the shit out of everyone, making them disinclined to help lest in return they be hung out to dry.

I also note the committee's confidential personal evaluations of the officers:

"Waincroft: out of his depth, has no business holding

a supervisory position. Recommend immediate demotion with incentives to retire.

"Hayes: less than middling officer long past his prime. Retirement to be actively encouraged.

"Puccio: sloppiest of the bunch, apparently ignorant of police norms and procedures. Recommend dismissal.

"Vasquez: sharp, helpful, contrite, the officer we deem least likely to have been responsible. Recommend mild punishment. This officer should be allowed a future with the Department.

"Farrow: a decent, experienced officer who, perhaps by chance, has had a less than stellar career. Since Waincroft was in command, we remain mystified by his insistence on taking responsibility for the loss. Because he seems less than fully committed to police work, retirement to be actively encouraged."

I walk down the slope to Polk, purchase a micro tape recorder and cartridges at Radio Shack, then stop at a gourmet store to buy a variety of organic fruits and vegetables and a loaf of City Stone Ground bread. I carry my bag of groceries back up to the walkway on the Larkin side of Sterling Park, ostentatiously leave it on the same bench where I left the beribboned Styrofoam box two days ago. As before I pirouette, knowing my savior, Drake, is watching from somewhere in the bush.

At home I eat an apple, then go to work, taking down every print, clipping, appointment slip and note pinned to my cork office wall. With the cork clean, I proceed to pin up photographs relevant to Tim's death, seeking some sort of order that will clarify the complexities by which I'm feeling overwhelmed.

A cluster of pictures of Tim go up first, casual shots I took of him on the Gulch, plus the nude of him doing the handstand, and my favorite, the glamour shot on Angel Island.

Following these I lay out my two main sequences, the one on Willow Alley where his head and limbs were found, the other the ground in Wildcat Canyon.

Above and below these sequences I place several of the police crime-scene photos Hilly supplied, and at the end of the row, a shot I took on the boat when we let Tim's ashes go.

I stand back for an overview. *There he is,* I think, in all the startling beauty and vitality of his life, and savage uncomeliness and stillness of his death.

On a separate section of cork I arrange a sequence that profiles the Gulch, street shots and portraits of several of the regulars—Crawf, Slick, Remo, Alyson, Doreen, a few others, and the one of Knob and his acolytes I took in The Werewolf. Above them I post shots I surreptitiously took of various unidentified prowling johns, and, connected to these but in a cluster all its own, the sequence of Marcus Crane at the gate of his and Sarah Lashaw's home.

In still another area I pin up pictures of the detectives, Shanley and Hilly Lentz, as well as my new comrade-in-arms, Joel Glickman. Nearby I arrange a sequence on the original T case, centered around the photo I took of Dad in front of City Stone Ground, surrounded by pictures I photocopied off of library microfilm of the other Sipple cops, plus the excellent press photo of Inspector Jonathan Topper Hale leaving the Hall of Justice the day of his disgrace.

On the opposite wall I pin up parallel sequences of Tim's studio when Crawf and I first visited it, and its chaotic state when I later returned to pack up his stuff. Back near the idyllic portraits, I tack up one of David deGeoffroy, one of the facade of Tim's mail drop and also (the only nonphoto in my show) the unidentified key I found tucked in the molding of Tim's flat.

Above the shot of Dad, I place one I made of Mom when I was at the Art Institute and first took up photography. Finally, for no reason I can think of, I add one of the detached self-portraits I shot of myself last week. Then I stand back again to see what I have wrought.

Things are connected, that much is clear, but no overarching pattern emerges, no theme that ties everything together.

Two torso cases fifteen years apart, similar in some respects, different in others: the recent victim (I'm trying to think of Tim objectively now) has a history in which cutting played a part.

I move closer to the wall, examine my before-and-after shots of his studio. I am, I realize, the only person with such pictures; except for me and Crawf, no one, including the cops, knows what the place looked like before it was tossed. I search the photos for crucial differences, objects which might have been removed. The big Angel Island print of Tim is gone; I noticed that before. Also, the curious sorting of the clothing. But where is his address book, assuming he had one—and what street hustler doesn't? Where are the personal things—family photos, letters, passport, birth certificate? Where, for that matter, are items I know he possessed, such as the decks of cards he used for his card tricks and the balls he carried in his backpack which he juggled on the ferry to Sausalito?

I don't see any of this stuff in either set of photos, but then such items would most likely have been stowed away. When Crawf and I were there we didn't make a search, and since, according to Shanley, such items didn't turn up, it seems safe to assume whoever tossed the place carried them off. But why?

There's something else that occurs to me as I study these photographs—the fact that the person who did the tossing entered with a key. So . . . someone had a key to Tim's studio, and, I note, my eyes falling upon the key I found, he had a key to someone else's flat as well.

Too great a leap? I don't think so. The key hidden in his molding didn't fit his door, but it matches his door key in design. A key to another apartment, perhaps one in the same building? The apparition I saw the day I moved his stuff—was that Ariane, having just left the building, heading off for a stroll?

I'm excited. Laying out my pictures, seeking visual connections, has led me to this fascinating thought. And,

I realize, I would never have come up with it if I hadn't intercepted David's letter and heard his Magician's Tale.

I pull out a blank white sheet of processed photographic printing paper, one of several I use for focusing when I make a print. With a grease pencil I inscribe the word *ARIANE,* then pin the sheet up between my photos of David and of Tim. She, I decide, is the missing piece . . . and there are other pieces missing as well: the link between the two cases, if indeed there is one, and the links between Marcus Crane and Knob and Tim.

Sasha calls me from the hospital. In the background I hear the sounds of the E.R., including those implausibly placid public address announcements by which surgeons are summoned to patch up horrendous wounds.

"I'm thinking about you," Sasha says.

"Nice thoughts?"

"Better than nice." He lowers his voice. "Highly desiring."

"Yes, I hear you're quite the ladies' man," I tell him.

"I used to be. Not anymore."

"Is this a recent change, Sasha?"

"Since last night."

"You're sure it's not just lust?"

"Oh, Kay—why so cynical?"

"All right." I relent. "You can come over tonight. Truth is I'm highly desiring myself."

I walk over to Van Ness, but the sunlight's so brilliant I decide to take a bus down to Market. From there I walk to Tim's building on Mission, enter the lobby, inspect the names on the register:

Perkins; Nakamura; Pannella/Rosenfeld; Lovsey; Swink; Yaegger; Sowards; two blanks—a typical San Francisco mix. Deciding to bring the number of vacancies to three, I pry out the black plastic strip for Lovsey.

On a hunch, I ring the buzzers opposite the blanks,

apartments 303 and 500. No responses back. I climb the stairs, find the door to 303, knock, then try the key from Tim's molding. It slips into the keyhole but doesn't turn and is difficult to extract. But in the door to 500, at the very top of the stairs, the key turns easily and opens the lock.

I enter. Suddenly, I'm lost in a snowstorm. The apartment, with its dazzling white walls and gleaming white floor, is so harshly lit, such a stark container of blazing light, that the rods in my retinas are instantly saturated.

I shut my eyes lest I go blind, fumble for my darkest shades, put them on. Then, slowly, I open my eyes. But even with the shades I'm lost in a blizzard. I shut down again, feel my way to the windows, grope for the venetian blinds, pull them closed. This time, though the room's still treacherously alive, I can see enough to understand that it's not light from the windows that's been blinding me but from a skylight that tents the room. I spot a pair of hanging ropes secured to a cleat on the wall, go to the cleat, untie the ropes, haul as hard as I can. Slowly a large drape rises to cover the glass. When I'm finished, ropes again secured, the room, though still well lit, is bearable at last.

It's a fine space, bigger than Tim's and, with its high slanted ceiling and skylight, perfect for an artist. But it would be the worst possible studio for me. So much light would kill my vision.

I pace about. I'm impressed by the condition of the place, the way everything's freshly painted, kitchen appliances shiny and perfectly flush with counters and cabinets, and the new white tiles in the bathroom joined by immaculate white grout. Hard to believe I'm in the same grungy building, not in some new high-rise near Opera Plaza. Someone's renovated this flat, and I can't believe it's landlord Murray Paulus, so annoyed Tim didn't give him notice prior to being killed. Yes, someone spent a lot of money fixing this place up, someone who either is about to move in or has recently moved out.

The buzzer sounds. At first I'm nonplussed. I'm a trespasser, have no right to be here. But in fact, I realize, since the place is empty I can't be accused of being a robber. I can claim I was looking for an apartment, noted the vacancy on the lobby register, climbed the stairs and found the door unlocked.

Better, I decide, to answer than have someone come up and find me hiding. I go to the wall, press the responder, then open the door a crack.

Footsteps in the stairwell. A woman's heeled shoes and gait. I've never found the stairwell so quiet, then recall that on other visits I heard operatic arias echoing down.

The steps approach. The person is one floor below. I tense as an attractive young woman comes into view. She's beautifully dressed in cashmere sweater and skirt, wears earrings and a necklace with a Celtic cross as pendant. She sees me too, approaches, smiles.

"Hi!" she says.

"Hi yourself."

"I was looking for . . ." Her voice falters.

"Yes?"

"For her, you know, but, like—hello!—I see she isn't here." She peers about, wide-eyed, taking in the emptiness. "Least not anymore," she adds.

I shrug to indicate I find the former resident's absence obvious.

"When was the last time you saw her?" I inquire.

"Oh, well, you know . . ." She smiles again, embarrassed. "Not too long ago, I guess." She ponders. "Maybe, four, five weeks, something like that."

She's young, nineteen or twenty, and her jewelry and Rolex tell me she's well-off. But there's something about her that belies the upper-middle-class suburban look. I check out her shoes. They're high-style fetishistic—black-and-chrome ankle-bondage straps, embedded steel tips and modified-for-daywear stiletto heels.

"How 'bout you?" she asks. "I mean—were you looking for her too?" I nod. "How long since you've seen her?"

I shrug again. "A while, I guess."

"Well . . ."

"Yes, well . . ."

She puts out her hand. "I'm Courtney Hill."

I put out mine. "Kay Farrow." We shake.

She squints at me. "Kay? Have I seen you around?"

"Maybe," I say. And then: "Since she's moved I guess there's no point standing here." I look at her. "Shall we escort each other down?"

I close the door. It clicks shut. When I try it again, it's locked.

"Looks like she really cleaned out," Courtney observes as we descend. She giggles. "Lock, stock and barrel."

I giggle too, though I don't quite get the joke . . . unless Courtney means to mock the cliché.

"How did you meet her?" she asks.

I shrug. "Just around, I guess."

"Yeah," she nods, "like so many. I met her at HardCandy. Of course I'd *heard* about her. Everyone has. Then one night someone pointed her out. I took one look, said to myself: 'What an incredible slut!' " Courtney glances at me. I smile and nod. "I'd never seen anything like her. Way she moved, came on. And the response she got! Like she was God's gift to us, you know." I nod again. "Like—*wow!*"

In the lobby I point out that there's a blank space opposite the buzzer for apartment 500.

"She kept it blank, least when I met her," Courtney says. Then she giggles. "I mean, what was she going to put in there anyway? 'Love Goddess'? 'Amoretto'?"

Amoretto. The word sears my brain. I feel my cheeks flush, my hands burn, as Courtney and I part on the sidewalk. *The Amazing Amoretto:* the name David deGeoffroy devised for Ariane when he contemplated devoting himself full-time to her career.

Apartment 500, I now know, was occupied by Ariane Lovsey. David was right, she *was* close. In fact, I realize, I may have only just missed her.

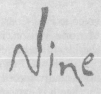

Nine

I want to find her now . . . if only to mourn with her
and tell her where her brother's ashes were scattered.
But I want far more, I want to know the secrets, how the
twins survived after they ran away, their whole story,
everything. Also I want to see this creature who so closely
resembles Tim. I long to photograph her face.

Courtney Hill has given me a lead: HardCandy. I know
the place though I've never been inside. Along with Eros
and ATF, it's one of the cutting-edge SoMa clubs where
hip young people go to dance, score, indulge fantasies of
decadence.

On my way home I plot my moves. I'll ask Sasha to
take me, or turn up on my own and ask for Amoretto, or
show around a photograph of Tim and ask if anyone's
seen a woman with his face.

I pause outside my building, then walk into Sterling
Park. I want to check if my bag of groceries is still on
the bench. It's not. In its place I find a piece of torn brown
paper bearing Drake's billet-doux: ''Thanks again.'' This
time the signature's a simple ''D.''

My phone is ringing as I come through the door. I'm
still thinking about Ariane as I pick up. The woman's

voice is East Coast and refined. She tells me her name is Marjorie Wilson, and before I can ask how I can help, she identifies herself as Sarah Lashaw's assistant.

I sit down. I'm not expecting this. Have my provocations finally forced forth some fruit?

"Sarah is extremely interested in your work," Marjorie gushes. "She wants very much to meet you. There's a project she'd like to discuss."

"What kind of project?"

"A photographic one, I imagine."

"Commissioned photographs?"

An awkward laugh. "It would be best to discuss that with her, don't you think?"

Since Lashaw's my suitor, I decide to have some fun. "I gotta tell you, Ms. Wilson, I think there may be a misunderstanding here."

"I assure you she's a great admirer."

"That's nice, but the fact is I no longer do commissioned work."

Another laugh. "Oh, I think she understands that, Ms. Farrow. I did the research on you and I can assure you I was thorough." Pause. "Do you ever get up to St. Helena?"

"Not often." In truth, I realize, it's probably been a couple of years.

"Sarah's asked me to invite you for lunch tomorrow. If that's not inconvenient."

"Tomorrow . . ." I stall to clear my head. "Don't know. I don't own a car."

"That won't be a problem. Our driver will pick you up and have you back in town by dark." A little pause. "Shall we say in front of your place tomorrow, eleven a.m.?"

I think a moment. No one in her right mind declines an invitation to lunch with Sarah Lashaw. As for a "project," it's hard to imagine it doesn't concern the photos I took of Crane.

"That'll be fine," I tell her. "How should I dress?"

"Oh, you know—country. We're all pretty casual around here."

I'm freshly bathed, wrapped only in a kimono, staring at the city through my telescope, when Sasha buzzes from downstairs. It's nearly midnight. I ring him in, then tilt the telescope up. It wouldn't do for him to find me snooping on the Judge.

He comes bearing gifts, a bouquet of roses in one hand, a split of iced champagne in the other.

"Is this courtship, Sasha?" I ask as I dodge into my kitchen to scrounge a pair of flutes.

"I'm a romantic," he answers from the other room. "Perhaps the last one," he adds as I return, glasses in hand.

I kiss him. I'm flattered, grateful too. It's been a long time since a man came to me with flowers and drink. Sasha's lips taste faintly of mint mouthwash. So thoughtful, handsome, hygienic! What more could a girl want?

He pops the cork with precision, spilling nary a drop. We sit and sip. He tells me he's had an easy night—no knife or gunshot wounds, two falls, one heart attack, one not serious stroke, a couple of broken arms.

"Sounds like bliss," I say.

He gazes at me. His eyes are incredible. I could easily get lost in eyes like his. I imagine many women have.

"Do you ever do the club scene?" I ask him.

"There's a Latino one I like. Venceremos in the Mission."

"How 'bout HardCandy?"

He smiles. "I hear it's wild."

"Been there?"

"Once," he admits. "My date insisted."

"Well, one night soon I'm going to insist too."

His eyes enlarge, he grins. I've surprised him . . . which is good. Now he's wondering if I do drugs, triad sex or, God help him, SM. Yes, poor Sasha, I can see, is falling ever deeper into lust. I set down my glass, take his hand, lead him into my bedroom, appropriately lit for another night of love.

I not only don't have clothing I consider "country," I'm not even sure what kind that is. Also, I'm angry at myself for inquiring as to the proper dress as if I care whether I blend in or not. Since I'll be damned if I'll cater to Sarah Lashaw, I squeeze into a pair of jeans, pull on a pair of cowboy boots, don my leather jacket, then thread the jeans with my only concession to fashion, a turquoise and silver concha belt I bought last winter in Santa Fe.

A dark Mercedes pulls up promptly at eleven. The driver is female; her name is Brit. She speaks with a Scottish brogue, is polite, formal, wears a sharply tailored black suit, white shirt, black necktie, black chauffeur's cap with shiny brim.

I feel almost kinky as I settle into the back seat, luxuriating against the butter-soft upholstery. Still, remembering that someone up north wants something from me, I vow not to allow myself to feel flattered.

The drive is uneventful . . . or perhaps so smooth and comfortable it lulls me into a reverie. After we cross the Golden Gate, I close my eyes and remember the feel of Sasha, his hairless silken chest and lovely satiny ass. I spent a lot of time riding his dark thighs last night, staring into the deep dark pools of his eyes. Even the condom he used felt sleek. All his moves were perfect. My South Asian Lothario!

There's something magical about the Napa Valley, particularly in autumn after the grape harvest, when the vines stand clean and bare. The air is fresh, the sky clear, the hills glint beneath the sun. It's paradise, a Northern California Eden. As we roll through the vineyards, I have trouble imagining this land could be more beautiful in color.

Before St. Helena, we cross over to the Silverado Trail, then wind through the hills. At one point, just past the sign for a vineyard named Stag's Leap, I'm amazed to see a magnificent full-antlered flesh-and-blood stag literally leap across the road.

A mile further we turn into a track between stone columns, then start to climb. We circle the hill, at the top reach a straight and formal alley of eucalyptus. At the end I spot the stone and clapboard house, scene of the lavish picnic depicted in *House & Garden*.

The house is beautiful, serene, perfect in its proportions, grand but not at all ostentatious. Its facade speaks of that mythical protective place called "home" where no unpleasantness intrudes—a place of inviolate security one can always return to, a fortress against the harshnesses of the world.

If one in ten thousand of us comes from a home like this I'd be much surprised. No rancor here, no parents quarreling over money, no dirty dishes in the sink, crumbs in the toaster, dust balls beneath the beds. Here the linens are changed daily, no one uses a bath towel twice, one is enveloped by the aromas of the garden, the tinkle of wind chimes, the babbling of a country brook.

Even as the car rounds the circle that ends the drive, I squirm at the smugness of it all. Casual indeed! In this dream house, I suspect, the look of every nook and cranny will be calculated for maximum effect.

Marjorie Wilson is waiting for me. She's not the efficient gray-banged type I expect, rather a clone of Brit the chauffeur—young, poised, well put together. It takes her but an instant to size me up.

"Brit was fast today. Sarah's still at her tennis lesson. Why don't we go down to the courts? We can wait there while she finishes up, or if you prefer, I'll show you the pool. We've all shapes and sizes of swimsuits if you'd care to take a dip."

I opt for the courts. We stroll through the front hall of the house, then into a perfectly proportioned living room decorated to the nines. A vase of fresh-cut flowers sits on every table. The huge stone fireplace is loaded with perfectly arranged white birch logs. We pass through a set of brass-hinged French doors to a flagstone terrace that

runs the length of the house. From here the views are
extraordinary, embracing the valley from Oakville to Cal-
istoga, a crazy quilt of vineyards between two rows of
wild-growth hills.

A clay tennis court is situated fifty yards below the
terrace. Marjorie guides me down to a shaded area furnished with cushioned wicker. Here, waiting on a table,
is a perfect frosted pitcher of fresh lemonade. She pours
me a glass while I watch Sarah Lashaw play out her steely
heart against her coach.

She's a powerful player—I see that at once. She has a
merciless serve, a mean two-fisted backhand, a somewhat
weaker forehand yet plenty strong enough. She's dressed
for exertion in a plain white V-neck T-shirt, white cotton
shorts, white socks with tassels and immaculate white tennis shoes. She wears one of those sunshades that consist
of a bill supported simply by a band, thus showing off
her locks of frosted hair. Her face and forearms are glazed
as she runs about retrieving every shot her shirtless muscular trainer pounds to her across the net.

She's also, I quickly learn, a woman who doesn't like
to lose.

"Well, cock-a-doodle-doo, Roy!" she hoots, when, at
the end of a sustained volley, her trainer smashes a shot
between her legs.

"Too fast for you?" he taunts.

"Never too fast, you wart!"

I glance at Marjorie. She meets my eyes and shrugs, as
if to acknowledge that, indeed, Mrs. Lashaw sometimes
does get riled while indulging in stressful sport.

I quickly gain the impression of an undercurrent between Lashaw and Roy. He's in his mid-twenties while
she's probably fifty-five, but he shows her no deference
or respect. On the contrary, he seems to enjoy flaunting
his superior power while showing off his well-developed
chest. Rather than playing the roles of employer and
trainer, they behave like lovers engaged in a stylized fight.
Yes! her tennis game would seem to say, *you're bigger*

*and stronger than me, but I can take whatever you dish
out and smack it right back in your face!*

"Deuce!" Roy calls out the score, then sets up to serve.

Whish! His shot aces by her. *Swish!* She swings at it
even though it's passed.

"Pee-yoo!" she exclaims, as Roy announces they're at
set point.

I raise my camera, start shooting as they play the point
back and forth, alternating shots down the line and cross-
court, forcing one another from side to side. Suddenly
Roy breaks the rally by rushing the net.

"Ho ho!" Lashaw shouts.

But he bats back her returns until he wears her down;
then he tips the ball across and watches amused as she
rushes and stumbles in a fruitless effort to snag it back.

"Game, set, match!" Roy savors the words, as Sarah
pulls herself up off the clay.

She brushes the dust from her hips, turns to him and
crows: "You'll pay for this later, Roy-boy."

Spotting me, she turns her back on him.

"Kay Farrow! How great to meet you!"

I gaze into the fabled eyes. She extends both hands as
if I'm a dear old friend. When I take hold, she pulls me
against her hard warm moist body so I can feel her extraordinary power.

Roy rates no further attention, not even an introduction,
as Sarah, with Marjorie two paces behind, walks me back
up to the house.

"We've lots to talk about," she says. "Just give me
ten minutes to shower and change, then we'll sit down to
lunch."

The feast is served on the terrace on a table laden with a
hand-embroidered cloth and gorgeous hand-painted ce-
ramic plates. Conventional pleasantries and San Francisco
gossip accompany scallops and crab over angel-hair pasta,
garden-fresh mesclun, raspberry sorbet, accompanied by
a local Chardonnay.

After the meal Marjorie excuses herself. Sarah leans forward as soon as we're alone.

"It's terrific to get to know you, Kay. I've long admired your work. Your show at Zeitgeist last year, those poor battered women, their eyes so proud—it really knocked me out."

An extremely handsome woman, she looks ten or fifteen years younger than her age. She's dressed in a prairie skirt and dark silk blouse. I try to imagine her wearing emeralds. To me, I believe, they would show as a bright midgray, slightly darker than her eyes.

"Marjorie says you had me researched."

Sarah smiles. "You don't believe I saw your show?"

"Did you?" I ask, meeting her eyes.

"Check the gallery guest book," she says merrily. "You'll see."

A good response. I'm also flattered . . . though I promised myself I wouldn't be. But how could my brand of art connect to anything in her life? I reach into my camera bag, flick my little tape recorder on.

"Why did you invite me?" I ask.

She stares directly at me. When she grins, engaging crow's-feet form around her eyes.

"I'd like to buy some of your pictures, Kay. Negatives as well as prints."

I shake my head. "I don't sell negatives. No photographer does. You must know that."

"I do, but in this case there'd be no need to keep them. It would be a condition of the sale, based on appropriate compensation, that the pictures would never be reproduced."

I can't believe she's being so brazen. Is she desperate, or testing me for weakness?

"I'm not a blackmailer, Sarah. I don't take pictures of people to sell them back."

"Of course not! I didn't mean to suggest—"

"But you did. You implied I can be bought. I can't. So if it's my pictures of your husband you want, neither prints nor negatives are for sale."

She fixes me with a fierce withering gaze, like the one she directed at Roy on the tennis court. It's not the charming grin of the society page she's showing now, but her true face, the one that announces its owner gets what she wants. It's a face I'd like to photograph so much I reach beside my chair for my camera. I pick it up, start to bring it to my eye, when I feel her hand upon my wrist.

"No pictures," she says quietly, in a tone all the more frightening for being so certain and still. She tightens her grip. My wrist begins to hurt. Our eyes lock.

"Take your hand off me," I demand.

She flashes the society page grin. "Of course, my dear." She lets go. "No need to get testy."

I lower my camera. "I won't take pictures of you without permission, not here in your house. But outside you're fair game just like everybody else. You're a public figure, as is Mr. Crane, especially when he cruises Polk Gulch in his Mercedes looking to rent himself a piece of male ass."

"Fine." She grins. "That's just fine. Got it all out of your system now?"

"Most of it," I say. "How 'bout you?"

"I'm doing fine too."

"Good."

"Let's talk straight."

"Yes, let's. Why did you ask me here? Surely you didn't think you could buy me off."

She nods. She wants me to understand she's impressed, that she respects my guts for standing up to her even in her own rigorously controlled milieu.

"My husband has a complicated nature," she explains. "He has his desires, as I have mine. Neither of us has ever done anything to intentionally harm another person. If we stray sometimes, make mistakes, then our transgressions are only the faults of passion and of love." She pauses. "Sometimes by error people get hurt. Whenever that happens we try to set things right. That might involve some form of payment to alleviate the injury. Of course there are wounds that money cannot salve, though in my experience a significant cash payment can go quite a way when coupled with a sincere expression of remorse. As you know, Kay, we all have our longings and desires. This world we live in is a difficult place. We can only do our very best not to make it worse.''

It is as pretty a speech as I have heard, and, delivered so frankly, calmly, without a waver of the eyes, contrived to soften even the harshest critic's heart. But my wrist, still smarting from her grasp, tells me this is a woman who will use any means, sweet or brutal, to get her way. So I take a moment to analyze what she's said, ferret out its rotten core. It doesn't take me long: *Our transgressions are only the faults of passion and of love*. Oh, yes! We only wound in the names of eros and amour! Never out of selfish lust, never because the flesh of another is for us but fodder! We buy bodies, and if the fragile souls within should sometimes break, it is but the flaw in the carnality all humans share.

"The hormone defense," I mutter.

She turns indignant. *"What?"*

"Everyone has his peccadilloes. But see, Sarah, I take pictures. I don't judge."

"Then what good, may I ask, do your pictures do?"

"You said my *Transgressions* show knocked you out."

"Surely you don't intend—"

"I'll tell you what I intend. A friend of mine, a street hustler, was killed. Savagely, brutally, without pity, most likely out of lust. Perhaps to someone like yourself a person who does that sort of work deserves whatever he gets. I don't see it that way. Anyhow, before he was killed I recorded his life on film, and that meant also documenting the life of the street where he worked. Your husband appears in a number of my shots soliciting minors for sex. He's well known on Polk Gulch. He cruises around there in his fancy car. He's what the street kids call a chicken hawk, which means he preys on underage boys. That's not a mere 'fault of love,' Sarah—that's a criminal offense. As you undoubtedly know, I trapped him with my camera the other day. The shots are great. At first he preens, tries to laugh me off, but in the end he looks like a cornered rat. Okay, what do I intend to do with those pictures? Right now I've no idea. If they're relevant to the murder of my friend, I'll publish them. If not . . . well, I may just publish them anyway. I probably wouldn't feel this way if, a few hours after our shoot, I hadn't been jumped from behind in the little park in front of my house. One of the men who jumped me (he also stole my best camera) is someone I've seen acting as flesh merchant for Mr. Crane. By the way, when your husband's out cruising he doesn't wear his toupee. I guess he thinks that's a good disguise. But still, for some reason, he likes to flaunt his car. Cars, you know, bear license plates. So, you see, it wasn't hard to track him down."

"That's it?"

"Pretty much."

The indignation in her eyes cannot be described. She is utterly, irrevocably outraged.

"It would appear there's no dealing with you."

I shrug. "Not on the terms you're used to."

"What terms then?"

I hand her my card. "Tell Mr. Crane there's no need to hide behind your skirts. Tell him to get in touch, we'll have a talk and, depending on how it goes, I'll see what I can do." I glance at my watch, show concern, suggest it's time for me to leave. "You can also tell him I want my Contax back . . . if, by chance, he knows where it is."

On the drive back to the city I sit in the front seat beside Brit. She's stiff, monosyllabic, until I ask her about the tennis trainer, Roy.

"Oh he's a lad, Roy is," Brit says, amused.

"Does he live at the house?"

"Has his own suite above the garage."

"Pretty sexy guy. He and Mrs. Lashaw—are they, you know . . ."

"I'm no gossip, ma'am."

But from her grin it would appear Sarah and Roy play all sorts of games.

Back home, agitated, I phone Sasha at the hospital, persuade him I'm too tired for a visit and suggest, in recompense, that we do HardCandy Friday night.

"Like a real date?" he asks.

"You got it, Sasha."

"Can we dress up?"

"The whole nine yards!" I promise.

I try to calm myself by meditating for a while, but I'm still too hyped by my day in the country. What should have been a pastoral interlude turned into a nightmare. In the process I've made a powerful enemy.

Feeling the need to regroup, I grab my camera and head out for the Gulch. But I'm careful as I cross Sterling Park; even with Drake watching out for me, I have no wish to be sandbagged again.

Tonight the Gulch is sweet, the air warm, the regulars posing in their usual places. I find Doreen lingering at the corner of Polk and Bush.

"Missing you, Bug," she says.

I tell her I've been trying to sort things out.

"Story of my life." She laughs. "Good luck!"

On Hemlock I spot Slick posing with a hustler I barely know, the one they call Sho because, Tim told me, he's three-quarter Shoshone Indian. Sho is handsome, grave, with dark skin, shoulder-length black hair parted in the middle and lovely quasi-Asian eyes.

"I hear you take pictures," he says when we're introduced. "I need some head shots, eight-by-tens, to get my modeling career off the ground."

I tell him I don't do glamour shots, but I'll be happy to shoot some outdoor candids if he thinks they'd help. We agree to meet the following afternoon at five. Just then a big Jaguar pulls up. The boys, nervous, move toward it.

"Gotta go, Bug. This is our date," Slick says.

I watch as they climb into the backseat, one dark, the

other albino, hired for the evening to do God-knows-what. It takes all my self-restraint to keep from taking pictures, but tonight I don't want to get anyone upset.

I walk for a while, stopping to schmooze with acquaintances, trying to regain my fascination with this tawdry strip. But though the territory is familiar, an important person is missing. I feel like a widow returning to a city where a great romance was born, hoping to find the same beauty in the streets, finding instead only piercing loneliness.

Knob is standing beside the door of an all-male video shop near Sutter, thumbs hitched casually in his belt. He's grinning at me, the grin of a cougar awaiting the nightly prowl of a yearling deer. *Will I pounce or won't I?* his grin seems to ask. And since I'm not feeling particularly yearlinglike this evening, I dare to stop and meet his eyes.

"Still stomping the Gulch, Bug?"

"Any reason I shouldn't?"

"Figured you'd gotten enough by now. Don't want to gild the lily, do we?"

What the hell is he talking about? Have Lashaw & Crane already put out another contract?

"Amoretto," I say. I don't know why; the name just springs into my head.

"Yeah, what about her?" Knob replies coolly.

I laugh, continue on my way, flabbergasted by his response. He didn't say "Who?" or "What?" or "Fuck off!" He said "What about her?"—which means he knows who she is.

Joel Glickman calls at eleven to say he's seen Hilly.

"She made me meet her at this western bar. She was the only woman there and I was the only straight guy. She said we were safer there than anyplace else. She says she meets you at The Duchess."

I laugh. "What'd you think of her?"

"Friendly, smart, straightforward enough . . . until experience proves otherwise."

"Is she onto something?"

"Too early, kiddo. With these case-in-progress deals it's barely one in five. Remember, this isn't a whistle-blow. She's got a theory. Maybe she's right, maybe not."

"But it's worth a shot?"

"Definitely." Joel pauses. "I want to see Hale."

Jonathan Topper Hale: how I'd love to photograph him! "Didn't he retire south?"

"Uh-uh, he's still in the area. Lives in Oakland. And, from what I hear, is still obsessed with Torsos."

"Does he know about Tim Lovsey?"

"I hope not. I want to be the one to tell him." Joel pauses again. "Wanna come along?"

Friday evening: When Sasha rings from downstairs I'm still dolling myself up. Maybe "dolling" isn't quite the right word, more like garnishing myself. I've applied several stick-on tattoos to my upper arms, the black New Age calligraphic kind. I've also painted my lips with black lipstick (if I'd used red it would appear black to me). My leather pants are secured by my concha belt. Now I'm snapping on a leather bracelet with chrome points. I buzz Sasha in, then return to self-adornment. I'm wearing a black lace bra, but can't find anything that looks good on top.

Sasha is even more decorous. No longer in his serious-young-physician mode, he wears a tight black muscle shirt, black spandex pants, a chain-link belt that hangs loose about his hips, and a black leather motorcycle cap embellished by another length of chain.

We preen for each other, then get down to business—how best to drape my torso. Sasha thinks the bra is all I need.

"Underwear as outerwear," he says, "that's the hot new look."

Actually it's a style that's five years old, but being un-fashionable doesn't bother me; I only wish to be desired.

"Want me to go bare belly?" I ask.

"Why not? Half the women at these clubs do."

"I don't know . . . I think I'll feel naked."

"Let me decorate you then."

I follow his instructions, remove my bra, then sit backwards astride a chair. He sits behind me and begins applying more temporary tattoos to my back. When he's done, he escorts me into the bathroom, where I have mirrors on opposite walls. Together we inspect his handiwork. I look like a Kandinsky from behind.

"Very futuristic," Sasha remarks.

Fine! I'll wear just the bra, my embellished skin taking the place of fabric. But Sasha has brought me a gift, a black leather collar with spiky points. He puts it on me lovingly as we both face the mirror. I like it. It matches my bracelet, says I'm kinky, and at the same time: *Don't get too close, my throat's inviolate.*

HardCandy, like most SoMa clubs, is housed in a former warehouse. There's something ominous about a stark windowless building on a dark empty street at night. There are piles of glossy trash bags up and down the block, and a homeless man huddled beside a grocery cart on the far side. A dozen snazzy motorcycles are lined up neatly beneath the lone streetlamp, while luxury cars of various makes are parked along the curb.

No sign designates the club, just a neon strip (Sasha informs me it's violet) that outlines the door. A short line of bizarrely made-up and festooned wanna-get-ins clings to the warehouse wall. I take a place at the end of the line while Sasha goes to its head to negotiate.

He returns to fetch me. The bouncer, a hairy guy in leather vest, doesn't crack a smile as he lets us in. Meantime the wanna-get-ins glare at us with hate.

"How'd you swing it?" I whisper to Sasha.

"Fifty bucks," he whispers.

Ouch!

We walk down a narrow, dark, oppressively low-ceilinged corridor until we come to a door padded with tufted leather. Suddenly it opens and music, heavy metal punk, smacks us like a blow across the face.

We step forward, the door closes behind; then, through a confusion of cries, flashing lights, air thick with the aroma of sweat and pot, we make our entrance into Hades.

Punked-out hairstyles, half-nude bodies, glistening writhing flesh—HardCandy has it all. Perhaps I'm too old, staid, insufficiently coked up, but this kind of bacchanalian extravaganza only hurts my ears. I'm not offended by it, rather I'm bored. But far be it from me to pass judgment. There are worthy people, I know, for whom the late-night scene is a narcotic, an aphrodisiac, a cheat against the drudgery of daily life. A night at HardCandy is a way to meet a lover, score dope, dance away excess energy and angst. It's a place to indulge all one's most decadent exhibitionistic and voyeuristic fantasies. Bottom line: It's our era's stylized version of that great and eternal human enterprise, the orgy.

On Sasha's advice I've left my camera at home; the taking of photographs and/or videos is forbidden here. Thus, being denied my usual means of response, I have no choice but to step out onto the floor and join the debauch.

Sasha, not surprisingly, is a fantastic dancer. He boogies so well I look good just following his lead. About the time I break a sweat, I feel the approval of others as they grant us extra space. We use it to get into a kind of twist-shag routine. When Sasha starts scissoring his fingers, I do the same.

Gaining the impression we're being discussed, I tune in to snippets of conversation taking place around:

"Great dancer," a female comments.

"She's not half bad herself."

"Good tats on that back."

"Dig the collar."

"See them before?"

"Uh-uh. But I like what I see."

"Fresh meat. Let's try and link up."

Sasha whirls me away, then separates again as we go

into a series of retro-fifties moves. The music pounds. Sweat runs off my body. I worry my tattoos will wash away. Then I decide to just go with the rush. Soon, feeling the intoxicating effect of rhythmic movement, I yield to the self-obliterating energy all around. *Let me become animal,* I will, and willing it, feel it start to happen.

We're sitting with four other people at a table on the balcony above the dance floor, sipping vodka and giggling at the goings-on in the passion pit below. We don't know the quartet we're with, but they know one another and are putting out feelers that they'd like us to join their circle.

Proper names, professions, backgrounds—such information is not exchanged. Here it's how you look, dress, dance, present yourself. In the stripped-down ambience of HardCandy, what you see is what you get.

I decide to drop a bombshell. I make my eyes large, then pronounce the magic word: ''Amoretto?''

Heads turn. Lips curl into smiles. Attention is deliciously paid.

''Seen her lately?'' a woman asks. Her eyes are made up like a raccoon's.

Heads shake.

''She's like disappeared,'' the other female says. This one's hair is arranged into spikes that rival the ones on my collar.

''You ought to say 'it.' Like—'*It* disappeared,' '' says the young man to my right, who sports heavily gelled silver hair.

The response to that is such wild mirth I'm led to believe he's spouted a witty line.

''Friend of mine''—it's Spiky Hair speaking again—''she went with 'it' one time. Says all of a sudden she-he-it started plucking coins from her cunt.''

''That's nothing!'' Raccoon Eyes says. ''This gay guy I know tells me she-he-it plucked them from his ass!''

Much tittering over that. Seems everyone has a story. The other male in the group, whose left eyebrow and ear bear multiple piercings, allows as how, since he's actually been to bed with the creature, he's the only one at the table who can authoritatively describe her/his/its genitalia.

"Okay, Kit," Silver Gel taunts, "let us in on the big secret."

Pierced Guy offers an enigmatic smile. "Amoretto's like one of those, you know, magical goddesses—she can change sex even while you fuck."

"I heard that too," says Spiky Hair. "You go to bed with a hen, wake up with a rooster."

"Like she does you with a strap-on?" Raccoon Eyes asks.

"No way!" Pierced Guy is adamant. "The cock's for real."

"Well, you ought to know!" Silver Gel elbows Pierced Guy in the ribs.

By this time Sasha is giving me a look. He leans over, whispers: "Who the hell are we talking about?"

I want to know more. "Could it've been twins?" I ask.

Pierced Guy screws up his face, spreads his hands. "Wish I knew," he says. "I was just too stoned to notice."

I take Sasha's hand, tell the others we're going back down to the pit. They're a little hurt, taking our departure as rejection, but I must rescue Sasha, who is, after all, a mere ladies' man. These bisexual kids we've been hanging with play in an entirely different league.

"Were you talking about someone human?" Sasha asks me on the stairs.

"Just some club-scene person I want to meet."

"Pulling coins out of pussies and asses. Weird!"

Poor Sasha! He knows all about the insides of people's bodies, but perhaps not so much about their fantasies.

The music here is too percussive, the lyrics to the songs screamed too loud. We've only been here an hour and a half, and already I feel burnt-out. Sasha's proven his skills on the dance floor. Now I'm ready to go home.

Outside, I ask the bouncer if Amoretto's been around.

"Not lately," he says in an ultraserious tone that tells

me he'll provide no more information. But on the way back to my apartment in Sasha's BMW, I consider the fact that when we sat down with strangers, they all knew who I was talking about. One even claimed to have spent the night with her. Knob also knew who she was. So, it would seem that Ariane is notorious in town, at least within a certain set—a fact of which I, in my isolated artist's life on the hill, have until this evening been unaware.

Back at my place, Sasha and I strip one another of kinky attire, then fall into bed. Though it would be my preference to apply rubbing alcohol and sponge off my tattoos, Sasha wants me to keep them on.

"I like you encrusted," he tells me, perhaps not the most romantic words to escape his sultry lips. But he's been good to me tonight, taken me where I wanted to go, so now it's my turn to give him a ride.

In the morning, still half deaf from the heavy metal assault, I pace about my apartment trying to collect my thoughts.

What do I know?

One, that Ariane lived in Tim's building.

Two, that she most likely moved out within the past week.

Three, that living so close, in possession of each other's keys, they surely saw each other a lot . . . yet Tim never let on that she existed.

Four, that just as he hustled on the Gulch, she had her own hustle going at the clubs.

Five, that they seemed to have played an erotic variation on David deGeoffroy's Zamantha Illusion, Ariane going to bed with someone, then switching places with Tim, thus freaking the new bedmate out.

Six, it would seem Ariane deliberately cultivated a bizarre reputation among club people as some sort of gender-bending mistress of legerdemain.

Seven, Ariane and Tim stole fifty thousand dollars from

David, and Tim boasted to me he had fifty thousand stashed—which has never turned up.

Eight, it's clear that Tim's hints there was a woman in his life I'd want to photograph were references to his twin, Ariane.

Nine, the day Tim was killed, when he set up a meeting with me, he sounded as if he was scared.

Ten, Ariane's apparent lack of interest in recovering her brother's body and subsequent disappearance suggests she too is scared, perhaps of meeting the same fate.

But what good does all this analysis do me? None . . . unless I can locate the girl. From the moment I heard of her I've wanted to meet her. Now I feel I must.

I look up Courtney Hill in the city phone directory. No listing. For all I know, she's from down the peninsula, East Bay or Marin. She's so young she probably still lives at home with her parents. Unless, of course, she's in college somewhere . . . in which case I might be able to find her.

I make a few quick calls: San Francisco State, Stanford, University of California at Berkeley. I'm prepared to make many more, but I luck out at U.C., where, I discover, a Ms. Courtney Dayton Hill is indeed registered as an undergraduate.

I leave a message at her dorm, then walk down to Marina Aikido for class. Today my workout partner is Flora, a Philippine diplomat's wife. We practice fiercely, throw one another well, blend energy, get into the flow. When we finish we realize we've been watched. After we bow, the class applauds.

At noon Courtney calls me back, says she just returned to dump her books and found my message. She recalls our encounter very well and was hoping she'd see me again. Yes, she'd be happy to get together and talk about Amoretto. We agree to meet that night at Kabul, an Afghan restaurant in Berkeley.

A little before five I walk over to the Gulch for my

photo-session date with the hustler, Sho. He's so beautiful this evening I'm nearly swept away. His hair's parted to the side, his eyes glisten, he wears a black T-shirt that goes perfectly with his dark skin. We walk down to Fort Mason, where I pose him on the lawn overlooking the piers. Wind off the Bay blows his hair across his face. I'm touched by his gestures as he brushes it off. I shoot out a roll, then tell him I have to go. Walking home, thinking of Tim, I feel my eyes tear up.

I take the cable car down to the end of Powell, there board the BART train for East Bay. The ride underwater is smooth and hushed. Emerging at the downtown Berkeley station, I walk swiftly to Telegraph Avenue, where I'm caught up in a swirl of student pedestrians, aggressive street peddlers, panhandlers and hostile handicapped people speeding around too fast in motorized wheelchairs. The smell here's the universal aroma of an off-campus street—cigarette smoke, coffee, frying grease going bad.

First to arrive at Kabul, I take a table facing the door. The lighting's dim, the furnishings sparse, the aroma sensuous, Eastern spices and roasting lamb. Most of the other diners are students. The prices for the specials, posted on a blackboard, strike me as ridiculously cheap.

Courtney shows up fifteen minutes later looking more like a student than on the day we met. She wears the same expensive wristwatch and Celtic cross pendant, but tonight she's shod in Nikes and dressed in a *CAL* sweatshirt and jeans frayed at the knees.

"Hi!" She's spunkier than before, in appearance at least more innocent. We exchange backgrounds. She's from Santa Barbara, her father's an attorney, mother a psychotherapist. She went to a private day school, applied to Stanford and Yale, was pleasantly surprised to be accepted at Cal.

"It's very competitive," she says, "but the kids are great—especially if you get along with Asian-Americans.

And of course my dad is happy, since tuition's practically free.''

She's majoring in rhetoric, which she knows is useless, unless, of course, she wants to make a career in academia, which, she assures me, touching the cross around her neck, she does not. She likes sports, is a member of the women's junior varsity tennis squad, active too in the Gay, Lesbian and Bisexual Students Association—which is how, she tells me, she found herself in the crowd that hangs around HardCandy on weekends.

She's smart, I discover, cheerful, offbeat, socially courageous and impressed by people with strong personal style. This, she explains, was why she was so attracted to Amoretto, but also, of course, because of the woman's aura of sluttishness and mystery.

"Was it the same with you?" she asks.

"Actually not," I say. "I was attracted to her brother."

She smiles knowingly. "Her animus. I never met him, though I heard the talk. There're people who think he doesn't exist, that she really changes sex. Isn't that like—totally *weird?*"

I agree.

"No question she's got her macho side. 'Watch out! I'm packing!' Such a turn-on, least for me. But mostly she's quiet, barely says a word. She kinda leads you in with her eyes. In my crowd it's a rite of passage to go to bed with her."

"Which is how you knew the studio?"

She nods, looks at me wistfully. "I'd really like to see her again."

"To sleep with her?"

Courtney shrugs. "Sure, if that works out. But actually just to get to know her better. She's just so fascinating, yet so . . . you know . . . mysterious."

"You say she doesn't talk that much?"

"I found her secretive. When I asked how she learned to do magic she smiled like I was crazy to ask. She wouldn't tell me where she comes from, her real name, anything. She either smiled or changed the subject or did

something to . . . you know, my *body*.'' Courtney grins.
''She had all this incredible apparatus up there. I mean,
some of that stuff was huge. I can't imagine how she
moved it out.''

When I ask exactly what apparatus she's referring to,
Courtney giggles.

''You know, those stocks and that incredible wheel!
God! Just seeing it made me weak in the knees!''

I recall her little joke when we met, the one about the
studio being cleaned out ''lock, stock and barrel.'' Now
that it makes sense, I laugh along with her.

''Was there any kind of . . . arrangement?'' I ask tim-
idly.

''Like what?''

''You said she provides this rite of passage. What does
she get out of it?''

Courtney gives me a quizzical look. ''Pleasure, I
hope!''

''Nothing else?''

''You mean like . . . money?'' I nod. ''How well do
you know her, Kay?''

I can see I've upset her, she's wary of answering more
queries. Since I seem to have fallen in her estimation, I
decide to tell her the truth.

She listens intently as I describe how Amoretto's
brother was a Polk Gulch hustler and how he was savagely murdered. I tell her that Tim lived in the same building as Ariane, that they were fraternal twins who as
children were part of a magician's troupe. Since Tim hustled for tricks, I hope Courtney will forgive me for asking
if Ariane did the same.

''Okay, now I see. Sure, you had to wonder about
that.'' She pauses. ''I've heard she charges a lot for
scenes. But I gotta tell you''—she peers into my eyes—
''she didn't ask me for a cent.''

Time to wrap things up. I ask if she'll let me know if
she sees Amoretto again or hears anything new about her.
I explain that I want to tell her what I did with Tim's

remains and talk to her about her twin brother, whom I loved.

Courtney agrees. In front of the restaurant we embrace. Then she walks back to her dorm and I to Berkeley station.

Ten

I'm sitting in the passenger seat of Joel's vintage VW beetle. We're crossing the Bay Bridge on our way to see retired inspector Jonathan Topper Hale.

"If he's not listed, how did you find him?" I ask Joel.

"Professional secret." Joel's smile is smug, but it doesn't take. He's too open, too generous, at least with friends. The toughness comes out when he thinks someone's covering up.

"Okay, kiddo, here's how. When Hale resigned a lawyer friend of his, Denis Roquelle, issued a statement. It's been fifteen years but he's still in practice . . . so I called him up."

Joel, I remind myself, is always thorough.

His car amuses me. Its sides are battered from years of street parking. Foam rubber dice hang from the rearview mirror. There's a picture of Ice Goddess Kirstin taped to the steering wheel. The back seat's covered with a tangle of old jogging shoes and empty soda cans. Joel calls this bug "Melvin." Generally it's a pain when a person insists on naming his car, but with Joel I'm in a forgiving mood. He's a true-blue former flower child; his hippie-days credentials are impeccable. In the aristocracy of Bay Area social movement people, Joel is nothing less than a prince.

We follow heavy truck traffic onto 580, exit at Grand Avenue, swing around Lake Merritt. Joel hands me a map of Oakland, tells me to navigate. It takes me a couple of minutes to orient myself. Meantime, by instinct, he finds the street.

It's straight and shady in a grid of other straight shady streets, the houses lined up, each in a different style, on identical-size lots. This is older white middle-class Oakland, a neighborhood for retired cops, teachers, civil servants. Here hedges are trimmed, lawns are well kept, each facade conceals a backyard barbecue and deck.

"Not what I expected," Joel says, as he stops in front of 4123.

I gaze at the house. "What did you expect?"

He shrugs. "Maybe something Gothic with a turret."

In fact it's a fifties-era split-level with a rusting netless basketball hoop installed over the garage. The front windows are all draped and the shades have been pulled upstairs.

We get out, Joel pats Melvin's fender, then we follow the walk to the front stoop.

The door chimes are off key. After a while a gray-haired woman in print housedress peers at us through the sidelight. Apparently satisfied, she unlatches the door.

"He's expecting you," she says in a monotone. "In his den."

She leads us through several dark rooms, ritually opening and shutting the doors as we pass through. The kitchen is dark and smells of burnt toast. She opens another door, shows us the basement stairs, gestures for us to descend.

Joel and I exchange looks and start down. The stairwell's dim. At the bottom we pass a lavatory, furnace room, malodorous laundry area, arriving finally at a wood-panel door. Joel signals me to turn on my tape recorder. He knocks. A moment passes, the door opens and we find ourselves face-to-face with Hale.

I wouldn't have recognized him on the street. He bears little resemblance to the stocky, authoritative man whose face glared out of the *Examiner* fifteen years ago. In that photograph he had clear eyes, thick black hair, a bushy black mustache. The man facing us now is gaunt, his hair is white and his mustache droops on either side of his mouth. His flesh has the pasty look of a person who rarely ventures outdoors. The famous detective, at his prime when he resigned, has cruelly aged.

"Come in." His voice is gruff, but I note wiliness in his eyes. "Glickman. Miss Farrow." No "Ms." from Inspector Hale; he's strictly a ma'am-Miss-Mrs.-type guy.

As he and Joel feel one another out, I make a quick study of the room. At first glance it appears ordinary, a den outfitted with recycled office furniture, books, framed nostalgia photographs, clippings and awards. But after a minute I feel claustrophobic, and then it occurs to me that the room is not only windowless but also cramped. There's too much in here, too many old clippings clustered on the walls, too many books jammed into the bookcases, too many moldy boxes of files strewn upon the threadbare rug. And, too, it seems ill proportioned, depth insufficient to width. Perhaps, I think, it's a metaphor for Hale's mind.

". . . Kay, here, will be doing the photos," Joel is saying. Hale, seated behind his desk, examines me carefully. "Some of the places where the torsos were found as they appear today. A portrait of you too, we hope."

Joel pauses, waiting for Hale to agree. But Hale is searching my eyes.

"The other principals too." Joel pauses. "Including Steele, if we can find him."

"Oh, you'll find him," Hale says. "Poke around in the garbage somewhere. Just be careful when a rattlesnake crawls out."

If Joel's mention of the reporter who exposed Hale is meant to rile him, it works. He squints and starts to knock his knees, causing his desk to shake.

"You're his daughter, aren't you?" Hale's eyes bore into mine.

"My father's Jack Farrow . . . if that's what you

mean." Hale nods. "Is that going to be a problem, Inspector?"

"How is old Jack?" Then, before I can respond: "Still baking bread up on Clement?"

"You know about that?"

"I know a lot of things." Hale's eyes turn cunning. "I keep track of them all."

"Who?" Joel asks.

"Everyone connected to it."

"It?"

"The T case, what'd you think?"

Joel smiles. "Roquelle says you're still interested in it."

"Interested? Consumed is more like it."

No obfuscation here. In a few choice words Hale has let us know why he agreed to meet.

"So," Joel says, "after all these years, what've you found out?"

"Maybe we'll get to that," Hale says. "First, I want to know why. What brings you to me now?"

"It seemed a good time to do a follow-up."

Hale shakes his head. "Follow-ups appear on anniversaries. There're no T case anniversaries coming up."

"All right, Inspector—there's a new case," Joel confides. "I'm going to tell you about it, but I expect something in return."

For the first time since we've met, Hale cracks a smile. "I show you mine, you show me yours—I remember how it goes." He turns to me. "Tell me something, young lady—do you think your dad's the one fumbled the evidence that night?"

"I've no idea," I say. "What do *you* think?"

"I think it was someone else. And I think your dad knows who."

Nothing I can reply to that. I spread my hands, expecting more. Hale winks at me, then turns back to Joel. "Let's start by establishing some ground rules," he says.

I listen as they hammer out an arrangement, defining "background only" and "off the record," talking of "embargoes" and "trial balloons." Hale is shrewd and his voice, at first so gruff, now takes on a more melodious tone. Perhaps he doesn't do much talking these days; his wife didn't strike me as much of a talk-and-listen type. Or perhaps he's energized by the chance to fence with a bright reporter once again. It's been years since anyone's asked his views, but he hasn't lost his press skills, the ones that led to his idolization as "San Francisco's smartest cop."

"Okay," says Joel, "we got rules, let's play."

Guy talk! I'm amused. Joel's the least jocklike man I know. He prides himself on not following sports, on not even knowing the names of local pro teams. But he's such a chameleon he'll say anything to build rapport.

He tells Hale about Tim, the discovery of his limbs and head on Hemlock, his torso in Wildcat Canyon. Hale acts mildly interested, not fascinated as we'd hoped.

Joel describes the marks: ". . . the number 'seven.' Tribal arabesques on his back, not tattooed but applied with paint. So, you see, there're similarities and differences. And of course fifteen years."

Hale smiles. "Who's the investigating officer?" When Joel names Shanley, Hale doesn't react. "Lots of new faces downtown. You'd think the man would have gotten in touch." He shakes his head. "They've no idea what I've been up to all this time. Nobody does. Except Alice." He points upstairs.

"Tell us, Inspector—what *have* you been up to?" Joel asks, trying to flatter out a revelation.

"Investigating," Hale says. "I'll show you."

He turns to me, winks again, the crafty wink of a man about to amaze. Then he stands, turns to the bookcase on the wall behind his desk, reaches forward and . . . behold! The bookcase parts in the middle to reveal another room of equal size behind. Now I understand why the office seemed so cramped—Hale divided the original space in half. I also understand why he insisted on dealing with us formally from behind his desk: he needed to guard his secret space.

As he beckons us into this den-within-the-den, I try to catch Joel's eye. But he's focused on the display inside, three walls covered with a complicated chart that puts to shame my own wall display at home. This is a real detective's flowchart: drawings, photos, maps, names, documents and queries connected by a network of strings tracking various investigative lines. Listening to Hale explain, I learn that the strings are of different colors—white tracking the chronological line, yellow the methodological, blue the evidentiary and red the psychological. In addition there are hundreds of thumbtacked cards bearing references to undisplayed material and research notes.

Hale picks up a pointer, starts to talk. It takes him nearly an hour to bring us up to speed. His presentation is brilliant, his command of the case dazzling. I'm struck too by the fluid way he speaks, weaving each thread with the others into a fully organized design.

"This," he concludes with a sweeping gesture, "is the case as explored by S.F.P.D. What I have shown you is everything they've got." He smiles, drops his pointer to his side. "But not everything *I've* got," he adds.

It's then that I take Hale's picture. He glares at me, surprised. As I take another, I feel his anger rise, prepare to take a third and am almost disappointed when unexpectedly he grins. I think a truth he knew as a cop has suddenly come back, one my father once revealed and which I never forgot: an arrested person who tries to cover his face inevitably looks guiltier than one who faces the press with head held high.

"Sorry," I tell him, "I couldn't resist."

"No harm done."

"None intended."

"But please, Miss Farrow, warn me before you shoot again."

I agree, not only because I'm a guest in his home, but because I know any pictures I may take later are unlikely to surpass what I have just caught: the retired detective, mad and smug in his secret knowledge, surrounded by a chart that perfectly expresses his obsession.

Having done what I was brought along to do, I put my camera aside and listen. Hale, in exchange for what Joel has told him, reveals two facets of his own investigation, making sure we understand there's plenty more he's keeping to himself.

"First, victimology. We know the identities of only two of the original victims: Gary Kendall and Robbie Sipple. Kendall's the one who had the gallbladder operation and Sipple's the one"—Hale glances at me—"rescued by your dad. Everyone knows what they had in common. Besides a certain physical look, which they shared with the other four, they'd sleep with anything in pants."

Hale, I note, doesn't wince the way Dad did when he mentioned that all the T case victims were gay. I'm surprised since Hale's of the generation of homophobic cops whose attitudes long stigmatized S.F.P.D.

"No one except me went the extra mile to dig up more, not just what they shared in terms of looks, age, orientation, but also what they were actually like, the way they carried themselves. Both were what's called 'cute'—not girlish necessarily, but good-looking and . . ."

"Androgynous?" I ask.

Hale nods. "So by extrapolation we can assume the other four were probably the same." Hale leans on his pointer. "Maybe not all that important, you say."

Joel looks up. "We're not saying that."

"True . . . but others did, the ones took charge after I left. In fact it *is* important, because cute's a special type, and not the most common around. Macho muscle, leather, preppy, poof, bear, queen—there're all these types, of which cute is merely one. And, like any kind of tribe, each has its hangouts and dating styles. Take The Gryphon, the bar where Sipple was picked up—that's known as a cute boy's pub. While I was still lead detective we covered it pretty well. Had Kendall ever been in there? Any regulars over the years who recently stopped coming in? The handsome, thirtyish guy who picked Sipple up— anyone seen him there before? No, no and no . . . but that was just one bar. So a year after I resigned, when it was obvious the official investigation was going nowhere fast, I worked up a list of cute boy spots around the city and started checking them out one by one.

"Sometimes I had trouble along the way. I'd been on TV a lot, people recognized me, many knew that I'd been hounded out of the Department. 'What do you want, Hale? We don't have to talk to you—you're not a cop anymore.' But I kept at it, kept smiling and talking, till I made the right connections. Ended up with my own private intelligence net. Pretty sweet, huh?"

Actually I have some difficulty imagining this crusty old man haunting a bunch of gay bars. Still I admire him for his persistence, even as I'm appalled by his lack of self-knowledge. "Hounded out" seems a pretty tame phrase; "found out" would be more accurate. But then, I remember, intimate self-knowledge is not a requisite for being a cop.

Hale tells us how, over time, he came to view three individuals as suspects. One had a particular fondness for tattoos, another had a medical background, which meant training in dissection, the third had neither tattoo nor butchering experience but was definitely handsome, and twice Hale followed him to The Gryphon where he picked up and took home cute young Robbie Sipple types.

Over the years Hale gave up on the handsome man; interviews with his pickups convinced him he was sane and gentle. The doctor died of AIDS in 1988, which left him with the tattoo freak.

"He was legendary in the tattoo underground," Hale tells us. "Then around the time of the Sipple incident, he just cold dropped out. Wasn't seen again. People said he moved away." Hale shrugs. "I've got his prints. I hope someday to make a match."

Which brings him, he says, to the second area he's willing to discuss—the missing evidence from Sipple's basement flat.

"When I was in charge I pulled the files of every man there that night, cops and paramedics alike. No matter what anyone says, I never thought that evidence was lost.''

"Way I heard it," I tell him, "you called the cops in and told them they were assholes.''

Hale smiles. "Which doesn't mean I thought they were. One of them took that material, and at least one other knows who did.''

"You're talking cover-up," Joel says.

"Conspiracy's more like it.''

"Conspiracy to do what?''

"Obstruct justice. What other damn kind of conspiracy could it be?''

Not only Hale's words but the gleam in his eyes tell me we're in paranoid country now, a murky land full of fogs and mists, where shadowy figures with nefarious aims scheme to thwart the honorable process of the Law. Frame-ups, hidden relationships, secret agendas, are at work. Sometimes, of course, the mist parts, the fog lifts and then, for an instant, you catch a glimpse of the master plot. Conspiracies are never simple. To penetrate one you must be as devious and sly as the conspirators. And sometimes, of course, a cigar is just a cigar, or, as in the case of Torsos, incompetent cops are merely incompetent cops.

"If someone covered up," Joel says, "there had to be a reason.''

Again a gleam in the eye accompanied by a knowing nod and the sweet tight-lipped smile of the insider.

"You're saying a cop did these killings?''

Hale shrugs. "You said it, not me.''

"Come on, Inspector," Joel goads, "tell us what you think.''

"What I think isn't important. Only what I can prove.''

I recall Hilly's notion, that only an insider on the T case could have known how to mark Tim's body.

"Seems to me," I tell him, "you've got conflicting theories: a tattoo freak into cute young men who suddenly dropped out, and a cop who got rid of evidence because maybe it implicated himself.''

This time the nod's even more knowing, the tight-lipped smile verging on a smirk.

"Let's just say that what may appear conflicting to you can, upon investigation, be resolved."

The way Hale bites off these final words tells us he'll have no more to say. He leads us from his inner chamber back into his office. Closing the bookcase doors, he turns to me.

"I've been to see your dad."

He lightly drops this news, perhaps knowing it will fall upon me like a bomb.

"Several times. He's always cordial. Makes a damn good loaf of bread." Hale nods toward the ceiling. "Alice says it's the best bread other side of the Bay."

"What did you see him about?" I ask, trying to keep my voice level, disguise the feelings roiling within.

"The bondage hood. He had a good look at it. I thought he might remember how it was made. He was helpful, made some sketches, even accompanied me to a couple custom leather shops where we looked at hoods with similar features."

So strange, I think, Dad didn't mention this . . . but then I had a feeling after our lunch that he'd left a great deal out.

"Earlier you said you thought he knew who lost the evidence."

Hale grins. "Did I say 'lost'?"

His coy little smiles annoy me, but I refrain from displaying irritation. Instead, feigning loss of interest, I turn my attention back to Joel. Hale's a control freak, a trait that undoubtedly served him well as he moved up the ladder at S.F.P.D. One thing, I know, a control freak can't abide is the notion he no longer dominates the room.

I figure Joel, being intuitive, will understand what I'm up to. But he still has questions of his own.

"What about the new case?" he asks.

"Copycat," Hale snaps.

"A copycat's got to know what to copy."

"The body painting? We had tattoo experts in. Word on the designs got around."

"So why did the killer use paint this time, and not tattoo?"

"Tattooing's difficult. You have to have tools and technique."

"Is it really so difficult, Inspector? Convicts do it without special tools. There're books that tell you how."

"It takes time."

"The new killer had time enough to cut the man up."

"We looked into that. An experienced butcher can cut up a human being in less than half an hour."

"Then why the number 'seven'?"

"An attempt to divert attention."

"Is that really what you think? If tattooing's so crucial to your theory—"

"Who says it is?"

"Excuse me—didn't you say so?"

"There're things I said and a lot I didn't. You came here with something interesting so I returned the favor."

Joel shrugs. "Then perhaps the real story isn't the old unsolved case. It's the retired cop who refuses to give up."

"How you play it's up to you," Hale says . . . but I can tell he's pleased.

Ending on a note of mild flattery—that's Joel's technique. He's not the sort to go for broke in one interview, risking refusal when he requests a second. Rather he's the methodical journalist who comes back again and again, building trust while each time subtly prying out a little more.

Out on the street, away from Hale's oppressive basement, I breathe in, then deeply exhale. The air here may not be so heady, but at least it's clear. The air down in paranoid country was thick and close.

We get back into Melvin. I study Hale's house as we pull away. It may not be Gothic, may lack a turret, but there's something sinister about a split-level on a sunny day with all the shades pulled and drapes drawn tight.

Joel doesn't speak until we're back on the freeway.

"You know, kiddo—whenever I'm with someone like that I find myself drawn in. But once I get away and think about what he said, it always starts sounding dumb."

"Hale creates a force field," I say. "Inside it we're his prisoners."

"Catch the smell in that kitchen?"

"Old Alice hates him. She burns his toast."

Joel laughs. "Takes an expert to burn toast, toasters being more or less infallible. Still, I wonder . . ." Joel strokes his goatee.

"What?"

"Why he did it?"

"The letters?"

Joel nods. "He had everything going for him, was at the peak of his career. Then he threw it all away for nothing."

"The old Greek formula for tragedy," I suggest. "Arrogant pride, a reckless act . . . nemesis."

"Like he willed his own downfall."

"He was a detective, Joel. He knew typewriters leave a signature, yet he went ahead and used his own. Perhaps unconsciously he wanted to fall off the high wire. Couldn't take the pressure. Better to work the T case alone from a secret basement room than face his people every day knowing sooner or later he'd have to admit he couldn't solve it."

Joel shakes his head. "Too rich for me, kiddo. Think of his disgrace, getting caught writing letters praising himself, ending his career as a laughingstock."

"But what if he does solve it? Then who has the last laugh?"

"Don't kid yourself. It's been fifteen years. How the hell's he going to solve it now?"

Eleven

Joel drops me at Third near the new Museum of Modern Art. I walk up Howard Street to the sharply angled doorway of Zeitgeist Gallery.

Zeitgeist presents itself as a showcase for young cutting-edge photographers. In L.A. it would be one of many; here it stands alone. The pristine white floor, white walls and ceiling Erector-set lights give it a drop-dead New York look.

The current show is of new work by Clury Bowen, huge color prints of masses of entwined yarn which, needless to say, I fail to appreciate. I may be the most conservative artist on the Zeitgeist roster, being more of a photojournalist than the kind of photographer who sets up scenes. The closest I came to that was in my "Watcher" series, for which I dressed a store mannequin in trench coat and fedora, then posed him in shadowy doorways along the Tenderloin. Shot from behind this "watcher," my pictures of raw street life were imbued with a noirish quality people liked. I sold many more "Watcher" prints than prints from *Transgressions*.

I find Zeitgeist's owner, Caroline Gifford, in her office off the gallery floor, bent over a light box studying transparencies. We smooch air. Caroline's dark hair is so thick it forms a cave around her face. She's plump, maternal, her eyes soft and mellow.

"Sorry I missed Clury's opening," I lie. "That *Guardian* review was mean." Caroline winces. "I'm here to show solidarity."

"Sweet, Kay. Clury'll be thrilled!"

In fact, like most artists I know, I'm as guilty of schadenfreude as the next. Also I don't get it about Clury's work. Why photograph the yarn? Why not just hang it directly on the wall?

Caroline and I spend a few minutes dishing art gossip—who got a grant, who didn't, who made a big sale, the sad tale of the local sculptor whose entire New York show went unsold. This gives me a chance to ask about various prominent Bay Area collectors, which in turn enables me to drop the name Sarah Lashaw. Caroline mentions she's been in the gallery several times.

"My show?" I ask.

"Not the opening. I'd remember. But maybe later on." Caroline grins. "There's a reason you're asking, Kay?"

I nod. "She had me over for lunch, boasted she'd seen the show, made a big point about having signed the book."

"Easy enough to check."

Caroline sends her assistant scurrying to the storage room to fetch the *Transgressions* guest book from the files. The girl, blotchy-faced and bony, returns with a spiral-bound filler, the kind Caroline inserts into the handmade leather portfolio she keeps with her price lists on the gallery desk.

Caroline opens it, starts reeling off the names of prominent local citizens—CEOs, socialites, successful venture capitalists. Caroline, in addition to her excellent eye, is a genius at cultivating collectors. She sees herself as a cultural ambassadress committed to ending visual arts provincialism in San Francisco. Photographs, she exhorts her wealthy friends, are art, and, isn't it great, they're also cheap!

"Ta-da!" Caroline shows me the signature: Sarah Lashaw, St. Helena. "Now own up—she wants to buy your work?"

"She tried to. I refused."

"*Kay!* Get real! If you can get some of your pictures onto *her* walls, we'll have a real breakthrough!"

"Forget it," I tell her. "What she wants to buy she wouldn't dare expose."

I taxi to City Stone Ground. Dad's out, but expected back soon. While I wait I hang out with the jovial Russian staff, and enjoy the great aroma, far less intense now than during baking time but still, for me, ambrosia.

Tamara, a stout, middle-aged Georgian woman, wants me to persuade Dad to put in a special oven so she can make her native crackling flat bread.

"They will sell, Kay. I promise. Like how does Jack say? Hot cakes. No?"

I take some pictures of the crew. A few late shoppers appear. When the last of the day's bread is sold, Peter, Dad's second, posts a sign, *SORRY, NO MORE BREAD,* on the door.

A few minutes later Dad appears. He's pleased to find me. I get a big hug, the staff gets thanks, he sends them home, locks up, then we walk together to his apartment.

He moved here a year after Mom took her life. He couldn't bear to stay on in the house where she had shot herself. He found a two-bedroom flat in a four-story rent-controlled building on Cherry Street, the second bedroom permanently reserved, he said, for me. In fact, having already flown the nest, I never once slept there. A few years later, after City Stone Ground started bringing in money, Dad bought the building, waited patiently for the resident families to move out, renovated the flats and is now a proud live-in landlord.

We sip vodka in the bay of his living room overlooking the pines of the Presidio. The room has a spare masculine look—huge TV, leather maroon recliners with seats worn smooth. No trace here of Dad's longtime girlfriend, Phyllis Sorenson. I've never understood whether they sleep here or at her place. Phyllis, a real estate top-producer, is fifteen years younger than Dad, an aggressive dyed-blond painted-nails divorcée. She finds me scruffy; I find her overgroomed. We don't get along too well.

"I saw Hale this morning."

I drop the bomb just as Dad settles in. I watch him carefully. As expected, he twitches his neck against his collar.

"Joel Glickman—you remember Joel, Dad?" He twitches again. "He set the interview up. Hale lives over in Oakland. His wife keeps the drapes pulled during the day. Whenever she leaves a room she shuts the door. His den, down in the cellar, is set up like a T case temple."

"Jesus!"

"He told me he's been to see you several times." Dad nods. "When we had dim sum that day, you didn't mention you'd made up."

Dad sniffs. "That what he says we've done?"

"He says you've been helpful to him, especially on the bondage hood."

"Helpful doesn't mean we're friends." Dad shuts his eyes. "Hale's a nut."

"A smart nut," I correct. "Sly, canny, the kind who can solve a tough case."

"Oh, he was good. In his prime, probably the best. But it's been a long time since he slipped."

"He's still obsessed with Torsos."

"I'm not surprised . . . since it ruined him."

"He thinks you know who took that hood from Sipple's."

Dad sniffs again. "Any chance did he mention the taker's name?" I shake my head. "Easy to make an accusation, Kay. A little harder to prove it."

"You don't deny it."

"That's what you want?"

Again he twitches, as if to free his neck from a too tight collar. It's a familiar gesture, one I remember well from my childhood. He'd do it whenever he got upset. I wonder if he does it now because, entangled in a subterfuge, he imagines his neck caught in a noose.

"Investigating me, are you?"

"I'm investigating the brutal murder of my friend. And since the T case is connected and you were part of that . . . well, your name keeps coming up." I meet his eyes. "Please, Dad—I need your help."

He drinks down half his glass, sets it on the floor. "Take it from an old cop—there's not a chance in hell the person who did in Tim is the original T killer."

"They say he knows things only cops knew at the time."

"There were lots of cops and it's been lots of years." He looks at me. "You want to know who lost that hood? Talk to the people who were there that night. Maybe now someone'll admit it."

"Waincroft, Hayes, Puccio, Vasquez."

His eyes enlarge. He's stunned I know their names.

"Still see any of them?"

"Rusty sees Vasquez sometimes. He's the only one of us survived in the Department. He's a lieutenant now, some kind of division chief. Truth is I try to avoid them."

"Still bitter?"

"It hurt to be driven out."

"You weren't dismissed."

He shakes his head. "They made retirement the only option. Funny thing—I never much liked being a cop, but I didn't like being forced to give it up." He smiles. "Even though it was probably the best thing could've happened to me, I wanted to make the decision in my own sweet time."

I know it's time to leave, that if I stay any longer we'll get into something neither of us can deal with. But as much as I want to go I can't. Rather I feel compelled to bring up the issue that, being unspoken so many years, makes us both uncomfortable.

He broaches it first. "The other day I told you I thought the end of my police career pushed your mother to—"

He pauses. "I imagine you've been giving that some thought."

I admit to him that I have.

"I shouldn't have said it. Regretted it soon as I did. See, Kay—I'm convinced sooner or later she would have killed herself. I'm certain it had nothing to do with me."

"Oh, Dad! Don't you see?"

"See what, darlin'? Tell me."

"The *way* she did it, like a ruined cop. It's as if she did it *instead* of you—like she thought maybe you might do it, so to keep you from doing it she did it herself."

"That's crazy!" He's twitching continuously now. His eyes, I notice, are moist. "I wasn't corrupt! I wasn't disgraced! I had no damn reason to eat my gun."

"Course not! But what if *she* thought so? You said she was depressed. Maybe she did it as an act of love, thinking if she did, then you wouldn't have to. In that way, you see, she did it *for* you."

He shakes his head. He can't stand hearing this. He gets up, starts pacing the room, flicks on the TV, snaps it off. I feel terrible. I've pushed him too far, broken our contract of silence.

"Jesus, Kay! I've tried not to think about it. People kill themselves—that's part of life. It's been hard enough to live with that without having to wonder why."

I make my voice gentle. "You have to deal with it. It'll always haunt you otherwise."

"But what you're saying, that she did it so I wouldn't—that's a heavy load to carry, darlin'. A very heavy load."

I have had to carry it too, I remind him. To be the daughter of a suicide is to have one leg kicked out from under you. You teeter, unsure of who you are and whether a gene of self-destruction isn't at work somewhere inside.

"Listen, Dad, I've got to ask you this. You're the best organized, most reliable man I know. How come you didn't secure that evidence or make sure it was secured by someone else?"

He throws up his hands. "Back to that! Give me a

break, darlin'. Even the best players sometimes drop the ball. Remember, I'd just brought a guy back to life. I lost my concentration, screwed up. I'd never forgive myself if someone else got killed. Thank God the killings stopped. Maybe the perp freaked, realizing how close he'd come. Or . . .'' He hesitates. There's a dreamy look in his eyes.

''What?''

''Just something that's crossed my mind over the years. Pretty ridiculous if you want to know.''

''Tell me.''

''Maybe the guy who tied up Sipple had nothing to do with the T case. It was a coincidence. Or maybe . . .''— he smiles at the notion—''the whole Sipple thing was just a plant.''

It's dark when I leave. Outside I feel as I did after visiting Hale: relieved to be in open air.

I stop at a discount pharmacy on Sacramento, phone Joel at home, tell him I think we ought to see the four other cops who were there the night the Sipple evidence was lost.

Joel says he's been thinking the same thing. ''But why only four?'' he asks.

''Because I just saw the fifth,'' I tell him. ''I'm still shaking from the encounter.''

''Calm yourself, kiddo.''

''How can I? He's my dad.''

I recount the conversation. It helps to share the pain. When I come to Dad's last words, the possibility Sipple wasn't connected or was a plant, Joel points out how interesting it is the way both Hale and Dad dummy up when trying to explain the loss.

Walking up Hyde to my building, I spot someone lingering in the shrubbery that demarcates the Alice Marble Tennis Courts. No danger—I'm on the sidewalk and the hedge here is extremely thick. I pause beneath a streetlight and peer into the darkness. Silence as I scan the bushes, searching out the eyes of the voyeur. A rustling of branches, then a face appears amidst the leaves.

"What're you doing there, Drake?"

"Waiting for you to come home safe."

He stares at me, then disappears. I hear him as he retreats into the shadows and the brush.

In the elevator, ascending to my floor, I wonder how much Drake knows about me, whether he's aware of Sasha's late-night visits. Is he infatuated with me or merely my self-appointed guardian? In either case, I resolve, I must remember to draw my blinds.

I fall to sleep around eleven, only to be awakened after midnight by the delicate touch of Sasha's hand upon my breast. I've given him my key, urged him to sneak in on me, throw himself upon me, take me harshly like a beast. He acknowledges my fantasy but says he can't bring himself to fulfill it. Too fine a gentleman is Dr. C. Patel. Even so, I like his style of lovemaking—slow, thoughtful, ever so chivalrous.

I don't open my eyes, instead present myself to him half somnambulant, moaning beneath his expert ministrations. He leaves me hours later as stealthily as he came, his sandalwood smell upon my body, the delicious taste of him upon my lips.

In the morning my mailbox yields a letter addressed to Tim, forwarded by Gordon from Mail From Home. It's postmarked San Francisco with no return address. I open it, find a note handwritten on the stationery of The Sultan's Tent, a posh boutique hotel near Alamo Square. The handwriting's familiar. Then I remember the postcard from Florence:

Gorgeous One:
    In town at last! Am here in my usual room awaiting your silken presence. I shall sing for four nights and then be ready for play. Please stay abstinent from the

*time you receive this. On the night of the seventeenth,
present yourself here at nine P.M., announce yourself as
"Carlo" . . . and violate me!*

Your devoted

J

P.S. I know I can count on your fine discretion!

I dig out the old postcard. It was signed "Jerome." I
pull my *Chronicle* out of the wastebasket, open it to the
arts section, check the listings. This week the San Francisco Opera is presenting *Tristan und Isolde.* Among the
scheduled singers: the American Wagnerian tenor, Jerome
Tattinger.

I spend the morning developing and printing the roll I
shot of Sho. With his sharp, triangular chin and modeled
Native American features, he's got the looks to make it
as a model. I select two of the images, one full-face, the
other a strong profile with the wind raising his hair. I
make him twenty prints of each, laborious work, but I
want him to succeed, find a way to make a living so he'll
no longer have to work the Gulch.

I try writing a note to Jerome Tattinger, something I can
safely leave for him at the Opera box office. After three
attempts I realize that nothing I can put on paper will be
discreet yet clear enough to gain me an audience. There
is, of course, an alternative: I can show up at The Sultan's
Tent in place of Tim. Though not especially crazy about
the idea, I don't rule it out.

Joel calls, excited. Hilly has left chalk marks signaling
she wants a meet. According to our contact code, three-
way meetings are to take place at ten p.m. at the Rough
Rider bar the evening following the day the marks are
left.

• • •

After dinner I walk down to the Gulch, looking for Sho to give him his head shots. I don't find him, instead come upon Slick in the classic one-foot-against-the-wall hustler's stance, which, suggesting loneliness, is so seductive.

Since he and Sho are buddies, I hand him the prints.

"Can I look at them, Bug?" When I nod he opens the envelope, gazes at the first shot and gasps. "You really make people pretty," he says, lightly touching his white eyebrows. He looks at me, then primps . . . as if I'm a mirror. "Could you make me pretty too?"

"You're already pretty."

"Yeah, like pretty . . . weird."

As someone who squinted a lot and couldn't see colors, I have no trouble imagining the kind of abuse Slick took as a kid. "Pink Eyes!" "Colorless!" The taunts were probably worse since to be albino is to wear one's affliction on one's face. Achromatopsia, at least, is a hidden malady.

I invite him for coffee. We walk a block to Roy's, the grungy place Crawf and I went after Shanley showed me Tim's head.

I ask Slick about his date with Sho and the man in the big Jaguar who picked them up.

"Guy's fussy, fussy." Slick pauses. "Tim used to go with him. I won't see him alone, tell you that."

"Because he's dangerous?"

Slick shrugs. "Any of Tim's old johns—I'm real careful now." He shows a sickly smile. "Don't wanna die."

Yeah . . . but suddenly I'm angry with Tim. So many things he didn't tell me, so many sides he didn't show— world-class opera singers, johns in Jaguars, a boyhood in a magician's troupe, a strange twin sister into bizarre sex for pay. I still want desperately to find out who killed him, yet now I wonder, did he really view me as a friend? I think he did, yet he held back so much . . . and that wounds me still.

• • •

When I arrive at Rough Rider, I find Joel alone nursing a beer, looking awkward in a new ill-fitting glossy black jacket.

I slip in beside him, peck his cheek, then check out the jacket . . . which, it turns out, isn't made of leather.

"Vinyl! Oh, Joel!''

"Looks good, huh?''

"No. And it doesn't feel good either. Where'd you get it?''

"Discount place. Eighty-nine ninety-five.''

"Figures. Why'd you bother?''

"I don't want to look out of place.''

I peer around. The joint is filled with tough-looking leathermen in motorcycle jackets with close-cropped hair and beards. Poor Joel! A Pulitzer prize, two decades as an investigative journalist, and he's still too cheap to buy himself a proper San Francisco disguise.

"Take it off before Hilly gets here,'' I advise, "unless you want her to take you for a dork.''

Joel barely has his jacket off and stuffed behind his back when Hilly shows up in tight jeans and body-molded vest.

"Hi guys!''

Tonight she's wired, less interested in flaunting her orientation than providing us with information. "First thing yesterday morning we have a meeting in Captain Charbeau's office. Shanley, me and a Lieutenant Vasquez from Vice Crimes.''

"Luis Cruz Vasquez?'' I ask.

Hilly nods. "Himself. So okay, the guys are talking. Being the junior detective in the room, I stay quiet. Shanley brings everyone up to speed, which is basically we got zilch, he's pursuing an a-john-did-it theory and I'm still working on connections to the old T case. At that point you'd think Vasquez would mention *his* connection . . . but he doesn't. Meantime Charbeau's getting antsy. After a couple minutes—this is why I signaled you guys—Charbeau says, like out of thin air: 'Why're we gang-banging this so hard?'

"We all look at him surprised. Shanley goes: 'What do you mean?' 'What I mean,' Charbeau says, 'it's just another cocksucker killing, right?' I go: *'Scuse me!'* They all turn to me with these Oh!—we-forgot-*she*-was-in-the-room expressions."

I find myself liking this direct, indignant Hilly more than the canny ambitious woman I've been dealing with.

"Charbeau's black, tough as hell. Now he realizes he's offended me. He starts to backpedal. 'Vice Crimes wants to help out. They know the hustlers and johns. Lieutenant Vasquez asked to sit in on account of the gay felony-prostitution angle.' Figuring that's enough to keep me from filing a grievance, Charbeau adjourns the meeting.

"Immediately Vasquez takes off down the hall, me chasing after. 'Hey! Lieutenant, Lieutenant Vasquez, sir! Please, sir, a precious moment of your time.' I finally catch him at the elevators. He glares at me, annoyed. 'Yeah, Detective, what's on your mind?' 'Just this, sir—' I sputter. 'I know you were there the night Sipple was attacked and I was wondering if you had any thoughts you'd like to pass on. Like who beside Hale's task force knew the details of the T killer's M.O.?'

"Vasquez, he's six one, stares down at me like I'm some kind of bug. 'Why don't you move your fanny back to the squad room, Detective, before I have a talk with your captain.' Just then the elevator opens, he steps in, stares straight ahead like I don't exist and pushes the button for the executive floor."

It's a good vignette, Joel says, atmospheric too, but, he tells Hilly, it doesn't prove there's any kind of cover-up. A hustler homicide is bound to annoy the Homicide Division chief, if only because such cases are rarely solved. As for Vasquez, it's understandable he doesn't want to be reminded of what was undoubtedly the nadir of his career.

"Still," I point out, "he came to the meeting. If he wasn't interested why did he bother?"

"I don't know," Hilly says, "but I'll tell you this—if

he'd used just two more words, like *'wiggle* your *juicy* fanny back to the squad room,' I'd have brought him up on a sex harassment charge."

After Hilly leaves, Joel, uncomfortable in the bar, offers to drive me home. In the car we discuss Hilly's story. He says she was right to call for a meeting; any documentation that police are dragging their feet only makes the Gulch story better.

Then, since we're going to be speaking to Vasquez, we discuss whether to reveal how much we know.

"Can't," Joel says. "Minute we do he'll know Hilly's the leak. He'll tell the others, they'll all be wary of her and Charbeau'll pull her off the case."

"So what do we do—act like we *don't* know he's aware?"

"Absolutely!" Joel smiles. "I'd love it if he lied."

We plan the interviews: I'll do the taping; Joel'll make the calls and set them up. After he drops me, I spend a couple of minutes walking the perimeter of Sterling Park, trying to catch a glimpse of Drake. No sign of him, so I enter my building, take the elevator up. The moment I step into the little vestibule on my floor, I realize something's wrong.

My door, which I always lock, is open an inch. I move toward it cautiously and, hearing nothing, push it open all the way. When I turn on my foyer lights I discover the lock's been jimmied. Then, peering inside, I see the mess.

Books and papers are scattered on the floor. All my living room furniture's upended. My telescope is broken like someone stamped hard on the tube. And there's a foul smell in the room. It takes me a moment to locate the source: a pile of excrement in the center of the rug, left by the invaders to show me their contempt.

I quickly check the other rooms. Nothing broken in the kitchen, but in my bedroom all the contents of my closets and drawers have been pulled out, ripped up and strewn. My underwear is in tatters, several pieces festoon my bedside lamp. My mattress has been gouged with a knife, my bedding ripped. In the bathroom I find my toilet clogged with condoms and tampons from the cupboard.

Sick in my gut, I check out my office. It's been hit the worst. My computer disks are gone, my computer screen is smashed, the keys of my keyboard have been pried loose and one of my screwdrivers has been jammed into the disk drive. My flat files have also been rifled, prints torn up, then piled on my light table, where they've been covered with some sort of tar. The flow chart I constructed has been ripped from the walls; all the pinned-up photographs are gone. In their place horrible words have been spray-painted onto the cork: *DIE!CUNT!DIE! DIE STINKING BITCH*. One of my self-portraits lies on the floor, eyes viciously cut from my face.

I rush to the darkroom. My enlarger's been vandalized, my enlarging lenses are missing, but the door of my negative safe is still intact. The one roll of negatives I was working with, the roll I shot of Sho, lies scrambled in the sink.

More insults spray-painted in here: *SUCK ME WHORE. EAT SHIT & DIE. FUCKING CUNT EAT SHIT*. The intruders' message is clear: We're brutal; we've violated you; to us your art is trash; our threats are sexual; our scatological attack is but a warning; next time we'll rip your body as we ripped your underwear.

I return to the living room, face the windows, cry out to the city, howl out my rage. I yell a few times, then, hands shaking, dial 911. Trying to keep my voice level, I tell the operator what's happened. She advises me not to touch anything and to wait downstairs if I'm afraid. Officers, she kindly assures me, are already on their way.

Still standing at my window amidst the debris, I look out at San Francisco. It appears so calm, still, beautiful behind the glass. The Bay too is still, reflecting the moon. Traffic on the bridges moves like molten metal. The Alcatraz light sweeps my face, paints my walls, moves on. Feeling frightened, alone, terribly vulnerable, I suddenly yearn for my father's embrace. Then, resolving to be strong, I decide that first thing in the morning I'll go out and buy myself a gun.

Twelve

K im Coates and David Choy, a pair of good San Francisco cops, show up eight minutes later. Both in their twenties, one black, the other Chinese, they arrive while I'm still photographing the damage.

They analyze the means of entry (Kim: "Hate to tell you this, Ms. Farrow—your front door lock is crap.") and the pattern of destruction (David: "Probable reason they didn't break dishes is fear of alerting the neighbors."). Apparently the only decent lock I have is the one on my negative safe, bought to protect against fire, not burglary.

Andy Lamott, landlord and resident manager, is the next to appear. He and his brother inherited the building; Andy now occupies the penthouse floor. He's a dignified, sweet-natured guy in his forties, not above performing such menial chores as shining the brass in the elevator cab and sweeping the sidewalk out front. Awakened by the rumpus, he appears in jacket and tie to apologize for my ordeal. Building security, he promises, will be immediately upgraded. He'll install a closed-circuit TV system, the motion-activated kind, to videotape all entrances and exits. And first thing in the morning he'll put a new security lock and alarm on my door.

"My brother and I, Ms. Farrow, are very proud of our building and equally proud of our distinguished tenants."

Such gallantry!

Sasha, turning up at midnight for fun and games, spots the patrol car out front. Storming in like a knight-on-white-charger, he's relieved to find me safe. He assists as, with Kim and David's permission, I scrape the shit off the living room rug. Then he flips my mattress and makes up the bed with fresh linen, while I gather up torn clothing, underwear, ruined prints and broken equipment into garbage bags. When Sasha's finished with the bed, he finds a can of touch-up paint in the kitchen and sets to work painting over the graffiti.

By this time the cops are finished. Kim tells me I'll be hearing from a detective in the morning.

"We take sexual threats of this kind very seriously," she says.

As soon as they're gone, I collapse into Sasha's arms.

"Soon, Kay," he says, wiping away my tears, "this ugliness will pass as water runs through sand."

Sasha, I decide, would make a terrific psychiatrist. I resolve to steer him toward this specialty away from his current preference, gynecology.

In the morning there's a sympathy note from the elderly couple who live downstairs. If this had happened in New York, I doubt anyone would have shown concern, but here in San Francisco we observe the old-fashioned amenities.

To forestall the intervention of another detective, I report the invasion to Hilly. And since it's legitimate police business, I phone her directly at the Hall of Justice.

She agrees there's an almost certain connection to the beating provoked by my follow-up on Tim's murder. Then Shanley comes on the line.

"Cowardly little shits!" he says when I repeat the story. He promises I won't have to deal with a new detective; he'll have my case attached to Tim's. "We told you to leave the investigating to us. Lay off now, Kay. Trust us to do our job.''

My next call's to Dad at City Stone Ground. He's horrified but quick to dissuade me from acquiring a gun.

''A threat mean as that, darlin'—of course you take it seriously. But with a good lock they won't get in again. Packing a gun—that's different, that's taking it to another level. You'll need a permit and, if it's going to do you any good, a firearm combat training course. You're better off living defensively for a while—staying off dark streets, and, when you go out, being sure to watch your back.''

Good advice, but I'm not so enamored of his next suggestion, echoing Shanley's, that I leave the matter to the cops.

''I'm not playing Nancy Drew here,'' I remind him. ''I'm a photographer working on a project.''

''Pretty dangerous project sounds like to me.''

''Yes, dangerous,'' I agree, ''but have you ever known me to chicken out?''

A brief pause while Dad thinks that over. ''Never, darlin'—I'm proud to say.''

''I'm going to keep on doing what I've been doing,'' I tell him, ''and we'll just have to see what they do next.''

Midmorning I contemplate walking down to Polk to buy a selection of organic fruits and vegetables for Drake. Then I decide that would look too much like a bribe. This isn't a game, I remind myself, and Drake's not a pet.

I repair empty-handed to 'our' bench in Sterling Park, take a seat and wait for him to show.

I sit there undisturbed for twenty minutes, straight-backed and apprehensive so he knows I'm waiting for him, not just resting my bones. From the excitement last night he's certain to know what happened and he may know a good deal more. So why is he keeping me waiting like this? Is he timid, afraid of getting involved? Or is he afraid I'll be angry with him for inadequately guarding my home?

I pass the time thinking about George Sterling, poet of the city for whom this park was named. There are San Franciscans who still call him "our Baudelaire" because of his famous couplet: "The blue-eyed vampire, sated at her feast / Smiles bloodily against the leprous moon." Born just after the Civil War, he was a great pal of Jack London and Ambrose Bierce. The latter wrote him: "You shall be the poet of the skies, the prophet of the suns." For years he was a local romantic literary figure. Theodore Dreiser described him as hovering over the city "like a burnished black holy ghost." In 1926, in his room at the Bohemian Club, he killed himself, like so many in his circle, with cyanide.

I hear a branch snap behind me.

"That you, Drake?"

"It's me." From his voice I can tell he's close, just a few yards behind the bench. I don't turn for fear of scaring him off.

"Want to sit with me awhile?"

He takes a seat at the opposite end, leaving an empty space between us. Knowing he's eyes-shy, I glance quickly at him, then away.

"I looked for you when I came home last night."

"I saw you."

"But you didn't show yourself." No response. "You know what I found upstairs?"

"They did bad things."

"Yes, Drake. They tore up my place, ripped my clothes, ruined my computer. They wrote awful things on the walls. Threatening things." Again, no response. "Did you see them?"

He whispers: "Yes."

"Want to tell me who they were?"

This time, when he doesn't answer, I turn to engage him. He's staring out across the path toward a clump of Leptospermum trees whose thick exposed roots undulate like serpents.

"Help me, Drake. Please."

He bites on his lip. The sun glints off his hair. "No cops," he says.

"No cops. Just you and me. I have to know so I can protect myself. You understand, don't you?"

Silence, then: "I went to college, Kay."

For a moment I'm puzzled, then I understand. I'm talking to him like he's a child, stupid and uneducated. He wants me to know he's not.

"Chemistry major," he adds. "I didn't graduate. Too much stress. But I got good grades." He sighs. "Maybe someday I'll go back and finish."

"Which college?"

"Reed," he says casually.

I believe him. He could be a brilliant boy, high-strung, mentally disturbed but with an I.Q. in the stratosphere. The streets of Berkeley are filled with emotional cripples, clever kids who somehow got off track. So why not also the Hermit of Sterling Park?

Time now to let him talk. I've made my plea; I can only hope he'll tell me what he knows. Meantime we engage in neighborhood gossip, not the kind I'd be likely to hear from anyone else, rather Drake's own odd angle on people as viewed through the prism of his madness.

"The white-haired lady with the schnauzer," he says, "the one who talks to her dog all the time?"

I nod.

"I've heard what she says to him. She talks about current events. She'll say, 'The situation in Russia is grave, isn't it, Leopold?' That's the dog's name. And then she'll wait for him to reply. He doesn't of course, but she pretends he does. Then she'll say, 'I'm not sure I agree with that view, Leopold. There's an economic aspect I think you've overlooked.' She'll talk to him like that for a whole hour, walking him around the park. Then she'll stop right in the middle of the conversation. 'Go on, Leo! Go on, boy! Make poopy for Mommy! Make good poopy now!' " Drake turns to me. "See, she calls him Leopold

when they're talking like intellectuals, but just plain Leo
when she remembers he's a dog.''

Drake continues with tales of other Russian Hill eccentrics. Our neighborhood has its share. Some of his vi-
gnettes are sad, others charming, all reflect his offbeat
view.

Suddenly he claps his forehead. He looks at me, then
away.

"Three of them. It was dark. I'm not sure, Kay, but I
think the same ones beat you up. One waited across the
street. He had a phone. The other two went in carrying
bags. Then I saw beams in your rooms.''

"Beams?''

"From flashlights, beams crisscrossing in the dark.
They were there ten minutes. When they came out the
three of them crossed here . . . and out this way.'' Drake
gestures toward the steep steps that lead down to Larkin.

"Did they pass close?''

"Maybe twenty feet.''

"Did you recognize them?''

Drake ponders. "One of them. I've seen him here a
couple of times. He comes into the park, watches your
place. He never sees me.''

"How do you know he watches my place?''

"I figured that out last night.''

"Can you describe him?''

"Stocky, muscular.'' Drake combs his fingers through
his scraggly beard. "Buzz cut, goatee. He's not a nice
man.''

You sure got that right! I think.

"Did he go upstairs?''

Drake shakes his head. "He was the one with the
phone.''

"If I showed you some pictures do you think you could
pick the men out?''

Drake smiles. "Like the police?''

"But not for them, Drake. Just for me, okay?''

"I'll try.''

"That would be a big help.''

"You're my friend," he declares.

I reach across the bench, take his hand. "I have to go. I've still got a lot to do."

He pulls his hand away. "One thing . . . ?" His voice sounds urgent. "The . . . mmmmman who cccccomes."

The stutter is new to me. Feeling his tension, I try to relax him with a smile.

"What man?"

"The dark one who comes to see you very late."

"That's Sasha."

"Is he your bbbboyffffriend?"

"Well . . ." I smile. "Come to think of it, I guess he is."

Drake smiles sweetly, apparently relieved the dark man is not a stalker. But leaving him, I realize he's not only my secret admirer, but also a kind of stalker himself.

Returning home, I find Andy installing my new lock and alarm. His handyman is in the bathroom unplugging my toilet with a plumber's snake. Inspired by these efforts, I go to work. My first call is to the Kavakian Carpet Cleaning Company to arrange a pickup and steam cleaning of my rug. Then I call Beds Unlimited and order a new queen-size mattress.

I call my favorite photographic supply house, order a new Beseler 45MXT enlarger with Aristo cold light head, 50mm and 75mm Rodenstock enlarging lenses, a new grain focusing scope and twenty boxes of assorted printing papers—all to be shipped by next-day air. I consider ordering a new Contax G1 but decide to put that off. Perhaps my stolen camera will turn up; meantime I'll keep working with the Nikon.

A new computer can wait; a telescope cannot. I phone Omega Optics and order a new Celestron. Now, with my credit card nearly maxed out, all I need is undies. I slip on a pair of shades and take the Hyde Street cable car downtown. At Nordstrom I go mad in the lingerie department, a first for me since I usually buy underwear at discount. On my way home, clutching my purchases, the cable car rattling up the hill, I realize my real work lies ahead—making hundreds of new prints to replace the ones destroyed. But no matter. There is satisfaction that my negatives, my capital, escaped unscathed.

Sasha's managed to switch night duty with another resident and will be by in an hour to pick me up. Since he was so sweet last night, I decide to please him. I apply lipstick and eyeliner, put on a black silk blouse and pants over my sexy new black lace bra and panties, and slip on black pumps instead of boots.

"Kay!" he exclaims when he arrives. "You're all dressed up for a date."

"Right," I tell him, kissing him on the lips. "A one hundred percent wowie-zowie date. Our first!"

He takes me to Eden Roc, a dinner club on Nob Hill. We make our entrance descending a curved staircase lit by deco-period sconces. The tablecloths are damask, the waiters wear tuxedos and there's a separate snack menu featuring luxury foods—smoked salmon, foie gras, varieties of caviar. Entertainment is provided by Sheila Hudson, an old-time torch singer, belting out classic world-weary tunes: "When My Baby Left Me"; "I Get a Kick Out of You."

Sasha says he's amazed at my manner, that I seem almost serene.

I tell him I am. "Being beaten up, then invaded—it's been bad, but not as bad as I'd have thought. I coped, survived, and here I am. I don't know why, but I'm feeling good."

"You're a brave girl, Kay."

"You can say that after you've seen me cry?"

"Nothing wrong with shedding a tear or two. I occasionally shed a few myself."

"You?" I gaze into his deep liquid eyes, eyes that never fail to move me. "What could possibly make you weep?"

Sasha smiles. "Lots of things—homesickness, missing my mother, my sisters. Also the miseries of the world, people who starve, patients I try to save and then must watch as they die. Then all the little rudenesses, incivilities, petty meannesses and cruelties of life. Human viciousness . . . as reflected in those awful writings on your walls. I had to paint them over, Kay—I couldn't bear leaving them there to poison your eyes." He smiles again. "I know what you're thinking: 'My hard little brown lover—he's perhaps not so tough as I thought. He's a'—how did Claude Rains describe Bogart in that film?—'a sentimentalist.' Maybe I am. It's not the worst insult, is it?"

I'm impressed, moved. "I think I'd call you a humanist, Sasha."

"Ah!" He smiles. "I like that even better!"

"I think I misjudged you."

"I believe you did." He gazes at me. "So tell me, how *did* you judge me until tonight?"

A tricky question. I have to be careful. "I found you charming." He nods. "Extraordinarily handsome." He bows. "Vain." He smiles. "Sexy." He demurs.

"But—?"

"But perhaps also, a little . . . superficial."

He grins. "Better than empty."

"You aren't either, Sasha. You're quite marvelous. You know it, and now I know it too."

He leans forward. "Tell me, Kay—do you think perhaps you might come to love me one day? Can you give me some small hope for that?"

I don't know what to say, so take the easy path. "Let's talk about it next spring," I suggest. "Meantime, see how things go."

A little later, Sasha again makes me see colors, rockets that shoot up, explode, branch out, shoot, explode and branch again until the blackness is flooded with brilliant sparks to which I add imaginary hues: jasper, henna, garnet, honey, beet red, blood red, blush . . .

"I fear for you," he whispers against my neck. "I want to protect you from all the dangers."

God! This gorgeous man's not only a sentimental humanist, he's a real old-fashioned romantic! Lucky me, writhing in his arms. What was it he called himself—my hard little brown lover? How about my silken-fleshed South Asian prince who licks me with his silver tongue and prongs me with his golden cock? My salty dusty Gujarati doctor who plays me like a flute, makes my body arch, fills my head with lovely rainbows?

In the morning, as soon as my new gear arrives, I set to work in the darkroom making prints. Not fine prints for exhibition, just legible images so I can again lay out my project on the wall. But first I create a mini rogues' gallery of Polk Gulch hustlers for Drake, all the usual suspects plus Tim, Crawf, Slick, Remo and, of course, Marcus Crane. When I'm done I separate out my suspects, then place them at random in the pack.

I work like a demon through the afternoon, stopping only to munch fruit. A little after seven, losing concentration, I decide to knock off for the day. In the middle of my shower, I suddenly realize today is the seventeenth. Tonight at nine Tim's devoted J. will be expecting him at The Sultan's Tent.

Should I or should I not attend the gentleman? I can make decent arguments either way. As I towel off I decide. Curiosity demands I go . . . and I know I'll despise myself for cowardice if I don't.

The Sultan's Tent has been carved out of the old Demoine Mansion, a Moorish fantasy of domes, arches, minarets built at the turn of the century by an eccentric sugar baron. Situated on a cul-de-sac off Alamo Square, it dominates the surrounding Victorians.

Heavily damaged in the 1906 earthquake, it was converted into a rooming house in the thirties. After decades of neglect, it was boarded up in the eighties after being declared uninhabitable by city authorities. Five years ago a pair of smart entrepreneurs bought it cheap, then spent a fortune on renovation. Regilding the domes, retiling the minarets, they turned it into a luxurious boutique hotel catering to visiting soloists, singers and conductors in town to perform with the San Francisco Opera and Symphony.

Dressed in my usual tough-girl garb, Nikon around my neck, I enter the main courtyard through an arch. At once the sounds of the street are replaced by the rustle of leaves, tinkle of wind chimes, murmur of running water. I'm in an ersatz Moorish garden planted with palms and aromatic plants. At its center is a marble fountain feeding a rectangular pool stocked with lily pads and carp.

Octagonal lanterns of perforated metal shed soft light upon the paths. I follow one to a terrace where two women in evening gowns sit on a swing couch conversing softly while puffing on attenuated cigarettes.

Seeing what looks to be a lounge, I pass through another arch, enter a domed room carpeted with overlapping Persian rugs. At the opposite side I find the reception desk. A clock above shows the time.

"How may I help you?" asks the snooty clerk. He wears a dark blazer bearing the hotel monogram, sports a blond pompadour and manicured nails.

"Jerome Tattinger please."

"You have an appointment?" I nod. He looks me over skeptically. "Whom shall I announce to Mr. Tattinger?"

"Tell him Carlo is here."

"*Carlo?*" He raises one eyebrow.

"You got it." I stare him down.

Snooty shrugs, picks up a phone, announces my arrival. "Very good, sir!" Snooty hangs up, shows me a leer. "He'll see you in his room . . . Carlo."

"Which room?"

"Mr. T. *only* stays in our Seraglio Suite. Two flights

up the curving staircase"—he gestures—"then through the red door surrounded by cherubs."

The red door looks black to me, but the cluster of cherubs gives me confidence. I pull a rope, hear the tinkle of a bell, then a warm bellow: "Enter, Gorgeous One!"

I take a deep breath and walk in. The first room, an oval, is dimly lit. Silk tenting covers the ceiling and cascades down the walls.

"In here! The sanctum sanctorum."

I cross the oval and peer into a second, smaller room, dark and also tented. A plump middle-aged male lies naked on the bed, facedown, rump up, legs spread, supported by pillows.

"Please . . . I can't wait . . . violate me, Gorgeous One!" he begs, twitching his butt. "Afterward we'll talk and drink."

Petrified, I remain in the doorway. I can't make out his face.

"Dammit, boy! What're you waiting for?"

"Tim's dead," I murmur.

Tattinger freezes. Then he flops onto his back. "I don't—Another game—" He sees me, screams, frantically covers himself with bedding. "I thought you were— Oh, God!" He spots my camera. "Please, no pictures. *Please!*"

"No pictures," I promise. "I mean you no harm. I was his friend. I found your note in his mail. I wanted to write you but was afraid someone would see the letter. So I came myself. I didn't mean to scare you. Really."

He peers at me. He's holding bedding to his chin. "Come closer, girl. Let me see your face."

I approach, curious to see his as well.

"Sit here on the side of the bed."

I sit.

His hair is thin on top, his face puffy, his jowls thick. Neither ugly nor particularly good-looking, I might take him for a banker if it weren't for the compelling quality of his voice.

"Your name?" I tell him. "Do you know mine?" I

nod. "You truly wish me no harm?" I nod again. "You gave me quite a start, young lady." The words roll from him. "Actually, when I heard your voice I thought you were someone else."

"Another woman?" He nods. "Amoretto?"

He smiles. "So you know her. Why didn't *she* come tonight?"

"She doesn't go out much these days."

"I see." He squints at me. "Tell me what happened . . . if you can."

As I tell him how Tim was killed and my commitment to discovering by whom, tears start pulsing from his eyes. I like him immediately for this display, also his lack of shame at being caught butt in the air.

"Let me hold you, dear." He reaches for me.

Without thinking I lie beside him. Immediately he wraps me in his arms. I feel his strength, then his body tremble as he sobs against my hair. Soon I'm sobbing too. I feel as I did with David deGeoffroy, relieved to be with someone with whom I can share my grief. It doesn't matter to me that Jerome Tattinger most likely met Tim on the street. All that matters is that he loved him enough that now, hearing he is no longer in the world, he weeps.

We lie this way for several minutes, soothing each other until finally we lie still.

"He was so beautiful. It hurts me to think of his body broken. You know, my dear, I sometimes imagine him when I sing, his face, the curve of his lips, those incredible eyes. His comeliness has been an inspiration to me. As it will continue to be. Something so special about that boy . . ."

I wait in the oval living room while he splashes water on his face. When he rejoins me he's wearing a dark silk dressing gown and monogrammed slippers, carrying a bottle of chilled champagne.

"A toast to his memory?"

I nod. He wraps the bottle in a napkin, pops the cork and pours us each a glass.

"Dear Tim, wherever you are, may you always have good cheer."

He clicks his glass against mine, then drains it off.

"I'm a not especially attractive fifty-eight-year-old man," he confesses. "Nevertheless, I like to think he held me in some esteem. Oh, I paid him for his services and we played all kinds of nasty games. I would grovel before him, beseech him to hurt me." He laughs. "He often did. But still there was something deep between us, something money can't buy." He refills his glass. "Intimacy, my dear. You see, in my foolish self-indulgent life I've lain with many boys, but with very few have I felt such trust."

I like listening to him. He is, I understand, a world-class singer renowned as much for his dramatic abilities as for the warm, sonorous timbre of his voice. To listen to him is to harken to him, for his voice is like a magnet.

He tells me he is on the road nearly the whole year long, fulfilling engagements in opera houses around the world. In each city he has a favorite hotel, usually a favorite suite, and in most a favorite boy he has selected after numerous tryouts and escapades.

"In Milano there's Roberto. In Paris . . . Jean-Louis. Hans in Vienna, Roger in London, Dick in New York. But the one I loved best was my beloved Tim, he of the green eyes and what I call the ephebe's girdle. He had such a slim hard pale hairless body, you know—such a big heart, such a tender touch. . . ."

Ephebe: the Greek word for adolescent male, the very word I used to describe Tim to myself. Hearing Jerome employ it, I share with him my conception of Tim as a gentle warrior of the city, perhaps doomed to being a sacrificial victim of its lust.

He loves my concept. It appeals, he tells me, to his Wagnerian taste for mysticism, melodrama, archetypes. Within half an hour he finishes off the rest of the champagne, then retreats to his sanctum sanctorum to fetch another bottle from the minibar.

"So you met Amoretto?" I ask when he returns.

He raises his eyebrows, grins fiendishly. "I did indeed!"

"She, Tim and you . . . ?"

"Yes, my dear, and, if you'll allow me, the word for what we did is . . . *partouze*. Oh, I know—on the vulgar street they call it a 'sandwich,' in the suburbs a 'threesome.' The mathematical types, I believe, say 'three-way.' I much prefer the French word. Listen to it again: *Par-touze* . . ." He enunciates slowly, drawing out each syllable. "Delicious the way it almost imitates the slippery sucky sounds one makes. So delightful, wicked, sinfully carnal and hedonistic." He burps. "Actually, I rather enjoyed the ordeal—which is not to say I'd want to partake again."

"It was Tim's idea?"

"Oh yes! Innocent little me—I would *never* have thought of *that!*" He grins, a mock expression of lechery. "He said he had this twin, which made me very excited. Then he mentioned the twin was a she, which caused a certain deflation, shall we say. But when I finally saw them together, how much alike they looked, and discovered how incredibly kinky she was . . . well, all I can tell you is that afterward I knew I'd had an—experience."

"And the two of them—with each other—?"

"That, my dear, was the best part! Brother and sister! Like Tristan and Isolde. The depravity of it! The absolutely scrumptious degenerate depravity!" He scowls. "Cost me a damn fortune too. A scene like that, you know, doesn't come cheap."

Jerome, intoxicated, is growing woozy, and I'm feeling hurt, for the dumbest reason too. I've discovered that Tim and Ariane did little numbers together for pay, and it pains me that in his copious confessions Tim never said a word. But then, I think, how could he? How would he have broached it? Perhaps he felt that such a confidence would cost him my respect. If so, how wrong he was. I would have loved him all the better for his openness.

I help Jerome to his bed, where he sprawls upon his

back. In the process his dressing gown slips open to reveal flaccid genitalia between pale hairy thighs. Immediately he begins to snore. Nothing musical about him now. I glance at his bureau, where I notice the score for *Tannhäuser*, a lavish gold wristwatch, a fine leather breast-pocket wallet, assorted coins and ten fresh new one-hundred-dollar bills perfectly aligned. This money, I assume, was intended for Tim in return for a night of delicious violation. Ah, well . . . Soon, I expect, Jerome will find himself a new companion here.

I tiptoe out, close the door, descend the curving stairs. At the reception desk, Snooty wide-eyes me as I pass.

"Lovely time with Mr. T.?" he snickers.

Perhaps he expects a tip. I walk by him without breaking my stride.

"Goodnight, *Carlo,*" he sneers.

I sleep poorly. Is it because I'm afraid of another invasion? I think rather it's because Sasha's on duty and cannot be here with me tonight.

The time's coming, I know, when I must sort out my feelings for him. Unfair, I know, to allow him to love me so earnestly without giving him something substantial in return. When we first started going out, I viewed him as a terrific companion with whom to share laughs, good talk, great meals, great sex. Then, somewhere along the line, my feelings began to change. Now I see him in a deeper way. Yes, I believe I could love him. So why didn't I tell him so at Eden Roc?

In the middle of the night I get out of bed, go to the living room, unpack my new telescope, set it up on the old tripod and aim it at the Judge's terrace across the way.

No lights on over there. It's far too late. He always retires early on weekday nights. Still, I use it to explore his terrace, the pots of geraniums, the porch furniture, the three-legged grill on which we used to cook, the round table and tightly woven straw cafe chairs where we sat when we ate outdoors.

I recall a birthday dinner I prepared for him, a ragout of lobster tails and a simple salad accompanied by my father's bread. Champagne. A tiny cake I bought at an Italian sweets shop in North Beach. One candle only to represent the day . . . but, lest we forget, fifty-four silver stars I picked up at a paper store enclosed with my birthday letter so that they spilled upon him when he opened it up.

Stardust, he called those fluttering glittering stars. And then he kissed me. That was the last birthday we celebrated. I think I knew then that though I loved him with all my heart, he merely enjoyed my company . . . and the pain of that revelation is with me still. He's fifty-six now. It's been nearly two years since we've spoken or met. I've seen him, of course, quite a few times—from here through a lens, with his friends, a new lover or two, or just lying in his swimsuit on his chaise on a Sunday afternoon, taking the sun while reading a brief.

They say that those who are abused become abusers in turn, that those upon whom suffering is inflicted will inevitably inflict it upon another even to a greater degree. This, I'm told, is a basic tenet of psychology—that we will do unto others as they have done unto us. Now, standing here spying on the Judge's empty terrace, I take no pleasure in the notion that Sasha may be harboring a love for me which, in his mind at least, I do not return.

I spend most of the morning working in the darkroom, then go out a little after eleven with my pack of mug shots to the bench in Sterling Park.

Again Drake keeps me waiting. Perhaps he's testing my patience, hoping I'll give up and leave. Undoubtedly he's watching me; to watch is his profession. But though he loves me in his strange way and sees himself as my protector, identifying my violators frightens him too much.

Sympathy enables me to wait him out. While I do I

imagine the silent war raging in his head: his every anti-
social instinct telling him not to get involved, while his
voyeur's love demands he do the gallant thing. Which
side will win, the self-sufficient hermit or the lovesick
knight? By remaining on the bench, I force the issue. He
must come to me or quit this park, his home.

Finally he shows up. The noon church bells have rung,
a distant work whistle has sounded . . . and he must see
by the still way I sit that I will stay here if necessary the
entire day.

"Kay."

His whisper startles me, seeming to issue from behind
my back. Drake has the ability of a Native American
tracker to emerge silently from the woods. He can, I believe, stand within yards of people without them even sus-
pecting that he's there.

"Drake." I softly pat the seat beside me. But just as
before, he perches at the far end of the bench.

"Sorry I'm late," he says. "I've been nervous."

"I understand." One of his feet, crossed over the other,
is shaking. "I brought the pictures," I tell him, "but you
don't have to look at them. Your choice."

"I want to help you," he says. "I'm scared, that's all."

"I promise you'll never have to talk to the cops, or
testify in court, or attend a police lineup, or do anything
beyond telling me honestly what you know."

I turn to him in time to catch his nod. How fragile he
is, I think. Perhaps he suffers from some mild form of
autism, not so serious as to warrant being hospitalized,
but painful enough so that encounters of any sort fill him
with severe anxiety, even dread.

"Are you ready or should we put it off? I can come
back later if you want."

"Let's do it now."

I nod, set my little stack of mug shots facedown between us on the bench. "What I'd like you to do, Drake,
is pick up the pack, turn it over and slowly look at each
picture in turn. If you recognize any of the three men you
saw that night, set those pictures aside. But look at them

all. You might not recognize any, or perhaps just one. That's fine. Don't try and please me—just tell the truth.''

With interpersonal skills like these, I think, I should have become a cop. Except I'm not sure I've been all that skillful, until Drake finally picks the photos up. Then I recall how in my adolescence I actually toyed with the notion of law enforcement work. Dad told me gently I could do many things in life, but, being color-blind, not that.

I decide not to watch Drake as he examines the faces, believing the less pressure I exert, the more conscientiously he'll perform. Instead I listen to the sounds of the park—the thunk of tennis balls on the courts above, singing birds, whispering grasses, the wind fluttering the leaves. The sound of the city is present too—muffled traffic, the faint ring and clatter of the Hyde Street cable car a block away, muted sounds from off the water, a special blend I've heard nowhere else. Every city, I believe, has its din. The din of San Francisco is music to my ears.

It's a quirky town of alleys, stairways, culs-de-sac, funny little houses clinging to the sides of hills, some built on stilts. Gulls wheel above the Embarcadero. Ferries crisscross the Bay churning trails of wake. Someone once said that this is a city that looks as if it were built by gods. In fact it was built by innumerable eccentrics, which accounts for its special combination of grandeur and charm.

''Kay.''

I turn back to Drake. The pack of photos is just where I left it on the bench. He is staring out, as he did the other day, across the gravel park path toward the pines.

Seeing that he has set no photos aside, I feel deflated. Either none of my suspects is guilty or Drake is incapable of singling them out.

''Hungry?'' I ask. ''Want me to get you some food?''

He turns to me. ''Aren't you going to ask?''

''What?''

''Did I see them?''

''Did you, Drake?'' I ask softly.

He nods. "All three. You'll find their pictures on the bottom."

He stands as I reach for the photos. I pick the pack up, turn it over, and at that moment he slips away. Suddenly I'm alone and he's gone . . . like a phantom who was never here.

Thirteen

Knob and his acolytes: the photos Drake pulled do not surprise me. Yet ambushing me at night in the park is one thing; not that hard to get away with. But breaking into and vandalizing my apartment—whatever possessed them to take such a risk?

As I walk home I think the matter over. It couldn't be our little run-in at The Werewolf; that was street stuff, bluster. Which brings me back to my theory they were paid to do it. Considering that both their attacks occurred after my confrontation with Crane and my rebuff of Sarah Lashaw, I return to the notion that Crane and Lashaw ordered me hit.

Fine! At least now I know whom I'm dealing with. And I'm prepared to take this escalation as proof Crane's got something serious to hide. Knob's a street hustler, the acolytes are punks, but Marcus Crane is acting like a man in trouble . . . and I must doubt that his fear of me is over a few fuzzy photographs showing him soliciting on the Gulch.

Entering my building, I glance at the security video camera. The lens is small but it gives me comfort. Upstairs, when I turn my key in my new lock, there's a sweet sound as the bolt is thrown. I shut the door behind me and disarm the alarm. If I fail to do so within fifteen seconds, a siren will start to shriek.

I go immediately to my darkroom, pull negatives of the shots I took of Crane in front of his house, print up the whole series on eight-by-ten paper, squeegee the prints, pin them up and look closely at his face.

Is this the face of a killer? Perhaps in the final shot. But is it also the face of a man who could cut his victim into pieces in Wildcat Canyon, paint up the torso, then haul the head and limbs back downtown?

I have doubts. Crane's too suave, his car's too nice; he's not the type to sully himself. Sure, he'd plunder a person's body, use him without qualm—but would he take pleasure in the blood, eroticize the butchery? I don't think so. Still, I must not forget, he is my enemy.

Joel calls. He's been phoning around trying to locate the four cops.

"We can't see Hayes—he's been dead five years. Classic gun-in-the-mouth cop suicide."

Even as I wince, I understand Joel has forgotten about my mother.

"Waincroft," he continues. "lives down in Santa Cruz. Night watchman at the pier amusement park. I finally got hold of him. Sounded like he does a lot of drinking. Says he wants to think it over before submitting to an interview."

From cop sergeant to night watchman—what a fall!

"Puccio's another story. You know Giordano's in North Beach?"

"Pizza and pasta joint. Great calamari salad."

"It's his mom's place. He's the maitre d'. Invited us over tomorrow for a late lunch after the crowd thins out."

"What about Vasquez?"

"Since he's still a cop, his interview'll have to be cleared through S.F.P.D. Public Affairs."

I tell Joel about the break-in, Drake's ID of the perps,

my hunch that Knob and his boys are working for Crane.

"I'm worried about you, kiddo."

"I can take care of myself."

"Maybe . . . but admit it, so far you haven't done too good a job."

He's right, which pisses me off. "So tell me, Joel—what would *you* do if three guys jumped you, then broke into your house?"

"Well," he says, "I guess I'd put in a new lock, then sign up for a martial arts class."

I print up my shots of Knob and his flunkies on polycontrast, quick-dry them with my hair dryer, place them in an envelope with my eight-by-tens of Crane, walk down to Marina Aikido, take a class and shower. Afterward I use the pay phone to call Maddy. She says it's okay to come over, so I walk on to her place on Alhambra.

She looks particularly fragile today, but I know better than to inquire after her health. Still I'm touched when, in the hallway, she takes hold of my arm. After we're seated on her couch, I notice the translucence of her skin, the thinness of her wrists, the delicacy of the cords that protrude from her neck. Her eyes, on the other hand, are sharp as ever.

"You look good, Kay," she says, "strong, confident. But you've been having trouble."

How well she knows me.

"That's why I've come."

She glances at my envelope. I open it, pull the photos, spread them out. "Not proof sheets this time, just prints."

Unlike other teachers I've had, slop prints don't bother Maddy. Technical stuff, she knows, can be taught by anyone. She concerns herself with how her students see.

"These are grab shots of hostile models," she says. "A couple are very good. This one"—she picks up the shot I took of Knob and his boys at The Werewolf, "and this"—she chooses the last in my series on Crane, the one in which he appears about to break. "But you've done a lot of work like this, Kay. You've learned how and you do it well. You shoot them straight and refuse to flinch." She looks at me, questioning. "But you didn't come to hear that. There's something else."

I ask her if she'll look closely at the pictures and tell me what they say to her about the people.

"I know this isn't what you usually do, Maddy, but you're so perceptive . . . and I need some good advice."

She waves her hand to shush me, resumes studying the prints. I watch her as she peers at their faces. I wonder why I have come to her for this when I could have easily shown the shots to Rita Reese. Rita is also shrewd about people; she could tell me whether Knob and Crane are truly dangerous. But Maddy is the only person I know who has come to her understanding of the world through black-and-white photography.

"This man"—she is studying my Crane series—"at first he doesn't know what to make of you. You confuse him, threaten him. He's accustomed to masking himself and at first he does it well. Quickly he comes to hate you. I'm sorry to tell you—his hate goes deep. It fills him. He is a man who can hate easily. Beneath his mask, you see, he's a man who hates himself."

She turns to me, shows her most sibylline smile. "Yes, your pictures are like stories." She pats me on the knee. "Proof of their power." She picks up the shots of Knob. "Not much here. He buys, sells, trades. One of your hustlers, I suppose, though there's something that separates him from others you've shown me. He's older, harder, tougher. He's got a vicious streak."

She picks up the Werewolf shot. "Here he looks different. He wants to show you his scorn, but, like the first man, he's afraid." She looks at me. "You know how, after we hurt people, we study them closely to see how deeply we have cut?" She taps her forefinger against Knob's face. "That's how he's looking at you here. But he doesn't find what he wants. Instead he sees strength— which surprises and awes him. Yes, he's afraid of you, Kay. And he will hurt you again if he can."

I feel sweat break out in my armpits.

"The two with him?" I ask.

"Kids."

"So you don't think they're bad?"

"Only in a gang. Then they'd pile on. But alone"—
she shakes her head—"they're cowards."

The sky is dark by the time I reach the Hampshire Arms.
The grunge on its granite facade is lost in shadow. The
same lackadaisical gum-chewing kid with bad skin is sitting behind the desk. He's the opposite of Snooty at The
Sultan's Tent. There they guard their guests; here they
regard them as whores and all their visitors as johns.

Doreen's in, Alyson's out. Doreen invites me up, but,
as usual, begs me first to walk around the block while she
cleans up. When finally I present myself the room is, also
as usual, *not* cleaned up, and redolent with booze.

Doreen sits at the dresser in a camisole applying eye
makeup. I notice a tightly curled jockstrap at her feet.

"Hey, Bug!" She pecks my cheek, then lightly strokes
my arm. "Great biceps, dearie. Get some tats, spike up
your hair, pierce your brows, go punk."

I sit on the bed, watch her skillful moves as she wields
her eyelash brush.

"Business is off. Soon the holidays'll come, then the
short cold days of winter. What I need now is a new john,
dearie—someone handsome and flush who'll take me to
Hawaii."

"I hope you find him, Doreen."

"Don't know." She shrugs. "Either I'm losing my
looks, or the pickin's are gittin' slim."

I show her my Werewolf photograph.

"Yeah, Knob and his flunkies. They don't look
pleased."

She turns back to the mirror.

"The flunkies—do they have names?"

"Price and Pride. Frick and Frack." She shrugs. "One

on the right's Tommy, one on the left—they call him Boat.''

"Boat?''

"Uh-huh.'' Doreen draws her eyebrows with an economy of motion that would do any girl proud. "I once asked him about that. He said his given name is Bato, which means something like 'Hey, kid!' in Serbo-Croat. His family lived in France, and the kids there starting calling him *Bateau*. Later, when he moved to the States, that got translated into Boat.''

"How old is he?''

"Fifteen tops. Jailbait. Tough on the outside, mushy as caramel underneath. It's that sweet candy part, dearie, that they like. Ass skin soft as a baby's, the puniest patch of body hair and cock hard as a spike.''

"Knob and his flunkies—what's the deal there?''

"Come on! You know! He rents them out, high prices too. Ever notice how he protects them, barely lets them out of his sight? He's their mom, they're his pussies . . . and come to think of it, the most valuable commodity on the Gulch.''

She finishes up her eyes, turns to face me, cocks her head. "Why so interested, dearie?''

"The three of them beat me up. And that's not the half of it.'' I tell her about the break-in, the things they wrote on my walls. The sexual insults shock her.

"Positive they did all that?''

"I've got a witness.''

"What're you going to do?''

"Still thinking about it.''

"Want some advice?''

I shrug.

"Leave it alone, Bug. Whatever hard feelings Knob had toward you, they're over now that he's put you down. But raise the stakes and he could do you serious harm. There're rumors about him, dearie—and none of them are nice.''

I thank her for her counsel, but don't commit either

way. In fact, I have a plan, but need more information before deciding whether it'll work.

"Tommy and Boat—any difference between them?"

"One's got lighter hair, but that's not what you mean." Doreen ponders. "Boat's softer than Tommy, more naive. Tommy's more your smartass type, Boat's more your runaway kid."

"Thanks, Doreen."

She looks into my eyes. "Think about what Mama told you, dearie—don't mess with Knob. He's the kind who'll squirt you with lighter fluid, toss in a match, watch you burn, lick his lips and walk off whistling a merry tune."

Knowing my new hotel-quality mattress has arrived, Sasha comes to me at midnight with a bouquet of irises, pocketful of ace bandages, twinkle in his liquid eyes and devilish plan.

Lovingly he ties my wrists to the bedposts, spreads my thighs, ties them back to the handles of the box spring, then produces a feather with which he tickles my parts. I giggle and squirm, thrash and laugh, my nipples swell, I go creamy until all I can think of in this rapture is requital.

"Please, please, please . . ." I moan.

But sweet dark Sasha enjoys inflicting pleasure. I writhe until I reach a point beyond endurance. Finally my lover comes upon me to deliver me from desire. I cry out, tremble, give myself up. I want to draw out every quantum of his passion, employ him to help me mount crest after crest of pleasure. And so I do until at last I arch, then fall back released.

It takes a long time for the vibrato in me to subside. Meantime Sasha, who smells as usual of sandalwood, whispers to me the erotic secrets of multiarmed Hindu deities and their consorts, fleshly means, he promises, we will use to join together and pierce our earthly prison.

"Insights! Revelations! Orgasms like bolts of lightning!"

"Sounds great," I tell him, burying my face in his

shoulder. "I'm crazy about you. You know that, don't you?"

I feel him quiver with delight.

Then, as an afterthought: "Next time, Doctor, I'm tying *you!*"

They have a wood-fired oven at Giordano's, the kind that fills the restaurant with an aroma of woodsmoke and baking pizza crust. The walls here bear a sooty patina, there are plain wood tables, creaky old chairs, a long bar frequented by local characters and an array of framed and inscribed photographs of movie stars and famous figures from the worlds of sports and California politics.

Joel and I are sitting with Enrico ("Call me Ricky") Puccio in the proprietor's booth opposite the cash register near the door. From here Ricky can greet his friends as they pass in and out. He's a short, stout, balding guy in his fifties, dressed in dark trousers, white shirt with French cuffs, and flamboyant tie. He doesn't look like an ex-cop, rather like what he is—an ebullient, happy, hospitable host at a very busy dining spot, adept at greeting guests.

I glance around. Though it's past two-thirty, most of the tables still are filled—tourists, people from the financial district, local store owners, North Beach regulars. There's a plate of olives in olive oil on every table, a basket of bread sticks and a bottle of wine from the Giordano family winery. The pastas and calamari salad here are famous. Another house specialty is the antipasto plate of fresh mozzarella with tomatoes, basil and roasted red pepper. But in the end it's the pizza that brings them in—the best pizza in town.

Ricky has stood to shake hands with a man I recognize, a lawyer friend of the Judge. When he rejoins us, he apologizes.

"Room'll clear out soon. Now eat and drink. When things settle down, we'll talk."

This suits me. I'm dying of hunger. But Joel is unhappy. He likes focused interviews. Today he's at the mercy of an extrovert.

I recall the evaluation of Puccio in the confidential Internal Affairs report: "Sloppiest of the bunch, apparently ignorant of police norms and procedures." *Well,* I think, *Ricky may have acted sloppy and dumb back then, but he runs a sharp operation now.*

Shortly after three, he joins us in a buoyant mood. I switch on my tape recorder.

"What can I tell you, guys?" he asks. Then, before Joel can reply, he touches my arm. "Give my best regards to your pop, Kay. Tell him to come in sometime and that his money's no good here. Tell him I like to feed old pals."

"As I told you," Joel says, "we're doing a piece on the T case. And that, of course, includes Sipple."

Ricky stares at Joel, then pops up, this time to speak to an elderly woman in the back.

Joel shakes his head. "He doesn't want to talk."

"Why's he seeing us?"

"Wants us to like him."

"Do we?"

"Not yet," Joel says.

Ricky returns scratching his head. "Sipple, Sipple—oh, yeah!" He beams. "Nearly forgot about that. Now why'd you bring it up? There's good things in this life like weddings and graduations, and there's crap like Sipple you want to forget happened. Know what I mean?"

But soon we get to it. Ricky's too loquacious, can't abide the silence that follows. So he starts off on a riff accompanied by an array of gestures and expressions sufficient to mime his feelings to the world.

"They called us buffoons! Know what that means to an Italian? Got any friggin' idea? Clowns, fools—it's what we yell at the politicians when they march them off to jail for graft. So don't be so sure we were all that stupid. Maybe we weren't stupid at all." Again Ricky touches my arm. "You know your pop, Kay. You know how smart he is. If he was stupid that night, then that was about the only time he was—right?'' He shakes his head vigorously. ''Maybe we were a few good cops doing a dirty job best we could.'' He shows a secretive grin. ''Maybe there was a lot more that happened back then than met the eye. . . .''

He doesn't tell us what that might have been. Rather he retells the story we already know, but from an outsider's point of view. All the while, there's a look of complicity in his eyes that implies we share a secret about the matter, which, by mutual consent, none of us will broach.

''Now let's take a look at who was there that night, all right? I'm talking about the sworn officers, no one else.''

Ricky takes a lick at his thumb, sticks it up.

''First we got Wainy Waincroft, straight-arrow sergeant, last of the true blue-flame believers. You don't make sarge being an asshole, least not in good old S.F.P.D. Sure, old Wainy had a temper, he could knock a guy around it came to that. Busted a few heads in his time, no doubt of it. Not a college man, no . . . but few in those times were. Ragged around the edges—you betcha! But stupid?'' Ricky shakes his head. ''I never heard anyone call Wainy stupid, not until Hale, that is.''

He prongs his forefinger.

''Next you got Billy Hayes. Squirrelish little guy, eyes like a rodent, but shiny, hear what I'm saying? Shiny little eyes, not dull. Billy was a boxer. Did you know? Was City Golden Gloves finalist in the bantamweight division, thought about turning pro, went into the cops instead. Boxed for us awhile as a welterweight. Was Potrero Station champ a couple years. Coached kids in the Activities League and they loved him for it. Sweetest little guy, Billy. Best hand-eye coordination you ever saw. He could pack one helluva wallop. So was he dumb?'' Ricky shrugs. ''Good clean record. Never lost any evidence, made his share of collars, but then boxers act like dummies sometimes, all that bobbin' and weavin', you know—all those punches to the head. Softens up your brain, they say, though funny no one ever noticed any softening in Billy till Inspector Jonathan Topper Hale—let's call him

'Halo' since that's what he puts around his head!—yeah, not till the old Halo himself brought it up.''

Ricky sticks up his middle finger.

"Jack Farrow. Truly kingly man. Worked bunko five, six years in Chinatown with Rusty Quinn, made more collars there than the Chink cops worked with 'em. Learned the lingo, built up a network, ended up with an army of deep throats up Stockton, down Grant. You didn't mess with old Jack. Sweet guy, but not one to take any crap. They say he could swing a nightstick good as anyone in Central. Course when they transferred him to Park Station, maybe he turned slow and dumb. Funny thing though—no one I ever spoke to noticed it.''

His ring finger rises.

"Me? Better let someone else tell you. My ma, the old stove out back—she taught me never toot my own horn.''

Ricky raises his pinky.

"Which leaves us with Louie Vasquez, number five. Kind of odd man out his being Hispanic and the way he approached the job. Now the squawk on Louie was that he acted real bright, going to college at night, betterin' himself, all spit and polish, shoes shined like mirrors. But the deeper squawk, the locker room skinny, was that Louie was an intriguer. Not too big on swingin' the stick, not Louie. More the gabby type. Yak, yak, yak. But when the shit hit the fan, they said, old Louie, he was more 'n likely to take off on those bright shiny shoes of his.''

Ricky places his hand flat down on the table, fingers spread as far as they will go. His nails, I note, are beautifully groomed, but his hand is quivering, the knuckles losing color as he presses down hard with his palm.

"Five guys,'' Ricky says, "Wainy, Billy, Jack, Ricky and Louie—and suddenly they all go stupid. Find important evidence in a capital case but don't recognize it as such. Lose said evidence because no one takes care to follow S.O.P. Five guys, competent guys, tankin' on the job. But funny, isn't it, that those five, all bright enough, all with good records, suddenly go flat all together. Like there's this contagious disease, know what I mean? This disease that strikes them all at once. And suddenly they're—what?—bunglers, screwups, buffoons. Yeah, I *do* think it's funny. Matter of fact, I wake up sometimes middle of the night and laugh so hard my wife gets mad. 'You dreamin' comedy again, Ricky?' she steams, kicking me in the shins. 'Shut up, *paesan'*, you'll wake Ma and the kids.' But it's still so friggin' funny I gotta bury my head in the pillow to stifle the guffaws.''

Joel and I sit gaping. The riff is finished. Ricky, knowing his performance has been splendid, rises in the manner of a grand seigneur. "Scuse me now, guys. Gotta consult with Ma out back. Your lunch is on the house. No tips neither. Your money's no good here—least not today!''

Later, outside on busy Columbus Avenue, I turn to Joel.

"Do you like him better now?"

"Actually, I do," Joel says. "He's got a way about him. The way he talks—it warms you up."

I walk through the labyrinth of narrow lanes that adjoin the financial district, short little streets lined with old low brick buildings which now house galleries and antique stores, specialty book shops, elegant architects' and attorneys' offices. Jackson Square, Gold Street, Balance, Hotaling, Gibb, Ils Lane—the core of what's left of the once-infamous Barbary Coast.

The late-afternoon light down here is sweet, shadows are long, you can hear your footsteps as they ring off the cobblestones. I wander here as I allow Ricky's words to float through my head, seeking to net some secret from the depths . . . a secret which floats so close I almost feel I can touch it, but which always, just as it comes within my grasp, slips elusively away.

I find myself thinking a lot about Ariane Lovsey. From what I've discovered, this woman is so powerful and strange as to make the other players I've met in this pursuit seem but ordinary folk. David deGeoffroy, Jonathan

Topper Hale, Jerome Tattinger, Sarah Lashaw—I've met vivid personalities, all bigger than life, spoken with them, entered their orbits. But the one who exerts the strongest force field is Ariane, Amoretto, the one I've never seen.

I'm spending nearly all my time in the darkroom now, printing out my negatives, assembling my pictures into some sort of visual order. Perhaps, I think, in the rarefied details of the photographs—the shadows, backgrounds, the very grain of the film—I will discover the hidden pattern that I seek.

I've always loved darkroom work, working with my minimalist palette of blacks and whites. I feel safe here, protected by the solid walls and door, eyes comfortable in the gloom where my vision is at its best. So much easier to work in dim confined space with paper, film and chemicals than to go outdoors with a camera and confront the inconsistencies of natural light. And, I know, cowardly too. It was Maddy who three years ago told me to get out and walk the streets:

"You want to photograph people, Kay? Go out and smell them. Get that close. Smell developer and acetic acid and you'll stay a studio photographer. Smell people and you'll start becoming a photojournalist."

Finally, midafternoon, three days after our lunch with Ricky, Joel calls to rescue me from my cell.

"We're going down to Santa Cruz. Waincroft's agreed to talk."

We take Route 1 along the coast; it's the slow way, but it's beautiful and will give us time to unwind and talk. We pass the seal rock beaches, turn south, and a little north of San Pedro Point pass some serious surfers riding awesome waves.

After Half Moon Bay there's barely any traffic, just

miles of empty road running along the coast, rocky portions alternating with state beaches named for the creeks that run down to them from the hills. There's heavy fog here, the road snakes and I feel good sitting next to Joel, breathing the thick salty darkening air. Better, I think, to chug along with him in Melvin than to recline against the butter-soft seats in the back of Sarah Lashaw's chauffeured limo.

"I haven't spoken to a soul since we lunched with Ricky," I tell him. "Thanks for rescuing me. I've been talking to myself."

"Not a bad person to talk with," Joel says. "Any thoughts on that lunch?"

"His five-finger exercise—it haunts me still."

"Join the club."

"He must've told us something. By any chance, did you figure out what?"

Joel shakes his head. "It was more of a mood thing, like they were all smart guys, suddenly they all went slack and that's really funny except it isn't. But I keep thinking there's another level."

"Me too."

What I don't tell him is that the real reason I locked myself in my darkroom for three full days was so I wouldn't run over to City Stone Ground, corner Dad and try to coax out an explanation.

The Santa Cruz Beach Boardwalk is the last beachside amusement park in California. Tattered, tacky, tawdry but proud, it clings to the water, attracting kids and old folks nostalgic for those pre-Disney days when a rollercoaster, carny music and cotton candy were all you needed to instill the blend of forced humor and melancholy summed up in the hollow word "amusement."

In my Art Institute days I did my share of picture taking here, roaming the boardwalk on weekends, catching images of the last hippies as they lurched, stoned, beneath signs depicting clowns with riotous smiles. Easy juxtapositions, art school stuff, but that was a time when nearly everything I saw through the viewfinder caught my eye. Busted windows, abandoned gas station pumps, feral street cats, overflowing trash barrels beneath thrashing palms—I would show Californians what they passed every day but didn't see, filtered through the fine artist's prism of my eye.

I soon got over it, learned the difference between picture taking and photography. Still, I know, sometimes an amateur will catch an image by accident so strong a pro could shoot a hundred rolls and still not equal it. Whenever I see a photograph like that I wonder again about what I'm doing. Which is why I need Maddy to coach me and keep me on my path.

Joel and I are standing outside a run-down Paddy bar called The Brogue two blocks back from the boardwalk on a street lined with raunchy motels. The gaunt and haggard man standing before us does not resemble the Lucius D. Waincroft I've been expecting. Time, I know, always takes its toll; Hale, I recall, looked far different than in his photographs. But the face of the Wainy now facing us is totally unlike the proud, stubborn sergeant's face that appeared in the row of mug shot photos published in the *Chronicle* under the headline "BUFFOONS." This man has rotten teeth, unshaven cheeks, burst capillaries streaking his nose. His eyes are milky, the left one twitching as he leers. When he bends toward me, I want to turn my back; instead I bow my head, forcing him to plant his kiss upon my hair.

"Do ye not know me, Kay? What a fine woman you've become!" His breath reeks of cheap booze and rum-soaked cigars. But now those milky eyes are filled with merriment. "Remember Uncle Wainy? I've known ye since you were a wee girl."

I have only the vaguest memory of him from childhood, being presented to him by Dad at cop picnics and sporting events. We used to attend those kinds of affairs before my mother turned agoraphobic, the first step in the decline that culminated in her suicide.

He studies me. "You've got your ma's sweet eyes, Kay. You truly do. Fine gal, Carlotta. I miss her . . . as I'm sure Jack and you must do. Most likely you think of her every day." He chucks my chin. "You've become an artist, I hear."

"Photographer."

"Yeah, sure, but that's an artist too, I understand."

As he turns to Joel the neon sign of The Brogue casts a shaft of light across his face—red light, I assume, though to me it appears as a glowing black bar. A dark uniform with some sort of security service patch on the shoulders hangs upon Wainy's emaciated frame.

I step back to take his picture. He poses grandly, Napoleon style, hand thrust deep inside his shirt. A heavy gun belt from which dangle the tools of his trade—field radio, flashlight, nightstick, holstered automatic—droops below his waist.

Flash!Whap! I catch an image: The Ruined Cop.

"Five of seven," he says, "time to go to work. Hope the two of you don't mind walking along with me. That way we can talk while I do my job."

As he leads us down to the waterfront, he explains that after Labor Day the amusement park is closed except on weekends. But that doesn't stop all sorts of riffraff from trying to force their way in from the beach.

At the gate he introduces us to another uniformed guard.

"Just going to show these young people the place, you don't mind, Mac," Wainy says.

The gatekeeper shrugs. We pass through the office, Wainy pulls his card, sticks it into a time clock, returns it to its slot, picks up his watchman's key, clips it to a chain attached to his belt, then motions us out to the kennel area, where he attaches a leash to the collar of an elderly black rottweiler, whom, he tells us cheerily, the guards have nicknamed Crud.

"Come on, Crudder. Come on, boy," he addresses the

creature in a singsong. "Another night, another dollar, doggie—off to make our rounds. . . ."

Soon we're walking along a spooky row of shuttered booths, dimly lit by occasional security lamps and the glow of street-lights beyond the fence. In season the booths here, faded signs tell me, offer soda, burritos, franks and taffy, or provide places where you can win a Kewpie by virtue of your marksmanship or by defeating an expert at guessing your weight and age. There are booths that sell horror masks, magic tricks, poopoo pillows, where you can be photographed beside cardboard cutouts of Bogie, Elvis, Marilyn, Reagan or the Pope. But tonight everything's closed down, the only sounds in this night-scape Crud's panting and the echoes of our steps upon the wooden walk.

"Hale! Seen him, have you?" Wainy hoots, his chuckles resounding along the corridor of shuttered shacks. "He came down a few times. Asked me to open up. Ha! I wouldn't say a word, sent him packing. Last time he begged me. 'Please, Wainy, *pleeeeease.*' Didn't mind seeing him grovel, I tell you. 'No,' I said, 'I'd rather die a ghastly death than tell *you* anything, you no-good bastard son of a bitch.' That was about a year ago. I think he got the idea. Hasn't been back any rate."

"What did he think you could tell him?" Joel asks.

"Where we stashed the evidence—what else?"

"*Did* you stash it?"

"Ha! That's what Hale thinks. Got a bug up his arse. Bug's been nibbling at his 'rhoids since the day it happened. Hated me 'cause I wouldn't take a polygraph. 'Now why should I take it?' I asked him. My lawyer told me: 'Don't even think about it, Wainy. They're going to bounce you out, let 'em. But don't give 'em ammo they can use to shoot you down.' Good advice, so I hushed up, never told 'em a thing. Then they tried to take my pension. Was in and out of court five years over that. Case was settled in the end, though not so well for me. Which is why I'm doing this damn job here. Isn't half bad actually. Pays for the booze and smokes at least."

He yanks on the leash. "Dammit, Crudder! Stop scamperin', you stupid mutt!"

But Crud, though old and overweight, pulls Wainy along faster than he wants to walk, forcing him to angle back like a thin man marching in the face of a ferocious wind.

"These hounds're damn near useless," he says. "Still the company insists we use 'em. They think big black dogs scare off invaders. Theory is kids who try and get in here from the beach side will hear the dogs and think twice. Ratfuck! Kids don't give a damn. They're wearin' wet suits anyway. They just stick some sleeping potion in hot dogs, throw them at the mutts, the mutts gobble them, next thing you know they're lyin' on their backs snorin' like there's no tomorrow."

The sight of Wainy trying to control Crud inspires me to take another picture. I step away to catch him in profile tilted backward as he fights the irresistible canine force.

"Poor Billy!" Wainy exclaims over the suicide of Billy Hayes. "After the cops he tried all kinds of work. Not like your pop, Kay—who could always make one helluva loaf. Billy didn't know nothin' 'cept boxing and law enforcement. He took up coachin', tried to develop a couple kids, but soon as he'd find a prospect some sweet-talkin' manager'd steal the kid from under his nose. So old Billy finally threw it in. Won't say I haven't thought occasionally of doing the same. Only reason I haven't is . . . curiosity. I'm always wonderin' what's going to happen next. Never find out, will I, if I chow down my gun?"

We enter the roller-coaster perimeter. Wainy uses his watchman's key to open the gate. Inside, the wood and steel structure looms above us like the skeleton of an enormous dinosaur.

"Couple of us here the other night," Wainy says, "caught ourselves one real live intruder." His milky eyes go cold. "Crud and the other fella's dog cornered him, then we surrounded him and beat him. Bloody pulp when we got done."

Wainy hee-haws, then shows a leer that chills my blood.

Does he think Joel and I will admire him for this? Is he trying to psych us, or doesn't he give a damn? Probably the latter, I decide. He's a wasted man living in an enclosed world of booze, mean memories and the beat we're walking with him now.

"Won't be able to work much longer," he says, a propos of nothing. "Got lung cancer. Eatin' me up inside. That's why I'm so thin." He turns his head, spits. "Wainy's never been a squealer, and I ain't startin' now. So you won't get nothin' out of me, not even on my deathbed you won't."

I glance at Joel in time to see his eyes catch fire.

"You're saying there *is* something to be gotten out of you?" he asks.

Wainy lets out with a crazed laugh. "You bet there is, friend!"

"Come on, Wainy," I plead. "Tell us. Who'll be hurt by it now?"

"Your dad for one. Why don't you ask him, Kay, see what he's got to say?"

"About what?"

"What'd you think, girl? *It.* Hear me? What the hell else we talking about? What're we doing, for Christ's sake? What'd you come down here for? Not to pay your goddamn respects. I know that. You came to ask 'bout the same thing Hale, that wheedling bastard, tried to sweet-talk an answer to. *It!* Stinkin' *it.* That stupid bag of—ha! give the man a Kewpie doll, Harry!—that bag of ever-lovin' shit-eatin' fuck-all *ev-eye-dense!*"

Though Joel keeps at him, plugging him with questions, Wainy's done answering for the night. He goes silent on us, leading us back toward the security gate, mumbling something about having to feed Crud his dinner.

"I'm not used to walking these boards with visitors," he mutters.

"Saying you know where that evidence is, Wainy?" Joel asks again.

But Wainy doesn't reply. He's finished with us, can't wait to see our backs. I try and stall him by asking him to pose again. He obliges but the humor of his Napoleon stance is lacking, as is the pathos when he was being dragged forward by Crud. Now he just stands there, blank, dejected, grim.

Then I get an idea.

"Take off your shirt," I tell him.

"Kidding me, Kay?"

"Uh-uh. Strip. I want to see some skin."

He hoots, but even so strips to the waist, handing off Crud to Joel.

"Great!" I tell him, focusing. "Now put the gun belt back on. That's right, the way it was. Just let it hang there. Yeah!"

Flash!Whap!Flash!Whap!

"Now do something, Wainy! Give me a show!"

He thinks a moment, perplexed. Then he gets a notion. He starts whistling, some sort of Irish ditty, then starts moving, raising his feet, pumping his arms, hopping.

Whap!Whap!Whap!Whap!Whap! I can't believe my luck. The man's dancing an Irish jig right there in the middle of the deserted amusement park. He's got the ribs of a concentration camp survivor and the expression of a lecher, and still he high-steps, while Crud, incredulous, sits on his haunches watching his mad master dance. My motor drive hums, my flash strobes the night as I freeze him in absurd postures against the stanchions and girders behind. I shoot till he's exhausted, wheezes, coughs, finally bends forward to let the drool run free.

"How you like them beans, girl?" he demands, crouched over, expectorating onto the boardwalk.

I like them very much, I tell him. And, to myself, I give a title to what I'm sure will be a remarkable series: "Wainy's Last Hurrah."

At the gate he bids us a sweet farewell.

"Kind of you to drive down and see me," he says to Joel. They shake hands, then Wainy turns to me, looks deep into my eyes.

"You're a grand-looking gal, Kay," he says. "Carlotta's eyes too. Such lovely music she could play. Break your heart with it she could. So beautiful it was to see her fingers rise and fall, the delicate way she caressed the keys. Be well and happy, that's what I wish for ye, Kay. I do."

And with that, teary-eyed, he kisses me in the center of my forehead, then turns away.

"Come on, Crudder boy. Time to chow down, doggie."

He strolls with the big black dog back toward the kennel while we stare after him from the other side of the gate.

Joel and I barely speak on our way north, the fast way this time, the one that mounts the hills, picks up Route 280 west of San Jose, then follows the freeway up the peninsula.

"This is getting interesting, Kay. I'm thinking—maybe Hale was right."

I don't respond because I know what he means—Hale's theory that there was some kind of obstruction-of-justice conspiracy in which Dad played a part. I really don't want to think about that. For one thing it strikes me as implausible. It was Dad, after all, who suggested we talk to the other cops. Why do that if he had something to hide?

"My father's the most honest man I know," I tell Joel. "All he's interested in is baking honest loaves of bread."

"Kay!" Joel sputters. "I wasn't—didn't mean—"

But of course we both know what he meant.

"Let's talk to Vasquez," I suggest. "Then, if you still want to interview Dad, I'll set it up."

San Francisco sparkles as we approach it from the back; I always think of the front of the city as the water side. The lit towers of the financial district stand like totems against the sky. A few minutes later, as we drive past the low buildings of SoMa, a distant growl of motorcycles rends the tranquil night.

This is reality, I think, thankful to be home. Wainy's world, so dark and menacing, frightened me more than I realized.

Joel drives me up Russian Hill through residential streets. I'm glad he doesn't choose Polk or Van Ness—I need quiet now, have no desire to pass through the Gulch.

"I'll never forget the sight of that old man," Joel says, "whistling and dancing on the boards. He knows he's a goner, but still he danced till he dropped." Joel turns to me. "A dance of death, do you think?"

"Or a dance of courage."

I ask him to drop me a block from my building. After he stops the car he takes my hand.

"Are you willing to follow this all the way, Kay—no matter where the trail leads? Because if you're not, that's fine. Just say the word. If you don't want to go on, I'll understand."

I shake my head. "I'll go all the way with you, Joel. But thanks for giving me the choice."

He kisses me. I get out, cross Hyde, then saunter along the hedge looking to see if Drake is watching me from within the park.

"Kay!"

His whisper cuts to my ears. I follow the sound until I see him standing in thick foliage beside the trunk of a Monterey pine.

"Thanks for waiting up for me."

"Will the doc be coming by tonight?"

I shake my head, and as I do, note Drake's relief.

Later, upstairs, safe in my flat, staring out at the Bay, I can still feel the press of Wainy's lips upon my forehead and the power of his scrutiny as he peered into my eyes.

Joel phones at noon. I take his call in the darkroom, where I'm working up prints of Wainy dancing his jig in the night.

"I spoke to S.F.P.D. Public Affairs. There'll be no

sanctioned interviews with Vasquez on the T case or anything else.''

''His decision or theirs?''

''Both I expect.''

''What do we do now?''

''Ambush-interview him tonight when he gets home.''

By five we're set up, sitting in Melvin, on the opposite side of Valley Street from Vasquez's 1930s house. The street is lined with nice well-kept homes set side by side on small well-tended lots. The Noe Valley is known for its excellent climate, warmer and far less foggy than Russian Hill. A neighborhood of affluent young marrieds, yuppies, conservative gays, it costs plenty to buy a home here. Vasquez, who Joel tells me is married with three kids, appears to be doing well.

I'm nervous sitting here, loaded camera and micro tape recorder in my hands, scrunched up in this uncomfortable little car. Especially as time passes, the sky darkens, and there is as yet no sign of our quarry.

''What if he doesn't show?'' I ask Joel.

''We'll wait till seven. If he doesn't turn up, we'll come back in the morning, try and catch him then.''

''I'm wondering—is it really all that smart to surprise a cop? What if he thinks we're threatening him and pulls his gun?''

''I'll identify us as press right away.'' He shows me his police press pass. ''Flash this in his face.''

''And if he walks by?''

''Whatever he does he'll give us a look.''

''Which is when I'm supposed to take his picture?''

''You got it, kiddo. Now sit back, keep your powder dry.''

Still I'm worried. What can Vasquez possibly tell us in a situation like this, in full view of his neighbors, with his family hovering just behind the door? Joel says we're here to show commitment to our story, and if Vasquez gives us a ''No comment,'' to put it squarely on the record. Still I'm nervous. I wonder how Dad would handle it. If Vasquez is smart, I think, he'll smile, invite us in, offer us Cokes, tell us he's sorry but under orders not to talk, then send us home with sincere regrets. And if he isn't smart, if we unnerve him? Then, I think, God save us from his wrath.

He turns up finally, just about the time I'm thinking he won't, parks his car, a new silver Taurus, in his driveway.

Joel touches my arm. "Go get him, kiddo!"

He's out his side before I can open my door. After that I move fast, nearly tripping as I cross the street, all the while struggling to keep up with Joel and intersect with Vasquez before he reaches his front stoop.

He feels ambushed all right. He stops to peer at us, alarmed. He's blocky and tall. I understand why Hilly felt intimidated. He has a head of thick black hair, wears heavy black-rimmed glasses, stands erect like a military man on parade.

"Joel Glickman, *Bay Area News!*" Joel speaks so fast the words run together.

"You were told—no interviews."

Vasquez starts up the front steps. I focus my camera ready to catch him when he turns.

"We've already talked to Hale, Ricky, Wainy and Jack," Joel says. "Only fair you get a chance to tell your side."

Vasquez wheels, furious.

Whap! My strobe glints off his glasses.

"Bastards!" The word comes out of him in a hiss.

"What's the problem, Lieutenant? We're going to write about this whether you cooperate or not."

"You're scum! Get out!"

Whap!Whap! Got him twice more!

" 'Journalist scum.' " Joel scribbles in his notebook. "Sir, can we quote you on that?"

Vasquez squints at me. "Who're you?"

"She's—"

I wave Joel off. "Kay Farrow, Jack Farrow's daughter."

Vasquez stares hard at me, like he's photographing me with his eyes.

"Your dad ought to spank your behind," he whispers, with an intensity that makes me tremble. Then he mounts the last two steps, enters his house and slams the door.

"He's bad," I tell Joel.

We're sitting in a bar on Church Street, the nearest one to Vasquez's house. I'm still shaking from the confrontation. Joel's trying to calm me down.

"I know what he said degraded you, Kay. But put it in context. How'd *you* feel if someone stuck a flash camera in your face?"

"I'm not talking about being degraded."

"What is it then?"

"He's a bad cop."

"Come on! He's head of Felony Prostitution. How bad can he be?"

"I don't care what he's head of," I say. "I've known cops all my life. I know what they're like. He's got bad cops' eyes. Hale, Ricky and Wainy didn't. They were only nuts."

Joel spreads his hands. "I'll give it a couple days, write him a note, see if he's changed his mind about an interview."

"He won't answer. Then you'll want to talk to Dad?"

Joel meets my eyes. "Don't you think I should, kiddo?"

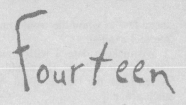

Fourteen

The time has come to see the Judge. It's been a long while since we've exchanged a word. My only sight of him has been through the lens of my telescope. As far as I know, he has not seen me.

I receive the summons midmorning. The phone rings, I pick it up, hear his voice. No secretary or clerk on first to announce the call, just that voice flowing from the receiver like rich warm honey. Hearing it, I feel my heart speed up.

"I've missed you, Kay."

It's the composed, rational, mellifluous voice that becalms all passion, melts all rage. A touch of cheer in it too. Today he's at his best, not judicial, stentorian or pompous. I hear the voice of the man I loved, the man who loved me, then betrayed me without even understanding how he had.

"I need your wisdom," he says. "I'd like to see you, tomorrow evening if possible. But if you don't feel up to it, or would rather postpone . . . of course I understand."

He wants *my* wisdom! Sweet Jesus!

He was always good at this, making me feel special, singled out from the multitude. To tell me I am among those few to whom he would turn for counsel is to make me feel exalted.

We make a date. I will come to his home at six tomorrow for a drink. He would make it for tonight if it weren't for the County Trial Attorneys Roast or some such affair.

"Justice, remember, Kay, is also politics," he reminds me.

"Yes, I remember," I tell him . . . and think: *You taught me so much.*

I have trouble concentrating on Sasha when he comes— for this is the night I am to tie *him* up. *Rope trick, rope trick*—the words keep flashing through my brain. I seem to be getting things mixed up: my sex life, bondage, trickery, David deGeoffroy and his magic show. Am I so confused I feel tied in knots? Or am I merely haunted by the image of a shower of dismembered limbs?

Thankfully I recover my concentration. Then Sasha and I start having fun. Wanting my bindings to be symbolic, I toss the ropes away.

"I'm not going to tie you," I tell him. "Tonight your shackles shall be composed of will."

He loves the discipline of the exercise, revels in it, thrashing and squirming as I gnaw. When he can't stand it anymore, dares to remove his wrists from the headboard, I admonish him ("Naughty, naughty!"), place his hands back where they belong and recommence the torturous raptures I'm inflicting upon his dusky flesh.

"You're terrible, Kay. Wicked!"

How can I not adore a man who calls me that?

"Yes, a love witch!"

I lap at the precise spot where he relishes it most and can endure it least.

"Lord Vishnu, save me!"

It's an act, but such a delightful one. We finally break down into giggles.

• • •

Normally I care nothing about clothes, but here I am before the mirror nervously trying combinations. Should I go as funky urban artist? The Judge used to like that look. How about stylish fashion photographer? That's how I was dressed the first time we met. Ingenue, the kid he fell for? I can probably put together a schoolgirl's outfit if I try.

I'm disgusted with myself for being so indecisive, though I know this is how people behave when they're dressing to meet an old lover for a drink. We want to make ourselves as attractive as possible in the hope that he/she will feel a twinge of regret. Could the Judge be worrying about his wardrobe too? No, not him; he's too confident and mature.

I finally decide on my "fine dining" outfit: black silk pants and blouse, black pumps, concha belt, silver earrings plus my liquid silver necklace from Santa Fe. I look good, I think, checking myself out before I leave. Actually it's hard for me to dress badly, since everything I own now is black, white or gray. Something I learned the hard way after years of making a fool of myself choosing clashing colors and wearing mismatched socks.

Darkness comes early these late-autumn days. I take a Union Street bus up to Grant. When I get off it's just six o'clock. Thinking it better not to arrive on time, I kill five minutes in an antique store, then meander north via Lombard toward his building on Telegraph Hill, catching the aroma of wild fennel and resin from the conifers and Monterey cypresses that surround Coit Tower.

The Judge's condo comprises the fourth floor and penthouse of a gray stone building, its facade broken by finely detailed bays.

Ascending, I notice lush new carpeting on the stairs. My pulse, I note, is steady. Pausing at the third-floor landing, I take the measure of my sangfroid. No gloss on my forehead, no trembling in my limbs. Excellent! Even though I feel vulnerable (this being one of those few occasions when I've chosen to go out without my camera), I also feel strong.

He's waiting for me in his doorway. Sparkling eyes, cleft chin, sleek combed-back hair. His neck is perhaps a bit more leathery than before, but that's appropriate for an ex-marine. The gray zone in his hair has expanded up his temples, but that only adds to the clubman appeal. He wears a dark blazer, chevron tie, striped shirt with pure white collar. Perfectly creased slacks, glowing shoes—he's the very image of a Man of Distinction stepping out of a Scotch whiskey ad.

"Kay!"

He gently pulls me to him, kisses me lightly on the lips.

"Been too long. So great to see you." He stands back. "You're looking great too!"

Dare I blush!

We take the spiral staircase up to the penthouse. The large Japanese plum blossom screen still adorns one wall, the Khmer bronze stands safe in its niche. The Judge, a collector of Far Eastern antiquities, heads the accession committee at the Museum of Asian Art.

He uncorks a bottle of Napa Valley Cabernet, pours us each a glass, then slides open the terrace doors. I step out, go immediately to the railing. He follows, stands beside me. The sky is black, the air clear, horizon broken by the elegant outline of the Golden Gate Bridge, its traffic flowing like a distant molten river in the night.

We stand in silence. I search Russian Hill, find my building, then the window through which I regularly aim my telescope. In his living room I noticed a small spotting scope on a tripod. I wonder: Does he use it to snoop on me?

"The view hasn't changed," I say. "The air here's sweet as ever."

"Have you?" he asks. I turn to him. "Changed?"

"I hope so." I peer at him. "How about you?"

He gives the matter judicial consideration. "I hope so too." Then gently: "Do you have a lover, Kay?" A little taken aback, I admit that I do. He nods wistfully. "Lucky guy."

"What are you telling me?" I ask.

"What I told you on the phone—that I've missed you. I loved you dearly, Kay. I'm sure I always will."

Not knowing how to respond, I merely nod. "Do you ever look over at my place?" I ask. "I look over here all the time."

He smiles, shakes his head. "I try not to indulge myself. Better to steer clear of might-have-beens." He smiles again. "But if occasionally my eyes do fall upon your windows, I always tip my hat . . . even when I'm not wearing one." He raises his hand to eye level to show me how he does it.

We go back inside. I sit down. He refills my glass, takes a seat on the opposing couch.

"Tell me what you've been up to?" he asks, in a manner so sweet and avuncular I let down my guard.

I tell him about my investigations into the old T case, my worries about Dad, that he may have been involved in something illegal. The Judge listens intently as I speak. At one point he gets up to turn on the exquisite Japanese lanterns that line the room.

I lean forward. "If it turns out there was obstruction of justice and Dad was involved . . . I guess what I'm asking is—can what I'm doing get him in trouble?"

Manicured fingers stroke the square cleft chin. "You're asking a legal question, Kay. I'm not your lawyer. I'm a federal judge."

"But surely you can tell me the law."

"I can . . . but should I? Is that really what you need from me tonight?" He pauses. "I think you need another kind of counsel. You want to know whether you should go ahead no matter the risk. Not the legal risk, but the risk to your integrity. Personal integrity's very important to you—I remember that."

"I was brought up to believe it's the most important thing about a person."

"Which is why I—" He smiles. "But I already told you."

Which is why I loved you: Is that what he doesn't want to say again?

"Nearly every lesson Dad taught had to do with truth and honor. There was one . . ." I tell the Judge the story, a bedside tale from my youth:

A man was sent out on a treasure hunt, the kind where you find a note that gives clues to the position of the next note, and so on, until finally you locate the treasure. In Dad's story the hunt takes up most of the hero's life. He is told that when he finds the treasure he will discover "the most valuable thing in all the world."

The man travels the globe, works out the clues, finds note after note, and after twenty years ends up less than a mile from where he started out. The last clue takes him to a rock beneath which, he's been promised, he will find the treasure.

He lifts the rock, digs beneath it, down five feet, ten, fifteen, but finds nothing. Feeling he's been tricked, he flings himself upon the ground. Then he notices that something's been carved on the bottom of the rock. Excited, he adjusts it to catch the light. There are five letters inscribed: *T-R-U-T-H*. Truly "the most valuable thing in all the world."

The Judge laughs. "Your dad's great. That's a terrific story. And I think in it you may find your answer too. You were taught that seeking the truth is a lifetime's work. I think you must pursue it now no matter how the chips may fall."

He's good tonight, the Judge is. I always thought he'd have made a great teacher. Now that he's shown me my answer lies within my query, I'm reminded of something similar Maddy once said: "We take pictures to discover what we can't see, the truth invisible to our naked eyes."

"You make it sound so simple," I tell him.

He smiles. "Most solutions are. Still I think you should consult a lawyer. I can give you several names. There may be some way of handling this whereby, depending on the outcome, the damage won't be too great.''

I thank him. We fall into silence. I'm waiting for him to tell me why he called. When he doesn't, I ask: ''That business about needing my wisdom—you were joking, of course.''

He smiles again. ''Perhaps wisdom wasn't the right word. Compassion—that's closer to what I meant.''

More silence.

''I don't understand.''

He looks slightly nervous now. ''You're involved in something, Kay—something you may have misunderstood.''

I tighten. ''If this is about—''

''Please!'' He raises his hand. ''No names. We can only speak of this if we don't use names. Agreed?''

I stare at him. ''If that's how you want it.'' I take a deep breath. ''What have I misunderstood?''

''It's not so simple. . . .''

''Most solutions are,'' I remind him.

He looks grim. I think: This may be the only time I've seen him at a loss for words.

''Sometimes people engage in acts,'' he says, ''acts that may strike others as wrong, immoral, but which are not as they appear. I mean, who among us has the right—'' He smiles. ''Pretty funny, I guess, coming from a judge. What I'm getting at, Kay, is . . . well, suppose someone takes a benign interest in a class of deprived young people who are living in a way we can't even imagine . . .''

''*Benign?*''

''You're smirking. Have I said something wrong?''

''I don't mean to smirk, but what you're saying is absurd.''

''Look, I know what you think, but believe me, you've got it wrong. It's a matter of preferences, nothing more.''

''Just preferences? Are you sure?''

''People like that, prominent people, don't relish having their private lives spread out for all to see. So, sometimes, they'll act in a self-protective manner, which, if you look at it from their point of view, makes perfect sense.''

"Just self-protective—is that really what you think?"

"Wait a minute, please.''

"No, you wait.'' I stand. "I can't believe this, can't believe it. We're not talking about the same people. We *can't* be. If you'd only come out straight and say their names.''

He shakes his head.

"Right. . . .'' I move to the bronze Khmer figure, stare into its expressionless face. "You're the one's got it wrong.'' I wheel, face him. "I've been beaten! My life's been threatened! Do you know that? Did they tell you *that*?''

He stares at me. "If that's true—''

"It is.''

"Then my advice is go to the D.A.'s people, tell them your story, leave it in their hands.''

"I can't do that yet. I've got no proof.''

A thin smile. Now he must feel he has the upper hand. "That could mean there's nothing to be proven.''

"There's plenty.''

"Then let the justice system take its course. For your own safety, Kay, stop playing Private Eye.''

I nod, walk over to the plum blossom screen, note the austere elegance of the design.

"I guess I don't really like that advice,'' I tell him.

He's surprised. "It's good counsel.''

" 'Playing Private Eye'—for me this is not a game.''

"I didn't mean to diminish—''

"I'm a photojournalist. A terrible crime's been committed. I'm investigating it. It's the subject of my book.'' I turn to him. "In your eyes I guess I'm still the pretty little art student with the too big camera around her neck.''

"I didn't mean to make you angry.''

"Who says I am? Though I admit the last time we met I was.''

"Because I had a meaningless fling with someone who meant nothing to me?''

"Because you made *me* feel meaningless. You still don't understand."

"You left me. I got my punishment."

"I got mine too . . . because I missed you more than I like to say."

"Look, Kay, I never claimed to be a paragon." He shakes his head. "I'm human, flesh and blood, with frailties like everyone else. You held me to a standard I couldn't meet. That was your verdict. Painful as it was, I had to accept it."

"Which is why I forgave you," I tell him, though his comments remind me so strongly of Sarah Lashaw's *mea culpa* I feel sick. "The person you showed me wasn't the person I wanted to be with, so for me it had to end. And, admit it—you were starting to get tired of me anyway. I wasn't getting younger. Yet you gave me so much that for all my anger I still treasured you in my heart."

God! I didn't come here to say all this. What kind of damn hole am I digging for myself?

"Listen," I tell him, "a few moments ago you shushed me. That hurt. I want to discuss this thing up front. I want to tell you my side of it. Then I want your advice."

He looks scared. "Don't!"

I stare at him. "You mean that?" When he nods, I nod back casually, my heart sinking inside.

He relaxes, smiles. We talk about our careers. I ask him if there's still a possibility he may move up to the appellate court.

"There's a chance I may move even higher," he says smoothly. "For obvious reasons I can't say more."

I nod. I'm satisfied. He has disappointed me, perhaps as I hoped he would. He has failed my integrity test, placed ambition above loyalty, making it possible for me to feel released. No longer need I long for him, wonder which pretty young woman he has lately seduced. And if he should manage to earn the high judicial appointment he seeks, I will hold close my knowledge that his rectitude's a sham.

"Have you ever been compromised?" I ask him boldly.

He stares at me as if I'm mad. "What kind of awful question is that?"

I meet his eyes. "Sorry. I just wondered, in view of what you've said. I mean, these people are your friends, you're in their circle. They're wealthy. They have political clout. Perhaps they checked around, found out we were once lovers, so they decided to approach you, persuade you to intervene."

"Act as a conciliator in a dispute between friends. Nothing wrong with that."

"No, except they lied to you, tried to use you. I'd think that would make you mad. But it doesn't seem to have had any effect, which tells me you believe their phony story—whatever it is."

"I don't take sides, Kay."

"That's right, you're a judge. And Justice is also politics."

Choking back tears, I quickly descend the spiral stairs. He follows, but before he can reach me I let myself out, then rush down to the street.

Now there are things I must do. I order a taxi from a pay phone, tell the driver to take me to the Castro.

In the Safeway on Market, I buy a box of chalk, walk over to the mailbox on Collingwood and Eighteenth, leave the mark that will tell Hilly I seek a meeting at eight the following night. Exhilarated at having set things in motion, I drop into a burrito joint for dinner. Then I taxi home, change clothes, grab my camera and go out again on foot to stalk the Gulch.

The fog has suddenly rushed in from the ocean, causing particles of water to accumulate in window screens. But despite the mist, the Gulch tonight seems especially alive, hustlers posing awaiting clients—who appear to be in scant supply.

I spot Sho beside the Korean barbecue in a classic stance, one leg bent so his foot is pressed against the building wall. I sidle up to him, ask what's going on.

"Police sweep," he says. "Scared off the johns. Usually takes a couple days for things to settle down."

I take up a position beside him, position my foot the same way, breathe in the cooking smells, enjoy the feel of the concrete wall against my back. Checking out the parade emerging and disappearing into inky mist, I sense an abundance of energy, hunger, testosterone.

I turn to him. I'm fascinated by the triangular shape of his face and the way it's framed by his long center-parted hair.

"Tell me, Sho—did you ever go out with the bald guy, the one drives the Mercedes coupe?"

He squints, asks why I'm asking.

"Just curious," I tell him. "What's his scene about?"

Sho smiles. "Can't tell you that, Bug."

"Hustler's secret?"

"You'd probably—" He screws up his face.

"—throw up? You think I'm that naive?"

He shuffles awkwardly. "It's just—it's hard to explain to a woman."

"Believe me, there's nothing I haven't heard about and little I haven't seen."

He shuffles again. "Rain probably told you."

I don't reveal how pleased I am to receive this confirmation that Tim knew Crane.

"I hear he can be mean," Sho finally says. "Depends on his mood. Different strokes for different folks. Never messed with me. Probably knew if he did I'd bust his nose."

So much for a "benign interest."

I'm content to leave it at that, but there's more Sho has to say.

"Rumor is he bashed a couple kids. Pissed everybody off. Some of the guys got together, agreed they wouldn't go out with him anymore. But, you know, there's no way to enforce something like that out here. Anyway, I'm sure he still finds what he's looking for, young and sweet. What he likes to do with them—I couldn't say."

"Knob rents him his boys, doesn't he? Tommy and Boat?"

Sho is surprised I possess such sensitive information.

"You're wired pretty good, Bug."

"Knob put you with him?"

Sho shuffles, shakes his head. "There're things I just can't say."

"Tim used to tell me stuff."

"Yeah . . . look what happened to him."

"You think he got offed because he talked too much?"

Now it's Sho's turn to shrug. "You don't mess with Knob and make a living on the Gulch," he says.

I thank him, saunter off into the gloom, chewing on this new bit of information. So Knob is king here, rules with a merciless hand. Tim never told me that, but then he was a freelance, and, in Sho's words—look what happened to him.

I join the parade, searching for Knob, but don't spot him on the street. Perhaps he's in one of the bars, doing a deal in the back of someone's car, or, unpleasant thought, tracking me even as I seek him out. I stop a couple of times, turn abruptly in the hope of catching sight of him behind. But the gloom's so thick I doubt I'd see him even if he were trailing me at fifty feet.

I ask myself: What makes me so important to Knob? For all I know, he administers beatings twice a week. But then I'm the only one here who carries a camera, a device that can document meetings between people who would deny they ever met.

Back home, setting down my camera, I realize I didn't take a single shot. An odd event, but then it's been a strange evening all around.

Approaching my telescope, I swing the tube from its usual position, trained on the penthouse of the Judge. I don't even bother to check the viewfinder to see if he's standing outside brooding over our final words. Rather I pick the whole apparatus up and move it to the bay window of the dining room. The view from here is only a smidgen different, but the new position will remind me I'll be taking a new perspective from now on.

The phone rings. I pick up.

"I'm in a pay phone." It's Hilly. She doesn't identify herself. "Got your message. I'll be there." She clicks off.

I smile; I do enjoy this cloak and dagger stuff, so perhaps the Judge was right. In a sense I *am* playing Private Eye . . . but then it no longer matters what he thinks.

Ariane: I dream of her, this woman I have never seen. I may have lost Tim, but it gives me hope that his twin, whom I'm convinced I will one day find, still walks the earth.

In the morning I wait around until eleven, then set out for Clement Street. I want to arrive just after the baking and Dad's prime business hours, yet catch him before he goes out on errands.

He's standing outside City Stone Ground when I arrive, talking to one of his suppliers. I study him as I wait: a huge friendly bear of a man in a white apron with smears of flour on his forearms and cheeks.

The staff is friendly. Everyone greets me. "Hi ya, Kay!" "Hi!"

Tamara brings me coffee and a slice of panettone. Peter stops to show me the new narrow crusty baguette. Kids, he tells me, love these long thin loaves; they pretend they're swords, fight duels with them.

Dad gives me a great hug. "Wanna have lunch?" he asks. "Chinese?"

I shake my head, suggest since it's a beautiful day, we pack a picnic and take it into the park.

He thinks that's a great idea, strips off his apron, goes to the refrigerator, extracts a half-bottle of rosé, packs two narrow baguettes into a canvas bag, then leads me down Clement two blocks to a Russian deli, where he purchases napkins, pickles, hard-boiled eggs, a little container of blackberry-and-green-coriander sauce, and a cold flattened Tabaka-style chicken which he orders cut up.

With these gastronomic treasures, we walk into the Presidio, find an empty picnic table overlooking the golf course and sit down to feast.

We make small talk for a while. He knows I've come for a reason, but for now we pretend we're on a pleasant father-daughter outing in the woods.

I ask after Phyllis. He tells me she's made a huge sale in Pacific Heights.

"Sold a floor of that fancy ocher building on Washington."

"Don't know it, Dad. Remember, I don't see colors."

He winces. The moment the words escape my lips I'm angry at myself for being bitchy.

"Sorry," I tell him. "That wasn't necessary. I had no right. You, who helped me more than anyone . . ."

He places his hand on mine. "I'm a fool to have forgotten, darlin'." He smiles. "It's the building next to the big Spreckels house."

"Sure, I know it."

"Sold it for two million eight. She'll split six percent— net eighty-four thou. Not bad."

I can tell he's not really excited by this; he repeats it by rote, as if straight from Phyllis Sorenson's lips.

"Phyl says she wants to blow some of it on a Christmas trip. She's got Hawaii in mind. When I told her I always spend my holidays with you, she said she'll invite you and her daughters along."

I can imagine how much fun that's going to be— Christmas in some big beachfront hotel, beholden to a woman I can barely stand, along with her two college-age daughters whom, having met only once, I hoped never to see again.

"Actually, Dad, I'm not sure that's such a good idea."

He laughs. "That's what I told her. So it's off."

"How're the two of you getting along these days?"

"So-so," he says. "Actually, I think we're getting kind

of tired of each other, wanna know the truth.''

I nod respectfully, not sure I'm happy about that. Though I don't care for Phyllis, I hate to think of Dad companionless.

"We went to see them," I say.

He looks up; he's nibbling on a Russian pickle. "If you don't mind my asking, darlin'—just who is 'we' and who is 'them'?"

"We is me and Joel. Them is Ricky, Wainy and Vasquez. Billy Hayes is dead."

He nods.

"You didn't mention that the other day."

"I didn't much feel like describing how it happened."

I nod to show him I understand. "Anyway, Vasquez refused to talk."

"Figures."

"Ricky and Wainy, on the other hand, they talked a lot."

Dad dips a piece of chicken into the blackberry sauce, places it in his mouth. He's so calm, so thoroughly at ease, I wonder if I'm onto something after all.

"They went off on riffs, the two of them. Lots of words but the underlying meaning wasn't clear." Again Dad smiles. "Still, thinking it over, I decoded some of it. You know, what they call the subtext."

"I believe I've heard that word, on public television I think."

"You're hilarious, Dad!"

He grins. "Humor, they say, can sometimes leaven the load."

I'm grateful he wants to lighten up. At least this time he isn't twisting his neck against his collar.

"What I got out of it is more like a theory. Because, you see, though they were drinking and talking crazy, they were also careful about what they said. Maybe they thought we were recording them." I pause. "In fact, I was."

"So, you got a theory, darlin', share it, why don't you?"

I lay it out for him, first Ricky's numerous references to each cop's propensity for violence.

"Billy Hayes's boxing skills, a hint that Vasquez might be cowardly. Wainy, he said, busted a few heads in his time. What he said about you is you could swing a night-stick good as anyone in Central Command."

"And himself?"

"He didn't say."

"Ricky knew how to be a brute."

"So that leaves us with a gang of five cops, four with tempers, capable of beating people up."

"That's good." Dad smiles. "I'm impressed. Go on."

"Ricky also made a point about how none of you were clumsy or dumb, none of you the type to bungle evidence. Yet somehow, by some mysterious process, you all seemed to become afflicted at the same time with this lose-the-evidence 'disease.' "

Dad laughs. "Disease—I like that. Kind of sums it up."

"What're you telling me?"

"Just listenin', darlin'. You're the one doing the tel-lin'."

I boil down Wainy's ravings. "First he boasted about how he and a fellow guard in Santa Cruz beat an amuse-ment park intruder to a pulp a few nights before. Then he claimed to be harboring a secret about Sipple, which, if he told it, could hurt people including you." Dad doesn't blink. "Finally he admitted this secret concerned the lo-cation of what he referred to as 'that bag of ever-lovin' shit-eatin' fuck-all ev-eye-dense.' "

"So, darlin', what'd you make of all that?"

"That Wainy's still got a violent temper and that the Sipple evidence wasn't neglectfully lost, but stashed."

"Putting that together with what Ricky told you, you come up with a pretty grim picture, right?"

"Jesus, Dad! Do I have to spell it out?"

"Only if you want to, darlin'."

"You could put it together for me, couldn't you?"

"I could," he says. "Let me think about it a little first."

Suddenly I realize that what he's just said is about as far as I've been prepared to hear him go. Anything more and I'm not sure I can take it, anything less and I'll leave with the feeling he's a liar.

"That was a load of crap you handed me the other day," I tell him. "About the guy who tied up Sipple maybe not even being the T killer. Or—what was your other theory? That maybe the whole Sipple incident was a plant—whatever that was supposed to mean."

Dad stares at me, not blinking.

"Why?"

"Why what, darlin'?"

"Why'd you try and mislead me?"

"If I did, you can be sure I had my reasons." He pauses. "Know something?" He smiles. "That I didn't succeed only makes me proud of you. Prouder than ever!"

I study him. He's showing me the face of a parent whose kid has just won a trophy. I realize he actually *is* proud his deception failed.

I want to scream! What's going on? I turn to him. He's staring into my eyes.

"What," I ask him, *"what the ever-loving hell did the five of you guys do?"*

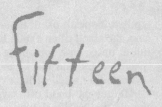

Fifteen

Even from the first moment Jack knew.

That wasn't what he told Hale of course. He admitted nothing, played stupid, figuring that was his only way out of the jam. Still, he maintained, he knew from the first moment he walked in, and so did the others when they arrived . . . but damned if any of them would admit it.

Soon as his eyes took in the scene—the nude kid bound, the tattoo equipment—he *knew*. He recognized the tattoo stuff because he and Rusty Quinn had worked bunko in Chinatown, and he'd been in a lot of tattoo parlors over those years. But it really wasn't that or anything else he consciously added up that told him this was a failed T killing. Rather it was the smell, the way the whole place stank of craziness and homicide.

First task, he knew, was save the kid . . . if he wasn't already dead. But even as he moved in to wrestle the black leather hood off his head, his eyes probed the edges of the room to make sure the T killer wasn't still there.

He wasn't. The room had an empty feel to it, yet there was this feeling of menace, too, something strong, powerful, that stank of hatred, cruelty, blood splashed and spilled, bones broken, tissue rent. There was a real smell too, the smell of an exotic brand of soap, sweet and spicy all at once, with something added to it, something unexpected, dark and black, and he knew what it was—the dark stifling smell of licorice.

He got the hood off, saved the kid, worrying even as he did that he'd pick up something awful from his mouth. Not HIV, for no one knew about AIDS back then, but something vile like gonorrhea or syphilis the kid was nurturing in the warm wet swamp pit of his throat, acquired from giving blow jobs at the baths or whatever they did in there—Jack didn't like to think too much about stuff like that.

Yet, despite his fear, he breathed for the kid, became his lungs until he felt him respond. Then he felt as good as he had in the twenty years he'd been on the force— because the best times for him had never been stopping a suspect or making a collar or sitting in a courtroom when a jury came in with a verdict. The good, the heady times were helping people, doing such small fine deeds as assisting a mother to find her lost child in the crowds on Stockton, or persuading some girl with dirty hair and scabs on her arms to get herself into detox before she caught pneumonia and died there on the Haight. This time it was saving this kid's life, because he hadn't the slightest doubt that if he'd walked up the hill instead of run, or taken his time about searching the flat before wrestling off the hood, the boy, who now lay before him spitting and puking, would be dead.

Maggie, the middle-aged landlady from upstairs, was watching from the basement doorway horrified. Maybe it was the kid's nudity or the choking and vomiting or just that something so sordid was taking place in her house. Whatever, he ordered her back upstairs to call for an ambulance and extra cops, and then, when she was gone, took the kid's head in his lap, mopped his face, told him he was going to be okay and asked who had tied him up.

The kid couldn't speak too well. He was in the twilight limbo state of a person who'd just crossed the line back from death. But he did manage to croak out a word that sounded like it was maybe a person's name, something like "Skelton," Jack thought, though he wasn't sure, and the kid was looking so distant and terrified he decided to let it rest awhile.

Then it occurred to him there'd be no chance to pursue it, for the whole thing would soon be out of his hands. The T case was the biggest game in town, was, as everyone in the Department knew, the exclusive no-intruders-allowed province of the elite investigative unit headed by the city's top cop and press favorite, Inspector Jonathan Topper Hale.

Billy Hayes was the first to show. The two of them always got along, so when Billy entered in that fighter's crouch he invariably used when he set foot in a room, as if entering a ring for a bout, Jack didn't say a word, just waited, curious how Billy would react. He wasn't surprised when Billy shot his bright blue little fighter's eyes around, took everything in, sniffed the air, blinked and said: "Bad, Jack. *Bad!*"

What was bad about it? Jack wanted to know. But before he could ask, Billy came out with it himself:

"It's the smell, ain't it—like you sniff sometimes around a gym when one fighter's beat up on another too hard, the murderous smell the trainers call 'the stink.' "

Billy checked the kid's pulse, then Jack pointed out what the perp had left behind—the hood with its elaborate trussings, so sinister and black, fraught with hazard, pungent with his victim's vomit and sweat; the tattoo gear, old stuff, crude, acquired most likely third or fourth hand, and the sooty smell that came out of the jar of black tattooing ink; the hypodermic syringe lying on the wooden stool, full of some colorless viscous fluid with a cotton swab tucked carefully beneath its tip; finally, that thing you couldn't see, the aroma lingering over everything, strong enough to cut through the smell of the vomit and the ink, the sweet-acrid licorice scent of the soap.

They sniffed it together without speaking, trying to track it to its source. It took them straight back to the kid, the skin of his torso though not his head or arms or legs. That's when Jack went into the bathroom to sniff at the soap in the depression of the sink. Nothing there, so he stuck his head through the greasy plastic shower curtain into the rusted sheet-metal stall, and this time he got a heavy hit. But the bar in the soap dish was ordinary, without a trace of the cloying odor, so he came back out, knelt beside the kid, said: "He washed you up first, didn't he— with his own soap too?"

The kid's eyes were glazed. He was done puking, but his pulse was still racing hard. The kid stared up at him, then gulped and nodded, and Jack felt the rush of having psyched a problem out, the kind of surge he figured a detective probably got every day but which was sweet and rare to him.

Just then the paramedics burst in. They took over the way they always do like everything is life-and-death, gave the kid oxygen, placed him on a gurney, covered him with a blanket and wheeled him out.

When they were gone Billy looked straight at Jack, fire in his squinty little eyes, then configured the forefingers of both hands so they formed a T.

Jack nodded, Billy smiled, and next thing Wainy and Ricky arrived, trailed shortly afterward by Luis Vasquez.

Wainy was half drunk and so was Ricky; they'd been hitting bars around lower Fillmore when they got the call. But soused as they were, they got real quiet when they walked in, smelled the smell, felt the vibes, sensed the solemnity between Billy and Jack.

No one touched the evidence or handed it around . . . though that was the story they would later tell. They were too smart, too experienced to do a damn fool thing like that. Rather they circled in, discussed it, then Wainy pulled out his leather-covered flask, took a snort, passed it around, and everyone, except Vasquez, took a snort as well.

They knew what they had: the first break in the biggest case of the decade, hard evidence, stuff the T killer had actually touched. And they knew soon as they called it in they'd be pushed straight out. Their names wouldn't appear in the papers. Though there might be some mention of patrolmen who'd stumbled into a scene, then dutifully turned it over to detectives, it would be Hale and his people who would be named and quoted and praised. There was nothing they could do about that and it rankled them hard, for to stumble into a crime scene like this, a scene so alive, filled with still-hot-from-the-perp's-hands evidence—this was what a good cop lived for, a chance to be a great cop, solve a great and gruesome case. And they knew soon as they called it in they'd be back to being plain patrol cops like before.

They stood around awhile bemoaning their lot. Griping about the injustice of it, they took more snorts from Wainy's flask. When they finished it off, Wainy went out to his car to retrieve the full bottle of Jack Daniel's he had stashed beneath his seat. When he came back his face was pink—he'd been hit by an inspiration. They didn't have to call the task force, he said, least not right away. If they wanted they had a few hours' cushion time to pursue the T case on their own. They were five smart cops, experienced cops who knew their way around the city, right? So here they were, standing in this Aladdin's cave of evidence. Was there any reason they couldn't solve this thing, track down the T killer, emerge as heroes and at the same time drive Hale and his crew of strut-around detectives nuts?

The bottle went around again, and by the time it made three circuits they were raring to go.

"So now let's take a little look-see here at what we got," Wainy said.

First there was the hood. Billy slipped on a pair of latex gloves and picked it up. They looked at the clasps. Solid stainless steel, not the cheap chrome stuff you usually see. The hood, butter-soft, had that smoky leathery smell. The sewing and riveting had been done by hand. No store tag inside. Made to order, had to be.

But if you knew a little about made-to-order SM gear, you knew the guys who fit and cut and riveted the stuff were proud of their work. Most of them had a private mark they put inside, their initials or some kind of signature. Since there was nothing in this hood, that could mean it had been made by the T killer himself.

The tattoo gear didn't tell them much. Old and most likely untraceable. But the ink could be traced. There was the manufacturer's name and a batch number right on the jar. A good phone detective could track that down in an hour.

The syringe was a job for the crime lab boys. They could tell what kind of juice was in it and lift the prints.

So how the hell were the five of them going to track this friggin' killer? Things were bleak; the bottle made another pass. When it reached Wainy again, he took a deep draft and, when he lowered his head, showed a canny smile.

"Hey," he said, "let's face it, we're not detectives, we don't work phones, lift prints, do lab analysis, we can't compete. But I say we got our own area of expertise— we know what real people do. We're patrolmen, so I say forget the detective crap and take a look at this from our angle, the real life street side we know better 'n anyone else."

That got them going. Even Vasquez got caught up in it. Wainy had set them on the track, they all had things to say, but finally it was Jack who laid it out.

It wasn't all that complicated when you looked at it, he said. Here was all this evidence left behind by a guy in a big hurry to get away. This guy, call him the T killer, had to be scared shitless, because now, for the first time after five perfect homicides, he was in a real predicament. All kinds of stuff that could be traced back to him was sitting here in this cellar. He had to know that if the right cops got hold of it, he might as well as turn himself in. Whether that happened would depend on a number of circumstances such as whether Robbie Sipple survived. But whatever the outcome, he owed it to himself to do his damnedest to get his stuff back. If he was lucky and the cops who'd gone in were as stupid as they looked . . .

then, maybe, there was a small chance he could retrieve it and get away clean. In which case, even though he'd goofed, his chances of escape would be astronomically enhanced. So, figuring it was that or the gas chamber, he just *had* to take the shot.

"Sure," Billy said, "that's what I'd do. I'd wait around till after we all leave, then break in and hope to hell that stuff is still here to take back."

Wainy and Ricky went along. Then, for the first time, Vasquez spoke up.

"If he's smart," Vasquez said, "he's still in the neighborhood, walking around, keeping an eye on the house. If a bunch of squad cars show up, he knows he's fucked. But if he sees us who came in go out again, he might just figure he's got a chance."

So where he's watching from? they asked one another.

"Could be he's got a car parked up the street," Ricky said. "Or just out pacing, walking the sidewalk, circling the block, maybe with a dog to give him cover."

The rest of them didn't think the dog idea made sense—a killer doesn't usually bring along a dog when he's going to snuff a guy. Still, they agreed, he could be out there walking, or circling in his car, or just parked like Ricky said. Problem was how to bait him, make him think all of them had left. Would he know how many of them had originally gone in? Not likely—the five of them arrived at four different times, then the paramedics showed, so even if he'd been watching, he probably couldn't have kept track.

"What we gotta do," Wainy said, "is four of us exit together like we're all done here for the night. One of us stays behind, in the closet or lav, radio on, ready to call if anyone comes in. Meantime the four of us hover a block or so away, say down on Waller or up on Carl Street. Then, when our buddy here gives the word, we all rush the hell back, grab the guy and shake the shit outa him till he spills."

Of course every one of them said he was best qualified to stay. Wainy and Billy meant it, Ricky and Jack played along, Vasquez didn't mean it at all. The way it ended up, they drew straws and Billy won.

He'd be fine, he said, when Wainy asked if he didn't want company. He had his billy club, gun, deadly-weapon fists and, best of all, the element of surprise. If the T killer returned, it would be because he was sure he had a chance, not because he suspected a trap. All Billy had to do was pounce the guy, cuff him, kick him couple times in the gut to subdue him, then wait for his pals to show up, which shouldn't take them more than half a minute.

Wainy and Ricky were the actors. They made the best show out on the street, upending the bottle, wiping their mouths on their sleeves, saying, "Goodnight, sleep tight, see you in the morning," that kind of crap. Vasquez and Jack played it straight, mumbling stuff like, "Drive careful now, give my love to Sue, thanks for another cruddy night on the job." Lots of glad-handing, arm-across-the-shoulder man-to-man cop garbage, then Wainy and Ricky stumbled into Wainy's car, while Vasquez and Jack casually wove their way down the street, and then up a block, where they took up positions inside an all-night grocery, radios on, waiting for Billy's call.

Was an hour and a half before it came. When it did it was quick and shrill, interrupted by static and firecracker sounds:

"Son of a . . . he's here! Fuckin' dipshit! Hurry, guys! *Shit! Take this, asshole!*"

Jack was rounding the corner of Frederick and Clayton when he saw Wainy's car pull in front of the house. Vasquez, he thought, was trailing, the way he had all evening, like he was calculating just how far he wanted to go in this thing. But Jack wasn't thinking about Vasquez just then. Seeing Wainy and Ricky rush down the outside steps to the flat, he ran fast as he could so he wouldn't be last one in to help.

Billy, as it turned out, didn't need any help. It was dim in there, no lights, just the barest amount of illumination coming through the high cellar window from the street, but it was light enough for them to see Billy had the guy down on the floor, was kicking the shit out of him, right foot, left foot, right! Left! Like he was dancing, skipping rope, doing him in the belly, kidneys, ribs, spine. And the guy—he was good-sized, a lot bigger than Billy, who had always been a lean welterweight—was moaning and writhing there the way Robbie Sipple had done just a couple hours before.

That, anyhow, was how it struck Jack: poetic justice, he thought, lungs still aching from the run. One guy nearly kills another, and now he's down there on the same floor nearly getting killed himself.

It was Wainy finally pulled Billy off, which wasn't so easy, Billy being in auto kick-him mode. Then Jack got down with the guy, turned him over as Ricky switched on the lights, so they could all get a good look at him for the first time.

What hit him first was the sweet-acrid licorice smell of the soap. But the guy was no sweet beauty anymore. He was a mess, nose cracked, one eye hanging out, teeth splintered, struggling to breathe, with some kind of awful stinkin' ooze trickling out of his mouth.

Jack looked up at Billy. "Jesus, what the hell did you do to him?"

"I dunno. Cracked him couple times with the stick, then smacked him around."

"Shit! The guy's losing it. He'll die on us we don't get him help quick."

Silence. Then Ricky spoke, almost in a whisper: "We can't get him help—you know that, Jack."

Which was true. No need to discuss it. They all knew it perfectly well. Whoever this guy was, T killer or not, if he died on them they'd all go down too. Not just Billy but all five of them; they knew the law, knew they were all accessories. They'd been parties to a conspiracy, the kind of cop conspiracy gets prosecuted hard: five rogue cops going against the rules, getting drunk, taking the law into their own hands. Moreover they'd held back material evidence in a capital case. They could get ten years for that, maybe twenty . . . unless, of course, they could come up with a story that would float.

A lot of booze had been consumed that night, but not one of them felt intoxicated then. The guy on the floor, whoever he was, was gasping out his life, and they all knew they'd better think up something fast or forget about having futures.

It was then that Vasquez emerged. The earlier portion of the evening he'd been the reluctant one, the outsider, nondrinker, the one none of them knew very well. He'd only walked in because he'd heard the call for officers and happened to be close at the time. He'd gone along with everything quietly, but now that they had trouble he took charge.

First thing, he instructed, they had to get the guy out of there fast, dead or alive, along with all the evidence. They needed to restore things to the way they'd been an hour and a half before, when they'd all pretended to leave. In the new version Billy didn't stay behind, he left with them, then they split up on the street and each went his separate way. No hanging around, no ruckus, no beating up the suspect. They all just went home, their only crime forgetting to bag, seal and log in the evidence.

The landlady had told Jack she was going to take sleeping pills, so it was doubtful she'd heard a thing. The street had been deserted, no one out there watching them come and go. At worst, Vasquez said, there might be some dispute about what time they left, and, of course, complaints that they'd bungled the crime scene. But everything would turn out when Robbie Sipple described the guy and Hale and his people searched him out. When they couldn't find him they'd assume he ran away after retrieving the incriminating evidence.

Not bad, Wainy said, when Vasquez finished. But what do we do with the guy?

Jack, who'd been kneeling beside him, checked his pulse, looked up at them and shook his head.

Deep-six him, Vasquez said. Dump him in the Bay and get rid of the evidence somewhere else. It'll work, he said, it'll be like the guy knew he was doomed, so he went and jumped off the fuckin' G.G. Bridge. So now let's get to it, he said, get him the hell out of here before someone happens along.

No need to discuss it. It was a decent plan, and their futures were at stake. But when they stripped the guy preparatory to wrapping him in one of Sipple's blankets, they couldn't believe what they found.

His body was covered with bizarre tattoos of a type none of them had ever seen: arm bones tattooed on his arms, leg bones on his legs, rib bones over his ribs, all in a brilliant raucous red. Just like a skeleton, Billy said, and then Jack remembered what Robbie had mumbled when he'd asked who tied him up. "Skelton," he'd thought he heard, but the word surely must have been "skeleton." It was a man with tattooed red bones all over his body, Skeleton-man, who'd done this awful thing. Which meant this dead man before them really *was* the T killer and that made Jack feel good. They hadn't killed some innocent guy, one of Sipple's friends who happened to wander in. No, thank God! They'd gotten the killer. Against all odds they'd planned and sprung a perfect trap.

The fog: Jack remembered how thick and cold it was by the time they reached the Presidio gate. There'd been no mist on the Haight, but when they got over to the Bay they found themselves in a swirl of it, so cold and damp it chilled him to the bone. Here they were, five cops, stinking of booze, cramped into Wainy's crummy car, driving wildly through the fog-bound forests of the Presidio, with a naked serial killer's body wrapped up inside the trunk.

It was crazy, Jack knew, but he couldn't think of an alternative. One thing to lose important evidence, another to beat a suspect to death. And it wouldn't matter that Skeleton-man actually *was* the T killer; in fact that probably made things worse. A suspect in a high-profile murder case, Hale in charge, then five rogue cops catch him and act as judge, jury and executioner—they'd never be forgiven. So he just breathed in the cold wet air, so close and thick he could chew it almost, and prayed they'd be able to get safely rid of Skeleton-man, and then all get home safe without being caught.

They were headed for Fort Point just below the bridge, the spot where in Hitchcock's *Vertigo* Kim Novak leaps into the Bay. The fort itself, that time of night, wasn't visible till they reached its base, and even there the bridge girders above were mostly lost in the fog that surged through the Golden Gate like billows of black smoke.

Wainy backed his car up to the seawall; he and Billy got out, opened the trunk and with Ricky's help carried Skeleton-man to the chain fence, each rusty link bigger than a man's hand. They carried him over, then onto the black boulders of the breakwater. Here they unwrapped him, then lowered him into the waves lapping and roiling like thick black oil. They watched as he floated off into the fog. The tide would carry him beneath the bridge, either into the shipping lanes or against the south tower barrier. Eventually he'd be washed ashore, probably somewhere on the Marin side. Naked, strangely tattooed, with no accompanying ID—the Coast Guard would figure him for a jumper. There was some talk then about whether they ought to leave his clothes up in a neat pile the way jumpers sometimes do as a final farewell to the world. Vasquez agreed that might make for a nice touch, but said they couldn't take the risk.

On the way back through the fog, they worked out their story. The point, Vasquez kept reminding them, was to keep it simple and as close as possible to actual events. Everything straight up till ten thirty P.M. Minimum amount of fabrication after that. It'd be okay, he said, if their stories differed slightly since cops' stories often do. But the essential points must be the same. If just one of them stumbled, he could bring the rest of them down.

It was then that Jack offered to take the greater share of the blame for forgetting to remove and preserve the evidence. He'd been first on the scene, he should have closed it down. He told them he'd long wanted out of

S.F.P.D. and so was willing to take the fall.

Back at Park Station, in the parking lot, Jack, realizing they'd yet to go through Skeleton-man's clothes, asked the others whether they didn't wonder who he was.

"Not me," Wainy said.

"Me neither." Ricky shook his head.

Vasquez turned away. Billy shrugged. It was Billy, they'd agreed, who would get rid of the clothing and evidence.

"And don't tell us what you did with them neither," Wainy instructed just before they all split up.

Jack intended to go straight home, but was too tightly wound. He needed some kind of transition and knew where he could find it—an ear into which he could confess his sins, a mouth from which absolution would flow.

He and Rusty had worked Chinatown five years, bunko most of that time, narcotics too for a while. Best beat in the city, people said, if you were smart and knew how to work it.

So maybe he and Rusty weren't so smart, or simply lacked desire. Corruption didn't suit them; they were interested in other things. For Rusty that meant getting laid, for Jack understanding how Chinatown worked. So even as they patrolled together, each pursued his interest in his own way.

Rusty befriended a string of gorgeous Asian prostitutes who took good care of him at the special Chinatown price for friends. Who could blame them? Wasn't Rusty's fault those beauties were turned on by a hairy Caucasian cop.

Jack learned some Cantonese, then started making friends, up and down Stockton, Grant, Jackson, Washington, the alleys—Ross, Pontiac, Stark, Old Chinatown—narrow dead-end streets where when you passed you could hear the slap of mahjong pieces against wood, and where, in cellars and on the upper floors, whorehouses, opium dens and gambling parlors were installed.

The partners got along well, in time became best

friends. So that night, when Jack felt his springs about to bust, it was natural he search Rusty out in half a dozen hangouts he frequented late at night.

He found him finally at Choi's Triple-X, a nudie-cutie live-action cabaret at the eastern end of Chinatown. Out in front of Choi's a busty sloe-eyed hawker-girl was leashed to a pagoda-shaped stanchion, enabling her to act as a warm-bodied gatepost without fear of being carried off by rowdy passersby.

There was a stripper worked here, one Becky Yee, who at the time possessed Rusty's heart. Jack found his old partner in her dressing room, holding one of her yellow silk stage garments to his mustache.

Sensing at once that Jack was in trouble, Rusty guided him to a beer joint around the corner. Immediately Jack began spilling out the evening's events, Rusty nodding, consoling, giving Jack succor to face his demons.

"A purely innocent occurrence," was how Rusty described Skeleton-man's demise. "No harm intended. Could've happened to anyone, Jack."

"Yeah, but we all knew Billy was violent," Jack said. "We shouldn't have let him stay."

"We're *all* fuckin' violent," Rusty countered. "Anyway it's not killing the guy that'll bring you trouble. No jury'll convict you for that. Vasquez steered you wrong. It's covering up, lying about it. If Hale smells a rat he'll be all over you. He'll follow you all to the ends of the earth . . . and then on to your graves."

Rusty's advice was terse: Once you take the cover-up route, you can't consider turning back. You brave it out, lie and bluster, and hope your story holds and none of your buddies breaks. The code of silence, he said, should get you through, and if no one ID's the body, or better, doesn't connect it to Sipple, the odds of things working out are probably four to one. What Jack ought to do now, he said, is go home, take a shower, get a good night's sleep. The next couple of days were going to be rough, so the better rested he was, the greater his chances of getting by Hale.

But there was something else Jack wanted to discuss: who the T killer was. They'd killed a man. It didn't seem decent not to know his name.

"You got his clothes, check them out."

Jack explained that Billy took them. "Look, I'm no detective," Jack said. "I don't know where to begin."

Rusty knew: "Start with the car. Walk the streets up there, chalk the tires, let a couple days pass and see which cars don't move. Then run their plates. I doubt he parked more 'n a block or two away."

When he finally got home, he found Carlotta asleep, but when he came out of the shower she was sitting up in bed.

"Nice evening with tootsie-baby?" she inquired. She had a way of hissing the word, which was why, Jack supposed, she used it instead of "girlfriend" or "lover."

There was no tootsie-baby, of course. They both knew that. It was just a little joke between them whenever he came home late. But tonight he wasn't in a joking mood, was too sloshed, wrapped up in his troubles. So he made a mistake, forgot to humor her, mumbled something about finding the quip stale.

She settled back under the covers, face creased with hurt. "Sometimes you're a real bastard, Jack."

"Sure," he acknowledged, "sometimes a damned unhappy one too."

Silence while he pulled on a fresh pair of boxers. He was going to slip into bed beside her, when she issued her retort:

"One of these days soon I'll stick my head in the oven. Or jump off the G.G. Bridge. Then maybe you'll look back and regret the hurtful things you said. . . ."

The mention of the bridge at that particular moment came close to pushing him over the edge. It was one o'clock in the morning, he'd saved one man's life, then been party to the killing of another. He was exhausted, but he didn't care—he wasn't going to lie down beside her now. Instead he went downstairs to the kitchen and set to work making a perfect, honest, truth-telling loaf of bread. He dozed while the dough rose, then fired up the oven and baked it off. When it came out it was beautiful—soft and chewy at its center with a gently shattering crust.

Though he wasn't due on duty till four p.m. the following day, he planned to go early to the Haight and start marking parked cars like Rusty said. But just as he was preparing to leave the house, he got a call from Wainy. They were wanted down at the Hall of Justice right away.

When he arrived he ran into the other four, along with Mercurio, the Park Station commander. Sipple had dropped dead a couple hours before, of a heart attack the doctors said. Meantime Hale's team had spotted the case, gone over to the crime scene and found a mess. Now they wanted the evidence Wainy had reported on the forms, and when he couldn't produce it, all hell broke loose.

First they were separated, placed in five small interrogation cubicles, then left alone to stew. During that time Jack thought about Sipple—how exhilarated he'd felt after saving the kid's life and how miserable now that all his efforts had been for naught. Then Mercurio came in and told him how serious the matter was. This was the T case and somebody'd better remember something fast or heavy discipline would be meted out.

Next a two-man team of detectives, T case investigators, hard jaws and flinty eyes, came in. Jack had to tell them his story three separate times, more time passed, then he and the others were herded into a conference room, seated opposite the entire T case task force. The detectives glared at them. Mercurio, arms folded, stood against the wall. Minutes passed then Hale entered. Jack, who only knew him from appearances on TV, found his eyes frighteningly pale. Hale didn't bother to introduce himself, just started to talk.

He didn't shout at them or scream, yet every word came

dripping with contempt. As the task force glowered, and Mercurio shook his head, the five of them endured the dressing-down. They had royally fucked up, and now because of that more innocent people would likely be killed. They had disgraced their shields, which they no longer deserved to wear, were meager examples of cops, everything an S.F.P.D. cop shouldn't be—stupid, clumsy, weak, inept, unreliable, undependable, totally unfit. If it were up to Hale he'd nail their hides to the front of the Hall, signs saying *DICKHEAD* hanging around their necks. Fortunately for them, their fates were in other hands. But he'd taken this opportunity to express the task force's scorn, hoping they would do the honorable thing and resign. He held no hatred for them, merely pity. At that he left the room, followed by his detectives. When everyone had gone, Mercurio informed them they were dismissed, then left them without a glance.

For Jack that half hour was the most humiliating of his life. The others, he guessed, felt the same. Billy sat low in his seat. There were tears in Ricky's eyes. Wainy looked broken—a functioning alcoholic, his whole life revolved around being a cop. Only Vasquez appeared unmoved. He was completing college at night, people said. Glancing at him after the dressing-down, Jack detected a frightening sangfroid.

They didn't speak as they filed out of the building. Word of what had happened quickly spread. Reporters clustered around peppering them with questions, peering at them in that curious way one stares at people in disgrace. They ran a gauntlet of cops, attorneys, handcuffed criminals, all stripping them with mocking eyes. Jack was trembling when he reached his car. Safe inside, he leaned over his steering wheel and wept.

Back at Park Station he was informed by his sergeant he'd been reassigned to desk duty pending a hearing. No way now could he risk going up to Frederick Street and placing chalk marks on the tires of parked cars. Too many

task force people milling around, too much visibility, too
many questions he wouldn't be able to answer if he was
seen. The only thing to do was sit at the bare desk, stare
at the wall, put in the hours, then go home to his wounded,
troubled wife.

She was on psychiatric leave from her job as school
music teacher; she'd broken down too many times in
class. When he came home he'd usually find her at her
piano, either sitting morose and still or else struggling
with the Schubert B-flat sonata, a piece that wandered and
ruminated in ways she could never resolve, so that she
constantly became lost within it, repeating sections over
and over for hours at a time. It was, Jack felt, the saddest
piece of music he ever heard, and, in her hands, so tearful
it filled the house with gloom.

He tried to counter this darkness with the aroma of
baking bread. He baked some magnificent loaves over
those weeks, bread making his only respite from Carlotta's melancholy and the forces crushing him down.

Every day he waited for Skeleton-man to show up,
searching the papers for one of those one-paragraph items
about an unidentified jumper washed to shore. Nothing.

At work he daily checked the missing persons lists,
looking closely at reports that mentioned tattoos. There
were no such reports.

What had happened? Had Skeleton-man drifted out to
sea, been devoured by ocean beasts, torn to pieces against
the rocks? Had he no lover, parents, siblings, friends, no
one who missed him and declared him missing? Had he
existed at all? That his body never turned up gave the
whole experience the hallucinatory quality of dream.

The summer passed. He, Wainy and the others avoided
one another. When they met by accident, they'd nod
grimly and move on. All appeared broken except for Vasquez, who, strangely, seemed to gain strength from the
debacle.

The next few months Jack and Carlotta rarely spoke,
he lost in wonderment at the sour way his life had turned,
she mired ever deeper in depression. Their friends avoided

them. It wasn't his disgrace, Jack understood, but the aura he and Carlotta cast. Carrying themselves like broken souls, they had become exemplars of despair.

When the I.A. report was leaked, Jack didn't waste time. He didn't like leaving in disgrace, but was determined to get out fast. He borrowed some money from his brother-in-law, arranged a bank loan for the rest and that October opened the City Stone Ground Bakery on upper Clement Street.

After the first day of business, exhilarated at last to be doing what he loved, he came home to find Carlotta slumped limply over the foot end of their bed. She had lain down, thrust her head back till it was upside down, stuck his spare revolver in her mouth and fired. Death for her had been instantaneous. But, perhaps the opposite of her intention, guilt over what she'd done would haunt him the rest of his life.

Years passed. The memory of that night of rescue and murder would fade, though the recollection of certain sensory impressions—the licorice smell of the soap, the thickness of the fog, the oiliness of the water—remained intense. And what could never fade was the image of Carlotta that faced him when he returned that first night from the bakery—the bizarre position of her head, the glassy stare in her eyes, the garbled agony of her mouth. Sometimes, early in the morning, when he worked dough in his hands, Jack would take a few moments to sculpt human features. Then as he mashed the dough back into a loaf shape, he would re-create the distortion of her face.

It was seven years before Hale approached him for the first time, late one afternoon walking nonchalantly into the bakery, purchasing a baguette, smiling slightly when Jack, handing him his change, recognized his face. This was a different Hale than the man who'd berated them down at the Hall that awful afternoon. He was a thin man now, his mustache was gray, his eyes and hair had lost their luster.

"How you doin', Jack?"

At first he was anxious; Rusty, after all, had warned him Hale would pursue them to their graves. And then, with Hale so amiable, he wondered if he'd stopped by to make amends. When he discovered what Hale wanted, he was shocked and horrified: the man was still working the T case on his own and had come to ask for help.

Thus began the series of annual visits that always set Jack on edge—Hale in his you-and-I-are-now-equals mode, stopping in to discuss the details of the hood. One year he asked Jack to make a drawing of it from memory, another year had him accompany him on a tour of custom leather shops. Word got back that Hale was also making unannounced visits to the others. Wainy said he enjoyed these encounters for the opportunity to play Hale for a fool. Ricky Puccio laughed them off. Billy Hayes found himself rattled. As for Vasquez, he was still in the Department, climbing steadily up the ladder. None of them knew whether Hale had taken to dropping in on him, but Jack doubted it. There was something about Vasquez that caused people to want to stay clear.

There was a cat-and-mouse aspect to Hale's visits, a message in his congeniality. His thin smile announced: *I know about the conspiracy, I know more than you think.*

Because the meetings were so widely spaced, they appeared to be made without pressure. But Hale's apparent lack of urgency became a form of pressure in itself. It was as if he was saying: "I have all the time in the world to get to the bottom of what you did. Sooner or later one of you'll break. Till then I'll be coming around."

One autumn day, ten years after Sipple, Billy Hayes wandered in. Jack's greeting was guarded, but Billy pretended he didn't notice. He asked Jack if he had time to talk. They strolled up Clement, past the little Asian groceries and hole-in-the-wall restaurants, then over to quieter California Street where there was a neighborhood bar Billy knew.

Here they talked about this and that, what each had been doing, Jack's success with the bakery, Billy's troubles as boxing trainer and promoter. Then Billy steered the conversation around to the event that had changed their lives—the accidental death of Skeleton-man and the puzzle of who he was.

Billy mentioned Hale's visits, how unnerving he found them, as if Hale already knew everything that had happened and was just waiting for one of them to spill. He said he'd been tempted several times to dig up the garbage bag containing Skeleton-man's clothing and the other evidence he'd hurriedly buried behind his garage, then throw the stuff into the ocean to be rid of it once and for all. He'd even, he admitted, prepared to excavate by the rear foundation wall several times, but each time lost his nerve before his shovel hit the dirt. It was as if, Billy said, so long as that sack remained in the ground, the whole haunting nightmare would stay on hold. But if he should ever bring it up, no matter his purpose, the consequences could not be foreseen.

Three weeks later, Billy shot himself. It was Hale's visits, Jack was certain, that drove him to it. That, Jack believed, was what Hale wanted from them all: Either give up the evidence, tell the story straight, or eat your guns—your choice.

A month later, Jack drove out to where Billy had lived on Railroad Avenue in South San Francisco. He told himself he wanted to see how Debbie Hayes, Billy's widow, was doing. But when he arrived he didn't get out of his car. Instead he paused in front of the house, then circled the block to locate the rear of the garage, set on a weed-choked strip that lined a dusty stretch of track. He stared for a while at the garage, a flat-roofed structure built of cinder blocks, then drove back home.

It bothered him that he knew where the stuff was hidden. He hadn't wanted that information, but back at the bar Billy had casually let it slip. Or perhaps not so casually, Jack thought—perhaps Billy had come by with the sole purpose of telling because he already had his suicide planned and wanted to pass on the burden first.

Whatever Billy's intent, Jack realized, he was now back in the nightmare. He not only knew what had happened, but now also knew where the evidence could be found. Evidence that not only would resolve the T case, lead to the identification of the T killer and satisfy Hale, but also would ruin people's lives, not least of all his own.

Or was he wrong?

That's what he wondered now that Kay had pried the story out of him. If she'd been right when she speculated that Carlotta had shot herself to lift from him the burden of his guilt, then perhaps Billy had killed himself for a similar reason—to take on responsibility for the awful act in which they'd all played a part.

But if that was true, then why hadn't Billy left a note addressed to Hale, confessing everything, telling where the stuff was stashed?

Carlotta hadn't left a note either.

So the truth was that in both cases Jack didn't know, and further, there was no way he could ever find out.

Sixteen

The shadows of the pines are long now, striping the close-cut grass. There's a chill in the air, a breeze from off the Bay that makes me cross my arms and huddle in my sweater.

Dad gazes past me . . . at a pair of golfers. I look at them too. One stands, hands on hips, while his companion prepares to swing. With the stroke the iron blade of the club catches the sun, transmitting a flash. Instinctively I blink . . . too late to save my rods from saturation. Several seconds later, when my vision clears, I find Dad searching my eyes.

"It rips my heart when the light hurts you," he says.

A great love for him wells up. I need to hold him close. I step behind him, wrap his massive torso, press my chest against his vast broad back.

I can feel him shudder. Through his cotton shirt the tips of my fingers detect the beating of his heart. He was always my supporter, builder of my confidence, telling me I could do anything I set my mind to. Yes, he taught me, I had a handicap, but not one that need hold me back. If I loved the night, that's when he'd take me out for walks, tell me stories, teach me to ride a bicycle. If the midday sun blinded me, he would play catch with me at twilight, take me to the beach at dusk, teach me to swim against the sunset.

"She must have been so wounded." He's speaking now of Mom. "She wouldn't have done it otherwise."

"And angry," I say. "Most likely at herself."

He shakes his head. "At me."

I don't understand it and never expect to. Who can comprehend her parents' marriage? All I know is that to kill oneself one must be possessed by an enormous rage. My heart goes out to both of them—to her for her ferocious anger, to him for all the ravages wrought by guilt.

"I meant what I said, Kay." I wait for him to explain. "So proud you didn't give up. I tried to confuse you. I didn't want you to know. But deep inside I hoped you'd figure it out."

"You taught me the importance of truth," I remind him. "So you see, I couldn't flinch."

I walk him back to his bakery. At the door we embrace. Then I walk down to Arguello and catch the 33 bus. It follows a singular route, along the rim of Golden Gate Park, meanders through the Haight and the hills north of Twin Peaks, finally depositing me at the corner of Castro and Eighteenth, the intersection known as Hibernia Beach.

It's magic time when I arrive, the sky still darkening, my favorite hour in the city. The Castro is alive, people going rapidly about their affairs while others linger against the sides of buildings or sit on benches observing the passing scene. An urgent young man with an AIDS petition gently importunes me. A smiling young woman, hair like straw, offers me condoms from a basket.

Autumn chill has not discouraged the exposure of flesh. Here skin is always king. Tank tops abound, bare arms exhibit tattoos, hair glows, eyes glisten, men and women alike wear shorts to display attractive legs. Still too early for my meeting with Hilly, I decide to float with the crowd. As I walk pairs of eyes meet mine, lock in, then release me with a smile. This is the way here, and most of the time these street gazes are more ironic than lewd, gazes of what-might-have-been, wistful admiration exchanged. For a moment our lives cross, we esteem one another's beauty, then move on. The world turns, the clocks advance, yet for an instant we pause to acknowledge we share the earth and that each of us lives under the tyranny of his desire.

I think of Dad's strange intersections that night fifteen years ago—breathing the breath of life into Robbie Sipple, kneeling beside Skeleton-man, feeling his life ebb away. Did Dad commit a crime? Did any of them besides Billy? Yes, of course, and I cannot condone what they did. But, with the possible exception of Vasquez, I forgive them. They've been punished enough.

I pause at a pay phone, dial Joel. Ice Goddess Kirstin answers.

"You are very missible here," she says in her Swedish-accented singsong. Does she mean I'm missed, admissible or merely miserable? Before I can ask she turns the phone over to Joel.

"We need to talk. I know where the Sipple stuff is stashed."

I can feel his excitement through the wire. "Your dad?"

"He told me everything. We can break the T case, Joel, but we have to protect him and the others by blaming it all on Billy Hayes. He didn't tell me to do that, but it's the only way. He didn't even say dig it up or don't, just told me what happened and where it's buried." I pause, out of breath.

"Can you come over?"

"I'm meeting Hilly in half an hour. I'll drop by soon as we're finished."

Hilly looks sloppy tonight, eyes tired, hair wild, not gelled. She's wearing a faded Grateful Dead T-shirt and grungy fatigues. I'm pleased she's not dressed hot.

We attract no attention in our corner of The Duchess; it's clear we're not here to play. The loud scene swirling around us is fun. I enjoy the spectacle of funky women on the make. It's only the smoke I dislike, but then Hilly explains that here a cigarette dangling from a (preferably bee-stung) lip is considered a luscious come-on.

"I'm beat," she informs me, applying her beer bottle to her brow. "Shanley gives me shit, Charbeau gives me shit. I'm onto something, but those oafs don't see it. It's a crappy life, Kay, being a cop."

"Want to tell me about it?"

"Not especially." She peers at me. "You called this meet. What's up?"

I wonder why she's being secretive. Is she irritated with me or just feeling testy?

"There's a pimp on the Gulch they call Knob," I tell her. "Don't ask me his real name—I've no idea. He wheels and deals, acts as middleman for underage hustlers. He hangs out with two kids, Tommy and Boat, runaways who think he's God."

"So?"

"They're the three beat me up in the park. Last week the kids vandalized my place while Knob stood lookout downstairs."

"Great! Swear out a complaint. I'll pick 'em up."

I explain why she can't, that my only witness is a park hermit terrified of the police. He won't testify and would be ineffective if he did.

"So what's the connection to Tim Lovsey?"

"Someone put Knob up to it, wanted me scared off. Why do that if he isn't the killer?"

"How do you know someone put Knob up to it?"

"Just a hunch. But I think there's a soft spot, the runaways. I hear the one called Boat is mushy. If you pick him up for soliciting, get him alone, put on pressure, there's a chance he'll break. So I was thinking—suppose you squeeze him, turn him against Tommy, then turn the two of them on Knob. With two witnesses ready to testify against him, maybe Knob'll say who ordered me hit."

She studies me. "You got it all figured out."

"Just a suggestion, Hilly."

"You think like a cop."

"Is that a compliment?"

She smiles, sips some beer. "You're talking about entrapment. That's tricky business. There're all sorts of niceties—coercion, legal representation, 'fruit of the poisoned tree.' And it gets trickier when you're dealing with juveniles." She pauses. "This Knob—tell me more about him."

I tell her what I heard from Doreen and Sho, that Knob's ruthless, and in effect rules the Gulch.

She nods. "Probably got a record. Too bad you don't know his name."

I show her the photo I took of him at The Werewolf. She examines it.

"Looks like he's been around."

"I could go through the mug books."

"That's slow and a lot of times doesn't work. Prints are better. I can run them through the Automated Fingerprint ID System, A.F.I.S., do a national screening."

"You want Knob's fingerprints? We'll get 'em!"

She brightens up, we bring our heads close, quickly hatch a plan. After a while the butch bartender appears with another round of beers. An anonymous person has sent them over.

"She doesn't want to be pointed out," the butch informs us, squinting down one eye, raising the corresponding nostril. "Said to say you guys look very friendly so she thought she'd act friendly too."

Joel owns a run-down Victorian on Roosevelt Park Hill, not far from where Sipple lived in the upper Haight. The place has what realtors call "good bones," plus a fine rear-window view across the city to China Basin. A dusty granddaddy palm, centerpiece of a jungle, obscures the front of the house. Making my way beneath it, traipsing through a mesh of vines, I nearly trip over an abandoned rake. Joel, no surprise, is not big on domestic upkeep. A feral cat scoots beneath the stoop, gazes up at me, meows.

I notice a mezuzah beside the door. Ice Goddess opens up. Her long hair is parted in the center; her large Nordic eyes sparkle with spirituality. Joel found this willowy young blonde shortly after Rachel Glickman dumped him, a week after their second daughter left home for college. Rachel, dark, homely, serious and brilliant, is a tenured professor of sociology at San Francisco State. Kirstin, fair, beautiful, bright only in the wattage of her smile, makes fabric collages and reads runes for pay.

"Hi, Kay!" she moos.

We embrace.

"Am I still missible?" I ask.

She stands back, perplexed. "Golly, I hope not!"

So . . . whatever she was trying to tell me earlier will remain a mystery to us both.

She leads me to Joel's office in the attic, a clone of his cubicle at the *Bay Area News*. No Pulitzer certificate here but a similar decor—cartoons posted on the walls, dog-eared books jammed top first into shelves, a chaos of clippings, manuscripts, articles in progress, an old manual Underwood on the desk. Joel claims to despise computers.

He listens, fascinated, as I recount Dad's saga. When I'm finished he reminds me of one of my exchanges with Hale.

"You pointed out he had conflicting theories," Joel says. "Remember what he said?"

I think back. "Something like . . . once you understand what happened the theories no longer conflict."

Joel nods. "A tattoo-freak cute-boy T killer and a cop who gets rid of unwelcome evidence. Two separate crimes. Which means Hale more or less figured it out. Amazing!"

Joel's right: it *is* amazing. Hale's statement, so cryptic at the time, now makes sense. So, I ask, does this mean we're going to tell him where the stuff is buried?

Joel muses. "Obsessed old detective, forced out of his job, works the case fifteen years, finally finds missing evidence. Eureka! The old T case is solved!''

"It's a good story, but I don't like it, Joel."

"Neither do I." He starts to pace. "Hale's a paranoid and paranoids are dangerous. He won't buy that Billy Hayes did it all alone. He'll want to string up everyone . . . including your dad." He pauses. "Which leaves us with Hilly. All she wants is glory. She's got no axe to grind, so we can probably make a deal with her up front.''

"We could just let it go, couldn't we?" I ask.

A knock on the door. Kirstin appears with a pot of herbal tea and three hand-painted Scandinavian cups.

"I am thinking your thirsts would use a good quenching,'' she says.

Joel smiles, the sweet my-heart-is-touched grin of an indulgent father whose daughter is showing off her goodness. Kirstin, I understand, is what he's always wanted: a shiksa innocent who reminds him of his time on the Haight—heroic days and nights of good dope, dumb talk and endless sex with doped-out girls wearing flowers in their stringy hair.

Kirstin pours the tea, settles on a hassock, exposes milky thighs. She sips, then, apropos of nothing, announces she and Joel have decided to make a baby. I turn to Joel; he glows with pride. Sure, it figures—he could use a second crack at youth. I've seen plenty of grayhaired men like him trotting around supermarkets with papooses on their backs, filling grocery carts with baby chow and Pampers.

He turns to me. "Could you bear to let it go?"

There's a side of me, I recognize, that could, that would just as soon leave buried evidence in the ground, especially as I now know that the T case has nothing to do with Tim. But there's another part of me that can't stand the notion of leaving things incomplete, that, like Dad, wants to know who Skeleton-man was.

"On what basis could Hilly get a warrant to dig?" I ask.

Joel smiles. "Tip from a confidential informant—you and me, kiddo. Not all that far-fetched. She's investigating the T case angle on the Tim Lovsey homicide. She starts asking around about the old case. Someone calls, tells her where the evidence is buried. She goes to a judge, says her source is reliable. Judge scowls . . . but lets her dig.''

Kirstin's tea tastes of bitter herbs. I can barely stomach it, but Joel sips as if it's ambrosia. I suddenly wonder if Kirstin holds him in thrall with more than sex, with spells and secret potions.

"What about Debbie Hayes, Billy's widow?"

"I doubt she knows anything, and even if she does she won't make a fuss. She's getting Billy's pension. She won't want to screw that up."

"So Billy goes down as the bad guy?"

Joel shrugs. "In a major sense he was."

Kirstin, following our dialogue like a spectator at a tennis match, doesn't have a clue as to what we're talking about. Still I sense she's hurt at being ignored. When I turn to thank her for the tea, she flashes me a grateful smile.

"If it all works out," Joel says, "we'll be handing Hilly fame beyond her dreams."

"And if that encourages her to get to the bottom of who killed Tim, she'll deserve it," I reply.

I've no idea where Drake gets his food; the groceries I leave for him couldn't sustain a child. Where does he find the water he needs—to drink, bathe, launder his clothes? Where does he sleep when it's cold, store his covers when it rains, go to the toilet, shampoo his hair? When he ventures out of Sterling Park, where does he go? How can he survive in a wood the size of half a city block?

The homeless, I understand, have survival strategies, holes and caches, stocks of booty. Some get by collecting aluminum cans, others barter, still others find saleable treasure scrounging trash. There are soup kitchens in church basements, shelters offering toilets and hot showers, and the urban parks where they reside can be gold mines to those who know how to live off the detritus of a wealthy town.

I sit with Drake side by side on a bench, he, as always, perched as far from me as he can get. Filled with feelings yet unable to form attachments, he likes me at a distance, even loves me in his way, but up close I frighten him, am too solid, too real. Better a fantasy woman glimpsed at night through a window from afar than a live palpable female person seated in broad daylight three feet away.

The trees break up the sunlight, scatter it upon his face. We talk about his future. He hopes to go back to school one day, resume the study of chemistry. He's from Oregon, misses the rain. His favorite color is green. He has a sister. Photochemistry is interesting. Do I use Kodak Dektol? Do I believe someone really wants me dead?

His non sequiturs touch me.

"Do you think someone does?" I ask.

He turns away, nods. "I do," he says gravely. "But he will have to kill me first."

We're cruising slowly along Polk in Hilly's old Volvo, the kind that in California seems to last forever. Hilly is driving, I'm in the passenger seat, an actor named Rob Mathews is in back.

Rob's in his forties, well groomed, dressed tonight like an affluent dentist. I met him a few years ago when I did some fashion photography for his wife, an ad exec. He's a member of the company at Berkeley Rep, specializing in middle-aged character roles. He's intrigued, he tells me, by the proposed gig.

"Never played a chicken hawk before," he says, stroking his mustache. "But how tough can it be? I like girls in their twenties, so why not boys in their teens?"

Hilly guffaws.

Rob leans forward. He's eager, wants to internalize the role. "How should I behave? Timid or bold?"

"Either way," I tell him. "Some guys are cocky, most are scared. They know if they get caught they'll lose everything, job, wife, kids. You gotta be obsessed to take the risk.''

Rob understands.

"There he is.'' I point out Knob as we cruise by. He's standing alone in his usual spot between Bush and Sutter, back propped against a wall beside an all-male video store.

"Looks mean,'' Rob says.

"*Is* mean,'' I tell him. I slink down in my seat in case Knob looks up.

Hilly asks Rob if he wants her to make another pass. Rob says that isn't necessary, he saw Knob clear enough. Hilly drives two blocks, turns the corner, cuts over to Larkin, stops.

"What's my best lead-in?''

I turn to Rob. He's cool. In his shoes I'd have the jitters.

I advise: "Tell Knob you hear he's the man to see. He'll probably pretend he doesn't know what you're talking about. If he asks who steered you to him, just say 'a friend.' If he insists on a name tell him you can't give it up, it's a matter of personal honor. He'll laugh . . . but that'll build his confidence. Offer to buy him a drink.''

Hilly hands him an envelope. "The photos inside are sterile. Hand them to him discreetly at the bar. Tell him this is the type of kid you want—young, long hair, smooth. Since you don't want him to think he's being set up, make a big point that for legal reasons you don't want a kid under eighteen. What you want is someone who *looks* underage. Can he fix you up?''

"Great! But what if he does?''

"He won't. Not tonight. Too risky,'' Hilly says. "You'll have to see him two or three times before he'll agree to do business. Show him you understand this, that you came by to get acquainted, build trust. The important thing is to get his prints on the photos. Don't worry if you touch them. We'll eliminate yours, go for what's left.''

Rob nods, gets out of the car. Hilly and I wish him luck

then take off. We've agreed to meet him in an hour at the Buena Vista. We drive for a time, threading through the Tenderloin. It's a weekday night; people are hanging out. The hotels down here don't rate neon signs. You can see the stains on the window shades even from the street.

"Jesus, what a gutter!" Hilly says.

"I don't know, it doesn't seem all that bad."

She glances at me. "Yeah, you can save that. You live up on Russian. No whores or homeless up there. The air's sweet. You got a pretty view. Every once in a while you come down, take a few pictures, then go back up. That's fine, Kay. But reality's down here where it stinks full-time."

"Ah," I say, "the cynical cop!"

"You bet!" She bites her lip.

I'm annoyed. I don't like being patronized. I decide to smack her back.

"Of course *you* don't slum around," I tell her. "With your cozy flat in the Castro, your cat, your lifestyle, your hot dyke bars. Give me a break, Hilly. I take a few pictures, you make a few arrests—after which we both go home. Frankly, I don't see the difference."

She chews on that as we run a gauntlet of addicts clustered around the door to a Cambodian restaurant.

"You're right. I'm feeling mean tonight. Sorry to take it out on you."

"What's the matter?"

"The job. Believe me, I could tell you a few things."

"Please do," I urge.

Again she bites her lip. Then it comes, the torrent. Charbeau, she tells me, has been riding her. Last week he called her in, told her she wasn't cutting it. When she asked what was wrong he said it wasn't her work, it was the way she strutted around. "I got nothing against female detectives," he told her, "fact I think they're great. What I can't stand is anyone, male or female, who fucks me up with a colleague."

She knew immediately he was talking about Vasquez. "You don't mess with a guy like that," Charbeau told her. "Whatever you think of him, you don't talk to him the way you did."

I ask if this goes back to the incident by the elevators.

Hilly shakes her head. "Something else. He blew up when I asked him about the soap."

She pulls into a bus stop, cuts the engine. Though I've no idea what she's going to say, I feel my pulse speed up.

"There's stuff I didn't tell you," she says. "I first noticed it out at Wildcat Canyon after Shanley sent you home. Timothy's torso had been washed with a very strong type of medicinal soap, so strong you could still smell it on him in the rain. Sweet and peppery. Like licorice."

The word sends a tremor across my chest.

"We decided to keep it quiet. Might turn out to be important. Then, when I went through the T case file, naturally I looked for references. Nothing until I got to Sipple. Remember, he wasn't carved, he died in the hospital of a heart attack. But a couple of the cops who found him—Hayes and your dad—mentioned a strong-smelling soap. So I got this weird idea: Here we got a copycat T killer homicide with several things out of whack—paint instead of tattoos, a big number 'seven' lest we miss the point, and the torso washed with scented soap . . . which resembled what happened to Sipple, but to no one else. Remember what I was looking for? Insiders who knew the T killer's M.O. But here we got this similarity to Sipple, but not to any of the rest. So I start thinking maybe the leak didn't come from the T case task force, but from someone who was just in on Sipple. Then's when I went to see Vasquez. Maybe he'd have an idea or two, maybe he wouldn't, but I wanted him to know he hadn't intimidated me when he told me to move my fanny in the hall."

Now I'm shaking. Could Hilly be right? What if Tim was killed by one of the five? Since it couldn't be Hayes or Dad, that leaves just three—Wainy, Ricky, Vasquez.

"The lieutenant tells me to close the door, doesn't invite me to sit. He stares at me very cold. I guess the asshole thinks I've come to apologize. He hears me out. When I'm done, he keeps staring at me like there must be more. I stare right back. No way am I going to blink. So our little staring contest goes on awhile, then he asks if I'm an ambitious cop. Sure, I tell him, I'm ambitious . . . to clear my cases just like everyone else. I'm investigating a homicide and I've come to him for help. If he doesn't choose to assist, fine, I'll go on about my work."

Hilly smiles. "I wasn't sure I had the balls to stand up to the guy. Now I'm wondering if standing up to him was so smart."

"Why?"

"Something scary about him. Way he looks at you like he's looking through you, through your eyes into your brain."

Vasquez. Suddenly my Crane theory doesn't look so neat. I prodded Crane, threatened to ruin his reputation, so why *wouldn't* he want me beaten and my photographic files destroyed? But that doesn't prove he was Tim's killer. How could he have known about the soap?

Vasquez knew. And then I remember something else, that Vasquez is in charge of Felony Prostitution. He could have known Tim. He could even have killed him. *But why would Vasquez do that? It doesn't make sense.*

Hilly's still talking. Meantime my head's swelling with heat.

". . . word on the lieutenant is he takes protection money, that he's got deals going all over town. On Polk Gulch, here in the Tenderloin, on Capp Street in the Mission, the real bottom of the barrel." She peers at me. "You're looking queasy, Kay. You all right?"

"Migraine," I lie. In fact, I feel as though the top of my head's about to blow off.

"Anyhow, makes you wonder, Charbeau standing up for a guy like that, while I'm just trying to do my job." She shrugs, glances at her watch. "What d'you say we head over to the Buena Vista, scope out Rob?"

• • •

We find him standing at the bar, enjoying a Scotch, displaying a victor's smile. No need to ask whether he got Knob's prints; he not only got them, he never touched the pictures himself, just handed the envelope to Knob, watched as he went through them, waited until he replaced them, then took the treasured envelope back.

"Not a bad guy once you get to know him," Rob says. "Brute type, but with a certain savage charm."

Hilly excuses herself; she wants to rush the photos to the fingerprint lab. I pick up the tab for Rob's drinks, then buy him dinner.

"You won't have to see Knob again," I assure him.

"I'm thrilled, Kay. Frankly, I was scared."

"I never would have known," I tell him.

Rob beams. "Must mean I'm a good actor."

Sasha spends the night. It's been days since we've seen each other. He's been on duty and I've been busy exploring the oddly connected trails of my life. Tim, Dad, Mom, the Judge, Ariane . . . Knob, Crane, Vasquez . . . and perhaps other strands I may be too close to or too blind to see.

Sasha, as it happens, bathes with perfumed soap, which imbues his skin with the aroma of sandalwood. I ask him why he likes it.

"Don't you?" he asks.

"Of course. Just curious why you chose it."

"Actually, I never much liked scented toiletries," he says. We're lying side by side naked in my bed, in contact from our shoulders to our calves. "Shaving soaps, men's fragrances, lotions. People give them as gifts. Usually I take one sniff, then pass the stuff on. But one day . . ." He stops. "This is embarrassing."

I nudge him. "Go on!"

"A lady I was seeing—"

"Lady?"

"She was. But so as not to offend you, we'll call her a woman. Anyway, I was staying over one night."

"As you're accustomed to do."

He nods. "And in the morning when I took a shower and used her soap it was scented with sandalwood and I liked it very much. So, though I never saw this lady, this woman, again—"

"As was also your custom."

He laughs. "Although we stopped seeing one another, having failed to fall in love, I did in fact fall in love with her bath soap . . . and have been using it ever since."

"Great story, Sasha!"

"Glad you like it, Kay. And I hope someday you too will look back and recall receiving a similar gift from me—a scent sniffed, a dish tasted, perhaps some little trick I've taught."

"Bed trick?"

"Wouldn't that be fine?"

"You're a great lover, Sasha. You know you are. I've learned a lot from you. Felt, you know, special things. I hope we're going to have a future together."

"We will," he says, firmly.

I turn, plant my elbow, prop my head on my fist, so I can look straight into his dreamy eyes.

"Here's my secret, Sasha. I'm speaking seriously now. My fondest wish is to see colors. And, surprise!—some nights with you I actually do. Oh, not real colors, of course. Sadly, that's not possible. But the equivalent, the *sense* of colors. It's hard to explain."

"I love what you're saying."

"It's like a flowering. Objects take on a different dimension. There's an unexpected depth, a richness . . . which is what I've always thought colors must endow. I dream more vivid dreams, see more brilliantly. The light opens up, hues are revealed."

I turn to lie on my back, stare up at the ceiling. "You see, I have ways of knowing colors—from music, passages in Wagner, Berlioz, Scriabin, Debussy, Rimsky-Korsakov. From literature too—the greens in Walt

Whitman, golds and yellows in Gerard Manley Hopkins, Conrad's reds and blues. I also know colors from the great painters. I look at the paintings and imagine . . . Poussin's blue, Degas's green, van Gogh's yellow, Rembrandt's brown.''

He leans over me to kiss my eyes.

"My mom was a music teacher," I continue. "She tried to teach me colors via correspondences with sounds—the chromatic scale, orchestral color, how harmony could be thought of as a kind of color-mixing too. We'd listen to records. She'd make analogies between the sounds of the different instruments and the intensities of different hues. The yellow sounds of the clarinets, violets of the oboes, reds of the trumpets. Crimson flutes. Dark blue cellos. Aquamarine violas. Pure blue violins. We'd spend hours listening. I tried to memorize the correspondences. The keys too. She told me D Major was purple, D Minor was tawny, A Major was green. In the end, unfortunately, her lessons didn't take. She was so disappointed I didn't have a good ear. Later she took my artistic ambitions as rejection. Music, you see, was such a perfect medium for a color-blind girl. She thought I went to art school just to spite her. She was wrong, of course. I found my way there, discovered black-and-white photography, a way of making pictures in which the line and shape take precedence over the field.''

I turn back to him. "Still, I wish I could have pleased her, Sasha. At least learned from her, learned the colors.''

"You're not blind, Kay.''

"Not at all. My whole life's about seeing—looking, peering, selecting, creating images. And who knows? If I *could* see colors, most likely my colors wouldn't be the same as yours. Scientists say it can take but the slightest difference in a chromosome, a single amino acid, to change the way a person perceives a hue. But never mind! I'm talking about the colors I *do* see. Sometimes I see them in my mind via sound and touch and smell, but the best time for me, the time I see them most beautifully, is when the two of us make love. All of which is my way of telling you, Sasha, that this woman already has a story to tell, for she has already received your gift. And—need I add?—still longs for more. . . ."

Midmorning I phone Dad: "You okay?"

"Sure, darlin'. You?"

"I'm doing good."

"Glad to hear it. What we talked about—that was bound to hurt."

"It cleared the air. Thanks for sharing it with me." I pause. "We'll probably try and dig up the evidence now. Unless you object."

A long pause. "Go ahead."

"You're sure?"

"Do what you have to do."

"Billy can take the rap. Joel says his widow won't be hurt."

"Poor Billy!"

"Poor you! But don't worry—we won't throw you to the wolves. Not Ricky or Wainy either. No guarantees for Vasquez."

"A word of advice, darlin'."

"Please?"

"Go for it, but watch out for Vasquez. He plays dirty, a dirty game."

The phone rings. It's Caroline Gifford at Zeitgeist.

"You won't believe this, Kay. I just got off a call from Sarah Lashaw. Says she wants to buy thirty or so prints, a representative selection of your work. Wants to come by tomorrow, make choices." Caroline pauses. "Isn't that fab?"

"No, sorry, Caroline, it's not."

"Hey, girlfriend, this is business! You can't refuse a serious buyer. We're talking twenty-five, thirty thousand dollars here."

"I understand, but, see, Lashaw isn't buying, she's

bribing, and I'm not in the bribe-taking business. Trust me on this?''

A silence. "Oh, I trust you all right. But I gotta tell you, Kay—sometimes it really hurts.''

I keep thinking of Ariane: Where is she now? To what extent was she involved in Tim's death? I've talked to David deGeoffroy twice since Tim's funeral, and each time he asks after her with special tenderness. I'm still convinced I haven't heard the whole story from him and will only learn the rest from her . . . if I'm fortunate enough to find her.

I think about the Lovsey twins going through adolescence on their own, and then the forces that must have driven them to work the street. I think of their deft hands and brilliant minds, their interchangeability, androgyny and charm, their love of juggling, tumbling, pulling coins and scarfs out of orifices, most of all of the bravery with which they faced the world. They never allowed themselves to feel degraded no matter the disdain in which their work was held. Magician-nighthawk purveyors of lust, gorgeous sensuous objects of desire, they entered the dark subconscious of the city, maintaining their dignity in the face of all its sleaze and scorn.

I walk into an old-fashioned professional building on lower Market, the kind with a cage elevator and echoing lobby. An elderly attendant with dragon breath operates the apparatus. The cage jerks and trembles its way up, depositing me on the eighth floor after numerous false stops.

The corridor here is lined with doors with bubble-glass panels bearing the names of tenants. Aromas ooze out of open transoms—mouthwash from the waiting room of Lawrence Fisher, D.D.S.; cigar smoke from the suite of Courter & Lee, Admiralty Insurers; stale coffee and pizza from the hole-in-the-wall workplace of Susan Marzik &

Associates, Private Investigations. But from my destination, the law office of J. F. Judd, Esq., Criminal Defense, there is no smell, no essence, no odor at all.

The receptionist, a middle-aged battle-axe with a bitter mouth, gives me the once-over as she snatches away my card. Five minutes later a squat bald man with canny eyes waddles out to greet me.

"Hi! I'm Judd," he says, escorting me to his office. "Thanks for dropping by."

"You were expecting me?"

He gestures me to the client chair. "I figure you came to settle Lovsey's account."

I examine him as he sits behind his desk. Late thirties, flashy tie, flabby jowls, grossly overweight.

"That's not why I'm here," I tell him.

"Look, the client's deceased. I'm open to settlement."

I'm not prepared for this, but what the hell? I offer him two hundred dollars.

While Judd thinks it over, I peer around. His office is a den of files, lawbooks, briefs and, on the walls, satiric Daumier barrister cartoons. He is, I quickly understand, small-time. No big murder cases here, just penny ante stuff—drug possession, solicitation, petty theft.

When I turn back he's studying my face.

"Beaten up, weren't you?"

Jesus! "Does it still show?"

He shakes his head. "Not at all."

"Then how—"

"Tim told me. Wanted me to nail the son of a bitch. I told him I'm a defense attorney, not a prosecutor, his friend should go to the cops. That was the last time we spoke. A day or two later he was killed." Judd shrugs and shakes his head.

Suddenly I feel heat rising from my chest to my head, the same sensation I felt when Hilly told me about Vasquez. *Ariane—it had to be! But who beat her and why?* Knowing I must anchor myself, I think of Rita's admonishment in aikido: *Find your center, Kay. Root yourself.*

"It wasn't me he was talking about."

"You said—"

"I was beaten afterwards." Judd raises his eyebrows. "Do you remember exactly what Tim said?"

Judd neither nods nor shakes his head, just continues to stare, waiting for me to explain.

"The night he was killed we were supposed to meet. He wanted my advice. He was upset, scared. Maybe what he told you had to do with what he was going to tell me."

Judd turns away. "Attorney-client privilege extends after death."

"But you already told me some of it. I'm just asking for the details."

He widens his eyes, body language for *What's in it for me?* I understand him perfectly: for chump change attorney Judd would sell his soul.

I make him an offer: "I'll settle Tim's account."

"In full?"

I nod. "Providing you tell me everything."

In fact, $1,250 will empty out my bank account. But then, I remember, I just turned down a fortune from Sarah Lashaw. I reach into my camera bag, whip out my checkbook, turn on my micro tape recorder at the same time. I write Judd a check, show it to him, then pull it back.

He smiles. "You wouldn't stiff me now, would you, Ms. Farrow?"

"Is that what you're used to—getting stiffed?"

"Unhappily, yes."

"You'll get this when you tell me everything, from the first time you met Tim Lovsey to the last time you spoke."

He studies me a moment, swivels around in his chair, starts to talk. It isn't an uninteresting story. Tim was picked up on Polk Gulch, got into a car, took a hundred bucks to receive a blow job from an undercover cop. A second after Tim accepted the money, the cop put him under arrest. Then it was off to the Hall of Justice, with a little conversation en route. What Tim needed, the cop advised, was a good lawyer to settle his case. When Tim said he didn't know any lawyers, the cop recommended

Judd, then stopped so Tim could phone him from a booth.

"Police officer scam," Judd explains. "Arrest a guy, tell him he needs a lawyer, steer him to one who knows how to deal. Everyone's protected—the cop gets paid off, the lawyer gets his fee, the arrestee gets his freedom and can't claim later he was solicited for a bribe."

"How much?"

"In this case five hundred. I negotiated it down from a grand."

"For which you billed him twelve-fifty."

"Of which my cut was seven-fifty. A fair fee, believe me. I was called out of bed."

"You're saying Tim never paid you?"

Judd shrugs. "He was a hustler. What'd you expect?"

I don't believe him. He wouldn't have listened to Tim's story about the beaten girl if he hadn't already been paid. I very much want to ask the arresting officer's name, but decide to hold off till I hear the rest.

"No jail, no bail, no court appearance," Judd continues. "The matter was privately settled. Then, like I mentioned, last month Tim calls me about this girl, says she's been badly beaten up. He's pissed, wants me to represent her, bring criminal charges against the guy, sue him, the works. When I tell him I don't do that kind of work, he says he'll find someone who does. Next thing, I read in the newspaper he's been killed."

"Did he say who beat the girl?"

Judd shakes his head.

"I think he did," I tell him. "And when you heard the name you got scared."

"Think whatever you like, missy. Twelve-fifty only buys so much."

Missy! What an asshole! "Well, you got me there, Mr. Judd," I tell him. "For me twelve-fifty's a stretch." I search his eyes. "It was a rich man beat the girl, wasn't it?"

Judd shrugs. Does he know I'm bluffing? Did he sell the news of Tim's intentions and by so doing get Tim killed? Is he such a cheap piece of crud that even after collecting on that, he sent the bill for twelve-fifty figuring he could squeeze it out of Tim's estate?

"You're not going to tell me. I understand. At least give me the name of the cop."

Judd smiles. "Too sweet a deal. I'm not about to mess that up."

"Fine." I stand. "Then you don't get paid." I tear up my check, sprinkle the pieces on his desk.

He opens his center drawer, brushes the pieces into it. "You're a welsher, missy, but your check taped back to-gether'll be enough to persuade a small claims judge."

"Fuck you! You're the one welshed. And now I'm going to fry your ass."

"What're you talking about?"

"Friend of mine, an investigative journalist, is going to turn you inside out—bank accounts, every case you ever tried or settled, who your friends are, which ones are cops. A sleazebag like you—something's bound to turn up. By the time we're done with you, you'll be disbarred."

"You can't prove a thing!"

I hold up my tape recorder. "I think I can." I start toward the door.

"Hey! Wait! We can work this out."

I turn. He's up now, menacing, coming around the side of his desk.

"Gimme that tape!"

I laugh. He lunges at me. I grasp his wrist, turn, throw him across the room. He crashes into his filing cabinet. When he rises I note that his forehead's cut.

"*Bitch!*"

"Have to do better than that, fatso."

He lunges again. This time I knife-hand the side of his neck, then back-fist him across the nose. He crumples to the floor. I stare down at him. He looks pathetic. I take his picture twice.

A knock on the door. It's Battle-axe. "Everything all right, Mr. Judd."

"Yeah, go back to work." He glares up at me: "I'll get you for assault."

"God, you're dumb!" I show him the recorder again. "It's still running. You attacked me. I defended myself. It's all on tape."

He touches his nose, winces. His eyes go meek. "What do you want?"

"Names. The rich man who beat up the girl, the cop who took the bribe."

"They'll kill me if I tell."

"Who's 'they'?"

"Listen, please—"

"*You* listen! You've been stupid. When I walked in here I didn't know about a beating. I just wanted to know who arrested Tim. You could have refused, written off your twelve-fifty, sent me on my way. Instead you got greedy, showed off, as much as admitted you sold Tim out. Now it's time to get smart. You've got my card. Tell me what I want to know or take what's coming to you. You got three days."

As I leave, old Battle-axe gives me the evil eye.

"Your boss needs help. Got bandages?" I ask. I bring my face close. "Does he often attack women? You really should speak to him about that."

Sasha wants us to spend Thanksgiving at an inn in the wine country or perhaps south in Pebble Beach or on Big Sur. The idea is to luxuriate—sleep late, make love on crisp linen sheets, eat breakfast in bed, bathe in a hot tub, take long romantic walks in the vineyards or on the beach. It sounds great. I give him my blessing. Three hours later he calls back. We'll have to spend the holiday in the city; every luxury place in Northern California's booked.

Not to worry, I tell him. My idea of a perfect Thanksgiving is to catch a movie, hit Chinatown for a platter of grilled salt-and-pepper shrimp, walk home holding hands, make love, snuggle close, then fall to sleep.

• • •

I stop at the farmers' market on the Embarcadero, peruse the produce, buy a bag of clementines, which have just come into season. Due to my achromatopsia, eggplants and tomatoes appear the same shade, namely black. But color-blindness, I feel, has its advantages, forcing me, unable to make quick decisions based on colors, to look carefully at shapes. Yes, it is the shapes of things—their forms, not their fields—that reach my eye. Color-blindness has taught me to look steadily, view the world, discern.

Tonight, playing with my telescope, studiously avoiding the terrace of the Judge, I reacquaint myself with my neighbors, then sweep the city searching for points of interest.

Alcatraz, the forbidding rock, fills my eyepiece. Then the apex of Coit Tower, and several office buildings downtown outlined in lights for the holidays. But, as always, it's the smaller structures of North Beach and Telegraph Hill that engage me, variegated cubes arrayed, stacked, fitting together like pieces in an intricate, superbly constructed puzzle. Doors, windows, streetlamps, houses, stores, churches, playgrounds, schools—the variety and complexity of shapes is music to my eyes.

I realize that what I love best about San Francisco, and have rarely found anyplace else, is that here all these forms and shapes add up to something I can grasp. Each piece, each part, fits together to make the whole. The city is a unity, and now I wish that the mysteries that taunt me, the maze of photos pinned to my office wall, will come clear as well.

In the morning I leave half my clementines on the bench for Drake, whom I haven't seen in two days. An hour later, when I go out again and cruise the spot, I find my package gone. I only hope it was Drake who took it, not some other denizen of Russian Hill. Since he has declared himself, as much as promised to protect me with his life, I figure the least I owe him is decent nourishment.

I meet Joel at the *Bay Area News,* then we saunter over to the Transcendental Cafe for lunch. The late-autumn light catches the varnished tarot cards that paper the wall, creating a reflective sheen. The resident swami sits at his usual table reading the fortune of a boy with tresses.

I fill Joel in on what Hilly told me about Vasquez and the scented soap, then play him the tape of my exchange with Judd. After listening to the noise of our fight, he gazes at me with mock awe.

"Gosh, Kay—you really *do* beat guys up!"

But he's confused about the rest, not clear on the identity of Tim's beaten friend. I tell him about Ariane, David deGeoffroy, the Zamantha Illusion, the twins' heist of deGeoffroy's savings, Ariane's strange identity as Amoretto, the key hidden in Tim's molding, and how I met Courtney Hill in Ariane's vacated flat.

"Dammit!" he exclaims when I'm finished. "Why didn't you tell me this before?"

"It didn't seem relevant and I didn't want to distract you. Then, yesterday, I realized it may have been the reason Tim was killed."

Joel nods. "What about Vasquez?"

"Suppose he was the cop who picked Tim up?"

"A lieutenant, commander of the felony prostitution squad?"

"Why not? He's got a nice house. I'm sure he can use some extra cash. Suppose he freelances after hours? Cops run scams all the time."

"Actually, now that I think about it, it's a good one too. Vasquez knows the streets, knows the pickup lines. Boys and girls—he goes after them all. They take his cash, he's got them cold. He doesn't even have to have sex with them if he doesn't want to. Just make the deal, fork over, snap on the cuffs."

"How can we be sure?"

"That'll be hard. But since both Hilly and your dad say he's dirty there's probably something there. Let me ask around, see what I can find."

"When do you want to tip off Hilly on the buried treasure?"

"Soon. Keep working with her, Kay. As for Judd"— Joel smiles—"that was a pretty good bluff: your friend the investigative journalist. Only trouble is . . . it would take me months."

"I think Judd'll call."

"I think so too. But be careful, kiddo. Knock a guy around, humiliate him like you did, you may end up facing a mad dog."

Hilly and I meet again at The Duchess. Tonight her hair is beautifully slicked back. She's glowing with triumph. She's got a match on Knob's prints.

"Your friend's a bad boy, Kay. Up to his ears in shit." She pulls out a computer printout, reads off a list of names:

"Raymond Crogan, a.k.a. Ray Crow, a.k.a. Ray 'Crow-bar,' a.k.a. Ray 'Knob' Cross. Arrests go back to his teens—stealing, pandering, soliciting, battery, attempted vehicular homicide . . . a few more. Get this: two California felony convictions, the first for burglary, two-year sentence, fourteen months served, the second for felonious assault upon a police officer—five years sentenced and served at Pelican Bay." Hilly looks up at me. "Bottom line, under California three-strikes law he's vulnerable."

"Meaning . . . ?"

"Beating up on you and stealing your camera was a big mistake. If a D.A. can prove it to a jury, he'll get twenty-five to life."

Great! I think, and then, how strange that Knob would take such a chance. Which may explain why he pulled the pillowcase over my head and sent his boys up to my flat while he stood lookout below.

"He must have been paid a great deal of money to take

chances like that," I tell her. "Knob may be many things, but he isn't stupid . . . and to risk life in prison to settle a score would be stupid beyond belief."

Hilly agrees. "Hiring out kids for sex is a felony too, and he does that every night. Which makes it even more risky. Unless—" She grins.

"What?"

"He's got protection."

Something about the smile on her face tells me she's tasting blood. What better vindication, after all, than to nail Vasquez for taking bribes?

"What're you going to do about it?" I ask, hoping to taunt her into action.

"I like your idea of hauling in Knob's boys, breaking them, turning them into witnesses. Trouble is . . . if I take this to Charbeau, he'll shoot me down or put Shanley in charge. And if I try it without authorization I'll get shit-canned even if it works."

She ponders. "Thanksgiving's coming up. Shanley and Charbeau'll both be out of town. I was going to drive down to L.A., spend the holiday with my folks, but now I got a better idea." She squints. "With everyone away I'll have the field to myself. If I handle things right, it could be over before anyone gets back."

Seventeen

Seven p.m., Thanksgiving night. A chill in the air. Mist clings to the streetlights while buoy bells and mournful foghorns float up to me from the Bay. I'm standing still and alert in the strip of park between Larkin and Hyde at the base of Russian Hill. The old clock tower at Ghirardelli Square is barely visible through the vapor.

I've chosen this location and also the hour, insisting the meeting take place after dark. Judd argued for Fort Mason Park in daytime, but I took a hard line, figuring that anything he wanted would not be good for me.

I wait under cover of a small grove of olive trees a hundred feet back from the street, beautiful ancient, gnarled specimens with thick black twisted trunks. Beneath these boughs the air smells good, sweet and loamy. And from here I can watch for Judd's approach.

The fog is heavy, this place is dark and isolated, there are no pedestrians and, it being a holiday, traffic is sparse. But I'm not worried. Having already physically defeated Judd, I have the psychological advantage. Moreover, in darkness my vision is far superior to his, and tonight, unlike the night I was sandbagged in Sterling Park, I'm on guard.

I know this territory well, traverse it regularly. Although a good two hundred feet below the summit of the hill, it is but three blocks from my building. I often walk down here via the Larkin steps, guided by the anise scent of wild fennel that grows so luxuriantly in the city. Anise, of course, is an olfactory cousin of licorice, that haunting aroma Dad smelled on Skeleton-man's body.

A mid-size Toyota approaches, slows, speeds away. Three minutes later it reappears. This time it pulls into a parking space on Bay, then hovers, lights and engine on. I tense; this must be him, the timing is right and the behavior appropriately peculiar. A minute passes, the driver cuts his engine, waits a few seconds, douses his lights and gets out.

I recognize him immediately, the aggressive waddle, extended paunch. He's even carrying an overstuffed briefcase the way a harassed lawyer should. I watch from my hiding place as he peers about, then paces back and forth, never straying far from his vehicle. Several times he stops, checks his watch, looks toward me and the trees above. Finally, nervously, he goes to the benches where I told him to wait, chooses one and sits, cradling his briefcase in his arms.

I peer around to be sure no one's lurking. I search the shadows beneath surrounding trees for human forms. I scan the crest behind, the flat fenced-off reservoir above, finally the backs of the buildings behind me on Chestnut Street, where several large view windows are dimly lit.

No uncommon movements, visible confederates, nothing extraordinary or out of place. This is a dog-walking area, but tonight the haze has confined evening strollers to residential streets. The only sound, beside the buoys and foghorns, is the erratic rumbling of the cable beneath the tracks on Hyde.

I stoop, step out from beneath the boughs, straighten up, stand still, scan my surroundings again. Judd, back to me, sits quietly on his bench. I'm eager to go to him, but hold myself back. Five minutes more, I decide, to be certain he's alone. Then I'll approach him from behind.

• • •

Judd moves as if to turn. "Don't!" I order. I hear the same labored breathing I heard in his office after I knocked him down. "Let's make this quick," I snap. "Give me the names."

"Yeah, and what do I get?" he asks, his voice whiny, shrill. "You hand over the tape, how do I know you didn't make a copy?"

"You don't. Which is why I won't be handing over the tape."

"What?" He's outraged. It comes back to me now—how much I dislike him. "I thought we had a deal." Again he starts to turn.

I place my hand on his sweaty pate, am revulsed at the touch. "Face front! We *do* have a deal. You give me the names, you don't get disbarred." He squirms beneath my palm. "Of course I've copied the tape," I tell him, "deposited it with friends . . . as I have all the incriminating photographs I took since I started delving into this vipers' nest."

"Why should I trust you, missy?"

How I loathe that word! Sensing he's stalling, I turn, check the trees behind, see nothing, focus again on the back of his head.

"My deal expires in twenty seconds. Talk or I'm walking away."

"You can't!"

"I am!" I retreat a step.

"Wait!"

"Talk!"

"Sure." Suddenly he turns, a light flashes and I go blind.

An extremely brilliant lamp, a strobe, has been fired point-blank at my face. Instinctively I start running up the hill, feeling my way blindly, scrambling, grasping desperately at gravel and weeds.

I open my eyes, see nothing, but hear someone climbing behind. Propelled by terror, I rush on as slowly my vision clears. At the top of the ridge, I turn and look down. I have but a split second to glimpse the scene below before lights flash again, twice this time, from two different points. Again blinded, I turn and rush forward, colliding with a fence.

I know where I am, at the fenced perimeter of the old underground Francisco Street reservoir, closed off by the Water Department because the roof is weak. I turn right, run along the fence, brushing one hand against the metal. There are at least two people chasing me and both have strobes. If I trip and fall, they'll overtake me. I must outrun them even though I can't see. If I can keep from looking back, I'll gradually regain my sight. But if I turn to face them, they will strobe me again, and then I'll be at their mercy.

The air's chilly but I sweat as I stumble along the path. I can see now, better every second, can also hear my pursuers' steps. Not Judd, I'm certain; he's a waddler, couldn't move this fast. Who are these people? Where did they come from? Then it hits me: they must have been hiding in Judd's car. He hid his strobe in his briefcase, fired it at me, then they got out with strobes of their own and chased me up the hill.

I scramble back down toward the olive trees, choose one, hit the ground, crawl on my belly beneath the branches until I reach the trunk. So long as they can fire off strobes, I don't have a chance. If I turn to fight, they'll blind me; if I try to hide, they have lamps to find me out.

I hear them now moving in the darkness. They know I'm in the grove. I catch a glimpse of one. He's holding a cell phone to his ear. They're conferring, coordinating their search. In a minute one of them will spot me. If I'm to survive I must move fast, gain back my advantage— superior vision at night.

I choose the one closest. In silhouette he looks familiar, but even with my sight restored I can't make out his face. I crouch, ready to rush him, waiting for him to turn his back. Rita said: *Use your camera as a ball and chain.*

Merge with it. I wrap the strap of my Nikon around my hand until there's but a foot of slack.

He steps closer, stops and stares. Now he's just fifteen feet away. When he turns, I charge. He hears me, raises his strobe. Swinging my camera, I knock it from his hands. On the reverse swing, I smack him in the side of the head. He goes down. I stamp hard on the strobe, hear the lens and bulb crack beneath my shoe. He groans, moves. I kick him, then hear a shout. His colleague is charging at me from below. I turn just in time to avoid another burst of light, dash back up the hill, stumbling on my own shadow as the strobe flashes again and again like a hot lash against my back.

Ping! Something nicks the earth beside me. *Ping!Ping!* Two more nicks, closer. Must be bullets! I scurry along the north-south reservoir fence, prepared to rush up the Larkin steps.

Suddenly another figure rises before me. I turn. Behind me the man with the gun is gaining fast. Cornered! I rush the new man, am about to strike him with my camera, stop just as the strobe behind me fires off. The light reveals Drake, illuminated like a ghost, his face chalk-white and flat. Confused, I drop my camera. Drake pulls me to him, pivots, pushes me down, then through an opening at the bottom of the fence.

We race across the asphalt. I'm terrified. I know the reason this area is fenced, the weakness of the roof, can feel it cave beneath my feet.

"We can't cross here!" I tell him. "We'll fall through."

Drake whispers: "Stay with me. You'll be safe."

He guides me to a wooden walkway that angles across the asphalt. I glance back, spot our pursuer wriggling beneath the fence.

Drake lifts up a flap of asphalt, pulls up boards, throws them aside.

"Down," he orders.

"Into the water?"

"It's empty. Go down, Kay. Feel for the ladder."

Ping!Ping! More shots. I find a footing on the ladder, scamper down, several times feeling Drake's heels as they scuff my head. Just as I reach the bottom, the silhouette of our pursuer appears in the hatch above. I jump for the floor. Drake leaps too, then yanks the ladder from the opening. It crashes down, raising a cloud of dust. I turn away and choke.

It's black down here, the floor is covered with debris and muck, there are pillars at regular intervals, the ceiling is twenty-five feet high and the smell is of old iron, rust and rot. Drake guides me toward the Hyde Street side. The man in the hatch opening is firing his strobe, trying to find us in the gloom. I flatten myself behind a pillar, draw in my legs, freeze. My vision has grown keen; I don't relish the thought of losing it. I shade my eyes, then peer around, taking care not to look directly at the strobe.

This reservoir, I recall, was built in the last century. For years there's been talk of making it safe, retrofitting it to withstand a magnitude-8 quake. Meantime it's been sitting here, a vast subterranean space, forest of old columns supporting a crumbling roof, dusty, unused, uninhabited by anything except rodents and an occasional vagrant.

In the distance I spot another ladder leading up to a second hatch. Our pursuer apparently sees it too, for he and his strobe disappear from the opening. I hear his footsteps on the roof. I whisper to Drake we must pull the second ladder down. Drake brings his finger to his lips. The ceiling creaks. He grins.

The groan of wood under strain. Splintering, then a scream as a huge piece of roof crashes down. An explosion of dust. I turn away. When I look back up, the night sky's visible. The man pursuing us has fallen through. When the echoes die, I hear his cries in the darkness, like the whining of an injured dog.

To approach or not? I hold Drake back; the man may still have his gun.

"Is there another way out?"

Drake nods, starts crawling. I crawl after him through the dust toward the sound of traffic on Hyde. By the time we reach the reservoir wall, the moans of our fallen pursuer have grown faint. Suddenly there's a roar as a cable car ascends. I think of myself with Sasha, just a few weeks ago, walking up this hill which I am now beneath, en route to our first kiss at my door.

Drake motions toward rungs built into the wall. He climbs, I follow, until we are at the top, parallel with the slanting sidewalk. We swing ourselves up, Drake pushes out a section of grillwork, then we crawl out between close-fitting struts. At last in the open, I gulp fresh inky fog.

"You saved my life, Drake." He's stunned when I take his face in my hands, plant a chaste kiss on his cheek. I feel him withdraw. When we were in danger there was contact; he grasped me, pushed and pulled me to safety. Now that we're safe, he retreats back into his solitude.

He lowers his eyes. "I am always watching out for you, Kay."

"I know." I gesture toward the reservoir. "He's still down there. I've got to call the cops."

He nods sadly.

"You won't stay?"

He shakes his head. "Be careful. The other one—"

"I'll be careful." I touch his hand. "Thanks."

He reenters the park. I watch as he skits along the reservoir fence toward Larkin, disappears in the fog. He will climb back up to Sterling Park, I know, hole up again among the trees and shrubs and from there gaze up at my window. I wish that one time at least we could hug one another, but I know this is something my secret watchman of the woods will not permit.

I walk up to Chestnut, find a pay phone. My finger trembles as I punch in Hilly's number. Thank God she's home! Excited, she hears me out. When I'm done she says: "I'm on my way." I replace the phone, venture carefully back toward my vantage point among the olive trees, noting that Judd's car is no longer on the street.

I'm looking for the other man, the one I hit in the head. There was something familiar about the way he moved I couldn't place. No trace of him now, but I do find my Nikon and the strobe I smashed. To my amazement Dad's old camera still works; beneath the black exterior it's solid brass.

I pick up the broken strobe, examine it. Brand-new. Judd brought them here expressly to blind and kill me. How did they know I'm photophobic? I look down at my hands; they're still shaking. I drop the strobe in the dust.

I feel no pity for the man I struck or the one lying at the bottom of the reservoir. I have no doubt that if they had caught me, they'd have heaved me through that very roof.

Three squad cars pull up, then Hilly in her Volvo. I tell her about Judd. A minute later a police rescue unit arrives, followed by an ambulance. Hilly joins them. I watch through the fog as men and women with flashlights go to the reservoir, peer down through the hole. A crew arrives with a portable block and tackle. Another crew sets up a generator and lights. Rescue workers descend. I start taking pictures, hear the crackle of police radios, watch as the injured body of my pursuer is hoisted up.

He's placed on a stretcher, rushed down to the ambulance. Hilly walks to where I'm standing. She's carrying another broken strobe and a .22 automatic in a Ziploc bag. There's some kind of attachment on the barrel. Hilly tells me it's a silencer.

"It's Vasquez," she says. "He can't move. Lots of broken bones." She stares at me, smiles, shakes her head. "Can you believe it, Kay—chief of Felony Prostitution shooting at an unarmed woman with an illegally silenced gun! Jesus hot fuckin' dog!"

I tell her why I'm not surprised, that I suspected he was Judd's partner in the scam.

She tells me Vasquez is crying for his lawyer, that she's sent a team to find Judd and arrest him, also put out a call to all hospital E.R.s to look out for the man I hit.

"There's plenty of blood," she tells me. "Looks like you whacked him good."

"I'm thrilled."

"Seen him before, Kay?"

"I think so. Can't remember where."

"It'll come to you." She steps closer, smiles again. "Last night I checked Knob's record at Pelican Bay. They try and train the boys up there, teach them a trade so they can find work when they get out. Guess what? His job was in the kitchen, apprentice meat cutter." She curls her lip. "They say near the end he got pretty good." She pauses. "I'm going to pick him up. Wanna come along?"

As we drive over the top of Russian Hill, followed by two squad cars, each containing a team of uniformed cops, I catch glimpses through lit windows of cheerful domestic scenes, families clustered in comfortable living rooms relaxing after Thanksgiving dinner. Down on Polk it's a different story, lonely singles sitting in all-night Chinese restaurants, staring at their food. In doorways the homeless lie like broken dolls, while the addicts in the alleys peer at us with haunted eyes.

After Bush Street we come upon hustlers. Hilly says she's surprised to see them out. I tell her what I learned from Tim, that around holidays business is always good, the streets filled with lonely johns, married men seeking rough trade, obsessed chicken hawks yearning for sweet boy-love in the night.

We spot Knob, standing with Tommy and Boat, beside the door of The Werewolf. Hilly drives a block, pulls over, confers with the cops in the squad cars, returns to talk to me. The cops, she says, will scoop up all three, separate them, run the kids down to the Hall of Justice, place them in cubicles. She'll take Knob in her car on a longer, slower ride around the city. Certain he'll ask for a lawyer, she wants to talk to him informally first. I can't come along, but I'm welcome to meet her later at the Hall.

"Aren't you afraid to be alone with him?" I ask.

Hilly grins. "He's already done one five-year stretch for felonious assault. I kinda doubt he wants to go back for life."

I walk home, shower, change and then, in an attempt to stop my hands from shaking, clean my camera and reload. The shaking's so bad I can barely get the fresh film aligned.

Calm yourself. Find your center, Kay.

I go to my office, look down through the window at Sterling Park. Drake's down there, I know, possibly, this very moment, gazing up at me.

I phone for a cab. On my way out the door, it suddenly comes to me—the identity of the third man with the strobe.

I return to my office, check the photos pinned to the cork. Yes, now I'm certain—it was Sarah Lashaw's lover and tennis coach, the man I know as Roy.

The receptionist at the Hall of Justice phones for Hilly. She comes down to meet me, glow of triumph on her face. I sign in, a guard hangs a visitor's ID around my neck, Hilly escorts me back up to the Homicide Division.

I tell her about Roy. She beams. "It fits. The house of cards is falling fast."

In her office she instructs the duty detective to call the Lashaw house in St. Helena, get the full name of the resident tennis coach. Then she takes me into a viewing room.

The cubicle on the other side of the one-way glass is small, oppressive like a cell. I think: Maybe this is the one where the T case detectives worked over Dad. Knob faces us. He doesn't look like king of the Gulch tonight. His eyes are puffy; there're bruises on his cheeks.

I turn to Hilly. "What'd you do to him?"

She grins. "Explained a few facts of life. Like whatever

happened he was going down, the only question being whether he'd get life or lethal injection.''

"Okay if I take his picture?"

"Be my guest."

As I trip the shutter, I think I see him wince.

"He's in recovery," Hilly says. "That's normal after a confession. Come on, I'll show you the videotape."

She escorts me to another room, equipped with TV monitor and VCR, gestures me to a chair, slaps in a tape, fast-forwards it, stops.

"Here's the good part," she says, restarting the tape at normal speed.

I lean forward. This, I feel, is a moment I ought to savor.

Knob, sobbing, desperate: "I *swear* I didn't kill him!"

Hilly's voice, sympathetic, calm: "But you know who did?"

Knob, crying, insistent: "Wasn't me!"

"But you did *something,* right?"

A moan, a nod: "Helped clean up, that's all."

"Clean up? What does that mean?"

"He was dead. I did some cutting. I *swear*—he was already dead."

Hilly freezes the frame.

She has things to do, leaves me alone to watch the rest of the tape. I stare spellbound as Knob tells how Crane became his most important client, the huge amounts of money Crane paid him to procure boys.

"He kept wanting them younger, prettier. I broke my ass trying to please the guy. Then he met Rain, liked him . . . which wasn't good for me. See, Rain worked freelance. He wouldn't cut me in."

"You hated Rain for that?" Hilly asks.

Knob winces, shakes his head. "Wasn't personal. Business, that's all it was. He stole my best client. It's tough out there."

"Tough?"

"I had expenses. I was paying out big to Vasquez."

"For what?"

"Protection. If I didn't pay, he'd run me off the street."

"You the only one who paid him?"

"No, everyone does. He knows everything going on, names of all the important johns, who pays how much and what they get for it. He knows Crane, takes money from him, too. Knew Rain. When Crane got in trouble with Rain, he was there to help."

"What kind of trouble?" Hilly asks.

"Rain stopped seeing him."

"Dropped him?"

Knob nods.

"Why?"

Knob shakes his head. "Didn't like the way Crane kept crowding him, I guess."

"You said Crane paid big."

"He did, but Rain didn't care. Last month he comes to me, asks me to find Crane someone else. 'Get the guy off my back, I'll give you a split,' he says. So then we were friends again."

"What happened?"

"Beginning of October, when Rain stopped seeing him, Crane started talking crazy. One night he tells me since he can't have Rain he wants the next best thing. I try to fix him up for a three-way with Tommy and Boat, but this isn't what he's got in mind. Turns out he wants Rain's twin, the girl."

Amoretto! I marvel at how her story keeps getting entwined with this. And certainly it makes sense: if Crane couldn't have Tim, he'd have his androgynous twin, Ariane. Boy, girl—small difference if the game was about possession.

Knob requires little prompting now. Studying his face, expressionless eyes, listening to his matter-of-fact tone, I'm mesmerized as much as repelled. I even think I catch a glimmer of relief. Cool and amoral as he is, Knob isn't a pure sociopath, just a Catholic boy gone bad, carrying a burden of guilt. To confess to Hilly is to seek absolution, a first step toward redemption. She wants so much to understand him; he tries so hard to make her understand.

After all, he keeps insisting, he didn't kill anyone, just helped clean up . . . and was thus but a bystander to the drama.

"Scene with the girl didn't work out. Way I heard, got nasty too. I think that was Crane's plan—belt the girl around, get Rain mad. Then Rain'd *have* to come see him." Knob laughs. "Oh, Rain got mad all right. Real mad. Said he was going to go after the guy, report him, sue his ass. I told him, 'Don't do that!' It's the number-one rule on the street. You don't tell on these guys. They got too much to lose—family, reputation, whatever. You threaten them, try and blackmail, they're as likely to kill you as pay you off.

"Not that Crane had the guts to kill anybody. Least I didn't think he did. More like he'd hire someone to do the job. There're plenty of guys on the Gulch, addicts and whatnot, they'll do anything you pay 'em enough."

But Knob had underrated Crane, who, as it turned out, was quite capable of killing Tim. Knob didn't know what happened, only that Crane came to him and Vasquez afterward with twenty-five thousand cash each to clean up and cover up the killing.

Right away Knob knew what to do—cut Tim up and dispose of the pieces. Then Vasquez got the bright idea of tying the Homicide Division up in knots. He'd wash Tim's torso with licorice-scented soap, then apply designs and the number "7" to make it look like a copycat T killing. Knob, figuring the head and limbs would never be found, bagged and dropped them into an alley Dumpster. Vasquez, hoping the tricked-up torso *would* be found, ditched it in open sight in Wildcat Canyon.

"So, see, I didn't kill anyone," Knob says, pleading for sympathy. "I'm bad, but not that bad. Like I said— the kid was dead. Guy offers you a bundle to clean up, what would you do? Huh?"

Hilly reappears to tell me Crane and Roy have just been picked up at Sarah Lashaw's San Francisco house. I'm impressed with the way she's handling things. Without a supervisor to slow her down, she's moved decisively. Now with Crane under arrest, I have to agree that yes, the house of cards is falling fast.

"The way it comes down," she says, "Vasquez and Knob were accessories after the fact. They'll both get life sentences for that. Crane'll get the needle, Roy and Judd'll do time for trying to kill you. It's all over now except for the trials."

I shake my head. The riddle is solved. Now that I know the story all the pieces fit: Crane, the Chicken Hawk, kills Tim to shut him up; Knob, the Butcher, cuts up Tim's body; Vasquez, the Bad Cop, ornaments Tim's torso to confuse the investigation.

But why did Crane have to kill Tim? Why not just pay him off? I think I know. Crane, I believe, tried to pay, but Tim refused his money. Ariane, his beloved twin, had been brutally beaten; no amount would stop him from bringing Crane down.

In the morning Joel and I attend the arraignments. The courtroom is packed with squabbling lawyers, bored cops, irritable bailiffs, terrified spouses, some with infants in their arms. Judge Helen Lesser, gray-haired and gaunt, presides.

The players perform like robots, each accused person approaching the bar with counsel, listening to, then answering the charge, followed by a brisk argument over bail, a quick decision by the judge, a stroke of the gavel, then a rapid march-off to the wings.

We sit through a string of minor cases: pickpockets, prostitutes, shoplifters, persons accused of peddling without a license. At one point Hilly approaches with an attractive young Asian-American woman whom she introduces as Assistant D.A. Patricia Chu. Pat Chu, Hilly tells us, will be prosecuting the Lovsey defendants. We shake hands, Pat returns to her table, Hilly whispers: "She's young but one of the best."

The clerk calls Luis Vasquez.

One Laurence Granby steps forward, former police officer, now shiny-suited defense attorney specializing in the representation of accused cops. His client, he tells Judge Lesser, cannot appear, being presently in the hospital recovering from a fall. He presents papers allowing him to plead in his stead.

The charges are read: attempted homicide; corruption; obstruction of justice; accessory after the fact to murder. Granby tells the judge that his client pleads not guilty. Mr. Vasquez, he argues, being a sworn law enforcement officer with strong ties to the community, should, upon his recovery, be released without bond.

Pat Chu, with just the slightest hint of a snarl, argues for confinement. Judge Lesser agrees, orders Vasquez transferred to the jail ward at Cal Med. "Next!" she tells her clerk.

J. F. Judd appears, accompanied by his former law partner, a rumpled old-timer named Jeremiah Waldroon. The charges: false representation; solicitation of corruption; conspiracy to commit murder. Waldroon asks for minimum bail. Judge Lesser sternly sets bond at $100,000.

Raymond Crogan, a.k.a. Knob, accompanied by public defender Wendy Aronson, is called next. Knob pleads guilty to the charge of accessory to murder. Pat Chu informs the judge that Crogan has agreed to testify against other parties in return for being allowed to plead to a single three-strikes offense. Since there can be no bail for a three-strikes offender, Judge Lesser sets a date for the formal plea and sentencing. Knob is led away.

Next up is Peter Royal, known to me as Roy, dressed in pressed chinos and tennis shirt, head swathed in bandages. His lawyer assists him in pleading not guilty to the charge of attempted murder, then asks for bail.

"My client," he pleads, "is the injured party here. Truth is, the person he's accused of trying to kill, tried to kill him . . . and nearly did."

Pat Chu explains that the victim, namely me, was acting in self-defense. She asks for $200,000 bond. Judge Lesser agrees, smacks her gavel, asks the clerk to call the next case.

The room becomes still. This is what everyone's been waiting for. Marcus Crane, toupeed, dressed in dark gray slacks, bespoke sports jacket and Pacific-Union Club tie, walks confidently to the bar, accompanied by J. Carter Hackford, possibly the best and certainly the most expensive defense attorney in San Francisco. The charge: first degree murder.

During the reading, Crane, head held high, stares straight ahead. But scanning the courtroom, I spot Sarah Lashaw. Our eyes meet. She glares raw hatred. I turn away.

Hackford argues for bond; the charge, he says, is based solely on the testimony of a lying street hustler and convicted felon. He lists various important corporate and charity boards upon which Mr. Crane sits, his role as scion of one of the city's oldest, most distinguished families, the lack of any criminal record and the absurdity of the notion that such a man would attempt to flee.

Pat Chu reminds the court that this is a capital case, describes the brutality of the crime, the overwhelming evidence and the fact that no citizen, no matter his station, is entitled to special privilege.

Judge Lesser agrees, remands Marcus Crane to the custody of the Sheriff's Department, to be held in jail pending a preliminary hearing.

Outside we're swarmed. TV and print reporters, photographers and videotape cameramen press close. Even though I'm wearing shades, I hold up my hand to protect my eyes.

The questions fly at me:

"Is it true Tim Lovsey was a hustler?"

"You took photos of Crane soliciting kids, right?"

"Why'd they want to kill you, Kay?"

Keeping silent, I try to work my way through, Joel gently pushing his press colleagues aside to create a path.

Suddenly the crowd parts, then deserts us. A far bigger attraction has appeared.

"Mrs. Lashaw—is it true your husband's part of a ring of chicken hawks?"

"Sarah! Did you know Mark Crane was gay?"

"How's your tennis coach involved?"

"Did you put him up to it?"

"How's it feel to be married to a child molester?"

The questions resound as Joel and I escape the crush. Out on Bryant Street, Joel turns to me, winks.

"You'll be on TV tonight, kiddo."

Sasha is on duty, so I go over to Dad's on Cherry Street to watch the evening news. Since I'm more interested in his reactions than in seeing myself, I study him as he waits for my appearance. He's nervous but also rooting for me, I can tell, actually looks proud when I come on.

"Oh, boy!" he says. "That's it, darlin'! Give it to 'em, give it to 'em good!"

Since, in the film clip, I speak not a word, it must be my silence that he likes.

"No, it's you, darlin'—your dignity, the way you move. Class! They recognize it. Now that Lashaw lady—she comes off like a tart."

I have to smile. His vocabulary's so quaint. Tarts, fairies, tootsie-babies—such archetypes populate his mind. But if he's an old-fashioned guy, his heart is big and his integrity intact. When the news segment is over, he flicks the set off.

"So what's next, darlin'? When're you planning on digging up Billy's stuff?"

"Joel thinks we should give it a month."

Dad nods. "Good idea. Wait till after the holidays at least."

Hilly, Joel, Ice Goddess Kirstin, Sasha and I meet to celebrate the publication of Joel's front-page story in the *Bay*

Area News. We assemble at the bar at Zuni, my favorite San Francisco haunt because of its food, conviviality and eccentric triangular flatiron space. When our table is ready we ascend to the balcony. Conversation and laughter bubble up to us as we eat. This, I think, is San Francisco at its best—happy, youthful, still a little wild.

Sasha's great. Everyone likes him. But as dinner progresses, Hilly slips into a funk. When Joel asks what's the matter, she says being without a date makes her feel odd-man-out.

"Jeez, Hilly," Joel says, "now that you're famous you'll get hit on all the time."

"Yeah," she says, brightening. Then just as quickly she deflates: "But then how'll I know it's me she likes and not just the true-blue image?"

A few days of euphoria, then the letdown. It's all wrapped up . . . except it's not. *Exposures,* I think, will work. I'll have a book, a coherent story with beginning, middle and end. But still there's something missing. In my anger and the passion of the chase, I forgot about my loss. Now I miss Tim terribly. His smile, eyes, beauty, the perfect planes of his face, the way he used to touch me when we talked. I long for closure, cannot find it. His twin, carrying at least some portion of his spirit, somewhere roams the earth. I know I must find her, that until I do I cannot rest.

Early December days are clear this year, the light oblique and sharp. Hard to imagine winter rains are coming soon. In daytime it's balmy, people walk around in jogging clothes. I spot a Santa Claus standing on the corner of Mason and Sutter ringing a bell in shorts. At night the air is crisp; the city sparkles beneath the moon. I study various neighborhoods through my telescope, recalling David deGeoffroy's certainty that Ariane must be nearby. Why hasn't she come forward? Surely she knows of the arrests. She also knows who I am and how to find me, but I have no notion of where to look for her.

• • •

Joel's call awakens me from a dream. I answer groggily, brain fogged with sleep.

"Crane's dead, killed himself."

"*What?*" My head clears fast. "*When? Where?*"

"Last night. In jail. He wasn't on suicide watch. He was acting so cocky the jailers left him alone. Somehow he got hold of a belt, used it to make a noose, got up on a stool, secured the belt to the window bars, kicked the stool away. They're pissing blood downtown. Hackford's yelling the cops railroaded an innocent man, hounded him unto death. Lashaw was just on the air fuming with indignation. It's all the fault, she says, of a sick, obsessed girl. That's you, kiddo. And a scummy journalist, me. She named us both."

"Jesus!"

"Don't worry. She and Hackford'll be sorry. I just got off the phone with Pat Chu. The D.A.'s office believes in the public's right to know. They'll release details of their case this afternoon."

At five I turn on my TV, watch the press conference live. Pat Chu is terrific, smooth, even-tempered, precise, and she presents a devastating brief. She's got it all, chapter and verse, even the gun used to shoot Tim, registered to Crane and found in Knob's hooch. She shows the knives Knob used to do the cutting, the wad of money he received from Crane, Crane's lease on the Washington Street pied-à-terre where he engaged in sexual acts with underage boys. Best of all, she offers serology reports showing that traces of Tim's blood were found in the love nest, on the carpet where he fell after he was shot and in the drain of the bathtub where the butchering was carried out.

"The evidence," she says, "is overwhelming, as Mr. Crane surely recognized. Naturally we deplore his suicide. We'd have much preferred to take our case to a jury. Still, we must surmise that Marcus Crane took his own life to spare himself and his family a blistering defeat at trial.''

Joel wants me to attend Crane's funeral, to be held in Grace Cathedral. I decline. I have no wish to stand outside in a vulture's pack of photographers ready to pounce when Sarah Lashaw appears.

I've had more than enough of that doomed, demented couple. Like specimen insects, they'll be pinned forever in my memory. Instead I spend those hours working quietly in my darkroom, where the safety light gives off a comforting glow.

An image emerging slowly from a sheet of photographic paper immersed in developer—the magic of it stirs me still. It's the same feeling I get when I look out at the city at night. I smile at the wonder of it, the mystery.

Two weeks before Christmas, Dad again asks me to join him, Phyllis Sorenson and her daughters on their holiday trip to Honolulu. But he doesn't demur when I remind him we agreed a joint vacation wouldn't work.

"I'll miss you, darlin'."

I tell him I'll miss him too.

"Just hate to think of you all alone."

"I won't be alone. I'll be with Sasha."

"That's right." A pause. "You know, I really *like* that boy!"

I thank him, but haven't the heart to respond that I wish I liked Phyllis as well.

In fact, Sasha, having learned his lesson at Thanksgiving, has reserved a room for us at Treetops in Big Sur. Our stay, he promises, will be "sybaritic." Needless to say, I can't wait.

December 16. Hilly stops by to return my Contax G1 and Zeiss 28mm lens, discovered in Knob's hooch in the Tenderloin, the little room he rented at the corner of Turk and Jones. Both are in as good shape as they were the night Knob grabbed them. I'm thrilled. I love this little camera which has served me so well, and am mystified Knob didn't try to sell it.

In fact, Hilly tells me, Knob kept everything—the pistol Crane told him to get rid of, the butcher knives he used, even Tim's clothing, wallet and keys. She thinks it's because, during the time he served in Pelican, Knob acquired convict traits—compulsive neatness, covetousness, an inability to throw anything away.

Just before she goes she slips me a transcript copy of his amended confession.

"It's got a few more details," she says.

I place it on my bedside table, then, uncomfortable with the notion of sleeping so close to it, hide it away in a drawer.

Still it oppresses me. Why, I wonder, can't I just sit down and read the damn thing? After all, it's an essential part of the story. If *Exposures* is to be a proper account, I must know everything that happened.

After three days I give in, take it to the living room, lie down on my couch and start to read.

Soon I'm enveloped. Then I come to the part where my life intersected with the described events. The night Tim was killed, when I went out to meet him on the Gulch, I spotted Crane—whom I dubbed Baldy at the time—speaking with Knob, then handing him a package I was sure contained drugs. A few seconds later, passing Crane, I noticed he was upset, but when I asked Knob what their conversation had been about, he shrugged the encounter off.

In fact, I now learn from Knob's amended confession, it was during that brief exchange that Crane paid him to get rid of Tim's body. A few minutes after receiving the money and the key, Knob went over to Crane's Washington Street pied-à-terre, hauled Tim's body into the bathroom, placed it in the tub and commenced his grisly work.

There is fascination in madness. Crane, according to Knob, was truly mad:

"... I'm in the bathroom cutting. Suddenly he comes in, this weird look on his face, says he wants to keep Rain's head. I ask him, 'What're you going to do with it, man? Make love to it, put it on the wall like a fuckin' trophy?' 'I want it!' he says. He tries to grab it out of the tub. I slap him down. 'Look,' I tell him, 'I got work to do, I don't need this kinda shit.' Vasquez comes in, pulls him into the other room, so I get on with the job. ..."

Yeah, the job.

The next day, the Friday before Christmas, I deliver my important gifts: a carry-on bag for Dad, not too imaginative but he'll need it for his trip; a handmade craftswoman's kaleidoscope for Maddy ("May you always see beauty, Maddy!"); the shell of a chambered nautilus for Rita ("For you, you hard-assed softy!"); a pad of play money for Caroline Gifford at Zeitgeist ("Next time, I promise, it'll be real!"); and a bottle of Courvoisier Extra for Rob Mathews ("With special thanks for your very special help!").

The day Sasha and I are to drive south, I prepare a holiday package for Drake: an assortment of the organic health foods he likes, plus Christmas cookies and a bottle of Italian egg liqueur. I wrap the whole thing up in foiled paper, tie it with a mix of ribbons, slip a couple of poinsettias beneath the bow, then place it on our bench.

I wait awhile, hoping he'll show himself. I want to tell him how things worked out and that now I'm out of danger. He doesn't appear. He's been so elusive the last couple of weeks, I wonder if something's wrong. I take a brief walk around the park, but find no trace of him. When I return to the bench the box is gone. He's here all right; he simply chooses not to show himself. That's fine. I call out, "Best wishes for the holidays, Drake," then return to my apartment to pack.

Treetops is a dream. Our suite is a detached house set up on stilts among the redwoods to protect their roots. We have a fireplace, hot tub, porch furnished with wicker chairs, huge bed made up with incredibly luxurious sheets arranged for perfect viewing of the Pacific.

At night we watch a cruise ship pass, lit up like a city. Then a thick fog hugs us in. In the morning we arise to find whales cavorting in the waves, blowing off fountains of spray. There's nothing to do here except eat, sleep, read, make love and receive deep Swedish-style massages from the staff.

On Christmas morning after breakfast, we take a long hike through the woods. At lunch we exchange gifts: a black silk dressing gown for Sasha, a small framed Indian tantric painting of a female warrior for me.

I'm overwhelmed. The drawing is exquisite. Sasha tells me it's colored, but he thinks the effect is more powerful in black and white.

"How do you know?" I ask.

"I photographed it first to see."

What a fabulous man! "I'm crazy about you, Sasha. I chose a black robe for you because you wear white all day."

He kisses me. We repair to our tree house to make love. After that a long soak in our hot tub, then a double massage as we lie side by side while a pair of tender-fingered masseuses knead our flesh. This, I think, must be what "sybaritic" means.

Before sleep, I look closely at the painting. It's less than a foot square, yet filled with energy. The woman warrior holds a sword in one hand, a shield in the other. At her feet lies a half-clad male.

I ask Sasha if there's a story to go with it. He says there're a hundred possible stories, and, to demonstrate, he'll tell me one.

"The warrior is you, Kay—powerful, indomitable, a woman of convictions, never to be trifled with. The man is your lover, me, 'slain' by your fierce beauty. We've made love all night. Now we recline declaring our love— you in your warrior's crouch, female power enhanced, I at your feet drained but in bliss.''

"Sasha," I tell him, "that's just wonderful."

January 8: foggy, wintry. Hilly, "based on information received from a confidential source," has secured a search warrant from Judge Henry Beck to dig up the area behind Billy Hayes's widow's garage.

Debbie Hayes doesn't act surprised when we show up— Hilly, Joel and me, a van carrying two cops and three criminalists with shovels, trailed by a backhoe and driver from Public Works.

Debbie's a big blowsy middle-aged woman with a Texas twang. Hard to imagine her with Billy, the lean, fast-talking welterweight. But she doesn't object or squawk or carry on. I get the impression she's cried lots of tears in her life and more or less expects disasters.

When I ask if I can take her picture, she invites me into the house. There's a display of family photos on the spinet, no sign in them of kids. I pose her holding a photo of young Billy to her chest, in which, in head-guard and trunks, he receives his Golden Gloves award. There's an expression of longing on her face that seems to deepen as I shoot. Afterwards she stands by the window staring out at the men.

"It's nice to have a bunch of guys around again. Billy used to bring his cop friends home. I miss those days."

She asks me if I think it'll be all right if she takes a case of beer out to the crew, or whether she should wait until they find whatever it is they're looking for.

Dusk comes early in January. It's dark and cold by the time the trench is dug, fifteen feet wide running along the rear of the garage. The backhoe operator had to take special care not to break into the foundation.

I shiver in my jacket as the criminalists start sifting dirt. They wear miners' lights on their helmets; the beams crisscross as they work the pit. A train passes behind the house, hissing its way south to San Jose. Neighborhood kids cluster around to watch. Not much conversation, just steady work by men anxious to finish a tough job and go home.

I keep my eyes on Hilly, wondering what she thinks, why she supposes Billy buried this stuff and to what degree she suspects Dad's involvement. We've tipped her off without telling her the entire story. In return for our tip, she's promised not to delve too deeply. As Joel puts it, she's chosen personal glory at the price of never understanding Billy's motivation. In this matter each of us has used the other: Hilly to greatly advance her career; Joel to break a terrific story; I, as best I understand myself, to preserve the symmetries; all of us to uncover the dead T killer's identity.

Photographing the scene, I try to capture its starkness, the sense I have that we're digging up a grave. A couple of times people call Hilly over, but in each instance the find turns out to be a stone.

Shortly after seven, a cop near the corner of the garage holds up a black polyethylene bag knotted at the top. Hilly takes it to the van, hands it to the chief criminalist. Miraculously, the plastic hasn't torn.

During the opening I fire off rapid frames. Behind me the men light cigarettes while herding against the chill.

Once the bag is opened an odor is released, earthy and, perhaps in my imagination, faintly tinged with licorice. I catch my breath as the criminalist pulls out a set of mildewed clothes, then the hypodermic, the tattooing gear, finally the awful ominous hood slippery with mold.

Hilly turns to me: "Do you believe this, Kay? Fifteen years in the ground?" She turns to the others. "Yes! *Yes!*" She whoops. They cheer, hug, congratulate. I photograph their faces, the pride, the gloat.

Joel sidles over. "Big moment."

"Absolutely," I agree.

"How do you feel?"

"Nervous. Afraid it'll backfire on Dad."

"Don't worry, kiddo. Hilly'll see he isn't hurt."

"How does she explain it then?"

"An old dead cop's perversity, something like that."

"What'll Hale think when he hears?"

Joel smiles. "That he's been screwed. You know, by the powers that be, the forces of darkness, the conspirators. He was methodical, did everything right, more or less figured out what happened. Only trouble was . . . he didn't know where to dig."

"Any regrets about not telling him?"

Joel shakes his head. "I like Hilly." His smile is sly. "I'm going to have the best cop source in town for years to come, I think."

I'm spending the better part of my days in the darkroom now, marking up proof sheets, printing my selections out. Twice a week, late in the afternoon, I drop by Maddy's to show her my work. She confirms some of my decisions, questions others, but never challenges my premise. Often she'll point out a new direction, a route into the story via an alternate set of images. Guided by her counsel, I make final choices, then return to the darkroom to work up exhibition-quality prints.

Some photographers I know hire a printer, but I like printing too much to farm it out. Choosing the paper, selecting contrast, exposure time, burning and dodging—I never find the process dull. And the fact that it's slow and must be done by hand adds to the pleasure. Available-light street photography is quick; one shoots fast, guided by instinct. Making prints is more like working with traditional art materials, paint or clay or wood.

The treasure trove discovered behind Debbie Hayes's garage yields nothing in the way of fingerprints. Perhaps Skeleton-man wore gloves or time or moisture eroded whatever prints were there. It doesn't matter; in the end it's the hood that takes hold of Hilly's mind.

Well on her way to earning Hale's old title "San Francisco's smartest cop," she and Joel try to run it down, trekking leather store to leather store, smoothly working their way into the Bay Area leathersex community.

Hilly's lesbianism and Joel's Pulitzer prize don't hurt, opening up doors which an ordinary team would probably not discover were there. Within days they are able to set up a meeting with several senior leather community people, aging experts on the arcane history of their scene. I'm invited, in my role as project photographer, to document the gathering.

Our host is Chet Bellows, a vivacious, charming, grizzled survivor of gay life. White-haired, in his late sixties, decked out in leather vest and worn black leather chaps, he greets us from the window of his Folsom Street loft, when we call up to him from the street.

"Catch!" he yells, throwing down the building key in what turns out to be a knotted sock. Hilly gracefully scoops it from the air, unlocks the building door. We enter a dark lobby, ascend in a freight elevator, then, upstairs, emerge into another world. The loft is spacious, beautifully furnished with antiques, there are good paintings by Bay Area artists on the walls, and case after case exhibiting a vast eclectic collection of books.

Chet introduces us around: David, Fred, Bill, Adam and Cindy, all dressed casually in gear. No giggling here, these are serious scene leaders, "wisepersons" Chet calls them, working on an oral-history project that will document gay and lesbian leather culture as it grew and changed in San Francisco over the past thirty years.

We help ourselves to beer, then Chet introduces Hilly, who explains what she's looking for and shows the gathering what she's got. The wisepersons are fascinated by the hood, which they pass among themselves, commenting on its fine craftsmanship and design.

"Stitching reminds me of Al Jameson's work," Cindy says. "Also the fittings look like his."

The hood makes another round. The men agree:

"Does look like a Jameson piece."

"What happened to Al?"

"Died of AIDS in '83."

"His old lover, Dan Fowler—he's still around. I saw him on line at the Castro Theatre a few weeks back."

"Dan'd know for sure."

"Shouldn't be hard to find him."

Chet Bellows goes to the phone, makes a couple of calls, reaches Fowler, who says he'll be happy to come over and give us his opinion on the hood.

While we wait for him, the group reminisces about the T case and what it meant to them at the time, how they feared a backlash from a normally tolerant city on account of the awful brutality of the crimes.

"We were scared," Cindy says. She's a friendly stout woman in her forties, short gray hair, pale eyes, beatific smile. "Back then most folks didn't understand what we do is the opposite of sadistic murder."

"Safe, sane and consensual," Adam adds. "A lot of folks still don't get it."

As they talk I'm impressed by their gentleness, intelligence, commitment to social justice. These are bright, friendly people who hold down sophisticated jobs: Chet's a retired professor of psychology, Cindy's a midwife, Fred's a computer programmer, Adam's an industrial designer in Silicon Valley, Bill's a flight instructor and David's an attorney. I can feel the strong bonds of affection between them, forged by years together on the barricades.

"We're queer and we love it," Chet tells us. "We're also a despised minority. We've found the best way to confront our detractors is with solidarity, openness and shared humanity. 'We're your children and you're ours'—that's the essence of our message."

Dan Fowler arrives. A tall, thin, bespectacled, weathered-face guy in his fifties, he wears faded jeans, boots, a wrangler's jacket, and carries a beaten-up attaché case.

"Oh, certainly—this is one of Al's," he says, taking hold of the hood. "His stitching, his fittings." Although the police lab removed the mold, they couldn't resuscitate the leather. Still Dan fondles it. "He always used best quality hide."

Dan opens his case, pulls out an oversize ledger, leafs through it. "I kept his old design-and-order book."

I catch Joel's eye, then we both turn to Hilly. She cranes forward as Dan stops several times to examine drawings of full-head hoods. Finally, he nods.

"Sure, here it is, order number S-H17." He drums his forefinger on the design, hands the ledger to Hilly. " 'S' is for special, 'H' is for hood. This was the seventeenth special-order hood Al made. It's all there—date, customer name and address."

I read the data over Hilly's shoulder: Burton Boyt Quint, 110 Moraga Street, San Francisco.

Hilly, Joel and I pile into Melvin, then drive off into the cold night to view Quint's old address. I'm thrilled, Hilly is frothing, Joel is trying to stay cool but I can sense he's excited too.

It's a miracle, we all agree, that Chet Bellows's group identified the deceased leatherworker, and that his surviving companion kept his order book as a memento of the man he loved.

Moraga is in the Sunset, the vast grid of residential streets south of Golden Gate Park that extends to the Pacific Ocean. It's often foggy here, perhaps the foggiest district in the city. Most of the homes are modest two-story flat-roofed cubes erected side by side, painted in what I'm told are pastel hues. The population now is largely Asian-American, but fifteen years ago there was more of a mix. Since Burton Boyt Quint has long since been fed to the fishes, our purpose is simply to find his building, gaze at it, take in the vibes.

It's a dollhouse sort of place, simple one-story bunga-low with garage on one side and narrow strip of lawn on the other. It's small, innocuous, and lonely on account of that extra bit of land on an avenue where nearly every other structure abuts its neighbors.

"Perfect place to do bad stuff," Joel says.

Hilly squints as she peers at the house. "Like cut guys up," she says.

Silence. In fact, it turns out, we're all thinking the same thing: What if some of the missing heads and limbs are buried beneath that grass or walled up in the cellar?

"You got your work cut out," Joel tells Hilly, "that is, if Quint's the one."

"He's the one." There's something prideful in her now. An enormous success is within her grasp. She can feel it, can already taste the spoils.

"What'll you do now?"

"Backtrack the name," Hilly says, "come up with a Social Security number. Check military, school, voting and car-registration records. Look through old phone books and trace the ownership of the house. We know the T killer had access to a car if only to carry and dump his torsos. What happened to it? What sort of job did Quint have? When did he disappear? Who *was* this guy?"

Joel looks at me. "There's one more thing we can tell you," he says to Hilly, "to help you stay on track. It's the only other thing we know and you must promise you'll never ask us how we know or reveal it to anyone."

Hilly agrees; how could she not, since we're offering her the keys to the law enforcement treasury? Joel describes the full-body red skeleton tattoo on the T killer's arms, legs and ribs. If Hilly can turn up someone who knew Burton Boyt Quint and recalls a tattoo like that, then, Joel tells her, she's found her man.

Long days in the darkroom trying to produce expressive prints. In a book of photographs, no matter how fine the gravure process, some quality is always lost. As I work I think of my tonal fields—glove-soft grays, glistening whites, velvety blacks—as my palette. In that limited but expressive range, I feel I can convey any color that exists.

Sometimes I stop work to think about the differences between the cases: Quint and the old T case; Crane's murder of Tim. Skeleton-man's crimes, brutal and sinister as they were, contained at least some mystery and passion. But what Crane did to Tim strikes me as utterly, irredeemably evil.

Sasha warms me. After difficult days, I revel in his arrivals at night. Then the feel of his hard dark body, silken skin, the look of his gorgeous deep liquid eyes. In bed he whispers sweet intimacies into my ear. I adore that he whispers, no matter that no one's around to overhear. It's as if we inhabit a country of our own, a dark secret country of love.

Why, I wonder, did it take me so long to come to love him? Surely not on account of any deficiency of his, Sasha being not only beautiful but wonderful as well. And, I tell myself, I must be careful not to blame the Judge. No, the fault was purely mine, my inability, my lack, something that froze up inside when Tim was killed, which only Sasha could warm and melt.

Hilly's making good progress, Joel tells me. If her investigation pans out, it'll be the crime story of the decade. Charbeau and Shanley no longer mess with her, are much too awed and scared. She's been on the fast track since she broke the Lovsey case. It's only a matter of time, they know, before she's given a command position. Joel says she's aiming for chief of Homicide, and if she solves the T case, she may just get it . . . and more.

I drop by Cherry Street to see Dad. There's a new openness between us, has been since he made what we both now smilingly refer to as his "confession." He tells me he's thinking of expanding his social life, which will mean cooling things down with Phyllis. He'd like to get out more, he says, meet new people. The notion of him dating makes me smile.

Drake has disappeared. I haven't seen him in days. Twice I leave him food packages; both times they remain untouched. Has something happened to him? Is he ill? Or has he simply moved away?

I wish he'd contact me, even as I know maintaining relationships is not his forte. Just as he used to glide in and out of the shadows, so now he seems to have drifted from Sterling Park. But to what sort of life? Though he was difficult to talk to, I miss him more than I'd have thought. And a good part of my sorrow comes from the knowledge that if he has left for good, I know no way to find him again.

Hilly has turned up a lot on Burton Boyt Quint, including the fact that he disappeared around the time Sipple was attacked.

His car, a 1979 Ford Mustang, probably stolen from the Haight, was discovered abandoned a few weeks later on Bluxome Street near the CalTrain depot. A Streets Environment tow truck dutifully pulled it to the pound, where, after the requisite thirty days, it was auctioned off.

Quint never renewed his California driver's license or car registration. A month and a half after his disappearance, his landlord, one Kam Yong Choi, had his furniture, clothing and possessions removed from the Moraga Street house, stored them 120 days and then, in accordance with California law, put them up for auction, the receipts to cover Quint's unpaid rent.

Quint worked in a print shop on upper Geary. The company disposed of its old employment records long ago. But one senior worker vaguely recalls him as "the quiet guy who one day stopped showing up."

No one on Moraga Street remembers him, but few of the neighbors were living there fifteen years ago. Landlord Choi passed away, the house was sold by his estate, is now the property of a wealthy Vietnamese who leases it out to an immigrant Chinese family, and has neither the interest nor the obligation to allow S.F.P.D. to take it apart.

Tattoos: Hilly wishes she could work that angle, round up old-timers in the tattoo community the way she and Joel gathered the wisepersons of leathersex. But since she has no justification for asking about a set of red skeleton tattoos, she's at a loss how to proceed.

Joel and I take her to dinner in North Beach, persuade her that her goal of nailing the T killer's identity down one hundred percent will probably not be met. What she should do now, Joel suggests, is write a report to the chief of police on everything she's discovered, making a strong circumstantial case that Quint and the T killer were one and the same. And if the Department chooses not to release it, Joel will write a front-page story depicting Hilly's quest to solve the city's most perplexing series of unsolved crimes.

"It'll almost be better than nailing Quint," Joel tells her. "You'll be seen as a dedicated detective who left no stone unturned. You followed the trail as far as it went. Most people will believe Quint's the guy, and that little shadow of doubt will make the saga even better."

Hilly mulls on that, decides she likes it. "It really *is* better," she says. "Like having a new lover, when there's still a little mystery left."

Judd's lawyer, Jeremiah Waldroon, makes a deal with Pat Chu: Judd will plead guilty to one count of solicitation of corruption in return for testimony against Vasquez. The agreement calls for Judd to serve two-to-six in the country club prison in Chino. In addition he'll permanently give up his right to practice law.

Peter "Roy" Royal, on the other hand, has not yet come to terms. Pat Chu is pressuring him to implicate Sarah Lashaw, but Roy is holding out, at least for now. Pat believes Lashaw is paying Roy to take the fall.

"God knows, she can afford it," Pat says.

. . .

The end of February brings heavy showers. The city is washed clean by days of driving rain. I find myself depressed. *Exposures,* which was going so well, has bogged down. The stream of images which, a month ago, seemed to flow so well, now strikes me as awkward, at times even forced. Tim's story is so complex there are times when even I get lost. I think of Mom, the last months of her life, trying over and over to play through Schubert's B-flat sonata, forever stumbling over the repeats, unable to find and play the climax.

Sasha tries to help. He suggests I get out of the house, start a new project or take time off, anything to stop staring out at the rain. I'm too isolated, he says, too wrapped up in work. I need stimulation, fun, something to make me laugh. I disagree. What I need, I think, is illumination, a flash of brilliant light.

The last day of the month, six p.m. Magic time is over. I'm gazing out at the dark sodden city. It's been a windy umbrella-shredding sort of day, about as miserable here as it can get.

The phone rings. Dazed, I pick up.

"Hi, Kay! It's Courtney Hill."

The voice is familiar, but for a moment I can't place the name.

"You said if I ever heard anything about Amoretto to let you know."

Suddenly I'm alert.

"This isn't definite . . . but then nothing about her is." Courtney laughs. "An ex-boyfriend of mine, part of our old HardCandy crowd, thinks he saw her down in Mexico a couple weeks ago. He was there on vacation, thought he saw her crossing the street. He called out to her, but she didn't turn. He tried to follow her, but it was night and then he lost her in the gloom. He isn't positive, mind you. She looked different, he says. Older maybe. But the way she moved—if it wasn't her, he says, it could have been her twin.''

I try to steady my voice. ''Where in Mexico?''

''Resort town up in the mountains, San Miguel de Allende. Cool place, full of expatriates. You might like it, Kay. They got some kind of art school there.''

Eighteen

After a dawn flight from San Francisco, total chaos in the Mexico City airport, then a four-hour bus trip, I arrive finally at San Miguel. It's five p.m., the sun is low, the light soft, magic time has just begun. Within minutes of starting out on my first exploratory walk I understand I've arrived at some kind of paradise.

The air here, scented by flowers, is cool and dry. The hills above town are ridged with ancient stone terraces; the plains below are studded with cacti. But it's San Miguel itself that seems enchanted. Striding its steep, narrow, cobblestone streets, I feel myself slipping into a trance state, spellbound by the aura of old Mexico—shadowed, timeless, serene.

Through partially opened doors I catch glimpses of courtyards, hear the gurgle of fountains, smell the rich aroma of blooming plants. By the time I reach the main square, the paseo has already begun. Mariachi musicians, pants embellished with silver disks, play a bullfighter's march, while hundreds of young people circulate along covered sidewalks before an approving audience of elders seated in cafes.

I start taking pictures. Grave young men in tight jeans

pace in one direction; smiling, beribboned girls move along in pairs in the other. It's a mating dance of quick glances, bold looks, flashing eyes. As the sun fails and the shadows lengthen, the intensity of this public courtship builds. A swarm of bats swoops into the air; a flock of cawing blackbirds settles on the tops of the pollarded laurel trees. The last rays of slanting light hit building facades, etching out details—baroque balconies, carved escutcheons—causing the walls to glow as if lit from within.

A three-legged dog limps across the *zócalo,* then disappears up a narrow street. Prowling the square, I suddenly find myself face-to-face with a bent old man. He's a commercial street photographer, packing up his huge view camera for the day. His portable stand, already shut, is plastered with snapshots—young couples posed stiffly before the soaring wedding-cake facade of the town cathedral.

Darkness falls, the air turns chilly, lights come on in branching iron streetlamps built like enormous candelabra. The courtship ritual reaches a peak. Bells start tolling; nuns scurry across the *zócalo* on their way to vespers. I huddle in my leather jacket, hands deep in my pockets. *Are you here, Ariane? How will I find you in this maze of angled streets, courtyards, barricaded doors?*

Setting out in the morning I devise a plan. I will explore the town block by block, resting in restaurants and cafes; after dark I'll hang out in bars and cantinas, and late at night at discos, the sort of places where, in San Francisco, Amoretto found her prey. I will give myself five days. San Miguel is small, compact. Unless Ariane is in seclusion, sooner or later our paths should cross.

Will I recognize her? I know she resembles Tim in posture and face, that her hair's the same length, that she's shorter but moves in a similar way. I recall how I mistook her on Mission Street the day I cleaned out Tim's studio. Yes, I think, if I see her I'll know her right away.

Eyes shielded by my heaviest shades, I commence my search, pausing every so often to peer into shops. The crafts stores don't interest me, but I'm impressed by the multitude of galleries. According to my guidebook, San Miguel is a town obsessed by art. For years I've heard about the Instituto Allende, which attracts painters from all over the world. When I find it, I'm touched; it's small, beautifully situated. San Miguel, I understand, is a city of colors—contrasting pinks, ivories, mustards, terra-cottas. Most likely it's these chalk hues that draw the artists. Still I'm content with the wondrous clarity of the light. The town strikes me as the perfect place for a surprise encounter, an unexpected meeting with a lover or an enemy.

Four days without success—I'm discouraged. At dusk, seated by the *zócalo,* nursing a coffee, I despair of accomplishing my mission. Exhausted by lengthy walks and late nights spent in earsplitting discos, I ask myself whether the time hasn't come to give it up. I'm here, after all, only because someone I don't know told someone else he *thought* he saw Ariane. Maybe he did, and she's moved on. Maybe she's here, and doesn't go out. Maybe she was never here and the sighting was a mistake. Still I'm haunted by the coincidence with Tim's remark that he would retire to San Miguel when he gave up working the Gulch.

Suddenly it comes back to me—the smile on his face when he told me he had a house picked out. I think: *That's it!* It *wasn't* just a fantasy; he and Ariane had it planned. They would come here together. Perhaps they already *owned* the house.

I struggle to recall Tim's description: church and jacaranda tree on the corner, sharp angle in a narrow street, old stone wall, carved wooden door with coat of arms above, courtyard "dripping with bougainvillaea," pots overflowing with flowers hanging from iron balustrades.

I grow excited. This is a place I *know,* a place I've passed numerous times! I sit back, try to visualize it, then understand my error. Of course I know it! It's a generic description applicable to nearly every block in town. All of San Miguel looks like that. Have I yet walked down a street here that doesn't?

What to do? I ask myself how Joel would find the house, or Hilly, San Francisco's new "smartest cop." It's easy: go to the registry of deeds, backtrack house sales, discover if anyone named Lovsey owns property here. I know I can't do that myself, but I can hire someone who can. Excited again, I gulp down my coffee and walk swiftly back to my hotel, where, with the assistance of the phone book, I find a single listing under the rubric *Agencias de Detectivos:* Julio Manolo Mondonado, *"especialista en investigaciones matrimoniales."*

Sitting in his shabby office across from the railroad station, I feel like a character in a cheap Mexican film. Manolo, on the other side of the desk, is a hulk, has a thick accent, an even thicker musklike scent, a lounge lizard's mat of shiny black hair and a mustache so wide, bushy and black as to rival the tail of a mink. But more offputting than his facial hair and odor is the complicated contraption of straps that crisscross his shirt, from which an enormous black revolver protrudes. I wonder: Is this what a Mexican client expects in a private eye?

"Call me Paco," he says, with a fake grin. My new friend, I surmise, fancies himself quite the ladies' man. A pale, anorexic young thing, introduced as María, sits slumped beside his desk interpreting and scribbling notes as we converse.

I peer around. The windows are filthy, the venetian blinds uneven and cracked. A dusty fan hangs lifeless from the ceiling. A huge, black, scarred, old double-door safe broods against one wall.

As I explain what I want, Paco leans back, grin fixed upon his face. When I'm finished, he sits straight again, furrows his brow, then quotes me the gringo price: "A thousand dollars U.S."

"That's crazy," I tell him, standing.

"Please, not so fast. We will make you a courtesy accommodation."

"How much?"

He strokes his chin. "If my operative takes care of it"—he gestures toward María—"for you, señora, two hundred cash up front. A very good price for a records search. Believe me, we don't need business here."

Still way too much, but I agree since it's a task I can't accomplish myself. Handing over the money, meeting María's submissive eyes, I smile at the notion that she's an "operative."

After a trek around town and a leisurely lunch, I find María waiting in the lobby of my hotel.

The moment she spots me she shakes her head. "No owner by that name," she says meekly. "I am sorry."

I thank her, turn to go upstairs, when I feel her tug at my sleeve.

I turn back.

"Perhaps I can help you, señora." Her English, I note, is very good.

"You have an idea?"

She shrugs her narrow shoulders. "Perhaps if you tell me your story I shall think of something that can be done." She peers into my eyes. "No extra charge." She pauses, then, beneath her breath: "He is a brute."

This remark wins me over. We adjourn to the hotel terrace, where she reveals that she's a graduate of the Xultan School of Investigatory Detection in Mexico City, that her dream is to someday own her own agency in Guanajuato and that meantime she's serving her apprenticeship with Manolo, whom she loathes.

"He is a womanizer, incompetent, ignorant, corrupt, but for now he is the cross that I must bear. He has no inkling of this, but one day soon, after I learn his secrets, I shall leave him and set up on my own. Then I shall become his rival. He will be surprised. I shall steal all his business. The beast will learn what it is to be vanquished by a woman, one who smiles sweetly while harboring rage within her heart.''

What have I stepped into here? María, waving her hand to dispel ugly thoughts, turns her attention back to me.

''At Xultan we learned that the most essential task of an investigator is to listen closely to the client. If you will kindly tell me your story, perhaps I shall hear something that will lead me to a solution.''

She's attentive to every nuance of Tim's description of the house, in the end agreeing there's insufficient specificity. In response to her question about the habits of the woman I seek, I describe Ariane's expertise in stage magic and kinky sex-for-hire.

''There is no such woman here,'' she says gravely.

''No commercial sex?''

''True, there is, but not like that. Also I would think that a woman who lived that kind of life would come to San Miguel to live differently.''

Certainly that's what Tim had in mind. I peer at María. I'm impressed. Perhaps I have underrated her and the Xultan School of Investigatory Detection of which she's such a proud diplomate.

''Purgation,'' she says. I stare at her. ''Our subject, to begin anew, may have felt a need to purge herself.''

''There's a place for that here?''

''Not in San Miguel, but nearby at Atotonilco. Men and women at separate times make pilgrimages to the *santuario* to cleanse themselves of sin. They stay a week. The food is simple. They sleep on stone floors, silence is required and many use *disciplinas,* little braided whips, to scourge themselves. Some wear actual crowns of thorns and approach the sanctuary on knees made bloody by sharp stones. The fascinating thing is that those who do this so enjoy it. You can see their pleasure''—María's eyes widen—''in their eyes.''

We set off by taxi. Our journey, less than ten miles, takes us by roadside bathhouses set up beside hot mineral springs. The village of Atotonilco is small and dusty, but the church is huge, looming above the plaza.

María leaves me alone in the gloomy echoing nave choked with statues and religious murals. She is off to the convent behind, photo of Tim in hand, to ask the nuns whether a foreign woman who resembles him has made pilgrimage in recent months.

Waiting, peering around the vast brooding space, I'm astounded by the many images of suffering. Saints exhibit bloody wounds; Christ figures display whip-marked backs. The paintings range in style from academic to na- ive, but there is one constant: an obsessive savoring of martyrdom and pain.

María returns. Yes, she says, a light-haired American, vaguely resembling Tim, did come on a woman's pilgrim- age in the autumn. Though thousands have since come and gone, several nuns remember her since it's so rare for a gringa to come as a pilgrim, and on account of the fervor with which she practiced her devotions.

At last, proof Ariane has been here! And if she is start- ing life anew, that may explain why I haven't seen her in the discos, and why she refused to recognize Courtney Hill's friend on the street. But, I realize on the road back to San Miguel, I'm no closer now to finding her than I was before.

"I'm so sorry," María says, when we part at my hotel. "I wanted so much to solve this case."

"You've helped me a lot, María." I press a hundred dollars into her hand. She tries to return it, but I insist. "You're on your way to becoming a fine detective. Save this, add to it and soon you'll have enough to open your own agency."

Her smile is so brilliant it could blind.

My final afternoon in San Miguel: I walk the streets, camera in hand, trying to capture the unique flavor of the town. During magic time I sit on a bench in the *zó- calo,* watch the paseo until the last light drains from the sky. Then I walk slowly back toward my hotel to pack, intending to depart for Mexico City on an early morning bus.

Church and jacaranda tree on the corner. For perhaps the twentieth time I pass that combination. *Sharp angle in a narrow street.* There're so many sharp street angles here. *Pots overflowing with flowers hanging from iron balconies.* All balconies here are iron, and nearly all support overflowing pots of flowers. *Carved wooden door with coat of arms above.* I have seen innumerable heraldic devices in San Miguel, from the elaborate coat of arms on the palace of the Counts of Canal, to crude little shields dangling above tourist shops.

But suddenly I realize that there's something else I know, something important I've forgotten. I stop, stand still at the bend in the street, close my eyes to allow the memory to flow back. Not something architectural like the street and balcony and coat of arms, rather something subliminal from another dimension appealing to another sense. Not visual but aural. Sound. Music—*yes!* Now I remember! Those operatic arias that flooded the stairwell in the building where the twins lived on Mission Street in San Francisco.

I hear an aria now when I strain my ears, faintly in the distance. Am I imagining? I backtrack a few steps, pause, listen, hear it again, faint still yet present. I move forward fifty feet, stop; I can no longer hear it. I walk back, pick it up again. Yes, it's real!

Slowly I circle the block. On the street behind I hear the music faintly at first but growing in volume as I approach an old walled house. Moving carefully, trying to position myself as close as possible to the source, I finally recognize the voice and song: Maria Callas singing *"Morrò, ma prima in grazia"* from *Un Ballo in Maschera.* It was Callas's voice too I heard in that tenement stairwell.

I approach the door. There's a coat of arms above. I push it open, enter a paved courtyard, solitary fig tree at its center surrounded by fallen fruit. The stone floor is illuminated by an electrified lantern hanging from a wall.

Immediately I'm suffused by the aroma of bougainvillaea. The opposite wall actually does seem to "drip" with it. Now the music is clearly audible.

Following the sound, I move to a set of stone stairs, mount them, find myself on a covered balcony overlooking the court. The song is full now, close, so very close. I approach a door, press my ear to it. It's coming from within, the room just behind.

I pause, step back, knock.

At first nothing, no reaction, no sound of approaching steps. The song, in fact, seems to increase in volume. I take in the lyrics: *". . . ma queste viscere, consolino i suoi baci—let his kisses console this body."*

Slowly the door opens. A slim young woman in silk robe stands poised in the doorway, a glowing room behind. She peers into my eyes, no trace of surprise on her face. Finally, slowly, she nods her head.

"I know who you are. You're Kay," she says quietly. She smiles as if expecting me, steps back so I can enter.

For a while we simply stare at one another while the music echoes off the high curved ceiling, a dark celestial canopy studded with gleaming painted stars. The floor too is dark, the wood glossy and rich; the stucco walls are white. No pictures on them, just an old wooden crucifix at one end, a stone fireplace at the other. Embers glow in the grate.

She sits very still, as if displaying herself. A dozen thick church candles, set in holders upon the floor, send flickering shadows across her face. She has, I note, the body of a model, but I'm frightened by what I see above: Tim's features, but with something added that makes her face distinctive—ferocity in the eyes and a devouring aspect to the lips and mouth. No perfect mirror image of her twin, she looks stronger, more savage.

"I thought one day you might turn up," she says, "if you cared enough . . . and since we've never met, I couldn't know." She smiles. "He spoke of you often. He liked you very much. I believe he even loved you in his way—which was curious, wasn't it? His way, I mean. He was so gentle." She shakes her head. "Not at all like me."

She gazes into my eyes. I look away. The furnishings in the huge room are sparse—a wooden table, several colonial-era chairs, nothing more.

"You look as I imagined, Kay. He described people very well. He could be funny too about people's flaws, but he never said a mocking word about you." She pauses. "We were lovers. I suppose you know that now." She pauses again. "It must have been very difficult to find me. You must be a clever person and have cared a good deal to take the trouble."

I gasp. She speaks too casually of things that to me are monumental—Tim's and my feelings for one another, my tortured quest for him that became a search for her.

"I know," she says, "you must think I'm awful." She shrugs. "Perhaps I am. But then who isn't really—when you come down to it? Shall I turn off the music? I'm sure you have questions. If not I can't imagine why you've come."

She moves to the table, flicks off the stereo. The great room goes silent. She pulls her chair up close so that we sit but a yard apart, places a footstool between us, rests her slippered feet upon it.

"Put yours up too," she urges.

I shake my head. She shrugs.

"I see my words have hurt you. I only wanted to let you know how much he cared. He told me so, and how tempted he was. But for people like us, you see, abstinence is always more expressive than seduction."

She pauses, shows me her full face in repose. She's so stunning, intense, I can't take my eyes off of her . . . and wish I could. I would like to get up now, leave. But if I do, I know she'll haunt me forever. Coming here in search of Tim, I've found someone entirely different. Yet physically she is Tim in female form. It's this contradiction that's got me so confused.

"Why didn't you claim him?" I ask.

"His body?" She tosses her head. "Timmy and I weren't into dead bodies much. We figured once you're dead that's it. Also I was hiding. A little later I fled." She shrugs. "Anyhow, I heard you had things well in hand."

"You could have called me."

She blinks. "I probably would have one day."

"We scattered his ashes at sea."

"Yes . . . that's fine."

"David deGeoffroy came."

She laughs. "Oh, I'm sure!"

I can't believe how disinterested she is, am angry too at her reaction that it was okay to leave town without a word since I had taken on the bereavement duties.

"What happened," I demand, "between you and Tim and Crane? How did all this come about?"

She turns away, and as she does her face seems to harden even more. Still her eyes, I note, are stunningly beautiful, deep, opaque, like Tim's. I wonder: Who is this woman and why do I feel so uneasy in her presence?

". . . they called Crane 'Dome' on account of his being bald, which he was too vain to show. A man hires hustlers off the street, then he's too embarrassed to take off his toupee." She sneers: "Pathetic! Anyhow, Dome fell hard for Timmy, which bored Timmy no end. One thing to be desired, another to have a client who's obsessed. Dome was crowding him, would have suffocated him if Timmy had given him half a chance. Dome wanted Timmy all to himself, offered to set him up in his love nest, make him his full-time pet. Timmy wasn't interested, didn't care about money—silly boy! He enjoyed the game too much, the hustle. Control was fine, but once they groveled he'd get bored. Too many new bodies to explore, fantasies to fulfill. So he turned Dome down. And that, it seems, made Dome very mad.

"One day he saw Timmy with a rival, another rich guy they called 'J.J.,' for Jaguar John—on account of how he picked up hustlers in his Jaguar. The next night Dome sought Timmy out on Polk, demanded he stop seeing J.J. Timmy laughed, told him he'd see whoever he liked, that J.J. had offered to take him to Key West over Christmas . . . which was true. Dome said he'd do better than that, take him to Paris, Rome, anywhere he liked. Timmy explained that wasn't the point, J.J. would take him to those cities too if he wanted . . . then let him hustle for himself. In fact, he told Dome, J.J. liked to watch him do it—which, I guess, infuriated Dome even more. Though, of course, he didn't show it. According to Timmy he went all wet-eyed and limp.''

This doesn't sound like the slick Marcus Crane I've observed. ''Was Crane really in love with him?'' I ask.

''As much as someone like that is capable of love.''

I think back to Knob's confession, the bizarre moment when Crane tried to take Tim's head. ''What happened?''

Ariane grins. ''Dome decided he wanted to do it with us both. We charged a grand for a Zamantha—that's what we called it. I guess David told you about our old Zamantha substitution trick. A Zamantha, as you can imagine, is a sex act in which the john starts out in the arms of one and ends in the arms of the other. People liked it. It freaked them out. We liked it too. It was fun, made us giggle.''

As Ariane speaks she glances occasionally at me, but most of the time stares past me at the crucifix. She is, I feel, talking primarily to herself, recalling events that took place just months ago as if they happened in the distant past.

''There were rumors about Dome, that he was violent. Still we decided to go ahead. He'd always been correct with Timmy, and during our Zamantha he was fine. We got him hot, got him off, twisted his brain into a pretzel. Afterward he was so grateful it made me want to puke.''

She stands, goes to the fireplace, tosses a fresh log upon the embers. Sparks fly. She gazes at them, smiles as she watches them die.

''Want a drink?'' she asks. ''Joint? All of the above?''

I shake my head. She shrugs. "Excuse me while I indulge."

She leaves the room, comes back with a snifter of cognac in one hand, a lit joint in the other, takes a short sip from the glass, a long drag from the joint, resumes her seat, smiles at me, continues with her tale:

"Few days later Dome goes to Knob, asks him to arrange a scene with me alone. You're willing to pay you get to play, so I go up to his love nest, we start getting into it, he makes a few suggestions, some I accept, some I don't, I make a few to him, we take it a little further and . . . suddenly he's out of control. Bam! He hits me! Bam! He socks me in the eye. I fall to the floor, then he's all over me, sitting on me, pinning back my arms, slapping me with his free hand.

"I'm not like you, Kay, not a fighter. Timmy told me you train in martial arts. Dome's big, powerful. The only way I know to get through a scene like that is go limp, take it till he tires. What I don't want to do is make it fun for him by crying out or begging him to stop. It was a while before he quit. Afterward I lay there hurting. Then he threw a bunch of money at me and told me to get out."

She takes a long drag from her joint.

"Back home, looking in the mirror, I was appalled. My face was a mess, both my eyes were black, my lips were all puffed up. I didn't go out much those next few days, just hunkered down at home.

"Soon as Timmy saw me he went bananas, announced the time had come for us to quit The Life. 'Why do we keep doing this?' he sobbed. 'We got money saved, our place down in San Miguel. We don't need this shit anymore.' But first he was going to stick it to Dome, go to the cops, file charges. 'He's married to this society bitch. I can ruin him,' stuff like that. I told him forget it, just spread the word and no one'll touch the guy again. But Timmy was furious. He loved me, introduced me to Dome in good faith. Dome injured me. Timmy wanted revenge."

She stands again, goes to the fireplace, takes a final drag

on her joint, flicks the butt on to the coals, then stands with her back to the fire.

"When I counted up the money Dome threw at me, it came to a fairly decent sum. I pointed out to Timmy that ruining Dome's reputation would hurt him, sure, but wouldn't do anything for us. On the other hand, reparation money would.

"Timmy didn't like that, said blackmail wasn't our style. I told him how silly that was, seeing as how we'd done things far worse. I also reminded him that, far as the cops and public went, I wouldn't be the most sympathetic victim in town. Finally he agreed to meet with Dome, squeeze him for as much as he could get. Take Dome for a bundle—that was the plan. Then be on our way."

She returns to her chair, sits, extends her feet toward the footstool, which, in her absence, I've been using to rest my own. My first instinct is to relinquish the space. Then, recalling David deGeoffroy's words about her need to dominate, I move my feet just a bit. She notices, smiles slightly to herself, carefully positions hers so they're beside mine, not quite touching but close.

"I was with him when he phoned you that afternoon," she says. "He was going to introduce us that night. He'd told me a lot about you, your work, what you were trying to do. He'd spoken of getting us together for weeks. After you photographed him nude, he had this notion you should shoot us nude together. He wanted that, and after I saw your photos, so did I."

She finishes off her cognac, bends to set down the glass, then partially straightens herself so our heads are just inches apart. I occupy her now. She no longer looks out across the room. Rather her eyes, filled with candle-light, bore into mine.

"I thought you could take some really great shots of us. You know, shots that would show people what we were really like. No one ever saw us clear. We were either this sordid incestuous pair or this weird couple who were so much fun to fuck. There're plenty of close twin sister-brother couples, but we knew we were special, did things no one else had ever done. Our mentalist routine, for instance. There'd never been another twin sister-brother act like ours. Then, when we grew up, became sex magicians, we offered our Zamanthas, a unique experience, providing bedazzlement, gender-bending rapture. We were King and Queen, God and Goddess. Who else offered anything like that?

"Sure"—she shakes her head—"we were paid for it! After all, that was our work. But for us it was so much more. We loved the street, anonymous sex, being so hugely *desired*. We were explorers discovering new ways of leaping out of our skins—transcending, exchanging, the one becoming the other, the other the one. Sister, brother, separate yet the same. Two! One! Two again!" She snaps her fingers. "Zamantha! Twins!"

She moans. "It couldn't go on too long. We both recognized that, knew one day we'd burn ourselves out. But always there was our plan to come down here, start out fresh and clean." She sniffs to mock the notion. "We even planned to write a memoir, the story of our adventures. Perhaps a little like Saint Augustine's, you know." She grins. "A confession of all our sins."

She leans back, eyes still locked to mine. She has me spellbound. We sit in silence for a time, then church bells start to toll. I wonder: Why did she send Tim off to blackmail Crane alone? The number-one rule of the street, Knob said: Never threaten a john or try to blackmail him; do that and you're as likely to get killed as paid.

"I waited two hours for him that night," I tell her. "Finally I gave up, went home. Crawf called me early in the morning, said the cops had found—"

"Sure. His head."

Though she winces I'm struck by her lack of affect. "Like the Zamantha," she adds. "Except this time it wasn't an illusion. The child wasn't made whole at the end."

"How did you hear?"

"Gulch telegraph, same as you. At first, when he didn't come home, I wasn't too concerned. We both did a lot of overnights. Then, early in the morning, when I got the word, it was already all over town.'' She smiles. ''I was on the landing just above when you and Crawf went into his flat. Soon as you left I went in myself.''

''It was you who cut up his bedroll.'' She nods. ''What were you looking for?''

''His passport, letters, money, an album of photos of us when we were kids. I took one of your portraits, too, the one he liked best, took it down, rolled it up. When I got here I had it framed.'' She smiles. ''Now it's hanging over my bed.''

''I'd like to see it,'' I tell her.

She brightens. ''My bed?''

''My photo above it actually. All the rest too, if that's all right.''

''Sure,'' she says, ''the grand tour.''

She smiles as if to herself, flicks the stereo back on. Again the voice of Maria Callas fills the room. Explaining that the apartment occupies an entire floor of a subdivided eighteenth-century mansion, she leads me from the living room into a sumptuously proportioned dining room, then into the kitchen. Here we pause while she refreshes her cognac, and fills a fresh snifter for me. Then on to the two studies, each furnished with a daybed, to which she and Tim could retreat when one or the other desired privacy. Finally to the doorway of a large dark room with fireplace. ''The bedroom,'' she announces, gesturing me in.

We enter. She lights a long match, applies it to wood set in the grate. Seconds later kindling erupts, the flames throwing our shadows upon the walls, also revealing various strange furnishings arranged like sculptures about the room—an open coffin on a platform, a sword box big as a steamer trunk, pieces of large-scale magical apparatus, a scaffold, a guillotine, a set of Pilgrims' stocks and a huge rotating wooden disk.

I'm taken aback. Looking around, I find Ariane sitting on a huge carved bed, watching me, enjoying my bewilderment. Above her head hangs my Angel Island portrait of Tim magnificently framed like an old master painting.

She tries to lure me. "Look!" she says, flinging herself back upon the bed, pointing upward at a skylight. "Lie down beside me, Kay. You'll see a wonderful sight. The moon, the stars—the sky's magnificent tonight."

But I decline, instead take a step backward, then raise my camera to my eye.

"Oh, yes! The Photographer!" she announces, amused. "Want me to pose, strip?"

"That won't be necessary." I prepare to shoot.

"No nudes . . . oh. . . ." She feigns disappointment, then, like David deGeoffroy, starts to pose.

"How's this?" She turns onto her belly, grins like a pinup girl. "Or this?" She curls back a leg. "Just tell me what you want and I'll do it. I'm like that, you know, happy to oblige."

I ignore her, start shooting, fascinated by the strange double portrait revealed by my strobe—Ariane writhing mock-seductively on the bed beneath the photo I took of Tim bare-chested on Angel Island late last summer.

She's disappointed, I can see, wants my full attention, is annoyed at my refusal to approach. Or perhaps she understands it's the image of them together that interests me, for suddenly she gives up the pinup poses, sits erect, rests her back against the carved backboard, draws up her knees, clasps her arms about them, then eyes me solemnly like an owl.

"This more like it?" she asks.

"Better." I crouch to enhance the drama of the shot. *Whap!* "Tell me something, Ariane—was it all that wise to send Tim to see Crane alone?"

"Huh?"

Whap! I shoot again, leaving my question hanging in the air.

"What're you talking about?"

As my strobe dies, I catch a flicker of anger in her eyes. "Something Knob said when he confessed."

"What?"

"That you should never try and blackmail a john, that's the number-one rule of the street."

Whap!Whap!Whap! I work the motor drive to catch the astonishment on her face.

"Dome killed Timmy for love," she says.

Whap! "How come you're so sure?"

I feel her studying me, evaluating my gullibility.

"It's clear enough."

Whap! "Clear how?"

"Since he knew he'd never have Timmy again, he made sure no one else would either."

"Oh, so that's it." I nod. "Then it wasn't fear of being blackmailed again and again, the worst nightmare of a john, especially when he's closeted and prominently married like Crane, dependent too on the wealth of his wife."

She tosses her head. "Dome had tons of money. He could easily have paid us off."

"So he killed Tim for love?"

She nods. "A kind of love."

Right, I think, *a kind of love.*

Through this colloquy, a feeling has grown in me, a suspicion so horrifying that at first I reject it as absurd. Perhaps Ariane knows what's in my head, for, as if to distract me, she suddenly exposes her torso by opening her silk robe, extracting her arms, then retying the arms of the robe at her waist.

I don't comment or react, recalling Maddy's theory that by leaving a portrait subject to his/her own devices, the photographer can inevitably force a revelation. *Fine,* I think, *go ahead! Show yourself! Perform!*

"This is what you want, isn't it?" she asks, standing beside the bed so that her bared upper body is parallel with Tim's. "I can imagine the caption too—'The Lovsey Twins: A Study in Narcissism and Incest.' "

Whap!Whap!Whap!Whap!Whap! I fire away, my strobe creating such potent light that soon it floods the rods in my eyes. No matter—I continue shooting blind, my Contax automatically adjusting exposure. For me the scene has become albescent, but in my blindness, the suspicion returns. Did she send Tim to his death? Could that be possible? What could have been her motive?

I shoot out the roll, stop, wait for my rods to clear, reload, Ariane watching me the entire time.

"Something's always bothered me," I tell her. "Maybe you can help me out?"

"Sure."

"Why didn't Tim tell me about you? Even casual acquaintances knew he had a twin, but he never said a word to me and I was supposed to be his friend."

"That hurt you?"

"Still does."

She shrugs. "Last summer we tried to separate. We'd tried it before, it didn't work, but still, last September, we tried again. It was just impossible, you know—needing each other so much, yet each of us wanting desperately to live his own life. Of course this time it didn't work either. A twinship like ours was too powerful, not something you can just walk out on, escape. Only death can release you." She pauses. "And sometimes even that won't do it. So, you see, if Timmy neglected to mention me, that was just his way, you see, his attempt."

As she talks on, I resume shooting, moving closer, framing her head and Tim's together, disengaging the motor drive, taking individual shots now, seeking moments when her expression matches his, moments too when she shows herself as his darker half.

She's speaking about David deGeoffroy, and what she's saying doesn't jibe with his Magician's Tale. In her version, their affair went on far longer than a few weeks. Even more surprising, it was merely an afterthought, she says, to David's seduction of and affair with Tim, his primary object of desire, which started a full year before the twins escaped.

"It was like I was this little puppy dog," she says bitterly, "and David was throwing me a bone so I wouldn't get jealous."

"What about Bev?"

"What about her?"

"Did she know what was going on?"

"Why would she?"

"I thought, since she was his girlfriend, she might have picked up—"

"Girlfriend! What a hoot! Bev was his stage assistant, not his lover. David deGeoffroy's a bisexual pedophile. How pitiful he can't admit it. How contemptible!" She guffaws. "Listen, we had no choice but to run away. As for stealing, we only took what was rightfully ours."

Suddenly the design I thought I'd grasped changes form. Like looking through a kaleidoscope, then giving it a tiny twist—inside, the pieces need only shift a bit for a completely different pattern to emerge.

The link I could never grasp, between the Lovsey twins as children and what they later became, now comes clear. From child magicians performing the disconcerting Zamantha Illusion, then passing the hat, they mutated to grown-up sex magicians performing Zamanthas for well-paying clients. Seduced in childhood, robbed of innocence, taught to fascinate—magic was the only way they knew to gain love, feel desired. David deGeoffroy taught them to perform sex as he had taught them to perform magic, forging a chain of shackles that would forever bind their souls.

Ariane's speaking now of their childhood, the imaginary universe they created, their fascination with magic which predated their fateful meeting with David. The best aspect of being twins, she says, was the fun of confusing others. Thus David's Zamantha Illusion was but a formal rendering of the switched-identity games they'd always played. If David hadn't entered their lives, she says, they'd probably have given the games up. But once they joined his magic show, the game became theirs for life. This, she tells me, was their glory and also their shame: their feeling that they were inseparable, caught up in a force field which bound them so tightly existence apart became impossible.

Another turn of the kaleidoscope, another new design. *There,* I think, is Ariane's motive. Sending Tim to Crane to do blackmail alone, she put his life at risk. If Crane killed him she'd be free; if Tim returned, they'd both be rich.

"I still miss him terribly," she moans, as if reading the awful thought in my mind.

"But isn't there a side of you that's also relieved?" I ask.

"*Oh, no!*" Her eyes enlarge. *Whap!* My camera, I think, will catch the truth: her lie.

"You want to know what he was really like," she whispers. "I can show you. You can know him through me."

We're resting in oversize chairs on either side of the bedroom fireplace. Music from the main room wafts to us, echoing off the plaster walls, the great voice of Maria Callas singing of the torments of love.

I'm tired now. I close my eyes. It's the cognac, I think, also my exhaustion, the fatigue that comes when a great quest ends in anticlimax. I feel myself slipping into a semisomnambulant state, like a person hypnotized, subordinate to another's power.

"Kay . . ." Her whisper, low-pitched, seductive, enters my ear, then, like a snake, seems to twist its way into my brain.

I don't want any part of what she's offering. The truth, I recognize, is that I find her sinister. Yes, I sought her out, hoping to find Tim again through her. But though I recognize there's much that's attractive about her—her strangeness, the intensity that fascinated her lovers at HardCandy, the fervor that struck the nuns at Atotonilco—still she's too hard, dark and frightening, too willful. I now see nothing of Tim in her, nothing at all.

"Come!" Her voice jars me. "Turnaround's fair play. You had your fun, took your pictures. My turn now. Time for a little magic." She glances at the array of magical apparatus across the room. "Yes, I think . . . *the wheel.*"

Even as she guides me to the great wooden disk, I feel apprehension. I only play along in the hope of getting more out of her—something she's holding back yet needs to confess, the burden of guilt that required such strenuous purgation at Atotonilco. Perhaps, I think, if I let her play out her little game, she'll open up and tell me what I need to know.

So, reluctantly, I accompany her, don't even resist as she helps me slip out of my shirt, spread-eagles me against the rough cork surface of the disk, then binds my ankles and wrists to the embedded steel rings. Funny, I think, how each of us has her weapon—mine my camera, hers this huge piece of magical apparatus.

After securing me, she stands back, squints critically, makes several small alterations in my position, then an adjustment that causes the wheel against which I'm pinioned to tilt back.

Suddenly feeling helpless, I try to wriggle free.

"Don't!" she advises, pressing firmly on my shoulders. "To make this work you're going to have to keep very still."

"What're you going to do?"

"Nothing too terrible." She smiles. "Actually, I think you're going to like it." Her eyes sparkle. "Timmy always did."

She gazes at me, lightly brushes her hand against my cheek. "I'm going to kiss you," she says.

She leans forward, presses her lips against mine, even as I twist my head away. She steps back, glances at me annoyed. I meet her eyes.

"That's not going to work, Ariane."

"Isn't it?"

I shake my head.

"Fine!" she snaps. "Have it your own way then."

She reaches forward, pulls a lever, there's a mechanical sound, then the disk starts to revolve. Moments later, turning, I feel a swelling in my head. Then, in panic, I understand I'm gazing at her upside down.

"Turn it off!" I yell.

"Hush! Timmy loved the wheel. You will too."

"I'm getting dizzy."

"You're right, it is turning too fast. Not to worry—I'll slow you down." She reaches forward, makes an adjustment. "There, that's better." I feel my rotation slow.

Pinned to this wheel, turning sluggishly before her, I feel like a captive set pitilessly upon a spit.

"You have to trust me now," she says, stepping back. "I never missed with him. I won't with you. At least I'll try not to," she adds with a smirk.

It's then that I see the knife in her hand, its blade catching light from the fire. She turns it so it flashes in my eyes. The brilliance blinds me. Then I hear it whoosh past my face.

My God! She threw it at me! She knows I know! She's going to kill me!

I blink rapidly to regain my sight. Just then a second knife plunks into the wood inches beneath my arm. I feel the wind as it passes. Then I rotate another quarter-turn. She throws another knife. Then, when I'm upside down again, another.

The cork scrapes my back as I freeze against it. I'm furious, terrified. I shut my eyes, order her to stop.

She ignores me, and still the knives come, landing all around me, beside my neck, torso, outlining my legs, whistling as they pass, vibrating when they hit the wood. I open my eyes. Ariane, oblivious to my terror, is concentrating entirely on her throws. Turning before her, I am, I realize, no longer a person in her eyes, have become merely a target.

"Go ahead, scream if you like," she says. "For some, they say, the screaming helps."

Understanding that's what she wants from me, to hear me scream, I resolve I'd rather die than give her the pleasure.

Whoosh!Plunk! Another knife lands, this time but an inch from my ear.

"That one was really close," she says. "Sometimes, I'd throw them that close to him. So close that for an instant both our hearts would stop. Afterward, when I let him down, he'd be slick with sweat and his body would tremble for half an hour.''

She bites her lip and throws another. This one lands beside my hand.

"One day," she says, "we were working on a new ending to the routine. Our concept was great—I'd fling the usual thirty or so blades as he revolved, then, the new finale, I'd throw a trick knife straight at his chest. It would penetrate to his heart, blood would gush and . . . blackout! The audience would go crazy, scream! We wanted so much to do it, but couldn't figure out how. So, just to see how it would look, I attached the front half of a broken knife right here.''

She approaches me, stabs her finger hard between my breasts.

"It looked so cool. Then, I remember, I found a red candle, lit it, dripped thick red wax all up and down his chest." She traces the path of the wax upon my flesh. "Just like blood. To see how it would look."

Another twist of the kaleidoscope, another shift in the pattern. She is, I realize, recounting Tim's Saint Sebastian fantasy, the one he expressed the day I photographed him nude.

She steps back from me again, further back than before. "Just four more," she warns me. "To the four points of the compass, as we used to say."

Whoosh!Plunk! Whoosh!Plunk! Two knives land quickly on either side of my chest. I can even feel the second graze my left breast as I turn.

Whoosh!Plunk! The third lands just above my head, cutting through my hair.

I think: The next will be the one. She'll go for my chest, my heart, the very place she stabbed me with her finger.

She lets me rotate a full turn, waits until I'm nearly upside down. Then . . . *Whoosh!Plunk!* The knife lands close up between my legs.

She leaves me to rotate several times before the motor

shuts off. When the wheel finally stops, I end up slightly off center, dripping, dizzy, outraged.

"You did well." She compliments me as she loosens my bonds. "No sissy stuff, whimpers, screams. Timmy always behaved well too. Brave, manly, you know." She sniffs.

Free at last, I shake my head to clear it, then find my shirt and put it on.

"You're angry with me?" she asks.

"Of course!"

"But, Kay—I thought you'd like it, the thrill, I mean. I was never going to hurt you, wanted to give you something to remember, that's all."

"You presumed too much," I tell her coldly.

She stands back. "You don't like me, do you?"

"Not much," I admit. "I'm finished here. I'm leaving."

"Please! Don't go," she begs. She lurches toward me. I step back. She stumbles, falls.

"What did I do wrong, Kay? Tell me?"

"Why don't *you* tell *me?*"

"What do you mean?"

I stare down at her, hating her.

"I'm waiting," I tell her. "But not for long."

She gazes up at me. Suddenly I find her pathetic. I address her with contempt:

"A few hard days at Atotonilco, maybe a half-baked confession to a priest. Lousy food, crawling around on stone floors, a few self-administered lashes of the *disciplina*—is that all it takes to purge your little soul of guilt?"

She starts to weep.

"Oh, please, Ariane—don't go sissy on me now."

"God," she whines, "what do you want from me? What do you *want?*"

"Spit it out!" I tell her.

"What?" She gazes at me, eyes watery, mouth slack, her beauty now all drained away. "That I sent Timmy to see Crane alone? Yes, that was wrong. But it was his choice too. We took a gamble and we lost. I see that now—''

"What do you see?"

"That I shouldn't have let him. He would have done whatever I wanted. I should have—''

"What?"

"—should have thought it through.''

"So why didn't you?''

"I don't know,'' she cries, "I don't know. I just don't know.''

"Oh, I think you do, Ariane. I think you know very well.''

She continues to stare up at me, then crumbles.

"I just wanted . . .'' she moans. "I thought . . . if I could finally be, you know . . . just be *alone.*'' Her body shakes as she sobs helplessly on the floor. "Was that so bad?''

Murder by omission. Gazing down with pity at her writhing form, I wonder what will become of her, whether she'll ever free herself of guilt. I shrug, pick up my camera, make my way through the apartment, descend the stone steps, cross the courtyard, open the heavy door that lets out to the street.

Dawn has just broken. I've been up, I realize, the entire night. As I slip outside, a burro carrying firewood plods by, escorted by a small boy wearing a huge sombrero. I walk swiftly to my hotel, shower, change clothes, pack, order a taxi, make it to the terminal just in time to catch the first bus out.

On the drive down to the plain, I ask myself if I was right to leave her like that, sobbing, so pathetic in her anguish. Is she evil? Probably, I think. Certainly she is mad and capable of evil acts. I know too there is nothing she can tell me that will further illuminate the mystery of the twins. I only hope that in the photographs I took, there will be one or two that will encapsulate their passion.

● ● ●

Late-winter rains batter San Francisco. This cool gray city of love turns gray indeed. Water, funneled into the streets, rushes down the hills. There is flooding, a sinkhole opens on Seacliff, a mud slide shuts down Route 101, cutting off Marin County for a day.

My own days now are constant, spent in the darkroom producing prints. Sometimes the work goes well, more often it turns difficult, in which case I walk down to the Marina, take an aikido class with Rita, then walk on to Maddy's for a consultation.

Spring comes, flowers bloom, the city feels young again. An unexpected postcard arrives from Portland. The message, written in block letters, is spare, succinct:

HI KAY! MOM DIED. I'M STAYING NOW WITH SIS. SEE-ING A SHRINK. MAYBE GOING BACK TO COLLEGE SOMEDAY. MISSING YOU AND RUSSIAN HILL. HOPE ALL GOES WELL.

DRAKE

I'm very happy to hear from him, to learn he's in care and safe.

Hilly calls, tells me she's tired of "jilling off," that she's now "out there" seriously searching for a lover. Giggling, she adds that to her immense surprise, at The Duchess at least, her newfound fame has cut no ice at all.

On Sundays Dad and I have gotten into the habit of taking long slow hikes at dusk. We vary our route, sometimes walking from Fort Mason through Crissy Field to Fort Point, other times exploring the shimmering upper forests of the Presidio, or striding along Baker Beach looking at old gun emplacements, then continuing on to Point Lobos, Lands End and the ruins of the Sutro Baths.

Today, striding the footpath between the Great Highway and the dunes, we marvel at the way the sun melts into the Pacific.

Dad mentions that Hale came by City Stone Ground on Friday and, for the first time in years, didn't ask about the leather hood. He looked hunched and haggard, Dad says, bought a couple of baguettes, made small talk, suddenly leaned forward, whispered, "You and your daughter betrayed me," then scuttled off.

We shake our heads over that, then walk on, keeping stride, relishing the moment when the sun slips away leaving only a glow behind.

"It's night now. Your time, darlin'," he says.

I look at him. There's still something unspoken, a question that's been nagging me for months. Now that it's dark I dare to pose it:

"When did Wainy see Mom play the piano?" I ask.

Dad's surprised. "He told you he did?"

"He spoke of the beauty of her fingers as they caressed the keys, told me I have her eyes."

"As you do, darlin'. As you do."

"You were close friends, then?"

He looks away. "Not me and him so much."

"Him and Mom?"

"Yeah. Sort of."

When he turns back, I see tears in his eyes. He must think the dark conceals them; otherwise he would not have faced me. He has forgotten how well I see at night.

"I must pity the man now he's such a wreck," Dad says. "Back then he was handsome. Hard to believe, I know."

What can I say? Is it any of my business, these intimate corners of my parents' lives—whom they loved, betrayed, the dangerous adulterous games they played? I don't like to think of Mom having an affair with Wainy, handsome or not, or with any other man, or Dad with another woman. But I can deal with it. I believe I've even come to love them the more for their weaknesses. Tim was flawed too, as are we all. For me now it's only the flaws that are worth photographing, not the smooth concealing masks. And so I turn back to the ocean, now just barely rimmed by the rapidly failing light.

Brave, wonderful Sasha comes to me at night, helps me to see "colors." On days when he's off, we draw the blinds and make love for hours. Then we go out to walk. San Francisco is a city of unexpected, suddenly revealed views. We climb and descend, always trying new routes, always delighting in the exquisite light as it hits a building or paints our shadows upon a wall.

Now, on nights when I'm alone, I never think about the Judge. Also on these warm spring nights I rarely look through my telescope. Rather I sit and gaze out with naked eyes, taking in a panoramic view. The city is whole for me now; I can see my future in it. I will wander its streets, take pictures of its people, and, though never seeing its colors, will feel them and by feeling come to know their beauty.

Tonight, again inspecting my final photographs of the twins, the ones I took in Ariane's bedroom down in San Miguel, I view them as the key images in my book.

Exposures, I now understand, is many things at once: murder story; horror story; story of good and evil; the story of a street hustler, his life and death; of Tim and Ariane Lovsey, the Zamantha Illusion by which they were formed and the world of illusion in which they lived. In the end it is also a story of light and shadow, black and white, and all the tones between: desire, love, fear, courage, greed and pain—the tale of my quest.

trick of light

David Hunt

Author of
THE MAGICIAN'S TALE

Putnam